WILLIAM PENN

ENCYCLOPEDIA *of* PENNSYLVANIA

Editor

Hiram H. Shenk, LL.D.

Associate Editor

Esther Shenk

HERITAGE BOOKS
2010

HERITAGE BOOKS
AN IMPRINT OF HERITAGE BOOKS, INC.

Books, CDs, and more—Worldwide

For our listing of thousands of titles see our website
at
www.HeritageBooks.com

A Facsimile Reprint
Published 2010 by
HERITAGE BOOKS, INC.
Publishing Division
100 Railroad Ave. #104
Westminster, Maryland 21157

Originally published
National Historical Association, Inc.
Harrisburg
1932

— Publisher's Notice —
In reprints such as this, it is often not possible to remove blemishes from the original. We feel the contents of this book warrant its reissue despite these blemishes and hope you will agree and read it with pleasure.

International Standard Book Numbers
Paperbound: 978-0-7884-0968-4
Clothbound: 978-0-7884-8421-6

Preface

IT IS the purpose of the editor to bring within the scope of this volume, Pennsylvania historical and biographical material hitherto inaccessible except to persons having leisure for extended research and also possessing adequate library facilities. The need for a publication of this kind is obvious alike to all research librarians throughout the entire country and to teachers of American History in the Commonwealth.

The selection of material naturally offers serious difficulties in a Commonwealth so rich and complex in its history. This applies alike to the elimination of subjects and to the length of the respective articles. It has been the aim of the editor to give relatively more space to subjects never before fully developed than to those hitherto adequately treated. Thus much space is given to Gerrymandering because it gives information of great interest on a subject never before exploited. The reader will find relatively brief sketches of men of international fame like Benjamin Franklin, a record of whose achievements can be found in any library.

It was at first planned to present herewith a complete bibliography but it soon became obvious that it would require compiling a list of all the general works on Pennsylvania History and Biography, together with all the county histories and the publications of the Historical Society of Pennsylvania, the Historical Society of Western Pennsylvania and the publications of the several historical societies throughout the Commonwealth.

Among the limitations imposed are the excluding of all newspapers less than one hundred years old; populations of towns less than five thousand and streams less than twenty miles in length.

The editor expresses his acknowledgment, first of all, to his daughter, Esther Shenk, Associate Editor, without whose assistance the work would have been impossible; to his daughter, Lucile Shenk, for the contribution of valuable sketches and for numerous suggestions.

PREFACE

The editor acknowledges his indebtedness to Messrs. Franklin Glassmoyer, Clinton Allen, Newton Burgner, Warren Lebo, and John Rank, students in American History at Lebanon Valley College; to Mrs. Mary C. Ramsey, Hazel Thatcher and Ruth B. Cunningham, of the Division of Archives, Pennsylvania State Library, and to the late Prof. J. J. Brehm, Prof. M. O. Billow and Prof. John F. Kob, of the Harrisburg Schools, for varied contributions. Thanks are also due to Miss Gladys Tantaquidgeon, Prof. Glenn Lehman, Mr. H. K. Deisher, the Rev. Dr. Thomas Reisch and Father John O'Donnel, for special contributions, and to Prof. J. A. Durrenberger, of the Georgia State Woman's College, for permission to use his recent article on Turnpike Roads.

THE EDITOR.

Encyclopedia of Pennsylvania

ABBEY, EDWIN AUSTIN, historical and mural painter, was born at Philadelphia, April 1, 1852. He attended Henry D. Gregory's School, in Philadelphia, and later studied drawing with Isaac L. Williams, and the art of drawing on boxwood for engraving with Van Ingen and Snyder. Still later he was a pupil of Christian Schussele at the Pennsylvania Academy. In 1871, he became an illustrator for Harper's Magazine. In 1874, he withdrew from Harper's and set up his own studio. During this time he illustrated for Scribner's. In 1876, he returned to Harper's, and in 1878, was sent by them to England. His sixteen drawings for Old Songs, in 1889, won him a first-class medal at the World's Exhibition in Paris. In 1902, he completed a frieze for the delivery room at the Boston Public Library, depicting the legend of the Quest of the Holy Grail, in fifteen panels. His last work was the decoration of the Pennsylvania State Capitol, at Harrisburg, which he completed in 1907. His historical paintings include "Richard of Gloucester and the Lady Anne," shown in the Royal Academy, in 1896, and "Columbus in the New World." He died August 1, 1911.

ABBOTT, ALEXANDER CREVER, hygienist. In 1900, professor of hygiene and director of the laboratory of hygiene at the University of Pennsylvania, Fellow of the College of Physicians, in Philadelphia. Born, Baltimore, Md., February 26, 1860. Educated, Johns Hopkins, Universities of Maryland, Munich and Berlin. Present professor emeritus hygiene and bacteriology and director of the School of Hygiene and Public Health of the University of Pennsylvania. Member of Philadelphia Board of Health. Author of "The Principles of Bacteriology" and "The Hygiene of Transmissible Diseases."

ABBOTT, CHARLES CONRAD, author and naturalist, graduated University of Pennsylvania, degree of M. D., 1865. In 1876, announced discovery of traces of man in Delaware River Valley, dating from close of glacial period, since verified. Member, American Philosophical Society of Philadelphia. Voluminous author. Born, Trenton, N. J., June 4, 1843.

ABELL, AURNAH SHEPERDSON, journalist; born, East Providence, R. I., August 10, 1806. With William M. Swain, and Azariah H. Simmons, he issued the first publication of the Public Ledger on March 25, 1836. Later he became associated with the Baltimore Sun, issuing the first number on May 17, 1837. He established a pony express by means of which foreign news could more quickly be received, was interested in establishing telegraphic communication with other parts of the world and in improvements in printing. He died at Baltimore, April 19, 1888.

ABERCROMBIE, JAMES, Episcopalian clergyman, who in a sermon preached at St. Peter's Episcopal Church, in Philadelphia, in August, 1800, referring to Jefferson, spoke of the danger to the community which would result from the election of an irreligious chief magistrate. He was severely criticized for this statement. Dr. Abercrombie, born about the year 1758, was for many years an associate rector of Christ Church, St. Peter's and St. James' in Philadelphia. He died in Philadelphia on June 26, 1841.

ABJURATION, OATH OF—*See* OATH OF ABJURATION.

ABOLITION OF SLAVERY IN PENNSYLVANIA—The Society of Friends were among the first abolitionists in America. Pennsylvania passed a law providing for gradual abolition of slavery, March 1, 1780, by a vote of 34 to 21, the author of which was George Bryan, a Justice of the Supreme Court. Under the act children of slave parents were to remain servants until twenty-eight years of age, like those persons bound by indenture. Twenty-four conventions of abolition societies were held between 1794 and 1829, and twenty of these met in Philadelphia.

ABOLITION PUBLICATIONS—Among the early writers against slavery in Pennsylvania were Ralph Andiford, Benjamin Lay, Anthony Benget, and John Woolman. Lay's book published in 1737 was entitled, "All Slave Keepers that Keep the Innocent in Bondage Apostates."

ABOLITIONISTS—On April 14, 1775, the first organized effort to educate public sentiment to abolish slavery in America was made in Philadelphia, with Benjamin Franklin, president and Benjamin Rush, secretary of the organization. The first petition favoring abolition to be presented to the United States Congress came from The Society of Friends (Quakers) in Pennsylvania, Colonizationists.

In December, 1833, the American Anti-Slavery Society was organized at Philadelphia during an abolition convention. Branches of this society were established throughout the states and the abolition movement became prominent throughout the nation. The adoption of the Thirteenth Constitutional Amendment after the Civil War, caused the society to disband.

ACADEMY, THE PHILADELPHIA, was founded in 1750 by Benjamin Franklin, following an investigation of a committee appointed by the City Council, into the advantages of erecting an academy in Philadelphia. In 1753, the academy became a "college" and in 1779, a "university." The University of Pennsylvania descended directly from the Philadelphia Academy.

ACADEMY OF FINE ARTS—*See* PENNSYLVANIA ACADEMY OF FINE ARTS.

ACADEMY OF MUSIC, in Philadelphia, early known as the American Academy of Music, was opened in 1857. The cornerstone for the building at the southwest corner of Broad and Locust Streets, was laid on July 26, 1855. For many years it was the only house where Italian opera was presented.

ACADEMY OF NATURAL SCIENCES OF PHILADELPHIA—Founded 1812. Excellent natural history collection, especially stuffed birds. Valuable scientific library.

ACADEMY OF THE SACRED HEART—The Institute of the Sacred Heart was founded at Amiens, France, in 1800, by Madame Sophia Barat, its object being chiefly the education of young ladies in boarding schools, and when practicable, in parochial and free schools. In 1847, the mansion and ninety-acre farm of F. Cowperthwait at Torresdale were purchased by the Religious of the Sacred Heart and an academy was opened under the direction of Madame Aloysia Hardey. The academy was incorporated in 1849.

ACADEMY OF SURGERY, in Philadelphia, was organized April 21, 1879, at a meeting held at the home of Dr. Samuel D. Gross. Dr. Addinell Hewson was elected president and Dr. J. Ewing Mears, secretary. The aim of the academy consists in "the cultivation and improvement of the art of surgery, the elevation of the medical profession, the promotion of the public health, and such other matters as may come legitimately within its sphere."

ACADIAN REFUGEES, commonly called "French neutrals," were forced to leave their homes in Nova Scotia because they refused to take the oath of allegiance to the British government. The first detachment of them arrived in Philadelphia on November 18, 1755, at a time when opposition to French, Canadians and Catholics was strong. Through the efforts of Anthony Benezet the Assembly agreed to provide for the refugees whose condition at the time of their arrival, was deplorable. In March, 1756, the Assembly passed a bill ordering that the Acadians be dispersed into Philadelphia, Bucks, Chester, and Lancaster Counties where they would be supported by public expense, for twelve months, until they secured homes. Because of the refusal of many authorities in these counties to receive them, they suffered greatly. Finally another bill was passed by the Assembly by which those of the refugees who were under age would be bound to employers and the aged, sick and maimed would be maintained at public expense. Many of the refugees were supported by the province until death.

ACHESON, EDWARD GOODRICH, chemist and inventor, was born at Washington, Pennsylvania, March 9, 1856. He attended the Bellefonte Academy and in 1872, at the age of sixteen, entered the employ of his father, an iron manufacturer. At an early age he became interested in chemistry and electricity. When he was seventeen, he invented a drilling machine for use in coal mining.

Among his later discoveries was that of carborundum, or silicide of carbon, and the method of producing artificial graphite. He died July 6, 1931.

ACRELIUS, ISRAEL, Lutheran clergyman and author, was born December 4, 1714, at Aster-Aker, Sweden. He entered the University of Upsala before he was thirteen years old and studied there until he was ordained to the ministry in 1743. In 1749, Rev. Acrelius was appointed pastor of the parish at Christina (now Wilmington), Delaware. His influence as provost of the church over the Swedish congregations in this country, was marked. He was sympathetic and helpful to the German Lutherans in Pennsylvania and was a friend of their leader the Rev. Henry Melchoir Muhlenberg. His "History of New Sweden" is invaluable in its account of the period of Swedish, Dutch and English rule in America. Because of ill health, Rev. Acrelius resigned his parish leaving for his home in Sweden in 1756. In 1757, he was appointed pastor in Fellingsboro in the diocese of Westeras. He died April 25, 1800.

ADAMS, HENRY A., JR., naval officer, was born in Pennsylvania. He was graduated from the United States Naval Academy and in 1856, participated in the engagement with the Barrier Forts, Canton River, China. On May 11, 1856, he was commissioned a lieutenant, on July 16, 1862, a lieutenant-commander and on July 25, 1866, a commander. He was on the steam sloop "Brooklyn" when it passed Fort St. Philip and Fort Jackson in 1862, and took part in the attacks on Fort Fisher. His death occurred February 1, 1878.

ADAMS, ROBERT, JR., lawyer and legislator, was born February 26, 1846, at Philadelphia, the son of Robert and Matilda Hart Adams. He was educated at the Philadelphia Classical Institute and the University of Pennsylvania, graduating from the latter institution with the A. B. degree, in 1869, and the A. M. degree, in 1872. He studied law with George W. Biddle, of Philadelphia, and was admitted to the bar in 1872. In 1871, he joined Prof. Ferdinand V. Hayden in his exploration of the Yellowstone region of western United States, and during his four years of research corresponded for two New York and two Philadelphia newspapers. Retaining his membership in the United States Geological Survey, he resumed his study of law, and in 1884, graduated from the Wharton School of the University of Pennsylvania with the B. F. degree. From 1882 to 1886, he was a representative in the State Senate. On April 1, 1889, President Harrison appointed him minister to Brazil. In 1893, he was elected to Congress, and on April 11, 1898, was acting chairman of the House Committee on Foreign Affairs, conducted through the House, and had charge in conference with the Senate, of the resolution by which, on April 19th, Congress declared Cuba independent. On April 25th, he introduced and passed through the House the resolution declaring war against Spain. After the downfall of Spanish power, he advocated the retention of the Philippines by the United States. He died June 1, 1906.

ADAMS COUNTY, named for president John Adams, was formed from part of York, January 22, 1800. Land area, 528 square miles. Population (1930), 37,128; (1920), 34,583. County seat, Gettysburg laid out in 1780.

ADDICKS, JOHN EDWARD, capitalist, was born in Philadelphia, November 21, 1841. Flour merchant, gas manufacturer, president of Bay State Gas Co., of Boston in 1884, controlling interest in Brooklyn Gas Co. in 1892; 1895-1903, in Delaware where he was Republican candidate for U. S. Senate—unsuccessful himself but succeeded in keeping first one and then both of the seats vacant.

AFRICAN INSURANCE COMPANY OF PHILADELPHIA was organized in 1810 by the negroes of that city. An office was opened at what was then 159 Lombard Street, with a capital of $5,000 in fifty dollar shares. This is believed to have been the first project of its kind in this country.

AFRICAN METHODIST EPISCOPAL CHURCH was organized in Philadelphia, in 1816, by colored members of the Methodist Episcopal Church. The first bishop of the church was the Rev. Richard Allen. The first church erected in this country for colored members of the Methodist faith was located at Sixth and Lombard Streets, Philadelphia. The African Church does not essentially differ in doctrine and government from the mother church. It is widely distributed throughout the United States. Membership in Pennsylvania (1926), 23,208.

AGNEW, DANIEL, jurist, was born in Trenton, N. J., January 5, 1809. From Trenton he moved to Pittsburgh; was district judge in 1851; judge of the Supreme Court, 1863; Chief Justice of the State in 1873; resigned in 1879. He is the author of "Our National Constitution," and "History of Pennsylvania," in addition to other works. He died at Beaver, March 9, 1902.

AGNEW, DAVID HAYES, surgeon and medical writer. Born November 24, 1818, died March 22, 1892. Many years professor of surgery at University of Pennsylvania; attended President Garfield, upon whom he made an important operation; published "Practical Anatomy" (1867), "Anatomy and Its Relation to Medicine and Surgery", "Principles and Practice of Surgery" (1878).

AGNEW, JAMES, British general in Revolutionary War, who commanded the 4th Brigade of the Royal Army during and after the siege of Long Island.

He was wounded at the Battle of Brandywine and was killed in the Battle at Germantown on October 4, 1777.

AGRICULTURAL SOCIETY OF PHILADELPHIA, known as the Philadelphia Society for Promoting Agriculture, was organized in 1805 and incorporated in February, 1809.

AITKIN, ROBERT, Philadelphia printer and publisher, born, Dalkeith, Scotland, 1734, came to America, 1769, and settled in Philadelphia where he was in turn bookseller, bookbinder and publisher. His publications included The Pennsylvania Magazine, 1775-1776, publications for the Continental Congress, and the first English Bible in America. Only 25 copies of this Bible are known to exist. Aitkin was active in the cause of independence and submitted to imprisonment for it in 1777. He died in Philadelphia in July, 1802.

AITKIN'S BIBLE, printed in Philadelphia, in 1781, was the first Bible ever printed in the English language in America.

AKE, JACOB, founder of Williamsburg, Blair County, formerly called Aketown. Realizing the necessity of educational training for the young he established what was probably the first school in Blair County and financed it himself. With the beginning of the subscription school about fifteen years later, this school was discontinued.

ALBRIGHT, JACOB, founder of the Evangelical Association, born near Pottstown, May 1, 1759, active Methodist minister among the Pennsylvania-Germans. Began reform work in eastern Pennsylvania about 1790, after which he traveled and preached in churches, barns and schoolhouses throughout Eastern Pennsylvania, Maryland and Virginia. Died May 18, 1808, and is buried at Newmanstown, Lebanon County.

ALBRIGHT COLLEGE, a coeducational institution at Reading, was formed in 1929 by the union of Schuylkill and Albright Colleges, both of which were under the control of the Evangelical Church. Schuylkill College at Reading was the outgrowth of Schuylkill Seminary and Albright College originated from Palatinate College, formed in 1867 and located at Myerstown. Courses leading to the A. B. and B. S. degrees are offered. Warren Floyd Teel is president of the college. Enrollment (1930-1931), 466.

ALCOTT, LOUISA MAY, novelist, was born, Germantown, November 29, 1832. Two years later her family moved to Boston and thence to Concord. Her father, A. B. Alcott, organized an infant school there, in which he used conversation as the principle method of teaching. Louisa Alcott was under the instruction of Thoreau for a time and served as a magazine writer and school teacher. During the Civil War she was a nurse in a Washington hospital. This latter experience gave her material for Hospital Sketches. The success of this literary venture induced her to write "Little Women," "An Old Fashioned Girl," "Little Men," and others not so well known. She died at Boston on March 6, 1888.

ALDEN, BRADFORD R., soldier, was born at Meadeville, in 1800. He graduated from West Point, in 1831, and was instructor there from 1833 to 1840. He was aide to Winfield Scott for two years and from 1845 to 1852, was commandant at West Point. He was detailed to the northwest in 1853, where he led an expedition against the Rogue River Indians who were uprising in Southwest Oregon. In a battle at Jacksonville on August 24, 1853, he was disabled and retired from service.

ALDEN, ISABELLA McDONALD, juvenile writer of Philadelphia, was born in Rochester, N. Y., November 3, 1841. She was educated at Ovid and Auburn, N. Y. In 1866, she married Rev. G. R. Alden. She is best known as the author of about 75 Sunday School juvenile novels, known as the "Pansy Books." She edited the juvenile periodical Pansy from 1873 to 1896. In addition she was a member of the staff of The Christian Endeavor World and The Herald and Presbyter, for many years. She resides in Palo Alto, California.

ALEXANDER, JOHN WHITE, artist, born at Allegheny City, October 7, 1856. He studied at the National Academy of Fine Arts in Munich and with Duverneck in Florence and Venice. In 1893, his paintings were exhibited in the Salon of the Champ de Mars. After that he was awarded gold medals by the Philadelphia Academy of Fine Arts, the Paris Exposition of 1900, and the Exposition at Buffalo, in 1901. Some of his productions appear in the Luxembourg Galleries and in the United States. Six lunettes depicting The History of the Book appear in the east hall of the Library of Congress at Washington. In addition, he is well known as a magazine illustrator in the United States where he was connected with the art department of Harper's for three years.

ALEXANDER, JOSEPH ADDISON, Princeton Biblical scholar, was born in Philadelphia, the son of Archibald Alexander, on April 24, 1809. After graduating from Princeton, in 1826, he became one of the founders of Edgehill Seminary. He studied extensively in foreign universities, became an outstanding American Bibliologist and Orientalist. Between the years 1838, and 1860, when he died, he was a professor at Princeton Seminary in the departments of Oriental and Biblical literature, church history and government, New Testament history and government. He was the author of several standard commentaries.

ALIQUIPPA, an Indian queen, who lived at the junction of the Monongahela and Youghiogheny Rivers, was visited by Washington at her request upon his return from Fort Le Boeuf in 1753. She was a leading Indian character and had much influence upon local tribes. The town of Aliquippa and various landmarks in Western Pennsylvania bear her name.

ALISON, FRANCIS, educator, was born in Donegal County, Ireland, in 1705; came to America in 1735. From 1755 until his death on November 28, 1779, he was vice-provost and professor of Moral Philosophy of the College of Pennsylvania. Numbered among his students are many who took prominent parts in the Revolution.

ALLAQUIPPA—See ALIQUIPPA.

ALLEGHENY, a section of Pittsburgh, located on the western side of the Allegheny River. By an act of legislature of 1788, the land on which the town is built was surveyed and in 1789, a portion of it was ordered to be divided into town lots, in order that a fund might be raised to pay the claims of Pennsylvania soldiers. Until June 16, 1906, when it was consolidated with Pittsburgh, Allegheny was an independent city.

ALLEGHENY COLLEGE, Meadville, is a co-educational institution organized in 1815 by the Presbyterian Church. In 1833, it was put under the control of the Methodist Church, under the condition that it be conducted as a nonsectarian institution. The college received the support of John Adams, Thomas Jefferson, James Winthrop and William Bentley. Enrollment (1930-1931), 640.

ALLEGHENY COUNTY was formed from part of Westmoreland and Washington, September 24, 1788. Name of Indian origin probably from Talligequi meaning "People of the cave country." Land area, 725 square miles; population (1930), 1,374,310; (1920), 1,185,808. County seat, Pittsburgh, laid out in 1765.

ALLEGHENY LITERARY MAGAZINE, THE, established in 1815, appears four times during the college year; edited by the students of Allegheny College, Meadville; circulation, 3,600.

ALLEGHENY PORTAGE—See PORTAGE.

ALLEGHENY RIVER—Tributary to Ohio River. Basin, Ohio; source, in Sweden Township, central Potter County; course, northwesterly through McKean County into New York forming a loop 50 miles long before reentering Pennsylvania in Warren County; mouth, at Pittsburgh; length, 314 miles. Indian name, probably a corruption of Alligewi-hanna, "stream of the Allegewi."

ALLEGIANCE, OATH OF—See OATH OF ALLEGIANCE.

ALLEN, ANDREW, a prominent member of the Whig Party, who was a member of the Continental Congress of July 4, 1776. Due to his failure to sign the Declaration of Independence he lost his reelection to Congress. Consequently he deserted the American cause, putting himself under the protection of Gen. Howe. He spent the last years of his life in England.

ALLEN, HARRISON, anatomist of Philadelphia, was born there on April 17, 1841. In 1861, he was granted the M. D. degree at the University of Pennsylvania, after which he was a surgeon in the United States Army during the Civil War. At the University of Pennsylvania, he was first professor of comparative anatomy and medical zoology and later of physiology. He was a member of the university faculty from 1865 until 1895, just two years before his death on November 14, 1897.

ALLEN, HORATIO, American engineer, who was born in Schenectady, N. Y., in 1802, made the first locomotive trip in America, with the "Stourbridge Lion," at Honesdale, in 1829.

ALLEN, RICHARD, negro clergyman, organized the first church for colored people in the United States, and was the first bishop of the African Methodist Episcopal Church. He was born in 1760 and died in Philadelphia, March 26, 1831.

ALLEN, WILLIAM, jurist, was one of the founders of the College of Philadelphia (University of Pennsylvania). From 1750-1774, he was Chief Justice of Pennsylvania. He bought and paid for out of his private funds the land on which the state house was built. He did not advocate the Revolution nor independence although he sympathized with the Colonists.

ALLENTOWN is the county seat of Lehigh County. It is located on the Lehigh Valley Railroad, Central Railroad of New Jersey and the Philadelphia and Reading Railroad, six miles southwest of Bethlehem and fifty-five miles northwest of Philadelphia. William Allen, Chief Justice of the Province of Pennsylvania, and father-in-law of Governor John Penn, founded it about 1752. He received land grants from the Penn family and after 1811, the town became progressive. It was the center from which Colonel James Bird warred against the Indians, and was the asylum for Philadelphians who were driven from that city during the Revolution. In 1799, the town received prominence when John Fries led the German inhabitants in the opposition to the "window tax." When Northampton County was separated from Lehigh, in 1811, Allentown was incorporated as Northampton Borough and became the Lehigh county seat. Deposits of iron ore, zinc, limestone, etc., aided in developing its wealth. After the organization of a water company, in 1828, a great obstacle to the development of the community was overcome. The original name Allentown was restored in 1838 and a special charter was granted in 1867. The same year, the Lutheran Church established Muhlenburg College, an institution for the education of young men. In addition, the Allentown College for Women, now Cedar Crest College, sponsored by the Reformed Church of America, is located on the southwestern border of the town.

City Government—In 1889, a charter was granted providing the triennial election of a mayor to preside over a council of two houses, the upper of 11 members, the lower of 22 members.

The leading manufactures are silk, iron, furniture, leather goods, cigars, textiles, miscellaneous machinery, barbed wire, cement, fire brick and auto trucks—258 factories, 1927, output $145,000,000. Population (1930), 92,563; (1920), 73,502.

ALLENTOWN FRIEDENS-BOTE (MESSENGER OF PEACE), THE, a German newspaper, was the second to be established in that city. The first was the *Independent Republican*, established in 1810. The *Friedens-Bote* was established September 28, 1812, by Joseph Ehrenfried and Henry Ebner in opposition to the War of 1812. It appears weekly and has a circulation of 11,316. It is sent to every part of the United States and throughout the world. Julius Bodisch is the editor.

ALLIBONE, SAMUEL AUSTIN, bibliographer and librarian, was born in Philadelphia, April 17, 1816. His most important work is a three-volume, Critical Dictionary of English Literature and British and American Authors, which required twenty years of work in compilation. In addition he served as both editor for the American Sunday-School Union and was librarian of the Lenox Library, in New York. He died in Luzerne, Switzerland, on September 2, 1889.

ALLUMOPEES OR SASSOONAN, head chief of the Turtle Clan of Delawares, who resided near Paxtang and later at Shamokin, now Sunbury. Some authorities maintain that he was the son of Tamanend. Upon his succession to the chieftainship sometime between May 19, 1712, and June 14, 1715, he attended conferences with the proprietors of Pennsylvania regarding the rights of white settlers to the land they occupied. He strongly advocated the renewal and continuance of the "Great Treaty" made between Tamanend and William Penn.

ALMANACS published in Pennsylvania include William Bradford's "Almanac," Philadelphia, 1685, believed to be the first in the Colonies; "Leed's American Almanac," Philadelphia, 1726; "Poor Richard's Almanac," by Benjamin Franklin, Philadelphia, 1732–1786; "Father Abraham's Almanac," Philadelphia, 1759–1799; "Agricultural Almanac," published by John Baer, Lancaster, for which calculations were made by Charles F. Egelman, of Reading, and later by Lawrence J. Ibach and Will R. Ibach, of Newmanstown.

ALTER, DAVID, scientist, was born in Allegheny Township, Westmoreland County, December 3, 1807, of Pennsylvania-German parentage. Beginning the study of medicine he was graduated from the Reformed Medical College of the United States in New York City in 1831. To attend this school he rode on horseback to Philadelphia, finishing his journey from there by railroad. He began the practice of medicine in Elderton, Armstrong County, and rose rapidly in his profession. He never under any circumstances prescribed whiskey for his patients.

In 1836 he invented an electric telegraph and in 1837 an electric motor. Numerous other inventions were made by him, but his greatest scientific achievement was the discovery of the spectrum analysis in 1853. He died September 18, 1881.

ALTOONA, city in Blair County, founded by the Pennsylvania Railroad, in 1849, is located 144 miles east of Pittsburgh, on the Pennsylvania Railroad. It is situated on an elevation of 1,182 feet above sea level, among the eastern Allegheny Mountains. The city is a typical American railroad center for the repair shops of the Pennsylvania Railroad are located there. Repair shops, freight classification yards, foundries and works for construction of cars and locomotives employ 16,000 men. The public schools have an enrollment of 15,167. The city was incorporated as a borough in 1858 and chartered as a city in 1868. In 1862, "Loyal War Governors," of Northern States, met there in the Logan House. The famous Horse Shoe Bend, an unusual feat of engineering, is located four miles west of the city. Population (1930), 82,041; (1920), 60,331.

ALTOONA CONFERENCE—A conference of governors of loyal states called by Governor Curtin in September, 1862. The conference was informal and private. The invitation and correspondence had been by telegraph, Curtin first asking the advice of Governor Andrew, of Massachusetts, whose reply was favorable. September 14, 1862, the call was signed by Governors Curtin, of Pennsylvania; Tod, of Ohio; and Pierpont, of West Virginia. The meetings were held at the Logan House. An address to President Lincoln was issued in which loyal support was pledged.

AMBULANCE—First used in Philadelphia during the Civil War. The firemen of that city supplemented hospital work for soldiers by arranging to meet vessels with wounded at the wharves and take them in spring wagons to local hospitals. The "Northern Liberties Engine Company" began the work and had a special ambulance constructed. Eventually more than thirty companies contributed $30,000 for this form of transport and served approximately 120,000 wounded.

AMERICAN ACADEMY OF POLITICAL AND SOCIAL SCIENCE, founded, Philadelphia, 1889; incorporated, 1891; publishes bi-monthly annuals.

AMERICAN ASSOCIATION FOR THE ADVANCEMENT OF SCIENCE was originally known as the Association of American Geologists, founded in Philadelphia, 1840. In 1842, naturalists were added to geologists and in 1847, the present name was assumed.

Members approximately 15,000 in 1927 from U. S. and Canada. In addition, 115 autonomous and independent associated organizations, 62 societies, 22 state academies.

Volumes of proceedings—published at intervals approximating four years and include directory of members.

Annual meeting during Christmas holidays. Headquarters, Washington, D. C.

AMERICAN BAPTIST MISSIONARY UNION—An organization of the Baptist Church, was formed in Philadelphia on May 18, 1814, as "The General Missionary Convention of the Baptist Denomination in the United States for Foreign Missions." Slavery became an issue so that in 1845, the Southern Bapitsts withdrew from the organization and it assumed the name by which it is now known. The aim of the organization was to carry the gospel through mission centers established all over the world.

AMERICAN BIBLE SOCIETY—*See* BIBLE SOCIETY.

AMERICAN ENTOMOLOGICAL SOCIETY was established in 1859, for the purpose of encouraging scientific study of insect life. The headquarters of the organization are in Philadelphia.

AMERICAN JOURNAL OF THE MEDICAL SCIENCES, THE, was established by Prof. Nathaniel Chapman as the *Philadelphia Journal of the Medical and Physical Sciences* in 1820. It took its present name in November, 1827, and appears monthly under the editorship of E. B. Krumbhaar, M. D. Lea and Febiger are the publishers. It is a professional organ with a circulation of 4,350.

AMERICAN JOURNAL OF PHARMACY, THE, published monthly by the Philadelphia College of Pharmacy and Science, was established in 1825. It is a professional organ. Ivor Griffith, Ph. M., is the editor. Circulation, 2,246.

AMERICAN MEDICAL ASSOCIATION was formed in Philadelphia, in 1847.

AMERICAN SUNDAY-SCHOOL UNION with headquarters in Philadelphia, had its beginning in the First Day Society, a Friend's organization there in 1791. This late 18th century society petitioned for free schools in Pennsylvania and led to the foundation, in 1817, of the Philadelphia Sunday and Adult School Union. The American Sunday-School Union grew out of this and allied

AMISH FAMILY, LANCASTER COUNTY

organizations in 1824. The object of this union has been the establishment of Sunday schools in neighborhoods where none exist and in communities where religious differences are closely drawn. Christians of various denominations contribute their services to the organization and it is managed entirely by laymen, although there are some clergymen connected with the administration of its affairs.

AMES, HERMAN VANDERBURG, university professor; born at Lancaster, Mass., August 7, 1865; graduated from Amherst College in 1888; attended the Graduate School of Columbia University, 1888-1889; graduated from Harvard University with the A. M. degree in 1890 and with the Ph. D. degree in 1891; did graduate work at Leipzig and Heidelberg, 1894-1895. He was instructor of history at the University of Michigan, 1891-1894; assistant professor of history, Ohio State University, 1896-1897; instructor, American Constitutional history, 1897-1903; assistant professor American history, 1903-1908; professor, American constitutional history since 1908 and dean of the Graduate School, 1907-1928, University of Pennsylvania. He also taught American History at the summer sessions of Columbia University, University of Wisconsin and University of California. Dr. Ames has served as a member of various committees of historical and educational organizations and from 1900-1903 was secretary of the Association of Colleges and Preparatory Schools of the Middle States and Maryland. He is the author of "The Proposed Amendments to the Constitution of the United States," which was awarded the prize of the American Historical Association in 1897. Dr. Ames lives in Philadelphia.

AMISH, a branch of the Mennonite Church originated in Europe about 1693, under the leadership of Jacob Ammon. They are sometimes called Aymonists, Aymish, Amish or "Hookers," because they wear hooks and eyes on their clothes instead of buttons. Because of religious persecutions in Europe they came to this country in the late seventeenth and early eighteenth centuries and settled in Lancaster, Union, Mifflin, Somerset and Lawrence Counties. They differ from the Mennonites in their practice of "avoidance" and "shunning," refusing to have business, social or religious relations with a member of their church placed under a ban for some religious offence. Because of their belief in the doctrine of peace some of their members were imprisoned at Reading at the time of the Revolution. They do not maintain church buildings, but worship in the homes and barns of members.

ANDAGGY-JUNGUAGH, Chief of the Conestoga Indians, who lived in Lancaster County. He represented his tribe at a council at Philadelphia on June 7, 1706, between Governor John Evans and the Chiefs of the Conestogas, Shawnees and Ganawese or Conoys.

ANDERSON, EDWIN HATFIELD, first librarian of Carnegie Library, Pittsburgh, was born in Zionsville, Indiana, September 27, 1861. After graduating from Wabash College and the New York State Library School, he was librarian in the Carnegie Free Library, Braddock, Pa., for three years. In 1895, he became the first librarian of the Carnegie Library in Pittsburgh of which he was the organizer. He was president of the Keystone State Library Association, 1901-1902, and served as a member of the Pennsylvania Public Records Commission and the Historical Archives Commission in 1903 and 1904. In 1906, he became director of the New York State Library and Library School. Since 1913 he has been director of the New York Public Library.

ANDERSON CREEK—Tributary to West Branch Susquehanna River. Sub-basin, Upper West Branch Susquehanna; source, in Huston Township, northwestern Clearfield County; course, southwesterly and southeasterly to West Branch Susquehanna River; mouth, at Curwensville; length, twenty-one miles.

ANDRE, JOHN, soldier, was born in London in 1751. At the age of twenty, he entered the English Army, was sent to Canada in 1774, and in November, 1775, was taken prisoner by Montgomery's expedition at St. John's and sent to Lancaster. Following the exchange of prisoners in December, 1776, he was raised to the rank of captain, made aide to Gen. Charles Grey, major in 1778, aide to Clinton and adjutant-general of the British forces in America in 1779. He was a popular member of Philadelphia society during the army's stay in that city in the winter of 1777-1778, and was the leading actor in the pageant known as the "Mischianza," given in honor of Howe upon his departure from the city.

Unfortunately, in 1780, Andre became seriously involved in the plans of Clinton and Benedict Arnold for the betrayal of West Point. In an attempt to carry papers containing the drawings of West Point from Arnold to the British lines, Andre, disguised as a civilian, was intercepted by three American soldiers practically within sight of the British lines near Tarrytown. The soldiers searched him, found the papers, and turned him over to Lieutenant Colonel Jamison. Andre was finally sent to Washington and because of his rank, did not suffer the customary immediate hanging. A military court, with Gen. Nathaniel Greene, as president, convicted Andre of being a spy and sentenced him to death on October 2nd. The decree was carried out and Andre was executed on that day at Tappan, N. Y.

ANNESLEY, JAMES, orphan son and heir of the Earl of Anglesey, Lord Altham, who was kidnapped in Dublin at the suggestion of his uncle, next of heir, sent to America about 1728, sold as a servant and taken to a place some forty miles west of Philadelphia. He attempted to run away but was always brought back and enslaved for a longer period of time. No credence was given his claims of his noble ancestry until the arrival, about twelve years later, of two men from County Wexford, Ireland, who confirmed James' story. He was taken to Philadelphia where he was brought to the attention of Robert Ellis, who in turn recommended him to Admiral Vernon. Vernon took him to England where friends financed him in the prosecution of the suit for his rights. James wrote "Memoirs of an Unfortunate Young Nobleman" in order to attract attention to his case. He did not win his suit and while funds were being raised for a renewal of his claims in 1760, he died.

ANNVILLE, first-class township in Lebanon County, founded by Abraham Miller, in 1762. For many years it was called Millerstown, but eventually became known as Annville for Ann Miller, wife of the founder. It is the seat of Lebanon Valley College, an institution under the control of the United Brethren in Christ. The population in 1930 was approximately 3,000.

ANTES, HENRY, pioneer settler, was born in Bavaria in 1701. With his father and mother, Frederick and Anna Catherine Antes, he came to America and settled in Philadelphia County. Upon his marriage to Christiana Elizabetha Dewees on February 2, 1726, Antes removed to what is now Frederick Township, Montgomery County, and with his father-in-law built a grist-mill and paper-mill at Crefeld, Germantown. Later he bought land in Frederick Township where he lived the rest of his life and in partnership with George Heebner, erected a grist-mill. In addition to his duties as a miller, Antes explored the wilderness and came to know the Indian. In 1736, he met Spangenberg, founder of the Moravian Church in this country, and the friendship between the two lasted for the remainder of their lives. Antes assisted the Moravians in their plans for the church organization by gathering his neighbors together for the purpose of worship. His house was the center of the Moravian efforts. He assisted in building the first house in Bethlehem and in the erection of grist-mills there, and until April, 1750, was an influential member of the Moravian Church. In that year the members of the church at Bethlehem introduced the wearing of the white surplice by the minister at the celebration of the Eucharist and Antes withdrew from the communion and rejoined the Reformed Church. However, in 1752, he accompanied Spangenberg to North Carolina to survey a tract of land the Moravians had bought for the purpose of settling a colony there. Antes assisted the London Society in its efforts to introduce English schools among the German settlers in 1754 and replied to the attack made in the same year by the King of England upon the German settlers of Pennsylvania, whom he accused of disloyalty. Antes died July 20, 1755. The Moravian service was read at his funeral and the address was delivered by Bishop Spangenberg.

ANTI-MASONRY—The opposition to the Masonic order in this country came as a result of incidents which followed the appearance of a book, published by William Morgan, of New York state, in 1826, in which, it is said, the secrets of the order were disclosed. An anti-masonic party was organized which soon became political instead of social. In 1832, a national Anti-Masonic convention was held at Philadelphia, and William Wirt, of Virginia, was nominated for president, and Amos Ellmaker, of Lancaster County, for vice-president. One of the leaders of the party in Pennsylvania was Thaddeus Stevens. A combination of Whigs and Anti-Masons elected Joseph Ritner, governor, in 1835. Prior to this an investigation into the secrets of Masonry was ordered but leaders like Governor Wolf refused to testify.—*See also* "BUCKSHOT WAR."

ANTI-SLAVERY MOVEMENT IN PENNSYLVANIA—In 1664, Plockhoy, in his plan for the government of his colony at Swanendael, declared that no slavery should exist there. The first protest against slavery was made by the Germantown Mennonites, sometimes called German Quakers, in 1688. The signers to the petition were Francis Daniel Pastorius, Garret Hendricks, Derich Op de Graeff and Abraham Op de Graeff. In 1774, the Society of Friends at the meeting in Philadelphia decided that Friends who held slaves beyond the time of the service of apprentices should be regarded as disorderly persons, and in 1776, slave owners were disowned by the Friends. Prior to this time hundreds of owners voluntarily manumitted their slaves. April 14, 1775, the first organized effort to educate public sentiment in favor of abolition of slavery in America was made in Philadelphia with Benjamin Franklin, president, and Dr. Benjamin Rush, secretary. The Act for the gradual abolition of slavery in Pennsylvania was adopted in 1780. In 1807, the General Assembly passed a joint resolution instructing the representatives in Congress to do all within their power to prohibit the importation of slaves into the United States. In 1819, the General Assembly passed a joint resolution against the admission of Missouri into the Union as a slave state. Governor Ritner, in 1836, wrote a strong message against slavery, and David Wilmot introduced into Congress the famous Wilmot Proviso, while Thaddeus Stevens delivered a most effective speech against the Fugitive Slave Law in the Compromise of 1850. Pennsylvania became a place of refuge for runaway slaves. In 1847, the General Assembly passed a law against kidnapping, making it a criminal offense for anyone claiming a runaway slave to capture him by the use of violence. After the passage of the Fugitive Slave Law, in 1850, there were many stations in the "Underground Railroad" established in Pennsylvania.—*See also* ABOLITION PUBLICATIONS; ABOLITION OF SLAVERY IN PENNSYLVANIA; ANTI-SLAVERY SOCIETIES AND NEGROES IN PENNSYLVANIA.

ANTI-SLAVERY PERIODICALS that were published in Pennsylvania include "The African Observer," by Enoch Lewis, Philadelphia, 1835; "National Inquirer," by Benjamin Lundy, Philadelphia, 1836; "Pennsylvania Freeman," by John G. Whittier, Philadelphia, 1838-1840.

ANTI-SLAVERY SOCIETY, THE AMERICAN, was organized in Philadelphia, December, 1833, by representatives from local and state societies of a like nature. The society stood for the abolition of slavery. The members differed on some major issues although the society eventually merged into the Liberty Party. Some of the original members continued as an organization until the 15th Amendment was adopted in 1870.

ANTI-SLAVERY SOCIETY, PENNSYLVANIA—See PENNSYLVANIA ANTI-SLAVERY SOCIETY.

ANTI-TRAMP ASSOCIATION, Abington and Cheltenham. An organization to secure protection against tramps and professional thieves was formed by the residents of Abington and Cheltenham, Montgomery County, on July 18, 1877.

AQUASHICOLA CREEK—Tributary to Lehigh River. Sub-basin, Middle Delaware; source, in Blue Mountain, Hamilton Township, Monroe County; course, southwesterly into Carbon County to Lehigh River; mouth, at Lehigh Gap; length, twenty-two and one-half miles.

ARCHBALD—A borough settled by Welsh miners in 1831, is located in Lackawanna County, ten miles northeast of Scranton. Population (1930), 9,587; (1920), 8,603.

ARCHER, BELLE, an actress, was born in Easton, in 1860. Before her marriage to Herbert Archer, in 1880, she was Arabella S. Mingle. She first appeared in Washington, D. C., with William Florence in "The Mighty Dollar," and subsequently was leading lady in presentations of "Pinafore," "Hazel Kirke," "Lord Chumley" and "Foresters." She divorced Archer in 1889, and died in 1890.

ARCHER, FREDERIC, founder of the Pittsburgh Symphony Orchestra, was born in Oxford, England, in 1838. He received his education at Oxford, London and Leipzig and became an outstanding organist in English and Scotch cities. He followed his profession in Brooklyn and Boston. In 1896, he founded the Pittsburgh Symphony Orchestra and was organist in the Church of the Ascension there for two years, until his death in 1901.

ARCHER, JOHN, was awarded first medical diploma granted in America when he graduated from the Philadelphia Medical College in 1768. He was a native of Maryland where he was born in Harford County, June 6, 1741. Prior to his study in Philadelphia, he graduated from Princeton in 1760. He served in the American Revolution, in the State Legislature, in Congress, and was a presidential elector from Maryland in 1801. He died in 1810 in his Maryland home after having contributed some results of medical investigations to the profession.

ENCYCLOPEDIA OF PENNSYLVANIA 19

ARCHIVES—Seven series of Pennsylvania Archives have been published; a publication not designated as Archives is called the Colonial Records, published by the State in 1851. The published Archives include the following subjects: First Series—12 volumes—edited by Samuel Hazard, 1853: 1664-1790, Letters, Petitions, Indian Deeds, with an account of Frontier Forts in Vol. XII. Second Series— 19 volumes—edited by William H. Egle, M. D., 1888: Vol. I, Minutes of Board of War; Vol. II, Names of Persons for Whom Marriage Licenses were issued in Pennsylvania previous to 1790, Persons Naturalized in Pennsylvania, Provincial Officers and Soldiers, Indian Traders, 1743-48 (Ed., 1876), and Ships' Registers; Vol. III, Oaths of Allegiance, Papers Relating to War of the Revolution, Memorials against Calling a Convention 1779, Minutes of the Provincial Deputies, Proceedings of the Provincial Conference, Officers of the State of Pennsylvania in the Revolution and under the Constitution, 1776; Vol. IV, Historical Notes (Whiskey Insurrection); Vol. V, Papers Relating to Colonies on the Delaware; Vol. VI, Papers Relating to the French Occupation; Vol. VII, Papers Relating to Provincial Affairs (Narrative of Marie Le Roy and Barbara Leininger); Vol. VIII, Marriages in Philadelphia, Carlisle, Chester, New Hanover, etc.; Vol. IX, Marriages in Philadelphia, Bethlehem, etc., List of Officers of the Colonies on the Delaware and the Province of Pennsylvania; Vol. X, Soldiers of the War of the Revolution, Flag of 1st Pennsylvania Battalion of Riflemen; Vol. XI, Soldiers of the War of the Revolution, Pulaski's Banner; Vol. XII, Muster Rolls of Pennsylvania Volunteers, 1812-14, with Papers and Documents; Vol. XIII, Soldiers of the War of the Revolution, Flag of Proctor's Westmoreland County Battalion; Vol. XIV, Soldiers of the War of the Revolution, 1775-1783, Standard of Philadelphia Light Horse, 1775, Flag of Hanover Associators, 1775, Picture of Fort McIntosh; Vol. XV, Journals and Diaries of War of the Revolution with lists of Officers and Soldiers, Map of Sullivan Expedition, Pennsylvania Pensioners, 1820, 1825; Vol. XVI, Boundary dispute between Pennsylvania and Maryland; Vol. XVII, Names of Foreigners who took Oath of Allegiance to the Province of and State of Pennsylvania, 1727-1775, with foreign arrivals, 1786-1808; Vol. XVIII, Documents Relating to the Connecticut Settlement in the Wyoming Valley, Prisoners at Wyoming; Vol. XIX, Minutes of the Board of Property of the Province of Pennsylvania. Third Series—30 volumes—edited by William H. Egle, M. D., 1894: Vol. I, Minutes of the Board of Property and other references to Lands in Pennsylvania; Vol. II, Minutes of the Board of Property, etc.; Vol. III, Old Rights, Proprietary Rights, Virginia Entries, and Soldiers Entitled to Donation Lands; Vol. IV, Draughts of the Proprietary Manors in the Province of Pennsylvania as Preserved in the Land Department of the Commonwealth; Vol. V, State of Accounts of the County Lieutenants during the War of the Revolution, 1777-....; Vol. VI (same as Vol. V); Vol. VII (same as Vol. V); Vol. VIII, Commissions issued by the Province of Pennsylvania with Official Proclamations; Vol. IX (same as Vol. VIII); Vol. X (same as Vol. VIII); Vol. XI, Provincial Papers, Proprietary Tax Lists of County of Chester for years

1765-66-67-68-69-71; Vol. XII, Provincial Papers, Proprietary Tax Lists of County of Chester for Years 1774, 1779-80-81, 1785; Vol. XIII, Provincial Papers, Proprietary and Other Tax Lists of County of Bucks for Years 1779, 1781-82-83-84-85-86; Vol. XIV, Provincial Papers, Proprietary and Supply Tax Lists and Tax Lists of the City and County of Philadelphia for the Years 1769, 1774, 1779; Vol. XV, Provincial Papers, Supply and State Tax Lists of the City and County of Philadelphia for Years 1779-80-81; Vol. XVI, Provincial Papers, Supply and State Tax Lists of the City and County of Philadelphia for Years 1781-82-83; Vol. XVII, Provincial Papers, Supply and State Tax Lists of the County of Lancaster for Years 1771-72-73-79-82; Vol. XVIII, Provincial Papers, Proprietary and State Tax Lists of the County of Berks for Years 1767-68, 1779-80-81-84-85; Vol. XIX, Proprietary, Supply and State Tax Lists of Counties of Northampton and Northumberland, 1772-87; Vol. XX, State and Supply Transcripts of the County of Cumberland for Years 1778-79-80-81-82-85; Vol. XXI, Returns of Taxables, County of York, 1779-80-81-82-83; Vol. XXII, Returns of Taxables for Counties of Bedford, 1773-84; Huntingdon 1798; Westmoreland, 1783-1786; Fayette, 1785-86; Allegheny, 1791; Washington, 1786; and Census of Bedford, 1784, and Westmoreland, 1783; Vol. XXIII, Muster Rolls of the Navy and Line Militia and Rangers, 1775-83, with Lists of Pensioners, 1818-1832, who served in the War of the Revolution; Vol. XXIV, Provincial Papers, Warrantees of Land in the Several Counties of the State of Pennsylvania, 1730-1798, Organization of Counties; Vol. XXV, Warrantees of Land in Several Counties of the State of Pennsylvania, 1730-1798; Vol. XXVI, Warrantees of Land in Counties of the State of Pennsylvania, 1730-1798; Vols. XXVII, XXVIII, XXIX, XXX, Index. Fourth Series—12 volumes—edited by George Edward Reed, 1900: Papers of the Governors. Fifth Series—eight volumes—edited by Thomas Lynch Montgomery, 1906: Vol. I, Roll of the French and Indian War, Pennsylvania Navy and Letters of Marque; Vol. II, Rosters of First American Troops in Revolutionary War, Muster Rolls of Fourth Pennsylvania Regiment, Continental Line; Vol. III, Muster Rolls of Revolutionary Troops, Pennsylvanians in Washington's Army; Vol. IV, Muster Rolls of Invalid Regiment and Depreciation Pay Lists; Pension Applications, Lists of Soldiers of the Revolution; Vol. V, Muster Rolls of Bedford, Berks, Bucks and Chester Counties (Rev.); Vol. VI, Muster Rolls of Cumberland County Troops (Rev.); Vol. VII, Muster Rolls of Lancaster County Troops (Rev.); Vol. VIII, Muster Rolls of Northampton and Northumberland Counties in the War of the Revolution. Sixth Series—14 volumes—edited by Thomas Lynch Montgomery, 1906: Vol. I, Muster Rolls of Philadelphia City and County Troops in the War of the Revolution; Vol. II, Muster Rolls of Washington, Westmoreland and York Counties in the War of the Revolution, Crawford's Expedition to Sandusky; Vol. III, Muster Rolls of the Militia, 1784-1790; Vol. IV, Muster Rolls of the Militia, 1790-1800; Vol. V, Muster Rolls of the Militia, 1800-1810; Vol. VI, Marriage and Baptismal Certificates of Lehigh and Lancaster Counties; Vol. VII, Pennsylvania Volunteers, War of 1812-14; Vol. VIII, Pennsylvania Volunteers, War of 1812-14; Vol. IX, Miscellaneous Papers, 1812-1814; Drafted Troops, 1812-14, Pensioners, 1812-14; Vol. X, Expenditures by the State of Pennsylvania on Account of the United States, 1812-14; Vol. XI, Election Returns to 1790; Vol. XII, Forfeited Estates, Inventories and Sales; Vol. XIII, Forfeited Estates, Inventories and Sales; Vol. XIV, Memorandum Book of Dr. John Ewing with Account of a Journey to Settle the Boundary of Pennsylvania, May, 1784. Seventh Series—five volumes—edited by Thomas Lynch Montgomery, 1914: Index to Sixth Series. Colonial Records—16 volumes—Minutes of the Provincial Council, the Council of Safety and the Supreme Executive Council.

ARMS OF PENN FAMILY—The motto of Admiral Penn, father of William Penn, was "Dum Clavum Teneam," meaning "While I hold the helm," or less literally "While I hold the helm the ship sails safely."

ARMSBY, HENRY PRENTISS, chemist, was born at Northbridge, Mass., September 21, 1853. He graduated from the Worcester Polytechnic Institute with the M. S. degree in 1871 and from Sheffield Scientific School of Yale University with the Ph. D. degree in 1874. During the next year he studied at the University of Leipzig in Germany, specializing in animal nutrition. From 1877-1879, he was a chemist at the Connecticut Agricultural Experimental Station; for two years he was vice-principal and professor at the Storrs (Conn.) Agricultural School, after which he became professor of agricultural chemistry at the University of Wisconsin. In 1886, he was made assistant director of the Agricultural Station. In 1887, he organized the Pennsylvania Agricultural Station, serving as its director for twenty years. From 1890 to 1902, he was dean of the School of Agriculture, and from 1907 to his death, he was director of the Institute of Animal Industry at the Pennsylvania Agricultural Station. He assisted in developing a respiration calorimeter for observation on farm animals. The results of his experiments are included in the following publications: "The Principles of Animal Nutrition with Special Reference to the Nutrition of Farm Animals" (1903), "The Nutrition of Farm Animals" (1917), "The Conservation of Food Energy" (1918), "The Animal as a Converter of Matter and Energy," prepared in 1925, after his death by C. R. Moulton. In 1918, he was sent to Europe by the United States as a member of the Inter-Allied Scientific Food Commission. His death occurred on October 19, 1921.

ARMSTRONG, JOHN, author and soldier, was born at Carlisle, on November 25, 1758. During the Revolutionary War he served as a member of the staff of General Gates. From 1804 to 1810, he served as United States Minister to France and after that in the same capacity in Spain. From 1813 to 1814, he was Secretary of War in Madison's Cabinet. He was the author of "The Newburg Addresses," written in 1783, and of "Notices of the War of 1812." His death occurred at Red Hook, N. Y., April 1, 1843.

ARMSTRONG COUNTY—Formed from part of Allegheny, Westmoreland and Lycoming, March 12, 1800. Named for General John Armstrong. Land area, 653 square miles; population (1930), 79,298; (1920), 75,568. County seat, Kittanning, laid out in 1804.

ARNOLD, ABRAHAM KERNS, soldier, was born at Bedford, March 24, 1837. After receiving military education at West Point, he was commissioned 1st Lieutenant, Fifth Cavalry, on July 17, 1862. He was promoted to the rank of captain and then to that of major and was awarded the Congressional Medal of Honor for the high character of his military services during the Civil War. He led expeditions against the Apaches in Arizona in 1879 and against the Crows in 1887. He commanded the Second Division of the 7th Army Corps in Cuba during the Spanish-American War.

ARNOLD, BENEDICT, Revolutionary patriot and traitor, was born at Norwich, Conn., January 14, 1741. His early training was of the most rigid New England type and at fourteen he ran away, joined the Colonial troops in the French and Indian War, was brought back, but again ran away, joined the troops and served on Lakes Champlain and George. When he was twenty-one he became a druggist and bookseller in New Haven and later sold horses and mules, travelling between Quebec and the West Indies. At the outbreak of the Revolution he organized a volunteer company, assisted in the defense of Fort Ticonderoga, captured the fort at St. Johns, and with his personal savings aided the Colonial service. In 1775, Arnold led an unsuccessful attack upon Quebec, and on January 10, 1776, was made a brigadier-general by Congress. His defense of Lakes Champlain and George and Fort Ticonderoga in 1776 upset the plans of Howe, the British general, and forced him to retreat temporarily to Canada. On September 19 and October 7, 1777, Arnold and his troops took part in the battles at Freeman's Farm and Bemis Heights. At the latter place Burgoyne surrendered and Arnold was wounded. In June, 1778, the British evacuated Philadelphia, and, upon the order of Washington, Arnold became commander of the city. Here he fell in love with and married Margaret Shippen, the belle of Philadelphia. Because of his attempts to maintain a brilliant social existence, he lived beyond his income and fell heavily into debt. He was also accused of using his military office for private gain and his soldiers for personal and menial duties. In December, 1779, he was tried by court martial and found guilty of some of the charges, among them being the violation of Articles of War in permitting a vessel to leave a port in the possession of the enemy and enter a port in the United States. They recommended a reprimand from Washington. About this time Arnold began his betrayal of the American cause, entering into correspondence with Sir Henry Chilton sometime in 1779. Through an elaborate code and spy system he was able to give valuable information to the British. In the summer of 1780, Arnold obtained command of West Point and with Major John Andre, the British adjutant-general, made plans for surrendering the fort to the

British. Andre's capture by the Americans in his attempt to reach the British lines after a conference with Arnold brought to light the latter's betrayal. Arnold immediately joined the British army, and at the conclusion of the war in December, 1781, with his family, sailed for England. Here he endured much unpopularity and ridicule, failed to procure active military service and entered into business ventures in which he was not successful. He died in London, June 14, 1801.

ARTIFICIAL TEETH—First manufactured in Philadelphia by Michael Poree, dental surgeon.

ARTISTS AND MANUFACTURERS, ASSOCIATION OF—Was organized in Philadelphia, in 1803, for the collection of statistics of domestic industry and the promotion of the arts and manufactures.

ASBURY, BISHOP, an early leader of the Methodist Church in America. He was first known as a "Superintendent" under John Wesley, founder of the denomination, but later took the title of bishop, which title has since been perpetuated.

ASHBURNER, CHARLES ALBERT, geologist, was born in Philadelphia, February 9, 1854. He graduated with honors from the University of Pennsylvania, was appointed Assistant State Geologist in 1875. He was an acknowledged authority on coal and natural gas fields. He became associated with the Westinghouse interests in Western Pennsylvania in 1886. He prepared more than twenty of Pennsylvania's State Geological reports and contributed widley to professional journals. He died in Pittsburgh, December 24, 1889.

ASHHURST, JOHN, president of the College of Physicians in Philadelphia. was graduated at the University of Pennsylvania Medical School in 1857. He served in the Civil War as a surgeon, in several Philadelphia hospitals and became president of the College of Physicians in Philadelphia in 1898. He was also a member of the medical faculty at the University of Pennsylvania. His most important publications included an "International Encyclopedia of Surgery" and "Lippincott's New Medical Dictionary." He died in 1900 at the age of 61 years.

ASHLAND, a borough in Schuylkill County, 12 miles northwest of Pottsville, is located in the heart of the great anthracite coal field. It was founded in 1850 and named for Henry Clay's home at Lexington, Ky. Mining is the principal industry, but the town also has machine shops, foundries, and factories. The State Miner's Hospital is located here. Population (1930), 7,164; (1920), 6,666.

ASSESSORS—Local officials who place a valuation on taxable property. Voters owning no property are assessed by them for their profession or occupation. They also prepare a list of the voters of the district and are present at elections for the purpose of giving information regarding the right of any person to vote. One of the duties is to list all children between the ages of six and twenty-one.

ASSOCIATE REFORMED CHURCH, a branch of Presbyterianism, formed in 1733, with Ebenezer Erskine as its leader, as a result of trouble caused by the revival of lay patronage. In 1752, the Associate Presbytery of Pennsylvania was formed under the leadership of two gentlemen, Gellatly and Arnot, sent from Scotland by the Anti-Burgher Synod. The Burgher Synod, in 1766, sent Rev. Telfair to America. He became pastor of the Burgher Congregation, Shippen Street, Philadelphia. An attempt was made by the Burgher Synods in this country to unite, but the Scottish Church would not permit it. In 1776, the old Presbytery in Pennsylvania divided into the Pennsylvania Presbytery and the Presbytery of New York. However, in October, 1782, the three Presbyteries met in Philadelphia and formed a synod called the Associate Reformed Synod of North America. Early Associate Reformed Churches were located in the Cumberland Valley and in Western Pennsylvania, from which point they became diffused throughout the United States.

ASYLUM, THE FRENCH SETTLEMENT IN—During the French Revolution the nobility of France were subject to so many horrors at the hands of the people that in the fall of 1789 many of them began to seek permanent refuge in America. Among the refugees were Antoine Omer Talon and Louis de Noailles (brother-in-law of Lafayette, who had fought for America during the Revolution and who had received Cornwallis' surrender). They founded a settlement in the valley of the north branch of the Susquehanna River in what is now Bradford County, which they called Azylum or Azilum. The town plot which covered three hundred acres was carefully laid out in the form of a parallelogram, with a large square in the center and houses for slaves along the bank of the river. On April 25, 1794, an Asylum Company was formed with Robert Morris as president and Omer Talon and Adam Hoops, agents. The settlers at Asylum lived in log houses more palatial than those of the other settlers in the new country. The community also included a school house, chapel, shops and a theatre. Great interest was displayed in landscape gardening and in the building of wide streets. Plans were made for the reception of the French queen, Marie Antoinette, but she was put to death before her friends were able to complete arrangements for her trip to America. The house built for her, known as the "Queen's House" and "La Grande Maison" was occupied by several families until 1840 when it was demolished. When Napolean was made Consul, in 1802, the French emigrants were pardoned and many of the Asylum settlers returned to their own country. Others moved to various parts of the new country. Thus ten years after it had been begun, Asylum was almost entirely abandoned.

ATHENEUM, PHILADELPHIA, originated in 1813 when several young men established rooms for reading and recreation. By the following year, when the articles of association were adopted, the membership had grown to one hundred. A room was opened over the bookshop of Matthew Carey at the corner of Fourth and Chestnut Streets. Later the Atheneum was moved to Philosophical Hall, remaining there for almost thirty years, in 1847, occupying its new building at 219 S. Sixth Street.

TIOGA POINT (1843)

ATHENS (FORMERLY TIOGA POINT)—The oldest village in Northern Pennsylvania that remains substantially as laid out by its founders. The land north of the old town plat, and between the two rivers, "Great" or Susquehanna, and the Tioga Branch, which is now the main center of Athens, was laid off in irregular lines and sold by the Susquehanna Company by numbers. The noted Tioga Treaty was held there, on the banks of the Susquehanna, November 23, 1790. Between these two rivers is a broad and level plain, and on this was the Tioga Point of the early settlers, a place of the most historic importance of any in Bradford County. Here was the Indian town, first of the Susquehannocks, and then of the Iroquois, until the Revolution. The grandest gathering of military forces which has ever been assembled in Northern Pennsylvania was witnessed here when the two armies of Sullivan and Clinton joined their forces to devastate the Indian country. The most important military operations of this campaign were held here and it was the base of supplies and the advance post of occupation. This was the most attractive part of the Susquehanna Company's purchase. Athens was incorporated as a borough March 27, 1831, and even later than that date letters were directed to Tioga Point.

ATHERTON, GEORGE WILLIAM, educator. Born, Boxford, Mass., June 20, 1837. Educated at Phillips Exeter Academy and Yale University. Was professor of political economy and constitutional law at Rutgers University, 1869-1882; admitted to bar of New Jersey in 1878; president of Pennsylvania State College, 1882-1906. Died Bellefonte, July 24, 1906.

ATLEE, SAMUEL JOHN, military officer, was born at Lancaster in 1739. At the age of sixteen, he entered the provincial service, obtaining command of a company under Col. Burd. He was present at Braddock's defeat and afterwards was twice taken prisoner, once by the Indians and a second time by the French. After eleven years of service, he studied law and practiced his profession until the beginning of the Revolution. In 1776, he organized the First Regiment of State Infantry, composed of men from the Pequea Valley, Lancaster County and from Chester County, and was appointed colonel. He served with honor at the Battle of Long Island, where he was taken prisoner and confined for eighteen months. From 1778 to 1782, he was a member of the Continental Congress. In January, 1781, he, with Gen. Sullivan and Dr. Witherspoon, was sent by Congress to conciliate the mutineers of the Pennsylvania Line. In 1784, he was a commissioner, representing Pennsylvania, at the treaty of Forts Stanwix and McIntosh, with the deputies of the Six Nations and the Wyandot and Delaware Indians. He was a member of the Pennsylvania General Assembly in 1782, 1785 and 1786, and died in Philadelphia in November, 1786.

ATLEE, WASHINGTON LEMUEL, surgeon; born, Lancaster, February 22, 1808. Specialized in ovariotomy and the removal of uterine fibroid tumors, being a pioneer in this field of surgery. Died September 6, 1878.

ATLEE, WILLIAM AUGUSTUS, judge, was born at Philadelphia, July 1, 1735. At an early age he removed to Lancaster where he studied law under Edward Shippen. He was admitted to the bar, August 3, 1758, and subsequently became one of the most eminent lawyers of his day. Upon the outbreak of the Revolution he became an ardent member of the Whig Party, and in 1776, was chosen chairman of the Committee of Public Safety of Lancaster. On August 16, 1777, he was appointed second judge of the Supreme Court of Pennsylvania, and was reappointed August 9, 1784. On August 17, 1791, he became president judge of the district comprising Chester, Lancaster, York and Dauphin Counties, which position he held at the time of his death on September 9, 1793.

AUDUBON, JOHN JAMES, ornithologist, was born in Louisiana and in 1798 moved to a farm on the Perkiomen near Schuylkill Falls, in Pennsylvania. Here he became interested in ornithology. In 1810, he sailed down the Ohio with his wife and child on a bird sketching expedition and subsequently spent much time in research of the forests of this country. He journeyed to England in 1826 in the interests of his publication, "The Birds of America," later returning to America at intervals for further study and research. He died in 1851.

AUGHWICK CREEK—Tributary to Juniata River. Sub-basin, Lower Juniata; source, formed by junction of Sideling Hill Creek and Little Aughwick Creek, near Maddensville, Springfield Township, Southeastern Huntingdon County; course, northeasterly to Juniata River; mouth, three miles southeast of Mt. Union; length, twenty-one and one-half miles.

AUSBUNDT, THE, Amish hymnal, the first edition of which was printed in Germany, in 1564, but its origin is in a group of hymns first sung by prisoners of the Anabaptist faith in Passan, Bavaria, in 1537. This edition now used only by conservative Amish was early accepted by South German and Swiss Mennonites. The tunes as well as the words have been handed down for the last four hundred years. Said to be the oldest hymnal in use in the United States.— *See* SMITH; THE MENNONITE IMMIGRATION TO PENNSYLVANIA.

AVERELL, WILLIAM WOODS, military officer, born Cameron, N. Y.' November 5, 1832. Educated at West Point. Was appointed Colonel of the Third Pennsylvania Cavalry at the beginning of the Civil War. Distinguished himself as a cavalry raider and commander and at close of war was brevetted major-general of volunteers. Died Bath, N. Y., February 3, 1900.

AVERY, OTIS, dentist, born Bridgwater, Oneida County, N. Y., August 19, 1808. Studied dentistry and practiced at Honesdale, for sometime being the only dentist between Honesdale and Utica, N. Y. At the time of his death at Honesdale, in 1904, he was the oldest practicing dentist in the United States.

AYMISH—*See* AMISH.

AYMONISTS—*See* AMISH.

BACH CHOIR, of Bethlehem, was organized in 1898, an offspring of the Bethlehem Choral Union, formed in 1882, by Dr. J. Fred Wolle, who continued to direct the new musical organization. Festivals were presented yearly from 1900 to 1905. In the latter year, Dr. Wolle became professor of music at the University of California. Upon his return, in 1911, the choir was reorganized and the yearly festivals continued. The organization has received the support of Charles M. Schwab, of the Bethlehem Steel Company, and of Edward W. Bok, of Philadelphia. Through the financial assistance of these men it has been possible for the choir to present concerts to large audiences in New York and Philadelphia. Through the Bach Choir, often termed the best in the

United States, Bethlehem has become an important center of musical art and Dr. Wolle a leading exponent of Bach.

BACHE, ALEXANDER DALLAS, scientist; born Philadelphia, July 19, 1806. Graduated from U. S. Military Academy in 1825, at the head of his class. Became professor of natural philosophy and chemistry at the University of Pennsylvania in 1828; was the organizer and first president of Girard College, 1836. Established a magnetical and meteorological observatory at Girard College and was appointed superintendent of U. S. Coast Survey, in 1843. Regent of Smithsonian Institution, 1846-1847; active member of U. S. Sanitary Commission during Civil War; president of National Academy of Sciences in 1863. Author of "Education in Europe"(1839), "Observations at the Magnetic and Meteorological Observatory at Girard College" (1840-1847), and Annual Reports of the U. S. Coast Survey. He died February 17, 1867.

BACHE, FRANKLIN, chemist, born Philadelphia, October 25, 1792; professor chemistry, Philadelphia College of Pharmacy, 1831; professor chemistry, Jefferson Medical College, 1841; author "System of Chemistry for Students of Medicine" (1819), and joint author Wood and Bache "Dispensatory of the United States" (1833). He died March 19, 1864.

BACHE, HARTMAN, military engineer, born Philadelphia, September 3, 1798. Entered U. S. Topographical Corps, in the work of which he was engaged for forty-seven years. Appointed brigadier-general, March 13, 1865; was retired March 7, 1867. Outstanding among his accomplishments were the building of the Delaware breakwater and the application of iron screw piles for the foundations of lighthouses on sandy shoals and coral reefs. He died October 8, 1872.

BACHE, SARAH, philanthropist; born, Philadelphia, September 11, 1744, the only daughter of Benjamin Franklin. Organized relief work during the Revolutionary War. Married Richard Bache. Died October 5, 1808.

BAER, JOHN, printer; born, Leacock Township, Lancaster County, January 31, 1795; learned the printer's trade in Columbia and Harrisburg; published Der Volksfreund und Beobachter; succeeded William Albright in the publication of the Agricultural Almanac, in 1848; after his death, November 6, 1858, the Almanac was published by John Baer's Sons.

BAILLY, JOSEPH A., sculptor; born, Paris, 1825; came to Philadelphia, in 1850. "Adam and Eve," "Eve and Her Two Children," and the marble monument of Washington in front of the State House are his productions. He died June 15, 1883.

BAIRD, ABSALOM, military officer; born, Washington, Pa., August 20, 1824; graduated from U. S. Military Academy; entered artillery department of the army in 1849, in active service from the Manassas Campaign in 1861, until after the surrender of Gen. Johnston's Army in 1865; commissioned brigadier-general of volunteers, April 28, 1862, and major-general, September 1, 1862, for service in Atlanta Campaign; major-general, U. S. Army, March 13, 1865, for services during the war; served as staff inspector-general from 1885 to his retirement in 1888. Died June 14, 1905.

BAIRD, HENRY MARTYN, author; born, Philadelphia, January 17, 1832. Graduated from University of City of New York, 1850; lived in Europe for several years; studied theology at Union and Princeton Theological Seminaries; professor Greek Language and Literature, City College of New York, 1859; author, "History of the Rise of the Huguenots," 1879; "The Huguenots and Henry of Navarre," 1886, and "The Huguenots and the Revocation of the Edict of Nantes," 1895.

BAIRD, ROBERT, historian; born, Fayette County, October 6, 1798; graduate of Jefferson College; corresponding secretary, American and Foreign Christian Union, 1849-1855, 1861-1863; author, "History of the Waldenses, Alligenses, and Vaudois," "History of the Temperance Societies," 1836; "Religion in America," 1844; "Protestantism in Italy," 1845. Died at Yonkers, N. Y., March 15, 1863.

BAIRD, SPENCER FULLERTON, naturalist; born, Reading, February 3, 1823; professor of natural sciences, Dickinson College, Carlisle, Pa., 1845; assistant secretary, Smithsonian Institution, 1850; U. S. commissioner of fish and fisheries, 1871; secretary of the Smithsonian Institution, 1878; founder of the National Museum; author, "Catalogue of North American Reptiles," 1853; "Birds of North America" (with Cassin and Lawrence), 1860; "Mammals of North America," 1858; "History of North American Birds" (with Brewer and Ridgway), 1874-1884.

BALD EAGLE, chief of the Wolf Clan of Delawares, for whom Bald Eagle Township in Clinton County, Bald Eagle Mountain and Bald Eagle Valley in Clinton and Centre Counties are named. His friendship with the British at the time of the Revolutionary War brought terror to the settlements on the West Branch of the Susquehanna. Among the savage deeds which he committed was the shooting of James Brady, son of Captain John Brady, near Williamsport, August 8, 1778. In June, 1779, the chief was killed by Samuel Brady, brother of John.

BALD EAGLE CREEK—Tributary to West Branch Susquehanna River. Sub-basin, Middle West Branch Susquehanna; source, in Taylor Township,

Southwestern Centre County; course, Northeasterly into Clinton County to West Branch Susquehanna River; mouth, near Lock Haven; length, fifty-one miles. Named for a famous Munsee chief, called Woapalanne, "Bald Eagle."

BALDWIN, HENRY, jurist and author; born, New Haven, Conn., January 14, 1780; graduated from Yale University in 1797; studied law and removed to Pittsburgh, where he began his practice; member of Congress for three terms; was appointed Justice of the Supreme Court in 1830; died Philadelphia, April 21, 1844.

BALDWIN LOCOMOTIVE WORKS were founded by Matthias W. Baldwin, who, while in partnership with David Mason, a machinist, in Philadelphia, began the construction of stationary steam engines, and later of locomotives.

BALLIET, THOMAS M., educator; born, March 1, 1852; educated at Franklin and Marshall College, Lancaster, and at Yale University; superintendent of public schools, Springfield, Mass., and associate editor of the "Pedagogical Seminary."

BALLOON ASCENSIONS—As early as 1842, John Wise, deemed "the American Aeronaut, par excellence," prepared to make his thirty-ninth balloon ascension, from Gettysburg. John McClellan, a young resident of the town who was anxious to make the ascension, upon learning that he would be unable to accompany Wise, paid the latter fifty dollars for permission to make the trip alone. Taking the affair as a joke, Wise accepted the money and allowed McClellan to enter the balloon. When he realized that the young man was serious in his intentions of riding alone, Wise became concerned and ordered McClellan to climb from his seat. The latter refused, cut the rope and was off, followed by hurried directions from Wise. The balloon traveled smoothly toward York, where McClellan was determined to stop. Upon reaching his destination the young man, attempting to follow directions by pulling at the valve rope, tugged so hard that the rope was pulled completely from its hinges. However, the balloon formed a parachute and McClellan reached the earth safely.

BANGOR, a borough in Northampton County, 14 miles north of Easton; located on Lackawanna, Lehigh and New England Railroads; industries, numerous slate quarries, silk, gloves, hosiery, and furniture. Population (1930), 5,824; (1920), 5,402.

BANK OF NORTH AMERICA was established in Philadelphia by act of Congress on May 26, 1781. Congress acting under the Articles of Confederation had no independent power to levy taxes. Robert Morris, who was then superintendent of finance, suggested that a bank be established to provide the government with funds. The bank was chartered on December 31, 1781, with $400,000 capital and the right to use promissory notes as legal tender for payment of taxes, duties, etc., to the United States. This plan aided in keeping veterans of the Revolutionary War in sympathy with the government in the trying years before the adoption of the federal constitution.

BANK OF THE UNITED STATES, THE, was established in Philadelphia, with branches throughout the country, by an act of Congress, February 8, 1791. The success of the Bank of North America and other similar institutions that had been the source of banking capital in the country before 1791, led Alexander Hamilton, secretary of the treasury under Washington, to propose the establishment of a national bank in his financial plan of 1790. The charter of this bank was limited to twenty years and in 1808, an application was made to congress for its renewal. Local banks increased in the era of the first national bank, so that although Albert Gallatin, secretary of the treasury, advised renewal the bill was defeated in the Senate. After the War of 1812, many local banks suspended specie payments and the financial condition of the country was such that a Second United States Bank was chartered on April 3, 1816, with popular approval. It opened in Philadelphia in 1817 under a twenty-year charter with $35,000,000 capital, $7,000,000 of which was subscribed by the United States and $28,000,000 by individuals. Government funds were deposited here and consequently the bank was in a position to discount readily and to aid commercial developments of the country. When Andrew Jackson became president, in 1829, he found the bank a potent influence in the financial affairs of the country and he believed that as such it was a dangerous institution. He frequently attacked the bank as failing to fulfill its purpose of establishing a uniform currency and also doubted its constitutionality. In 1832, Jackson recommended the removal of public funds from the bank and the sale of the bank stock held by the United States. Congress refused to follow this recommendation and after its adjournment the president asked William Duane, then secretary of the treasury, to withdraw the government deposits and place them in designated State banks. Duane refused to follow Jackson's directions and was dismissed. Roger B. Taney succeeded him and in October, 1833, removed the deposits. The panic that followed only served to impress Jackson with the dangerous power of the monied institution that he had destroyed. In 1836, the operations of the bank ceased with the expiration of the charter. Experience taught the business men of the country the importance of conservative banking and as a result the states developed legislation that protected the public and encouraged commercial enterprises at the same time.

BAPTISTS IN PENNSYLVANIA—"Thomas Dungan, an old minister, came from Rhode Island to the Colony of Penn, in 1684. He gathered a church at Cold Spring, near Bristol, Bucks County, 'of which,' says Morgan Edwards, in 1770, 'nothing remains but a graveyard and the names of the families that belonged to it—the Dungans, Gardners, Woods, Doyles, etc.' He died in 1688, and was buried at Cold Spring.

"The second church founded in Pennsylvania was the Lower Dublin, or Pennepek. In the year 1686, Elias Keach, of London, a wild young man, arrived in Philadelphia. He dressed in black and wore bands to pass for a minister. He obtained an opportunity to preach in the house of a Baptist in Lower Dublin, and when he had spoken for some time he 'stopped short, looked like a man astonished, and the audience concluded that he had been seized with some sudden disorder.' But they speedily learned that he was deeply convicted of sin. He went to Father Dungan, of Cold Spring, who pointed him to Jesus; he soon had peace in believing, and he was baptized and ordained by Mr. Dungan. He formed a church of twelve persons at Pennepek in January, 1688, and became their pastor. He labored with burning zeal, and, considering the difficulties, with astonishing success, through Pennsylvania and New Jersey, and established missions at 'the Falls (Trenton, Burlington, Cohansey, Salem, Pennsneck, Chester, and Philadelphia),' and he maintained preaching at Cold Spring and Middletown. He had the zeal of an enthusiast, and 'he was considered the chief apostle of the Baptists in these parts of America.' He returned to his birthplace in 1692, but the missions in several cases became churches, and the spirit he planted in these communities created the Philadelphia Association a few years after he left the colony.

"The Great Valley Church was constituted in 1711. The Brandywine Church was formed in 1715. The Montgomery Church was organized in 1719. The Tulpehocken Church was founded in 1738, and the Southampton in 1746. The Philadelphia Church had an existence either as a branch of Lower Dublin or as an independent community from 1698, the former is the more probable. But in 1746, to settle doubts on this question and to protect legacies, the church was formally incorporated. The New Britain Church was organized in 1754, and the Vincent in 1770.

"Since our national independence was secured, about 200 churches have arisen in the counties east of the Susquehanna River and its North Branch. Some of these became extinct, or changed names and locations, so that a clear and complete sketch of them all, however interesting, would be entirely impracticable in this work.

"The first known English Baptist preacher on the Susquehanna was the first person named as slain in the first Wyoming Massacre, in 1763. He was William Marsh, a New England Separatist, but came from Wantage, N. J., into Pennsylvania. The first church was formed in Pittston, in December, 1776. The first Baptists in Northern Pennsylvania were from Connecticut, Rhode Island, Massachusetts, Virginia, New York, and New Jersey. They were Revolutionary soldiers and pioneers of the settlements, both ministers and private members.

"A portion of Southwestern Pennsylvania was taken up by Virginians. There were Baptists among them, and a church was founded at Aughwick, Huntingdon County, in 1776; at Konoloway, Bedford, in 1764; at Sideling Hill, Fulton, in 1790; at Turkeyfoot, Somerset, in 1775; at Great Bethel (Uniontown),

Fayette, in 1770; at Goshen, Greene, in 1773; at Peter's Creek, Washington, in 1773; at Pigeon Creek, in 1775; Loyalhanna, in 1775; Forks of Yough, in 1777. Enon Church arose in 1791; Beulah, Cambria County, in 1797; Pittsburgh, in 1812."—Baptist Encyclopedia, Vol. II, by Cathcart.

BAPTISTS OR BRETHREN, GERMAN, commonly called Dunkers or Tunkers, but now Church of the Brethren, originated in Germany, in 1708, under the leadership of Alexander Mack. Because of persecutions they moved to the Rhine Valley, to Holland, and finally to America, the first group arriving in Philadelphia in the fall of 1719. Ten years later, another group, accompanied by Mack, arrived. They organized the first church in this country in Germantown, on December 25, 1723. From Germantown they went to Oley, Skippack, Conestoga and other sections of the state. The Brethren are characterized by their plainness of garb, the plainness of their church buildings, and their refusal to take an oath, to fight or to go to law. In connection with the Lord's Supper they hold a Love Feast, at which the ceremonies of feet washing and passing of the holy kiss are observed. They adhere to baptism by immersion and strongly oppose infant baptism. In 1926, the Brethren were distributed throughout New Jersey, Pennsylvania, Ohio, Indiana, Illinois, Michigan, Wisconsin, Iowa, Nebraska, Kansas, Maryland, District of Columbia, Virginia, West Virginia, Kentucky, Tennessee, Washington and California, having in Pennsylvania a membership of 5,222.—See BRUMBAUGH; HISTORY OF THE CHURCH OF THE BRETHREN.

BAPTISTS, SEVENTH DAY, a religious organization founded by Conrad Beissel, who came to America from Germany, in 1720. Beissel was at first a Presbyterian, but tending toward the pietistic he came under the influence of the Dunkers or German Baptists upon his arrival in this country. Believing that the church erred in the observance of the first day as the Sabbath, he withdrew, and founded a settlement on the banks of the Cocalico Creek, in Lancaster County. For a time he lived alone, but was gradually joined by men and women, interested in the formation of a monastic society. In May, 1733, the first of a group of buildings, still standing at what is now Ephrata, was erected. The Seventh Day Baptists are strict in their observance of the seventh day as the Sabbath. They also observe baptism by trine forward immersion, and foot washing in connection with the Communion service. With the death of their leader the organization declined. In 1926, the membership totaled 144, and included four church buildings, all located in Pennsylvania.—See also EPHRATA CLOISTER.

BARD, JOHN, physician; born near Philadelphia, February, 1716; practiced in Philadelphia for several years, then moved to New York. Was elected first president of the New York Medical Society, in 1788; was directly responsible for establishment of a hospital on Bedloe's Island where ship's passengers suffering from contagious diseases could be cared for; died March 30, 1799.

BARD, SAMUEL, physician; born, Philadelphia, April 1, 1742; practiced at Philadelphia and New York; founded the medical school of King's College, now Columbia University, where he was dean of the faculty; served as president of the New York College of Physicians and Surgeons, the successor of the Medical School of King's College; died May 24, 1821.

BARD, THOMAS ROBERT, politician; born at Chambersburg, December 8, 1841. In 1864, he went to California in the interests of Thomas A. Scott. In 1892, was the only Republican elector for California. Was unanimously elected to United States Senate, February 7, 1900, serving until 1905; died Heuneme, California, March 5, 1915.

BARKER, GEORGE FREDERICK, physicist; born, Charlestown, Mass., July 14, 1835; graduated from Sheffield Scientific School, Yale University, 1858, and from Albany Medical College, 1863; member of faculty, Harvard University, Yale University, Wheaton College and Western University of Pennsylvania, now University of Pittsburgh, 1859-1872; Professor of Physics, University of Pennsylvania, 1873-1900; was United States Commissioner at the International Electrical Exhibition in Paris, 1881. Here he received the Legion of Honor decoration, with rank of commander. He died in 1910.

BARKER, WHARTON, financier and publicist; born, Philadelphia, May 1, 1846; graduated from University of Pennsylvania, 1866; became associated with banking firm of Barker Brothers & Co., becoming special financial agent of the Russian government. In 1869, founded the Penn Monthly, a periodical dealing with political, economic and social conditions; proposed the names of Garfield and Harrison for the presidency and opposed a third term for General Grant; became candidate for president of the Populist Party, in 1900. While in Russia was interested in development of coal and iron mining there, also directed the building of four cruisers for that country; favored a commercial union of all American nations and opposed all temporary arbitration treaties; died Philadelphia, April 8, 1921.

BARNARD, GEORGE GREY, sculptor; born, Bellefonte, May 24, 1863; educated at Chicago Art Institute and at the Ecole Nationale des Beaux Arts, Paris, 1884-1887; received a gold medal at the Paris Exposition in 1900; was for many years professor of Sculpture at Art Students' League, New York; among his works are: "Brotherly Love," "The Two Natures" (in the Metropolitan Museum), "The God Pan" (Central Park), and "The Hewer." He also executed a group of statues for the state capitol at Harrisburg. His home is in New York.

BARNARD, ISAAC D., military officer and lawyer, was born at Chester, in 1791. He left his study of law with William Graham at Chester, to enlist in the War of 1812. He was commissioned captain of the 14th U. S. Infantry, served with distinction at Fort George and in June, 1813, was advanced to the rank of major. Later he rendered valuable service at La Cole's Mill, with Izard's Army at Plattsburg and at the Battle of Lyons' Creek. At the conclusion of the war in 1815, Barnard continued his law study and was admitted to the bar on May 1, 1816. He advanced rapidly in his profession, serving four years as deputy attorney general of Chester County. In 1820, he was elected to the State Senate. He became major-general of the 3rd Division of the Pennsylvania Militia about 1824, and assisted in receiving Lafayette on his visit to Pennsylvania. Governor Shulze appointed him Secretary of the Commonwealth in 1826, and shortly afterward he was elected to the United States Senate where he served until 1831. Barnard died in West Chester, February 18, 1834.

BARNARD, SAMUEL, a native of England, came to America in 1819, and settled in Susquehanna County. He compiled a "Pollyglott Grammar of the Hebrew, Chaldee, Syriac, Greek, Latin, English, French, Italian, Spanish, and German languages, reduced to one common rule of syntax, and an uniform mode of declension and conjugation as far as practicable." This grammar was published in 1825 and among the subscribers was President John Quincy Adams. Barnard presented Gen. Lafayette with a specially bound copy. Barnard's death occurred in 1850 in Kentucky.

BARNES, JOSEPH K., surgeon; born Philadelphia, July 21, 1817; attended medical school, University of Pennsylvania; served as assistant surgeon during Mexican War; served in office of surgeon-general at the outbreak of the Civil War; appointed medical inspector with rank of colonel, 1863; became brigadier-general in September, 1863; promoted to rank of major-general, U. S. Army, 1865; served as surgeon-general from 1864-1882; died Washington, D. C., April 5, 1883.

BARRETT, BENJAMIN FISK, Swedenborgian clergyman; born, Dresden, Maine, 1808; graduated from Bowdoin College, in 1832; pastor of Swedenborgian Church in New York, Cincinnati and Philadelphia; author, "Life of Swedenborg," "Letters on the Divine Trinity," "Catholicity of the New Church," "Episcopalianism," "New View of Hell," "Swedenborg and Channing," "Heaven Revealed"; died at Germantown, Philadelphia, August 6, 1892.

BARTLETT, WILLIAM HOLMES CHAMBERS, soldier and scientist; born, Lancaster County, 1809; educated at West Point, where he was assistant professor from 1827-1829; employed in the construction of Fort Munroe and Fort Adams; assistant engineer at Washington, 1832-34; assistant professor, West Point, 1834-36; professor of philosophy, West Point, 1836-71; member,

Natural Academy of Sciences; author, "Treatise on Optics," "Synthetical Mechanics," "Acoustics and Optics," "Analytical Mechanics," "Spherical Astronomy"; died February 11, 1893.

BARTON, BENJAMIN SMITH, naturalist; born, Lancaster, February 10, 1766; student of natural sciences and medicine at Philadelphia, Edinburgh and London; received his medical degree at Gottingen; practiced medicine in Philadelphia; professor, successively, of botany, natural history, materia medica, and theory and practice of medicine at University of Pennsylvania; died Philadelphia, December 19, 1815.

BARTON, WILLIAM PAUL CRILLON, botanist; born, Philadelphia, November 17, 1786; nephew of Benjamin Smith Barton; attended Princeton University and the Medical School of the University of Pennsylvania; was surgeon in United States Navy; became professor of botany in Jefferson Medical College, in 1815; author, "Flora of North America," "Vegetable Materia Medica of the United States," "Compendium Florae"; died February 29, 1856.

BARTRAM, JOHN, botanist; born, Chester County, March 23, 1699; founded the first botanical garden in America at Kingsessing. He is called the "father of American botany." Corresponded with European botanists; is often spoken of as "The greatest natural botanist in the world." Died September 22, 1777.

BARTRAM, WILLIAM, botanist and ornithologist; born, Kingsessing, February 9, 1739, a son of John Bartram; published "Travels Through North and South Carolina, and East and West Florida," the result of five years of study in the southern states; died at Kingsessing, July 22, 1823.

BASCOM, FLORENCE, geologist; was born at Williamstown, Mass., the daughter of Dr. John Bascom. She attended the University of Wisconsin and the Johns Hopkins University, being the first woman to receive a degree from the latter institution. She was graduated from the University of Wisconsin, in 1882, with the degrees of B. A., and B. L., in 1884, was granted the B. S. degree, and in 1887, the M. A. by the same institution. In 1893, when she received the Ph. D. degree from Johns Hopkins University, she was the first woman to receive that degree from an American college. From 1896 to 1905, she was associate editor of the "American Geologist." Later she was a professor at Bryn Mawr College and in 1899, was appointed Supervisor of the Geological Survey of Chester County. Since 1909, she has been geologist of the United States Geological Survey.

BATES, DAVID, poet; born, 1810. His poems of which "Speak Gently" is the most generally known, were published in 1848 under the title "The Eolian." He died at Philadelphia, January 25, 1870.

BATES, SAMUEL PENNIMAN, historian; born, Mendon, Mass., January 29, 1827; principal, Meadville Academy, Meadville, superintendent of schools, Crawford County, 1857-1860; deputy state superintendent of schools, 1860-66; state historian, 1866-73; author, "Lives of the Governors of Pennsylvania," "Lectures on Mental and Moral Culture," "History of the Battle of Gettysburg," "History of the Battle of Chancellorsville," "History of Colleges in Pennsylvania"; died, 1902.

BATTLE AXE, THE—A religious sect of Southeastern Pennsylvania.— See THEOPHILUS; THE BATTLE AXE.

BATTLE OF THE KEGS—An incident which occurred January 7, 1778, during the period of the Revolution. The provincial troops constructed kegs, filled them with gunpowder and floated them down the Delaware to destroy the British ships. The kegs were so constructed that as soon as they touched the bottom of a ship, a spring lock would cause the explosion. Only the buoys which floated the kegs could be seen. This affair called forth a poem, "The Battle of the Kegs," by Francis Hopkinson.

BATTLES IN PENNSYLVANIA DURING VARIOUS WARS INCLUDE—French and Indian War: Great Meadows, May 28, 1754; Fort Necessity, July 4, 1754; Monongahela, July 9, 1755; Grant's Defeat, September 14, 1758; Loyalhanna, October 12, 1758; Bushy Run, August 5 and 6, 1763.

Revolutionary War: Brandywine, September 11, 1777; Paoli, September 20, 1777; Germantown, October 4, 1777; Wyoming, Wyoming Massacre, July 3, 1778; Indian Hill, September 29, 1778; Minisink, July 22, 1779; Fort Freeland, July 28, 1779; Lime Hill, April 14, 1782; Crooked Billet, May 1, 1778.

War of 1812: Lake Erie, September 10, 1813.

Civil War: Hanover Junction, June 30, 1863; Gettysburg, July 1-3, 1863.— See also under separate heading—GETTYSBURG, BATTLE OF.

BAUSMAN, BENJAMIN, German Reformed clergyman; born, Lancaster, January 28, 1824; founded St. Paul's Reformed Church, Reading, in 1863, and served as its pastor until his death in 1909. Was editor of The Guardian, 1867-1882, and Reformirter Hausfreund, 1882; author, "Sinai and Zion," "Wayside Gleanings in Europe," "Bible Characters," "Catechetics and Catechetical Instruction," "Precepts and Practice"; died Reading, May 8, 1909.

BAYARD, SAMUEL, jurist; born, Philadelphia, January 11, 1767, son of Col. John Bayard; graduated from Princeton University, in 1784, as valedictorian of his class; practiced law in Philadelphia until 1791. In that year he was appointed clerk of the United States Supreme Court; from 1794-1798, he served as agent in London, prosecuting American claims before the British admiralty court; from 1798-1803, he was presiding judge of Westchester County; practiced law in New York, 1803-1806. After that time he retired to Princeton, N. J. He was one of the founders of Princeton Theological Seminary, the American and New Jersey Bible Societies and the New York Historical Society; died May 12, 1840.

BEAN, BARTON A., ichthyologist; born, Bainbridge, May 21, 1860; educated at Academy, Smyrna, Del., and at Millersville State Normal School, special study in ichthyology; assistant curator of fishes, U. S. National Museum, January 4, 1881-1895; acting curator, Division of Fishes, April 1, 1895, to date (1930); author of various works of research on the fish including, "Review of the Venomous Toadfishes;" "Coloration of Fishes;" "Descriptions of New Rays from Deep Water off the South Carolina Coast" (with H. W. Fowler); "Notes on the Genus Lepomic" (with Alfred C. Weed); "Fishes of Indian River, Fla.;" "Fishes of District of Columbia;" "Fishes of Bahama Islands;" "History of the Whale Shark;" "Report of Fishes of Wilkes' Exploring Expedition and the Fishes of Maryland;" papers on Fishes in Proceedings U. S. National Museum and bulletins of Fish Commission; contributor to "*Shooting and Fishing*" and "*Forest and Stream.*"

BEAN, TARLETON HOFFMAN, ichthyologist; born, Bainbridge, October 8, 1846; graduated Columbian University, Washington, D. C., 1876; received M. S. degree, Indiana University, 1883; editor, Proceedings and Bulletins of the United States National Museum at Washington, 1878-1886; editor, "Reports and Bulletin of the U. S. Fish Commission," Washington, 1889-1892; assistant in charge of division of fish culture, United States Fish Commission, 1892-1895; curator, department of fishes, U. S. National Museum, 1880-1895; became director of N. Y. Aquarium, 1895-1898; director of forestry and fisheries, U. S. Commission to Paris, Exposition of 1900; represented U. S. Fish Commission at World's Columbian Exposition in 1893, and at the Atlanta Exposition in 1895; was appointed director of forestry and fisheries of the U. S. Commission to the Paris Exposition of 1900; chief of the fish, game and forestry departments at St. Louis Exposition, 1902-05; was honored by being made chevalier, Legion of Honor, and officer of Merite Agricole, France; knight of the Imperial Order of the Red Eagle, Germany; Order of the Rising Sun, Japan; member of the American Forestry Association, American Fisheries Society, Danish Fisheries Society and Biological Society of Washington; author and contributor to "*Forest and Stream;*" died December 28, 1916.

BEATTY, CHARLES, pioneer minister, traveled throughout Pennsylvania preaching to the frontier settlers and the Indians. His journal recording the events during a two months tour which he made in the state is valuable for its description of the country in the period following the French and Indian War.

BEATTY, JOHN, legislator; born, Bucks County, December 10, 1749; attended Princeton University and studied medicine with Dr. Rush, of Philadelphia; served in the army during the Revolutionary War, attaining rank of colonel; delegate to Continental Congress, 1783-1785; speaker of the House; member of the convention which adopted the Federal Constitution; member of Congress, 1793-1795; Secretary of State of New Jersey, 1795-1805; died Trenton, N. J., May 30, 1826.

BEAUX, CECILIA, artist; born, Philadelphia; pupil, William Sartain, the Julien School and the Lazar School, Paris; LL. D., University of Pennsylvania, 1908; A. M., Yale University, 1912; was four times awarded the Mary Smith prize, Pennsylvania Academy of Fine Arts; awarded gold medal at Paris Exposition, 1900; gold medal, Philadelphia Art Club; Dodge prize, National Academy of Design; bronze and gold medals, Carnegie Institute; gold medal of honor and Temple Gold Medal, Pennsylvania Academy of Fine Arts; Saltus Gold Medal, National Academy Design, 1913; medal of honor, Panama, 1915; gold medal, Art Institute, Chicago, 1921; gold medal, American Academy, Arts and Letters, 1926. Her work is shown at Pennsylvania Academy of Fine Arts; Toledo Art Museum; Metropolitan Museum, New York; Brooks Memorial Gallery, Memphis; John Herron Art Institute, Indianapolis; Boston Art Museum; Art Institute, Chicago; Corcoran Gallery, Washington, D. C.; exhibited at Champs de Mars, 1896, and at Societaire des Beaux Arts; director, American Federation of Arts, 1930.

BEAVER, JAMES ADDAMS, soldier and governor, was born in Millerstown, Perry County, October 21, 1837. He attended Pine Grove Mills Academy, Centre County, and graduated from Jefferson College in 1856. Afterwards he entered the law office of Hon. H. N. McAllister, at Bellefonte, and was admitted to the bar when he was barely twenty-one years old. He entered the practice of his profession as the partner of Mr. McAllister. At the outbreak of the Civil War he entered the army as first lieutenant of the Bellefonte Fencibles. He was wounded in several engagements but persisted in reentering the front at Ream's Station before he had fully recovered from a severe wound in the side received at Petersburg. Subsequently he received a wound which necessitated the amputation of his right leg. He attained successively the rank of lieutenant-colonel of the 45th Regiment, colonel of the 148th Regiment and was brevetted brigadier-general of volunteers for his meritorious conduct at Cold Harbor. After the war he resumed his law practice in the firm of McAllister and Beaver, at Bellefonte, and attained prominence in his profession. As president of the board of trustees of Pennsylvania State College, he instituted changes in the management of that institution which placed it on a sound financial footing, and which secured for its various departments much necessary equipment. For many years he was president of the Pennsylvania Y. M. C. A. General Beaver was one of the stalwart 306 who in the Republican National Convention of 1880 supported General Grant for a third term. From 1887-1891 he was governor of Pennsylvania. He died January 31, 1914.

BEAVER—A borough and county-seat of Beaver County, located on the Ohio River. The town was laid out in 1791 by the surveyor-general of the State under the direction of the Governor. By an act of March 29, 1802, Beaver was incorporated as a borough. Two years earlier when Beaver County was formed the town was designated as the county-seat. Beaver College, an institution under the Methodist Episcopal Church, founded in 1853, as the "Beaver College and Musical Institute," was located here until in 1925, it purchased Beechwood School, united the two institutions and moved to the Beechwood plant at Jenkintown. Population (1930), 5,665; (1920), 4,135.

BEAVER COLLEGE, for women, located at Jenkintown near Philadelphia, is the result of the union of two institutions, Beaver College, founded in 1853, and chartered by the Commonwealth of Pennsylvania, in 1872, and Beechwood School, founded in 1911. In 1925, Beaver College purchased the plant and operation of Beechwood and combined the faculty of the two schools. The present institution offers courses leading to a degree in Education, Liberal Arts, Public School Music, Music, Fine Arts, Speech Arts, Expression, Journalism, Health Education, Kindergarten—primary, Home Economics, Domestic Arts, Commercial Education and Secretaryship. Two-year courses in these fields are also offered. Lynn H. Harris, Ph. D., is president of the college. Enrollment (1930-1931), 485.

BEAVER COUNTY—Formed from part of Allegheny and Washington, March 12, 1800. Named for Big Beaver Creek within its borders. Land area, 429 square miles; population (1930), 149,062; (1920), 111,621. County seat, Beaver, laid out in 1791.

BEAVER FALLS, a borough in Beaver County, situated in the valley of the Big Beaver Creek. The town was laid out in 1806, by Isaac Wilson and Company, who erected a forge and charcoal furnace there; was early called Brighton and Old Brighton for Brighton, England, the home of two brothers who had surveyed the land on which the town was built; later the name was changed to Beaver Falls, for the falls in the creek. In 1868, the town was created into a borough. The Harmony Society, who purchased the land on which the town is located, at sheriff's sale in 1859, was largely responsible for the industrial prosperity of the community. Chief among the industries are the manufacture of chemicals, glass, terra cotta and fire-clay products, planing mill products, metals and metal products. In 1930 College Hill borough and Beaver Falls borough consolidated as Beaver Falls City. Population (1930), 17,147.

BEAVER (LITTLE) RIVER (INCLUDING NORTH FORK)—Tributary to Ohio River. Sub-basin, Main Ohio; source, North Fork in Mahoning County, Ohio; course, North Fork; southeasterly, crossing state boundary through Lawrence County into Beaver County; then southwesterly, crossing state boundary into Ohio to Little Beaver River; mouth, North Fork: at St. Clair, Ohio, main stream: at Smith's Ferry, near Pennsylvania-Ohio boundary; length, North Fork: in Pa., 21 miles. Main stream: from St. Clair, Ohio, to mouth, 7.5 miles. Indian name, Tankamahkhanne, "little beaver stream."

BEAVER RIVER—Tributary to Ohio River. Sub-basin, Main Ohio; source, formed by junction of Mahoning and Shenango Rivers, in Central Lawrence County, 2.5 miles southwest of New Castle; course, southeasterly into Beaver County to Ohio River; mouth, at Rochester; length, twenty-two and one-half miles. Indian name, Amahkhanne, "beaver stream," or Amahkwi-sipu, "beaver river."

BEAVER RUN—Tributary to Kiskiminitas River. Sub-basin, Lower Allegheny; source, in Salem Township, western central Westmoreland County; course, northerly to Kiskiminitas River; mouth, at Paulston; length, twenty miles.

BEDFORD, GUNNING, patriot; born, Philadelphia, about 1730; served as lieutenant in the French War; served as major in Revolutionary War; was wounded at White Plains; became muster-master-general in 1776; was a delegate to the Continental Congress; was elected governor of Delaware, in 1796; died September, 1797.

BEDFORD, GUNNING, lawyer; born, Philadelphia, 1747; graduated from Princeton University, in 1771; studied and practiced law; served as aide-de-camp

BEDFORD SPRINGS (1843)

to Gen. Washington; representative from Delaware to Continental Congress, 1783-1786; became state attorney-general and United States judge for district of Delaware; died March 30, 1812.

BEDFORD—County-seat of Bedford County, located on the Raystown branch of the Juniata River, on the site of the provincial forts called variously Raystown or Camp Raystown, and Fort Bedford. The present town was laid out by an order of the Governor issued May 5, 1776.

PUBLIC SQUARE IN BEDFORD (1843)

BEDFORD COUNTY—Formed from part of Cumberland, March 9, 1771. Named for English Duke of Bedford. Land area, 1,029 square miles; population (1930), 37,309; (1920), 38,277. County-seat, Bedford, laid out in 1766.

BEDFORD GAZETTE, THE, was established September 21, 1805, by Charles McDowell who advocated "Constitutional Republicanism." It is issued on Friday of each week and adheres to the principles of the Democratic Party. Samuel G. Levy is the editor. Circulation, 1,200.

BEDFORD INQUIRER, THE, was established as the *True American* by Thomas R. Gettys, in July, 1812. It took its present name in 1888. Politically, it has been successively Democratic-Republican, Whig and Republican. It appears every Friday under the editorship of A. M. Gilchrist. Circulation, 1,800.

BEECH CREEK—Tributary to Bald Eagle Creek. Sub-basin, Middle West Branch Susquehanna; source, formed by junction of North and South Forks, in Snow Shoe Township, northern central Centre County; course, easterly, by a circuitous route, to Bald Eagle Creek, forming Clinton-Center County boundary for last nine miles; mouth, at Beech Creek; length, twenty-three and one-half miles. Indian name, Schauweminsch-hanne, "beech stream."

BEISSEL, JOHANN CONRAD, founder of the Community of the Seventh Day Baptists at Ephrata; was born at Eberbach, Germany, 1690. At an early age he was apprenticed to a baker who was also a musician and taught the boy, who showed talent, to play the violin. At an early age, too, he showed an interest in the pietistic, advocating celibacy for the man who desired to devote his life to the church. Because of his religious views he was banished from the Palatinate and in 1720 with two friends, Stiefel and Stuntz, came to America. Beissel went to Germantown, where for a year he studied the weaver's trade under Peter Becker, a Baptist and organizer of the Church of the Brethren. In 1721, Beissel and Stuntz formed a cloistered settlement in Muehlbach, Lebanon County. Soon afterward Beissel was baptized by Peter Becker and seven years later he founded a settlement at Ephrata, Lancaster County, the members of which were unmarried men and women. A number of well known people of that period, among whom was Conrad Weiser, were at different times followers of Beissel. The wife of Christopher Sauer, the printer and publisher, left her husband to join the settlement and later became a Prioress. Peter Miller, a graduate of Heidelberg, succeeded Beissel as head of the sect upon Beissel's death which occurred July 6, 1768.

BELL, JAMES MONTGOMERY, soldier; born, Williamsburg, October 1, 1837; served with distinction throughout the Civil War; member of 86th Ohio Infantry; brevetted for services in Battles at Wilderness and Ream's Station, Va.; entered regular army in 1866 as 2nd lieutenant, 7th cavalry; participated in Cheyenne and Arapahoe War, 1867–1869; Sioux Wars, 1876–1881, and the Nez-Perces War, 1877; received brevet-commission of lieutenant-colonel as a reward for services against the Indians at Canon Creek, Montana, September 13, 1877; commanded army in Southern Luzon, Philippine Islands, 1900–1901; was appointed brigadier-general of volunteers, January 20, 1900; appointed brigadier-general, United States Army, September 17, 1901; retired October 1, 1901; died September 17, 1919.

BELL, LIBERTY—The bell known as the Liberty Bell because of the fact that it was rung at the public reading of the Declaration of Independence at the the State House in Philadelphia on July 8, 1776, was obtained by an Act of the Provincial Assembly on October 16, 1751. After it had proclaimed American liberty it was rung on various occasions, which included anniversaries of the signing of the Declaration of Independence, the birthday anniversaries of Washington, the surrender of Cornwallis on October 24, 1781, the deaths of distinguished citizens, the arrival of Lafayette to Independence Hall on September 29,

1824, and the visits of other distinguished men. The Liberty Bell is kept in Independence Hall, Philadelphia.

Other bells in Pennsylvania which may be called Liberty bells because they proclaimed the country's liberty to their respective communities were the Zion Reformed Church bell at Allentown; the court house bell at Chester; the court house bell at Easton; Trinity Lutheran Church bell and First Reformed Church bell at Lancaster; Berks County court house bell at Reading and York County court house bell at York.—*See also* J. B. STOUDT "LIBERTY BELLS OF PENNSYLVANIA."

BELLEFONTE—A borough and county-seat of Centre County. The town was laid out by Col. James Dunlop and James Harris, Esq., in 1795, and was named Bellefonte for the beautiful spring within its boundaries. Bellefonte Academy, located here, was incorporated January 8, 1805, and situated on lots set aside by the founders of the town for educational purposes. The principal industries of Bellefonte are the manufacture of matches, brass and bronze products, machinery, and the quarrying of limestone.

BENEZET, ANTHONY, Quaker philanthropist; born, St. Quentin, France, January 31, 1713; came with his family to Philadelphia from London, in 1731; opposed slavery, advocated emancipation and education of the negro, opening an evening school for colored students; died Philadelphia, May 3, 1784.

BENNER, PHILIP, merchant and ironmaster; was born in Chester County, May 19, 1762. During the Revolution his father, a Whig, was imprisoned by the British. Philip served through the war as a private, under Gen. Anthony Wayne. At the end of the war he took charge of a store in Vincent Township, Chester County, and engaged in the iron business at Coventry in the northern part of that county. In 1792, he moved to Centre County where he erected a house and saw-mill at Spring Creek and two years later built probably the first forge in that county, later a slitting mill and still later another forge and nail mill. He developed an iron trade with Pittsburgh, and conducted stores at Bellefonte and in Ferguson Township. He was one of the founders of Bellefonte and was interested in civic improvements and in the development of facilities for transportation. As a result of his interest in politics he founded, in 1827, the Centre Democrat. His industry was largely responsible for the prosperity of Bellefonte. He died July 27, 1832.

BENNETT, JOSEPH M., philanthropist; born, Johnstown, N. J., August 16, 1816; became interested in clothing business in Philadelphia at age of sixteen; gave forty acres of land in Fairmount Park for a Methodist Orphanage, in 1880, and contributed to its support; founded the Hays Home; contributed largely to the University of Pennsylvania, Deaf and Dumb Institute and to the Methodist Deaconesses. Of his property estimated at $3,000,000, he gave $1,000,000 to charity, bequeathed $500,000 to the University of Pennsylvania for its proposed College for women; died September 29, 1898.

BENNETT BRANCH—Tributary to Sinnemahoning Creek. Sub-basin, Upper West Branch Susquehanna; source, in Huston Township, Northwestern Clearfield County; course, northeasterly, through Elk County, into Cameron County; thence southeasterly to Sinnemahoning Creek; mouth, at Driftwood; length, thirty-seven miles.

BERKS COUNTY—Formed from parts of Philadelphia, Chester and Lancaster, March 11, 1752. Named for English shire, Berkshire. Land area, 865 square miles; population (1930), 231,717; (1920), 200,854. County-seat, Reading, laid out in 1748.

BERMUDIAN CREEK—Tributary to Conewago Creek. Sub-basin, Lower Main Susquehanna; source, in Tyrone Township, Northern Adams County; course, southeasterly into York County to Conewago Creek; mouth, one-half mile south of Roler; length, twenty-three and one-half miles.

BERNADOU, JOHN BAPTISTE, naval officer; born, Philadelphia, November 14, 1858; educated at the Naval Academy, Annapolis; commanded the United States torpedo boat Winslow in the Spanish-American War; was wounded in an engagement off Cardenas in 1898. He has written "The Development of the Resources of the United States for the Production of War Material," "The Development of Smokeless Powder," "A Trip Through Northern Korea, in 1883-1884." He died in 1908.

BETHLEHEM IN 1790

BETHLEHEM, a city in Northampton County, founded in 1741, by Moravians led by Count Zinzendorf. It is the seat of Lehigh University, Moravian Seminary and College for Women, Moravian College and Theological School, and Moravian Preparatory School. The famous Bach Choir originated here. The Bethlehem Steel Company employs more than 6,000 workers, and the other industries of the city include the manufacture of furniture, hosiery, silk, and silk goods and cigars. Population (1930), 57,892; (1920), 50,358.

BETHUNE, GEORGE WASHINGTON, Dutch Reformed clergyman and poet; born, New York, March 18, 1805; was pastor of churches at New York City, Philadelphia, Brooklyn, Rhinebeck and Utica, N. Y.; author, "British Female Poets," "Lays of Love and Faith," an edition of Isaak Walton's "Compleat Angler," numerous religious works and hymns; died Florence, Italy, April 27, 1862.

BEVERIDGE, JOHN, educator, in 1758, became professor of languages in the Academy and College of Philadelphia. He originally taught a grammar school in Edinburgh where Thomas Blacklock, the blind poet, was one of his pupils.

BEYER, SAMUEL WALKER, geologist; born, Clearfield, May 15, 1865; B. S., Iowa State College, 1889; Ph. D., Johns Hopkins University, 1895; instructor, Iowa State College, 1891-1895; assistant professor, 1895-1898; professor, geology and mining engineering, 1898 to date (1930); vice-dean, engineering division, 1908-1917; dean, 1917-1918; dean, Industrial Science division, 1919 to date (1930); geologist, Iowa Geological Survey, 1892 to date (1930).

BIBLE, THE, was first printed in Pennsylvania, in 1743, at Germantown, by Christopher Sauer. It was a German edition in quarto. In 1782, the first edition in English appeared in quarto form by Robert Aitken, a Philadelphia printer.

BIBLE CHRISTIANS, or Bryanites, a branch of Methodism, were formed by William O'Bryan, a Cornwall preacher, and follower of Rev. William Cowherd, in 1815. Rev. Cowherd was not in favor of sects and maintained that his principles were taken directly from the Bible, hence the name, Bible Christians. In 1807, he advocated the doctrine of abstention from the flesh of animals as food, and total abstinence from all intoxicating liquors. In 1817, forty-one members of the Bible Christian Church under the leadership of two ministers, Rev. James Clarke and Rev. William Metcalfe, emigrated to America. Rev. Metcalfe and some of his followers came to Philadelphia, where the minister opened a day school and academy. Services were held at various places in Philadelphia until in 1823, the society purchased a lot of land where, on December 21, 1823, a meeting-house was opened and dedicated.

BIBLE SOCIETY was established in Philadelphia as an unsectarian organization on May 7, 1808. Its aim was "to distribute the Bible in the native speech of those who may be disposed to read it." The first president was Bishop White. On January 10, 1810, the society was incorporated as "The Bible Society of Philadelphia." In 1840, the name was changed to "The Pennsylvania Bible Society."

BIDDLE, ANTHONY JOSEPH DREXEL, author, explorer, and lecturer; born, Philadelphia, October 1, 1874; educated in private schools in Philadelphia and at Heidelberg, Germany; lived in Madeira Islands studying conditions there; became member of staff of Philadelphia Public Ledger; became editor, Philadelphia Sunday Graphic, 1895; head of publishing house of Drexel Biddle, 1897-1904; founded movement known as Athletic Christianity; founder and president, Drexel Biddle Bible Classes which include 200,000 members in the U. S., England, West Indies, Ireland, Scotland, West Africa, South Australia and Canada; with A. E. F. in France as captain United States Marine Corps, 1918; major, U. S. Marine Corps Reserve; was in charge of U. S. Marine Corps combat team, exhibiting at Sesqui-Centennial, Philadelphia, 1926; instructor, individual combat, U. S. Marine Corps Basic School; Amateur boxing champion; author, "A Dual Role and Other Stories," "All Around Athletics," "An Allegory and Three Essays," "The Froggy Fairy Book," "The Second Froggy Fairy Book," "Shantytown Sketches," "Word for Word and Letter for Letter," "The Flowers of Life," "The Madeira Islands," and "The Land of the Wine."

BIDDLE, ARTHUR, lawyer; born, Philadelphia, September 23, 1852; admitted to bar in 1878, and after some years became a member of his father's law firm; author, "Treatise on the Law of Stock Brokers," "Treatise on the Law of Warranties in the Sale of Chattels," "The Law of Insurance"; died March 8, 1897.

BIDDLE, CLEMENT, Revolutionary soldier; born, Philadelphia, May 10, 1740. He entered his father's shipping and importing business at an early age, and in 1771, his name appears as one of the partners of the firm. With his brother, Owen, he signed the iron importation agreement of 1765. In 1775, he helped to raise in Philadelphia a company of volunteers known as the "Quaker Blues"; on July 8, 1776, Congress appointed him deputy quartermaster-general for the militia of Pennsylvania and New Jersey, with the rank of colonel; he participated in the Battle of Trenton and was asked by Washington to receive the swords of the surrendering Hessian officers; he took part in the battles of Brandywine, Germantown and Monmouth, and in 1776, was made aide-de-camp to Gen. Greene. In July, 1777, Gen. Greene appointed him commissary-general of forage, and in 1781, at the request of Gen. Greene, Biddle was made quartermaster-general of the state militia with the rank of colonel. After the war he returned to his business as merchant and importer in Philadelphia. In 1788, he was made a justice of the court of common pleas and in 1789, Washington appointed him United States Marshal of Pennsylvania. He died July 14, 1814.

BIDDLE, JAMES, naval officer; born, February 28, 1783; educated at University of Pennsylvania; entered navy in 1800; served as midshipman in war against Tripoli; taken as prisoner and spent 19 months in confinement; served as lieutenant on the *Wasp* in War of 1812; was again held prisoner after capture of the Wasp by the *Frolic*, but in the exchange of prisoners, Biddle was returned and became commander of *The Hornet*, capturing the British brig *Penguin* in March, 1815; was made captain in 1815. Congress rewarded him for his services by presenting him with a gold medal. Was commissioner to Turkey and China in 1845, negotiating the first treaty between United States and China; served in Mexican War; died October 1, 1848.

BIDDLE, NICHOLAS, naval officer; born, Philadelphia, September 10 1750. After a short career in the merchant service he entered the British navy, serving for some time as midshipman in Admiral Sterling's Sloop-of-war, *Portland*. Upon the refusal of his application to be transferred to one of the ships sent out by the Royal Geographical Society, in 1773, under Capt. Phipps, afterward Lord Mulgrave, to discover the polar limits of navigation, he left the navy and went on board one of the ships of the expedition. Here he and Horatio Nelson, who also left the navy to join the expedition, were made coxswains. Upon his return to England, Biddle resigned his commission, returned to Philadelphia and offered his services to the Continental Congress. He was given command of the "*Franklin*," a galley, fitted out by the Pennsylvania Committee of Safety for the defense of the Delaware in August, 1775, but in December of that year was given command of the brig "*Andrea Doria*," with the rank of captain; he joined the squadron of Esek Hopkins, commander-in-chief of the naval forces of the United Colonies, with which he took part in the expedition against New Providence. After this, while cruising on the North Atlantic, he distinguished himself by capturing a number of armed transports, two of them carrying four hundred Highlanders destined for service in the British Army. On his return from the cruise, Captain Biddle was appointed to the command of the *Randolph*. He was wounded in an engagement between that vessel and the *Yarmouth*, a British vessel in 1778, and perished when the *Randolph* was blown up on March 7, 1778.

BIDDLE, NICHOLAS, financier; born, Philadelphia, January 8, 1786; attended University of Pennsylvania; graduated from College of New Jersey; became secretary to John Armstrong at Princeton, in 1801; United States minister to France, 1804; later was secretary to James Monroe when he was United States minister to England; was elected a member of the Pennsylvania Legislature, in 1810; was appointed a director of the United States Bank, in 1819; became president of the bank in 1823; was a lawyer, having been admitted to the bar in 1809; was interested in literature, being a member of the "Tuesday Club," organized by Joseph Dennie to encourage contributions to the *Port Folio*, the first periodical devoted to the making of an American literature. In 1839, he retired to his country home "Andalusia," on the Delaware where he devoted himself to intellectual and social interests. Among his guests were distinguished European exiles. He died February 27, 1844.

BIDDLE, RICHARD, lawyer; born, Philadelphia, March 25, 1796; admitted to the bar in Pittsburgh; was member of Congress, 1837-1841; died Pittsburgh, July 7, 1847.

BIG FOOT—Indian well known for his encounter with Adam Poe, probably in 1781.

BIG RUNAWAY, THE—The name given to the flight of the settlers in the year 1778, after the Indian massacre near where Williamsport is now located. The settlements above Muncy were all abandoned and Fort Muncy, Freeland's Fort and all the intermediate forts were abandoned about the same time. Practically the entire valley of the West Branch was evacuated.

BIGLER, WILLIAM, governor of Pennsylvania and senator; was born at Shermansburg, Cumberland County, January 1, 1814. His father, discouraged by misfortune, died when William was small. At the age of fourteen, William entered the printing office of his brother, John, at Bellefonte. In 1833, equipped with a second-hand printing set and twenty dollars, he moved to Clearfield where he established the Clearfield Democrat. In 1836, he married Maria J. Reed, entered the lumber business as a partner of his father-in-law and amassed a fortune. In 1841, he was elected to the State Senate, serving for six terms, twice as speaker. In 1851, he was elected governor of the state, and was renominated in 1854, but failed of election. As governor he opposed the wholesale chartering of banks and the passing of "omnibus bills." Following his defeat for reelection he was made president of the Philadelphia & Erie Railroad Company, and in 1856, was elected to the Senate of the United States. He advocated the nomination of Buchanan; favored Buchanan's Lecompton Policy and opposed secession in 1860-1861. He retired in 1861 and spent the last years of his life as a railroad promoter and capitalist in Clearfield. He died August 9, 1880.

BINGHAM, JOHN A., politician; born, Mercer, 1815; became a lawyer; member of Congress from Ohio, 1855-1863 and 1866-1873; appointed military judge-advocate in 1864 by President Lincoln; subsequently President Lincoln appointed him solicitor of the United States Court of Claims; was special judge-advocate in trial of the assassins of President Lincoln; served as United States minister to Japan, 1873-1885; died Cadiz, Ohio, March 20, 1900.

BINNEY, HORACE, lawyer; born, Philadelphia, January 4, 1780; graduated from Harvard University in 1797; became a lawyer; served as member of Congress; director of United States bank; outstanding among his legal cases was his defense of the City of Philadelphia against the executors of Stephen Girard; died August 12, 1875.

BINNS, JOHN, politician and editor; was born in Dublin, Ireland, December 22, 1772. He was associated with William Godwin and other agitators in London, having been imprisoned several times before 1801 for political reasons. In September, 1801, he arrived in America, going at once to Northumberland which was then the community of those who desired to live independent lives and which Coleridge and Southey at one time thought seriously of joining. From 1802 to 1807, he published the Northumberland Republican Argus, and in 1807, moved to Philadelphia where he published the Democratic Press. He opposed the election of Andrew Jackson to the presidency in 1828, favoring John Quincy Adams. Because of his antagonism against Jackson and his tactless expressions of it he encountered trouble. His home was attacked by a mob and because of financial difficulties he was forced to discontinue his paper. Frequently because of his direct and personal attitude in political matters he became the center of bitter controversy. He was well known as an orator and claimed that before he was sixty he never wrote out a speech before delivering it. He published "Binn's Justice," a manual of Pennsylvania law, and "Recollections of the Life of John Binns, Written by Himself." He died June 16, 1860.

BIRCH, THOMAS, painter; born, London, England, July 26, 1779; came to United States in 1793 and settled in Philadelphia; devoted himself to portrait painting until 1807 when he became interested and attained great success in marine painting. In 1811, he was an exhibitor at the first annual exhibition of the Society of Artists, at the Pennsylvania Academy of Fine Arts. During the War of 1812, his attention was called to the artistic possibilities of the sea fight. His paintings depicting sea fights are "Engagement of the Constitution and the Guerriere," now at the Naval Academy at Annapolis, "The Wasp and the Frolic," and "The United States and the Macedonian." Birch also designed several coins for the United States mint. He died January 14, 1851.

BIRD, FREDERIC MAYER, Episcopal clergyman; born, Philadelphia, June 28, 1838; served as Episcopal rector at Spotswood, N. J., 1870-1874; chaplain and professor of psychology, Christian evidences and rhetoric, Lehigh University, 1881-1886; chaplain, Lehigh University, 1893-1898; was known as a hymnologist and the collector of one of the most valuable musical libraries in the United States; was associate editor of Chandler's Encyclopedia; editor, Lippincott's Magazine, 1893-1898; died South Bethlehem, April 3, 1908.

BIRD, ROBERT MONTGOMERY, novelist; born, Newcastle, Del., 1803; became a physician but soon discontinued his practice and devoted his entire time to literature; author (Plays), "The Gladiator," "Oraloosa," and "The Broker of Bogota" tragedies; novels, "Calavar," "The Infidel," "Hawks of Hawk Hollow," "Sheppard Lee," "Nick of the Woods," or the "Jibbenainosay," "Adventures of Robin Day," and "Peter Pilgrim," a collection of tales and sketches; died Philadelphia, January 22, 1854.

BIRNEY, DAVID BELL, military officer; born, Huntsville, Ala., May 29, 1825; studied law in Cincinnati and began to practice in Philadelphia in 1848; entered Union Army at opening of Civil War; was commissioned colonel of 23rd Pennsylvania volunteers, 1861; major-general, May 23, 1863; noted for his achievements in battles of Yorktown, Williamsburg, Fredericksburg, Chancellorsville, and Gettysburg; died October 18, 1864.

BISON IN PENNSYLVANIA—Many traditions concerning the Bison in Pennsylvania have been handed down from generation to generation. More accurate details appear in the account of an English traveler, Thomas Ashe, who wrote from Erie, December, 1806, relating the story of an old man who was visited regularly by buffaloes. Morgan in his "Annals of Harrisburg," quotes one Peter Snyder as relating how a buffalo appeared among a herd of cows and was finally driven into a stable and killed about the year 1792.

BISPHAM, DAVID S., baritone singer; born, Philadelphia, January 5, 1857; educated at Haverford College; studied music in England and Italy; made his debut as the Duc de Longueville in "The Basoche," in London, 1891; became leading baritone of the Royal Opera Company, Covent Garden, London, and the Metropolitan Opera Company, New York; was most successful in Wagnerian operas; left the stage and became a successful concert soloist; advocated use of English in opera; died October 2, 1921.

BLACK, JAMES, lawyer; was born September 23, 1823, at Lewisburg. He was educated at the Lewisburg Academy and was admitted to the Lancaster County Bar in 1846 and became a leading temperance advocate. He was responsible for the first State Prohibition Convention in Pennsylvania, held in Harrisburg in February, 1867. February 22, 1872, he was nominated for the presidency of the United States on the Prohibition ticket, being the first candidate of that party for the presidency. He died December 16, 1893.

BLACK, JEREMIAH SULLIVAN, jurist and statesman, was born January 10, 1810. He was educated in the local schools and at the Academy in Bridgeport. At the age of seventeen, he entered the office of Chancey Forward, a leader of the Somerset County Bar. Admitted to practice, December 3, 1830, he rose rapidly in the legal profession and in 1842, he was appointed, by Governor Porter, judge of the courts of the 16th Judicial District, including Franklin, Bedford and Somerset Counties. In 1851, he was elected to the Supreme Bench of the state and was reelected in 1854. The first three years he served as Chief Justice, having been selected by lot. A supporter of Buchanan for the presidency, he became Attorney-General, and upon the resignation of Cass as secretary of the State, he succeeded to that position. At the close of the administration he retired to York, and was appointed United States Supreme Court Reporter in December, 1861. He was a great defender of Christianity; was a member of the Constitutional Convention of 1873. He died August 19, 1883.

JEREMIAH S. BLACK

BLACK BOYS, A company of young men under the leadership of Capt., James Smith, who, about 1760, assisted in the defense of the frontier. They dressed like Indians, wearing red handkerchiefs in place of hats, and painting their faces. Smith, who had been captured by the Indians but who escaped, taught them Indian customs, so that they could more easily deal with their enemy. The organization was sponsored by the settlers who paid the volunteers for several months of service. The company demanded that all traders submit to an examination of their goods, fearing that the Indian upon receiving supplies of ammunition would continue his outrages. On one occasion when traders from Philadelphia to Fort Pitt refused to have their goods examined, the Black Boys killed their horses and burned their supplies, consisting of blankets, shirts, vermilion, lead, beads, wampum, tomahawks, scalping knives, guns, powder, etc.

BLACK CREEK—Tributary to Nescopeck Creek. Sub-basin, Lower North Branch Susquehanna; source, in Foster Township, Southeastern Luzerne County; course, southwesterly to Gowen; thence northerly to Nescopeck Creek; mouth, at Tank; length, twenty-four miles.

BLACK HUNTER—See JACK, CAPTAIN.

BLACKLICK CREEK—Tributary to Conemaugh River. Sub-basin, Lower Allegheny; source, formed by junction of North and South Branches near Vintondale, on Indiana-Cambria County line; course, westerly, through Indiana County to Conemaugh River; mouth, two miles northwest of Blairsville; length, twenty-nine and one-half miles. Indian name, Naeskahoni, Nees-ki-u, "black"; mahony, "a lick."

BLACK LOG CREEK—Tributary to Aughwick Creek. Sub-basin, Lower Juniata; source, in Tuscarora Township, southwestern Juniata County; course southwesterly into Huntingdon County to Aughwick Creek; mouth, at Rock Hill; length, twenty-five and one-half miles.

BLACKMAR, FRANK WILSON, university professor and economist; born, W. Springfield, November 3, 1854; Ph. B., University of the Pacific, 1881; A. M., 1884; Ph. D., Johns Hopkins University, 1889; professor of mathematics, University of the Pacific, 1882–1886; professor, history and sociology, 1889–1899; sociology and economics, 1899–1912; sociology, 1912 to date (1930); dean of Graduate School, 1896–1922, University of Kansas; president, Kansas Conference Social Work, 1900–1902; member, Phi Beta Kappa; author, "Federal and State Aid to Higher Education in the United States," 1890; "Spanish Colonization,," 1890; "Spanish Institutions in the Southwest," 1891; "The Study and History of Sociology," 1890; "The Story of Human Progress," 1896; "Economics," 1907; "History of Higher Education in Kansas," 1900; "Charles Robinson, the Free State Governor of Kansas," 1902; "The Elements of Sociology," 1905; "Economics for High School," 1907; editor, "Cyclopedia of History of Kansas," 1912; "Outlines of Sociology," 1914, 1923; "History of Kansas State Council of Defense," 1921; "Justifiable Individualism," 1922; "History of Human Society," 1926.

BLAINE, EPHRAIM, soldier, grandfather of James Gillespie Blaine, served in the Revolutionary War, first with the rank of colonel and later as commissary-general; was on intimate terms with his superior, General Washington. Due largely to his efforts the American Army during its winter at Valley Forge was prevented from starving. He died at Carlisle in 1808.

BLAINE, JAMES GILLESPIE, statesman; was born January 31, 1830, at West Brownsville. His paternal ancestors were Scotch-Irish stock from Londonderry, Ireland, who settled later in the Cumberland Valley, his grandfather, Ephraim Blaine, having been prominent in the War of the Revolution. At the age of thirteen, Blaine entered Washington College and after graduation taught in Kentucky and later in the Pennsylvania Institute for the Blind at Philadelphia where he also studied law. Having married Harriet Stanwood, whose family resided in Augusta, Maine, he became connected with the Kennebec Journal and was henceforth a resident of that state. Joining the Whig Party he became a Republican in 1856 and also one of the secretaries of the National Convention in that year; later he served in the Legislature of Maine and entered Congress in 1863. In 1869, he was elected Speaker and in 1876, became United States Senator. Of magnetic personality he was a candidate for the presidency at the Republican National Conventions of 1876 and 1880, but was not nominated until 1884 when he was defeated by Cleveland by a narrow margin. In 1881, he became Secretary of State under Garfield but resigned upon the accession of Arthur. Retiring to private life he wrote "Twenty Years of Congress." Declining the presidential nomination in 1888, President Harrison appointed him Secretary of State, March 4, 1889, which position he resigned June 4, 1892. He died January 27, 1893.

BLAIR COUNTY—Formed from part of Huntingdon and Bedford, February 26, 1846. Named for John Blair. Land area, 535 square miles; population (1930), 139,840; (1920), 128,334. County-seat, Hollidaysburg, laid out in 1820.

BLISS, PHILIP PAUL, singing evangelist; was born in Clearfield County, July 9, 1838. He attended Towner's Singing School in Towanda and the Normal Academy of Music at Geneseo, N. Y. For a time he taught music in Bradford County and about 1865 became associated with Root and Cady, of Chicago, conducting concerts and musical conventions throughout Illinois. Later he joined Dwight L. Moody and Major D. W. Whittle in evangelistic work. His compositions have been collected under the following titles, "The Charm," "The Song-Tree," "The Sunshine," "The Joy" and "Gospel Hymns." The best collection, written jointly with Ira Sankey, includes "Hold the Fort" and "Let the Lower Lights be Burning." Bliss died December 29, 1876, in a vain effort to extricate his wife from a train wreck.

BLISS, TASKER HOWARD, military officer, was born at Lewisburg, December 31, 1853. He attended Lewisburg Academy and the University at Lewisburg (now Bucknell University). In 1875 he graduated from the United States Military Academy and in 1884, was graduated with honors from the United States Artillery School. In 1875, he was commissioned 2nd lieutenant, 1st artillery; in 1880, 1st lieutenant; brigadier-general, volunteers, 1901; brigadier-general, United States Army, 1902. In 1884, he was recorder of the board appointed by the president to report on military value of interior waterways of the United States; from 1885-1888, was professor of military science at the United States Naval War College; served as military attache at United States Legation, Madrid, 1897-1898; in 1898, during the Porto Rican Campaign, was chief of staff to Maj.-Gen. James H. Wilson; was collector of customs at Port of Havana and chief of Cuban Customs Service, 1898-1902; in 1902, was appointed special envoy to Cuba to negotiate a treaty between Cuba and the United States. Bliss was a member of the Joint Army and Navy Board, and of the General Staff, U. S. A., commandant of the Army War College and member of the Army General Staff and president of the War College. From 1905-1909, he was stationed in the Philippines; during the Mexican uprising in 1911, he was in command of a provisional brigade on the Mexican border. On November 20, 1915, he was commissioned major-general, U. S. A., and in October, 1917, was appointed chief of staff of U. S. A., with rank of general. He was legally retired December 31, 1917, but by order of the president continued in active service. He served as a member of the Allied Conference, 1917; of the Supreme War Council in France; and was a member of the American Commission to negotiate peace in Paris, 1918-1919. By an act of Congress, May 20, 1918, he was appointed brevet-general. He died, 1931.

BLOODY SATURDAY—Refers to Saturday, August 14, 1875, when a great many depredations were committed in the Mahanoy Valley by the Molly Maguires, a band of outlaws who inhabited the coal regions of the state. Among the crimes committed on this day was the murder of Thomas Gwyther, Justice of the Peace, at Girardville.

BLOOMSBURG, county-seat of Columbia County, was founded in 1769 by James McClure. The town has machine shops, iron furnaces and foundries, and manufactories of wool, silk, carpets, furniture, bricks, hosiery, matches, etc. It is the seat of the Bloomsburg State Teachers' College. Population (1930), 9,093; (1920), 7,819.

BLOOMSBURG STATE TEACHERS' COLLEGE—On the recommendation of Dr. James P. Wickersham, State Superintendent of Public Instruction, the Bloomsburg Literary Institute became a state normal school, February 19, 1869. It went under the name, Bloomsburg Literary Institute and State Normal School until it was purchased by the state in 1920. It is now known as the State Teachers' College, at Bloomsburg. The principals and presidents from its organization to the present time are: Henry Carver, 1869-1871; Charles G. Barkley, December 20, 1871-March 27, 1872; John Hewitt, March 27, 1872-June, 1873; T. L. Griswold, 1873-1877; D. J. Waller, Jr., 1877-1890; Judson P. Welsh, 1890-1906; D. J. Waller, Jr., 1906-1920; Charles H. Fisher, 1920-1923; G. C. L. Riemer, 1923-1927; Francis B. Haas, 1927-..... Bloomsburg is situated on the Sullivan Trail, forty miles from Wilkes-Barre.

BOBS CREEK—Tributary to Dunning Creek. Sub-basin, Upper Juniata; source, in Portage Township, southeastern Cambria County; course, southerly, through Blair County, into Bedford County to Dunning Creek; mouth, at Reynoldsdale; length, twenty-one miles.

BOEHM, HENRY, minister, was born in Lancaster County, June 8, 1775, the son of Martin Boehm. When he was twenty-five, he became an itinerant preacher of the Methodist Church, traveling in Maryland and Virginia, and later in Pennsylvania where he established churches of the Methodist faith in Reading and Harrisburg. He preached in both German and English and before 1810 had preached in German in fourteen different states. For a time he traveled about with Bishop Asbury and later was appointed to pastorates in Pennsylvania and New Jersey. Largely through his efforts, the Methodist Church was established among the Pennsylvania Germans. He died December 28, 1875, having preached several times after his one hundredth birthday.

BOEHM, JOHN PHILIP, clergyman, was born at Hochstadt, Germany, in 1683. Before emigrating to America with his family in 1720, he was a schoolmaster of the Reformed congregation at Worms and at Lambsheim. Upon his arrival in this country he settled as a farmer in Whitpain Township, Philadelphia (later Montgomery) County. Being a member of the Reformed Church he regularly gathered together the people of his community and held religious services. Gradually he held services at other places until the time came when the territory which he covered on his ministerial visits extended from the Delaware to the Susquehanna and from Philadelphia to the Blue Mountains. Among the many troubles which he faced was that brought about by the arrival in this country of Rev. George Daniel Weiss, an educated and properly ordained minister of the Reformed Church who denounced Boehm as a farmer, unqualified for pastoral work. The Classis of Amsterdam, when appealed to, declared Boehm's position as valid, and he was ordained in New York, in 1729. Another source of trouble was the visit of Count Zinzendorf, who attempted to organize the various congregations into one. On September 29, 1747, the Coetus of Pennsylvania was formed and Boehm was elected president. Shortly before his death he was relieved of most of his pastoral duties, having been succeeded by Michael Schlatter. He died at Hellertown, April 29, 1749.

BOEHM, MARTIN, bishop, was born November 30, 1725, the son of Jacob Boehm, one of the Mennonites from the Palatinate who settled in Conestoga Township, Lancaster County, early in the eighteenth century. The son, Martin, like his father, engaged in farming, although religion was his chief interest. In 1756, he was chosen by lot as preacher of the Mennonites. In 1759, he became a bishop of that church. Boehm, however, liked to express his religious fervor emotionally and the Mennonite Church did not encourage such expression. Consequently he broke away from the orthodox manner of worship, and before 1800 severed relations with the church. At some time between 1766 and 1768, Boehm met William Otterbein. They were chosen as the first bishops of the Church of the United Brethren in Christ at the first annual conference in Baltimore in 1800. Later, Boehm was also associated with the Methodist Church. For a number of years Methodist ministers held meetings at his home and finally a Methodist church was built on land belonging to the Boehms. He traveled throughout Southern Pennsylvania, Maryland and Virginia, holding services in meeting-houses or barns. He died March 23, 1812.

BOKER, GEORGE HENRY, poet and dramatist; born, Philadelphia, October 6, 1823; graduated from Princeton University, 1842; studied law; was United States minister to Turkey, 1871-1879; author, plays, "Calaynos," 1848; "Anne Boleyn," 1850; "Francesca da Rimini," "The Betrothed," "All the World's a Mask"; poems, "Poems of the War," 1864; "Konigsmark and Other Poems," 1869; "The Book of the Dead," 1882; "Sonnets," 1886; died Philadelphia, January 2, 1890.

BONBRIGHT, DANIEL, educator; born, Youngstown, 1831; graduated from Yale University, 1850; studied at University of Berlin, Bonn and Gottingen, 1856-58; afterwards became professor of Latin language and literature, Northwestern University, Evanston, Ill.; dean of faculty of liberal arts, 1899-1902; acting president, 1900-1902. He died November 28, 1912.

BOONE, DANIEL, explorer, born in Bucks County, February 11, 1735. At an early age he, with his father, removed to North Carolina. In May, 1759, with five companions, Boone explored the Kentucky forests. He was captured by Indians there but escaped and returned home in 1771. Two years later he took his family to Kentucky where they were in constant danger of attacks by the savages. Consequently in 1775, Boone built a fort on the Kentucky River at the present site of Boonesboro. Upon several occasions the Indians were driven back, but in 1778 Boone was captured by them, taken to Chillicothe beyond the Ohio River and eventually to Detroit. He was adopted as a son by an Indian family but escaped and returned to his home. Again the Indians attacked the Boone Fort and at different times two of Boone's sons were killed. In 1782, Boone accompanied General Clarke on his expedition against the Indians in Scioto, Ohio. He moved to Missouri in 1795, settling on the Osage Woman

River and devoting his time to hunting and trapping. He died in Charette, Mo., September 26, 1820.

BORIE, ADOLPH EDWARD, merchant and financier, was born at Philadelphia, November 25, 1809, the son of a French merchant and manufacturer. He graduated from the University of Pennsylvania in 1825, after which he studied and traveled in Europe. He entered his father's mercantile business in 1828, at a time when Philadelphia's foreign trade was extensive. The firm traded with Mexico, the West Indies and the Far East, engaging particularly in the silk and tea trade. From 1848 to 1860, Borie served as president of the Bank of Commerce. In 1843, he was Consul to Belgium. At the outbreak of the Civil War, he stood firmly on the side of the Union, and during the war assisted in recruiting and equipping a number of regiments. In 1869, as a result of his friendship for General Grant he was appointed Secretary of the Navy, but he resigned the office in June of the same year. Borie was a philanthropist and a patron of the arts and learning. His collection of paintings has received a good deal of recognition. While on a world tour with former President Grant, Borie became ill, left the party and died in Philadelphia on February 5, 1880.

BORWIER, JOHN, jurist; born in Codogran, France, in 1787. When he was fifteen years old his family, French Quakers, moved to Philadelphia. He became a citizen of the U. S. in 1812; worked for a time in a book store; edited a newspaper in Brownsville, and finally studied law after which he was admitted to the bar in 1818. In 1822, he began legal practice in Philadelphia. He made numerous contributions to legal literature including a complete analysis of Blackstone's "Commentaries," a "Law Dictionary, adapted to the Constitution and Laws of the United States of America, and the Several States of the American Union," a new edition of Bacon's "Abridgement of the Law," and "Institutes of American Law." He died in Philadelphia, November 18, 1851.

BOUQUET, HENRY, military officer, was born in 1719, at Rolle, Canton Vaud, Switzerland. In 1738, two years after entering the service of the States General of Holland, he was commissioned a lieutenant. In the war of the Austrian succession he served the King of Sardinia with such distinction that he was made captain-commandant with the rank of lieutenant-colonel of the Swiss Guards. In 1748, he with other officers received from the French the evacuated forts of the low countries, and later traveled through France and Italy with Lord Middleton. Upon his return he devoted himself to the study of the science of warfare.

In 1756, Bouquet came to America as lieutenant-colonel of the first battalion of the Royal American Regiment, and was successful in recruiting the German settlers in Pennsylvania. In 1758, he became a colonel and served under Brigadier-General John Forbes in his expedition against Fort Duquesne. Due to his patience and his knowledge of the science of militarism, and of people, he was in large part responsible for the erection of new forts and for the completion of the Forbes Road, the first direct route across the Alleghenies. As a result the French lost their control of Fort Duquesne. Until the end of the war, Bouquet served under Stanwix and Monckton, having charge of Forts Pitt, Venango, and Presqu Isle.

In Pontiac's Conspiracy in 1763, he quelled the Delawares and Shawnees by drawing up his troops in a circle and making it appear to the savages that one section had retreated. The Indians consequently rushed through the ranks and were crushed by a bayonet charge. The savages came to respect Bouquet after the skirmish. In 1764, he commanded the southern of two expeditions sent to deal with the Indians. He forced them to return all prisoners and was responsible for the general peace that followed. He received the public thanks of the king, and in 1765, was made brigadier and given the command of the southern district. He died at Pensacola on September 2nd of that year.

HENRY BOUQUET

BOWMAN, ALEXANDER HAMILTON, soldier, was born in Wilkes-Barre, May 15, 1803. He graduated from West Point in 1825 and entered the engineer corps. He was a member of the faculty at the military academy for a time, teaching geography, history and ethics. He was an assistant engineer in constructing defenses and improvement of harbors and rivers along the Gulf of Mexico and supervised the construction of Fort Sumter. He served as chief engineer of the Construction Bureau of the United States Treasury for the erection of customs houses, post-offices, etc. During the Civil War, he was superintendent of the United States Military Academy and was one of the engineers detailed to make effective defenses in Boston in 1865. He died a lieutenant-colonel of the engineer corps on November 11, 1865, in Wilkes-Barre.

BOWMAN, JOHN GABBERT, college president, was born at Davenport, Iowa, May 18, 1877. He studied at the State University of Iowa and at Columbia where he became an instructor in English in 1905. From 1907 to 1911, he was secretary of the Carnegie Foundation for the advancement of teaching and then became president of Iowa State. In 1921, he was elected as chancellor of the University of Pittsburgh and developed a building program including the erection of a "Cathedral of Learning." He lives in Pittsburgh.

BOWMAN, THOMAS, clergyman and educator, was born in Berwick, July 15, 1817. He was educated at Dickinson College from which he graduated in 1837. He entered the ministry of the Methodist Church and organized Dickinson Seminary at Williamsport where he was president for ten years. In 1858, he was chosen president of Indiana Asbury University, now De Pauw University, and served there until 1872, when he became a bishop of the Methodist Church. He traveled extensively through the mission fields of the church in Europe, Asia and South America. He died March 3, 1914.

BOWMAN CREEK—Tributary to North Branch Susquehanna River. Sub-basin, Upper North Branch Susquehanna; source, in Fairmont Township, northwestern Luzerne County; course, northeasterly into Lycoming County to North Branch Susquehanna River; mouth, near Tunkhannock; length, twenty-six miles.

BOYD, JAMES P., lawyer and author, was born in Lancaster County, December 20, 1836. He graduated from Lafayette College in 1859, was admitted to the practice of law in 1863, and eventually became editor of several Philadelphia newspapers. He is the author of "Lalecca," "Envious Merchant," "Building and Ruling of the Republic," "History of the Crusades," "Bible Dictionary," "Paris Exposition," "Men and Issues," and biographies of Grant, Sherman, Sheridan, Blaine, Harrison, McKinley, and Emperor William I. He edited "Triumphs and Wonders of the Nineteenth Century," "Medicology," "Manual of the Nation," and was associate editor of the World's Drama and Analytic Reference History. His death occurred in 1910.

BOYE, MARTIN HANS, chemist, was born in Copenhagen, Denmark, December 6, 1812. He graduated from the University of Copenhagen in 1832. In 1836, he came to the United States where he made discoveries, with other scientists, of several chemical compounds and of perchloric ether in 1841. In 1844 he graduated from the medical school of the University of Pennsylvania and in 1845 discovered the first process for refining cotton seed oil. From 1845 to 1859, he taught chemistry in the Central High School, Philadelphia. His

HUGH HENRY BRACKENRIDGE

publications include, "Pneumatics, or the Physics of Gases," and "Chemistry, or the Physics of Atoms." He died March 5, 1909.

BRACKENRIDGE, HENRY MARIE, jurist and author, was born in Pittsburgh, May 11, 1786. He studied law under his father, Hugh Henry Brackenridge, and was admitted to practice in 1806. He was appointed deputy attorney general for the territory of Orleans after a hazardous journey from Pittsburgh on the Ohio and Mississippi Rivers in a keel-boat in 1811. In 1812, he became district judge of Orleans and was instrumental, because of his linguistic attainments, in the settlement of the Louisiana and Florida purchases. His most important literary contributions are, "Views of Louisiana," "The Voyage to South America," "Recollections of Persons and Places in the West," "History of the Western Insurrection in Western Pennsylvania." He died January 18, 1871.

BRACKENRIDGE, HUGH HENRY, jurist and author, was born in Scotland, in 1748. When five years of age, he came to the United States and attended Princeton University where he graduated in 1771. On this occasion he wrote, in collaboration with Philip Freneau, a practical dialogue, "The Rising Glory of America." He was a chaplain during the Revolutionary War and afterward made Pittsburgh his residence. He became a prominent member of the legal profession in Western Pennsylvania. His motives and actions in the series of meetings connected with the Whiskey Insurrection have been the source of much criticism and conjecture. As a vindication of his position in the affair he published "Incidents of the Insurrection in Western Pennsylvania," one of the best sources of information on the events of the period available. In 1799, he was appointed to the Supreme Court of Pennsylvania. His best literary work is "Modern Chivalry, or the Adventures of Captain Farrago and Teague O'Regan, His Servant," a political satire. He died in Carlisle on June 25, 1816.

BRADDOCK, EDWARD, military officer, was born in Perthshire, Scotland, about 1695. In 1710, he entered the Coldstream Guards, the regiment of his father, Major-General Edward Braddock, as ensign, rising rapidly in rank from ensign to lieutenant of the grenadier company, then to captain-lieutenant with army rank of lieutenant-colonel, next to captain, later to second major with army rank of colonel, still later to first major and eventually to lieutenant-colonel of the regiment. Subsequently he served with the British Army for forty-three years, accompanying the second battalion of the Coldstreams to Ostend in July, 1745, and serving during 1745-1746 under Cumberland in the suppression of the Jacobite rebellion. He became colonel of the 14th regiment in 1753, and in the following year as major-general he was made commander-in-chief of His Majesty's Forces in North America. With two British regiments he arrived at Hampton, Va., in February, 1755.

In America, Braddock faced many difficult problems. Provisions, laborers, money and ease of transportation were lacking, and jealousies between the colonies were constantly growing. Braddock had been ordered to proceed westward and attack Fort Duquesne. It was therefore necessary that a road to the west be built. This task was accomplished by 1,400 British regulars, and a smaller number of provincial troops from Virginia, Maryland, North Carolina and South Carolina. The road, which later became the National Highway, was the first to cross the Alleghenies.

When the army reached Little Meadows it divided, Braddock with 1,400 men moving towards the fords of the Monongahela River. Due to his ignorance of open fighting Braddock was unable to properly organize his troops and on July 9, 1755, eight miles from Fort Duquesne he was bitterly defeated, by French, Canadians and Indians. Braddock himself was wounded in the arms and lungs and died on July 13, 1755, four days after the battle.

BRADDOCK'S DEFEAT—The Colonial troops, led by Gen. Edward Braddock, were defeated in July, 1755, in an attempt to take Fort Duquesne from the French and Indians. Braddock himself was mortally wounded and Washington, who accompanied the general, had his clothes pierced by bullets and two horses killed under him.

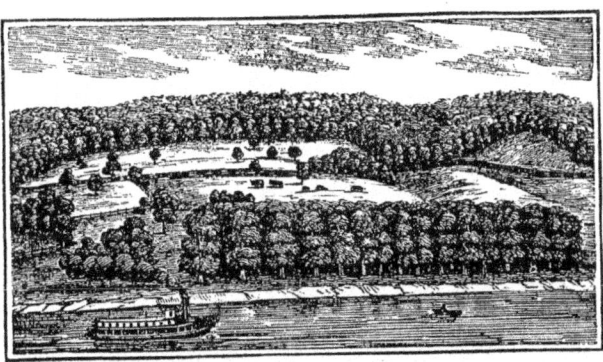

BRADDOCK'S FIELD (1843)

BRADDOCK'S ROAD, built in 1755, to carry provisions to Gen. Edward Braddock's Army in the vicinity of Fort Duquesne, was a further development of the road opened by George Washington in his campaign to the west in 1754. The road partly followed a trail blazed by Nemacolin, a Delaware Indian, for the Ohio Company, and led from Fort Cumberland to the forks of the Ohio River. The National Highway closely follows the Braddock Road from Cumberland, Md., to the eastern slope of Chestnut Ridge.

BRADFORD, ANDREW, printer, was born in Philadelphia, about 1686. He began publication of the Philadelphia, "American Weekly Mercury," in December, 1719, and from 1712 to 1725, was the only printer in Pennsylvania. He employed Benjamin Franklin when he came to Philadelphia in 1723. In 1732, he was Philadelphia's postmaster and conducted a book store at the "Sign of the Bible," on Second Street, in 1735. In 1738, he moved to No. 8 Front Street, to a house which became the printing establishment of his descendants for a century. He died November 23, 1742.

BRADFORD, WILLIAM, Pennsylvania's first printer, was born in Leicester, England, May 20, 1663. A member of the Quaker faith, he emigrated to America in 1682 or 1683, and settled on the present site of Philadelphia. He published an almanac in 1687 and in 1692 was arrested for libel in connection with publication of the writings of George Keith, the source of dissension among Quakers. Bradford was not convicted when brought to trial but incurred the displeasure of leading Quakers. He moved to New York and on October 16, 1725, published the "New York Gazette," first newspaper there. For more than fifty years he was printer for the government of the province of New York, and for thirty years the only printer there. In 1728, he established a paper mill at Elizabeth, N. J., to aid his work. He died in New York, May 23, 1752.

BRADFORD, WILLIAM, jurist, was born in Philadelphia, September 14, 1755. He graduated from Princeton in 1772 and then began the study of law. He served in the Revolutionary War and became a lieutenant-colonel when ill health caused him to resign after two years' service. He was admitted to the bar in Philadelphia in 1779 and in 1780 was made attorney-general of Pennsylvania. After the adoption of the federal constitution he was appointed to the Supreme Court, August 22, 1791. On January 28, 1794, after Edmund Randolph became Secretary of State, Bradford was appointed Attorney-General of the United States. His most important contribution to jurisprudence was "Inquiry How Far the Punishment of Death is Necessary in Pennsylvania." He died August 23, 1795.

BRADFORD, a city in McKean County, 15 miles northwest of Smethport, formerly called Littleton for Col. Little, who settled there in 1837. It is located in a region rich in coal, oil and natural gas. Its chief industries are machine works, chemical, boiler, vacuum cleaner, furniture, gas engine, cutlery, and brick and tile works. Population (1930), 19,306; (1920), 15,525.

BRADFORD COUNTY—Formed from part of Luzerne and Lycoming, February 21, 1810. Before that time known as Ontario. Named for William Bradford, second attorney-general of the United States. Land area, 1,145 square miles; population (1930), 49,039; (1920), 53,166. County-seat, Towanda, laid out in 1812.

BRADY, CYRUS TOWNSEND, author, was born in Allegheny, December 20, 1861. He was graduated from the United States Naval Academy in 1883, and in 1890 was ordained a clergyman of the Protestant Episcopal Church. From 1899-1902, he was rector of St. Paul's Church, Overbrook, Philadelphia, resigning to devote his entire time to writing. He served in the Spanish-American War as a chaplain. Included in his writings are "Stephen Decatur," "American Fights and Fighters," "Commodore Paul Jones," "Colonial Fights and Fighters," "Border Fights and Fighters," "In the War with Mexico," "Indian Fights and Fighters," "The True Andrew Jackson," "Northwestern Fights and Fighters," "On the Old Kearsarge."

BRADY, HUGH, military officer, was born in Northumberland County, in 1768. In March, 1792, he entered the United States Army as an ensign; was with Wayne in his western expedition; was made lieutenant in 1794; captain in 1799. He left the army for several years but was recalled in 1808 by President Jefferson. As colonel he fought in the Battle of Chippewa, distinguishing himself for his bravery there and at the Battle of Niagara Falls, where he was wounded. From 1835 to the time of his death, he held the command at Detroit, where he displayed diplomacy in his dealings with Canada. In July, 1822, Brady was brevetted brigadier-general and in May, 1848, major-general. He died at Detroit, April 15, 1851.

BRADY, JAMES, son of Captain John and Mary Brady and brother of Captain Samuel Brady, was fatally wounded by the Indians, August 8, 1778, and died at Sunbury, on August 13th.

BRADY, JOHN, military officer, was born in 1733, near Newark, Del., the son of Hugh Brady. He removed with his parents to Pennsylvania and at the outbreak of the French and Indian War entered the colonial service. He was commissioned captain of the 2nd Battalion of the Pennsylvania Regiment on July 19, 1763, and took part in Bouquet's expedition in 1764, serving as captain in the 2nd Pennsylvania Battalion. In 1768, he and his family moved to Standing Stone (now Huntingdon), in the following year to Lewisburg and in 1776 to Muncy, where Brady built a half-fortified residence, afterwards called Brady's Fort. During the Revolution he took part in the Battle of Brandywine, where he was wounded. In 1775, he was with Colonel Plunkett in his expedition to the Wyoming Valley to quell the uprisings of Connecticut settlers, concerning a land dispute. He was commissioned major of Plunkett's Battalion in March, 1776, and captain in the 12th Regiment of the Pennsylvania Line in October of that year. While he was not engaged in military pursuits he surveyed land in the Cumberland, Buffalo and White Deer Valleys. He was killed by Indians on April 11, 1779, while with Colonel Hartley on the west branch of the Susquehanna.

BRADY, SAMUEL, colonial officer, was born at Shippensburg, in 1758, the son of John Brady and grandson of Hugh Brady, who early emigrated from Ireland. About 1775, Samuel Brady joined a company of volunteer riflemen and marched to Boston; in 1776, he was made first lieutenant of Capt. Thomas Doyle's Company of Lancaster County men; after the Battle of Monmouth, he was promoted to a captaincy and was ordered west under General Brodhead. The news of his father's death at the hands of the Indians incensed him and he vowed vengeance against them. In 1780, Brodhead sent him to Sandusky, Ohio, to examine the place and to investigate preparations of the British and Indians for their defense. He spent his entire life in avenging the death of his father and the stories of his adventures are many.

BRANDYWINE, BATTLE OF—An engagement of the Revolutionary War, took place near the Brandywine Creek in Chester County, September 11, 1777. The Hessian troops under Knyphausen marched to Chadds Ford at daybreak where they made a feint of attacking. At the same time the greater part of the British troops under Cornwallis marched about 12 miles up the Brandywine, crossed the forks and turning southward came in the rear of Sullivan's division of the American troops. A delay in the movements of Washington's men resulted from conflicting information given by Sullivan concerning the British. Finally definite word came that Cornwallis' men were forming on Osborne's Hill about a mile in Sullivan's rear. Sullivan formed his division into a line across the main road at the Birmingham Meeting-House. Almost before the Americans were in position, Cornwallis commenced his attack. Sullivan's men were greatly outnumbered and were easily routed. Upon receiving word from Sullivan concerning the approach of the British, Washington ordered Greene to leave Wayne in defense of Chad's Ford and to march to the assistance of Sullivan. Taking a strong position in Sullivan's rear Greene withstood the repeated attacks of the enemy until nightfall and the end of firing. In the meantime Wayne, unable to resist Knyphausen and his men, retreated to Chester from whence he marched on to Germantown.

The defeat of Washington's Army was due to lack of men, equipment and proper discipline. Among the wounded was Lafayette, whose leg was badly injured.

BRANDYWINE CREEK—Tributary to Delaware River. Sub-basin, Lower Delaware; source, formed by junction of East and West Branches in East Bradford and Pocopson Townships, Chester County; course, southeasterly into State of Delaware to Delaware River, being Chester-Delaware County boundary by three miles; mouth, near Wilmington, Del.; length, in Pennsylvania, 9.5 miles.

BRANDYWINE CREEK, EAST BRANCH—Tributary to Brandywine Creek Sub-basin, Lower Delaware; source, in Welsh Mountain, Chester County, near Berks-Chester County boundary; course, southeasterly to Brandywine Creek; mouth, at junction with West Branch; length, twenty-five and one-half miles.

BRANDYWINE CREEK, WEST BRANCH—Tributary to Brandywine Creek. Sub-basin, Lower Delaware; source, in Welsh Mountain, near Honey Brook, Honey Brook Township, Chester County; course, southeasterly to Brandywine Creek; mouth, at junction with East Branch; length, thirty-one miles.

BRANDYWINE BATTLEFIELD (1843)

BRECK, JAMES LLOYD, clergyman, was born at Philadelphia on June 27, 1818; graduated from the University of Pennsylvania in 1838 and from the General Theological Seminary in New York in 1841. He was active in the development of the Episcopal Church in Wisconsin, Minnesota, and California and for a time was engaged in missionary work with the Chippewa Indians. He fostered the educational work of the church and died at Benicia, California, March 30, 1876.

BRECK, SAMUEL, was born in Boston, July 17, 1771. He was educated aboard and in 1792, with his family, moved to Philadelphia. From 1817 to 1821, he was a State Senator and in 1823 was elected to Congress but failed of re-election. He strongly opposed slavery, in February, 1821, introducing into the Senate a bill for the emancipation of all slaves within the state. He was the founder of the Society of Sons of New England. He died August 31, 1862.

BREESE, KIDDER RANDOLPH, naval officer, was born in Philadelphia, April 14, 1831. In 1846, he entered the navy, served during the Civil War with Porter's Flotilla that attacked New Orleans and Vicksburg. During the campaign in the west he was lieutenant commander on the Mississippi in 1863 and 1864.

In 1865, he was captain of the fleet that attacked Fort Fisher. In 1874, he was commissioned captain. His death occurred September 13, 1881.

BRENEMAN, BARAM ADAM, chemist, was born at Lancaster, April 28, 1847. He was educated at Pennsylvania State College, graduating in 1866. He served there as instructor and then became full professor of chemistry in 1869. He lectured and was professor of industrial chemistry at Cornell from 1875 to 1882. Later he went to New York City to engage in industrial research. He invented a process for rendering iron non-corrosive and made special investigations on water and its contaminations. He died May 10, 1928.

BRENNAN, THOMAS FRANCIS, Catholic bishop; born at Tipperary, Ireland, in 1853. He received his education at Allegheny College, Meadville, and in European universities. He engaged in missionary work in Pennsylvania, and subsequently was bishop of Dallas, Texas, auxiliary bishop of Newfoundland and auxiliary bishop of Albano and Frascati, Italy.

BRETHREN IN CHRIST, CHURCH OF, also called River Brethren. A religious sect founded by Jacob Engel who lived near Marietta in Lancaster County. He united with the Mennonite Church at the age of twelve, but at the age of eighteen became much concerned about the method of baptism. Coming to the conclusion that the proper method of baptism is by immersion, he and a few of his followers baptized each other and at the home of Henry Engel, about a mile east of Schock's Mills, Jacob Engel was elected bishop. These events took place about the year 1779. Engel died in 1832. Up to about 1850, the religious service was held in the homes of the members; love feasts were held in barns. A schism arose in the church when York County followers and the followers of Mathias Brinser broke away and the official name Brethren in Christ was adopted. They were called River Brethren not because they baptized in the river but because the founder and his followers were Mennonites who lived near the river. Because the Brethren in Christ use many of the practices of the Dunkards, they are usually associated in the popular mind with this sect.

BREWSTER, BENJAMIN HARRIS, lawyer, was born in Salem County, N. J., October 13, 1816. After graduating from Princeton in 1834, he studied law in Philadelphia, where he was admitted to the bar in 1838, practicing for half a century. In 1867, he became attorney-general for Pennsylvania and in 1881 President Arthur gave him that position in his cabinet. He assisted in the settlement of the Cherokee Indian claims in 1846 and in the prosecution of the "Star Route" conspirators later. He died at Philadelphia, April 4, 1888.

BREWSTER, FREDERICK CARROLL, lawyer, was born in Philadelphia, May 15, 1825. After graduating from the University of Pennsylvania, he studied law and was admitted to the bar in 1844. He was in turn city solicitor, and judge of the Court of Common Pleas in Philadelphia, and Attorney-General of Pennsylvania. He was successful in the Stephen Girard will case and in securing a Supreme Court decision on the Chestnut Street Bridge case. He made numerous contributions to jurisprudence and died at Charlotte, North Carolina, December 30, 1898.

BRIDGES, ROBERT, author; born, Shippensburg, July 13, 1858. He was educated at Princeton, was a member of the staff of the New York Evening Post, assistant editor of Scribner's Magazine and wrote book reviews for Life, signing himself "Droch." He edited Scribner's from 1914 to 1930 and is now literary adviser and a member of the National Institute of Arts and Letters. He is the author of "Overheard in Arcady," "Suppressed Chapters," "Bramble Brae" (collected verse), and editor of "The Roosevelt Book." He lives in New York City.

BRIGHTLY, FREDERICK CHARLES, lawyer and author, was born at Bungay, England, on August 26, 1812. He came to Philadelphia in 1831, and was admitted to the bar in 1839. He had an excellent law library and in 1870 retired to write. His compilations are valuable and include "Reports of Cases Decided by the Judges of the Supreme Court of Pennsylvania," "Equitable Jurisdiction of the Courts of Pennsylvania," "Leading Cases on the Law of Elections," etc. He died at Germantown, January 24, 1888.

BRINTON, DANIEL GARRISON, surgeon, archaeologist and ethnologist, was born at Thornbury, May 13, 1837. He served as a surgeon during the Civil War and from 1867 to 1887 was editor of the "Medical and Surgical Reporter." In 1884, he became professor of Ethnology at the Academy of Natural Sciences, Philadelphia, and in 1886, professor of American Linguistics and Archaeology at the University of Pennsylvania. He edited "The Library of Aboriginal American Literature" in addition to other works. He died in Atlantic City, New Jersey, July 31, 1899.

BRINTON, JOHN HILL, surgeon, was born in Philadelphia, May 21, 1832. He was educated at the University of Pennsylvania and Jefferson Medical College, graduating from the latter institution in 1852. He served in the Civil War as a surgeon and in 1882, became professor of the practice of surgery and clinical surgery at Jefferson. He has written extensively on medical service in the United States Army. He died March 18, 1907.

BRISTOL, a borough in Bucks County, 21 miles northeast of Philadelphia; settled in 1681 and originally called Buckingham, is an industrial town manufacturing carpets, hosiery, steel and leather goods, worsted, cast-iron pipe, wall paper and foundry products. It is also a trading center, being located in a rich fruit and truck farming region. Population (1930), 11,799; (1920), 10,273.

BRODENSTRAW CREEK—Tributary to Allegheny River. Sub-basin, Upper Allegheny; source, in Chautauqua County, southwestern New York; course, southwesterly into Erie County, Pennsylvania; thence southeasterly into Warren County to Allegheny; mouth, at Irvine; length, in Pennsylvania, thirty miles.

BRODHEAD, DANIEL, colonial officer, was born September 17, 1736, in New York state. In the following year his family moved to Brodhead Manor in Bucks, now Monroe, County, and in 1773, Daniel went to Reading where he was deputy surveyor-general. He was a delegate to the Pennsylvania Convention at the beginning of the Revolution and raised a company of riflemen to join Washington. He was commissioned lieutenant-colonel of the 4th Pennsylvania Regiment after the Battle of Long Island and was made colonel of the 8th Pennsylvania Regiment in March, 1777. In March, 1778, he was made commander of the troops at Pittsburgh and with 600 men marched up the Allegheny and subdued the Indians in that section. For a time Brodhead was successful in treating with the Delaware Indians, but in 1781 he was compelled to use forcible means to quell them. Following his trial by court martial as the result of a dispute with Col. John Gibson, Brodhead was acquitted but removed from command by Washington. He was brevetted brigadier-general at the close of the war and afterward served as surveyor-general of Pennsylvania. He died at Milford, November 15, 1809.

BRODHEAD, JOHN ROMEYN, historian, was born in Philadelphia, January 2, 1814; was graduated from Rutgers College in 1831, and admitted to the bar in 1835. In 1839, he was attached to the American Legation at The Hague. At this time the Legislature of New York appointed him to obtain original documents relating to the history of the state. The results of his three years of research among the archives of Holland, England and France have been published by the state of New York, edited by E. B. O'Callaghan. From 1846-1849, Mr. Brodhead was secretary of the American Legation in London; he was naval officer of New York from 1853-1857. He died in New York City, May 6, 1873, leaving unfinished his History of the State of New York, the first volume of which was published in 1853 and the second in 1871.

BRODHEADS CREEK—Tributary to Delaware River. Sub-basin, Upper Delaware; source, in Pocono Mountains, Barrett Township, northeastern Monroe County; course, northeasterly into Pike County; thence southerly into Monroe County to Stroudsburg; thence easterly to Delaware River; mouth, near Delaware Water Gap; length, twenty-nine miles.

BROOKE, JOHN RUTTER, military officer, was born at Pottsville, July 21, 1838. He entered the army as captain of a volunteer regiment in the Civil War in 1861. He resigned in 1866 with the rank of brevet major-general, became a colonel in 1879, a brigadier-general in 1888, and major-general in 1897. He distinguished himself during the Spanish-American War at Porto Rico where he commanded the 1st Provisional Army Corps. He helped to arrange the cession of that island to the United States, and in 1898 became military and civil governor of Cuba. In 1900, he became commander of the military department of the East. He was retired in 1902 and died at Philadelphia, September 5, 1926.

BROOKE-RAWLE, WILLIAM, lawyer, was born in Philadelphia, August 29, 1843; was graduated from the University of Pennsylvania in 1863. Shortly after he joined the Union Army and was commissioned lieutenant and later captain of the 3rd Pennsylvania Cavalry. He was brevetted major and lieutenant-colonel. He was agent of the Penn estates in Pennsylvania and treasurer of the Philadelphia Law Association. He died December 1, 1915.

BROOKVILLE, borough and county-seat of Jefferson County, was laid out in 1830 and incorporated as a borough in 1834. It was named Brookville because of the many brooks that flowed from the surrounding hills. The town is located in a region where coal and natural gas are abundant. Agriculture and dairying are important industries. Other industrial establishments are: railroad car and locomotive shops, glass mills, planing and flour mills, furniture, mirror and glove factories and brick and tile works.

BROTHERLY LOVE, city of—See PHILADELPHIA.

BROWN, CHARLES BROCKDEN, novelist, was born in Philadelphia, January 17, 1771. He was the first American novelist and the first American to make literature a profession. He is the author of "Wieland," "Ormond," "Arthur Mervyn," "An Address to Franklin," and "An Address to Congress on Foreign Commerce." He died at Philadelphia, February 22, 1810.

BROWN, DAVID PAUL, lawyer, orator and dramatist, was born in Philadelphia, September 28, 1795. For a short time he studied medicine with Dr. Benjamin Rush, but in 1813, after Dr. Rush's death, began the study of law. He was admitted to the bar in September, 1816, and afterward to the bar of the Supreme Court of Pennsylvania, the district and circuit courts and the Supreme Court of the United States. With his professional achievements came his success as an orator, and as a man of letters. Among his plays are "Sertorius" or "The Roman Patriot," produced at the Chestnut Street Theatre, Philadelphia, December 14, 1830, and "The Prophet of St. Paul's," played at the Walnut Street Theatre, Philadelphia, on March 20, 1837. He died July 11, 1872.

BROWN, JACOB, military officer, was born in Bucks County, May 9, 1775, of Quaker ancestry. He taught school and surveyed Ohio public lands. He became a pioneer in Jefferson County, New York, and during the War of 1812, became a militia-general, brigadier-general and finally major-general. He participated in the campaigns at Sackett Harbor, Chippewa, Niagara Falls and Fort Erie. He received recognition for his services from Congress and after the war continued as a major-general. In 1821, he became first in command of the federal army and died at Washington, D. C., February 24, 1828.

BROWN, JOHN, abolitionist, was born in 1825 or 1826; moved from Hudson, Ohio, to Richmond Township, Crawford County. In 1828, he became postmaster at Randolph, now New Richmond. He was a leader in erecting school houses and formed an Independent Congregational Society, January 1, 1832. He operated a tannery during his residence there. In 1835, he moved to Franklin Mills, Portage County, Ohio. In 1859, he made Chambersburg the basis for his operations against Harper's Ferry, and under the name of "Dr. Smith," engaged ostensibly in preparing for the development of minerals in Maryland. After the capture of Harper's Ferry and Brown's arrest there, one of his followers, Capt. John E. Cook, was arrested at Mont Alto.

BROWNE, WILLIAM HARDCASTLE, author and lawyer, was born in Philadelphia on November 14, 1840. He began the practice of law in Philadelphia in 1865 and made valuable contributions to the legal profession in some of his compilations, such as, "Digest of the Law of Divorce and Alimony in the United States," "Law of Negligence in Pennsylvania," and "Law on Decedents' Estates in Pennsylvania." He died in 1906.

BRULE, ETIENNE (STEPHEN), explorer, was born in Champigny, France, in 1592. In 1608, he came with Champlain to New France. There he lived with the Indians, learning their languages and became of great help to Champlain as an interpreter. In 1615, Champlain sent him on a journey to the Andastes who lived on the headwaters of the Susquehanna River. He explored that river to the point where it flows into the Chesapeake Bay, and is said to have been the first white man to set foot in Pennsylvania. Brule spent the remainder of his life among the Hurons where, because of his dissipation, he was killed in 1632, by the Bear Clan of the tribe and his remains eaten by the savages.

BRUMBAUGH, MARTIN GROVE, governor and educator, was born in Huntingdon County, April 14, 1862. He attended Juniata College where he received the B. E., M. E., B. S., and M. S. degrees. In 1894, the University of Pennsylvania granted him the A. M. degree and in 1895, the Ph. D. degree. From 1884–1890, he served as county superintendent of schools for Huntingdon County and from 1895–1906, was president of Juniata College. In the latter year he became superintendent of the schools of Philadelphia, resigning his position as professor of pedagogy at the University of Pennsylvania, which position he held from 1895-1900, and again from 1902-1906. At the May, 1914, primaries Brumbaugh was nominated for the governorship of the Commonwealth. He was elected to that office in November, serving from January, 1915, to January, 1919. During his term of office the Workmen's Compensation act was passed and made effective, child labor and woman's labor was limited, continuation schools were established and an effort to abolish toll roads and toll bridges was begun. In 1924, Brumbaugh was again called to the presidency of Juniata College, which position he held at the time of his death on March 14, 1930.

BRUSH CREEK—Tributary to Connoquenessing Creek. Sub-basin, Main Ohio; source, in Pine Township, northern Allegheny County; course, northwesterly, through Butler County, into Beaver County to Connoquenessing Creek; mouth, three miles southeast of Ellwood City; length, twenty-two miles. Indian name, Achweek, "brushy, or overgrown with brush."

BRUSH CREEK—Tributary to Turtle Creek. Sub-basin, Monongahela; source, in Hempfield Township, western central Westmoreland County, four miles north of Greensburg; course, southwesterly to Jeannette; thence northwesterly to Turtle Creek; mouth, at Trafford; length, twenty miles. Indian name, Achweek, "brushy, or overgrown with brush."

BRYANT, HENRY GRIER, explorer and geographer, was born at Allegheny City, November 7, 1859. He graduated from Princeton in 1883, and from the law school of the University of Pennsylvania in 1886. He conducted an expedition to Grand Falls, Labrador, in 1891, and in 1892 was second in command of the Peary Relief Expedition. In 1897, he explored the Mount Saint Elias region of Alaska. In 1912, he explored the St. Augustine River, Labrador. He served as president of the Geographical Society of Philadelphia at various times since 1897, of the Association of American Geographers, The American Alpine Club, the Contemporary Club, and is a fellow of the Royal Geographic Society in London. He is an honorary member of many European professional organizations. He contributed to various professional magazines and attended various international geographical congresses as a United States delegate. He lives in Philadelphia.

BRYN MAWR COLLEGE, for women, was founded at Bryn Mawr, a Philadelphia suburb, in 1880, by Joseph Taylor. The college was opened for instruction in 1885. Courses leading to the A. B. degree are offered and there is a large graduate school. Marion Edwards Park is president of the College. In 1931, there were 453 students and 86 teachers.

BUCHANAN, JAMES, 15th president of the United States, was born April 23, 1791, at Stony Batter in what was then Cumberland County, now

Franklin County. His father was James Buchanan, a native of the county of Donegal, Ireland, and his mother, Elizabeth Speer, the daughter of a farmer, then of York, now of Adams County. Buchanan studied Latin and Greek in Mercersburg in a school taught by the Rev. James R. Sharon, and afterwards by a Mr. McConnell and Dr. Jesse Magaw. In the fall of 1807, he entered the Junior Class of Dickinson College, graduating in 1809. Moving to Lancaster, he began the study of law in the office of Mr. Hopkins and was admitted to practice in 1812; enrolled as a volunteer for the defence of Baltimore in the War of 1812; October, 1814, he was elected a member of the House of Representatives in the General Assembly of Pennsylvania and was reelected. Beginning his career as a Federalist, he began to turn to Democratic principles while in the General Assembly as evidenced by his change of attitude on the bank question, becoming hostile to that institution. Resuming the practice of law, he alone defended Judge Walter Franklin on articles of impeachment against him in the Senate. October, 1820, elected to Congress from the district composed of Lancaster, Dauphin and Lebanon Counties, taking his seat on Monday, December 5, 1821. He served during the 17th, 18th, 19th, 20th and 21st Congresses, and announced after the election of 1828, that he would decline reelection. In the 21st Congress, as chairman of the Judiciary Committee, he made a minority report, January 24, 1831, on a proposition to repeal the twenty-fifth section of the Judiciary Act of 1789, which gave the Supreme Court appellate jurisdiction by writ of error to the State courts in cases where the Constitution, treaties and laws of the United States are drawn in question, causing rejection of the bill. Offered mission to Russia, May, 1831, by President Jackson, and negotiated only commercial treaty United States has ever had with Russia; returned November, 1833; appointed Delaware River Commissioner; elected to the United States Senate to succeed William Wilkins, December 6, 1834, and took his seat, December 15, 1834. As senator he ably defended President Jackson on the French Spoliation Claims Controversy, on the Resolution of Censure and the Bank question; appointed Secretary of State by President Polk, he conducted the delicate negotiations with great skill; retired to private life and the practice of law on the accession of President Taylor in 1849; purchased Wheatland, the summer residence of Wm. M. Meredith; prominent candidate for Democratic Presidential nomination in 1852, but defeated by Franklin Pierce; appointed by the latter Minister to England in 1853; signed Ostend Manifesto under direction of the government; returned to United States, April, 1856; nominated for the Presidency at Cincinnati and elected in November; inaugurated March 4, 1857; pursued a vigorous foreign policy, but was faced with the difficulties in Kansas, and criticized for recognizing the Lecompton Constitution; opposed the right of Search by England and defended the New American doctrine of expatriation of which he was the first exponent; vigorously opposed the methods used in the Covode investigation; faced severe crisis in the secession of the Southern States after the election of Lincoln; appointed Peter McIntire of Pennsylvania collector of the Port of Charleston, but Senate refused to confirm him; retired

JAMES BUCHANAN

to private life March 4, 1861; wrote a defense of his administration; president of the Board of Trustees of Franklin and Marshall College, Lancaster, from its organization in 1853 until a short time before his death, which occurred June 1, 1868. Buchanan never married, his brilliant niece, Harriet Lane, performing the duties of mistress of the White House during his presidency.

BUCKALEW, CHARLES ROLLIN, senator and diplomat, was born at Fishing Creek, Columbia County, December 28, 1821. He studied law, was admitted to the bar and practised his profession at Bloomsburg. From 1845-1847, he was district attorney of Columbia County and from 1850-1856, was a state senator. In 1854, he was sent to Paraguay as treaty commissioner and in 1857 was a member of the commission appointed to revise the United States penal code. Subsequently he served as chairman of the State Democratic committee and during President Buchanan's administration was United States minister to Ecuador. From 1863-1869, he was a member of the U. S. Senate, having defeated Simon Cameron of Lancaster County. He was a leader in the Democratic opposition to the attempted impeachment of President Johnson, and as senator served on the committees of Indian Affairs, Foreign Relations, Post-Offices and Post Roads, etc. Upon the expiration of his term he again served as state senator, was an unsuccessful candidate for governor in 1872, and was elected member of the House of Representatives in 1886. He died at Bloomsburg, May 19, 1899.

BUCKHART, WILLIAM ARMSTRONG, agriculturist, was born at Oswego, N. Y., December 26, 1846. At an early age he showed a marked interest in science. After completing his studies in the public schools he earned enough money, by working as a market gardener and trucker, to pay his way through the Agricultural College of Pennsylvania, where he graduated in 1868 with the degree of Bachelor of Science in Agriculture. From the time of his graduation until 1871, he did graduate work at his Alma Mater and at Harvard University and engaged in gardening and trucking in Oswego. In 1871, he became professor of Botany and Geology at the Agricultural College of Pennsylvania now Pennsylvania State College. In 1874 he received the A. M. degree from that institution, and in 1904, the degree of Doctor of Science. He was acting dean of the School of Agriculture from 1903 to 1906, and vice-president of the college for ten years. He established the forestry course at the college, contributed the results of many agricultural experiments to the bulletin published by the institution, and was a popular lecturer on scientific subjects. He died December 3, 1912.

BUCKNELL UNIVERSITY, at Lewisburg, was organized in 1846, under the auspices of the Baptist Church, as the University of Lewisburg. During the year 1863, when the Confederates invaded Pennsylvania, the institution was closed, and professors and students joined an emergency company. In 1882-

1883, women were admitted to the college and in 1884-1885, degrees were open to women. The first degree was conferred upon a woman in June, 1885. In 1886, the name of the institution was changed to Bucknell University, in honor of the late William Bucknell of Philadelphia, for many years chairman of the Board of Trustees. The university offers courses leading to the A. B. and B. S. degrees and graduate courses leading to the A. M. and M. S. degrees. The university conducts a summer session, an extension division, and a school of music. Dr. Emory William Hunt is president of the institution. The student body in 1930-1931 was distributed as follows: College, 1,185; Summer Session (1930), 442; Extension Division (1929-1930), 502.

BUCKS COUNTY was one of the three original counties established when the province was first settled in 1682. The others were Philadelphia and Chester. The name is an abbreviation of the English Buckinghamshire. Land area, 608 square miles; population (1930), 96,727; (1920), 82,416. County-seat, Doylestown, laid out in 1778.

BUCKS COUNTY INTELLIGENCER, THE, of Doylestown, is a Republican weekly newspaper that appears each Friday, and was established in 1804. It has a circulation of 950, which is supplemented by the publication of evening editions daily except Sunday since 1886. George S. Hotchkiss is the editor, and the Intelligencer Company, Inc., the publishers. The daily edition has a circulation of 5,375.

BUCKSHOT WAR, THE—In 1838, Governor Joseph Ritner was defeated for reelection by David R. Porter, of Huntingdon, by a majority of 5,540 votes. Threats to contest the election were made by Stevens and Burrowes and it was decided to investigate the alleged frauds. The Legislature which met December 4, 1838, was Anti-Masonic and Whig in the Senate, while both parties claimed a majority in the House. Rival speakers were elected in the House, Thomas S. Cunningham, of Beaver County, by the Anti-Masons and Whigs, and William Hopkins, of Washington County, by the Democrats. Both speakers occupied seats on the platform and both factions adjourned to meet the next day, but the Anti-Masons and Whigs met in the afternoon and some spectators who were the friends of the Hopkins party went up to the platform and carried the speaker down into the aisle. Overcome by superior numbers, the Cunningham House adjourned to what later became Lochiel Hotel. The Senate was also forced to adjourn, the speaker, Chas. B. Penrose, jumping out of a window twelve feet high. With this menacing situation, Governor Ritner called out the militia, under General Patterson, and requested President Van Buren to order United States Troops from Carlisle to the scene. This the President refused to do. The Senate recognized the Democratic wing of the House and the Buckshot War came to an end. The ammunition for the infantry was buckshot cartridges. It is said that some of these cartridges were made at the headquarters of the Cunningham men and sent by a negro to the arsenal to be used on the mob; that the negro was caught and forced to give up his cartridges to the enemies of the administration who distributed them among their friends as mementoes. From these facts the name Buckshot War was derived.

BUFFALO—*See* BISON.

BUFFALO CREEK—Tributary to Allegheny River. Sub-basin: Lower Allegheny; source, in Fairview Township, eastern Butler County, two miles east of Chicora; course, southerly, in eastern Butler and western Armstrong Counties, to Allegheny River; mouth, at Freeport; length, thirty-three miles. Indian name, Sisiliehanna, "buffalo stream."

BUFFALO CREEK—Tributary to West Branch Susquehanna River. Sub-basin: Lower West Branch Susquehanna; source, in Hartley Township, western Union County; course, easterly to West Branch Susquehanna River; mouth, at Lewisburg; length, twenty-one miles. Indian name, Sisiliehanna, "buffalo stream."

BUFFALO CREEK—Tributary to Juniata River. Sub-basin: Lower Juniata; source, in Madison Township, western Perry County; course, north-easterly to Juniata River; mouth, near Newport; length, twenty-six and one-half miles. Indian name, Sisiliehanna, "buffalo stream."

BUFFALO CREEK—Tributary to Ohio River. Sub-basin: Main Ohio; source, in East Finley Township, southwestern Washington County; course, northwesterly into West Virginia to Ohio River, crossing state boundary; mouth, at Wellsburg, W. Va.; length, in Pennsylvania, twenty-one and one-half miles. Indian name, Sisiliehanna, "buffalo stream."

BUILDING AND LOAN ASSOCIATIONS were first begun in the United States at Frankford, near Philadelphia, under the name Oxford, Provident Building Association in 1831. Cooperation for philanthropic reasons was the original aim of the organization which used similar British societies as models.

BULL, JOHN, Colonial officer, was born June 1, 1731, in Providence Township, Montgomery County. On May 12, 1758, he entered military service, was commissioned captain, and sent to Fort Allen at what is now Weissport, Carbon County. In the Forbes expedition against Fort Duquesne he rendered notable service. Later, Bull lived at what is now Norristown where he owned a plantation and mill and in January, 1775, and June, 1775, was a delegate to the Provincial Conference. He was a member of the Board of War, 1777, was one of the commissioners at the Indian Treaty at Easton in January, 1777, and was elected to the Assembly in the same year. In May, 1777, he became colonel of the 1st State Regiment of Foot and in July was commissioned Adjutant-General of Pennsylvania. In December, he succeeded Gen. James Irvine as commander of the 2nd Brigade of Pennsylvania Militia. He assisted in the defense of Philadelphia in 1778-1779. He moved to Northumberland in 1785 and died there, August 9, 1824.

BULL, OLE BORNEMANN, violinist, was born at Bergen, Norway, February 5, 1810. His playing brought him much success in both Europe and America. In his business ventures he was unsuccessful, losing all his money in an attempt to found a Norwegian colony in Pennsylvania. Later he settled in Cambridge, Mass., maintaining a summer home in Norway. He died in Norway, near Bergen, August 17, 1880.

BURD, EDWARD, lawyer, was the son of Colonel James Burd and Sarah Shippen Burd, the daughter of Judge Edward Shippen, of Lancaster. Edward Burd attended the Philadelphia Academy, now the University of Pennsylvania, and was admitted to the practice of law in Pennsylvania. In 1772, he came to Reading where he entered upon his profession, and soon afterward was appointed prosecuting attorney to the Crown in the newly created Northumberland County. In 1775, he joined the Reading Company of Riflemen, and participated in the Battle of Long Island where he was wounded and taken prisoner. Upon exchange of prisoners he returned to Reading. In 1778, he removed to Philadelphia where he assumed the office of prothonotary of the Supreme Court, which position he held until 1805. Burd married Elizabeth Shippen, the sister of Margaret Shippen (wife of Benedict Arnold). He died in Philadelphia in July, 1833.

BURDETTE, ROBERT JONES, humorist, was born at Greensboro, on July 30, 1844. He served in the Union Army during the Civil War, then moved to the middle west where he became popular as a humorist in connection with the Burlington, Iowa, "Hawkeye," to which organ he contributed. In 1888, he was licensed to preach in the Baptist Church. His works include "The Rise and Fall of the Moustache and Other Hawkeyetems," "HawkEyes," "Schooners that Pass in the Dark," "Chimes from a Jester's Bells" and "Old Time and Young Tom." His collections of verse parodies are "Smiles Yoked with Sighs" and "The Silver Trumpets." He also wrote a "Life of William Penn" for Henry Holt's series of the lives of American Worthies. He died November 19, 1914.

BURROWES, THOMAS HENRY, politician and educator, was born at Strasburg, November 16, 1805. He was educated privately, attended Trinity College, Dublin, a Quebec Classical School, and Yale College. Later he studied law under Amos Ellmaker, of Lancaster, and was admitted to the bar in 1829. From 1831-1832, he was a member of the lower house of the Pennsylvania legislature, and became so influential a member of the Whig party that he was able to assist Joseph Ritner in his election as governor in 1835, and secure for himself the appointment as Secretary of the Commonwealth which included the office of State Superintendent of Schools. With Thaddeus Stevens and Theophilus Fenn, Burrowes managed the administration of Governor Ritner. The Buckshot War came as a direct result of Burrowes refusal to recognize the defeat in 1838 of the Anti-Masonic Whig party of which he was state chairman. The Anti-Masonic Whigs claimed that their defeat came as the result of fraud at the Philadelphia polls. Burrowes in a proclamation of October 18, 1838, asked the people to consider the defeat as a victory. Consequently Ritner in his attempt to seat the defeated Anti-Masonic Whigs of Philadelphia in the House of Representatives was forced to call in the State Militia. The militia refused to assist as did President Van Buren, when appealed to. The Democrats, accompanied by a large mob, therefore, came into possession of the Senate and Burrowes left office through a window in the rear of the Senate Chamber.

During Ritner's administration, Burrowes revised the school law of 1834, and organized and developed the free school system of the state. He founded the Pennsylvania School Journal in 1852, edited it for eighteen years, was state superintendent of schools from 1860-1863, organized Soldier's Orphan's Schools after the Civil War and at the time of his death, on February 25, 1871, was president of the Pennsylvania Agricultural College.

BURROWS, WILLIAM, naval officer, was born in Kensington, Philadelphia, on October 6, 1785. He served in the war with Tripoli and was commander of "The Enterprise" in its activity against the British "Boxer" on the Maine Coast. Burrows and the British commander were killed there and buried together at Portland. Burrows was honored for his heroism and victory when Congress ordered a medal struck in his memory.

BUSHKILL CREEK—Tributary to Delaware River. Sub-basin: Upper Delaware; source, in Blue Mountains, Moore Township, northwestern Northhampton County; course, southeasterly to Delaware River; mouth, at Easton; length, twenty miles.

BUSHKILL (BIG) CREEK—Tributary to Delaware River. Sub-basin: Upper Delaware; source, Pecks Pond, in Blooming Grove and Porter Townships, southern central Pike County; course, southwesterly and southeasterly to Delaware River, crossing Pike-Monroe County three times and being the boundary for last three miles; mouth, near Bushkill; length, twenty-two miles.

BUSHY RUN, BATTLE OF—In the Pontiac War, on August 5, 1763, was fought, within the present Penn Township, Westmoreland County, the Battle of Bushy Run. Pontiac's conspiracy having been reported to the authorities, the officers and men at Fort Pitt became alarmed. Colonel Henry Bouquet, then on official duty at Philadelphia, was ordered to the relief of the Fort. July 1st Bouquet and his Highlanders reached Carlisle and spent eighteen days there collecting provisions, horses, oxen and wagons. On July 25th, he was at Fort Bedford. He arrived at Fort Ligonier, August 2nd; leaving his wagons and oxen at this place, he moved forward with 350 pack horses. He pushed on to Bushy Run intending to rest his troops there and meet the enemy the next day at the defile of Turtle Creek, but about 1 o'clock in the afternoon of August 5th, a fierce attack was made on the advance guard and Bouquet soon discovered that his little army was surrounded. The fight continued until darkness and the troops were forced to spend the night without water even for the wounded. On the morning of August 6th, the enemy, confident of victory, renewed the attack. Bouquet then resorted to strategy and withdrawing the advance line, all his army suddenly fell back as if in retreat. The Indians, confident of victory, rushed from the woods in pursuit and were themselves surprised by the fire of Bouquet's men from all sides. The Highlanders then fell upon them with bayonets and were masters of the field. The Indians lost 60 of their number, including several chiefs. The English loss was 50 killed, 60 wounded and 5 missing. "The Battle of Bushy Run," says Poole, "both for its military conduct and its political results, deserves a place among the memorable battles in America. The Indians fought with a courage and desperation rarely seen in Indian warfare, and the English troops with a steadiness and valor which was due to their training as regulars and the direction of so able a commander. The tidings of this victory broke the spirit of the Indian conspiracy, and the reports were received with rejoicing in all the English colonies." For this victory, Bouquet received a formal letter of thanks from the King.

BUTLER, RICHARD, military officer, was born in Ireland and came to America before 1760. He served during the Revolutionary War, as a lieutenant-colonel in the Pennsylvania ranks and of Morgan's rifle corps in 1777. In 1787, he was agent for Indian affairs in Ohio, and on November 4, 1791, was killed in a battle in that state while serving as major-general with St. Clair in his expedition against the Indians.

BUTLER, THOMAS, military officer, was born in Pennsylvania in 1754; served in most of the outstanding battles in the middle states during the Revolution. His gallantry in the battles of Brandywine and Monmouth merited him the thanks of Washington and Wayne. While with St. Clair in his expedition against the Indians in 1791, he was wounded twice. He died at New Orleans, September 7, 1805.

BUTLER, ZEBULON, soldier, was born in Connecticut. He was a member of a committee of three under whom the New England settlement in the Wyoming Valley was made. He served as an officer during the Revolution and led the settlers in the massacre of Wyoming, in July, 1778. He died in Luzerne County in 1795.

BUTLER, a borough and county-seat of Butler County, located on Conoquenessing Creek in the flourishing coal, iron, oil and natural gas region of western Pennsylvania. The town was first settled in 1778, and was incorporated in 1803. The chief industries are the manufacture of glass, silk, buttons, paints, metal beds, and oil-well supplies. Population (1930), 23,568; (1920), 23,778.

BUTLER COUNTY, formed from part of Allegheny, March 12, 1800. Named for General Richard Butler. Land area, 790 square miles; population 1930), 80,480; (1920), 77,270. County-seat, Butler, laid out in 1803.

BUTTZ, HENRY ANSON, educator and clergyman, was born in Middle Smithfield, on April 18, 1835. After graduating from Princeton in 1858, he entered the Methodist ministry; in 1880, he became president of Drew Theological Seminary at Chester. He has written extensively and is the editor of "Epistle to the Romans in Greek," "The New Life Dawning," by B. H. Nadal, "The Student's Commentary—The Book of Psalms," by Dr. James Strong. He died October 6, 1920.

BUTZ, GEORGE C., botanist, was born February 1, 1863, at New Castle. He attended New Castle High School and Pennsylvania State College where he graduated in 1883. From then until 1887, he engaged in floriculture in New Castle, was president of the Y. M. C. A. there, and was a landscape gardener in San Jose, Calif. On July 1, 1887, he became horticulturist of the Pennsylvania State College Agricultural Experimental Station. He performed many valuable experiments with both ornamental and economic food plants, and became widely known as a scholar, teacher and lecturer. He died December 14, 1907.

BYERLY, WILLIAM ELWOOD, mathematician, was born in Philadelphia, December 13, 1849. He attended Harvard, graduating in 1871, and held the chair of mathematics there from 1881-1913, in the latter year becoming professor emeritus. Prior to 1881, he was an assistant professor at Cornell and Harvard. He made many contributions to professional journals and is the author of the following works: "Elements of Differential Calculus," "Elements of Integral Calculus," "Problems in Differential Calculus," "Treatise on Fouriers' Series and Spherical, Cylindrical and Ellipsoidal Harmonics," "Problems in Differential Calculus," "Generalized Coordinates," "Introduction to the Calculus of Variations." Mr. Byerly lives at Cambridge, Mass.

BYERS, SAMUEL HAWKINS MARSHALL, soldier and author, was born at Pulaski, July 23, 1838. During the Civil War, he served in the Union Army for four years; was taken prisoner in the Battle of Chattanooga and spent fourteen months in Libby and other prisons. Later he was a member of Gen. Sherman's staff. From 1869-1884, he was consul at Zurich, Switzerland, and in 1885, was consul-general to Italy and later to Switzerland. In addition to his poem "March to the Sea," he is the author of "Switzerland and the Swiss," "Iowa in War Times," "Twenty Years in Europe," "With Fire and Sword," and "A Layman's Life of Jesus." He has also contributed to many magazines. Mr. Byers lives at Los Angeles, California.

CADWALADER, GEORGE, lawyer and soldier, was born at Philadelphia, in 1804. Before 1846, he engaged in the practice of law, but during the Mexican War, he became a brigadier-general of volunteers and served with distinction at Chapultepec. Between the end of the Mexican War and the outbreak of the Civil War in 1861, he resumed his law practice, and then became major-general of Pennsylvania volunteers during the latter conflict. He was placed in command at Baltimore, served with Patterson's expedition to Winchester in 1861, and was a member of the board that directed the operations of the Union Army. He wrote, "Services in the Mexican Campaign of 1847." His death occurred at Philadelphia, February 13, 1879.

CADWALADER, JOHN, soldier, was born at Philadelphia, January 10, 1742. He was placed in command of a battalion during the Revolution and became brigadier-general. He participated in engagements at Trenton, Monmouth, Brandywine and Germantown. He was the organizer of eastern Maryland's militia in 1777, and in 1778 he apprehended Thomas Conway who was plotting against Washington. Cadwalader died at Shrewsburg, February 10, 1786. In 1800, his daughter married Lord Erskine.

CALDWELL, ALEXANDER, business man, was born at Drake's Ferry, in Huntingdon County, on March 1, 1830. He was educated at public and private schools before 1847, when he entered a company commanded by his father for service in the Mexican War. His father was killed at one of the gates to the entrance of Mexico City and he returned to Pennsylvania where he entered the banking business at Columbia. The outbreak of the Civil War took him to Kansas in 1861 where he engaged in transportation of supplies to military posts, fostered bridge and railroad building, represented Kansas in the United States Senate as a Republican from 1871 to 1873. He organized the Kansas Manufacturing Company which yearly produced seven thousand wagons; was in charge of the Idaho and Oregon Land Improvement Company, and president of the First National Bank of Leavenworth. His death occurred May 19, 1917.

CALDWELL, MERRITT, educator, was born at Hebron, Maine, on November 29, 1806. He was educated at Bowdoin College and became professor of mathematics and English literature at Dickinson College. He was the author of "Manual of Elocution," "Philosophy of Christian Perfection," "Christianity Tested by Eminent Men," "The Doctrine of the English Verb."

CALIFORNIA STATE TEACHERS' COLLEGE is an outgrowth of an academy founded at California, Pa., in 1852. In 1865, this academy was chartered by the state to become the Southwestern Normal College. The school became state owned in 1914 and a teachers' college in 1929.

California is located thirty-five miles south of Pittsburgh, sixteen from Uniontown, twenty-five from Washington, Pa., twenty from Waynesburg, and sixty-six from Somerset.

CAMBRIA COUNTY, formed from part of Huntingdon, Somerset and Bedford, March 26, 1804. Named for Cambria Township. Land area, 717 square miles; population (1930), 203,146; (1920), 197,839. County-seat, Ebensburg, laid out in 1806.

CAMERON, JAMES, military officer, was born at Maytown, Lancaster County, March 1, 1801. He learned the printing trade from his brother, Simon, and by 1827, was associated with John Brandon in the publication of the Lycoming Gazette, at Williamsport. After the sale of the Gazette, Cameron returned to Lancaster County and published The Political Sentinel. In 1839, he became superintendent of motive power of the Columbia Railroad and in 1843, was appointed deputy attorney-general at Lancaster. Upon the completion of the Northern Central Railroad, he was made an officer of the company, and removed to near Milton. At the outbreak of the Civil War, he became commander of the 79th New York Regiment of Volunteers with rank of colonel. He was killed at the Battle of Bull Run, July 21, 1861, being the first Pennsylvania officer to be killed in the Civil War.

CAMERON, JAMES DONALD, capitalist and politician, was born at Middletown, on May 14, 1833, the son of Simon Cameron. He was educated at Princeton and after his graduation in 1852, engaged in business. In 1861, he became vice-president, and in 1863, president of the Northern Central Railroad, continuing in office until 1874. President Grant made him Secretary of War in 1876, and the following year he succeeded his father as United States Senator from Pennsylvania. He was returned to office in 1879, 1885 and 1891. In 1879, he was elected Chairman of the Republican National Committee. He died August 30, 1918.

CAMERON, SIMON, statesman, was born at Maytown, in Lancaster County, on March 8, 1799. He learned the trade of printer and in 1820, edited a Doylestown paper, and in 1822 was engaged in printing in Harrisburg. He became interested in internal improvements through banking contacts that he developed and encouraged railroad building. He served as adjutant-general of

SIMON CAMERON

his state, and in 1845 and 1849, was United States Senator, elected by the Democratic party. He became a member of the Republican party when it was organized and in 1856 was again elected United States Senator. He was considered as candidate for both the presidency and the vice-presidency at the Republican National Convention in 1860 and in 1861 President Lincoln appointed him Secretary of War. In January, 1862, he resigned from the cabinet to become minister to Russia. Within a year he gained Russian support for the Union and retired from active life until 1866, when he was returned to the Senate. He became chairman of the committee of foreign affairs and retired in favor of his son, James Donald Cameron, in 1877. He died at Maytown, June 26, 1889.

CAMERON COUNTY, formed from parts of Clinton, Elk, McKean and Potter, March 29, 1860. Named for United States Senator, Simon Cameron. Land area, 392 square miles; population (1930), 5,307; (1920), 6,297. County-seat, Emporium, laid out in 1861.

CAMMERHOFF, JOHN CHRISTOPHER FREDERICK, bishop, was born near Magdeburg, Germany, on July 28, 1721. He came to America after being educated at Jena and consecrated as a Moravian bishop in London. He assisted Bishop Spangenburg in the new world and preached extensively in New York and Pennsylvania where he met with much success among the Indians. He died at Bethlehem on April 28, 1751.

CAMPBELL, ALEXANDER, founder of "The Disciples of Christ," was born near Balbymena, County Antrim, Ireland, on September 12, 1788. He emigrated to the United States in 1807 and was connected with the work of the Presbyterian Church until 1812, when he and his father, Thomas Campbell, withdrew, were baptised by immersion and organized several congregations that united with a Baptist Association. They acknowledged the Bible as the sole source for rules of faith and practice. As a result they met with much opposition from the Baptist element in 1827. Alexander Campbell was ejected from their association. About this time his evangelistic work and lectures gained a following for him and he organized a sect commonly known as the Campbellites and officially called "The Disciples of Christ." The first Church was organized on Brush Run, Washington County. This organization became prominent among dissenters from Presbyterian and other Protestant churches in western Pennsylvania and Virginia. Campbell founded Bethany College, in Bethany, West Virginia, and died there, March 4, 1866.

CAMPBELL, BARTLEY, dramatist, was born at Allegheny City, on August 12, 1843. He established the Pittsburgh Evening Mail, in 1868, and "The Southern Magazine," at New Orleans. His plays that met with most success included "My Partner," "Fairfax, or Life in the Sunny South," "The Galley Slave," "Matrimony," "The White Slave," "Siberia" and "Paquita."

They appeared in New York and English theatres. He died at Middletown, New York, July 30, 1888.

CANACHQUASY (Captain New Castle), probably the son of Queen Aliquippa. During the French and Indian War, he rendered valuable service to the English. At a meeting of the Provincial Council, on August 22, 1755, Governor Morris gave him the name New Castle, because in 1701, his parents had presented him to William Penn at New Castle.

CANALS—The Union Canal is believed to be the oldest work of the kind in the United States. The idea of connecting Philadelphia with the western waters, by means of a continuous water navigation, was first projected by William Penn himself, in 1690. The route proposed by Penn was that now occupied by the Union Canal. The first actual survey of this route was made by a committee of the American Philosophical Society, 1770. The leading man in executing this survey was William Smith, D. D., Provost of the University of Pennsylvania. The same route was again surveyed a little later by David Rittenhouse, the astronomer, under the direction of the Legislature. The Revolutionary War suspended all further operations until 1790, when an association was formed for the purpose of improving the inland communications of the State. The leading members of this association were Robert Morris, the financier; David Rittenhouse and Dr. Smith, already mentioned; Thomas Mifflin, the governor, and other men of that stamp, well known in the early history of the State. They projected an extended plan for connecting Philadelphia with the Ohio and Lake Erie, by means of slack water navigation and canals. Their plan was to improve, by these means, the navigation of the Schuylkill up to Reading; thence by canal through the Lebanon Valley, and along the route of the Tulpehocken and Swatara Creeks to the Susquehanna; thence westerly to Pittsburgh.

The consultations and inquiries of this association led to the formation of two companies, both of which were incorporated by the Legislature. The first of these was called "The Schuylkill and Susquehanna Navigation Company." It was incorporated in 1791, with a capital of $400,000. Its object was to construct a canal from the Schuylkill at Reading, to Middletown on the Susquehanna, along the route first projected by Penn, and afterwards surveyed by Smith, Rittenhouse and others. This canal, as compared with those now made, was a mere ditch, suited to the accommodation of boats carrying from seven to ten tons each. Several miles of the most expensive part, across the summit level at Lebanon, were completed within three or four years after the organization of the company.

The second company was incorporated in the year 1792, under the title of the "Delaware and Schuylkill Navigation Company," also with a capital of $400,000. Its object was to construct a canal, a little to the north of the city of Philadelphia, from some point on the Delaware near Kensington, across towards the Schuylkill, to a point near Fairmount, and thence to make a water communication, partly by canal and partly by dams, up the Schuylkill to Reading, there to connect with the work first mentioned. This company proceeded to excavate a large part of the bed of their canal, from a point near the Schuylkill River, Second and Fairmount, up to Peters' Island, where the Columbia bridge now stands. It also made considerable progress in the work near Norristown.

The two companies had completed about fifteen miles of the most difficult and expensive parts of the canal, comprising numerous locks, deep cuttings, heavy embankments, and much rock excavation, when commercial difficulties obliged them to suspend operations, after having expended upon the enterprise upwards of $450,000. Though nominally and legally distinct, the two companies consisted of nearly the same stockholders and managers, and Robert Morris was president of both. In 1811, they were reorganized, and formally united under the title, which they continued to bear, of the "Union Canal Company." The War of 1812 again put a stop to all enterprises of this kind, nor were active operations renewed until 1821.

Between the last named year and the year 1827, the canal was carried forward to completion, and opened for navigation. On Friday, June 15th, of that year (1827), the "Lebanon Beobachter" (Lebanon Observer), a German weekly, established in 1817 as "Der Unpartheyischer Berichter" (Unpartisan Newsbearer), but in 1826, changed to "Der Beobachter," as above, contained this item (here translated):

"On last Monday all the citizens of this town and vicinity had the privilege of seeing the first boat, the 'Alpha,' come up the Union Canal from Tulpehocken (Myerstown), and remain over night at North Lebanon. The following morning it started on its journey westward, and passed through the tunnel. This was the first vessel of the kind to pass through a place over which corn and potatoes were growing, and hay was being made. It is a handsome and well built boat, and is 65 feet long."

Thus was signalized the completion at last of this wonderful waterway, 137 years after its inception. The canal at once became, and for many years remained, a great traffic line, but declined in trade progressively year by year after 1858, on account of the opening that year of the Lebanon Valley R. R. (Reading to Harrisburg). That line, tapping the same sections as the canal, gradually absorbed the latter's traffic, so much so that by the year 1884, the canal was without any trade, and in the fall of that year the last boat passed through it.

One of the earliest canals in Pennsylvania was built on the western side of the Susquehanna River, around the Conewago Falls, at York Haven. It was dedicated by Governor Thomas Mifflin, November 22, 1797. The canal was a mile in length, forty feet wide and four feet deep. It had two locks which lowered the nineteen feet of fall. This canal was in use until the railroad from Baltimore was extended to Harrisburg in 1850.

Work on the Pennsylvania Canal was begun on July 4, 1826. It was built along the eastern side of the Susquehanna and extended from the mouth of the Juniata River to the mouth of the Swatara Creek at Middletown. Later it was extended to Columbia and was called the Eastern Division of the Pennsylvania

Canal. The canal was forty feet wide, four feet deep with locks seventeen feet wide and ninety feet long. On July 4, 1826, work was also begun on the western end of the canal, extending from Pittsburgh to the mouth of the Kiskiminetas. At the same time a canal designed to connect Pittsburgh with Lake Erie, extending from French Creek to Conneaut Lake, was started. Later the Pennsylvania Canal was extended to Lewistown and up the Susquehanna to Northumberland.

CANBY, WILLIAM MARRIOTT, botanist, was born at Philadelphia, in 1831. He became interested in botany as an avocation and collected a herbarium of more than 30,000 plants, now owned by the New York College of Pharmacy. A smaller collection is in the possession of the Delaware Society of Natural History. Canby was connected with the Northern Pacific Transcontinental Survey as botanist. He died in 1904.

CAPTAIN JACOBS, chief of the Delaware Indians, who soon after Braddock's defeat took up arms against Pennsylvania. He lived principally at Kittanning, in Armstrong County, but also resided near Mount Pleasant, Westmoreland County, and near Lewistown, where Colonel Buchanan, to whom he sold land, gave him the name of Captain Jacobs, because of his close resemblance to a German settler in Cumberland County.

CARANTOUAN, a town of the Carantouannau (Susquehannas), referred to by Champlain as able to muster more than eight hundred warriors. Located at Spanish Hill, in Athens Township, Bradford County, near Waverly, N. Y. Champlain in his fight against the Iroquois sent his interpreter, Etienne Brule, to visit Carantouan. Later he followed the Susquehanna River to its mouth and returned to Carantouan.—*See also* BRULE.

CARBON COUNTY, formed from part of Northampton and Monroe, March 13, 1843. Named for anthracite coal deposits there. Land area, 406 square miles; population (1930), 63,380; (1920), 62,565. County-seat, Mauch Chunk, laid out in 1815.

CAREY, HENRY CHARLES, political economist, was born at Philadelphia, December 15, 1793. He became a partner with his father, Matthew Carey, in a bookselling, publishing firm in 1814, continuing there until 1835. He became an ardent supporter of the protectionist theory in economics on the principle of temporary expediency of the idea that the growth of population was self-regulating; opposed Ricardo's theories on the law of diminishing returns. His best known publications are "The Principles of Political Economy," "The Credit System in France, Great Britain and the United States," "The Past, the Present and the Future," "The Principles of Social Science," "Letters on Political Economy," and "The Unity of Law." He died at Philadelphia, October 13, 1879.

CAREY, MATTHEW, writer and bookseller, was born at Dublin, Ireland, on January 28, 1760. He came to Philadelphia in 1784 where he began publication of The Pennsylvania Herald. He extended his publishing activities and included book-selling In 1814, he produced "The Olive Branch" intended to promote peace between rival political parties of the War of 1812 period. Its popularity is evidenced by the fact that it appeared in ten editions. He also produced "Irish Vindications" and "Essays on Political Economy." He died at Philadelphia, September 16, 1839.

CARLISLE, a borough and county-seat of Cumberland County, is located eighteen miles west of Harrisburg, and was founded in 1783. During the Whiskey Rebellion, in 1794, Washington made his headquarters here and the Confederates invaded the town in 1863. Carlisle is the seat of Dickinson College, a co-educational institution, founded in 1783. The industries include the manufacture of silk, cotton, shoes, hosiery, paper boxes, carpets, and chain and switch works, machine shops and axle works. Population (1930), 12,596; (1920), 10,916.

CARLISLE INDIAN SCHOOL—See UNITED STATES INDIAN TRAINING AND INDUSTRIAL SCHOOL.

CARNEGIE, ANDREW, manufacturer and philanthropist, was born at Dunfermline, Scotland, November 25, 1835, the son of William and Margaret Morrison Carnegie. William Carnegie was a handloom weaver and his wife, the daughter of a shoemaker and tanner, but from both lines the son, Andrew, inherited a certain dissatisfaction with things as they are and a desire to progress, economically, socially and intellectually. The introduction of the factory system making it impossible for the elder Carnegie to secure work, he with his wife and sons, Andrew and Thomas, came to America in 1848 and settled with a group of their own countrymen, including a number of relatives who had arrived in America some years earlier, in Allegheny. William Carnegie obtained employment in a cotton factory and Andrew became a bobbin boy in the same factory at $1.20 a week. Because of his industry and his intense desire to succeed, Andrew advanced rapidly. From bobbin boy and engine tender, he became a telegraph messenger, then an operator, and later private secretary to Thomas Scott, of the Pennsylvania Railroad. In 1860, he succeeded Scott as superintendent of the Pittsburgh division of the railroad. During his connection with the railroad he introduced Pullman sleeping cars. At the time of the Civil War, he assisted Scott who was assistant secretary of war in charge of military transportation, transported the first troops to Washington and was in charge of the organization of the telegraph department.

With the Civil War the iron industry in America grew. The war brought demands for railway supplies and war materials of various kinds. Carnegie became an iron master, resigning his position with the railroad, in 1865, that he might devote all his time to the new venture. In addition to iron manufacturing,

ANDREW CARNEGIE

he became interested in oil, steel, railroad securities and other forms of business enterprise. Carnegie was audacious in his business dealings, and because of this characteristic became the pioneer in American "big business." He was an excellent judge of men and therefore a competent organizer. In 1882, Henry Clay Frick, a genius in the coke industry, joined Carnegie, becoming chairman of Carnegie Brothers, Limited, in 1889. Until the Carnegie Company was absorbed by the United States Steel Company it was a limited partnership, all shares being held by active members; thus Carnegie demonstrated his democratic business principles, and his hatred of "speculation." During periods of depression he improved and enlarged his plant, taking advantage of low prices and at the same time encouraging prosperity.

However, in spite of his vast business enterprises, Carnegie continued an interest in literary and cultural pursuits which had manifested themselves in his boyhood. He was a friend of Matthew Arnold, who visited him in 1883, of William E. Gladstone, Lloyd George, Theodore Roosevelt, James G. Blaine, Richard Watson Gilder, Mark Twain, Elihu Root and other political and literary notables. He was a frequent contributor to such magazines as the *Nineteenth Century* and *North American Review*. In 1886, he published a book, "Triumphant Democracy," the purpose of which was to show the superiority of Republican institutions over the monarchial and particularly of American institutions over the English. Later he obtained control, through purchase, of a number of English newspapers through which he advocated the establishment of a British republic. In June, 1889, Carnegie's article "Wealth," appeared in the North American Review. Shortly afterward Gladstone had it republished in William T. Stead's *Pall Mall Gazette* under the title "The Gospel of Wealth." In this article Carnegie maintained that the wealthy man should regard himself merely as a temporary guardian of the money he held and that the surplus funds should be distributed to institutions and organizations that sponsored the public welfare.

Upon the sale of the Carnegie Company to the United States Steel Corporation, in 1901, Carnegie immediately devoted $5,000,000 to a pension and benefit fund for employees of the Carnegie Company. In further upholding his principle of public distribution of surplus wealth, Carnegie gave away a total of $350,000,000. The greatest gifts were to the Carnegie Corporation of New York, to public library buildings, colleges, churches (for the purchasing of organs), Carnegie Foundation for the Advancement of Teaching, Carnegie Institute, Pittsburgh; Carnegie Institution of Washington, Hero Funds, Endowment for International Peace, Scottish Universities Trust, United Kingdom Trust, and the Dunfermline Trust. Among other honors which he received were honorary degrees of many colleges and universities, and his election as Lord Rector of the Universities of St. Andrews and Aberdeen. He died at "Shadowbrook," his summer home in Massachusetts, on August 1, 1919.

CARNEGIE INSTITUTE OF TECHNOLOGY, located in Pittsburgh, was founded by Andrew Carnegie, who on November 15, 1900, offered the city money with which to establish a technical school, under the condition that the city provide a suitable location for the institution. The offer was accepted in 1901, a site was selected and ground for the new buildings was broken in April, 1905. In October, of that year, the "Carnegie Technical School" was opened for the admission of students. The name was changed to the Carnegie Institute of Technology on April 20, 1912. The institution includes college of engineering, college of industries, Margaret Morrison Carnegie College and College of Fine Arts. Dr. Thomas Stockham Baker is president of the institute. Enrollment in all colleges (1930), 2,550.

CARPENTER, CYRUS CLAY, soldier and politician, was born in Harford, Susquehanna County, November 24, 1829. At ten years of age, he was left an orphan and became apprenticed to a tailor. In 1854, he went to Fort Dodge, Iowa, where he served as a government surveyor. He held various offices in educational, military and political life and climaxed his career by serving as governor of Iowa for four years following 1872. He died at Fort Dodge, May 29, 1898.

CARPENTER, SAMUEL, an early trader, settled in Philadelphia. He held a number of government positions, and was an active member of the Society of Friends. He died in 1713.

CARPENTER'S HALL, Philadelphia, meeting-place for the Continental Congress; was built in Chestnut Street between 3rd and 4th Streets just before 1770. It was intended to be used as a meeting-place for the local Carpenter's Guild and for public meetings. It has become immortal because of the business transacted there that culminated in the formation of the United States.

CARSON, HAMPTON LAWRENCE, lawyer and publicist, was born at Philadelphia, on February 21, 1852. He graduated at the University of Pennsylvania in 1871, and rapidly gained prominence as a lawyer and lecturer, becoming a member of the faculty of the law school at his Alma Mater. His best known productions are, "History of the Supreme Court of the United States," "The Law of Criminal Conspiracies as Found in American Cases," and "History of the One Hundredth Anniversary of the Promulgation of the Constitution of the United States." Died July 18, 1929.

CASSATT, ALEXANDER JOHNSTON, railway president, was born at Pittsburgh, December 8, 1839. He was educated at Heidelburg and at Rensselaer Institute. In 1859, he began his career in railway development as a civil engineer and became connected with The Pennsylvania Railroad as a roadman in 1861. He became general superintendent, general manager of the lines east of Pittsburgh, third vice-president, first vice-president, director and in 1899, president of the Pennsylvania System. One of his most outstanding accomplishments was the construction of the Pennsylvania Terminal in New York. He died December 28, 1906.

CASSATT, MARY, artist, was born at Pittsburgh, May 22, 1845. In 1875, she went to Europe and studied in Spain and France. She exhibited some of her works in New York City and Paris and has gained prominence as an etcher. She died June 14, 1926.

CASSELMAN RIVER—Tributary to Youghiogheny River. Sub-basin: Monongahela; source, formed by junction of North and South Branches in Garrett County, Maryland, four miles south of state boundary; course, northeasterly, crossing state boundary into Somerset County to Meyersdale; thence northwesterly to Rockwood; thence southwesterly to Youghiogheny River; mouth, at Confluence; length, in Pennsylvania, fourty two miles.

CASSIN, JOHN, ornithologist, was born at Chester, on September 6, 1813. After 1834, he lived at Philadelphia and became interested in ornithology as an avocation. He contributed to the *Proceedings* and *Journal* of the Philadelphia Academy of Natural Science. He was a recognized authority on bird life throughout the world. He published "Birds of California and Texas." "Mammalogy and Ornithology of the Wilkes' Exploring Expedition" and "Ornithology of Gilliss' Astronomical Expedition to Chile." He died at Philadelphia, January 10, 1869.

CATAWISSA CREEK—Tributary to North Branch Susquehanna River. Sub-basin: Lower North Branch Susquehanna; source, in Hazel Township, southern Luzerne County; course, southwesterly into Schuylkill County; thence northwesterly to Mainville in Columbia County; thence southwesterly to North Branch Susquehanna River; mouth, at Catawissa; length, thirty-six miles. Indian name, Ganawese, another name of the Conoy.

CATFISH CAMP, a tract of land in Washington County, on which the borough of Washington now stands. This land, with two other tracts, was the first surveyed and sold after the opening of the land office of Pennsylvania for the sale of lands west of the Allegheny Mountains and south of the Ohio River. A Council of War was held here on January 28, 1777.

CATHOLIC CHURCH, THE—The first parish of the Catholic Church in Pennsylvania was organized in 1720 by the Rev. Joseph Wheaton. The first priest to visit Pennsylvania, as far as is known, was the Rev. John Pierron, of Canada, who traveled through the state in 1673-1674. In 1733, the first Catholic Church was organized with a congregation of twenty-two Irish and fifteen

Germans. A German who came to America in 1683 with Daniel Pastorius, founder of Germantown, was the first Catholic resident of Philadelphia. Before the Revolution, and for many years after it, St. Mary's Parish, Philadelphia, was the largest Catholic Parish in the United States. In 1782, a parochial school was organized in that parish. Later, the German Jesuits established schools at Goshenhoppen, Berks County; at Lancaster, Hanover and other places. The first Catholic school in western Pennsylvania was established at Sportsman's Hall, Westmoreland County, after 1787. Later, the Benedictines built St. Vincent's Abbey and College there. A Catholic settlement was formed in Cambria County by Father Demetrius Augustine Gallitzin in 1799, and in 1800 a school was begun at Loretto. In 1811, the first Catholic Church in Pittsburgh was built, and a convent and academy were established there in 1828. The church organized schools at Pittsburgh, in 1835; McSherrytown, in 1830; Harrisburg, in 1828; and Pottsville, in 1836. Bishop Challoner in a report to the Propaganda in 1763 gave the number of missionaries in Pennsylvania as five and the number of Catholics as six or seven thousand. In 1808, the diocese of Philadelphia was erected, and in 1843 that of Pittsburgh. The diocese of Philadelphia became an archdiocese in 1875. In 1926, there were in Pennsylvania 2,124,382 members of the Roman Catholic Church.—See also CONEWAGO CHAPEL.

CATLIN, GEORGE, traveler and artist, was born at Wilkes-Barre, on June 26, 1796. He practised law for a time and then established a studio for portrait painting in Philadelphia. In 1832, he began to make special studies of the American Indians and traveled extensively throughout North and South America. He introduced groups of American Indians to European courts. The Catlin Gallery in the National Museum at Washington, D. C., is named for him and includes 500 portraits from life of American Indians. He died at Jersey City, New Jersey, December 23, 1872.

CATTEL, WILLIAM CASSADAY, educator and clergyman, was born at Salem, New Jersey, on August 30, 1827. He graduated from Princeton in 1848 and from the Theological Seminary there in 1852. He taught Latin and Greek at Lafayette from 1855 to 1860 and became president of that institution in 1863. He served in that capacity for twenty years and became an important figure in the educational work of the Presbyterian Church. On February 11, 1898, he died at Philadelphia.

CATTELL, JAMES McKEEN, psychologist, was born at Easton, May 25, 1860. In 1880, he graduated from Lafayette College and subsequently studied at the universities of Leipzig, Paris, Geneva, and Gottingen. He taught at the University of Leipzig, University of Pennsylvania and Columbia University, where he was professor of experimental psychology from 1891 to 1917. He served at various times as editor of "*The Psychological Review,*" "*Science,*" "*Scientific Monthly,*" "*School and Society,*" "*The American Naturalist,*" and

"*American Men of Science.*" In 1929, he was president of the International Congress of Psychology. He is the author of many psychological researches and lives at Garrison-on-Hudson, New York.

CAVES—Particularly in the limestone region of Pennsylvania are caves abundant. Their histories are mingled with tradition to such an extent that it is difficult to distinguish fact from legend. Eleven Pennsylvania caves have been exploited. They are the Alexander Caverns, in Mifflin County; Crystal Cave, five miles west of Kutztown, Berks County; Hipple Cave, Bedford County; Historic Indian Cave, Franklinville, Blair County; Indian Echo Cave, Hummelstown, Dauphin County; Lost Cave, Hellertown, Northampton County; Onyx Cave, Berks County; Penn's Cave, Brush Valley, Centre County; Seawra Cave, Mifflin County; Veiled Lady Cave, near Centre Hall, Centre County; Woodward Cave, Centre County. Alexander Caverns including a dry cave and a wet one (the latter accessible only by boat) were discovered in 1926, and immediately commercialized by the owner who formed a small company. Crystal Cave was discovered in 1871, by William Merkel, who was quarrying limestone near there. It was opened to the public in 1873 and is the first cave to be commercialized in the state. Hipple Cave was discovered several generations ago, but was not opened to the public until 1928. Historic Indian Cave was probably discovered by the Indians long before the arrival of the white man. David Lewis, the robber, frequented it, in the early nineteenth century. In 1928, the cave was commercialized. Indian Echo Cave was discovered many years ago, but was not opened to visitors until 1929. Lost Cave, discovered in 1883, by men quarrying limestone, was opened in 1930. Onyx Cave, known since 1872, was made ready for visitors in 1923. Penn's Cave, a traditional Indian retreat, was prepared for public inspection about 1885. It is the only cave in the state through which visitors are taken by boat only. Seawra Cave was opened in 1928. Veiled Lady is surrounded by tradition. It receives its name from a white formation inside the entrance. Woodward Cave, another Indian haunt, was opened to the public in 1925. Undeveloped caves in the state are: Arch Spring, in Blair County; Bear Cave, Westmoreland County; Bethlehem, under the Sun Inn, in Bethlehem; Carpenter, Northampton County; Coburn, Centre County; Conodoguinet, Cumberland County; Delaney, Fayette County; Driebelbis, Berks County; Durham, Bucks County; Frankstown, Blair County; Hartman, Monroe County; Maiden Creek, Berks County; Mammoth Spring, Mifflin County; Mapleton, Huntingdon County; Naginey, Mifflin County; Needy, Franklin County; Port Kennedy, Montgomery County; Redington, Lehigh County; Reese, Franklin County; Williamson, Franklin County.

CAVES AS HOMES OF SETTLERS—In the early days of the Province many settlers lived in caves in Philadelphia and vicinity. These caves were not all made by passengers who came over with William Penn. The Indians dug some, the Swedes may have dug others. Dr. Mease in his "Pictures of Philadelphia" gives the opinion that the name Schuylkill, "hidden river," came from the fact that many Maryland settlers lurked on the banks, concealing themselves from the Dutch and probably from the Indians, but this is considered doubtful. Caves existed in 1685 along the shores of the Schuylkill and Delaware Rivers and complaints reached the ears of Penn in reference to drinking and loose conduct in these caves. Penn ordered them vacated and held for other tenants immigrating under similar circumstances. These caves are matters of interest to the antiquarian. It is not unlikely that some of these excavations, if not the most of them, had been made for the Indians, for their counter quarters. The falling in of any part of the river bank would expose the burrowing of muskrats and other animals and suggest the enlargement of same by the Indians for their own use. Caves were used for defense and concealment in case of raids by hostile tribes. In 1682, about one-third of the population of Philadelphia wintered in them after enlarging and making them more comfortable. In 1685, these caves became low resorts and one Joseph Knight was refused the continuance of his traffic and the caves finally filled in by throwing upon them the banks upon which they were built.

CEDAR CREST COLLEGE, for women, at Allentown, is a non-sectarian institution, established in 1867. Enrollment (1930-1931), 180.

CELERON'S EXPEDITION—In the summer of 1749, Celeron de Bienville was sent by the Governor-General of New France down the valleys of the Allegheny and the Ohio to take formal possession of the region drained by these rivers for the King of France. Descending Conewango Creek to the Allegheny, Celeron, on July 29th, buried a leaden plate on the bank of the river. Other leaden plates were buried mostly at the mouths of tributary streams. At or near Pittsburgh he met Queen Allaquippa and at Logstown he ordered the raising of the French flag to replace the English one.—*See* Sipe: THE INDIAN WARS OF PENNSYLVANIA.

CENTENNIAL EXHIBITION, held in Philadelphia from May 10, to November 10, 1876, as a World's Fair on the occasion of the 100th anniversary of the American Declaration of Independence.

CENTRE COUNTY, formed from part of Mifflin, Northumberland, Lycoming and Huntingdon, February 13, 1800. Named because of geographic location in state. Land area, 1,146 square miles; population (1930), 46,294; (1920), 44,304 County seat, Bellefonte, laid out in 1795.

CENTRE DEMOCRAT, THE, a weekly newspaper was established in 1827 at Bellefonte by General Philip Benner. Thomas Simpson was its first editor and publisher. At one time it was an organ of the Know-Nothing Party.

It appears every Thursday, is Democratic in politics, and is edited by Cecil A. Walker. Circulation, 6,500.

CENTRE REPORTER, THE, of Centre Hall, is a Democratic weekly newspaper that was established in 1827. It appears every Thursday and has a circulation of 970. S. W. Smith and E. E. Bailey are the editors and publishers.

CHALKLEY, THOMAS, an early religious leader He settled in Pennsylvania from where he traveled about throughout the colonies, holding meetings. He died at Tortola, November 4, 1741.

CHAMBERSBURG, a borough, and the county-seat of Franklin County, located 49 miles southwest of Harrisburg. It was settled in 1730, by Benjamin Chambers, and was originally called Falling Creek. On July 30, 1864, during the Civil War, General McCausland, with the Confederate Cavalry, entered the town, demanding tribute money to the amount of $100,000 in gold. The money not being received the Confederates burned the town which was shortly afterwards rebuilt. Chambersburg is the seat of Wilson College for women and of Penn Hall, a girls school. Included among the town's industries are the manufacture of machinery, hosiery, furniture, wool, dresses, paper, iron, engines, boilers, soap, silk and iron castings. The shops of the Cumberland Valley Railroad are located here. Population (1930), 13,788; (1920), 13,171.

CHAPMAN, HENRY CADWALADER, physician, was born in Philadelphia, on August 17, 1845. In 1867, he graduated from the medical school of the University of Pennsylvania and spent the three succeeding years studying in Europe. Upon his return he settled in Philadelphia where he developed a large practice and lectured at both the University of Pennsylvania and Jefferson Medical College. In addition, he was curator of the Philadelphia Academy of Sciences. His published works include "Evolution of Life," "History of the Discovery of the Circulation of the Blood," "Medical Jurisprudence and Toxicology." He died September 7, 1909, at his summer home in Bar Harbor, Maine.

CHARLEROI, a city in Washington County, on the Monongahela River, 40 miles south of Pittsburgh. It was settled in 1890 and incorporated in 1891. Mining is the principal industry and there are also manufactories of glass and shovels. Population (1930), 11,260; (1920), 11,516.

CHARTERS AND CONSTITUTIONS OF PENNSYLVANIA—Pennsylvania has been governed by seven organic laws: three charters and four constitutions. The charters of 1682, 1683 and 1701, given by William Penn; and the constitutions of 1776, 1790, 1838 and 1873. The charters of 1682 and 1683 are in the custody of the Department of Archives, Pennsylvania State Library; the charter of 1701 is not in the Archives. The constitutions of 1776, 1790,

1838 and 1873 are in the custody of the Secretary of the Commonwealth.—*See also under each charter and constitution.*

CHARTIER, PETER, Indian trader. He was the son of Martin Chartier, a Frenchman, and a Shawnee squaw. It is said that Peter Chartier also married a Shawnee squaw. He traded with the Shawnees near Washington Borough, Lancaster County, and later at Paxtang and near the present town of New Cumberland, Cumberland County. Still later he is said to have moved to the valley of New Conococheague, and about 1730, began trading with the Shawnees on the Conemaugh and Kiskiminetas and later on the Allegheny. About 1744, Chartier with about four hundred Shawnees joined the French in Canada. Several years later the Indians apologized to the New Colonial Authorities for their desertion but Chartier, himself, never returned to Pennsylvania. Chartier River in Westmoreland County and Chartier's Creek in Washington and Allegheny Counties are named for him.

CHARTIERS CREEK—Tributary to Ohio River. Sub-basin: Main Ohio; source, in South Franklin Township, southern Washington County; course, northeasterly into Allegheny County to Ohio River; mouth, at McKees Rocks; length, fifty-two miles.

CHAUVENET, WILLIAM, astronomer and mathematician, was born at Milford, on May 24, 1820. He graduated from Yale and became instructor in mathematics in the navy, serving on U. S. S. Mississippi in 1841. Subsequently he held positions at the United States Naval Academy and at Washington University at St. Louis, Missouri, of which institution he became chancellor. He was the author of "Spherical and Practical Astronomy," and "Elementary Geometry." On December 13, 1870, he died at St. Paul, Minn.

CHEST CREEK—Tributary to West Branch Susquehanna River. Sub-basin: Upper West Branch Susquehanna; source on Cambria-Allegheny Township boundary, central Cambria County; course, northerly into Clearfield County; thence northwesterly to West Branch Susquehanna River; mouth, at Mahaffey; length, thirty-six miles.

CHESTER, a city and port in Delaware County, on the Delaware River, 15 miles south of Philadelphia, is the oldest town in the state. It was settled in 1643 by Swedes and given the name Upland. The city is noted for its ship and boat building. Other industries are the manufacture of chemical products, leather and rubber goods, textiles, metals and metal products. Population (1930), 59,164; (1920), 58,030.

CHESTER COUNTY was one of the three original counties established when the province was first settled in 1682. The others were Philadelphia and

Bucks. Chester County was named for Cheshire, England. Land area, 777 square miles; population (1930), 126,629; (1920), 115,120. County-seat, West Chester, laid out in 1786.

CHEW, BENJAMIN, jurist, was born in Maryland, November 29, 1722. He studied law in Philadelphia under Andrew Hamilton and later went abroad to study at the Middle Temple. Returning to Philadelphia in 1743 at the time of his father's death, he was admitted to the Supreme Court Bar in September, 1746. He practiced in New Castle and Dover, Delaware, but returned to Philadelphia about 1754. From 1755 to 1769, he served as attorney-general; in 1756, he became Speaker of the Assembly of the lower counties and in 1765, was made register-general of Pennsylvania. In 1774, he became chief justice of the Supreme Court of Pennsylvania, which office he retained until the outbreak of the Revolution. After the Signing of the Declaration of Independence he did not show proper patriotism and with John Penn was paroled for a time, living at Union Iron Works, N. J., until Congress ordered his return without parole. Chew and Washington were on friendly terms and the president attended the wedding of Chew's daughter, Peggy, and Col. John Howard at Chew House, Germantown. Judge Chew died January 20, 1810.

CHEW MANSION, or "Cliveden," at Germantown, the country house of Judge Benjamin Chew, figured prominently in the Battle of Germantown. On October 4, 1777, Lieutenant-Colonel Musgrave, a British officer, with six companies, took possession of the residence and turned it into a fortification, from which he led a successful attack upon the American troops.

THE CHEW MANSION

CHEYNEY, EDWARD POTTS, historian, was born at Wallingford, on January 18, 1861. He studied at the University of Pennsylvania in the undergraduate and graduate schools, traveled extensively, studying and occupying himself in research in German universities and in the British Museum. He is professor of European History at the University of Pennsylvania and has become an acknowledged American authority on social and economic life in England. His best known contributions are "Social and Industrial History of England," "European Background of American History," and "Readings in English History." He lives in Philadelphia.

CHEYNEY TRAINING SCHOOL FOR TEACHERS—From 1842, this institution, known first as the Institute for Colored Youth of Philadelphia, and after 1913, as the Cheyney Training School for Teachers, devoted to training colored men and women for professional work in colored schools, was conducted as a private corporation, administered solely, and supported principally, by members of the Society of Friends. Realizing that a growing institution like this would require increasing resources which no limited corporation could supply, the management requested an examination and appraisal of the school by the State with the idea of cooperation and articulation with the general State system. The required improvements were made and it opened as a standardized Normal School, September 13, 1920. In 1921, the whole property was transferred to the Commonwealth by regular act of the General Assembly. Cheyney is located twenty-two miles from Philadelphia.

CHICKIES (BIG) CREEK—Tributary to Susquehanna River. Sub-basin: Lower Main Susquehanna; source, in Rapho Township, northwestern Lancaster County; course, southwesterly, by a circuitous route, to Susquehanna River; mouth, at Chickies; length, twenty-five and one-half miles.

CHILDS, GEORGE WILLIAM, publisher, was born at Baltimore, Maryland, on May 12, 1829. Until July, 1849, when he became connected with R. E. Peterson, bookseller, he had spent fifteen months in the U. S. Navy, and had engaged in the confectionery business. In May, 1863, he founded the *American Publishers' Circular and Literary Gazette*, edited by R. Shelton Mackenzie. He purchased the Philadelphia Public Ledger, in December, 1864, and was successful in his management of it. Childs wrote "Recollections of General Grant" and "Recollection of George W. Childs." His death occurred February 3, 1894.

CHILLISQUAQUE CREEK—Tributary to West Branch Susquehanna River. Sub-basin: Lower West Branch Susquehanna; source, in Madison Township, western Columbia County; course, southwesterly, through Montour County, into Northumberland County to West Branch Susquehanna River; mouth, at Chillisquaque; length, twenty-four miles. Indian name, corrupted from Chililisuagi, "place of snow-birds."

CHILLOWAY, JOB, a friendly Delaware Indian, frequently acted as interpreter for the whites and Indians.

CHRIST CHURCH, PHILADELPHIA, was established about 1695 as the "Church in Philadelphia," and was the first Protestant Episcopal Church in that city. The first building was erected in 1697, and Christ Church, probably located on the present site on Second Street, early became the leader of all others in Philadelphia. All the lieutenant-governors under the proprietaries, except William Markham, and all the proprietaries after William Penn were members of this church. The governor's pew, more elaborately ornamented than the rest, was occupied by the proprietaries of the province, later by the President of Congress and still later by Presidents Washington and Adams. The church was the scene of many patriotic sermons during the Revolution and it was here that plans for the organization of the Protestant Episcopal Church in the United States were made. Among the eminent Philadelphians who are buried in the graveyard of Christ Church at the corner of Fifth and Arch Streets, are Benjamin Franklin; Francis Hopkinson, signer of the Declaration of Independence; Peyton Randolph, president of the First Continental Congress, and Dr. Benjamin Rush.

CHRISTIANA RIOT, occurred at Christiana, Lancaster County, in 1851, when a number of Maryland citizens attempted to seize a fugitive slave there. There was a fierce skirmish in which the leader of the pursuing party, Edward Gorsuch, was killed. Castner Hanway, a Quaker, was charged with treason for refusing to assist the United States Marshal in ending the riot, and Elijah Lewis, also a Quaker, was charged with riot and blood shed.

CHURCH, SAMUEL HARDEN, college president, was born in Caldwell County, Missouri, January 24, 1858. He attended the Western University of Pennsylvania, Bethany and Yale. In 1884, he was recognized by Governor Hoadly, of Ohio, for suppressing riots in Cincinnati. He served as superintendent of transportation for the Pennsylvania Railroad and later as vice-president of the lines west of Pittsburgh. He is vice-president of the Union Steel Casting Company, president of Carnegie Institute in Pittsburgh, and a trustee of the Carnegie Corporation of New York. He has been active in the interests of the Republican party and is a member of many honorary clubs and orders at home and abroad. He contributes to many periodicals and is the author of works of literature, drama and history, among them, a "Short History of Pittsburgh," "History of the Pennsylvania Railroad Lines West of Pittsburgh," "The American Verdict on the War." He lives in Pittsburgh.

CHURCH OF GOD—Grew out of religious revivals held during 1825 among German Reformed congregations in Harrisburg, Shiremanstown, Lisbon, Mechanicsburg, Churchtown, New Cumberland, Linglestown, Middletown, Millerstown, Lebanon, Lancaster, Shippensburg, Elizabethtown, Mount Joy,

Marietta and other places. German Reformed Church members divided; some laymen and ministers, including Rev. John Winebrenner, adopted the apostolic plan set forth in the New Testament and established spiritual, free, independent churches made up of believers or Christians without creed, ordinances, laws, etc. Finally ministers agreed to cooperate and organize. Met in October, 1830, in Harrisburg, and appointed John Winebrenner, of Harrisburg, speaker, and John Elliott, of Lancaster, clerk. Decided to make purpose of organization the promotion of the conversion of sinners; the establishment of churches upon the New Testament plan and the supplying of the destitute with the preaching of the gospel. The Bible is the only authoritative constitution, ritual, creed, catechism, etc., of the Church of God. Each congregation is responsible for its own affairs and is not subject to a central organization. The denomination is thus loosely united in elderships. Biblical references are given to answer questions as to faith and practice of the Church of God. The one thing that distinguishes members from other Protestant Churches of Pennsylvania, and which they hold in common with the German Baptists and other plain people is as follows: "She believes in three positive ordinances of perpetual standing in the church, viz : Baptism, Feet-washing, and the Lord's Supper. In the ceremony of baptism an expression of faith should precede immersion." Each eldership holds an annual meeting of all teaching elders within bounds. Cooperation, not legislation, is the aim of eldership meetings.

CIRCULAR HUNT—It was customary in the period from 1820 to 1840 for large groups to ascend mountains and drive game before them into the valley on the opposite sides of the mountains and engage in wholesale slaughter as the surrounded game attempted to escape. This was called a circular hunt and was very popular in certain sections.

CIVILITY, CAPTAIN, a chief of the Conestogas, who were descended from the Susquehannas. Was active in maintaining friendly relations between the Indians and the provincial government, from 1710 to 1736. He attended conferences at Conestoga in 1710, at Philadelphia in 1718, 1720 and 1736. His name appears in correspondence of provincial governors Keith and Gordon.

CLAPHAM, WILLIAM, Colonial officer, was born in England, July 5, 1722. He entered the army as an ensign and was sent to America during the French and Indian War. In 1756, he was commissioned to organize a battalion to erect Fort Augusta and in 1763, he took part in Bouquet's expedition to the west. On May 28, 1763, Clapham, his wife and three children were murdered by the Indians at their home on the Sewickley Creek near the present town of West Newton.

CLARION, borough and county-seat of Clarion County. The town was laid out in 1840, although a settlement had been begun there previous to that time. Clarion was incorporated as a borough, April 6, 1841, and was named for the county in which it is located. It is located in the vicinity of coal mines and oil and natural gas wells and has manufactures of glass, brick, cement block and toilet preparations. Clarion State Teachers College is located here.

CLARION COUNTY, formed from part of Venango and Armstrong, March 11, 1839. Named for the Clarion River within its borders. Land area, 601 square miles; population (1930), 34,531; (1920), 36,170. County-seat, Clarion, laid out in 1840.

CLARION STATE TEACHERS' COLLEGE was opened April 12, 1887. Until February 8, 1916, when it was purchased and taken over by the State, it was under the joint control of the State and stockholders. In 1928, the institution was granted the authority by the State Council of Education to confer the degree of B. S. in Education, and in the following year became a Teachers' College. The college is situated in Clarion, Clarion County.

CLARK, EDWARD, architect, was born in Philadelphia, in 1822. He became an assistant to Thomas Walter under whom he studied and in 1865, became chief architect of the United States Capitol. He held the latter position until his death in Washington, January 6, 1902.

CLARK, FREDERICK THICKSTUN, novelist, was born in Pennsylvania, in 1858. He is the author of "A Mexican Girl," "In the Valley of Havilah," "On Cloud Mountain," "The Mistress of the Ranch."

CLARK, WILLIAM ANDREWS, mining engineer and politician, was born near Connellsville, January 8, 1839. His family moved to the west and he at one time was identified with mining development throughout the country and became the largest individual metal producer in the world. He was later a resident of Montana and represented that state at the Philadelphia Centennial in 1876. He was Montana's Masonic Grand Master in 1877, Major in the Nez Perce War against Chief Joseph, president of the constitutional convention that admitted Montana to the union, and was elected to the Senate of the United States in 1901 having resigned after a previous disputed election in 1898. He died March 2, 1925.

CLARK, WILLIS GAYLORD, poet, was born in Otisco, New York, on March 5, 1808. He became an editor of the Columbian Star, in 1830, but came to Philadelphia a short time afterwards to publish the Philadelphia Gazette. A complete edition of his poems was edited by his brother in 1847. He died in Philadelphia on June 12, 1841.

CLARK CREEK—Tributary to Susquehanna River. Sub-basin: Lower Main Susquehanna; source, in Rush Township, northeastern Dauphin County;

course, southwesterly to Susquehanna River; mouth, two miles west of Dauphin; length, twenty-eight miles.

CLARKE, CRESTON, actor, was born in Philadelphia on August 20, 1865, the son of John Sleeper Clarke. He was educated abroad and made his stage debut in London in 1882, becoming a prominent tragedian. As a playwright he is well known for "The Last of His Race." He died in 1910.

CLARKE, HELEN ARCHIBALD, author, was born in Philadelphia, November 13, 1860. She graduated from the music department of the University of Pennsylvania in 1884, and began writing for periodicals in 1887. She collaborated with Charlotte Porter in founding *Poet Lore*, a literary journal maintaining high standards. She became an acknowledged authority on Browning, editing his work and contributing articles on his life and work to various literary organs. In addition, she became a composer of piano music and a contributor to musical periodicals. Her writings include "Browning's Italy: a Study of Italian Life and Art in Browning;" "Browning's England: a Study of English Influences in Browning;" "Longfellow's Country;" "Hawthorne's Country;" "The Poet's New England;" "Browning and His Century." She died February 8, 1926.

CLAYTON, POWELL, soldier and diplomatist, was born at Bethel, on August 7, 1833. He was educated at Bristol and studied civil engineering, going to Leavenworth, Kansas, in 1859. He served as captain in the Union Army during the Civil War and in 1864, became brigadier-general of volunteers. After the war ended he moved to Arkansas and rose to prominence there as governor in 1868, United States Senator from 1871 to 1877, minister and then ambassador to Mexico after 1897. In 1912, he moved to Washington, D. C., where he resided until his death on August 25, 1914.

CLEARFIELD (1843)

CLEARFIELD, county-seat of Clearfield County, is located in the west central part of Pennsylvania on the west branch of the Susquehanna River. It was settled in 1805 and incorporated as a borough in 1840. The industries include the manufacture of sewer pipe, machinery, refrigerators, cut glass, silk velvet, wagons, swings, foundry products, tanned leather, etc. Clearfield is located in an agricultural region, rich also in deposits of coal, fire-clay and limestone. Population (1930), 9,221; (1920), 8,529.

CLEARFIELD COUNTY, formed from part of Huntingdon and Lycoming, March 26, 1804. Named for Clearfield Creek within its limits. Land area, 1,142 square miles; population (1930), 86,727; (1920), 103,236. County-seat, Clearfield, laid out in 1805.

CLEARFIELD CREEK—Tributary to West Branch Susquehanna River. Sub-basin: Upper West Branch Susquehanna; source, in Munster Township, eastern Cambria County; course, northeasterly into Clearfield County to West Branch Susquehanna River; mouth, near Clearfield; length, sixty-two miles.

CLEARFIELD REPUBLICAN, THE, originally the Pennsylvania Banner, was established in 1827 by Christopher Kratzer and George S. Irvin. It appears every Friday; is Democratic in politics, and John F. Short is the editor and publisher. Circulation, 2,270.

CLINTON COUNTY, formed from part of Lycoming and Centre, June 21, 1839. Probably named for Governor De Witt Clinton of New York. Land area, 878 square miles; population (1930), 32,319; (1920), 33,555. County-seat, Lock Haven, laid out in 1833.

CLOCK-MAKERS, EARLY—About 1720, as the demand for clocks in this country increased, clock-makers settled in Philadelphia. Thirty years later clock-making had become an industry of importance. Among the early clock-makers in Pennsylvania were Joseph Ellicot, born in England in 1732, who later emigrated to this country and settled in Bucks County. His son, Andrew, born in 1754, in 1792 surveyor-general of the United States, was also a clock and mathematical instrument-maker. Benjamin Morris, Solomon Parke, Henry Wismer, Hugh Ely, Gotshalk, William Mans, Septimus Evans, Jacob, Peter, Benjamin, George, Samuel and John Solliday were all noted clock-makers of Bucks and Montgomery Counties.

CLOVER CREEK—Tributary to Frankstown Branch. Sub-basin: Upper Juniata; source, in Woodbury Township, northeastern Bedford County; course, northeasterly into Blair County to Frankstown Branch Juniata River; mouth, near Cove Forge; length, twenty-two miles.

CLYMER, GEORGE, statesman, was born in Philadelphia, in 1739. He became a merchant and was prominent in public life of the colony before 1775, when he became a treasurer of the Continental Congress. In 1776, he became a member of that body and signed the Declaration of Independence, the 38th man to write his name after that of John Hancock. He was a member of the Constitutional Convention and was influential in bringing the legislature of Pennsylvania to adopt the Federal Constitution. In 1788, he served as a member of the first Congress and in 1791 was appointed by President Washington as supervisor of the 14th district of Pennsylvania for collecting excise duties on spirits. The unpopularity of the excise led to the Whiskey Insurrection and Clymer resigned. He was appointed member of a commission to secure a satisfactory treaty with the Cherokee and Creek Indians of Georgia. He died at Morrisville on January 24, 1813.

COATES, FLORENCE EARLE, poet, was born in Philadelphia, July 1, 1850. She was educated in New England private schools, at the Convent of the Sacred Heart, in Paris, and studied music in Brussels. In 1872, she was married to William Nicholson who died five years later, and on January 7, 1879, she married Edward Horner Coates. Collected editions of her poems appeared in 1898 and in 1916. Other collections of her poems are, "Mine and Thine," "Lyrics of Life," "The Unconquered Air and Other Poems," and "Pro Patria." She died in Philadelphia on April 6, 1927.

COATESVILLE, a borough in Chester County, on the main line of the Pennsylvania Railroad between Harrisburg and Philadelphia. It was settled about 1800 and incorporated in 1867. Coatesville is an industrial center having iron and steel works, machine shops, steel-plate mills, boiler works, brass and iron factories, silk mills, a tube mill and tobacco, phosphate and automobile factories. Population (1930), 14,582; (1920), 14,515.

COBERN, CAMDEN McCORMACK, Methodist clergyman, was born at Uniontown, April 19, 1855. He was educated for the ministry at Allegheny College and at the Theological School of Boston University. In 1876, he entered his profession and contributed "Ancient Egypt in the Light of Modern Discovery," "Ezekiel and Daniel, a Critical Commentary," "The Stars and the Book," "Bible Etchings of Immortality," "The New Archaeological Discoveries and Their Bearing Upon the New Testament and Upon the Life and Times of the Primitive Church," to Biblical literature. He died in May, 1920.

COCALICO CREEK—Tributary to Conestoga Creek. Sub-basin, Lower Main Susquehanna; source, in Mill Creek Township, eastern Lebanon County; course, southerly into Lancaster County; thence southerly, by a circuitous route, to Conestoga Creek; mouth, one mile southwest of Brownstown; length, twenty-six miles.

COCHRAN, JOHN, physician, was born in Sadsbury, September 1, 1730. He was a pupil of Dr. Francis Allison and studied medicine under Dr. Thompson of Lancaster. He entered the British Army as surgeon's mate at the time of the French and Indian War and was with Bradstreet in his march against Fort Frontenac. During the Revolution he enlisted for hospital service and with Dr. Shippen made plans for the establishment of military hospitals. His accomplishments in the treatment of smallpox patients and of the wounded brought him to the attention of Washington. He became a physician and Surgeon-General in the middle department on April 10, 1777, and later chief physician and surgeon. He died at Palatine, N. Y., April 6, 1807.

COCOLAMUS CREEK—Tributary to Juniata River. Sub-basin: Lower Juniata; source, in West Perry Township, southwestern Snyder County; course, southeasterly, through Juniata County, into Perry County, to Juniata River; mouth, near Millerstown; length, twenty-one and one-half miles.

CODORUS CREEK, WEST BRANCH—Tributary to Codorus Creek. Sub-basin: Lower Main Susquehanna; source, at Bandanna, West Manheim Township, southwestern York County; course, northeasterly to join South Branch and form Codorus Creek; mouth, three miles southwest of York; length, twenty-three and one-half miles.

COFFIN, WILLIAM ANDERSON, painter, was born at Allegheny, on January 31, 1855. In 1874, he graduated from Yale and for three years following studied art in the United States. In 1877, he went to Paris and remained as a student of Leon Bonnat for five years. He returned to New York where he opened a studio in 1882 and became art critic for the New York Evening Post and the New York Sun successively. He became a landscape painter of note and in 1891 received Webb prize of the Society of American artists and in 1898 was the gold medallist of the Philadelphia Art Club. His work won other awards in Europe and the United States. The best known paintings are "The Rain" (in the Metropolitan Museum), "The Close of Day" and "The Hayfield." He died October 26, 1925.

COHEN, KATHERINE M., artist, was born in Philadelphia, on March 18, 1859. In early life she was privately educated and her talent for art was directed at the School of Design, The Pennsylvania Academy of Fine Arts, Students' Art League under Saint Gaudens and in Paris studios. Her work is varied, including sculptural figures and bas-reliefs, paintings of figures and landscapes. Her outstanding productions are, Portrait of General Beaver for the Smith Memorial in Fairmount Park, Philadelphia, "The Israelite," "Priscilla," "Romola," "Rabbi-ben-Ezra," and "Lorna Doone." She died at Philadelphia, December 14, 1914.

COHEN, SOLOMON SOLIS, physician, was born in Philadelphia, on September 1, 1857. He attended Central High School there, and Jefferson Medical College, where he graduated in 1883. In 1888, he lectured in clinical medicine at Jefferson, and in 1890 became professor of clinical medicine and therapeutics at Philadelphia Polyclinic and College of Graduates in Medicine. In 1898 and 1899, he served as president of the Philadelphia County Medical Society. His contribution to medical literature includes the edition of "System of Physiologic Therapeutics" and original works entitled "Therapeutics of Tuberculosis" and "Essentials of Diagnosis." He is also the author of "When Love Passed By" and other verses, including translations from Hebrew poets of the middle ages. Mr. Cohen lives in Philadelphia.

COIT, JAMES MILNOR, educator, was born at Harrisburg, on January 31, 1845. He was educated at Hobart College and developed an interest in scientific pursuits. He was associated with industrial work for several years in Cleveland and in 1886 became master in natural sciences at St. Paul's School in Concord, New Hampshire. His connection with this institution continued for more than a quarter of a century, during which time he attained an enviable record in scientific circles of the country. In 1909, he engaged in research work at the University of Munich, later becoming head of the Coit School for American boys in Munich. He is author of, "Manual of Chemical Arithmetic," "Treatise on the X-rays and Their Relation to the Medical and Surgical Sciences," and "Liquid Air." Coit died at Munich, January 5, 1922.

COKE— In 1835, William Firmstone, a native of England, made good forge pig iron for one month at the end of a blast at Mary Ann furnace, in Huntingdon County, with coke from Broad Top coal. This pig iron was taken to a forge three miles distant and made into blooms. In 1837, F. H. Oliphant made a quantity of coke pig iron at Fairchance furnace, near Uniontown, Fayette County. For many years anthracite coal was the favorite blast furnace fuel next to charcoal, but after 1850, the use of coke in the manufacture of pig iron became general. In 1849, there was not one coke furnace in blast in Pennsylvania. In 1856, there were twenty-one furnaces in western Pennsylvania, and in 1869, more pig iron was made with coke than with charcoal, and in 1875 more than with anthracite. In 1907, more than 98 per cent of the country's total production of the country's pig iron was made with coke, either by itself or in combination with anthracite or raw bituminous coal. Pennsylvania produces more coke than all the other states combined.

COLEMAN, LEIGHTON, Episcopal bishop, was born in Philadelphia, May 3, 1837. He graduated from the General Theological Seminary, was ordained for the Episcopal ministry, served as rector in important centers and became bishop of Delaware in 1888. He was a frequent contributor to newspapers and the author of, "History of the Lehigh Valley," "The Church in America," "A History of the American Church." He died December 14, 1907.

COLEMAN, LYMAN, educator, was born at Middlefield, Massachusetts, on June 14, 1796. He graduated at Yale in 1817 and later tutored there while studying theology. He served as a Congregational minister for a time and in 1842-1843 studied in German universities. He taught in the language departments at Amherst and Princeton and traveled extensively in the Orient until 1861 when he became professor of Latin and Greek at Lafayette College in Easton. In 1868, he took the chair of Latin and after more than twenty years of service there, he died in Easton, March 16, 1882. Among his literary contributions are translations and original works of which the following are outstanding: "Antiquities of the Christian Church," translated from the German; "The Apostolical and Primitive Church," "Prelacy and Ritualism."

COLEMAN, ROBERT, iron master, born near Castle Fin, Ireland, November 4, 1748. In 1764, he came to Pennsylvania and became a clerk for James Old, iron master, first at Quittapahilla Forge, near Lebanon, and afterwards at Reading Furnace. He married a daughter of James Old and was for more than a quarter of a century the leading iron manufacturer of Pennsylvania.

COLLEGEVILLE, borough in Montgomery County, 27 miles northwest of Philadelphia, located on the Perkiomen Creek and the Philadelphia and Reading Railroad, is the home of Ursinus College, a co-educational institution, founded in 1870, by the German Reformed Church.

COLONIAL RECORDS OF PENNSYLVANIA—See Archives.

COLONIZATION SOCIETIES were formed by the young men of Philadelphia and Pittsburgh for the purpose of relieving slaves of bondage, and of establishing colonies for them in Africa. The Young Men's Colonization Society of Philadelphia was founded about the year 1834, and shortly afterwards 126 slaves of good character were established at Bassa Cove on the southern border of Liberia.

COLUMBIA, a borough in Lancaster County, located on the Susquehanna River, was founded by Quakers in 1726 and was originally called Wright's Ferry. The Pennsylvania, and the Philadelphia and Reading Railroads connect it with Harrisburg 26 miles northwest, and with other cities. In 1789, Columbia was suggested as a site for the national capitol and in 1863 the bridge across the Susquehanna River connecting it with Wrightsville, York County, was burned so that armies of the Confederacy might not have access to that route to Philadelphia. A new bridge, excellently constructed and one of the longest in the United States, was completed in 1930. The town is a center of industry. Here are manufactured boilers and engines, foundry and machine shop products, lace, shirts, silk, wagons, glass, automobiles and lumber. Population (1930), 11,349; (1920), 10,836.

COLUMBIA COUNTY, formed from part of Northumberland, March 22, 1813. Named for Christopher Columbus. Land area, 479 square miles; population (1930), 48,803; (1920), 48,349. County-seat, Bloomsburg, laid out in 1802.

COMMERCIAL LIST AND MARITIME REGISTER, THE, was established in Philadelphia, in 1826. It is edited by Harry C. Daniels; is devoted to commerce, finance and marine subjects; appears weekly on Saturday and is published by the Commercial List Publishing Company.

COMMISSIONERS—County Commissioners, three in number, are the business managers of the county; to them is intrusted the care of its public property, the court house, the almshouse, the jail and the county bridges. They have the authority to lay the county tax, and may be appealed to when a person thinks the assessors have placed too high a valuation on his property. They have charge of printing the ballots for elections and are the custodians of the ballots after they are cast and counted by the election boards.

In voting for Commissioners, electors may cast ballots for only two of three candidates in order to permit minority representation.

COMMON PRAYER BOOK SOCIETY OF PENNSYLVANIA was founded in Philadelphia, December, 1817, with William Tilghman as president. Its object was to supply poor Episcopal congregations with prayer books.

CONCORDIA SOCIETY—An organization of German settlers, was formed about 1833, its object being the establishment of a community in which all would give and share equally. The difficulties which the early settlers encountered, suggested the formation of such an organization. The members consisted of farmers and tradesmen. Plans were made for the purchase from the city of Philadelphia of 14,000 acres of land lying on both sides of the west branch of the Susquehanna River, partly in Centre and partly in Lycoming County.

CONEMAUGH (LITTLE) RIVER—Tributary to Conemaugh River. Sub-basin: Lower Allegheny; source, in Cresson Township, eastern Cambria County; course, southwesterly to join Stony Creek and form Conemaugh River; mouth, at Johnstown; length, thirty-one and one-half miles. Indian name, Conunmoch, "otter."

CONESTOGA CREEK—Tributary to Susquehanna River. Sub-basin. Lower Main Susquehanna; source, in Caernarvon Township, southern Berks

County; course, southeasterly to Morgantown; thence southwesterly into Lancaster County to Susquehanna River; mouth, at Safe Harbor; length, sixty-one miles. Indian name, Kanastoge, "at the place of the immersed pole," or Andastoegue, "people of the cabin pole."

CONESTOGA (LITTLE) CREEK—Tributary to Conestoga Creek. Sub-basin: Lower Main Susquehanna; source, in Penn Township, northwestern Lancaster County, near Manheim; course, southerly to Conestoga Creek; mouth, one and one-half miles northeast of Safe Harbor; length, twenty miles. Indian name, Kanastoge, "at the place of the immersed pole," or Andastoegue, "people of the cabin pole."

CONESTOGA HORSES—Horses of unusual type as to size, bred in the Conestoga region, Lancaster County, from which they received the name.—See CONESTOGA WAGON.

CONESTOGA INDIANS—Historic tribe of Indians in Pennsylvania occupying village of same name in 18th century. The name is derived from "Kanastoge," "at the place of the immersed pole," and is of the Iroquoian group. It was first mentioned by Capt. John Smith, in 1608, and he describes them as a people of gigantic size and living not far from the location of the Indian fort near Conestoga.

CONESTOGA MASSACRE—On the morning of Wednesday, December 14, 1763, a number of armed men, known as the Paxton Boys, attacked the Indian village of Conestoga, in Lancaster County, killed women and children and a few old men, among them the chief, Sheehays. The majority of the Indians were absent from the settlement at the time of the attack. The authorities at Lancaster sent for the survivors and placed them in the newly erected work-house for safe keeping. On the 27th of December, 1763, between two and three o'clock in the afternoon, the Paxton Boys rode into the town and proceeded to the work-house where they broke open the door and killed all the Indians.—See also PAXTON BOYS.

CONESTOGA WAGON received its name from the valley of that name in Lancaster County inhabited by Mennonites. It was covered with canvas, and had a curve in the bottom which helped to prevent the slipping backward and forward of the contents when going over the mountains. It came into use about 1760. In 1789, Dr. Benjamin Rush described the Conestoga wagon and horses as follows:

"A large strong wagon (the ship of inland commerce), covered with a linen cloth, is an essential part of the furniture of a German farm. In this wagon, drawn by four or five horses of a peculiar breed, they convey to market, over the roughest roads, 2,000 and 3,000 pounds' weight of the produce of their farms.

In the months of September and October, it is no uncommon thing, on the Lancaster and Reading Roads, to meet in one day fifty or one hundred of these wagons on their way to Philadelphia, most of which belong to German farmers."

The Conestoga wagon formed an important factor in the commerce of Pennsylvania to the time when canals and railroads became the main avenue of traffic. The manufacturers of the Conestoga wagons protested vigorously against the railroads.

CONEWAGO CHAPEL—The oldest Catholic Church in the United States is Conewago Chapel, which was built in 1787, the year in which the Constitution of the United States was adopted. It is situated in Conewago Township, Adams County, twelve miles east of Gettysburg, within a few hundred yards of the Little Conewago Creek, in a most beautiful, picturesque, fertile, rolling farming country. The chapel is large and imposing, constructed of native stone, 125 feet long, 45 feet wide, 38 feet high, with a transcept 85 feet long, a steeple 87 feet in height from the comb of the roof and with a seating capacity of eight hundred. It was built by the Rev. James Pellentz, S. J., who was born in Germany, in 1727, and died February 3, 1800, at Conewago, where he is buried beneath the sanctuary. The first church on the present site was built in 1721 and enlarged in 1740. The Jesuit Fathers founded the Conewago Chapel Parish and remained in charge for almost two hundred years, withdrawing therefrom in 1901. Conewago is considered the Mother Parish of all the Catholic churches in Pennsylvania, because the Jesuits established practically all the early churches in the State from there, including those in Harrisburg, Lancaster, York, New Freedom, Carlisle, Chambersburg, Gettysburg, Bonneauville, Littlestown, Hanover, McSherrystown, New Oxford, Paradise, South Mountain and Loretto.

CONEWAGO CREEK—Tributary to Susquehanna River. Sub-basin: Lower Main Susquehanna; source, in South Mountain, Franklin Township, northwestern Adams County; course, easterly into York County; thence northeasterly to Susquehanna River; mouth, at York Haven; length, seventy-six and one-half miles. Indian name, Guneunga, "they have been gone a long time," or Ganowungo, "at the rapids."

CONEWAGO CREEK—Tributary to Susquehanna River. Sub-basin: Lower Main Susquehanna; source, in West Cornwall Township, southern Lebanon County, near Mt. Gretna; course, southwesterly to Susquehanna River, forming Dauphin-Lancaster County boundary for last eleven and one-half miles; mouth, at Falmouth; length, twenty and one-half miles. Indian name, Guneunga, "they have been gone a long time," or Ganowungo, "at the rapids,"

CONEWAGO (LITTLE) CREEK (or PARADISE CREEK)—Tributary to Conewago Creek. Sub-basin: Lower Main Susquehanna; source, in Jackson Township, southwestern York County; course, northeasterly to Conewago

Creek; mouth, two miles north of Manchester; length, twenty-three and one-half miles. Indian name, Guneunga, "they have been gone a long time, "or Ganowungo, "at the rapids."

CONNEAUT CREEK—Tributary to Lake Erie. Basin: Erie; source, in Summit Township, western Crawford County; course, northerly into Erie County to a point two miles north of Albion; thence southwesterly into Ohio at Kingsville; thence northeasterly to Lake Erie; mouth, at Conneaut, Ohio; length, in Pennsylvania, thirty-five and one-half miles. Indian name, a corruption of Gunniate, "it is a long time since they are gone."

CONNOLLY, DR. JOHN, was born in Lancaster County, about 1750. He was well connected and married a daughter of Samuel Semple, a noted Pittsburgh lawyer. In 1774, Lord Dunmore chose Connolly as his agent. The latter is accused of fomenting the boundary dispute between Virginia and Pennsylvania, and of bringing on the border troubles with the Indians. At the rupture between England and the Colonies, Connolly adhered to the former. He was arrested in Maryland (early in 1775) and relieved of treasonable correspondence. After that he was kept a prisoner until 1781, when escaping to Canada he plotted a descent upon Pittsburgh, and the next year led a force which destroyed Hannastown. Later (1788-1789), he was concerned in English intrigues to capture New Orleans, and visited Kentucky with that purpose; but was recognized, and expelled from the country.

CONNOQUENESSING CREEK—Tributary to Beaver River. Sub-basin: Main Ohio; source, in Concord Township, northern central Butler County; course, southwesterly to Renfrew; thence westerly into Beaver County; thence northwesterly into Lawrence County to Beaver River; mouth, one mile west of Ellwood City; length, fifty-nine miles. Indian name, Gunachquenesink, "for a long way straight."

CONOCOCHEAGUE CREEK—Tributary to Potomac River. Basin: Potomac; source, in Menallen Township, northwestern Adams County; course, westerly, by a circuitous route, to Chambersburg; thence southwesterly to junction of Back Creek at Williamson; thence southerly, into Maryland, to Potomac River; mouth, at Williamsport, Md.; length, in Pennsylvania, fifty-six miles. Indian name, a corruption of Guneukitschik," indeed a long way."

CONOCOCHEAGUE CREEK, WEST BRANCH—Tributary to Conococheague Creek. Basin: Potomac; source, in Fannett Township, northern Franklin County; course, southwesterly to Richmond Furnace; thence southeasterly to Conococheague Creek; mouth, four miles southwest of Greencastle; length, fifty-three miles. Indian name, a corruption of Guneukitschik, "indeed a long way."

CONODOGUINET CREEK—Tributary to Susquehanna River. Sub-basin: Lower Main Susquehanna; source, in Peters Township, western Franklin County; course, northeasterly into Cumberland County to Susquehanna River; mouth, at West Fairview, opposite Harrisburg; length, ninety-nine miles. Indian name, a corruption of Gunnipduckhannet, "for a long way nothing but bends," or "winding river."

CONSHOHOCKEN, a town in Montgomery County, 13 miles northwest of Philadelphia, on the Schuylkill River, was founded in 1830 and incorporated as a borough in 1852. Its principal manufactures are blast furnaces, rolling mills, woolen and cotton mills, pottery, rubber, and surgical implement works. Population (1930), 10,815; (1920), 8,481.

CONSTABLE—The word literally means count of the stable or master of the horse. A constable in Pennsylvania is an official in a township, borough, ward, or city elected or appointed to guard the public safety and conserve, defend and enforce the public peace, with power to summon any person or persons to his aid, to perform the ministerial and executive offices of alderman, magistrates and justices of the peace; to attend the sessions of the criminal courts, make returns and have the custody of juries, and to discharge other functions assigned to them by law.

The Duke of York's Laws in force in Pennsylvania provided for the election of constables prior to the landing of William Penn.

There are four classes of constables in Pennsylvania: (a) high constable, (b) constable, (c) deputy constable, and (d) state constabulary or members of the state police.—*See* Dill: CONSTABLES' GUIDE.

CONSTITUTION OF 1776—June 18, 1776, a number of men met in Philadelphia and issued an address to the people of Pennsylvania proposing the election of representatives for the purpose of holding a convention to frame a constitution for Pennsylvania. This was done in pursuance of a resolution of the Continental Congress, May 15, 1776, recommending to the several colonies the adoption of a new government. The convention met in the State House, Philadelphia, July 15, 1776, and completed its labors September 28, 1776. The constitution was never submitted to the people for ratification. It provided for a legislative body with only one house and a plural executive, called the Executive Council, of which the chief officer was the President. It also provided for a Council of Censors. The names of the signers of this Constitution follow: B. Franklin, President; John Morris, Jr., Secretary; Chester County—Benj. Bartholomeoo, Thoe. Strawbridge, Robert Smith, Samuel Cuningham, Jno. Macky, John Fleming; Lancaster County—Philip Marsteller, Thomas Porter, Bartram Galbraith, John Hubley, Alexr. Lourey; York County—Jas. Edger, Jas. Smith; Philadelphia City—Ty. Matlack, Frederick Kuhl, James Cannon, George Schloser, Dav. Rittenhouse; Philadelphia County—Robert Loller, Joseph

Blewer, Jno. Bull, Wm. Coats; County of Bucks—Jno. Wilkinson, Saml. Smith, John Keller, William Van Horne, John Grier, Abram V. Middleswart, Jo. Kirkbride; Cumberland County—John Harris, Jonathan Hoge, Wm. Clark, Robt. Whitehill, William Duffield, James Brown, Hugh Alexander, Jas. McLene; Berks County—Jacob Morgan, Gabriel Heester, Benjamin Spyker, Valentine Eckert, Charles Shoemaker, Thos. Jones, Jr.; Northampton County—Simon Drisbach, Jacob Orndt, Peter Burkhalter, Jacob Strowd, Heigal Gray, Abraham Miller, John Ralston; Bedford County—Benjn. Elliot, Thomas Coulter, Joseph Powel, John Bird, John Cune, Jno. Wilkins, Thomas Smith; Northampton County—Wm. Cook, Jas. Potter, Robt. Martin, Matthew Brown, Walter Clark, John Kelly, James Crawford, John Weitsel; Westmoreland County—James Barr, Edward Cook, James Smith, John Moore, John Carmichael, John McClelland, Christoph Lobengier.

CONSTITUTION OF 1790—Because of serious difficulties in the Constitution of 1776, an act was passed September 15, 1789, calling for a convention to revise the Constitution. This convention met November 24, 1789, and continued in session until February 26, 1790, and then adjourned in order that the public might have an opportunity to study the Constitution. The convention reassembled August 9, 1790, and on September 2, 1790, formally proclaimed the new Constitution. This Constitution made no provision for its own amendment. The names of the signers follow: Thomas Mifflin, James Wilson, Hilary Baker, William Lewis, Thomas M'Kean, George Gray, William Robison, Jr., Robert Hare, Enoch Edwards, Samuel Ogden, Thomas Jenks, John Barclay, Abraham Stout, William Gibbons, Thomas Bull, James Boyd, Edward Hand, Robert Coleman, Sebastian Graff, John Hubley, John Brechbill, Henry Miller, Henry Slegle, William Reed, Benjamin Tyson, Benjamin Pedan, Matthew Dill, William Irvine, James Power, Joseph Hiester, Christian Lower, Abraham Lincoln, Paul Groscop, Baltzer Gehr, Samuel Sitgreaves, John Arndt, Peter Rhoads, Joseph Powell, John Piper, Charles Smith, Simon Snyder, William Findley, William Todd, Alexander Addison, John Hoge, David Redick, James Ross, John Smilie, Albert Gallatin, James M'Lene, George Matthews, James Morris, Lindsay Coats, Jonathan Shoemaker, John Gloninger, William Brown, Alexander Graydon, Timothy Pickering, Andrew Henderson, John Gibson, Thomas Beale, John Sellers, Nathaniel Newlin.

CONSTITUTION OF 1838—In 1835, the General Assembly submitted to the electors the question of calling a convention to propose amendments to the Constitution. The vote being favorable, a convention was called May 2, 1837. After adjourning several times, its labors were completed February 22, 1838. The new Constitution was adopted by a vote of 113,971 to 112,759. This Constitution was amended 1850, 1857, 1864 and 1872. The names of the signers follow: Danil Agnew, Wm. Ayres, M. W. Baldwin, Ephraim Banks, John Y. Barclay, Jacob Barndolar, Chas. A. Barnitz, Andrew Bedford, Thos S. Bell,

James Cornell Biddle, Libbius L Bigelow, Saml. C. Bonham, Chas. Brown, Jeremiah Brown, William Brown, Pierce Butler, Samuel Carey, George Chambers, John Chandler, Jos. R. Chandler, Ch. Chauncey, Nathaniel Clapp, James Clarke, John Clarke, William Clark, Saml. Cleavinger, A. J. Cline, Lindley Coates, R. E. Cochran, Thos. P. Cope, Joshua F. Cox, Walter Craig, Richd. M. Crain, Geo. T. Crawford, Cornelius Crum, John Cummin, Thomas S. Cunningham, William Curll, Wm. Darlington, Mark Darrah, Harmar Denny, John Dickey, Joshua Dickerson, Jacob Dillinger, Jas. Donagan, J. R. Donnel, Joseph M. Doran, James Dunlop, Thomas Earle, Robt. Fleming, Walter Forward, John Foulkrod, Joseph Fry, Jr., John Fuller, John A. Gamble, William Gearhartt, David Gilmore, Virgil Grenell, William L. Harris, Thomas Hastings, Ezra S. Hayhurst, Wm. Hays, Abm. Helffenstein, M. Henderson, Wm. Henderson, Wm. Hiester, William High, Jos. Hopkinson, John Houpt, Jabes Hyde, Charles Jared Ingersole, Phs. Jenks, George M. Keim, James Kennedy, Aaron Kerr, Jos. Konigmacher, Jacob Krebs, H. G. Long, David Lyons, Wm. P. Maclay, Alexr. Magee, Joel K. Mann, Benjn. Martin, John J. McCahen, Thomas McCall, E. T. McDowell, James McSherry, W. M. Meredith, James Merril, Levi Merkel, Wm. L. Miller, James Montgomery, Christian Meyers, D. Nevin, Wm. Overfield, Hiram Payne, Matthias Pennypacker, James Pollock, James Porter, James Madison Porter, Saml. A. Purviance, E. C. Reigart, A. H. Read, Geo. W. Riter, Jno. Ritter, H. Gold Rogers, Samuel Royer, James M. Russell, Daniel Saeger, John Mervin Scott, Tobias Sellers, G. Seltzer, George Smith, Henry Scheetz, George Shillets, Thomas H. Sill, George Smith, Wm. Smyth, Joseph Snively, Jno. B. Sterigere, Thaddeus Stevens, Jacob Stickel, Ebeneser Sturdevant, Thomas Taggart, Morgan I. Thomas, James Todd, Thomas Weaver, Jacob B. Weidman, R. G. White, Geo. W. Woodward, R. Young, John Sergeant, President.

CONSTITUTION OF 1873 was adopted by a convention November 3, 1873. This convention was called pursuant to the Act of April 11, 1872. The Act calling the convention provided that the bill of rights was not to be changed. The convention, however, decided that it was an original body and proposed several changes. The Constitution was ratified at a special election, December 16, 1873, and went into effect January 1, 1874. One of the changes in the Constitution is the prohibition of special legislation. The Constitution has been frequently amended. The names of the signers follow: George A. Achenbach, John E. Addicks, Wm. H. Ainey, Hamilton Alricks, G. W. Andrews, Wm. H. Armstrong, Wm. J. Baer, Joseph Baily, John M. Bailey, William D. Baker, Thos. B. Bannan, Geo. G. Barclay, John Bardsley, James P. Barr, Lin. Bartholomew, M. C. Beebe, Wm. Bigler, C. A. Black, Chas. O. Bowman, Charles Brodhead, J. M. Broomall, R. Brown, C. R. Buckalew, John C. Bullitt, Saml. Calvin, John H. Campbell, Henry C. Carey, Lewis C. Cassidy, Pearson Church, Silas M. Clark, Thos. E. Cochran, Wm. L. Corbett, George N. Corson, Jno. P. Cronmiller, James W. Curry, A. G. Curtin, Theo. Cuyler, Geo. M. Dallas, Wm. Darlington, Wm. Davis, R. M. de France, S. C. T. Dodd, A. B. Dunning,

Matthew Edwards, M. F. Elliott, Jas. Ellis, Thos. Ewing, A. C. Finney, A. M. Fulton, Josiah Funck, John Gibson, John Gilpin, Henry Green, J. B. Guthrie, Jno. G. Hall, William B. Hanna, Edward Harvey, Malcolm Hay, T. R. Hazzard, Jos. Hemphill, James H. Heverin, Geo. F. Horton, Thos. Howard, Chas. Hunsicker, D. Kaine, E. C. Knight, R. A. Lamberton, Aug. S. Landis, Geo. V. Lawrence, Wm. Lilly, W. E. Littleton, Wayne MacVeagh, Thomas MacConnell, Joel B. McCamant, Wm. McClean, Jno. McCulloch, Morton McMichael, John McMurray, Frank Mantor, Jno. J. Metzger, Samuel Minor, Lewis Z. Mitchell, James W. M. Newlin, Jerome B. Niles, G. W. Palmer, Henry W. Palmer, Henry C. Parsons, D. W. Patterson, T. H. Baird Patterson, Joseph G. Patton, Dan. S. Porter, Lewis Pughe, Andrew A. Purman, John N. Purviance, Saml. A. Purviance, John R. Reed, And. Reed, Levi Rooke, Geo. Ross, C. M. Runk, Saml. L. Russell, J. McDowell Sharpe, J. Alexander Simpson, H. G. Smith, Henry W. Smith, Wm. H. Smith, M. Hall Stanton, Jno. Stewart, Thomas Struthers, Benjamin L. Temple, Wm. J. Turrell, Henry Van Reed, J. M. Wetherill, Jno. Price Wetherill, Saml. M. Wherry, David N. White, Harry White, Geo. W. Woodward, Edward R. Worrell, Caleb E. Wright.

CONVERSE, JAMES BOOTH, Presbyterian clergyman, was born in Philadelphia, April 8, 1844. He graduated from Princeton University in 1865 and from Union Theological Seminary, Virginia, 1870. Ordained as a Presbyterian minister, 1871; served as minister and evangelist from 1879-1888. Edited "*Christian Observer*" 1872-1879, and "*Christian Patriot*," 1890-1895; contributed frequently to magazines and newspapers and wrote "A Summer Vacation Abroad," "The Bible and Land" (an argument favoring single tax); "Uncle Sam's Bible, or Bible Teaching About Politics" and "There Shall Be No Poor." He died at Morristown, Tenn., October 31, 1914.

CONWAY CABAL, a scheme planned by Generals Gates, Mifflin and Conway, for the purpose of placing Gates in Washington's position as commander-in-chief. A faction of the Continental Congress, strongly in favor of the plan, was responsible for the appointment of a new war board. Without Washington's knowledge, the board suggested and Congress approved an invasion of Canada. Lafayette was put in command of the expedition. He remained in Albany for three months waiting for men and supplies and finally returned to Valley Forge, having been ordered by Congress to abandon the expedition. Thus the intrigue ended. A large part of the conspiracy was enacted at York when the Continental Congress was in session there.

CONWELL, RUSSELL HERMAN, clergyman and educator; born, Worthington, Mass., February 15, 1842. He studied law at Yale and Albany Law Schools; served as an officer in the Federal Army during the Civil War; was immigration officer of Minnesota in Germany, 1867-1868; foreign correspondent, New York Tribune and Boston Traveler, 1868-1870; practised law in Boston,

1870-1879. In 1879, he was ordained to the ministry of the Baptist Church, from 1881-1891 serving as pastor of Grace Baptist Church, Philadelphia, and from 1891 until his death as pastor of the Baptist Temple. He founded Temple University, Philadelphia, in 1888, and became its president. In 1891, he founded the Samaritan Hospital. He became well known as a lecturer particularly for his "Acres of Diamonds," which he delivered more than 5,000 times. His publications include "Life of Bayard Taylor," "Why the Chinese Emigrate," "Woman and the Law," "Acres of Diamonds," "Life of C. H. Spurgeon," "Present Successful Opportunities," "Lives of the Presidents," "Life of James G. Blaine," "The New Day," "Sermons for Occasions," "Why Lincoln Laughed," "Life of John Wanamaker." He died December 6, 1925.

COOK, JOEL, journalist; born, in Philadelphia, March 20, 1842; admitted to the bar in Philadelphia, 1863; became a journalist; was war correspondent with Army of the Potomac, 1862-1863; member of editorial staff of the Philadelphia Public Ledger in 1865; financial editor, 1883; president of City National Bank, Philadelphia; elected Representative in Congress, 1907, dying in 1910, before the expiration of his term. He wrote, "The Siege of Richmond, May-June, 1862," "A Holiday Tour in Europe," "An Eastern Tour at Home," "Brief Summer Rambles near Philadelphia," "England, Picturesque and Descriptive," "America, Picturesque and Descriptive."

COOKE, JAY, financier, was born in what is now Sandusky, Ohio, on August 10, 1821. At fourteen he became clerk in a store, later he secured a position in St. Louis, and in 1837, became a clerk on a canal packet line in Philadelphia. In 1839, he came into the employ of E. W. Clark & Co., Philadelphia bankers, leaving the firm after the Panic of 1857 and establishing the banking house of Jay Cooke and Company. During the Civil War, Cooke became financier for the government, opening an office at Washington that he might better care for the business interests of the country. In 1866, at the conclusion of the war, he established a branch in New York and in 1870 became resident partner of a house in London. On September 18, 1873, due to a series of misfortunes, Cooke's banking house was forced to close. Later because of successful investments he was able to recover the property he lost. He died February 16, 1905.

COOPER, ELLWOOD, horticulturist; born, Lancaster County, May 24, 1829. Was in business in Port au Prince, Haiti, for ten years, in 1870, engaging in fruit raising in California. He became the first manufacturer of olive oil in the United States and invented machinery for manufacture of olive oil, hulling and pitting almonds, and hulling and washing English walnuts. He was president of California State Board of Horticulture, 1885-1903, and president of Santa Barbara College for three years. He wrote, "Statistics of Trade with Haiti," "Forest Culture and Eucalyptus Trees," "Treatise on Olive Culture."

COOPER, JAMES, senator; born, Frederick County, Maryland, May 8, 1810; graduated from Washington College, Pennsylvania, 1832; studied law; practiced at Gettysburg; member of Congress, 1838 and 1840; member of state legislature, 1843-1848; United States senator, 1849; during Civil War, he commanded the Maryland volunteers; was made brigadier-general, May 17, 1861. At the time of his death, March 28, 1863, he was commander of Camp Chase, Columbus, Ohio.

COOPER, THOMAS, physicist and politician, was born in London, October 22, 1759. Educated at Oxford where he studied law and medicine, and was admitted to the bar. He entered politics and was sent by the Democratic clubs of England to those in France. In France he favored the Dirondists, but before their downfall managed to return to England. In France, he learned how chlorine could be made from salt and he became a bleacher and calico printer in Manchester. His business proving unsuccessful he came to America, became a Democrat and opposed the administration of John Adams so strongly that he was tried for libel because of a newspaper attack on the president. He was sentenced to six months' imprisonment and $400 fine. In 1806, he was land commissioner in Pennsylvania and was so successful in his treatment of the difficulties between Connecticut residents and the settlers of Luzerne County in regard to land, that he was appointed judge, only to be asked to leave the office in 1811. Subsequently he was professor of chemistry at Dickinson College, and professor of chemistry and political economy at Columbia College, S. C. In 1820, he became president of the latter institution, serving until his retirement in 1834, when he undertook the revision of the statutes of South Carolina, dying May 11, 1840, before the completion of the task. He published among other things a collection of political essays: "Medical Jurisprudence" and "Lectures on the Elements of Political Economy."

COPE, EDWARD DRINKER, zoologist and paleontologist, was born in Philadelphia, July 28, 1840. At thirteen, he entered the Friends' School, at Westtown, near West Chester, and at eighteen, announced his intention of becoming a naturalist. From 1859, when he published his first paper on "Primary Division of the Salamandridae," he devoted much time to the writing of scientific papers, which were published in the proceedings of the Philadelphia Academy of Natural Sciences and the American Philosophical Society, of both of which organizations he was a member. He published in all, 1,281 papers on scientific subjects. His research centered about the fish, amphibians, reptile, mammalia and philosophy. In 1864, he became professor of natural science at Haverford College and later was elected to the chair of geology and paleontology at the University of Pennsylvania. In 1879, he was awarded the Bigsby gold medal by the Geological Society of London and received the Ph. D. degree from Heidelberg University on its 500th anniversary. He was president of the American Society of Naturalists in 1895 and at the time of his death, April 12, 1897, was president-elect of the American Association for the Advancement of Science.

COPE, GILBERT, historian, was born in East Bradford Township, Chester County, August 17, 1840, a direct descendant of Oliver Cope, one of the first Englishmen to purchase land from William Penn. Oliver Cope came to America in 1683 and settled in New Castle County in what is now the State of Delaware. Gilbert was educated at home, at the Friends' School, West Chester, and at the Friends' Boarding School, Westtown. When he was seventeen, he displayed an interest in genealogy and began research work incident to the publication of a history of the Cope family. In later years he devoted himself to the preservation of Quaker records and Chester County archives, and in 1905 and 1907, visited London for the purpose of copying a number of volumes of early Quaker registers of England and Wales for the Genealogical Society of Pennsylvania. He was one of the founders of the Chester County Historical Society, and from 1911–1912, served as president of the Pennsylvania Federation of Historical Societies. His historical collections, including original papers, genealogical data, books, maps and newspapers, are in the possession of the Historical Society of Pennsylvania. Cope died December 17, 1928.

COPE, THOMAS PYM, merchant; born, Lancaster County, August 26, 1768. Imported goods in his own vessels in 1807; established first line of packets between Philadelphia and Liverpool, in 1821. Was interested in the civic development of Philadelphia, encouraging and being to a great extent responsible for the construction of the Pennsylvania Railroad, introduction of the Philadelphia water supply from the Schuylkill, completion of the Chesapeake and Delaware canal and the establishment of the Mercantile Library. He remained in Philadelphia at the time of the yellow fever and smallpox epidemics of 1793 and 1797 and assisted in caring for the afflicted. He was elected to the State Legislature in 1807. His death occurred at Philadelphia on November 22, 1854.

COPPÉE, HENRY, educator; born, Savannah, Ga., October 13, 1821; was a soldier in Mexican War, 1846–1848; instructor at West Point, 1848–1849 and 1850–1855; professor of English literature and history at University of Pennsylvania, 1855–1856; president of Lehigh University, 1866–1875; professor of history, Lehigh University, 1875–1895; died Bethlehem, March 21, 1895.

CORBIN, MARGARET, heroine, was born in Franklin County. After her husband had been killed at Fort Washington she took his place behind the cannon and was herself severely wounded. She died in Westmoreland County, about 1800.

CORNPLANTER, chief of the Senecas, born between 1732 and 1740. His Indian name was Garganwahgah or Gyantwachias meaning "The Planter." He was sometimes called John O'Bail, the name of his father, who was a white trader. His mother was a Seneca. During the Revolutionary War, Cornplanter and his tribe fought for the English cause but at the conclusion of the war their sympathies were with America. In October, 1784, he attended the treaty between the Six Nations and the United States at Fort Stanwix (Rome, N. Y.). He also attended the treaties of 1789, 1797, and 1802, thereby becoming unpopular with the Senecas and endangering his life. In 1790, the Seneca chief with his half-brother, Half-Town, visited Philadelphia for the purpose of laying before President Washington, his personal friend, certain complaints of the Senecas against Colonel John Gibson. During the War of 1812, Cornplanter offered his services to the United States of which he was always a staunch friend. His assistance, however, could not be accepted. The Seneca chief died at Cornplanter Town, Warren County, on February 18, 1836.

CORNSTALK, a Shawnee chief, sometimes identified with Tamenebuck (Taming Buck), was born about 1720. He followed Peter Chartier and took sides with the French in 1744 and in 1748 met with other deserter chiefs at Lancaster to ask Pennsylvania authorities forgiveness. He lived in the valley of the Scioto River and opposed the sale of lands claimed by the Iroquois to European settlers. In Lord Dunmore's War that followed, he led 1,000 Indians, against his judgment, in attack on General Andrew Lewis' division that was to protect settlers. He maneuvered his forces brilliantly and in November, 1774, brought his chiefs to an understanding with Virginia and made an eloquent appeal at the conference urging peace. In 1777, he warned Moravian missionaries on the Pennsylvania frontier that the Indians were going to the aid of the British. While on this mission he and his son, Ellinipisco, were killed by enraged soldiers over the protests of the Moravians.

SITE OF OPENING FIRE—BATTLE OF BRANDYWINE

CORNWALL ORE HILLS comprise three mountains of magnetic iron ore near Lebanon. Cornwall came into possession of Peter Grubb who built the Cornwall furnace in 1742. Later, Robert Coleman became the chief proprietor and the property is now owned by the Bethlehem Steel Company. In Israel Acrelius' History of New Sweden, written in 1756, appears the following statement:
"Cornwall, or Grubb's ironworks, in Lancaster County. The mine is rich and abundant, forty feet deep, commencing two feet under the earth's surface. The ore is somewhat mixed with sulphur and copper. Peter Grubb was its discoverer."

CORONER, a county official, whose duty it is to investigate cases of mysterious death, as in instances where murder or suicide is suspected. He is authorized to empanel a jury of six persons. If a vacancy occurs in the sheriff's office, the coroner acts until the Governor makes an appointment.

CORRY, a city in Erie County, about 26 miles southeast of Erie, was settled in 1860. It is located in a region rich in petroleum deposits. The manufactures of the city are iron products, locomotives, engines, leather goods, corsets, furniture, radiators, shovels, wrenches, brushes, toys, etc. Dairying, flour and feed mills and brick works are other industries of the city. The state fish hatchery is located here. Population (1930), 7,152; (1920), 7,228.

CORSE, JOHN MURRAY, military officer; born, Pittsburgh, April 25, 1835; educated at West Point; began the practice of law in 1860; enlisted in Union Army at opening of Civil War; was made brigadier-general in 1863; was with Sherman on his march to the sea. Following the war, he served as collector of internal revenue in Chicago and subsequently became postmaster of Boston. He died, Winchester, Mass., April 27, 1893.

CORSON, HIRAM, educator; born, Philadelphia, November 8, 1828; professor of rhetoric and English literature at St. John's College, Annapolis, 1866–1870; professor of English language and literature, Cornell University, 1870–1903; professor emeritus, 1903–1911. He is the author of "Handbook of Anglo-Saxon and Early English," "An Introduction to the Study of Robert Browning," "Jottings in the Text of Hamlet," "Lectures on the English Language and Literature," "The Aims of Literary Study." He died in 1911.

COSGROVE, HENRY, Roman Catholic prelate; born in Williamsport, 1834; ordained priest, 1857; pastor, Davenport, Iowa, Church, 1862; vice-general, 1882; bishop of Davenport, 1884; died 1906.

COUDERSPORT, town and county-seat of Potter County, located on the Allegheny River, 110 miles southeast of Erie. Chief among the manufactured products of the town are furniture, rubber goods, mangle rollers, condensed milk and barrel headings.

COUNCIL OF SAFETY, was elected July 23, 1776, by the Convention which met in Philadelphia. Its purpose was to perform the executive duties of the State government, formerly discharged by the Committee of Safety. David Rittenhouse became chairman of the council and Jacob S. Howell, secretary.

COUNTRY GENTLEMAN, THE, a monthly agricultural magazine, was established in 1831 in Philadelphia. It has a wide circulation throughout the world and is published by the Curtis Publishing Company. Circulation, 1,701,399.

COVODE, JOHN, congressman; born, Westmoreland County, March 17, 1808, the son of a farmer of Dutch ancestry; became successively a coal dealer, woolen manufacturer and railroad owner; entered politics as a Whig; elected to Congress by Anti-Masons in 1854; reelected as a Republican in 1856, serving until 1863; appointed chairman of committee to investigate passage of Lecompton bill; member of committee on conduct of the war; elected to Congress in 1868; became chairman of Republican State Committee of Pennsylvania in 1869; died January 11, 1871.

COVODE INVESTIGATION—In the Thirty-Sixth Congress, during President Buchanan's administration, charges were made to the effect that the president had used corrupt influence to secure votes for the admission of Kansas under the Lecompton Constitution. The leader was John Covode of Pennsylvania. A committee was appointed to investigate the charge and by a partisan majority decided against the president. No action was taken, but President Buchanan protested in a vigorous message.

COWAN, EDGAR, United States senator; born at Greensburg, Westmoreland County, of Scotch-Irish ancestry, September 19, 1815; graduated at Franklin College, New Athens, Ohio, 1839; admitted to the bar of Westmoreland County in 1842. He began his political career as a follower of Andrew Jackson, but joined the Whig party in the Harrison campaign of 1840, and in 1856 supported John C. Fremont, the Republican candidate for president. In 1861, he defeated David Wilmot in the Republican Caucus as a candidate for the United States Senate to succeed William Bigler, because he was more conservative than Wilmot; he defeated Henry Foster, his Democratic opponent. As a senator he was a strict constructionist of the Constitution and supported the conservatives during the war and during the period of reconstruction. In the contest between President Johnson and Congress, he supported the President, for which he virtually was read out of the party. President Johnson appointed him Minister to Austria in 1867, but the Senate refused to confirm his nomination. Retiring to private life, he continued the practice of law. He stood high as a lawyer and scholar. He died August 31, 1885.

COWAN, FRANK, lawyer and author, was born at Greensburg, December 11, 1844. He attended Mt. Pleasant and Jefferson Colleges, received the M. D. degree from Georgetown Medical College in 1869, studied law and was admitted to the bar in 1865. He toured the world and in 1884-1885 was in Korea, before that country had made any treaties with foreign nations. His writings include "Zomara, a Romance of Spain," "The City of the Royal Palm, and other Poems," "Fact and Fancy in New Zealand," "Dictionary of Proverbial Phrases Relating to the Sea," "Australianisms." He died in 1905.

COWANESQUE RIVER—Tributary to Tioga River. Sub-basin: Upper North Branch Susquehanna; source, in Bingham Township, northeastern Potter County; course, southeasterly into Tioga County; thence northeasterly into New York to Tioga River; mouth, in New York; length, in Pennsylvania, forty miles. Indian name, Gawunshesque, "overgrown with briers."

COWANSHANNOCK CREEK—Tributary to Allegheny River. Sub-basin: Middle Allegheny; source, in South Mahoning Township, northwestern Indiana County; course, westerly into Armstrong County to Allegheny River; mouth, at Gosford, two miles north of Kittanning; length, twenty-four miles. Indian name, a corruption of Gawunschhanna, "brier-stream."

COXE, TENCH, economist; born, Philadelphia, May 22, 1755. He became interested in political economy and devoted his life to study and writing on this subject. He encouraged manufacture and is sometimes called the father of the cotton industry. In 1788, he was a member of the Continental Congress, served as Commissioner of the Revenue from 1792-1797, and as Purveyor of Public Supplies from 1803-1812. He is the author of "Inquiry into the Principles on which a Commercial System for the United States should be Founded," "Examination of Lord Sheffield's Observations on the Commerce of the American States," "View of the United States of America," "Thoughts on Naval Power and the Encouragement of Commerce," "Memoir on Cultivation, Trade, and Manufacture of Cotton," "Statement of the Arts and Manufactures of the United States for the Year 1810" (the first industrial census of the country). He died at Philadelphia, July 17, 1824.

COYLE, JOHN PATTERSON, Congregational clergyman; born, East Waterford, May 3, 1852; graduated from Princeton University in 1875 and was instructor in Latin there from 1877-1879; entered the ministry of the Congregational Church and from 1882-1895 was pastor of churches in Ludlow, Mass., New York, North Adams, Mass., and Denver, Colo.; author, "The Spirit in

Literature and Life," "The Imperial Christ"; died in Denver, Colorado, February 21, 1895.

CRAIG, ISAAC, military officer, was born near Hillsborough, County Down, Ireland, in August, 1742. He came to America, arriving at Philadelphia in 1768 and engaged in the carpenter trade until 1775. At the beginning of the Revolution he served in the American navy, first as Lieutenant of Marines and during the winter of 1785-1786, as Captain of Marines, serving on the Andrea Doria, commanded by Captain Nicholas Biddle. He early distinguished himself in assisting in the capture of British vessels carrying ammunition and provisions, and was on board the Andrea Doria when the Island of New Providence was taken by the Americans and a large supply of military stores seized. Shortly after this event Craig left the navy and in December, 1776, was made a Captain of Artillery, under Col. Thomas Proctor. He took part in the capture of the Hessians at Trenton, and distinguished himself in the Battles of Princeton, Germantown and Brandywine. In 1779, he served under Gen. Sullivan in his expedition against the Indians, and in March, 1782, upon the conclusion of his active military service, was commissioned major by Congress. He spent the remainder of his life in Pittsburgh and died October 14, 1826.

CRAMER, MICHAEL, author and minister of Methodist Episcopal Church; born, Schaffhausen, Switzerland, February 6, 1835; graduated from Ohio Wesleyan University, 1860; chaplain in United States Army, 1864-1867; United States Consul at Leipzig, 1867-1870; United States minister to Denmark, 1870-1881; United States minister to Switzerland, 1881-1885; professor of systematic theology at Boston University, 1885-1887; professor of church history at Drew Theological Seminary; professor of philosophy at Dickinson College, 1897-1898; served as associate editor of the *Theological Quarterly Review*, and contributed articles to the *Methodist Review*, *German Theological Review*, etc. Died, Carlisle, January 25, 1898.

CRAMP, CHARLES HENRY, shipbuilder; born, Philadelphia, May 9, 1828. Graduated from Central High School, Philadelphia; entered the employ of his father, William Cramp, owner of ship yards. Incorporated and became president of firm of William Cramp and Sons, which company is now the largest of its kind in the United States. Cramp built ships for use in the Civil War, assisted in rebuilding the United States navy and the United States merchant marine. His company has an extensive foreign business, fulfilling contracts for the governments of United States, Russia, Japan, Argentina and Chile, and having a marked influence upon the development of the modern navy. Cramp died in Philadelphia, June 6, 1913.

CRAWFORD, JOHN MARTIN, physician and surgeon, was born at Herrick, October 18, 1845. He graduated from Lafayette College, 1871; from

Pulte Medical College, Cincinnati, 1878, and from Miami Medical College, 1881. He was professor of physiology, microscopy and physical diagnosis at Pulte Medical College, 1881-1889; consul-general of the United States to Russia, 1889-1895, and Commissioner of the World's Fair, 1892-1893. He became interested in the economic and literary life of Russia and Finland, editing and translating a five volume edition of "The Industries of Russia," making the first English translation of "The Kalevala," Finland's national epic, and lecturing on the Finns and their literature and on Russia and Russian folk-lore. He was president of several banks and a director of industrial and manufacturing companies. He died August 4, 1916.

CRAWFORD, WILLIAM, Colonial officer, for whom Crawford County is named. He and his family came to Pennsylvania from Berkeley County, Virginia, in 1768, and settled near Connellsville, Fayette County. In 1758, he served in Forbes' expedition as a captain. Colonel Crawford was an intimate friend of General Washington and one of the bravest soldiers of Colonial times. Alone he raised a regiment at the beginning of the Revolutionary War and held the commission of colonel in the Continental Army. In 1782, as leader of an expedition against Wyandott and Moravian Indians, he was taken prisoner, and burned at the stake.

CRAWFORD COUNTY, formed from part of Allegheny, March 12, 1800. Named for Colonel William Crawford. Land area, 1,038 square miles; population (1930), 62,980; (1920), 60,667. County-seat, Meadville, laid out in 1795.

CREDIT MOBILIER, a corporation chartered by the Pennsylvania Legislature in 1859 as the Pennsylvania Fiscal Agency, was reorganized in 1867 by Oakes Ames for the purpose of aiding in constructing the Union Pacific Railroad. High public officials were charged with accepting stocks as reward for political influence. As a result representatives Oakes Ames and James Brooks were censured by the House of Representatives. Pennsylvania demanded that taxes be paid on the dividends of the stock of the corporation, and the Auditor-General, with his counsel associated with Attorney-General prosecuted the claim in the Dauphin County courts and recovered verdicts against the Credit Mobilier. The supreme court reversed the judgment of the lower court.

CROGHAN, GEORGE, trader, was born in Ireland. He was educated at Dublin and came to America sometime between 1740 and 1744. Apparently he was first licensed as an Indian trader in Pennsylvania in 1744. In 1746, he lived in Silver Spring Township, Cumberland County. During that year he was made a counsellor of the Six Nations at Onondaga and in March, 1749, was appointed a justice of the peace for Cumberland County. As early as 1746 and 1747, he had gone on trading expeditions as far as the southwestern border of Lake Erie. His influence over the Indians brought him to the attention of Conrad Weiser, through whom he entered the Colonial service. He was directly connected with Conrad Weiser's mission of 1748, the French expedition under Celeron de Bienville, in 1749, the organization of the Ohio Company of Virginia, in 1749, Christopher Gist's expedition for the Ohio Company in 1750, the Virginia Treaty at Logstown, in 1752, Washington's mission to Fort LeBoeuf in 1753, his expedition of 1754, the building of Fort Duquesne, Braddock's expedition in 1755, and Gen. Forbes' final expedition in 1758. The French and Indian War ruined Croghan financially. His trading posts were destroyed and in 1753 he moved to Aughwick, now Shirleysburg. He died at Passyunk, August 31, 1782.

GEORGE CROGHAN

CROOKED BILLET, BATTLE OF—After Washington's withdrawal from Whitemarsh, he placed General John Lacey in command of one thousand Pennsylvania Militia, January 9, 1778. Lacey established his headquarters at the Crooked Billet Tavern, Bucks County, which was located in the present town of Hatboro. May 1, 1778, he was attacked by British troops, including loyalists under Lieutenant-Colonel Abercrombie, part of whose command was made up of Simcois Rangers. Lacey's force was surprised and lost 26 killed, 8 or 10 wounded and 58 missing.

CROOKED CREEK—Tributary to Allegheny River. Sub-basin: Middle Allegheny; source, in Rayne Township, central Indiana County; course, westerly, by a circuitous route, into Armstrong County; thence northwesterly to Allegheny River; mouth, at Rosston; length, fifty-eight miles. Indian name, Woak-hanne, "crooked-stream."

CROOKED CREEK—Tributary to Tioga River. Sub-basin: Upper North Branch Susquehanna; source, formed by junction of Hornby Hollow and Daggett Hollow, in Chatham Township, northwestern Tioga County; course, easterly and northeasterly to Tioga River; mouth, at Tioga; length, twenty-one miles. Indian name, Woak-hanne, "crooked-stream."

CRUM CREEK—Tributary to Delaware River. Sub-basin: Lower Delaware; source, near Malvern, Willistown Township, Chester County; course, southeasterly into Delaware County to Delaware River; mouth, two miles northeast of Chester; length, twenty-one and one-half miles. Indian name, Ockanickon, possibly referring to an Indian tribe.

CUMBERLAND COUNTY, formed from part of Lancaster, January 27, 1750. Named for English county of Cumberland. Land area, 528 square miles; population (1930), 68,236; (1920), 58,578. County-seat, Carlisle, laid out in 1751.

CURTIN, ANDREW GREGG, war governor, was born at Bellefonte, April 22, 1815. He received his preparatory education in the schools of his native town, in the Harrisburg Academy, and under the instruction of the Rev. David Kirkpatrick in the Academy at Milton. He began his legal studies under the direction of William W. Potter, Esq., a leading member of the Centre County Bar and concluded his legal studies at the Law School of Dickinson College. Entering into partnership with John Blanchard he rose rapidly in his profession. Becoming interested in politics he delivered many speeches for Henry Clay in the presidential campaign of 1844. In 1848 and 1852, his name was placed on the Whig electoral ticket and he was a popular speaker for both Taylor and Scott.

In January, 1855, Governor Pollock appointed Curtin, Secretary of the Commonwealth. As ex-officio Superintendent of Schools, his services called forth favorable comment from the friends of education.

In 1860, he was nominated by the Republican Convention as its candidate for Governor and his victory in October foreshadowed the election of Lincoln in November.

His firm stand for the National Government in his inaugural address of January, 1861, greatly strengthened the spirit of union in the north. He was reelected in 1863, although in ill health. One of his greatest achievements as Governor was the calling of a conference of loyal governors at Altoona, September 24, 1862.

In 1869, he was appointed Minister to Russia. Antagonized by the dominant Cameron influence of Pennsylvania he joined the Liberal Movement in 1872, and from 1881-1887 served his district in Congress as a Democrat. He died at Bellefonte, October 7, 1894.

CUSHING, FRANK HAMILTON, ethnologist; born, North East, July 22, 1857; at the age of nineteen, was curator of the ethnological exhibit at the Centennial Exposition at Philadelphia; was with Powell's expedition to New Mexico; lived with Zuni Indians, and as a result of his study of them wrote, "My Adventures in Zuni," "and "Zuni Folk Tales"; was in charge of excavations in Arizona in 1881 and discovered archaeological remains in Florida in 1895; became connected with the United States Bureau of Ethnology in 1897; died, Washington, D. C., April 10, 1900.

CUSSEWAGO CREEK—Tributary to French Creek. Sub-basin: Upper Allegheny; source, in Franklin Township, southwestern Erie County; course, southerly into Crawford County to French Creek; mouth, at Meadville; length, twenty-eight miles. Indian name, Custaloga's town, Custaloga, the head chief of the Munsee tribe.

CUSTOMS HOUSE—The first federal building used for a customs house in Philadelphia was opened July 12, 1819, on Second Street. This building was occupied until 1845, when the United States Bank Building, on Chestnut Street, between Fourth and Fifth, was used. By the Charter of Charles II to William Penn, Penn and the settlers in the province were permitted to import and export goods by land or sea subject to the king's customs and to the act of navigation. The first collector of customs in Pennsylvania, under the king, was Maj. William Dyer, who served in that capacity in Pennsylvania and New Jersey and as surveyor-general for all the king's colonies in America.

DA COSTA, JACOB MENDES, physician; born in Saint Thomas, W. I., February 7, 1833. He was early educated abroad and in 1852 graduated from Jefferson Medical College, Philadelphia. Later, he returned to Europe where he continued his studies in Paris and Vienna. He entered upon the practice of his profession in Philadelphia, specializing in clinical medicine and pathology. In 1863, he became lecturer at Jefferson Medical College, and in 1872, professor of theory and practice of medicine, retaining that chair until 1891 when he became professor emeritus. Da Costa was one of the most noted clinical teachers of his time. Among his contributions to medical literature are: "Harvey and His Discovery"; "Modern Medicine"; "The Physicians of the Last Century"; "The Scholar in Medicine"; and "Medical Diagnosis," which has been translated into several languages. Da Costa died at Villanova, September 11, 1900.

DAHLGREN, JOHN ADOLPH, naval commander; born in Philadelphia, November 13, 1809. In 1826, he entered the United States Navy as a midshipman; in 1837, was advanced to the rank of lieutenant; in 1855, to commander, and in 1863, was made rear admiral. He was the inventor of the Dahlgren gun, which he perfected at the navy yard at Washington. In 1862, he was made chief of the Bureau of Ordinance. In July, 1863, he took command of the South Atlantic squadron and with the land forces of Gen. Gillmore reduced Fort Sumter to a heap of ruins. In 1864, he cooperated with Gen. Sherman in the capture of Savannah. After the evacuation of Charleston he moved his vessels up to that city. Admiral Dahlgren, besides being the inventor of a cannon, introduced into the navy the highly esteemed light boat-howitzer. He was the author of several works of ordinance which became text-books. He died in Washington, D. C., July 12, 1870.

DAHLGREN, ULRIC, artillery officer; born in Bucks County, 1842, the son of Rear Admiral John A. Dahlgren. At the outbreak of the Civil War he became aide, first to his father and later to Gen. Sigel and was Sigel's Chief of Artillery at the second battle of Bull Run. He distinguished himself in an attack on Fredericksburg and at the battle of Chancellorsville and on the retreat of the Confederates from Gettysburg he led the charge into Hagerstown. He lost his life in a raid undertaken for the purpose of releasing National prisoners at Libby Prison and Belle Isle, near King and Queen's Court House, Va., March 4, 1864.

DAILY ADVERTISER, THE AMERICAN—The first daily newspaper on the western hemisphere, was established at Philadelphia, December 21, 1784, by Dunlap and Claypoole, as a branch of the Pennsylvania Packet, founded in 1771, by John Dunlap. The Daily Advertiser was later published by Zachariah Poulson as Poulson's Advertiser, and in 1839 was merged into the North American.

DAILY EXPRESS—A publication issued during the cholera epidemic in Philadelphia, its purpose being to give a daily report of cholera cases. The paper was first issued on August 1, 1832, but after a few weeks was discontinued.

DALE, RICHARD, naval officer; born near Norfolk, Va., November 6, 1756; went to sea at twelve years of age, and at nineteen, commanded a merchant vessel. He was first a lieutenant in the Virginia navy, as midshipman, in 1776. He was captured in 1777, and confined in Mill Prison, England, from which he escaped, but was recaptured in London and taken back. The next year he escaped, reached France, joined Paul Jones and soon became lieutenant of the Bon Homme Richard, receiving a wound in the famous battle with the Serapis. He continued to do good service to the end of the war, and in 1794 was made captain. He commanded the squadron ordered to the Mediterranean in 1801, and in April, 1802, returning home he resigned his commission. He spent the latter years of his life in ease in Philadelphia, where he died February 24, 1826. He is buried in Christ Churchyard, Philadelphia.

DALLAS, ALEXANDER JAMES, statesman; born in the island of Jamaica, June 21, 1759; left home in 1783, settled in Philadelphia, and was admitted to the bar. He soon became a practitioner in the Supreme Court of the United States. He wrote for newspapers, and at one time was the editor of the Columbian Magazine. He was appointed Secretary of State of Pennsylvania in 1791 and was engaged as paymaster of a force to quell the Whiskey Insurrection. In 1801, he was appointed United States Attorney for the Eastern Department of Pennsylvania and held that place until called to the cabinet of Madison as Secretary of the Treasury in October, 1814. In 1815, he also performed the duties of the War Office and was earnest in his efforts to reestablish a national bank.

He resigned in November, 1816, and resumed the practice of law. He died in Trenton, N. J., January 16, 1817.

DALLAS, GEORGE MIFFLIN, diplomatist; born in Philadelphia, July 10, 1792; was the son of A. J. Dallas. In 1813, he was admitted to the bar and soon after entered the diplomatic service. In 1831, he was elected a United States Senator from Pennsylvania; was United States Minister to Russia, 1837-1839, and in 1844, was elected Vice-President of the United States. In 1846, his casting-vote as president of the Senate repealed the protective tariff of 1842, though he had previously been considered a Protectionist. His course on this question aroused much indignation in Pennsylvania. He was United States Minister to Great Britain from 1856 to 1860. His principal published writings were posthumous, and include "Series of Letters from London" (1869), and "Life of A. J. Dallas" (1871). He died in Philadelphia, December 31, 1864.

DALZELL, JOHN, lawyer, was born in New York, April 19, 1845. He received his education at Yale University, after which he studied law, was admitted to the bar, and practiced his profession in Pittsburgh, where he had moved with his family in 1847. He rapidly achieved success serving as attorney for the Pennsylvania Railroad, the Westinghouse Company and other corporations, and becoming one of the most brilliant lawyers of the Pittsburgh bar. In 1887, he was elected to Congress and was subsequently reelected for fourteen successive terms. While a representative in Congress he served as chairman of many important committees. He died October 2, 1927.

DANVILLE—Borough and county-seat of Montour County on the Susquehanna River, 56 miles northeast of Harrisburg. Among its industries are iron and steel works and silk mills. Danville is the site of a state hospital for the insane. The town was laid out in 1792 and was originally called Dan's Town, for the son of the first settler. Population (1930), 7,185; (1920), 6,952.

DARBY, WILLIAM, geographer; born in Pennsylvania in 1775, served under General Jackson in Louisiana; was one of the surveyors of the boundary between Canada and the United States. Among his works are: "Geographical Description of Louisiana"; "Geography and History of Florida"; "View of the United States"; "Lectures on the Discovery of America," etc. He died in Washington, D. C., October 9, 1854.

DARBY—Borough of Delaware County, five miles southwest of Philadelphia. Its industries are the manufacture of silk, cotton, woolen and worsted goods and filters, tanks and tools. Darby was first settled about 1660 and has a public library established as early as 1743. Population (1930), 9,899; (1920), 7,922.

GEORGE M. DALLAS

DARBY CREEK—Tributary to Delaware River. Sub-basin: Lower Delaware; source, in Easttown Township, eastern Chester County; course, southeasterly into Delaware County; thence southwesterly to Delaware River, being Philadelphia-Delaware County boundary for two miles; mouth, at Essington; length, twenty-four miles.

DARKE, WILLIAM, military officer; born in Philadelphia County in 1736; served under Braddock in 1755 and was with him at his defeat; entered the patriot army at the outbreak of the Revolution as a captain; was captured at the Battle of Germantown; was subsequently promoted to colonel and commanded the Hampshire and Berkeley regiments at the capture of Cornwallis in 1781. He served as lieutenant-colonel under Gen. St. Clair, and was wounded in the battle with the Miami Indians, November 4, 1791. He was repeatedly a member of the Virginia Legislature and as a member of the Convention of 1788, voted for the Federal Constitution. He died in Jefferson County, Virginia, November 26, 1801.

DARLEY, FELIX OCTAVIUS CARR, artist; born in Philadelphia, June 23, 1822. His illustrations of literary masterpieces gave pleasure to thousands and made him famous. His best works comprise his drawings to accompany the text of "Rip Van Winkle"; "Sleepy Hollow"; "Courtship of Miles Standish"; "Scarlet Letter"; "Evangeline"; the novels of Cooper, Dickens and others, besides many special pictures. His book, "Sketches Abroad with Pen and Pencil" (1868), is well known. During the Civil War he delineated many characteristic scenes. Some of the more elaborate pictures on the United States government bonds were made by him, and also the beautiful designs of the certificate of stock given as evidence of subscription for the Centennial Exhibition in 1876. Mr. Darley went to Europe near the close of the war, studied models in Rome and returned with a portfolio full of personal sketches. He died in Claymont, Del., March 27, 1888.

DARLING, HENRY, clergyman; born in Reading, December 27, 1823; graduated at Amherst College in 1842; ordained to the ministry of the Presbyterian Church in 1847; published "Slavery and the War" (1863), etc. He died in Clinton, N. Y., April 20, 1891.

DARLINGTON, JAMES HENRY, Protestant Episcopal bishop. Born in Brooklyn, N. Y., June 9, 1856. He was educated at New York University where he graduated in 1877 and at Princeton Theological Seminary where he graduated in 1880. He became assistant rector of Christ Church, Brooklyn, in 1882 and from 1883–1905 was rector of that church. In the latter year, he assumed the office of bishop of the diocese of Harrisburg, which position he held at the time of his death on August 14, 1930. Bishop Darlington edited The Hymnal of the Church, In Memoriam, Little Rhymes for Little People. He wrote "Pastor and People" (1902), and Verses by the Way, and was the composer of hymn tunes, instrumental music and a symphony, The Sea and the Sea Gulls.

DARLINGTON, WILLIAM, botanist; born in Birmingham, April 28, 1782; was a soldier in the War of 1812 and a member of Congress, 1815-1817 and from 1819-1823. He published a descriptive catalogue of plants in Pennsylvania, "Flora Cestrica" (1837-1853); "Mutual Influence of Habit and Disease" (1804); "Agricultural Botany" (1847); and in 1853 a genus of pitcher plant found in California was named in his honor, Darlingtonia Californica. He died at West Chester, April 23, 1863.

DARRAH, LYDIA, heroine; place and date of birth unknown; lived in Philadelphia in 1777. One of the rooms in her house was used by the British officers who planned to surprise Washington's army. She overheard their plans and early in the morning of December 3rd, left her home ostensibly for the purpose of purchasing flour, but in reality to give warning to Washington. After a walk of several miles in the snow she met one of Washington's officers, to whom she revealed what she had overheard. Through this timely information Washington was prepared and the British expedition proved to be a failure.

DASHIEL, ROBERT LAURENSON, clergyman and educator; born, Salisbury, Md., June 25, 1825. He graduated from Dickinson College in 1846, subsequently serving various pastorates of the Methodist Church in Maryland and New Jersey. From 1868-1871, he was president of Dickinson College. He died at Newark, N. J., March 8, 1880.

DAUPHIN COUNTY—Formed from part of Lancaster, March 4, 1785; named for hereditary title of the eldest son of the French king, Louis XVI. Land area, 522 square miles. Population (1930), 165,231. County-seat, Harrisburg; laid out in 1785.

DAVENPORT, EDWARD LOOMIS, actor. Born in Boston, November 15, 1814. He made his debut on the stage in 1836 at Providence, R. I., as Parson Will in "Sir Giles Overreach." Two years later he played in Philadelphia, achieving success in comedy, melo-drama and tragedy. In 1847, he went to England, playing Claude Melnotte in "The Lady of Lyons," with Mrs. Mowatt as Pauline. Upon his return to the United States in 1854, he traveled about playing Shakesperian roles and in dramatizations of Dicken's novels. He became manager of the Howard Athenæum, Boston, in 1859, and of Chestnut Street Theatre, Philadelphia, in 1869. He died at Canton, Pa., September 1, 1877.

DAVENPORT, WILLIAM, mathematical instrument maker, maintained a shop at 43 South Front Street, Philadelphia, from 1802-1804. The Peabody

Museum, Salem, Mass., contains a brass surveyor and compass, marked "Wm. Davenport, Maker, Philadelphia."

DAVIDSON, WILLIAM, military officer, was born in Lancaster County in 1746; was appointed major in one of the North Carolina Regiments at the outbreak of the Revolution; took part in the battles of Brandywine, Germantown and Monmouth; commissioned brigadier-general. Was at Cowan's Ford, N. C., February 1, 1781, when the British Army under Cornwallis forced a passage; during the fight General Davidson was killed.

DAVIES, THOMAS FREDERICK, Protestant Episcopal bishop. Born, Fairfield, Conn., August 31, 1831. He was rector of Saint Peter's, Philadelphia, until his consecration as bishop of Michigan, in 1889. He died at Detroit, Mich., November 9, 1905.

DAVIES, THOMAS FREDERICK, Protestant Episcopal bishop, was born in Philadelphia, July 20, 1872, the son of Thomas Frederick Davies, bishop of Michigan. He graduated from Yale University in 1894 and from the General Theological Seminary, New York, in 1897. After his ordination as priest in 1898 he served as assistant rector of the Church of the Incarnation, New York, 1897-1900; rector, Christ Church, Norwich, Conn., 1901-1903; rector, All Saints', Worcester, Mass., 1903-1911; and in 1911 became bishop of Western Massachusetts. His home is in Springfield, Mass.

DAVIS, CHARLES BELMONT, author, was born in Philadelphia, January 24, 1866, the son of Rebecca Harding Davis and brother of Richard Harding Davis. He attended Lehigh University and was United States Consul at Florence, Italy. He died December 9, 1926.

DAVIS, NOAH KNOWLES, author. Born in Philadelphia, May 15, 1830. He received his education at Mercer University, Ga., and in 1873 became professor of philosophy in the University of Virginia. He is the author of "The Theory of Thought"; "Elements of Deductive Logic"; "Elements of Psychology"; "Judah's Jewels" (a study in Hebrew Lyrics); "Elements of Ethics"; "Synopsis, of Events in Life of Jesus of Nazareth"; "The Nazarene." He died at Charlottesville, Va., May 3, 1910.

DAVIS, REBECCA BLAINE HARDING, writer, was born in Washington, Pa., June 24, 1831. She is the author of several novels which include "Life in the Iron Mills"; "A Story of Today" (later published as "Margaret Howth"); "A Law Unto Herself"; "Waiting for the Verdict"; "Dallas Galbraith"; "Natasqua"; "Frances Waldeaux"; "Doctor Warrick's Daughters," and "Silhouettes of American Life." She was a frequent contributor to periodicals. Her death occurred September 29, 1910.

DAVIS, RICHARD HARDING, author, was born in Philadelphia, April 18, 1864, the son of Rebecca Harding Davis. He was educated at Lehigh and Johns Hopkins Universities. Was a war correspondent in Cuba in 1898 and in South Africa in 1900. He became popular as a short story writer. His collections of short stories include: "Gallegher"; "Van Bibber and Others"; "The Exiles and Other Stories"; "The Lion and the Unicorn"; "Ranson's Folly"; "The Scarlet Car"; "Once Upon a Time"; "The Man Who Could Not Lose"; "The Red Cross Girl"; "The Lost Road"; "The Boy Scout." He is also well known for the following novels: "Soldiers of Fortune"; "The King's Jackal"; "Captain Macklin"; "The Bar Sinister"; "Vera the Medium"; "The White Mice." Davis died at his home at Mount Kisco, N. Y., April 11, 1916.

DAVIS, WILLIAM MORRIS, geologist and geographer, was born at Philadelphia, February 12, 1850. He received his education at Harvard University and from 1870-1873 was assistant astronomer in the Argentine National Observatory at Cordoba. In 1876, he became a member of the faculty of Harvard University, teaching at first astronomy and geology and later physical geography. He was made Sturgis-Hooper professor of geology at Harvard in 1899 and retained this position until 1912, when he became professor emeritus. In 1911, he was elected president of the Geological Society of America and in 1912 was made a Chevalier of the Legion of Honor. Among his published works are: "Elementary Meteorology"; "Physical Geography"; "Whirlwinds, Cyclones and Tornadoes"; "Journey Across Turkestan"; in Pompelly's "Explorations in Turkestan." He has also contributed many articles to the *American Journal of Science* and other periodicals. His home is in Cambridge, Mass.

DEAN, HENRY CLAY, lawyer and minister, was born in Fayette County, in 1822, a descendant of a Maryland family who came to America with Lord Baltimore. He graduated from Madison College, Pa., later taught school, studied law and was admitted to the bar. Still later he gave up law to enter the ministry. He studied theology and was ordained to the ministry of the Methodist Church of Virginia. For four years he served an itinerant circuit in Virginia. In 1850, he moved to Iowa and after living at various other places for short periods, finally moved to Putnam County, Missouri. He was eminently successful as an orator, possessing much natural ability. At one time he served as chaplain of the United States Senate. He died in 1887.

DECATUR, STEPHEN, commodore, was born at Newport, R. I., in 1751. He served during the Revolution as commander of several privateers. At the beginning of the war with France in 1798, he commanded the Delaware, cruised about the American coast and the West Indies and captured several French privateers. He commanded a squadron in 1800 with the Philadelphia as his flagship. He died at Philadelphia, November 14, 1808.

DECATUR, STEPHEN, commodore, was born in Sinepexent, Maryland, January 5, 1779. He was the most conspicuous figure in the naval history of the United States for the 100 years between Paul Jones and Farragut. He was well educated at the Episcopal Academy and at the University of Pennsylvania. He was appointed a midshipman in the navy by President Adams, April 30, 1798. At the outbreak of the Tripolitan War, in command of the schooner, Enterprise, he captured the bomb ketch Mastico, December 23, 1803. In this ketch, renamed the Intrepid, he destroyed the frigate Philadelphia in the harbor of Tripoli. The phrase, "the most bold and daring act of the age," accurately described this undertaking. For the burning of the Philadelphia he was commissioned captain, and at the age of twenty-five, was placed in command of the frigate Constitution. In 1816, he was appointed naval commissioner and on March 22, 1820, he was killed in a duel with Commodore James Barron. He is buried in St. Peter's churchyard, Philadelphia. Loyalty to his country was the very breath of life to Decatur.

DECLARATION OF INDEPENDENCE—On July 4, 1776, the Continental Congress adopted a resolution declaring the colonies independent of Great Britain. The document was not signed until several days afterward. At the meeting of the Continental Congress in the state house (now Independence Hall) at Philadelphia on July 1st, Pennsylvania's seven delegates to the Congress voted against independence, but on July 4th, five of them voted in its favor. Pennsylvania's delegates who signed the declaration were: Robert Morris, Benjamin Franklin, Benjamin Rush, John Morton, George Clymer, James Smith, George Taylor, James Wilson, George Ross. On July 8th the Declaration of Independence was publicly read from the platform of the observatory of the state house by Captain Hopkins of the navy.

DE HAAS, JOHN PHILIP, military officer, was born in Holland about 1735, a descendant of an ancient family of northern France. He came to America in 1750; was an ensign in the French and Indian War; participated in a sharp conflict with Indians near Pittsburgh and was colonel of the 1st Pennsylvania Regiment in 1776. He served in the American army in Canada, and afterwards at Ticonderoga. He led his regiment from Lake Champlain to New York, and participated in the battle on Long Island in August, 1776. In February, 1777, he was promoted to brigadier-general. The latter years of his life were passed in Philadelphia where he died June 3, 1786.

DE LANCEY, WILLIAM HEATHCOTE, Protestant Episcopal bishop, was born in Westchester County, N. Y., October 8, 1797. He graduated from Yale University in 1817 and subsequently studied theology and became a minister in the Episcopal Church. He was made provost of the University of Pennsylvania in 1828 and served in that capacity for five years. He died in 1865.

STEPHEN DECATUR

DELAND, ELLEN DOUGLAS, writer, was born at Lake Mahopac, N. Y., September 3, 1860. For some time she lived in Philadelphia, moving to Boston in 1901. Her books include: "Oakleigh"; "Malvern"; "In the Old Herrick House"; "A Successful Venture"; "Alan Ransford"; "Katrina"; "Three Girls of Hazelmere"; "Josephine"; "A Little Son of Sunshine"; "The Friendship of Anne"; "Miss Betty of New York"; "The Girls of Dudley School"; "The Fortunes of Phoebe"; "Country Cousins"; "Cyntra"; "The Waring Girls"; "Clyde Corners," and "The Secret Stairs." She died February 22, 1923.

DELAND, MARGARETTA WADE (Campbell), novelist, was born at Allegheny, February 23, 1857. In 1880, she married L. F. Deland and went to live in Boston. Some of her novels are: "John Ward, Preacher"; "The Old Garden and Other Verses"; "Old Chester Tales"; "Good for the Soul"; "Dr. Lavendar's People"; "The Common Way"; "The Awakening of Helena Richie"; "An Encore"; "The Way of Peace"; "The Iron Woman"; "The Voice"; "Partners"; "The Hand of Esau"; "Around Old Chester"; "The Rising Tide"; "The Vehement Flame"; "New Friends in Old Chester"; "The Kays." Her home is in Cambridge, Mass.

DELAWARE COUNTY—Formed from part of Chester, September 26, 1789. Named for the Delaware River that forms the eastern boundary of the state. Land area, 185 square miles. Population (1930), 280,264. County-seat, Media; laid out in 1849.

DELAWARE WATER GAP (1843)

DELAWARE RIVER (INCLUDING WEST BRANCH)—Tributary to Delaware Bay. Basin: Delaware; source, the east and west branches head in the Catskill Mountains of eastern New York, and unite at Hancock, N. Y., on the Pennsylvania-New York boundary, to form main stream; course, southwesterly and southeasterly to Port Jervis, N. Y.; mouth, at Deep Water Point, Del.; length, total, 375 miles. The name is derived from that of the Governor of the English Colony at Jamestown, Lord de la Warre. The Indian name of the river was Lenapewihittuck, "river of the Lenape," and Kit-hanne, "great stream," also Kit-hit-tuck, "a large river."

DELAWARE WATER GAP—A town in Monroe County on the Delaware River, 65 miles northeast of New York. The Delaware River passing through the Kittatinny range of the Appalachian Mountains forms a gorge about three miles long, and it is from this gap that the town takes its name. Because of its location, Delaware Water Gap has become a popular summer resort.

DENNIE, JOSEPH, journalist, was born in Boston, August 30, 1768. He published "The Farrago" (1795), essays on life and literature. From 1796-1798, he edited with great success the Farmer's Weekly Museum at Walpole, N. H. In this appeared his essays signed "The Lay Preacher," whose droll and easy style made him popular. In Philadelphia (1801) assisted by Asbury Dickens, he founded the "Portfolio," which he edited till his death under the pen-name of "Oliver Old School." Two collections of his writing have been published: "The Lay Preacher, or Short Sermons for Idle Readers" (1796), and "The Lay Preacher" (1817). He died in Philadelphia, January 7, 1812.

DENNY, WILLIAM, governor, arrived in Pennsylvania, August 20, 1756. His authority was limited because of the domination of the Proprietors. He was required to withhold his assent from every bill for the emission of money that did not place the proceeds at the joint disposition of the Assembly and the Governor. He was also forbidden to pass any bill increasing the paper currency above forty thousand pounds, unless Proprietary rents were paid in sterling money. Denny was severely criticized for his adherence to the demands of the proprietaries. Finally when his personal needs became so great he signed a bill taxing the Proprietary estates and because of this action was recalled in October, 1759.

DENSLOW, WILLIAM WALLACE, illustrator, was born in Philadelphia, May 5, 1856. He studied art at Cooper Institute and at the National Academy of Design, New York. He was a prolific illustrator since 1872, at first being a traveling illustrator for the leading American newspapers. Among his works are the pictures: "What's the Use"; "Victory"; and "The Heathen Chinee." He died March 27, 1915.

DEPRECIATION CERTIFICATES—Under an act passed December 18, 1780, it was provided that in view of the fact that "the United States have not been able to comply with their engagements heretofore made to the officers and private men of the Pennsylvania Line," the Supreme Executive Council was authorized to appoint three auditors to settle the depreciation pay accounts of the officers and men from January 1, 1777, to August 1, 1780. The auditors were given power to estimate in specie all sums of continental money received by the soldiers and to issue certificates which are to be considered equal in specie. The proceeds from confiscated estates were to be applied to this purpose.

DERR, LOUIS, physician, was born at Pottsville, August 6, 1868. He graduated from Amherst College, in 1899, and later studied at the Massachusetts Institute of Technology and at Harvard Graduate School. In 1892, he became assistant in the department of physics at Massachusetts Institute of Technology and in 1909 attained a professorship. From 1893-1898, he was instructor of physics at Boston University and from 1895-1908 taught the same subject at the Boston Normal School of Gymnastics. He contributed various papers to scientific journals and published "Notes on the Principles of Dynamo and Transformer Design"; "Photography for Students of Physics and Chemistry." He edited the "Cyclopedia of Engineering," and in 1907 became assistant editor of "Chemical Abstracts." He died May 11, 1923.

DERRY CHURCH—A Presbyterian Church, near Hershey, Dauphin County, the oldest church in the Lebanon Valley, was established by the Scotch-Irish about 1724. The sessions house erected in 1732 and used as an academy, is still standing.

DEVIL'S DEN—A peculiar formation of large rocks from six to fifteen feet high thrown together in confusion and yet so arranged as to leave between them passages that are accessible, was located on the Battlefield of Gettysburg about 500 yards west of the summit of Little Round Top. At this place the Confederate sharp-shooters for some time prevented the Federal Army from placing their artillery on Little Round Top. A stream of water, called Plum Run, flows between Devil's Den and Little Round Top. Later the Federal Artillery was brought into play upon this stronghold of sharp-shooters and Devil's Den was held by the Federal Army. This occurred on the second day's fight at Gettysburg.

DEWEES, WILLIAM POTTS, physician, was born in Pottsgrove, now Pottstown, May 5, 1768. He attended several courses of medical lectures at the University of Pennsylvania, and in 1793 began practice in Philadelphia. Here he achieved for himself a high reputation, especially in the department to which he devoted particular attention, mid-wifery, previously much neglected in America. He published "Inaugural Essays"; "System of Mid-Wifery," of which latter many editions have been printed. "A Treatise on the Physical and Medical

Treatment of Children"; "A Treatise on Diseases of Females"; "Practice of Medicine" (1830). In 1826, he was elected adjunct professor, and in 1834 professor of obstetrics and diseases of women and children in the University of Pennsylvania. He died May 18, 1841.

DEWITT, MOSES, surveyor and pioneer, assisted in running the Pennsylvania boundary. He was born in Ulster County, N. Y., October 15, 1766, and died in Onondaga County, that state, August 15, 1794.

DICKENS, CHARLES, the English novelist, visited Pennsylvania during his tour of America in 1842. His impressions of his visit are set forth in his "American Notes," from which the following is quoted: "The journey from New York to Philadelphia is made by railroad and two ferries; and usually occupies between five and six hours. . . . It (Philadelphia) is a handsome city, but distractingly regular. After walking about it for an hour or two, I felt that I would have given the world for a crooked street. . . . My stay in Philadelphia was very short, but what I saw of its society I greatly liked. Treating of its general characteristics, I should be disposed to say that it is more provincial than Boston or New York, and that there is afloat in the fair city an assumption of taste and criticism, savouring rather of those genteel discussions upon the same themes, in connection with Shakespeare and the Musical Glasses, of which we read in the 'Vicar of Wakefield.'" Of his trip over the old Camel Back Bridge crossing the Susquehanna to Harrisburg, Dickens wrote: "We crossed this river by a wooden bridge, roofed and covered in on all sides, and nearly a mile in length. It was profoundly dark; perplexed, with great beams crossing and recrossing it at every possible angle; and through the broad chinks and crevices of the floor the rapid river gleamed, far down below, like a legion of eyes. We had no lamps; and as the horses stumbled and floundered through this place, towards the distant speck of dying light, it seemed interminable. I really could not persuade myself, as we rumbled heavily on, filling the bridge with hollow noises, and I held down my head to save it from the rafters above, but that I was in a painful dream."

From Harrisburg, Dickens left for Pittsburgh, crossing the Alleghenies on the Portage Railway. He describes his journey as follows:

"On Sunday morning we arrived at the foot of the mountain, which is crossed by railroad. There are ten inclined planes; five ascending, and five descending; the carriages are dragged up the former, and let slowly down the latter, by means of stationary engines; the comparatively level spaces between being traversed, sometimes by horse, and sometimes by engine power, as the case demands. Occasionally, the rails are laid upon the extreme verge of a giddy precipice; and looking from the carriage window, the traveler gazes sheer down, without a stone or scrap of fence between, into the mountain depths below. The journey is very carefully made, however; only two carriages traveling together; and, while proper precautions are taken, is not to be dreaded for its dangers.

"It was very pretty traveling thus at a rapid pace along the heights of the mountains in a keen wind, to look down into a valley full of light and softness; catching glimpses, through the tree-tops, of scattered cabins; children running to the door; dogs bursting out to bark, whom we could see without hearing; terrified pigs scampering homeward; families sitting out in their rude gardens; cows gazing upward with a stupid indifference; men in their shirt sleeves, looking on at their unfinished houses, planning out tomorrow's work; and we riding onward, high above them, like a whirlwind. It was amusing, too, when we had dined, and rattled down a steep pass, having no other moving power than the weight of the carriages themselves, to see the engine, released long after us, come buzzing down alone, like a great insect, its back of green and gold so shining in the sun that if it had spread a pair of wings and soared away, no one would have had occasion, as I fancied, for the least surprise. But it stopped short of us in a very businesslike manner when we reached the canal; and before we left the wharf, went panting up this hill again, with the passengers who had waited our arrival for the means of traversing the road by which we had come."

DICKENS, JOHN, clergyman, was born in London, August 24, 1747, emigrated to America, 1770. Was licensed to preach by the Methodist Church, 1777. His appointment as "Book Steward" in Philadelphia, 1790, was the beginning of the Methodist Book Concern, afterwards removed to New York City. He edited and published the "Armenian Magazine" and the "Methodist Magazine." He died in Philadelphia, September 27, 1798.

DICKINSON, ANNA ELIZABETH, reformer, was born in Philadelphia, October 28, 1842. She made her first appearance among public speakers in 1857, and spoke frequently on temperance and slavery. During the Civil War, she was employed by the Republican National Committee to make addresses and after its conclusion she lectured on reconstruction, woman's suffrage, and woman's work and wages. She wrote the plays "The Crown of Thorns" and "Mary Tudor" and for several years from 1867 she appeared on the dramatic stage.

DICKINSON, JOHN, publicist, was born in Maryland, November 13, 1732, the son of Chief-Justice Samuel D. Dickinson. He studied law in Philadelphia and at Temple in London and practiced his profession in Philadelphia. In the Pennsylvania Assembly, to which he was elected in 1764, he showed great legislative ability and was a ready and vehement debater. At the same time he wrote much on the subject of British infringement on the liberties of the colonies. He was a member of the first Continental Congress, and wrote several of the state papers put forth by that body. Considering the resolution of independence unwise, he voted against it and the Declaration, and did not sign the latter document. This made him unpopular. In 1777, he was made a brigadier-general of the Pennsylvania militia. He was elected a representative to Congress from Delaware in 1779 and wrote the "Address to the States" put forth in that year.

He was successively president of the states of Delaware and Pennsylvania (1781-1785), and a member of the convention that framed the National Constitution (1787). Letters from his pen, over the signature of "Fabius," advocating the adoption of the national constitution appeared in 1787, and another series on our relations with France appeared in 1797. Mr. Dickinson assisted in framing the constitution of Delaware in 1792. He died in Wilmington, Del., February 14, 1808.

DICKINSON COLLEGE, a co-educational institution at Carlisle, was founded in 1783 and named for John Dickinson. The first board of trustees included John Dickinson, James Wilson and Dr. Benjamin Rush. In 1913, Metzger Female Institute, opened in 1881, was discontinued, and part of the endowment given to Dickinson College under condition that Metzger Institute become the woman's department of Dickinson. Dickinson School of Law was established in 1834, by Hon. John Reed, then President Judge of the Cumberland County Courts. Enrollment (1930-1931), 575.

DICKSON, SAMUEL HENRY, physician, was born in Charleston, S. C., September 20, 1798. After his graduation from Yale University in 1814, he studied medicine. In 1824, he became a member of the faculty of the newly organized medical college at Charleston, which he had aided in establishing. From 1858 to his death on March 31, 1872, he was professor of practice of medicine in Jefferson Medical College, Philadelphia. He wrote "Manual of Pathology and Practice of Medicine"; "Elements of Medicine"; "Essays on Pathology and Therapeutics"; "Essays on Life, Sleep, Pain, Etc."

DICKSON CITY—Borough in Lackawanna County, five miles north of Scranton, is located in a coal mining region. It has foundries, machine shops and silk mills. Population (1930), 12,395; (1920), 11,049.

DILLER, JOSEPH SILAS, geologist, was born at Plainfield, in 1850. He attended Harvard and Heidelberg Universities and from 1881-1883 was with the Assos Expedition as geologist. In 1883, he joined the staff of the United States Geological Survey. He died November 13, 1928.

DOANS, THE—Royalist family of outlaws who lived in Bucks County. Their hatred of the patriots following the Revolutionary War was so bitter that they committed many depredations. The most serious of these was their robbery of the Bucks County treasury at Newtown on October 22, 1781, a few days after Cornwallis' surrender. The family was eventually exiled to Canada. Aaron and Joseph Doan served against the United States in the War of 1812. Another member of the family continued his outrages in Canada and was finally hanged for rebelling against the Canadian government.

DOCK, CHRISTOPHER, an early schoolmaster, came to America in 1714. In 1750, he wrote an essay on school teaching, entitled "Schulordnung," which is the earliest American book on that subject. He taught school at Germantown, Salford and Skippack and died in his schoolhouse at the latter place.

DODDRIDGE, PHILIP, lawyer and statesman, was born in Bedford County, in 1772. He attended school in Charlestown (now Wellsburg), W. Va., in 1797 was admitted to the bar in Brooke County, and eventually settled in Wellsburg. From 1815-1816 and from 1822-1823, he was a member of the House of Delegates of the Virginia Legislature, was a leader in the Virginia Constitutional Convention of 1829-1830, and from 1829 until his death, November 19, 1832, was a member of Congress.

DODDS, ALEXANDER, editor, was born at Allegheny, April 5, 1874. In 1890 he graduated from Duff's College, Pittsburgh, and subsequently entered the field of journalism. He was associate editor of The Builder, Pittsburgh, 1894-1896; night editor of the Pittsburgh Dispatch, 1902; associate editor of the Telegraph, Sharon 1902-1904; night editor of the Gazette Times, Pittsburgh, 1905-1908; managing editor, Christian Science Monitor, 1908-1914; managing editor, Los Angeles Herald, 1914-1916. He died November 30, 1920.

DOMESTIC SOCIETY, THE PHILADELPHIA, was incorporated March 2, 1805. Its aim was to relieve a business depression brought about by unemployment. At the time of its organization about five hundred weavers were out of employment. The Society assisted all in finding positions.

DONALDSON, WASHINGTON H., aeronaut, was born in Philadelphia, in 1840. In early life he was by turns a gymnast, a ventriloquist, a conjurer, and a tight-rope walker. A hotel proprietor presented him with a balloon, whereupon he became an aeronaut, and made himself famous all over the United States by his daring and wreckless ascensions. On July 15, 1875, he made an ascension from the lake front in Chicago and neither Donaldson nor his balloon was ever seen thereafter.

DONEGAL CHURCH—A Presbyterian church in Donegal Township, Lancaster County, organized about 1719 or 1720 by Andrew Galbraith who came to America with Penn in 1718. The church was the scene of many events of historic importance, the greatest of these taking place in the churchyard when on a Sunday morning in June, 1777, the congregation formed a circle about an oak tree, and placing their pastor, Rev. Farquhar (who persisted in praying for the King, according to the established order of church service), inside, made him cheer for the cause of the colonies. The congregation then renewed their pledge to freedom's cause. The old oak, still standing, is known as "The Witness Tree."

DONNELLY, ELEANOR CECILIA, author, was born in Philadelphia, September 6, 1838. She is a sister of Ignatius Donnelly. Among her many volumes of verse are: "Out of Sweet Solitude"; "Domus Dei"; "Legend of the Best Beloved and Other Poems"; "Crowned with Stars"; "Hymn of the Sacred Heart"; "Children of the Golden Sheaf and Other Poems." She has also written several prose works, including "Life of Father Felix." She died April 30, 1917.

DONNELLY, IGNATIUS, prose writer, born in Philadelphia, November 3, 1831. He was prominent in Minnesota politics, but was best known as an author. Among his writings are: "An Essay on the Sonnets of Shakespeare"; "Atlantis, the Antediluvian World" (1882); and "Ragnarok" (1883). In "The Great Cryptogram" he endeavors to prove that Francis Bacon was the author of Shakespeare's plays. His best known novel is "Cæsar's Column." He died in Minneapolis, January 2, 1901.

DONNELLY, SAMUEL BRATTON, printer and labor leader, was born at Concord, November 7, 1866. He attended Shippensburg Normal School and taught rural schools in Franklin County from 1883-1886. In the latter year he learned the printing trade and later served as president of the New York Typographical Union and of the International Typographical Union, Indianapolis. He was commissioner on the New York City Board of Education, 1901-1908, and from 1908-1913 was a public printer at Washington. In 1913, he served for a second time as secretary of the Joint Board of the New York Building Trades Employers' Association.

DOOLITTLE, CHARLES LEANDER, astronomer, was born at Ontario, Ind., November 12, 1843. For twenty years, after 1875, he was professor of mathematics and astronomy at Lehigh University. From 1895-1912, he was professor of astronomy at the University of Pennsylvania, and in 1912 became professor emeritus there. He made valuable contributions to practical astronomy, on which subject he wrote a text-book for use in advanced courses. He died March 3, 1919.

DOOLITTLE, ERIC, astronomer, was born at Ontario, Ind., July 26, 1869. He graduated from Lehigh University in 1891 and during the following year was instructor in astronomy there. He was instructor in astronomy at the State University of Iowa, 1892-1893; assistant professor of astronomy, University of Pennsylvania, 1896-1912; professor of astronomy and director of the Flower Astronomical Observatory, University of Pennsylvania, 1912. He contributed to both theoretical and practical astronomy and the results of his work in the latter field have been published in several volumes by the University of Pennsylvania. He died September 21, 1920.

DOS PASSOS, JOHN RANDOLPH, lawyer, was born in Philadelphia, 1844, of Portugese descent. He studied law; served in the Federal army during the Civil War, and after practicing law in Philadelphia for some time went to New York in 1867, where he was very successful in the criminal branch of practice. Later he became an authority upon banking, corporate and financial law. He has written considerably. Among his published works are: "A Treatise on the Laws of Stock Brokers and Stock Exchanges" (1882); "The Interstate Commerce Act" (1887); "Commercial Trusts"; "The Anglo-Saxon Century" (1903). He died January 27, 1917, in New York City.

DOUBLEDAY, ABNER, soldier, aided greatly in the success of the Battle of Gettysburg. On September 25, 1917, a bronze statue of General Doubleday was unveiled on the Gettysburg Battlefield. Gen. Doubleday published several reminiscences of the Civil War, among them being "Chancellorsville and Gettysburg."

DOUGHERTY, DENIS J., cardinal, was made the first American bishop of Nueva Segovia, Philippine Islands, in 1903. Prior to that he was connected with St. Charles' Seminary, Overbrook. In July, 1918, he was made archbishop of Philadelphia and in 1921 cardinal priest. He lives in Philadelphia.

DOUGHTY, THOMAS, landscape painter, was born in Philadelphia, July 19, 1793. He was apprenticed in his youth to a leather manufacturer, and afterwards carried on the business on his own account. A growing taste for art, however, induced him to become a painter. He practiced his profession for many years in the United States, and also in London and Paris. He died in New York, July 24, 1856.

DOUGLAS, JAMES, mining engineer, was born at Quebec, Canada, 1837. In 1858, he graduated from Queen's University, Kingston, Ontario, after which he taught chemistry for a time in Morrin College, Quebec. He moved to Phoenixville, Pa., in 1875, where he became eminently successful as a mining engineer. Among other offices which he held were the presidencies of several mining corporations and railroads. He did much original work, with Dr. T. Sterry Hunt, in hydrometallurgy of coppers. In addition to many articles and reports on mining engineering, Douglas published "Canadian Independence"; "Imperial Federation and Annexation"; "Old France in the New World"; "New England and New France." He died June 25, 1918.

DOUGLASS, EPHRAIM, Revolutionary soldier, spent his early life in the Cumberland Valley near Carlisle, the son of Adam Douglass. He located at Pittsburgh about 1768. In 1771, he engaged in the Indian trade; was appointed quartermaster of the 8th Regiment, Pennsylvania Line, September 12, 1776; was taken prisoner at Bond Brook, New York; was exchanged in November, 1780;

was sent by the government upon a special secret mission among Indian tribes of the northwest, returning May, 1782. From September 1, 1782, to April, 1783, he served as Intendant of the British prisoners at Philadelphia. June 7, 1783, he set out on a mission to the Indians at Sandusky, Detroit, Niagara and Oswego. October 6, 1783, he was appointed prothonotary and clerk of the courts of Fayette County, which position he held until December, 1808, when he resigned. He was chief burgess of Uniontown from April 4, 1796, to May, 1797. He was appointed treasurer of the county in 1789. In April, 1793, he was commissioned brigadier-general for the county of Fayette. He died July 17, 1833.

DOVE, DAVID JAMES, Philadelphia schoolmaster, began his work as master of English in the Academy and College of Philadelphia in January, 1751, and in August of the same year announced in the Pennsylvania Gazette that he would open a school for young ladies at the Academy, a position he held until 1753.

DOWNINGTOWN, borough in Chester County, 33 miles west of Philadelphia. Among its industries are brick yards, knitting mills, machine shops and paper mills.

DOYLESTOWN, borough and county-seat of Bucks County, 34 miles north of Philadelphia. It is located in a rich agricultural region, is the center for local trade, and includes among its industries hosiery, silk and worsted mills, manufactories of wagons, farm implements, soap, woolens and cabinets, and a foundry.

DRAKE, EDWIN LAURENTINE, oil well operator, was born in Greenville, Greene County, N. Y., March 29, 1819. When he was eight years old he moved with his parents to Vermont and there attended the public schools. He was employed at different times as hotel clerk, store clerk, railway express agent and railroad conductor. He gave up the latter position because of ill health and having previously bought stock in the Pennsylvania Rock Oil Company, was engaged by that company to visit its property on Oil Creek, near Titusville, Crawford County, and to investigate certain of the company's business matters. He went to Titusville, in December, 1857, and a few weeks afterward returned to New Haven with the suggestion that drilling for oil should be begun immediately. As a result the Pennsylvania Rock Oil Company leased to Drake and another stockholder lands for this purpose. The new company was known as the Seneca Oil Company and Drake was its president. Drilling was begun at once and on August 27, 1859, after nineteen months of hard work and persistent effort, oil was struck at a depth of sixty-nine feet. Aside from offering the first proof of the existence of oil reservoirs in the earth's surface, Drake originated the use of pipe on bed rock to prevent the filling in of the hole made by the drill. Drake died at Bethlehem, November 8, 1880. A monument has been erected to his memory at Titusville by the citizens of that city and the Commonwealth of Pennsylvania has taken over the original oil well.

DRAKE, SAMUEL, actor, with a theatrical company, including N. M. Ludlow and Miss Denney, gave the first regular theatrical performance ever seen in Pittsburgh in 1815. They traveled from Olean, N. Y., to Pittsburgh by flatboat on the Allegheny.

DRAWBAUGH, DANIEL, inventor, was born at Eberly's Mills, Cumberland County, about three miles southwest of Harrisburg, in 1827, of Pennsylvania-German stock. Following his father's trade of a blacksmith, he showed unusual ingenuity, and at the age of fourteen made a gun along original lines. He became locally famous as the inventor of an automatic sewing machine, a machine for boring spoke tenons, and one for sawing tenons, and a barrel stave jointing machine patented in 1851. An automatic grinding machine was next invented, then followed machines for making shingles, patented in 1855. He invented and patented four improvements in nail plate feeding, and later a tack machine. He invented devices in the field of photography, and a machine for alphabetic telegraphing. It is claimed that Drawbaugh had 125 patents to his credit. His most famous invention is that of the telephone. He made experiments as early as 1866 and his friends claim that he made a successful telephone as early as 1874, but delayed applying for a patent until later. The Bell Company successfully contested his claim in the courts for Bell took out his patent in 1876. The final decision in favor of Bell was rendered by the Supreme Court, March 18, 1888, three justices dissenting.

DRAYTON, WILLIAM, politician, was born in South Carolina. From 1825–1833, he represented his native state in Congress. Later he moved to Philadelphia and in 1839 became president of the United States Bank, succeeding Nicholas Biddle. He died at Philadelphia, May 24, 1846.

DREW, JOHN, actor, was born in Philadelphia, November 13, 1853. He made his stage debut at his father's theatre in Philadelphia and afterwards appeared in plays with Edwin Booth and Fanny Davenport. He achieved greatest success as Petruchio in "The Taming of the Shrew," and as Charles Surface in Sheridan's "School for Scandal." In 1879, he was leading man in Augustine Daly's Company at Daly's Theatre in New York and in 1892 went to Europe with the same company, where he traveled about playing in "The Masked Ball"; "The Butterflies"; "A Marriage of Convenience"; "One Summer's Day"; "The Liars"; "Richard Carvel"; "His House in Order"; "Inconstant George"; "Much Ado About Nothing"; "The Tyranny of Tears"; and "The Will." He died July 9, 1927.

EDWIN LAURENTINE DRAKE

DREW, JOHN, comedian, was born in Dublin, Ireland, September 3, 1825. He made his first stage appearance at the Bowery Theatre, New York, in 1845. Subsequently he appeared in other American cities as well as in England and Australia. He was at one time manager of the Arch Street Theatre, Philadelphia. His death occurred at Philadelphia, May 21, 1862.

DREXEL, ANTHONY JOSEPH, banker, was born in Philadelphia, in 1826. He became the head of the well-known firm of Drexel and Company, Philadelphia, having been identified with it from the age of thirteen. He was zealous in promoting science and art, especially music, and contributed largely to philanthropic and educational interests. The Drexel Institute of Arts, Science and Industry, Philadelphia, dedicated December 18, 1891, was established by him, the building costing over $600,000 with an endowment fund of $1,000,000. He died in Carlsbad, Germany, June 30, 1893.

DREXEL INSTITUTE OF ART, SCIENCE AND INDUSTRY, was founded at Philadelphia in 1891, by Anthony J. Drexel. The courses offered are fine and applied arts, engineering, commerce and finance, mechanical drawing and machine construction, domestic science, library science, mathematics, physics, chemistry and English. Each department has day and evening classes. Enrollment (1930–1931), 1,640.

DRIFTWOOD BRANCH. Tributary to Sinnemahoning Creek. Sub-basin: Upper West Branch Susquehanna; source, in Jones Township, northeastern Elk County; course, southeasterly into Cameron County to Sinnemahoning Creek; mouth, at Driftwood; length, thirty-one and one-half miles.

DRINKHOUSE, EDWARD J., clergyman and author, was born in Philadelphia, in 1830. In 1850, he became a minister of the Maryland Conference of the Methodist Protestant Church, but later was forced to retire because of poor health. He moved to California and in 1865 graduated from Toland Medical College, San Francisco, with the M. D. degree. He was editor of the "Methodist Protestant" for eighteen years and wrote "History of Methodist Reform Synoptical of General Methodism, 1703 to 1898, with Special and Comprehensive Reference to Its Salient Exhibition in the History of the Methodist Protestant Church." He died in 1903.

DROPSIE COLLEGE, was founded at Philadelphia in 1895, by Moses Aaron Dropsie, for the advanced study of Hebrew and cognate subjects.

DROWN, THOMAS MESSINGER, educator, was born at Philadelphia, March 19, 1842. Following his graduation from the Medical School of the University of Pennsylvania in 1862 he studied chemistry at Yale, Harvard and Heidelberg Universities. He was professor of analytical chemistry at Lafayette

College from 1874-1881 and afterwards for ten years was professor of the same subject at the Massachusetts Institute of Mining Engineers. In 1895, he became president of Lehigh University. Dr. Drown made valuable contributions to chemical science in quantitative analysis, both in metallurgy and in sanitary chemistry. He was one of the founders of the American Institute of Mining Engineers and at different times served as its secretary and president. He died at Bethlehem on November 16, 1904.

DRUM, RICHARD COULTER, military officer, born in Pennsylvania, May 28, 1825; joined the army in 1846 and served in the Mexican War, being present at the siege of Vera Cruz and the actions of Chapultepec and Mexico City. He was commissioned colonel and assistant adjutant-general, February 22, 1869; was promoted to brigadier-general and adjutant-general, June 15, 1880; retired May 28, 1889. He died October 25, 1909.

DRYSDALE, WILLIAM, journalist and author, was born in Lancaster, July 11, 1852. In 1876, he was editor of the Philadelphia Times and for over 20 years was on the staff of the New York Times, acting as its foreign correspondent (1877-1899). He was a popular writer of juvenile stories, and his books have had a wide circulation. They include: "Proverbs from Plymouth Pulpit" (1887); selections from the writings and addresses of Henry Ward Beecher; "The Princess of Montserrat" (1890); "The Mystery of Abel Forefinger" (1893); "The Young Reporter" (1895); "The Fast Mail" (1896); "The Beach Patrol" (1897); "Help for Ambitious Boys" (1899); "Help for Ambitious Girls" (1900); "The Treasury Club" (1900); "Pine Ridge Plantation" (1901); "The Young Consul" (1901). He died at Cranford, N. J., September 20, 1901.

EBENSBURG (1843)

DUANE, WILLIAM, politician, was born in 1760, near Lake Champlain, N. Y. He received his education in Ireland and after learning the printing trade, went to India. He was financially successful there, but because of his opposition to the local government was seized and his property taken. Duane was sent to England where he became editor of the General Advertiser, later merged with the London Times. In 1795, he returned to America where he became editor of the Aurora, published in Philadelphia. He gained the favor of Jefferson who maintained that Duane through his paper was largely responsible for Jefferson's election to the presidency of the United States. President Jefferson appointed Duane a lieutenant-colonel in 1805. During the War of 1812 he served as adjutant-general. After his retirment from the editorship of the Aurora in 1822, Duane traveled in South America. He is the author of "A Visit to Colombia"; "Military Dictionary"; "Handbook for Riflemen"; "Handbook for Infantry." He died at Philadelphia, November 24, 1835.

DUANE, WILLIAM JOHN, politician, was born at Clonmel, Ireland, May 9, 1780, the son of William Duane. In 1833, President Jackson appointed him Secretary of the Treasury, but he was shortly afterwards removed from office because he refused to allow the government deposits to be withdrawn from the United States Bank without the approval of Congress. He died at Philadelphia, September 26, 1865.

DUBBS, JOSEPH HENRY, clergyman and educator, was born at North Whitehall, October 5, 1838. After his graduation from Franklin and Marshall College in 1856 and from Mercersburg Theological Seminary in 1859, he entered the ministry of the Reformed Church, holding various pastorates. In 1875, he was elected to the chair of history and archaeology at Franklin and Marshall College. His published works include: "Historic Manual of the Reformed Church"; "Home Ballads and Metrical Versions"; "Why am I Reformed"; "Leaders of the Reformation"; "The Reformed Church in Pennsylvania." He died in 1910.

DUBOIS, borough in Clearfield County, about 80 miles northeast of Pittsburgh, was settled in 1873 and incorporated as a borough in 1881. It is located in a coal mining area and numbered among its industries are manufactories of mining and agricultural implements, railroad shops, machine shops, glass and clay works, blast furnaces. Population (1930), 11,595; (1920), 13,681.

DUCHÉ, JACOB, Episcopalian clergyman, read the prayers at the meeting of the First Continental Congress in Carpenter's Hall, Philadelphia, September 4, 1774. Rev. Duché, the son of Jacob Duché, of Huguenot ancestry, was born in 1738, studied at the Philadelphia College and at Class Hall, Cambridge. After he was ordained to the ministry in England in 1759, he became pastor of St. Peter's, Philadelphia, and also taught at the Philadelphia College. During the

Revolution he wavered in his loyalty to the colonies, at one time urging Washington to desert his cause and betray his fellows. In December, 1777, Duché's property was confiscated and Duché went to England, followed a short time afterward by his family. In 1792, upon his return to this country, Washington permitted Duché to call upon him. He died January 3, 1798.

DUFFIELD, GEORGE, Presbyterian clergyman, was born at Strasburg, July 4, 1794. He held prominent Presbyterian pastorates in Philadelphia, New York and Detroit and was active as a leader of the "New School" Presbyterians. He died at Detroit, Mich., June 26, 1869.

DUFFIELD, GEORGE, clergyman and hymn writer, was born at Carlisle, September 12, 1818. He graduated from Yale University in 1837 and from Union Theological Seminary, New York, in 1840. He became a minister in the Presbyterian Church, held several pastorates and wrote the well-known hymns: "Blest Saviour, Thee I Love," and "Stand Up, Stand Up, for Jesus." He died at Bloomfield, N. J., July 6, 1888.

DUFFIELD, JOHN THOMAS, mathematician, was born at McConnellsburg, February 19, 1823. He was graduated at Princeton in 1841 and at the Theological Seminary there in 1844. At that college he was successively tutor in Greek, 1845, adjunct professor of mathematics, 1847, and professor of mathematics in 1856, which last post he held for several years. Among his scientific writings are: "The Discovery of Gravitation"; "The Philosophy of Mathematics." He died at Princeton, N. J., April 10, 1901.

DUFFIELD, WILLIAM WARD, military officer, born in Carlisle, November 19, 1823. He graduated at Columbia College in 1842; served with gallantry in the war with Mexico. In 1861, he was made colonel of the 9th Michigan Infantry; in 1862, he captured the Confederate force at Lebanon. He was brevetted major-general of volunteers in 1863; was compelled by his wounds to resign. He was superintendent of the United States Coast and Geodetic Survey in 1894-1898. Published "School of the Brigade and Evolutions of the Line." He died in 1907.

DUNGLISON, RICHARD JAMES, physician, was born at Baltimore, November 13, 1834, the son of Robley Dunglison. In 1852, he graduated from the University of Pennsylvania and in 1856 from Jefferson Medical College. He was surgeon in Philadelphia military hospitals during the Civil War but soon afterwards discontinued his practice and entered the field of literature. His contributions to medical literature are valuable. From 1880-1889, he edited the College and Clinical Record and contributed many articles to medical publications. He also edited the Philadelphia Medical Times and these works of his father: "History of Medicine"; and "Medical Lexicon." He translated Guersant's "Surgical Diseases of Children" and wrote "The Practitioner's Reference Book"; "Elementary Physiology"; "The Present Treatment of Disease." He died at Philadelphia, March 4, 1901.

DUNGLISON, ROBLEY, physician, was born at Keswick, England, January 4, 1798. He studied medicine at London and Erlangen and in 1824 became professor of Medicine at the University of Virginia. In 1833, he became professor of Therapeutics at the University of Maryland and in 1836 professor of the institutes of Medicine in Jefferson Medical College, Philadelphia. He made numerous valuable contributions to medical literature including a "Dictionary of Medical Science and Literature." He died at Philadelphia, April 1, 1869.

DUNKARD CREEK. Tributary to Monongahela River. Sub-basin: Monongahela; source, formed by junction of Pennsylvania and West Virginia forks, near state boundary in Wayne Township, southern Greene County; course, northeasterly, crossing state boundary twelve times, to Monongahela River; mouth, near Lock No. 8; length, thirty-six miles.

DUNKARDS—See BAPTISTS, OR BRETHREN, GERMAN.

DUNLAP, JOHN, printer, was born in Strabane, Ireland, in 1747. He learned the printing trade from his uncle who was in business in Philadelphia and at the age of eighteen began the publication of the Pennsylvania Packet. This was made a daily paper in 1784 and was the first daily issue in the United States. The title was afterwards changed to the North American and United States Gazette. As printer to Congress, Mr. Dunlap printed the Declaration of Independence. He died in Philadelphia, November 27, 1812.

DUNMORE, FOURTH EARL OF (John Murray), was born in Scotland in 1732. He was appointed governor of New York in 1770 and in 1772 served Virginia as its last colonial governor. His energetic efforts to defend the western frontier were responsible for the Indian War known as Dunmore's War.

DUNMORE, borough in Lackawanna County, two miles northeast of Scranton, was settled in 1835 and incorporated as a borough in 1862. It is situated in a coal mining region. Other industries are silk and iron manufacturing. The State Oral School for the Deaf and Dumb is located here. Population (1930), 22,627; (1920), 20,250.

DUNMORE'S WAR, an Indian war, which occurred in 1774 as a result of a controversy between Governor Dunmore of Virginia and the Penns. Dunmore insisted on taking possession of Fort Pitt in order to intimidate Pennsylvania, punish the Indians and maintain the sovereignty of Virginia beyond the Ohio. About this time a hunting party from the settlement at the mouth of the Kanawha was attacked by wandering Cherokees. Under the leadership of Michael Cresap the hunters attacked Indian towns on the Scioto and murdered the family of John Logan, Mingo chief. Logan immediately sent a declaration of war to Cresap. The Mingoes and Shawnees were aided by the Delawares, Wyandots and other tribes. The frontier prepared to defend itself by erecting stockades and block-houses. A company of rangers, paid by residents of Westmoreland County, was organized and dividing into squads patrolled the region from Ligonier Valley to a few miles east of Pittsburgh. With the victory of Colonel Andrew Lewis, sent by Dunmore to the mouth of the Kanawha, the war ended.

OLD WELSH CHURCH AT RADNOR (1843)

DUNNING, JAMES, prominent Indian trader. Dunning's Creek and Dunning's Mountain, Bedford County, were both named for this trader. Robert Dunning, another trader, lived near Carlisle where the Indian trail from Harrisburg ran to his home, crossed to McAllister's Gap, then to Path Valley and then to Crogan's Gap (now Sterritts Gap).

DUNNING CREEK—Tributary to Raystown Branch. Sub-basin: Upper Juniata; source, in Napier Township, western Bedford County; course, northeasterly and southeasterly to Raystown Branch, Juniata River; mouth, near Beford; length, twenty-six miles.

DUNNING'S SLEEPING PLACE—Name of station on Indian Trail from Bedford to Pittsburgh near head of Brush Creek in Westmoreland County. It was named for James Dunning.

DU PONCEAU, PETER STEPHEN, lawyer, was born in the Isle of Rhé, France, June 3, 1760. Prior to 1777, when he came to America as private secretary and aide-de-camp to Baron Steuben, he had taken ecclesiastical orders, but abandoned that life in 1755 and went to Paris where he taught and acted as translator. For two years after his arrival in America he served in the army at Valley Forge. In 1779, he became secretary to Mr. Livingston, Secretary of Foreign Affairs. When the war ended Du Ponceau studied law, established a practice in Philadelphia and attained prominence in his profession. He was greatly interested in the introduction of the silk worm into America and with M. d'Homergue, of Nismes, France, established a filature in 1831. Du Ponceau died April 1, 1844.

DU PONT, ELEUTHERE IRENEE, scientist, was born in Paris, France, June 24, 1771, the son of Pierre Samuel Du Pont de Nemours. He emigrated to the United States in 1799; bought a tract of land near Wilmington, Delaware, where he established the powder works which have since been maintained by the Dupont (modern form) family. He died in Philadelphia, October 31, 1834.

DUQUESNE, borough in Allegheny County, about ten miles from Pittsburgh, was settled in 1885 and chartered in 1891. Its industries are manufactories of iron and steel. Population (1930), 21,396; (1920), 19,011.

DUQUESNE UNIVERSITY, at Pittsburgh, organized by the Holy Ghost Fathers in 1878, was originally called Holy Ghost College. In 1911, the name was changed to Duquesne University. The institution has a law school, school of speech arts, school of accounts, finance and commerce, school of pharmacy and school of music, in addition to the College of Arts and College of Science. Enrollment (1930-1931), 2,880.

DUTCH IN PENNSYLVANIA—In 1616, Cornelius Hendrickson from Monnikendam on the Zuyder Zee discovered the mouth of the Schuylkill River and first saw the site of Philadelphia. The Dutch made an unsuccessful settlement along the South River in Delaware about 1631 and other settlements were made along the North River and the Schuylkill.

DUTCH CHURCH—See REFORMED CHURCH IN AMERICA.

DUTCH REFORMED CHURCH—See REFORMED CHURCH IN AMERICA.

EAKINS, THOMAS, artist, born in Philadelphia, July 25, 1844. He was professor in several art schools. Among his paintings are many American domestic scenes and portraits. His best work is "Clinic of Prof. Gross," now at Jefferson Medical College. Other paintings are: "Chess Players," at the Metropolitan Museum of N. Y.; "The Cello Player," Pennsylvania Academy of Fine Arts. Part of the Brooklyn Soldiers' and Sailors' Monument at Trenton was designed by him. He died June 25, 1916.

EAST STROUDSBURG, borough of Monroe County, 23 miles north of Easton in the vicinity of the Pocono Mountains. It is the seat of a State Teachers' College and a manufacturing center for boilers, glass, silk, hosiery, etc. Population (1930), 6,099; (1920), 4,855.

EAST STROUDSBURG STATE TEACHERS' COLLEGE was founded about 1893 as a Normal School. In 1920, it passed entirely under state control and in June, 1926, became a Teachers' College, although the name was not officially changed until the following year.

The town of East Stroudsburg is located in the Pocono Mountains 23 miles north of Easton.

EASTERN PENITENTIARY, at Philadelphia, was established as a result of an act of Legislature of March 21, 1821, providing for the erection of a State Penitentiary within the limits of Philadelphia County and City. The buildings were completed in 1829.

EASTON, city, county-seat of Northampton County, located at the confluence of the Lehigh and Delaware Rivers. The city, an original outpost and trading center of the early settlers with the Indians, was formally laid out in 1752. It was incorporated as a borough in 1789 and chartered as a city in 1887. Lafayette College is located here. Among the manufactures of the city are iron, mining machinery, drills, railway supplies, agricultural implements, textile belting, mill and furnace equipment, etc. Population (1930), 34,468; (1920), 33,813.

EBENSBURG, borough and county-seat of Cambria County, was founded by the Rev. Rees Lloyd, who came to this country from Wales in 1795, and in the following year settled on the site of the town. Ebensburg was laid out in 1806 and was incorporated as a borough, July 15, 1825. It is a residential town, noted as a summer and health resort and for the beauty of its scenery. Coal mining and agriculture are industries of the vicinity.

ECLECTIC MEDICAL COLLEGE OF PHILADELPHIA was incorporated February 25, 1850. The degree of doctor of eclectic medicine was granted to those attending two courses of medical lectures and completing a prescribed course of study. Because of bad management the institution was never progressive.

ECONOMY—A communistic society founded by George Rapp, of Wurtemburg, Germany, who in 1803, with three or four followers, visited America in search of a location suitable for a colony. They purchased a tract of land near Zelionople, in Butler County, and in 1804 three shiploads of colonists came over, most of whom spent the winter in Philadelphia and Baltimore, although a number joined Rapp in the work of building a town, which received the name of Harmony.

His followers in Philadelphia and Baltimore then joined him and February 15, 1805, they organized into an association on the principle of communism. All possessions were put into a common stock and a simple and uniform style of dress was adopted. In 1807, as the result of a revival they abjured matrimony and gave up the use of tobacco. In 1814, they moved to New Harmony, Indiana, having disposed of their property in Butler County at great sacrifice, including about six thousand acres of land. The Indian tract comprised about thirty thousand acres of unimproved government land and there was developed a large trade with the southwest. In 1817, one hundred and thirty additional members were admitted and the book containing the record of contributions was burned to promote equality. Their numbers were reduced by the fever and ague and another migration was decided upon. They sold their town to Robert Dale Owen who here established his famous Owenite Community, having then been head of a community in Lanark, Scotland.

Having built a steamboat the followers of Rapp removed in detachments to their final settlement at Economy, Beaver, Pa., where a town with streets sixty feet wide, intersecting at right angles, was laid out. Ample space between houses was given for gardens, and grape vines were grown on the houses. Mulberry trees were planted and raw silk was produced. The Duke of Saxe-Weimar visited Economy in 1826 and wrote an interesting description of the community.

A crisis came when Cont Leon, an eccentric individual, claiming to be a divine messenger, arrived with much pomp, attended by his minister of justice in full military dress and about forty followers. Dissensions arose and Leon and his followers were forced to withdraw to the village of Phillipsburg (now Mona) which they purchased but where they soon became bankrupt, and made a demand on the Harmony Society. In April, 1823, a mob of eighty persons entered Economy, took possession of the hotel and made their demands but without

ECONOMY (1843)

success. They then fell on Leon and he and some of his followers were shipped to Alexandria, La., where he died of cholera in 1833. After the death of Rapp, the most influential member was Jacob Henrici whose death occurred December 25, 1892. Litigation followed and the Society was dissolved. At the session of the General Assembly in 1919 an act was passed and signed by Governor Sproul authorizing the transfer of the property to the Pennsylvania Historical Commission. The tract of four acres includes the Great House (the home of Rapp and Henrici), the Music Hall, the old Wine Cellar, the Carpenter Shop and several dwelling houses.

EDDY, THOMAS, philanthropist, was born in Philadelphia, September 5, 1758. He made a fortune in the insurance business in 1790; was instrumental in having a bill, establishing a penitentiary system, passed in 1796; had charge of erecting first building and for four years was its director. Was one of the originators of New York Savings Bank; promoter of Erie Canal. He received title of the "American Howard" for these labors. In 1801, he published "State Prison of New York." He died in New York, September 16, 1827.

EDGE, WALTER EVANS, statesman, was born in Philadelphia, November 20, 1874. He was educated in Philadelphia; worked on *Atlantic Review* of Atlantic City, N. J.; became identified with banking; served in Legislature of New Jersey, 1901–1904; was alternate delegate-at-large to Republican National Convention, 1908, and again served in the New Jersey Legislature from 1912–1916. He served during the Spanish-American War in the 4th New Jersey Volunteers and was afterward made a captain in the National Guard. Was governor of New Jersey from 1917–1919, when he resigned to enter the United States Senate. He was re-elected to the Senate, 1925–1931, but resigned. He has been Ambassador to France since November, 1929.

EDINBORO STATE TEACHERS' COLLEGE was organized January 29, 1861, an outgrowth of a school for higher learning, founded in 1856. In September, 1921, the Edinboro State Normal School opened an extension department in the city of Erie. In 1926, the State Council of Education authorized the school to confer the degree of Bachelor of Science in Education, and in 1927 by authority of the General Assembly the name of the institution was changed to the State Teachers' College at Edinboro.

The town of Edinboro is located in Erie County, a short distance from the city of Erie.

EGAN, MAURICE FRANCIS, diplomat, was born in Philadelphia, May 24, 1852. He graduated at LaSalle College, studied law under John I. Rogers, in Philadelphia, but later adopted literature as a profession. He was professor of Literature and English at University of Notre Dame; minister to Denmark, 1907–1918 (U. S. bought Virgin Islands during his term of office); declined an appointment to Greece by President Cleveland and the ambassadorship to Vienna tendered by Presidents Taft and Wilson. He published "Ten Years Near the German Frontier"; "Confessions of a Book Lover"; "Recollections of a Happy Life." His death occurred January 15, 1924.

EGAN, MICHAEL, first bishop of Philadelphia, was probably born in Ireland in 1761 although the exact place of his birth has never been determined. When he was about forty, he came to America and succeeded Father Antoine Garnier as assistant priest at Lancaster. In April, 1803, he became one of the pastors of St. Mary's Church, Philadelphia, and upon the erection of the See of Philadelphia, was consecrated bishop. He died July 22, 1814.

EGLE, WILLIAM HENRY, historian, was born in Harrisburg, September 17, 1830, of Swiss and Palatine ancestry. He was educated in the public and private schools of Harrisburg and at the Harrisburg Military Institute. He learned the printers' trade and was connected with the Pennsylvania Telegraph. Later he entered the medical department of the University of Pennsylvania graduating in March, 1859. He practiced in Harrisburg until called to field hospital service during the Civil War. In 1887, he was appointed State Librarian, a position he held until January, 1899. Among his historical works are the "Historical Register," two volumes; "History of Dauphin and Lebanon Counties"; "Pennsylvania Genealogies"; "Notes and Queries," twelve volumes; "History of Pennsylvania." He was co-editor of the second and third series of Pennsylvania Archives. He died February 19, 1901.

EIN SCHALL UND GEGANSCHALL DER WAHRHEIT, UND DES GESUNDTEN VERSTANDES CHRISTLIEBENDER SEELEN IN DIESAM AMERICANISCHER LAND THEIL was the first religious magazine in this country. It was established in February, 1746, by Christopher Sauer, of Germantown; later became a monthly but was finally discontinued.

"ELBETRITCHES"—Hunting elbetritches has been a favorite sport among Pennsylvania Germans. On a cold morning an unsophisticated person is asked to assist in hunting elbetritches and is stationed on the top of a hill holding a bag while others of the party promise to drive the imaginary creature into the receptacle, but proceed at once to their homes leaving the victim of the joke holding the bag. Some authorities define elbetritch as a mythical bird. Dr. E. E. S. Johnson says the origin of the word dates far back into the mythology of Europe, always meaning an awkward simple person who has been taken in by the elbe.—*See* PA. GERMAN MAGAZINE, VOL. 7, p. 122.

ELDER, JOHN, Presbyterian clergyman, was born in Edinburgh, Scotland, January 26, 1706. After graduation from the University of Edinburgh, he studied for the ministry and in 1732 was licensed to preach. Some years later he came to

PUMP OF WELL 85 FEET DEEP, DUG BY HAND AT ECONOMY (163)

America and settled in Pennsylvania to which province his father had emigrated a few years earlier. In this country Rev. Elder became a member of the New Castle Presbytery and later of the Donegal Presbytery. Subsequently, on November 22, 1738, he was ordained and installed as pastor of Paxtang and Derry Presbyterian Churches. During the French and Indian War, Elder organized his parishioners into companies, of which he was the captain; for at least two years every man who attended Paxtang Church, and the minister himself, carried rifles. The organization came to be known as the "Paxtang Boys." The Whitefield Controversy which preceded the French and Indian War in this country, brought Rev. Elder face to face with difficult problems. He opposed the "great revival," consequently some of his church members withdrew and he was left in charge of the "old side" members of Derry. Later, Paxtang and Derry were reunited and Rev. Elder served as their pastor until his death on July 17, 1792.

ELIZABETHTOWN COLLEGE, a co-educational institution at Elizabethtown, Lancaster County, was incorporated in 1899 by the German Baptist Brethren Church. The college was opened on November 13, 1900, with an enrollment of six students. Enrollment (1930-1931), 540.

ELK COUNTY, formed from part of Jefferson, Clearfield and McKean, April 18, 1843; named for Elk Creek and the elks within its borders. Land area, 806 square miles; population (1930), 33,431; county-seat, Ridgway, laid out in 1843.

ELLET, CHARLES, engineer, was born at Penn's Manor, Bucks County, January 1, 1810. He was educated at the Polytechnic School, Paris; built first wire suspension bridge in the United States, at Fairmont, Philadelphia. In 1845, he built a suspension bridge at Niagara Falls adapted for railway purposes; he also constructed a suspension bridge at Wheeling, W. Va. During the Civil War he had charge of equipment of Mississippi River steamboats as rams. He defeated a fleet of Confederate rams, but died of wounds June 21, 1862.

ELLICOTT, ANDREW, surveyor and mathematician, was born in Bucks County, January 24, 1754. He married when he was twenty-one, moved to Maryland and shortly afterward joined the Maryland militia, rising to the rank of major. As early as 1782 he published a series of almanacs known as "The United States Almanack." In 1784, he was appointed member from Virginia of the surveyors to continue the Mason and Dixon line, which had been discontinued in 1767. Later he taught mathematics in a Baltimore Academy, served a term in the Maryland Legislature and was a member of the Pennsylvania Commission for running the western and northern boundaries of the state and surveying the islands in the Ohio and Allegheny Rivers. In 1798, he was appointed by the federal government to fix the southwestern boundary of New York, concerning which there was much dispute. At that time, Ellicott made the first topographical study of Niagara River. He published the first map of the District of Columbia in 1793, from 1791 until that year having been occupied with surveying land ceded by Maryland and Virginia for the seat of the national government. Governor Mifflin appointed him a commissioner with two others, to lay out the town of Erie, then Presque Isle, and he planned a road through the Pennsylvania wilderness from Reading to Erie. In 1796, he received the commission to survey the frontier between the United States and Florida. "The Journal of Andrew Ellicott, Late Commissioner on Behalf of the United States, 1796-1800," published at Philadelphia in 1803, contains his report, with maps, etc. In 1813, Ellicott became professor of mathematics at West Point, where he died August 28, 1820.

ELLICOTT, JOSEPH, engineer and land agent, was born in Bucks County, a brother of Andrew Ellicott, November 1, 1760. With his family he removed to Maryland in 1774. After 1780 he taught school and in 1785 assisted his brother Andrew, from whom he learned surveying, in locating the western boundary of Pennsylvania; in 1789, he again assisted his brother in fixing the southwestern boundary of New York State and later in surveying the city of Washington. The federal government employed him to run a boundary between Georgia and the Creek Indian Territory in 1791. In 1794, he became connected with the Holland Land Company, at first as explorer in northern Pennsylvania and later as agent. He planned the opening of roads, division of the land into townships, the survey of the townships into lots, and the granting of deeds and mortgages. Ellicott founded the city of Buffalo, advocated the construction of the Erie Canal, and for a time served as canal commissioner and as director of early surveys. He died August 19, 1826.

ELLIS, WILLIAM THOMAS, journalist, was born in Allegheny, October 25, 1873. He was educated in public schools; was on the staff of Philadelphia newspapers until 1894 when he became editor of an International Christian Endeavor publication; was editorial writer for Philadelphia Press, 1903-1908; wrote Sunday-school lessons and contributed to religious periodicals; lectured before religious bodies. From 1917-1918, he was war correspondent on Persian, Caucasus, Roumanian and French fronts; foreign correspondent for New York Herald and associated newspapers, 1919; represented Chicago Daily News and associated newspapers at Conference on Limitation of Armaments at Washington, 1921-1922; was in Near East for Saturday Evening Post and other magazines, 1923. He is the author of "Men and Missions"; "Billy Sunday, the Man and His Message"; "Advertising the Church"; "Bible Lands Today." His home is at Swarthmore.

ELLMAKER, AMOS, jurist, was born at New Holland, Lancaster County, February 2, 1787. After graduating from Yale and completing a law course under Judge Reeves, at Litchfield, Conn., he studied law under Thomas Elder, at Harrisburg, and in 1808 was admitted to the bar. He served as deputy attorney-general of Dauphin County, 1809-1812; was a representative from Dauphin County in the State Legislature, 1812-1814; and in 1815 was appointed president judge of the Harrisburg district. From 1816 to 1819, he was attorney-general of Pennsylvania. He moved to Lancaster in 1821 and practiced his profession there. In 1832, he was the candidate of the Anti-Masonic Party for the vice-presidency of the United States. He died at Lancaster, November 28, 1851.

EMPORIUM, borough and county-seat of Cameron County. The earliest settler in Emporium was John Earl, who built the first house there in 1810. The town was laid out in 1861 and was incorporated as a borough in October, 1864. For several years it was called Shippen for Shippen Township in which it is located, and which was named for Edward Shippen, an early settler. According to tradition it was later named Emporium, meaning market or trade center, by an agent of the Holland Land Company, who in 1785 camped on the present site of the town as he came up the Driftwood branch of the Sinnemahoning Creek by boat. The industrial establishments of the borough include a blast furnace, cast iron pipe works, lumber and flour mills and incandescent lamp, radio tube and dynamite factories.

ENDLICH, GUSTAV ADOLF, lawyer, was born in Berks County, January 29, 1856. He was educated in Germany and at Princeton; admitted to the bar in 1877; member of the United States Assay Commission in 1897; 1906-1910 was president of board of trustees of Muhlenberg College; edited magazine, *Criminal Law Reporter*, and published numerous articles on legal subjects. He died February 11, 1929.

ENGLISH, THOMAS DUNN, author, was born in Philadelphia, June, 1819. He graduated at University of Pennsylvania Medical School, 1839, and in 1842 was admitted to the bar. He afterwards engaged in journalism; practiced medicine in what is now West Virginia, 1852-1857. During the years 1859 to 1879 he divided his time between New York City and Fort Lee, N. J. Was a member of the New Jersey State Legislature; wrote and published many popular writings, some of which are: "Ambrose Fecit, or the Peer and the Printer"; "American Ballads"; "The Boys Book of Battle Lyrics"; "Jacob Schuyler's Millions"; "The Rules of Order Governing Public Meetings." He also wrote about twenty plays for Palmo's Opera House, New York. His death occurred at Newark, N. J., April 1, 1902.

EPHRATA CLOISTER—In 1732 or 1733, John Conrad Beissel, a native of Eberbach, Germany, who came to this country in 1720, founded at Ephrata, Lancaster County, a settlement known as the German Religious Society of Seventh-Day Baptists. Among other doctrines Beissel advocated celibacy and the observation of the seventh day of the week for rest and religious worship. The first to join Beissel in his community were Martin Brener, Samuel Ecker-

ALMONRY, SAAL AND SARON, BUILT IN 1730, 1738 AND 1740, RESPECTIVELY, AT EPHRATA CLOISTER

ine, "Brother Jethro," and Anna and Maria Eicher. A granary was built, large brick ovens for the baking of bread were constructed and the almonry, a stone building erected in 1730, was used to feed the poor without charge. In 1735, the Kedar was built on the hill called Mount Zion. This building contained a large room for religious worship and other small rooms for the use of the brethren and sisters. Zion, a larger building, was built on the same hill in 1738; in 1741, Periel, another large building, was erected to be used as a meeting-house; Saron, a house for married men and women who had renounced matrimonial vows, was built in 1744. The Saron was later occupied by the women of the community. Bethania, a large building for the use of the brethren, was erected in 1746. Around it were clustered the school-house, printing office, almonry, bakery, etc. The houses used by the monks and sisters were rudely constructed, with extremely low ceilings, narrow passages, low and narrow doorways, and cells containing a rude cot, a small cupboard and one window, eighteen by twenty-four inches. The brethren of the community used wooden blocks for pillows; each cell had its hour-glass, and the walls of some of the cells, and of the chapels were covered with large sheets of paper on which were written German text passages of Scriptures and verses of original poetry by Beissel.

The brethren and sisters adopted a form of dress similar to that of the Capuchins. They wore a cowl and gown, white in color, linen in summer and woolen in winter. The cowl of the two sexes differed slightly, otherwise, with the exception of the skirt and trousers they were garbed similarly. Both brethren and sisters were barefooted except in the coldest weather. Their diet was almost entirely of vegetables. They never ate meat, butter, cheese or milk.

Because of the industry of its members the Ephrata community prospered. A paper mill for the manufacture of material for use in the printing press was erected, as was also a saw-mill, flour-mill, fulling-mill, etc. The printing press, one of the earliest in this country, was first used about 1742 or 1743.

The various arts, especially that of singing, were fostered by the community. In 1742, Father Friedsam began a singing school. The music used was composed by Beissel, and it was not long before the pupils became noted for their performances.

During the Revolution many wounded were cared for at the Ephrata Cloister. In September, 1777, a few days after the Battle of Brandywine, four or five hundred wounded were taken to Ephrata and placed in an improvised hospital there. Bethania was one of the buildings used for hospital purposes.

After the death of Beissel in 1768, Peter Miller, known as Brother Jabez, took charge of the community. From this time the organization slowly declined until only a few members remain. The question of the ownership of the property is in controversy.—*See also* BAPTISTS, SEVENTH-DAY.

EPISCOPAL CHURCH—*See* PROTESTANT EPISCOPAL CHURCH.

ERIE, city and county-seat of Erie County, located on Lake Erie, 85 miles southwest of Buffalo, 100 miles northeast of Cleveland, is situated on the site of Presque Isle, a French fort built in 1749. The town was laid out in 1795, incorporated as a borough in 1805 and chartered as a city in 1851. Commodore Perry had his headquarters here during the War of 1812 and it was here that the fleet, with which he defeated the British in the Battle of Put-in-Bay, was built. Erie has the largest land-locked harbor on the lake, and because of its location is a noted shipping and manufacturing center. Its manufactures include iron, steam engines, machinery, stoves, leather, furniture, electrical supplies, paper, etc. Lumber, coal, iron ore, petroleum and other products are shipped from the city by boats plying between Erie and other ports on the Great Lakes. Population (1930), 115,967; (1920), 93,372.

ERIE COUNTY, formed from part of Allegheny, March 12, 1800. Named for Lake Erie on which it is located. Land area, 781 square miles. Population (1930), 175,277. County-seat, Erie, laid out in 1795.

ESPY, JAMES POLLARD, meteorologist, was born in Westmoreland County, in 1786. He graduated at Transylvania University in 1808; practiced law; was professor of languages at Franklin Institute, Philadelphia, 1817-1853. He originated the theory of atmospheric disturbance due to the rising of air rarefied by heat. Was appointed meteorologist for the War Department in 1842, and instituted the first system of daily weather observations and maps tracing the progress of storms. He died in 1860.

EVANGELICAL CHURCH, was founded about 1800 by Jacob Albright, of Pottstown, for whom the organization was originally named. In 1796, Albright, having felt a call to the ministry, began to travel about through Pennsylvania, preaching to the German settlers. Four years later he and a band of followers organized the Evangelical Association. The new church accepted many of the customs of the Methodists in which church Albright was at one time a minister. At first the services were entirely in German, later in English and German, and finally in English. Churches were organized in Bucks, Berks, Northampton, Northumberland and Centre Counties and eventually the denomination spread into the central states, from New England to the Pacific Coast, and north into Canada.

In 1891, a division occurred, resulting in the establishment of the United Evangelical Church. However, on October 14, 1922, in the General Conference of the Evangelical Church, the two churches were united under the name of the Evangelical Church. A few organizations of the United Evangelical Church refused to merge and retain the original name.

The Evangelical Church is Arminian in doctrine and its articles of faith are to a great extent like those of the Methodist Episcopal Church.—See also EVANGELICAL CONGREGATIONAL CHURCH.

EVANGELICAL CONGREGATIONAL CHURCH is an outgrowth of the Evangelical Association founded in eastern Pennsylvania in 1800 by Jacob Albright. The schism came as a result of differing opinions regarding certain fundamental principles of church polity, and official acts affecting ministers and members of the organization. The first General Conference of the United Evangelical Church was held at Naperville, Ill., November 29, 1894. In 1922, when the majority of the delegates to the General Conference of the church voted to unite with the Evangelical Church, the East Pennsylvania Conference of the United Evangelical Church refused to vote. Later at a meeting of the East Pennsylvania Conference it was decided to continue the United Evangelical Church.

In both doctrine and organization the church resembles the Methodist Episcopal. Its membership, although largest in Pennsylvania, extends throughout the western states.—*See also* EVANGELICAL CHURCH.

EVANS, HENRY CLAY, legislator, was born in Juniata County, 1843. Served in 41st Wisconsin Infantry in Civil War, afterward settled in Chattanooga, Tenn. Was a member of Congress, 1889-1891; First Assistant Postmaster General, 1887-1893; 1894, elected Governor of Tennessee, but the election was not upheld by the Legislature, on a recount, occasioned by the charge of irregular balloting. Was Commissioner of Pensions, 1897-1902; United States Consul General at London, 1902-1905; Commissioner of Education and Health, Chattanooga, Tenn. He died in 1921.

EVANS, OLIVER, inventor, was born in Delaware. At an early age he came to Philadelphia where he made the first steam dredging machine used in this country. Put on wheels this machine moved on land and when fitted with propellers could be navigated on the water.

EVERHART, BENJAMIN MATLACK, botanist, was born in Chester County, April 24, 1818. After a successful business career he retired, in 1867, and devoted his time to the study of botany. He became a recognized authority on cryptogamic botany. Published noted work on American fungii, describing about 5,000 species. With W. A. Kellerman he founded and edited *The Journal of Mycology* to which he contributed many articles. Several new specimens of fungi have been named after him. He died September 22, 1904.

EWING, JAMES, pathologist, born at Pittsburgh, in 1866. Graduated at Amherst College and three years later at College of Physicians and Surgeons of Columbia University. Studied in Vienna and upon his return taught in Columbia, 1893-1899. In the latter part of 1899 was appointed pathologist at Cornell, which position he still holds. He is ex-president of Association for Cancer Research. His publications include: "Clinical Pathology of Blood," articles in identity; "The Signs of Death," and "Sudden Death," in Text Book of Legal

Medicine and Toxicology; on "Blood, etc.," in Text Book of Legal Medicine; "Neoplastic Diseases." He lives in New York City.

EWING, JAMES CARUTHERS, educator, born in Rural Valley, June 23, 1854. Graduated from Washington and Jefferson College, 1876; studied at Western Theological Seminary and was ordained to the Presbyterian ministry in 1879. Went as missionary to India, 1884-1888, and became professor in Theological Seminary there. Was president of Forman Christian College in Lahore, 1888-1918; dean of Faculty of Arts, 1890-1907; Vice-Chancellor of University of Punjab, 1910-1917. For his educational work in India he received from Edward VII of England the Kaiser-i-Hind gold medal (1907), and from George V, The Citation Companion of the Indian Empire (1915). He died August 20, 1925.

FAIRCHILD, HERMAN LEROY, geologist, born at Montrose, April 29, 1850. He was graduated at Cornell University, in 1874; was secretary of the New York Academy of Science, in 1885-1888; became president of the Rochester Academy of Science, 1889; secretary of the Geological Society of America, 1890-1906; vice-president in 1898, and president in 1912. He was professor of geology at the University of Rochester from 1888-1920 and professor emeritus since 1920. He is the author of "History of the New York Academy of Sciences"; "Revision of Le Conte's Elements of Geology"; "Geologic Story of the Genesee Valley and Western New York." His home is in Rochester, N. Y.

FAIRMOUNT PARK—A park in Philadelphia, having an area of 3,411 acres and being the largest municipal park in the United States. It extends along both banks of the Schuylkill for about five miles and from the confluence of the Schuylkill and Wissahickon Creek it continues up the latter stream through a romantic glen for six miles. Five acres of an estate belonging to Robert Morris during the War of Independence and known as "Fair Mount" or "The Hills" were purchased by the municipality for a "city waterworks and for park purposes," in 1812, and from this beginning the park grew to its present dimensions by purchases and gifts. There are many beautiful buildings, and statues and other works of art in the park which are the gift of the Fairmount Park Art Association.

FAIRS—In order to promote industrial enterprises in Philadelphia, William Penn established fairs. The first of these was held in 1686 when ten dollars worth of goods was sold. Fairs were held twice a year, in May and in November. They became extremely popular but resulted in gambling, drinking and races, and in 1783 were discontinued.

FAITH HEALING—A form of "mind cure" characterized by the doctrine that while pain and disease really exist, they may be neutralized and dispelled by faith in Divine power also with the aid of some intermediary. Faith cures, more commonly known as "pow-wow," were and still are practiced throughout the Pennsylvania-German counties of Eastern Pennsylvania; viz., Berks, Bucks, Lancaster, Lebanon, Lehigh, Montgomery, Schuylkill, and York.—See also POW-WOWING.

FALCKNER'S CURIEUSE NACHRICHT VON PENNSYLVANIA, the book that stimulated the great German emigration to Pennsylvania. A set of seventy-three questions relative to the voyage to America, the conditions of the country and its inhabitants, submitted to Daniel Falckner, the learned scholar and pietist, after he had returned in 1698 or 1699 from a pilgrimage to the colony of Pennsylvania. These questions were written by August Herman Francke, the celebrated divine and scholar, who together with Spencer was then the head of the Pietistical movement in the Lutheran Church in Germany. The questions were replied to by Falckner in writing, giving the results of his own experience and observations. Later on, twenty-one additional pertinent questions were propounded to him as to certain conditions in the New World, and answered with an equal degree of frankness.

FARMER, REV. FATHER, a Jesuit, was the first Catholic priest, and probably the first Catholic to hold civil office in Pennsylvania. By an act of the state legislature of 1779, reorganizing the College of Philadelphia, new trustees were appointed one of whom, according to the act, was to be "The Senior Minister of the Roman Churches in Philadelphia."

FARQUHAR, NORMAN VON HELDREICH, naval officer, was born at Pottsville, April 11, 1840. He was graduated from the United States Naval Adademy, in 1859; was acting master in the African squadron engaged in suppressing the slave trade, 1859-1861; and, during the Civil War, served in the North Atlantic blockading squadron. He commanded the Trenton when she was wrecked at Apia, Samoa, in 1889, when he succeeded in saving all his crew of 450 men and officers except one; became chief of the Bureau of Yards and Docks, in 1890, and commandant of the Norfolk navy yard. He was promoted rear admiral in 1899. He died in Jamestown, R. I., July 3, 1907.

FAULKNER'S SWAMP, in Montgomery County, was named for Daniel Faulkner who came to Pennsylvania in 1694 and who helped to settle Germantown.

FAYETTE COUNTY, formed from part of Westmoreland, September 26, 1783; named for the Marquis de la Fayette. Land area, 796 square miles. Population (1930), 198,542. County-seat, Uniontown, laid out in 1767.

FEBIGER, CHRISTIAN, military officer, born on Funen Island, Denmark, in 1747; entered the American army in April, 1775; was in the Battle of Bunker Hill, accompanied Arnold to Quebec, a few months afterward, where he was made a prisoner; and served faithfully throughout the war. He led one of the attacking columns at Stony Point (July, 1779); at Yorktown he commanded the 2nd Virginia Regiment with the rank of lieutenant-colonel. From 1789 till his death, September 20, 1796, in Philadelphia, Colonel Febiger was treasurer of the State of Pennsylvania.

FEBIGER, JOHN CARSON, naval officer, born in Pittsburgh, February 14, 1821; was a grandson of Col. Christian Febiger of the Revolutionary Army; was appointed midshipman in the navy in 1838; became commander, July 16, 1862, and was assigned to the steamer Kanawha of the Western Gulf blockading fleet. On May 5, 1864, while in command of the Mattabeset, of the North Atlantic Fleet, he participated with the little squadron under Captain Melanchthon Smith in defeating the Confederate ram Albemarle, in Albemarle Sound, N. C., and was commended for his bravery and skill in that engagement. He was promoted rear admiral February 4, 1882, and died in Londonderry, October 9, 1898.

FEDERAL CONVENTION, THE—The representatives of twelve states assembled in convention at Philadelphia in the summer of 1787 to prepare a constitution of government for the United States of a national character. George Washington, a delegate from Virginia, was chosen president, and William Jackson, secretary. This convention was composed of some of the most illustrious citizens of the new republic: Franklin, Dickinson, Rutledge, Washington, Robert Morris, James Wilson, Madison, Patrick Henry, etc. The Pennsylvania delegates were Thomas Mifflin, Robert Morris, George Clymer, Jared Ingersoll, Thomas Fitzsimons, James Wilson, Gouverneur Morris, and Benjamin Franklin.

FEDERALIST PARTY—See POLITICAL PARTIES.

ALBERT GALLATIN'S MANSION, FRIENDSHIP HILL

FEDERATION OF LABOR, AMERICAN—The first convention of the American Federation of Labor met in Pittsburgh in November, 1881. The call for this congress was the result of a meeting held at Terre Haute, Indiana, August, 1881. The call was addressed and sent to all the trade and labor unions of United States and Canada. Delegates began to arrive in Pittsburgh, Saturday, November 12th, and by Monday night between fifty and sixty delegates had arrived. The corresponding secretary, Mr. W. M. Moore, had reported on November 6th that fifty-five organizations had responded. Among them were printers, painters, cigar makers, molders, carpenters, shoemakers, plasterers, seamen, iron and steel workers, marine and pastry cooks, window glass workers, spinners, cigar packers, bookbinders, cap finishers, boot makers, furniture workers, cap coverers, horsesmiths and granite cutters.

FELLENBERG SCHOOL, THE, was founded in Philadelphia in 1822 by Von Fellenberg, a follower of Pestalozzi, who maintained, among other theories, that manual labor should be combined with a classical education. The school, which had one hundred and thirty pupils, was awarded a medal at an exhibition at Franklin Institute, for proficiency in the plaiting of straw for hats and bonnets.

FELTON, SAMUEL MORSE, engineer, was born in West Newbury, Mass., July 17, 1809; was graduated at Harvard in 1834; was connected with the Fitchburg Railroad until 1851, when he became president of the Philadelphia, Wilmington, and Baltimore Railroad. It was he who successfully planned the secret passage of Lincoln from Harrisburg to Washington and thereby defeated a deep laid plot to capture the President-elect. When communication through Baltimore was impossible (April, 1861), he devised a plan for transporting troops via Annapolis. He died in Philadelphia, January 24, 1889.

FELTON, SAMUEL MORSE, railroad president, was born at Philadelphia, February 3, 1853. He attended Massachusetts Institute of Technology and became a railroad worker, beginning as rodman and rising to the position of general manager of several different railroads between 1873–1885. From 1893–1895, he was president of the Louisville Southern and the Alabama Great Southern Railroads; 1890-1899, Cincinnati, New Orleans and Texas Pacific Railroads; 1899-1907, Chicago and Alton; 1907-1909, Mexican Central; 1909-1925, Chicago Great Western. He died March 11, 1930.

FEMALE BENEVOLENT SOCIETY OF LANCASTER, founded in 1816 for the purpose of procuring and making clothing for the poor, visiting the sick and infirm and administering to their wants.

FERGUSON, ELIZABETH, patriot, was born in Philadelphia, in 1739, a daughter of Dr. Graeme, of Graeme Park, near Philadelphia. She became famous during the Revolution by a futile mission which she took good-naturedly. She was a cultivated woman and enjoyed the friendship of many eminent persons. Her husband was on the British side, but she held the esteem and confidence of both Whigs and Tories. Johnstone, one of the peace commissioners sent over here in 1778, finding they could do nothing with the Congress, employed Mrs. Ferguson to sound Gen. Joseph Reed as to his disposition to aid the royal government and revolting colonies to be reconciled. Johnstone instructed her as to what she should say and she did it without losing the esteem of anyone. Her estate was confiscated but the State of Pennsylvania returned part of it to her in 1781. After the war she applied herself to literature and philanthropy. She died in Montgomery County, February 23, 1801.

FERRIS, BENJAMIN, historian, for many years a resident of Philadelphia from where he removed to Wilmington where he died in 1867. He is the author of "History of the Early Settlements on the Delaware, from Its Discovery to Its Colonization under William Penn."

FETTEROLF, ADAM H., educator, was born at Perkiomen, November 24, 1841. He was educated at Ursinus College; became vice-president of Girard College in 1880 and president in 1882.

FILSON, JOHN, pioneer and early historian, was born in Chester County, in 1747. He was the first historian of Kentucky, having published a history and map of that state in 1784. The Filson Club of that Commonwealth is named for him. Filson was one of the founders of the city of Cincinnati, in the site of which he purchased a one-third interest. While in the vicinity of Cincinnati, which he called Losantiville, he disappeared and is believed to have been killed by the Indians.

FINDLAY, JAMES, soldier and congressman, was born in Franklin County, October 12, 1770. With his wife he moved to Virginia in 1793, later to Kentucky and eventually to Cincinnati, Ohio. At the opening of the War of 1812, Findlay, who held the rank of brigadier-general in the state militia during the Burr conspiracy, commanded the 2nd Ohio Volunteer Infantry, with rank of colonel. He was at the surrender of Gen. William Hull, at Detroit, was praised for his services by Gen. Hull and raised to rank of major-general in the state militia. In June, 1812, he began the construction of Fort Findlay, named for him, upon the site of which the present town of Findlay, Ohio, is located. From 1824 to 1833, he was a representative of the Democratic party in Congress. Later he was a Democratic nominee for governor, but was defeated. He died December 28, 1835.

FINDLAY, WILLIAM, governor, was born at Mercersburg, Franklin County, June 20, 1768. In 1797, he was elected a member of the House of Representatives of Pennsylvania. He was again elected to the House in 1803 where he advocated the removal of the state capital from Lancaster to Harrisburg, a proposition which was not carried out until 1812. Upon his election to the office of State Treasurer, Findlay resigned his seat in the House. During nearly four out of the eleven years that Findlay held this office the United States was at war with England. In 1817, Findlay was nominated as the Republican candidate for Governor and was subsequently elected to that office. During his administration the building of the capital was begun and the corner-stone was laid by him. In 1820, he was again nominated for the office of Governor but failed of reelection, being defeated by Joseph Hiester. In 1821, he was elected to the United States Senate where he served the entire term. Upon the expiration of his term of office he was appointed Treasurer of the United States Mint, at Philadelphia, by President Jackson. He died at Harrisburg, November 12, 1846.

FINDLEY, WILLIAM, Congressman, was born in North Ireland, in 1741, a descendant of one of the signers of the Solemn League and Covenant of Scotland. In 1763, he came to America, joined a Scotch-Irish settlement near Waynesboro, Franklin County, and worked as a weaver, school teacher and farmer. During the Revolution he joined the colonial army and rose to the rank of captain. About the close of the war he moved to Westmoreland County near the present site of Latrobe. Here he held numerous public offices, was a member of the council of censors, 1783-1790, and delegate to the state constitutional convention of 1789-1790. In 1791, he was elected to Congress serving continuously until 1817 with the exception of four years, from 1799-1803, when he was a member of the state senate. Findley was a clever politician, and through his wide acquaintance influenced public opinion throughout the state. Washington consulted him about frontier problems and he was prominently identified with the Whiskey Insurrection of 1794, at first advocating resistance to the government and later encouraging obedience of the law. His "History of the Insurrection in the Four Western Counties of Pennsylvania," is an attempt to vindicate his own position in regard to the affair. He died April 5, 1821.

FINE, HENRY BURCHARD, mathematician, was born at Chambersburg, September 14, 1858. He graduated from Princeton in 1880, received the Ph. D. degree from the University of Leipzig in 1885 and upon his return to Princeton was made assistant professor of mathematics there. In 1891, he became Dod professor of Mathematics which position he held until his death on December 22, 1928. Fine declined President Wilson's offer to appoint him ambassador to Germany and a member of the Federal Reserve Board. He is the author of the following text-books: "The Number System of Algebra"; "College Algebra"; "Coordinate Geometry" (with Henry Dallas Thompson), and "Calculus."

FIRST DAY OR SUNDAY-SCHOOL SOCIETY—This society organized in Philadelphia, in 1791, was designed to give instruction on Sunday "to needy children." This organization was interdenominational. Bishop White, of the Episcopal Church, was president.

FISHER, JOHN S., governor, lawyer, was born in South Mahoning Township, Indiana County, May 25, 1867. In 1886, he graduated from the Indiana State Normal School; later taught in the public schools; studied law, and was admitted to the bar in 1893. Until elected governor of the Commonwealth, he practiced law in Indiana as a member of the firm of Cunningham and Fisher. He was a member of the Pennsylvania Senate, 1901-1909; chairman of the Capitol Investigating Committee which brought to light frauds connected with the furnishing of the State Capitol; became State Commissioner of Banking in 1919, and was a member of the commission on Constitutional Amendment and Revision for Pennsylvania. He was a delegate to the Republican National Convention at Chicago in 1916 and delegate-at-large to the Kansas City Convention in 1928. From 1927-1931, he served as governor of Pennsylvania. His administration was marked by unusual building activity, a definite plan for building extension and improvement having been developed, which included the completion of the North Office Building, The Soldiers' and Sailors' Memorial Bridge and the Farm Show Building. His home is in Indiana, Pa.

FISHER, JOSHUA FRANCIS, author, born in Philadelphia, February 17, 1807; was graduated from Harvard College, in 1825; studied law but never practised. His publications are: "An Account of the Early Poets and Poetry of Pennsylvania," "Private Life and Domestic Habits of William Penn," "The Degradation of Our Representative System and Its Reform," "Reform of Municipal Elections," and "Nomination of Candidates." He died in Philadelphia, January 21, 1873.

FISHER, REDWOOD S., statistician, born in Philadelphia, in 1782. He edited a New York daily newspaper and wrote "The Progress of the United States of America from the Earliest Periods, Geographical, Statistical, and Historical," and was editor of a "Gazetteer of the United States." He died in Philadelphia, May 17, 1856.

FISHER, SYDNEY GEORGE, author, was born in Philadelphia, September 11, 1856; was graduated from Trinity College in 1879; studied law at Harvard and was admitted to the bar in 1883. He is the author of "The Making of Pennsylvania," "The True Benjamin Franklin," "The Evolution of the Constitution of the United States," "The True William Penn," "The True Daniel Webster," "The True History of the Revolutionary War," etc. He has also written many articles on questions of public interest and on nature study. He died at Essington, near Philadelphia, February 22, 1927.

FISHING CREEK—Tributary to North Branch Susquehanna River. Sub-basin: Lower North Branch Susquehanna; source, formed by junction of east and west branches, in Sugar Loaf Township, northeastern Columbia County; course, southerly and southwesterly to North Branch Susquehanna River; mouth, at Rupert; length, twenty-nine and one-half miles. Indian name, Na-mee-si-ponk, "it tastes fishy."

FISHING (BIG) CREEK—Tributary to Bald Eagle Creek. Sub-basin: Middle West Branch Susquehanna; source, in Greene Township, southeastern Clinton County; course, southwesterly and northerly, by a circuitous route, to Bald Eagle Creek; mouth, at Mill Hall; length, thirty-three and one-half miles. Indian name, Na-mee-si-ponk, "it tastes fishy."

FISHING (LITTLE) CREEK—Tributary to Fishing Creek. Sub-basin: Lower North Branch Susquehanna; source, in Jordan Township, southeastern Lycoming County; course, southeasterly into Columbia County; thence southwesterly to Millville; thence southeasterly to Fishing Creek; mouth, two miles northwest of Bloomsburg; length, twenty miles. Indian name, Na-mee-si-ponk, "it tastes fishy."

FITCH, JOHN, metal craftsman and inventor, was born in Hartford County, Conn., January 21, 1743. He learned the rudiments of brass working and founding as a clock maker's assistant and when he was twenty-one established his own brass shop in East Windsor. Because of financial and domestic difficulties he left his family in 1769 and settled in New Jersey where he was successful in the brass and silversmith business. During the Revolution he entered the army and attained the rank of captain. Subsequently, having made money in the tobacco trade, he invested in Virginia land warrants, secured a surveyor's commission and in 1780 surveyed lands along the Ohio River. On a second expedition in 1782 he was captured by the Indians, turned over to the British and held prisoner in Canada. Upon exchange of prisoners he settled in Bucks County, Pennsylvania, where he devoted his time to the invention of a steamboat. The State Legislatures of New Jersey, Pennsylvania, New York, Delaware and Virginia permitted him to build and operate steamboats on the waters of those states. Securing the financial support of wealthy Philadelphians he constructed a 45-foot boat, propelled by a series of twelve paddles and operated by steam power, which he launched on the Delaware on August 22, 1787. He constructed two larger boats which made regular trips on the Delaware. His fourth boat was destroyed by a storm while in course of construction, and Fitch's company decided to withdraw their support. Fitch went to France where he again failed to secure financial support, later he returned to America and about 1796 removed to Kentucky where he died on July 2, 1798. Because of his failure to pay any attention to the economic side of steam navigation he lost all financial support and Robert Fulton is considered as the father of navigation by steam.

FITLER, EDWIN HENRY, manufacturer, was born in Philadelphia, December 2, 1825. He studied law under Charles E. Lex, in Philadelphia, but leaving that profession took a position in the cordage house of his brother-in-law, George J. Weaver. At the age of twenty-three, he became a partner in the firm and by 1870 he had purchased the majority of interests and the firm name was changed from Weaver, Fitler and Co. (Philadelphia Cordage Works), to Edwin H. Fitler and Company. Under his management the business prospered and at the time of his death the factory was one of the largest cordage works in the United States. Fitler was elected mayor of Philadelphia in 1887 and served until 1891. At the Republican National Convention at Chicago, in 1888, he was nominated by a number of delegates for the presidency of the United States. He died at his country home near Philadelphia, May 31, 1896.

FITZSIMMONS, THOMAS, merchant and soldier, was born in Ireland. He emigrated to America and settled in Philadelphia where he engaged in the mercantile business. He was captain of a company during the Revolution; was for many years a member of the Assembly; was a delegate to the Continental Congress, 1782–1783, and a member of the Federal Congress, 1789–1795.

FLAG, THE PENNSYLVANIA—There is no evidence to prove the existence of a strictly provincial flag. By act of April 9, 1799, provision was made for a state flag bearing the coat of arms of the Commonwealth. The governor, by a joint resolution of May 26, 1861, was required to procure regimental standards with the arms of the Commonwealth. The Act approved June 13, 1907, states that the official flag of the Commonwealth "shall be of blue, same color as the blue field in the flag of the United States, and of the following dimensions and design: The length, or height, of the staff to be nine feet, including brass spearhead and ferrule; the fly of the said flag to be six feet, two inches, and to be four feet six inches on the staff; in the center of the flag there shall be embroidered in silk the same on both sides of the flag the coat of arms of the Commonwealth of Pennsylvania, in proportionate size; the edges to be trimmed with knotted fringe of yellow silk, two and one-half inches wide; a cord, with tassels, to be attached to the staff at the spearhead, to be eight feet, six inches long, and composed of white and blue silk strands."

FLANDERS, HENRY, lawyer, born in Plainfield, N. H., February 13, 1826; practiced law in Philadelphia after 1850. He is the author of "Lives of the Chief Justices of the United States," "Memoirs of Cumberland," "Exposition of the United States Constitution," "Adventures of a Virginian," etc. He died April 3, 1911.

FLAX CULTURE IN LANCASTER COUNTY. In obedience to their early teaching the Scotch-Irish settlers, some English Friends and a few Germans, all felt the necessity of raising a crop of flax to furnish clothing, etc., and the cultivation and manufacture of flax continued from the days of the pioneers down to the middle of the nineteenth century. The industry was probably at its highest period of production about 1820.

FLETCHER, BENJAMIN, English colonial governor. He was appointed by William and Mary, in 1692, as governor of New York. When William Penn was deprived of his proprietary rights he acted as governor in Pennsylvania (1693-1694). He was possessed of violent passions, was weak in judgment, greedy, dishonest and cowardly. The recklessness of his administration, his avarice, his evident prostitution of his office to personal gain, disgusted all parties. The Quaker-governed Assembly of Pennsylvania thwarted his schemes for obtaining money for making war on the French. He was, at last, forced to resign from his post in New York and many charges were made against him.

FLINT, HENRY MARTYN, author, born in Philadelphia, March 24, 1829; studied law and settled in Chicago where he edited the "Times," in 1855-1861. He was the author of a "Life of Stephen Douglas," "The History and Statistics of the Railroads of the United States," and "Mexico under Maximillian." He died in Camden, N. J., December 12, 1868.

FLOOD, THEODORE L., Methodist clergyman, born at Williamsburg, February 20, 1842. He served the Federal Army in the Civil War; entered the Methodist ministry and after an active pastorate of fifteen years became connected with the Chautauqua movement. He edited the "Chautauqua Assembly Herald," which began its monthly issue at Meadville, in 1877, and became the "Chautauquan," in 1880. He retired from its editorship and ownership in 1899. He was active in various denominational and commercial enterprises and was an unsuccessful Republican candidate for Congress in 1892.

FORBES, JOHN, military officer, was born in Dunfermline, Scotland, in 1710. He studied medicine, was admitted to practice, but preferred the military profession. He enlisted in the Second Royal North British Dragoons, the Scots Greys. He served in the war of the Austrian succession and in 1745 was made a lieutenant-colonel of the army. In 1757, he was lieutenant-colonel of his regiment, and in February, 1757, was made a colonel and accompanied his regiment to Halifax. In December, 1757, he became a brigadier-general in America and was assigned by Gen. Abercromby, at Pitt's orders, to command the expedition against Fort Duquesne. His force consisted of Montgomery Highlanders, a detachment of Royal Americans, and some 5,000 provincials from Pennsylvania, Virginia, Maryland and North Carolina. He decided, against the advice of Washington, to cut a new road from Raystown to Fort Duquesne instead of taking Braddock's route. Throughout the entire campaign Forbes suffered serious illness and from September on he followed the advance of his army in a litter. Appreciating the importance of winning the French Indians, he approved the negotiations of Christian Frederick Post. On November 25th, five months after the expedition started, Forbes entered Fort Duquesne, which was named Pittsburgh at the suggestion of Gen. Forbes in a letter to William Pitt. He died in Philadelphia, March 11, 1759, and his body was buried with military honors in the chancel of Christ Church.

FORBES EXPEDITION—William Pitt issued orders of the King of Great Britain on December 30, 1757, appointing Brigadier-General Forbes to command the expedition against Fort Duquesne. March 20, 1757, Gen. Forbes wrote to Governor Denny, from New York, giving directions concerning the raising of troops in Pennsylvania. At this time he also made plans for a place of rendezvous at Raystown, Fort Bedford. Forbes decided to build a new road through the mountains from Raystown, Fort Bedford, to Fort Duquesne. Among the officers in this expedition were Sir John St. Clair, Col. Henry Bouquet, Col. John Armstrong and Major Grant. A base of supplies was established at Fort Loudon, but the rendezvous of the troops was at Raystown, Fort Bedford. Gen. Forbes was careful to protect his entire line of march to his base of supplies and to protect his front by the erection of breast works. Col. Bouquet was always in advance and was efficient in carrying out the orders of Gen. Forbes. An unfortunate event occurred on September 14, 1758, on what is known as Grant's Hill in the city of Pittsburgh, in which Grant was severely defeated and the expedition seriously endangered. Attacks made at Fort Ligonier, Loyal Hanna, were repulsed and Gen. Forbes left Loyal Hanna, November 17th, with 4,300 effective men. The General continued, seriously ill, carried in his litter, but determined to finish his work. On the 24th, the French commander, Captain Delignery, saw it was useless to attempt to hold the fort, for he was deserted by his Indian allies, and set fire to the buildings and went down the Ohio River. Forbes occupied Fort Duquesne the next day and on December 3rd, left for Fort Ligonier where he remained until the 27th. He reached Carlisle on January 7, 1759, and from there went to Philadelphia where he was received with great honor. The marker placed by the Pennsylvania Historical Commission at Bouquet's Block House bears the following inscription:

"Fort Duquesne, end of Forbes Road, occupied by Gen. Forbes, November 25, 1758, and by him named Pittsburgh. His victory determined the destiny of the great west and established Anglo-Saxon supremacy in the United States. 'His name for ages to come will be dear to Americans and appear with lustre among contemporary worthies in the British Annals'—Col. Hugh Mercer to Col. Bouquet, March 21, 1759."

FORBES ROAD, a military road built by Gen. John Forbes, a British officer, who was sent to western Pennsylvania to capture Fort Duquesne. Upon the advice of Col. Bouquet and others, he decided to cut a new road from Fort Bedford, formerly Raystown, to Fort Duquesne, instead of making his base of supplies Fort Cumberland and using the old Braddock Road. Washington was opposed to marching by any other route than the old Braddock Road, but Gen. Forbes decided, against the advice of Washington, to cut a road through the mountains by the northern route.

The Pennsylvania Historical Commission has recently marked this road by placing thirteen major markers, the majority of which are on the Lincoln Highway. These markers are at Bedford; The Forks at Bonnet's Tavern; Shawnee Cabins, Schellsburg; at the eastern slope of the Allegheny Mountains; McLean's Fort at the foot of the Allegheny Mountains; Edmund's Swamp; the Encampment at Stony Creek, Stoyestown; at the eastern approach of Laurel Ridge; Fort Ligonier; 12 Mile Run, near St. Vincent's Monastery; at Murraysville on the William Penn Highway; at Peterman's, three miles west of Murraysville, and at the old Bouquet Block House, Pittsburgh.

The length of this road was 104 miles and it was completed during the year 1758.—*See also* FORBES, JOHN, AND FORBES EXPEDITION.

FOREST COUNTY, formed from part of Jefferson and Venango, April 11, 1848; another part of Venango was added by legislative act, October 31, 1866. Named for forests within its boundaries. Land area, 424 square miles. Population (1930), 5,180. County-seat, Tionesta; laid out in 1852.

FORNEY, JAMES, military officer, was born in Lancaster, January 17, 1844; educated at Georgetown University; second lieutenant U. S. Marine Corps, 1861; promoted captain, 1864; colonel, 1892; brigadier-general, 1894, and retired the same year. He saw service during the Civil War at the capture of New Orleans and the attacks on Vicksburg, Baton Rouge, and Galveston. During the Spanish War he was the commander of the camp where 1,700 officers and men of Admiral Cervera's fleet were confined. He died February 2, 1921.

FORNEY, JOHN WEISS, journalist, was born in Lancaster, September 30, 1817; purchased the Lancaster "Intelligencer," in 1837, and three years later the "Journal," which papers he amalgamated under the name "Intelligencer and Journal." He was clerk of the National House of Representatives in 1851–1855; started the "Press," an independent Democratic journal, in Philadelphia, in 1857, and upon his reelection as clerk of the House of Representatives in 1859 he started the "Sunday Morning Chronicle," in Washington. Among his publications are: "Anecdotes of Public Men," "Forty Years of American Journalism," and "A Centennial Commissioner in Europe." He died in Philadelphia, December 9, 1881.

FORREST, EDWIN, actor, was born in Philadelphia, March 9, 1806. While still a boy he began performing female and juvenile parts. His first appearance on the professional stage was on November 27, 1820, in Philadelphia, in the title role of "Douglas." After a long professional tour in the west during which he undertook several Shakespearian characters, he filled engagements in Albany and Philadelphia, in 1826, where he met with remarkable success, owing to his superb form and presence and his natural genius. His chief characters were Othello, Macbeth, Hamlet, Richard III, Metamora, and Spartacus. He visited Europe several times. In 1858, Forrest announced his retirement from the stage but appeared at intervals till 1871. He was a man of literary culture and accumulated a large library rich in Shakespeare which was destroyed by fire January 15, 1873. He left his Philadelphia home and a considerable portion of his large fortune for the establishment of an asylum for aged and indigent actors. He died in Philadelphia, December 12, 1872.

FORSHEY, CALEB, goldsmith, was born in Somerset County, July 18, 1812. He was professor of mathematics and civil engineering in Jefferson College, Mississippi, and from 1851–1853 was engineer in charge of the government survey of the Mississippi delta. Though opposed to secession he became lieutenant-colonel of the Confederate engineers upon the withdrawal of Texas from the Union. He died in Carrolton, La., July 25, 1881.

FORSYTH, GEORGE ALEXANDER, military officer, was born at Muncy, November 7, 1837. He served with distinction in the Civil War; was brevetted colonel for gallant services at Five Forks and brigadier-general in 1868 for his action in an engagement with hostile Indians. He was a member of the board of officers to inspect the armies of Europe and Asia in 1875–1876, and on staff and frontier service till 1890, when he was retired on reaching the age limit. He published "Thrilling Days in Army Life," and "The Story of the Soldier." He died at Rockport, Mass., September 12, 1915.

FORT ALLEMANGLE, a frontier fort of the French and Indian War, located in Albany Township, Berks County.

FORT ALLEN, a regular fort established by the Provincial Government where the town of Weissport now stands. As a result of the defeat of General Braddock the frontiers were devastated by unfriendly Indians and the massacre at Gnadenhutten had occurred. A systematic plan of defense was considered necessary and Benjamin Franklin and James Hamilton were selected to carry it out, and in December, 1755, Fort Allen was determined upon. Fort Allen was named in honor of Judge William Allen, father of James Allen, who laid out Allentown. It was garrisoned for five years, 1756–1761, and after the expiration of that period was occasionally occupied by soldiers.

FORT ALLEN (Washington County), near the line between Smith and Robinson Townships, erected probably in 1774.

FORT ALLEN, Hempfield Township, Westmoreland County; a fort built by Christopher Truby and others and known as Truby's Block House in the

Dunmore War in 1774. The Pennsylvania Historical Commission has marked this site.

FORT ALLISON, was located west of Chambersburg, near the later site of McCauley's Mill, in Franklin County.

FORT ANDERSON, a fort erected in 1778, in the county of Huntingdon.

FORT ANTES, erected by Lt.-Col. Henry Antes, in 1778, opposite the present Jersey Shore, on Nippenose Creek. It was defended by Col. Antes until Col. Samuel Hunter ordered him to vacate it when the military authorities considered it hazardous to defend the forts in this section. Fort Antes was said to be a refuge for the Fair Play men as well as for those on the south side of the river.

FORT APPLEBY, a fort in Armstrong County, on the site of the old village of Kittanning.

FORT ARMSTRONG, a stockade, erected by Lt.-Col. Stephen Bayard, just below the present town of Kittanning, in June, 1779, naming it in honor of Gen. John Armstrong.

FORT AUGUSTA, a frontier fort of exceptional strategic value, located at Shamokin, now Sunbury, where was located the largest Indian town south of Tioga Point. Friendly Indians repeatedly urged the erection of a fort at this point which is the confluence of the north and west branches of the Susquehanna. In October, 1755, a number of inhabitants met at John Harris' and signed the petition for a fort at Shamokin as a protection against the French and Indians. A similar petition was signed at Conrad Weiser's on the same day. Governor Robert Hunter Morris, March 29, 1756, commissioned Lieutenant-Colonel William Clapham to recruit a battalion for this purpose, which battalion was known as the Augusta Regiment. The regiment rendezvoused at Harris' Ferry and on June 12th orders to march were given. A stockade was built at Halifax, which place the regiment left July 1st, reaching Shamokin, July 6th, and immediately began the construction of the fort which was named Augusta in honor of the daughter of King George II. The plans were drawn by E. Meyer, engineer for the British Government. On September 23rd, Col. Clapham informed Governor Denny that the fort was almost finished. Col. Clapham was succeeded by Col. James Burd, whose journal is a valuable contribution to the history of the period. Expeditions to various points were sent out from this fort. During the Revolution it was the headquarters of the Military Department of the Susquehanna, and was the depot of supplies for the Hartley and Sullivan Expeditions. The magazine is the only part of the fort that has been preserved.

FORT BARR, located on a branch of the Loyalhanna, about 5½ miles southeast of Fort Wallace (Westmoreland County).

FORT BEELOR, erected about 1774, in Washington County, at Candor, Robinson Township.

FORT BINGHAM, Tuscarora Township, Juniata County. This fort destroyed June, 1756, rebuilt about 1760 by Ralph Sterrett, an Indian trader.

FORT BOONE, located about one mile above Milton, Northumberland County.

FORT BOSLEY, erected during Revolutionary War where Washingtonville, Montour County, now stands.

FORT BRADY, located near the town of Muncy, Lycoming County.

FORT BRINK, located about three miles above Bushkill, Pike County. Erected probably during French and Indian War.

FORT BROWN, East Hanover Township, Dauphin County, erected about 1775.

FORT BURD (Fort Redstone), erected during the autumn of 1759, by Col. James Burd.

FORT CHAMBERS, Col. Chambers built a large stone house at Falling Springs, now Chambersburg. It was surrounded by water from the spring, the roof was of lead and was also stockaded. This fort was known as Chambers' Fort, built in 1730.

FORT CHERRY, Mt. Pleasant Township, Washington County, probably erected about 1774. It is situated on Little Raccoon Creek.

FORT CHRISTINA, erected by the Swedes, near the mouth of the Minequas Creek; named in honor of Swedish Queen, Christina.

FORT COXE, in Peter's Township, Washington County, built about 1774.

FORT CRAWFORD, located on east bank of the Allegheny where the town of Parnassus, Westmoreland County, now stands. Was erected during the summer of 1778 by Col. Wm. Crawford.

FORT CROGHAN, in Cumberland County, was erected as a trading-house, and was located on the Conodoquinet, eight miles from Harris' Ferry (Harrisburg), where the Indian trader, George Croghan, lived.

FORT CROSS, was located at Conococheague, Franklin County.

FORT CUMBERLAND, located where the city of Cumberland, Maryland, now stands on Will's Creek.

FORT DILLOW, located in Hanover Township, Washington County, in the summer of 1782. Was built by Matthew Dillon & Son.

FORT DODDRIDGE, erected in 1773, three miles west of West Middleton; built by John Doddridge, father of Rev. Dr. Doddridge, author of "Doddridge's Notes."

FORT DUPUI, erected on the property of the Huguenot settler, Samuel Dupui, on the site of the present town, Shawnee-on-the-Delaware, in Monroe County. The first of a chain of forts, built about 1755.

FORT DUQUESNE, a colonial fort on the present site of Pittsburgh, at the junction of the Allegheny and Monongahela Rivers. The work was begun in 1754 by a party of Virginians sent out by Governor Dinwiddie. They were driven away by the French and Indians before completing the fort. It was then finished by the French and named Duquesne. After being burned by the French in 1758 it was rebuilt by the English and at the suggestion of Gen. Forbes named Pittsburgh. Of the large fortifications built by the English before the Revolution, only a block house now remains. This is owned and preserved by the Daughters of the American Revolution.

FORT DURKEE, erected by Connecticut settlers in what is now the city of Wilkes-Barre, in the spring of 1769.

FORT EVERETT, erected near the town of Lynnport, Lehigh County, about 1755.

FORT FAYETTE, erected by Gen. Wayne (Mad Anthony), where the Western National Bank in Pittsburgh now stands, June, 1792.

FORT FETTERS, located where Duncansville, Blair County, now stands, about 1777.

FORT FRANKLIN, Schuylkill County, near Snydersville; erected about 1756.

FORT FRANKLIN, Venango County, erected in the spring of 1787 by detachment of United States troops under Capt. Jonathan Hart.

FORT FREELAND, located about four miles east of Watsontown, Northumberland County, a small fort near Muncy Hill.

FORT FREELAND, BATTLE OF, on July 28, 1779, Captain John MacDonald, a New York Tory, with a detachment of British and Seneca Indian Allies arrived near Fort Muncy from the vicinity of Wyalusing. Their object was to divert the army of Sullivan then on its famous march to the Iroquois country in New York. From Fort Muncy they marched toward Fort Augusta and came in conflict with the garrison at Fort Freeland where the inhabitants of the neighborhood had fled for protection. After a gallant defense Captain MacDonald's third demand for surrender was accepted, after which Captain Hawkins Boone arrived too late for relief. As a result of this campaign 108 settlers were killed or led away as prisoners of war by the British army.

FORT FROMAN'S-FORMAN'S, stood within the present town of Canonsburg, Washington County.

FORT GARARD, Greene County, about seven miles west of Greensboro, about 1774.

FORT GRANVILLE, near Lewistown, Mifflin County, was erected in 1755-1756. The fort was twice attacked by Indians. It was destroyed on July 30, 1756, when in command of Lieut. Edward Armstrong, who was killed. The entire garrison was either killed or taken captive.

FORT HALIFAX, at mouth of Armstrong Creek, one-half mile above the present town of Halifax on east bank of Susquehanna River, in Dauphin County. Built about 1755.

FORT HAMILTON, on site of Stroudsburg, in Monroe County, built 1755.

FORT HAND, erected in 1777, near Bell Township, Westmoreland County.

FORT HANNASTOWN, sometimes called Fort Reed, is located in Westmoreland County, and was built about 1773.

FORT HARTZOG, erected in 1778, near the site of the present town of Marklesburg.

FORT HENRY, at Dietrick Six's, near Millersburg, Berks County. This fort is sometimes called Busse's Fort from its commanding officer, also the Fort at Dietrick Six's.

FORT HOLLIDAY, erected in Blair County about 1777. Adam and William Holliday settled where the town of Hollidaysburg now stands about 1768.

FORT HORN, eastern part of Clinton County, erected prior to 1777.

FORT HUNTER, erected about 1755, on the east bank of the Susquehanna River, at the mouth of Fishing Creek, six miles north of Harrisburg.

FORT HYNDSHAW, located in the Minisink Region, Monroe County, about one mile from the Delaware River and near the Pike County line. Erected during 1756, under the direction of Franklin.

FORT JACKSON, near Waynesburg, Greene County.

FORT JENKINS, located on the north shore of North Branch of Susquehanna, midway between Berwick and Bloomsburg, in Columbia County.

FORT JENKINS, located within the present limits of the town of West Pittston.

FORT LEAD MINES, erected in 1778 in what is now Tyrone Township, Blair County; also called Fort Roberdeau.

FORT LE BOEUF, erected in the year 1753 by the French, located where Waterford, Erie County, now stands.

FORT LE BOEUF, EIRE COUNTY, BUILT, 1796

FORT LEBANON (also known as Fort William), not far from the present town of Auburn, in Schuylkill County.

FORT LIGONIER, at Ligonier, Westmoreland County, the first English fort west of the Allegheny Mountains, was built in 1758, by order of General John Forbes, and was named in honor of Lord John Ligonier. It was at this fort that Forbes with Washington, Bouquet and John Armstrong, organized an army of 7,850 men, marched against Fort Duquesne, which was evacuated November 25, 1758, thereby overthrowing the French and establishing English supremacy in the region. Here Colonel Bouquet reorganized the expedition for the relief of Fort Pitt.

FORT LINDLEY, erected in 1773 (the strongest fort in Washington and Greene Counties), near Prosperity.

FORT LOUDEN was erected in the winter of 1756, by Col. John Armstrong. It was situated a mile southeast of the town of Fort Louden, in Franklin County. During the expedition of General John Forbes, in 1758, and that of Colonel Henry Bouquet, in 1763-1764, the fort was used as a rendezvous for troops and as a base of supplies. In 1765, it was the scene of the exploits of Captain James Smith and his "Black Boys."

FORT LOWTHER was erected at Carlisle in 1753.

FORT LYTTLETON, located at Sugar Cabins, in the northeastern part of Fulton County.

FORT McCLURE, located within the limits of Bloomsburg, about the spring of 1781.

FORT McCORD, a private fort, erected in the autumn of 1755. Located several miles northeast of Fort Loudon, Franklin County, also near Yankee Gap in the Kittatinny Mountains west of Chambersburg. The fort was destroyed in April, 1756.

FORT McCORMICK, near Neff's Mills, Huntingdon County.

FORT McDOWELL, located where McDowell's Mill, Franklin County, now stands.

FORT McFARLAND, Amwell Township, Washington County, erected probably as early as 1772.

FORT McINTOSH, located on the bluff overlooking the Ohio where Beaver now stands; erected in 1778.

FORT McKEES, east shore of Susquehanna, in southern part of Northumberland County.

FORT MACHAULT. The French in April, 1754, erected Fort MaChault, at Venango (Franklin County). The English referred to it as the French Fort at Venango. In 1760, after the close of the French and Indian War, the English erected Fort Venango, near where Fort MaChault had stood.

FORT MANADA, one of the chain of forts erected about 1755, located at Manada Gap, Dauphin County.

FORT MENNINGER, located on the west bank of West Branch of the Susquehanna at the mouth of White Deer Creek, Union County.

FORT MIFFLIN, a United States military post, on Mud Island in the Delaware River. It was built in 1771 as one of the defenses for Philadelphia, and figured in numerous engagements of the Revolution. It was captured by Gen. Howe in November, 1777.

FORT MONTGOMERY (Fort Rice), in Lewis Township, Northumberland County. Erected by Col. Weltner's German Regiment in autumn of 1779.

FORT MORRIS, at Shippensburg, Cumberland County.

FORT MUNCY, located about four miles from town of Muncy, Lycoming County. Erected in spring of 1778 by Col. Thos. Hartley.

FORT NORRIS, located about one mile southeast of Kresgeville, Monroe County.

FORT NORTHKILL, located near Straustown, Berks County.

FORT PALMER, located in Fairfield Township, Westmoreland County.

FORT PATTERSON, located in the Tuscarora Valley at Mexico, Juniata County.

FORT PENN, erected on the site of present town of Stroudsburg, Monroe County.

FORT PITT (Fort Dunmore), erected in 1759 by Gen. John Stanwix. Gen. Stanwix remained at the fort until 1760, which was finally completed in 1761 under Col. Bouquet. In the summer of 1773, Fort Pitt having been abandoned by the King's orders, was repaired, and given a new name, Fort Dunmore.

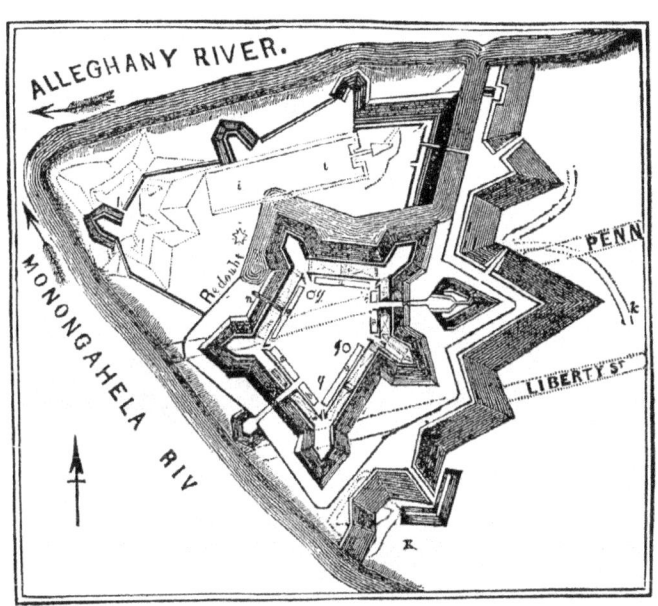

PLAN OF FORT PITT

FORT POMROY (POMEROY), erected during Revolutionary War by Col. James Pomroy. Located about a mile from Barr's Fort in the Derry settlement, and about one-half mile from Millwood Station on main line of P. R. R., in Westmoreland County. Fort raided during spring of 1781.

FORT PRESQU' ISLE. In the summer of 1753, Fort Presqu' Isle was erected by the French coming from Canada. The city of Erie now stands here.

FORT RALSTON, in the Irish settlement of Northampton County, about five miles northwest of Bethlehem. Erected about 1755.

FORT RECOVERY, erected by Col. James Wilkinson in 1793. Town in Mercer County by the same name now occupies the site where this fort stood.

FORT REED, located where Lock Haven now stands.

FORT REED, located at Hannastown, Westmoreland County.

FORT RICE, located on Buffalo Creek, in Donegal Township, Washington County. Last invasion in western Pennsylvania by a large body of Indians was the attack upon Fort Rice in 1782.

FORT ROBERDEAU—See FORT LEAD MINES.

FORT ROBERDEAU

FORT ROBINSON, erected about 1755 in Sherman's Valley, Perry County.

FORT RYERSON, near the present site of Ryerson Station, Greene County.

FORT SCHWARTZ, erected during the Revolutionary War on the Susquehanna, about one mile above the present town of Milton, Northumberland County.

FORT SHAWNEE, located south of the present town of Plymouth, Luzerne County.

FORT SHIELDS, located near the town of Alexandria, Westmoreland County, in 1777.

FORT SHIPPEN, erected about 1773 at Col. John Proctor's, in Unity Township.

FORT SHIRLEY, located at Shirleysburg, Huntingdon County; completed before 1756.

FORT SMITH, located on the Swatara, in Bethel Township, Lebanon County

FORT SQUAW, situated a short distance southeast of Somerfield, Somerset County.

FORT STANDING STONE, now Huntingdon.

FORT SWAN, located in Greene County.

FORT SWATARA, located in the vicinity of Swatara Gap, or Tolihais Gap, Lebanon County.

FORT SWEARINGEN, in Springfield Township, Fayette County.

FORT TEETER, erected probably as early as 1773 in Independence Township, Washington County.

FORT TRENT. On February 17, 1754, William Trent began the erection of a fort on the forks of the Ohio River. The unfinished fort was taken possession of by the French.

FORT ULRICH, near Annville, Lebanon County (1755).

FORT VAN METER, Greene County.

FORT VANCE, located about one mile north of the present village of Cross Creek, Washington County.

FORT WALLACE, located near Blairsville, Indiana County.

FORT WALLACE, was located at Muncy, Lycoming County.

FORT WALLENPAUPACK, on creek of the same name between Pike and Wayne Counties.

FORT WELLS, erected in 1789 in Cross Creek Township, Washington County

FORT WHEELER, built on banks of Fishing Creek, about three miles from Bloomsburg, Columbia County, in 1778.

FORT WILKES-BARRE, located on site now occupied by the court house at Wilkes-Barre. This fort was taken by the Indians and burned July 4, 1778.

FORT WIND GAP, was located near Wind Gap, Northampton County.

FORT WINTERMOOT, was located one mile below Fort Jenkins, Luzerne County.

FORT WOLF, Washington County.

FORT ZOLLARSVILLE seems to have been an Indian earthwork, erected in what is now West Bethlehem Township, Washington County.

FORTY-FORT, a protective work erected by the Connecticut settlers in Wyoming Valley, in 1769. It was the rendezvous of the Americans when the valley was invaded by Tories and Indians on June 3, 1778, and was surrendered on the following day.

FOSTER, STEPHEN COLLINS, song writer, was born in Pittsburgh, July 4, 1826. He was educated at Athens Academy, Bradford County, and at Jefferson College. He composed the music and wrote the words of more than one hundred and twenty-five songs and melodies. Among the best known are "Old Folks at Home," "Old Dog Tray," "Old Black Joe," "Massa's in de Cold Ground," "My Old Kentucky Home." He died in New York, January 13, 1864.

FOULKE, SAMUEL, member of the Colonial Assembly of Pennsylvania, 1761-1768; was born December 4, 1718. He was a member of the Society of Friends and during the Revolution was "disowned" by the society because of his sympathetic attitude toward the war, and his avowed allegiance to the colony. His journal written while he was a member of the Colonial Assembly of Pennsylvania, gives an interesting account of the period. He died January 21, 1797.

FOURTH OF JULY, THE AMERICAN, natal day, so designated because of the Declaration of Independence on July 4, 1776; it is also known as Independence Day. The signing of the Declaration of Independence took place in Independence Hall, Philadelphia. See also DECLARATION OF INDEPENDENCE.

FRANKLIN, BENJAMIN, statesman, was born in Boston, Mass., January 17, 1706. His father was an Englishman and his mother the daughter of a Quaker poet. He learned the art of printing with his brother, but when they disagreed he left Boston, sought employment in New York, but not finding any went to

BENJAMIN FRANKLIN

Philadelphia. In 1729, he established himself as a printer in Philadelphia. He was the chief founder of the Philadelphia Library in 1731. He became clerk of the Provincial Assembly in 1736 and postmaster of Pennsylvania the next year. He was the founder of the University of Pennsylvania and the American Philosophical Society in 1744, and was elected a member of the Provincial Assembly in 1750. In 1753, he was appointed deputy postmaster for the English-American colonies; and in 1754 he was a delegate to the Colonial Congress of Albany in which he prepared a plan of union, which was the basis of the Articles of Confederation. As early as 1746, he began investigations and experiments in electricity and the publication of these procured for him membership in the Royal Society and the degree of LL. D., from Oxford and Edinburgh in 1762. In 1764, he was sent to England as agent of the Colonial Legislature, in which capacity he afterwards acted for several other colonies. In Congress he advocated, helped to prepare and signed the "Declaration of Independence." In the fall of 1776, he was sent as ambassador to France. To him was chiefly due the successful negotiation of the treaty of alliance with France and he remained there until 1785. In 1786, he was governor of Pennsylvania and in 1787 helped to frame the constitution. He died in Philadelphia, April 17, 1790.

FRANKLIN, SAMUEL RHOADS, naval officer, was born in York, August 25, 1825, was appointed midshipman August 10, 1847, and was promoted successively until he became rear-admiral on January 24, 1885. He was retired in 1887. Most of his forty-six years of service was spent at sea. During both the Mexican and Civil Wars he was active in the most important operations. He was president of the International Marine Conference and is the author of "Memories of a Rear Admiral." He died February 24, 1909.

FRANKLIN, WILLIAM, Royal Governor, was born in Philadelphia, in 1729, the only son of Benjamin Franklin. He held a captain's commission in the French War (1744-1748). From 1754-1756 he was comptroller of the Colonial post-office, and clerk to the Provincial Assembly. In 1762, he was appointed governor of the province of New Jersey. Because of his loyalty to the crown he was arrested in 1776 and sent to Connecticut, where for more than two years he was strictly guarded, when, in November, 1778, he was exchanged. He remained in New York, and was active as president of the Board of Associated Loyalists until 1782 when he sailed for England, where he was allowed by the government $9,000 and a pension of $4,000 a year. He died in England, November 17, 1813.

FRANKLIN, WILLIAM BUEL, military officer, was born in York, February 27, 1823. He was graduated from West Point in 1843. He served on the staff of General Taylor at the Battle of Buena Vista (in the Mexican War) and was brevetted first lieutenant. In May, 1861, he was appointed colonel of the 12th Infantry. He was in the hottest of the fight at Bull Run; was promoted brigadier-general of volunteers in September, and appointed to the command of a division of the Army of the Potomac. He did excellent service in the campaign of the Virginia Peninsula and on July 4, 1862, was promoted to major-general. In March, 1865, he was brevetted major-general in the regular army. He resigned in 1866 to engage in manufacturing. He died in Hartford, Conn., March 8, 1903.

FRANKLIN, a city and county-seat of Venango County, located on the Allegheny River at the mouth of the French Creek, 123 miles north of Pittsburgh. It was settled in 1753 and incorporated in 1795. Franklin is located in the center of an extensive oil region; other industries are the manufacture of asbestos goods, air compressors, boring machines and drills, office blanks and books, etc. Population (1930), 10,254; (1920), 9,970.

FRANKLIN COUNTY, formed from part of Cumberland, September 9, 1784, named for Benjamin Franklin. Land area, 751 square miles; population (1930), 65,010; county-seat, Chambersburg; laid out in 1764.

FRANKLIN INSTITUTE, was founded at Philadelphia, in 1824, for the encouragement of scientific research. The Institute investigates discoveries, processes and inventions and reports on various scientific matters such as docks, boiler explosions, water power, metal testing, fire prevention. It awards the Franklin Medal to noted scientists; the Elliott Cresson Medal for discovery or original research; the Howard N. Potts Medal for outstanding work in science or the arts; the Edward Longstreth Medal of merit; the Certificate of Merit and the Boyden Prize for experiments relating to rays of light, etc. The Institute publishes the "Journal of the Franklin Institute," established in 1828. Its hall, located on Seventh Street, between Market and Chestnut, contains offices, a lecture hall, laboratories, a library and a School of Mechanic Arts.

FRANKLIN INSTITUTE, JOURNAL OF THE, was established by the Franklin Institute of Philadelphia, in 1826. It is devoted to the development of science and mechanics, and appears monthly. It was first edited by Thomas P. Jones, professor of Natural Philosophy and Mechanics, under the name of the *Franklin Journal*. In 1828, it took its present name. Dr. Howard McClenahan is the editor. Circulation, 2,554.

FRANKLIN AND MARSHALL COLLEGE, a men's college, at Lancaster, was formed in 1852 by the union of Franklin College, founded at Lancaster, in 1787, and Marshall College, founded at Mercersburg, in 1836. Franklin College was named for Benjamin Franklin who displayed his interest in it by contributing liberal sums of money to its endowment and by attending the opening. Marshall College was founded by the Reformed Church in the United States at the time when the theological seminary of the church was removed from New York to

Mercersburg. Because of financial troubles Marshall College did not prosper. Franklin and Marshall College, under the control of the Reformed Church of the United States, is a flourishing institution. Courses leading to the A.B., B.S., A.M., and M.S. degrees are offered. Enrollment (1930-1931), 750.

FRANKLIN REPOSITORY, THE, a Republican newspaper, was established at Chambersburg, in June, 1790, by William Davidson, of Philadelphia, and was originally called the *Western Advertiser and Chambersburg Weekly Newspaper*. Through the activities of Colonel A. K. McClure, one time proprietor, it became a leading political organ of Pennsylvania. On May 15, 1931, it was merged into *Public Opinion*, established in 1869. It is issued each evening, on Sunday and weekly. Shirley J. Zarger is the editor. Circulation, 4,800.

FRANKS, REBECCA, daughter of David Franks, a prominent Philadelphia Jew, was one of the belles of the Revolutionary period. Brilliant, witty, attractive, clever in repartee, she outshone all others in the social gatherings of the period, and in particular at the Meschianza, the entertainments given at Philadelphia on May 18, 1778, by the British officers of Gen. Howe, prior to his return to England. On a certain occasion when Lieutenant-Colonel Jack Stewart, of Maryland, an officer in the Continental Army, called on Miss Franks, wearing a red coat, he remarked, "I have adopted your colors, my princess, the better to secure a kind reception, deign to smile on a true knight." Miss Franks did not reply directly, but turning to her friends said, "How the ass glories in the lion's skin." Later she married General Sir Henry Johnson of the British Army, who was defeated and captured by General Wayne at the Battle of Stony Point.

FRANKSTOWN BRANCH—Tributary to Juniata River. Sub-basin: Upper Juniata; source, formed by junction of Beaverdam Creek and Boiling Spring Run, in Greenfield Township, southern Blair County; course, northeasterly to Water Street, forming Blair-Huntingdon County boundary for four miles; thence southeasterly into Huntingdon County to Juniata River; mouth, near Ardenheim; length, fifty-six and one-half miles.

FRAZER, JOHN FRIES, scientist, was born in Philadelphia, July 8, 1812, the grandson of Gen. Persifor Frazer, of the Revolution. He was graduated from the University of Pennsylvania in 1829 with highest honors and afterward completed courses both in law and medicine. With Professor A. D. Bache he made the first researches on magnetics in the United States. He succeeded Professor Bache as professor of natural philosophy and chemistry in the University of Pennsylvania, serving until his death; and from 1855-1868, also as vice-provost. In 1857, he received the degree of LL.D., from Harvard. He was an active member of the American Philosophical Society, the Academy of Natural Sciences, and the Franklin Institute, and one of the charter members of the National Academy of Sciences. He died in Philadelphia, October 12, 1872.

FRAZER, PERSIFOR, geologist, was born in Philadelphia, July 24, 1844, the son of John Fries Frazer. He was graduated from the University of Pennsylvania in 1862 and served during the Civil War in the South Atlantic squadron (1862-1863) as aide, United States coast survey; in the cavalry during the Gettysburg campaign and as ensign in the navy to the end. He taught in the University of Pennsylvania, 1870-1874. Was the first foreigner to receive the degree of Docteures Sciences Naturelles, which also gave him the decoration of the Golden Palms of the Academy. He served as vice-president, representing the United States in the International Geological Congress of 1888, in London, and of 1897, in St. Petersburg. He also wrote extensively for scientific periodicals and published five volumes of reports of the Geological Survey of Pennsylvania of which he was assistant geologist, 1874-1882. He died in 1909.

FREE QUAKERS, or the Monthly Meeting of Friends, were those members of the Society of Friends who had taken an active part in the Revolution and who, after the war, were denied their usual rights and privileges. In 1781, they organized this society of their own to distinguish themselves from those of their brethren who had disowned them.

FREE SOCIETY OF TRADERS IN PENNSYLVANIA, was organized in 1682 for the purpose of establishing "honest and industrious trade" in the province.

FREELAND, a borough in Luzerne County, about thirty miles southwest of Scranton. It is situated in the anthracite coal region, and in the center of good farming land. The chief manufactures are lumber, mining and farm implements, and foundry products. Population (1930), 7,098; (1920), 6,666.

FRENCH CREEK—Tributary to Allegheny River. Sub-basin: Upper Allegheny; source, in Chautauqua County, southwestern New York; course, southwesterly, through Erie County, Pennsylvania, into Crawford County, to Meadville; thence southeasterly, through Mercer County, into Venango County, to Allegheny River; mouth, at Franklin; length, in Pennsylvania, seventy-eight miles.

FRENCH CREEK—Tributary to Schuylkill River. Sub-basin: Lower Delaware; source, in Union Township, southern Berks County; course, southeasterly into Chester County to Schuylkill River; mouth, at Phoenixville; length, twenty-two miles.

FRENCH AND INDIAN WAR, a fourth intercolonial war between the English and French Colonies in America was begun in 1754, in which the Indians bore a conspicuous part. Much of the fighting took place in western Pennsylvania; some of the outstanding forts were Forts Le Boeuf, Venango, Duquesne and Necessity. Another outstanding outcome was the defeat of General Braddock. In northeastern Pennsylvania, in the Wyoming Valley, a dreadful massacre occurred.

FRICK, HENRY CLAY, manufacturer, was born at West Overton, December 19, 1849. He began commercial life in a small coke business which grew to be the largest in the country and became president of the H. C. Frick Coke Co. He was prominent in putting an end to the Homestead strike (1892). Was president of the Carnegie Steel Company from 1892 to his death, also a director and officer in numerous other business enterprises. On his death in 1919, he bequeathed his New York mansion with its art collection to the city. He bequeathed also a handsome park to the city of Pittsburgh.

FRIENDS, SOCIETY OF, commonly called Quakers, originated in England in the middle of the seventeenth century under the leadership of George Fox. Fox, who was born in Leicestershire, in 1624, emphasized the spiritual and discountenanced all form in Christianity; he believed in the doctrine of the inner light; that divine power within the individual will make it possible for him to live according to God's will.

A few members of the Society of Friends were in Pennsylvania before Penn, one of their persecuted leaders, who acquired it in payment of a debt due by the Crown to his father. Within three years there were 7,000 members of the organization in the province and it was not long before Pennsylvania became a place of refuge for persecuted Friends. They practiced toleration in their dealings with the Indians, thus following the policies of both Penn and Fox, and actively opposed slavery. In the early part of the nineteenth century, divisions in the church resulted from differences on certain points of doctrine. The Society of Friends known as the Hicksite Friends, or Quakers, developed in 1827, when the Philadelphia Yearly Meeting divided. Influential members of the Philadelphia division opposed certain teachings of Elias Hicks, a minister of the Society. Thereafter the conservative division has been generally known as the Orthodox Friends and the liberal as the Hicksite. Other divisions of the Society of Friends are the Wilburite group, formed in 1845, and the Primitive, an outgrowth of the Wilburite.

The largest of the four divisions is the Orthodox. They differ from the doctrines of other Christian denominations in their belief in the immediate personal teaching of the Holy Spirit or the "inner light," in the absence of the outward forms of worship, such as baptism and the Holy Supper; in the manner of worship and appointment of ministers and in the doctrine of peace or non-resistance. In 1926, there were 11,829 members of the Society of Friends in Pennsylvania.

FRIES, JOHN, rioter, was born in Bucks County, in 1764. During the window tax riots in Northampton, Bucks, and Montgomery Counties, in

1798-1799, Fries headed the rioters, liberated several prisoners whom the sheriff had arrested, and in turn arrested the assessors. Fries was arrested and tried on the charge of high treason, pronounced guilty, and sentenced to be hanged in April, 1800. President Adams issued a general amnesty which covered all the offenders. Subsequently Fries moved to Philadelphia where he became successful in the tinware business. He died in 1825.

FRIENDS' MEETING HOUSE, CATAWISSA (1843)

FRIETCHIE, BARBARA, the subject of a poem by John Greenleaf Whittier was born in Lancaster, December 3, 1766. On September 12, 1862, when the Union troops entered Frederick, Md., which was then the home of Barbara Frietchie, the aged woman stood by the window watching their passage and waving the American flag. The troops noting her loyalty and extreme age shouted to her and Major-General Reno asked for her flag. She refused, but gave him another. In his poem Whittier has added romance to fact so that today Barbara Frietchie is known and loved as a national heroine.

FUGITIVE SLAVES.—*See* UNDERGROUND RAILROAD.

FULTON, ROBERT, inventor and engineer, was born in Little Britain, Lancaster County, in 1765. He was apprenticed to a jeweler in Philadelphia at an early age, and, in addition to his labors at this trade, he applied himself to painting. At the age of twenty-two, he went to London where he studied painting under Benjamin West; but after several years he abandoned art and applied himself wholly to mechanics. From 1794, when he obtained a patent from the British government for an inclined plane, to 1806 he spent his time abroad devoting himself to new projects and inventions. In 1803, while in Paris, he constructed a small steamboat, and his experiments with it on the Seine were attended with great success. He returned to New York in 1806 and pursued his experiments there. In 1807 he launched on the Hudson his steam vessel, the "Clermont," which made a successful start in the presence of thousands of astonished spectators. From this period, steamers came into general use upon the rivers of the United States. He died in New York, February 24, 1815.

FULTON COUNTY, was formed from part of Bedford, on April 19, 1850. Named for Robert Fulton, inventor of the steamboat. No railroads traverse this county. Land area, 403 square miles. Population (1930), 9,231. County-seat, McConnellsburg; laid out in 1786.

FURNESS, HORACE HOWARD, author, editor, and Shakespearian scholar, was born in Philadelphia, November 2, 1833; was graduated from Harvard (1854) and from the University of Halle, Germany, 1856. He studied law in Philadelphia and was admitted to the bar in 1859. His great work in literary scholarship was contributed as editor of the Variorum edition of Shakespeare's plays, among which are: "Romeo and Juliet," "Macbeth," "Hamlet," "King Lear," "Othello," "Merchant of Venice," "As You Like It," "Antony and Cleopatra." In recognition of this achievement he was awarded honorary degrees by Columbia, Yale, and Harvard, and, in 1905, was elected member of the American Academy of Arts and Letters. He died August 13, 1912.

FUTHEY, JOHN SMITH, historian, was born in Chester County, September 3, 1820; was admitted to the bar in 1843 and was district attorney for five years. In 1879, he became presiding judge of the district. He is the author of many historical works including "Historical Collections of Chester County," "Historical Address on the One Hundredth Anniversary of the Paoli Massacre," etc. He died in 1888.

GABB, WILLIAM MORE, palaeontologist, was born in Philadelphia, in 1839. In 1862-1865, he was director of the palaeontological section of J. D. Whitney's geological survey of California, and later made surveys in Santo Domingo (1868) and Costa Rica (1873). He published Volumes I and II of the "Geological Survey of California," 1864, and monographs on the topography and ethnology of Costa Rica and the geology and topography of Santo Domingo in the "Transactions of the American Philosophical Society" and Petermann's "Mittheilungen." He died in 1878.

GALLATIN, ALBERT, statesman and financier, was born in Geneva, Switzerland, January 29, 1761. He was educated there and had the advantage, through family connections, of meeting many literary and social leaders of Europe, among them, Voltaire. In 1870 he came to America, spent some time in Maine where he furnished supplies for the Colonial Army. Later he was engaged to teach French at Harvard College. The possibilities of the Ohio Valley attracted

ROBERT FULTON

him, and he made several journeys to western Virginia, Ohio, and Pennsylvania as a surveyor. In 1786, he took up land in Monongahela County, Virginia, which is now southern Fayette County, Pennsylvania. With friends, he established New Geneva and built "Friendship Hill" where he later entertained Lafayette. He had great real estate investments here, and built a glass factory and gunsmith shop. He adhered to Republican principles in government and became a leader of the opposition in Pennsylvania to the policies of Hamilton. He attended the convention at Harrisburg in 1788 of citizens who opposed some of the articles of the United States Constitution. He became a member of the state legislature and was a member of the Constitutional Convention that framed the state constitution of 1790. Perhaps he is best known for his activities during the famous "Whiskey Insurrection" when he was at first in favor of using extreme methods in opposing the enforcement of the federal excise law. As conditions grew serious, and persons and property were attacked, his legal mind asserted itself, and he did everything in his power to bring about peaceful negotiations with the federal and state governments. In this he was successful and made up for what he termed his "first political sin." Meanwhile he had been elected by the state legislature to represent Pennsylvania in the United States Senate in 1793, but was denied his seat on the question of citizenship. From 1795 to 1801 he served in the House of Representatives. After that he became a national figure and had little time to spend in Pennsylvania. Jefferson chose him to be secretary of the treasury in 1801 and he remained there until 1813 when he was sent to Ghent, Belgium, to negotiate with British representatives for peace following the War of 1812. From 1815 to 1823, he was minister to France, and in 1826 was ambassador to England. His work in the treasury was so efficient that several succeeding presidents invited him to take that post, but he refused. He retired in New York in 1827 and devoted himself to literary and historical pursuits. He was first president and a founder of the Ethnological Society of America, and contributed articles on Indian life to various publications. Albert Gallatin died on August 12, 1849, in New York City.

GALLAUDET, THOMAS HOPKINS, educator, was born in Philadelphia, December 10, 1787, and was graduated from Yale College in 1805, where he was a tutor for a while. He prepared for the ministry at Andover Theological Seminary and was licensed to preach in 1814. He was interested in the deaf and dumb and in 1817 he began his labors with them in a class of seven. He became one of the most useful men of his time, labored incessantly for the benefit of the deaf and dumb, and was the founder of the first institution in America for their instruction. It was located in Hartford, Conn., where Dr. Gallaudet resigned the presidency of his institution to become chaplain for the Connecticut Retreat for the Insane in 1833 which office he held until his death, September 9, 1851.

GALLITZIN, PRINCE DEMETRIUS AUGUSTINE, clergyman, was born in The Hague, Holland, December 22, 1770, where his father was Russian

ALBERT GALLATIN

ambassador. In 1792, he came to America to travel but determined to become a Roman Catholic priest. He was ordained a priest March 18, 1795, and was the first priest who had both received holy orders and been ordained in the United States. In 1800, he purchased 20,000 acres in the present Cambria County which he divided into farms and offered to settlers on easy terms. Although constantly hampered by lack of money to carry out the grand schemes he contemplated, his colony soon took root and soon sent out branches. He died in Loretto, May 6, 1841, the foundations of which he laid.

GALLOWAY, JOSEPH, Loyalist, was born near West River, Anne Arundel County, Md., 1730. He was a member of the Pennsylvania Assembly in 1764 and at one time Speaker, and with Franklin advocated a change of the government of Pennsylvania from the proprietary to the royal form. As a member of the first Continental Congress he was conservative in his views, yet his line of argument in his first debates tended towards political independence. He proposed a plan of colonial government which was rejected. After the question of independence began to be seriously agitated he abandoned the Whig, or Republican, cause and became an uncompromising Tory. When the British Army evacuated Philadelphia, in 1778, he left this country with his daughter and went to England where he died August 29, 1803.

GARMAN, SAMUEL, naturalist, was born in Indiana County, June 5, 1843. He was graduated from the Illinois State Normal University in 1870 and became assistant in herpetology and ichthyology in the Museum of Comparative Zoology, Cambridge, Mass., in 1873. His works include "The Reptiles and Batrachians of North America," "Chalydoselachus," "The Evolution of the Rattlesnake." He died September 30, 1927.

GEARY, JOHN WHITE, military officer and governor, was born in Mount Pleasant, Westmoreland County, December 30, 1819. He served as lieutenant-colonel of a Pennsylvania regiment of volunteers in the Mexican War. He went to San Francisco in 1848 and was the first mayor of that city. Upon his return to Pennsylvania he was made territorial governor of Kansas in 1856, which office he held a year. Early in 1861 he raised and equipped the 28th Regiment of Pennsylvania Volunteers. In 1862, he was promoted brigadier-general. He did good service throughout the war, becoming, at the end of Sherman's march to the sea, military governor of Savannah and brevet major-general. In 1866, he was elected governor of Pennsylvania and held the office within two weeks of his death in Harrisburg, February 8, 1873.

GEDACHTNISS TAG, September 24, 1734—The Schwenkfelders established their Gedachtniss Tag or Memorial Day to commemorate their escape from persecution. This day has since been regularly observed as a day of thanksgiving by the members of this sect.

GENERAL MAGAZINE AND HISTORICAL CHRONICLE, THE, the first magazine established in America, was begun by Benjamin Franklin in January, 1741. The publication, designed "for all the British Plantations in America" was discontinued after about six months.

GENET, CITIZEN, French minister to the United States, 1793-1794, arrived in Philadelphia in May, 1793. A decided Republican, Genet received among other favors from the United States the assurance of her protection of French possessions in America. The French minister was royally entertained in Philadelphia, but his popularity affected him in such a way that his personality soon became overbearing. On May 18, 1793, when he was officially presented to Washington, he noticed a bust of Louis XVI at the entrance to the president's residence, and complained that because Louis had been beheaded some time before by order of the French government, the presence of his likeness was an insult to France. Genet caused a number of difficulties for Washington and Congress, at one time violating the proclamation of American neutrality between France and her enemies. Finally as his insolence increased his recall was requested, and on February 22, 1794, M. Fauchet, the new minister, arrived in Philadelphia.

BIRTHPLACE OF STEPHEN C. FOSTER

GENEVA COLLEGE, a co-educational institution, under the control of the Reformed Presbyterians was founded at Northwood, Ohio, April 20, 1848. In 1880, the college was removed to Beaver Falls where buildings were erected upon a plot of land donated to the college by the Harmony Society. Enrollment (1930-1931), 500.

GEORGE, HENRY, political economist, was born in Philadelphia, September 2, 1839. He was educated in the public school of his native place, and after working in a store for a short time went to sea and served as a cabin boy for fourteen months. In 1858, he went to British Columbia in search for gold, but meeting with disappointment he went to San Francisco, where he and two others published a paper the "Journal." In 1872, he was a delegate to the convention which nominated Horace Greeley for the presidency. In 1880, he went to New York and the following year to Ireland to write up the land question for several newspapers. In 1889, he visited England and in 1890 Australia. In 1897, he was nominated for mayor of Greater New York but died October 29th of that year during the campaign.

GERHARD, BENJAMIN, born at Philadelphia, in 1812; was graduated at Dickinson College, in 1828; studied law under Joseph R. Ingersoll, and was admitted to the bar in 1832. He was later a trustee of the University of Pennsylvania; a vestryman of St. James' Church; a member of the American Philosophical and Historical Societies and of the Episcopal Corporation for Widows. During the Civil War he was provost-marshall of the city of Philadelphia to superintend the draft. He was one of the founders of the Union League. He died June 18, 1864.

GERHART, EMANUEL VOGEL, clergyman, was born in Freeburg, Snyder County, June 13, 1817. He entered the ministry of the German Reformed Church in 1842. From 1851-55, he was president of Tiffin College, Ohio, and from 1855-1866, of Franklin and Marshall College, Lancaster. He was professor of theology at the theological seminary at Lancaster from 1868. He published "Philosophy and Logic," "Institutes of the Christian Religion." He died in Lancaster, May 6, 1904.

GERMAN AND ENGLISH GAZETTE, was established in Philadelphia in 1751. Was printed in both English and German at the German Printing Office on Arch Street.

GERMAN PENNSYLVANIA JOURNAL, THE, is believed to have been the title of a newspaper in the German language which was printed in Philadelphia as early as 1742. It was published by Joseph Crillins, who was also supposed to have kept a winter evening German school.

GERMAN PRINTING OFFICE, was established in Philadelphia as early as 1755 by a society formed in London for the purpose of "promoting religious knowledge among the German emigrants in Pennsylvania." This printing office published school books, religious tracts and a newspaper.

GERMAN SOCIETY, established in Philadelphia in 1764 by citizens of German birth to urge the Legislature to make such reforms as were necessary to protect the Germans who were brought to this country. This society also supplied relief to the poor and distressed Germans brought to the city of Philadelphia.

GERMAN UNION BOND SOCIETY, an organization that purchased 35,000 acres of land in Elk County from the United States Land Company in 1842. In the fall, thirty-one families settled there and in 1843 thirty-three more families joined the settlement.

GERMANTOWN, settled by German immigrants as early as 1683, marking the landing in this country of a race whose influence can never be accurately measured. Lots were drawn in Pastorius' Cave on October 24, 1683, for the future homes of these pioneers in the then unbroken forest. Francis Daniel Pastorius was the agent of the Frankfort Land Company and there were fourteen families who came with him and were the first inhabitants of Germantown, which was properly named as a German settlement. One of the most important and epoch-making battles of the War of the Revolution was fought here. It was on two occasions the home of the first president of the United States and of the members of his cabinet. Germantown was temporarily the seat of the state government and was the home of the First National Bank.

GERMANTOWN TELEGRAPH, THE, appears every Friday and was first issued by Philip R. Freas, on March 17, 1830. John J. McDevitt, Jr., is the editor, and the Germantown Publishing Company, Inc., are the publishers.

GERMANTOWN, BATTLE OF, October 4, 1777. Howe having captured Philadelphia, stationed his army across the Germantown Road north of the city and east of the Schuylkill. He shortly detached part of it to reduce the forts which blocked the Delaware below the city. Washington planned the capture of the weakened army, starting after dark on the evening of the 3rd of October. His right under Sullivan and accompanied by himself, with six brigades, was to move down the main street and crush the British left; the Pennsylvania Militia was to march along the river and take it in flank; the left under Greene was to divide, three brigades under himself taking the British right in front and flank while two others were to move to the east and come up in its rear. This, it was hoped, would compel surrender. At sunrise a heavy fog came up and left all darker than ever. The British advance bodies were overwhelmed by the Americans and the battery captured, but Colonel Musgrave took shelter in former Chief Justice Chew's house, and after an unsuccessful attempt at breaching it with the light guns, the Americans left a brigade to besiege it and moved on. Despite this delay and the warning to the British, both their wings soon began to give way before the American onset. But in the fog, Wayne and Sullivan had turned considerably east and came in front of Stephen, who took them for the enemy and attacked them in the rear. Wayne's men were driven against the next left of Sullivan's remaining brigades, a panic started and a general retreat began. The British took the offensive and reinforced by Cornwallis, from Philadelphia, pressed the Americans hard; but the latter soon regained composure and retired in good order, though one regiment of Greene's was surrounded and captured. The Americans, however, brought away several captured cannon and all their own and their wounded. Their loss in killed and wounded was 673, the British 535. Stephen was accused of being drunk, courtmartialed, and dismissed from the army. Although the plan failed, the ultimate results were very great. The audacity of the Americans in attacking the British so soon after the defeat at Brandywine, determined largely the French Alliance.

GERRYMANDERING IN PENNSYLVANIA—It is commonly supposed that Gerrymandering had its origin in Massachusetts in 1812, when Governor Gerry signed an apportionment bill which divided the state into oddly-shaped districts for the election of senators. From this the practice was named, but the scheme of districting a state for partisan purposes actually had its origin in Pennsylvania. In order to substantiate the contention that gerrymandering was known and practiced prior to 1812 it is essential to examine some political maneuvers during the earlier days of our colonial history. W. T. Rout says that the beginning of political strife in Pennsylvania came in 1695, when the Anglicans succeeded, against the wishes of the Quakers, in establishing the First Christ Church in Philadelphia. Jealousy existed and increased between the two groups because of the desire for what each claimed was a just share in the government of the colony. The Anglicans were stronger in Philadelphia city, while in the rural section the Quakers predominated. Hence it is natural to find the early strife as existing between the inhabitants of the city on one hand and the people of the rural section on the other. The original charter of 1683 did not prescribe any separate representation for Philadelphia city nor did the charter under Markham, in 1696, but in the Charter of Privileges of 1701, Penn made a provision that Philadelphia may have two separate representatives if they so desired, within three years thereafter, when they had become an incorporated city.

The outcome of this concession by Penn was that in 1705 the Assembly permitted the Delaware counties to withdraw and then proceeded to establish new representation for the colony. Each of the three counties remaining, Bucks, Chester and Philadelphia, were given eight members instead of four while the representation for Philadelphia city remained at two, as established by the Law of November 27, 1700.

This failure to increase the number of representatives for Philadelphia city was a clear case of discrimination, because it was growing rapidly and threatened the political well-being of the colony. From that time to the present day the struggle for political advantage between Philadelphia and the rest of Pennsylvania has become more marked than ever. So we can rightly say that in Pennsylvania, the birthplace of the monster, an attempt to make representation more equal resulted in the gerrymander which is in itself just the antithesis of fair representation.

Having secured a hold upon the Assembly through the Charter of Privileges the Quakers saw to it by laws of their own making that the city and western counties were kept in the minority for a long period of time. This was done largely by making the voting requirements such that proportionately more Quakers would qualify than any other element. The principal suffrage qualification in 1705 was put at 50 acres of land or 50 pounds value of property, real or personal. This kept the Quakers in almost complete control of the Legislature until the beginning of the Revolution. Lists of taxables for Philadelphia city in 1754 also in 1767 show about 15% of the taxables qualified to vote by possessing fifty pounds or over, out of a taxable population of 3,885. In the east the danger to Quaker power arose from the number of counties. By keeping down the voters of Philadelphia city and erecting new western counties slowly there would be little danger of dethroning the Quakers.

Previous to the Revolution the voice of the unqualified voters became so loud that reluctantly the Assembly increased representation for some of the western counties. The enmity had been increased by the failure of the Assembly to vote money and men for protection of the frontier counties against Indian attacks at the time of the French and Indian War. Under pretense of justice, but more for self-preservation, the Assembly voted additional representation, in 1776, but it was too late. The Revolutionary Party had already seized the government and Quaker authority came to an end. The first thing was the establishment of a state constitution. The suffrage requirements were made more lenient and constituted only an age limit of 21 years, residence of one year in the state prior to election and payment of taxes. On account of the war this new Constitution was never ratified by a vote of the people and with the beginning of our new National Government in 1789 came also another State Constitution in 1790 into which was written a provision that has been considered the first restriction on gerrymandering. Our Revolutionary forefathers in Pennsylvania who had finally gained control of the government were going to see to it that it should not pass from them through any arbitary arrangement of counties by their political opponents. The particular provision to which reference has been made was Article 1, Section VII, concerning the choice of State Senators.

"When a district shall be composed of two or more counties they shall be adjoining neither the city of Philadelphia nor any county shall be divided in forming a district."

The main point of disagreement between the Federalists and Anti-Federalists arose at the time of the adoption of the Constitution in 1787. The Federalists, headed by Hamilton, wanted a strong national government, while the Anti-Federalists, led by Jefferson, wished more power delegated to the states and to the people. Under Washington's supreme leadership the Anti-Federalists did not challenge the Federalists for state control of politics. The conduct of the

Adams administration in dealing with foreign affairs aroused the national mind, and his absolute negligence in appointing any Pennsylvanians to prominent offices, brought forth a storm of protest from the Keystone State. The results of this was seen in 1800 when the Jeffersonian tide so completely submerged Federalism that the control of state politics rested safely within their hands almost without interruption for over a quarter of a century and not until after the close of the Jacksonian Era did the Democrats surrender, to their opponents the Whigs. If the opposing party threatened as they did on several occasions, a rearrangement of districts or a new ratio of apportionment would take care of the danger. The chief concern rested with representation in the State Senate and Congress of the United States since they were each represented by members chosen from groups of counties forming districts, while the State Assembly was composed of representatives, at least one from each county, prior to 1790. After that a new county could not have a separate member in the Assembly unless it had a population agreeable to the ratio then established.

There was no provision in the Constitution of 1790 for grouping counties to form a representative district and likewise no restriction of the same. When the Democrats became supreme in 1800 they proceeded to re-district the state for both state and national representation.

Apportionments for State Senate and House of Representatives were required by the Constitution every seven years, and for Congress every ten years. The state was apportioned for Senators and Representatives in 1801. Instead of having twelve senatorial districts as before, with twenty-four members, they formed eighteen districts, electing twenty-five Senators. This was necessary in part at least to take care of the ten newly erected counties, that had been erected in 1800.

The first and possibly the most notorious gerrymander came in 1802, when the Congressional apportionment of April second became a law. The former act had provided for twelve districts electing thirteen members. In the election of 1800 the Democrats had elected ten Congressmen and the Federalists three. By the proper arrangement of districts under the apportionment of 1802 the Democrats saw to it that not a Federalist was elected to Congress in 1802. The districts that elected Federalists in 1800 were the third, composed of counties of (Chester and Delaware); the seventh (Lancaster), and the tenth (Bedford, Somerset, Franklin and Huntingdon). Chester and Lancaster were put into the third district with Berks which had gone Democratic by over 2,500 votes in 1800. Delaware was put in with Philadelphia city, which was doubtful, and Philadelphia county overwhelmingly Democratic. The tenth district was taken care of in this manner. Huntingdon, a Federalist county, was put in with Dauphin, Cumberland and Mifflin, to form the fourth district.

The result in the 1802 election was that eighteen Democratic Congressmen and not a single Federalist represented Pennsylvania in the National Government, yet about one-third of the people of Pennsylvania were Federalists.

Another point worth mentioning here pertains to the ratio. Instead of raising the ratio to at least 35,000 or 36,000 as they might have done, the Democrats chose to keep that at 33,000 and make plural districts where possible.

Little change occurred in districting the state in 1808 and 1812, although the Embargo and the War with England seriously threatened the Administration Party, and thereby reduced the majority, but following the so-called successful war with England in 1812, there came a lull in party strife. The Whigs, who in 1812 had not supported the war, were without good leadership and consequently little influence. In 1820, by a close vote the people had repudiated Governor Findlay, a Democrat, for his unwise expenditures and maladministration and elected Hiester, a Federalist. During his term the apportionment act of April 2, 1822, became a law. It had been made originally to discriminate against Lancaster County and Delaware County, but for such violations of the Constitution of 1790 Governor Hiester vetoed the bill April 1, 1822, and his veto, together with a formal protest to the State Legislature by representatives from Berks, Philadelphia and Delaware Counties, caused the Legislature to reconsider the bill and amend it. It was then signed by him April 2, 1822. This is the first instance in which a governor vetoed an apportionment bill.

The plural district system was by now creating a great deal of concern among our Congressmen, and in April, 1832, Webster was chosen as chairman of a committee to investigate elections and apportionments. This committee reported that the system was unfair and that Congress should make some provision by which apportionment should be done on a purely mathematical basis relative to the strength of parties. Before the National Government took any action on the proposal made by Webster's committee, the people of Pennsylvania remodeled their Constitution in 1838 and went a step farther than they had gone in 1790 in eliminating the gerrymander. The provisions of 1790 were retained, and another clause was added which required that—"no district be formed of more than one county or city in case such a combination should entitle the district thus formed to more than two senators."

The first Federal restriction on gerrymandering was the Apportionment Act of June 25, 1842, which provided that Congressmen should be elected by "single member districts composed of compact and contiguous territory." The Federal Act of 1842 was the first to recognize the justice of districts and in order to prevent or limit gerrymandering the contiguous territory clause was added.

An amendment to the Pennsylvania Constitution in 1857 was directed towards what had been unfair methods in the choice of state representatives. The provisions were specific and required that any county of 3,500 taxables may have separate representation in the state assembly; second that no more than three counties shall be joined in forming a legislative district; third, no county shall be divided, and fourth, any city of sufficient number of taxables to entitle it to two representatives shall have a separate representation and shall be divided into convenient districts of contiguous territory of equal taxable population as near as can be and each district shall elect one member.

Some apportionment acts which resorted to more or less gerrymandering may be mentioned here. The one of June 16, 1836, by which the Democrats were accused of being unfair to Delaware County in the choice of state senators. This was referred to by Governor Porter at the time he vetoed the "infamous" Apportionment Act of March 25, 1843. In the latter act it was charged that at least 125,000 citizens of Pennsylvania were deprived of rightful representation, and were mere tax payers. In 1850, the Democrats got a chance to return some of the Whig favors of 1843 and that year experienced the most clamor in the State Legislature as the Whig minority protested so violently both in speech and through the press that Governor Johnston prepared an elaborate statistical veto to what he considered a violation of the Constitution, which deprives citizens of their most precious right.

In 1852, the Whigs took advantage of their return to power and redistricted the state for Congressmen. This was the last apportionment before the Civil War, and since that time neither of the two big parties have dared to gerrymander the state similar to the ones mentioned.

In 1873, there was added to our Constitution of that year the provision that apportionment was to be made according to the total population instead of taxables. Now it is difficult, although not impossible, to gerrymander the state.

GETTYSBURG, borough and county-seat of Adams County, 35 miles southwest of Harrisburg, was founded about 1783 by James Gettys. In 1806, it became an incorporated borough. Gettysburg is the seat of a Theological Seminary of the Lutheran Church, founded in 1826, and of Gettysburg College, under the control of the Lutheran Church, founded in 1832. One of the most notable battles of the Civil War was fought here on July 1, 2, and 3, 1863. The battlefield has been transformed into a national park and the national cemetery dedicated by President Lincoln on November 19, 1863, contains 3,629 graves. Population (1930), 5,584; (1920), 4,439.

GETTYSBURG, BATTLE OF. After the defeat of the Army of the Potomac at Chancellorsville, May 3, 4, and 5, 1863, Lee decided upon a second invasion of the north. With his right holding his defenses at Fredericksburg, he advanced his left under Ewell into the Shenandoah Valley. Hooker threw his cavalry across the Rappahannock; Ewell defeated Milroy at Winchester and entered Pennsylvania. Hooker started in pursuit of Ewell and concentrated at Frederick City, Maryland, June 25th to 27th On the morning of June 28th, General Hooker was superceded by Major-General George Gordon Meade, a Pennsylvanian, who was a tried and capable soldier. Ewell had reached Carlisle and was threatening Harrisburg, Jenkins' cavalry coming within eight miles of that city, while General Meade occupied Wrightsville. Meanwhile, on June 28th, two confederate soldiers were killed at McConnellsburg, in Fulton County, in a brief engagement. A. P. Hill's corps of Lee's army was at Fayetteville on the 29th. Meade moved northward from Frederick with promptness and threatened Lee's communication. He selected the line of Pipe Creek for his defense. Major General D. N. Couch was sent to Harrisburg where he organized the Department of the Susquehanna. He put up fortifications on the opposite side of the river. President Lincoln issued a call for fifty thousand men from Pennsylvania to repel the invasion, and Governor Curtin issued a proclamation calling upon the citizens to protect the Commonwealth. June 30th, J. E. B. Stuart encountered Kilpatrick in Hanover and was repulsed.—(See HANOVER, BATTLE OF.) On July 1st, the first and eleventh corps met the advance of Lee's army under A. P. Hill on the north of Gettysburg. In this engagement General John F. Reynolds, of Lancaster, lost his life, and the Federals were driven through the town. A short time after the death of General Reynolds, General Winfield Scott Hancock assumed command of the advance and held the strategic position at Cemetery ridge to which point Meade, at Hancock's suggestion, ordered the army forward from Pipe Creek. The first day ended, therefore, with Meade's army driven through Gettysburg to Cemetery Ridge. The struggle of the second day was desperate in an attempt on the part of the Confederate left wing, under Ewell, to dislodge Meade's right from Culp's Hill, which was only partially successful. July 2nd also witnessed the struggle for the possession of Little Round Top, which was secured from the Federals by the foresight of General Warren. On the same day a desperate engagement took place in the Peach Orchard where the salient of Sickles' was attacked by Longstreet and Sickles was driven back and the Federal line rectified. Meade called a council of war at which it was determined to hold the position. On July 3rd, Meade's right successfully attacked Ewell on Culp's Hill. Lee had failed to secure a victory on either flank and Meade's army was protected by strong field works. Against the advice of Longstreet, Lee massed one hundred and fifty guns along Seminary Ridge and at one o'clock in the afternoon opened fire. Two hours later Pickett's division of Longstreet's corps attacked Meade's center on Cemetery Ridge and succeeded in penetrating fifty yards beyond Hancock's line. Hancock was wounded but the attack failed and the "High Water Mark of the Rebellion" had been reached. In Meade's rear a desperate cavalry engagement was won by Gregg against the attack of Stuart. Lee spent July 4th and the greater part of July 5th in preparing to withdraw his army. Meade decided not to attack his opponent but to be content with pursuit; he had marched his army from Frederick, Md., to Gettysburg and had fought a three days' battle in six days' time. Meade's army lost in this battle 23,000 men out of 93,000 engaged; the Confederates 22,500 out of 80,000 engaged, beside 5,100 prisoners.

GETTYSBURG COLLEGE, formerly Pennsylvania College, was founded in 1832 at Gettysburg. Originally a college for men, the institution later became co-educational. Enrollment (1930-1931), 650.

GETTYSBURG COMPILER, THE, which appears every Friday, is a Democratic newspaper which was established September 16, 1818, by Jacob LeFevre. The present editor is W. Clarence Sheely.

GETTYSBURG STAR AND SENTINEL, THE, was established in 1800. It has a circulation of 1,350; is issued on Saturday; is Republican in politics, and is edited by Richard Wolff, and published by the Times and News Publishing Company.

GIBBON, JOHN, military officer, was born near Holmesburg, April 20, 1827. He was graduated from West Point in 1847 and served to the close of the Mexican War in the artillery. During the Civil War he was chief of artillery to General McDowell till May, 1862, when he was promoted brigadier-general of volunteers. His brigade was in constant service, and he was soon promoted colonel, United States Army, and major-general, United States Volunteers; he was brevetted major-general, United States Army, March 13, 1865. He was in command of the Yellowstone expedition against Sitting Bull in 1876; he fought Chief Joseph and the Nez Perces Indians in 1877 when he was severely wounded. He published "The Artillerist's Manual." He died in Baltimore, Md., February 6, 1896.

GIBBONS, ABIGAIL HOPPER, philanthropist, was born in Philadelphia, December 7, 1801. She was the wife of James Sloan Gibbons and was the chief founder of the Isaac T. Hopper Home. During the mob riots of 1863 her home was among the first to be entered by the mob because of her abolition sympathies. The appointment of police matrons in station houses in New York City and the establishment of the Reformatory for girls and women in New York were due mainly to her personal efforts. She died in New York City, January 10, 1893.

GIBBONS, JOSEPH, abolitionist, was born in Lancaster, August 14, 1818, and graduated from Jefferson College in 1845. With his father he was one of the principal conductors of the "underground railroad," through which institution they helped hundreds of slaves to freedom. He died in Lancaster, December 8, 1883.

GIBSON, GEORGE, military officer, was born in Lancaster, October 10, 1747. On the breaking out of the Revolution he raised a company of 100 men at Fort Pitt, who were distinguished for their bravery and as sharp-shooters, and were called "Gibson's Lambs." They did good service throughout the war. A part of the time Gibson was colonel of a Virginia regiment. In the battle, November 4, 1791, in which St. Clair was defeated, Colonel Gibson was mortally wounded, dying in Fort Jefferson, Ohio, December 14, 1791.

CHIEF JUSTICE JOHN BANNISTER GIBSON

GIBSON, JOHN, soldier, was born in Lancaster, May 23, 1730, a brother of George Gibson. He was in Forbes' expedition against Fort Duquesne and acted a conspicuous part in Dunmore's War in 1774. He commanded a Continental regiment in the Revolutionary War. He was made a judge of the Common Pleas of Allegheny County, and in 1800, Jefferson appointed him secretary of the Territory of Indiana. He died near Pittsburgh, April 10, 1822.

GIBSON, JOHN BANNISTER, jurist, was born at Cumberland, in November, 1780, the son of Col. George Gibson of the Revolutionary army who was killed at the defeat of St. Clair in 1791. In order to educate her son, John, Ann West Gibson, widow of Col. Gibson, made many sacrifices. She ran the mill, erected by her husband, taught school, in order that her children and those of the vicinity might receive the necessary education, and performed the additional tasks of mother and housekeeper. John Bannister Gibson graduated from Dickinson College and afterward studied law under Judge Duncan, being admitted to the bar in 1803. In 1812, he was appointed president judge of the Court of Common Pleas for Tioga County and in 1816 was appointed by Governor Snyder associate justice of the Supreme Court of Pennsylvania. He became chief justice in 1827 and held that position for twenty-three years. He died in 1853.

GIBSON, WILLIAM, surgeon, was born in Baltimore, March 14, 1788. He attended Princeton and the University of Pennsylvania, and was graduated from the University of Edinburgh. In 1819, he became professor of surgery at the University of Pennsylvania. He published "Institutes and Practice of Surgery," in 1824, and died at Savannah, Ga., March 2, 1868.

GIDDINGS, JOSHUA REED, statesman, was born in Athens, October 6, 1795. His parents moved to Ohio, and in 1812 he enlisted in a regiment under Colonel Hayes, which was sent on an expedition against the Sandusky Indians. In 1826, he was elected to the Ohio Legislature and in 1838 to the United States Congress. From early life he was known as an active abolitionist. While in Congress he was very active in anti-slavery measures. He published a selection of his speeches and "The Rebellion: Its Authors and Causes." He died in Montreal, Canada, where he was United States Consul-general, May 27, 1864.

GIHON, ALBERT LEARY, sanitarian, was born in Philadelphia, September 28, 1833. He was appointed assistant surgeon of the U. S. Navy in 1855 and took part in the attack and capture of the barrier forts, near Canton, China, in 1856, and served throughout the Civil War. He was promoted medical director in 1895 and was retired with the rank of commodore the same year. He published "Practical Suggestions in Naval Hygiene," "Need of Sanitary Reform in Ship Life," "Sanitary Commonplaces Applied to the Navy," and was editor of "Annual of the Medical Sciences" for six years. He died in New York, November 17, 1901.

GILBERT, DAVID McCONAUGHY, clergyman, was born in Gettysburg, February 4, 1836. He was graduated from Pennsylvania College, 1857, and ordained to the ministry of the Lutheran Church, in 1860. His publications include: "The Lutheran Church in Virginia, 1776-1876," "The Synod of Virginia, Its History and Work," "Muhlenberg's Ministry in Virginia, a Chapter of Colonial Luthero-Episcopal Church History."

GILDER, WILLIAM HENRY, explorer, was born in Philadelphia, August 16, 1838. He served through the Civil War and received the brevet of major at its close. In 1878, he was appointed second in command of the expedition to King William's Land and while so engaged made a sledge journey of 3,251 miles, the longest on record. In 1881, he was with the "Rodgers" expedition to look for the "Jeannette." After the "Rodgers" was burned he journeyed from Bering Strait across Siberia, a distance of 2,000 miles, in the depth of winter, and sent a dispatch of the misfortune to the Secretary of the Navy. He published "Schwatka's Search" and "Ice-Pack and Tundra." He died in Morristown, N. J., February 5, 1900.

GILLESPIE, ELIZA MARIE, philanthropist, was born near West Brownsville, Washington County, February 21, 1824. In 1853, she became a member of the congregation of the Holy Cross and after a novitiate in France was appointed a superior of the St. Mary's Academy in Bertrand, Mich., in 1855. Later she transferred the academy to St. Mary's, Ind. During the Civil War she directed from Cairo, Ill., an important hospital work for Federal soldiers. Upon the separation of the congregation of the Holy Cross in the United States from the order in Europe she served for two terms as superior. She died in Notre Dame, Ind., March 4, 1887.

GILLMORE, JAMES CLARKSON, naval officer, was born in Philadelphia, July 10, 1854. He was graduated from the U. S. Naval Academy in 1875. On January 14, 1899, he was ordered to Manila, where he was assigned to the "Yorktown." In April of the same year, he and seven others were captured while scouting at Baler, Luzon. After spending over eighteen months in captivity and suffering great privations the party was rescued in the mountains near Cagayan by Col. Luther R. Hare, in December, 1899.

GILPIN, HENRY DILWOOD, lawyer, was born in Lancaster, England, April 14, 1801. He was graduated from the University of Pennsylvania in 1819 and began law practice in Philadelphia in 1822. He was Attorney-General of the United States 1840-1841, and published "Opinions of the Attorney-Generals of the United States from the Beginning of the Government to 1841," and edited "The Papers of James Madison." He died in Philadelphia, January 29, 1860.

GIRARD, STEPHEN, philanthropist, was born near Bordeaux, France, March 24, 1750. In 1769, he settled in Philadelphia and engaged in various trades. Later in 1780-1790, he formed a partnership with his brother, John, and for some years continued a most successful trade in the West Indies. He became interested in the first U. S. Bank in Philadelphia and in 1812 had purchased the controlling interest and building. The bank continued to do business under the name of Girard Bank and soon became one of the foremost financial institutions in the country. He was a man of peculiar habits, ill-tempered and repellent in manner, but with all generous in charity. He left $5,000,000 for the erection and maintenance of a college for male white orphans. During the rage of yellow fever in Philadelphia he was ever present in relieving the afflicted, both by his free-giving and by his personal care. He died in Philadelphia, December 26, 1831.

GIRARD COLLEGE, Philadelphia, is an institution for the education of poor white orphan boys, founded by the will of Stephen Girard, and opened January 1, 1848. By provision in the will no ecclesiastic, missionary, or minister of any sect whatever is to have any connection with the college, but the officers of the institution are required to instruct the pupils in the purest principles of morality, leaving them to adopt their own religious opinions. The beneficiaries are admitted between the age of six and ten years; are fed, clothed, and educated; and between the ages of fourteen and eighteen are bound out to mechanical, agricultural, and commercial occupations.

GIRTY, SIMON, partisan, was born in Pennsylvania, about 1750. He was a spy for the British at Fort Pitt in 1774. When the Revolutionary War broke out he became a leader of the Indians and took part in numerous atrocities. In 1778, he went to Detroit, inciting the Indians on the way to hostility against the United States. He was present when Col. William Crawford was tortured to death by the savages, and it is alleged that he manifested joy in Crawford's agony. In 1791, he was present at the defeat of St. Clair and while Gen. William Butler lay wounded he ordered an Indian to kill and scalp him. He also took up the cause of the British in the War of 1812. He died in Canada about 1815.

GIST, CHRISTOPHER, pioneer land agent for the Ohio Company of Virginia, was born after 1705, the son of Richard, a surveyor, and one of the commissioners who laid out the city of Baltimore, and Zipporah (Murray) Gist. Christopher Gist resided in North Carolina when he was first employed by the Ohio Company. That organization employed him, in 1750, to explore and report upon the lands on the Ohio River and its branches. His reports are valuable sources of information on the life and customs of the Indians with whom

STEPHEN GIRARD

he came in contact as well as records of his own achievements as a diplomat. In 1752, he selected a site for a home not far from the present site of Brownsville. His career became linked with that of Washington when he accompanied the latter on a journey to the French at Fort LeBoeuf, with messages from Governor Dinwiddie, of Virginia, warning the French against further encroachments in Pennsylvania. During the journey which was made in mid-winter, Gist saved Washington's life on two occasions. Later, Gist participated in the battles at Great Meadows and at Fort Necessity under Washington. He served as General Braddock's guide on the fatal expedition against the French and Indians at Fort Duquesne. After Braddock's defeat he commanded a company of Virginia and Maryland scouts in defense of the frontier. He was the second explorer to traverse Kentucky and served as an Indian agent for a time. His death resulted from small pox, in 1759, in either South Carolina or Georgia.

GLADDEN, WASHINGTON, clergyman, was born at Pottsgrove, February 11, 1836. He was ordained in 1860; was editor of "The Independent," 1871-75, and "Sunday Afternoon," 1875-82. He was a successful lecturer and writer for many years and was an authority on Protestantism in the United States. He died July 2, 1918.

GLASS MANUFACTURE—At an early period attempts were made to manufacture glass in or near Philadelphia. Soon after 1683 a glass and pottery house was established at Frankford by English Friends. About 1657, Henry William Steigel, a German, conducted a flint glass factory. In 1763, "Baron" Steigel began to manufacture glass at Elizabeth Furnace, Lancaster County. Later he made a trip to Bristol, England, then a center of glass making and brought with him, upon his return, English and German glass workers. He established the town of Manheim, Lancaster County, and built a glass factory there. Steigel glass, which is today of great value, is characterized by fine discrimination in the use of beautiful and artistic patterns, lightness of weight, thinness of texture, resonance and brilliance of surface.

In 1769, Richard Wistar moved his glass works from New Jersey to Philadelphia. He manufactured glass lamps and bottles.

Albert Gallatin established the first glass works in western Pennsylvania in 1787 on the Monongahela River, about sixty miles above Pittsburgh. Here and at Pittsburgh, where the first factory was built in 1795, window glass alone, was made.

GLIKKIKAN, was the principal counsellor of the Delaware Chief Packauke, whose castle was near the site of Edenburg, Lawrence County. In the summer of 1769, Glikkikan made a journey to the Moravian Mission on the east bank of the Allegheny for the purpose of refuting the doctrine of Christianity, in which he failed. Sometime afterwards, being converted, he made another visit to the mission, stating he desired to embrace Christianity. The Moravians accepted a tract of land, also his invitation to move to the Valley of the Beaver in April, 1770, settling where the town of Moravia, Lawrence County, now stands. Soon after, he became a devout Christian and so continued until his death, which took place in the Massacre of Gnadenhuetten, Carbon County, November 24, 1755.

GLORIA DEI CHURCH, or Old Swedes' Church, on Swanson Street, Philadelphia, was dedicated July 2, 1700, by Rev. Eric Biork. The first pastor of this Swedish congregation was Rev. Andrew Rudman.

GLORIA DEI (OLD SWEDES') CHURCH

GNADENHUETTEN MASSACRES, THE—The first white settlement in Pennsylvania, north of the Blue Mountains, was a Moravian mission at Gnadenhuetten, near the present site of Lehighton. An outgrowth of the settlement at Bethlehem, Gnadenhuetten was laid out in 1746 under the supervision of Christian Rauch and Martin Mack. Three years later the congregation of the mission numbered five hundred, a great many of whom were Indians. At the time of the French and Indian War, the savages were so embittered against the settlers that even some of those who had come under the influence of the Moravians were incensed and left the mission to join forces with their fellows. On the evening of November 24, 1755, the missionaries at Gnadenhuetten were surprised by a band of hostile Indians, their Pilgerhaus burned to the ground, and eleven of its inmates killed outright or burned to death. On January 1, 1756, another Moravian mission known as Neu Gnadenhuetten, located where Weissport now stands, was burned to the ground. The residents of the town had fled some time previously.

GOBIN, JOHN PETER SHINDEL, lawyer, was born in Sunbury, January 26, 1837. He became a brevet brigadier-general in the Civil War; brigadier-general of United States Volunteers in the war against Spain (1898); lieutenant-governor of Pennsylvania, 1898; commander of the National Guard of Pennsylvania during the coal strike of 1902; commander-in-chief, G. A. R., in 1897–1898, and Past Grand Master, Knights Templar of the United States. He died in 1910.

GODEY'S LADY'S BOOK, the oldest publication of its kind in America, was begun at Philadelphia by Louis A. Godey, in July, 1830. Because of its colored fashion plates, an unusual feature at that time, it rapidly gained in popularity until it attained a circulation of 100,050 a month. As a literary publication its standards were always of the highest. Among its contributors were: Poe, Longfellow, Holmes, Bayard Taylor, James T. Field, Emma Willard, Charlotte Cushman and Harriet Beecher Stowe.

GODFREY, THOMAS, inventor, was born in Bristol, in 1704. He was by trade a glazier, and became a self-taught mathematician. In 1730, he communicated to James Logan, who had befriended him, an improvement on Davis' quadrant. In May, 1742, Logan addressed a letter to Dr. Edmund Hadley, in England, describing Godfrey's instrument. Hadley did not notice it, when Logan sent a copy of this letter to Hadley, together with Godfrey's account of his inventions, to a friend, to be placed before the Royal Society. Hadley, the vice-president, had presented a paper a year before, describing a reflecting quadrant like Godfrey's. They both seem to have conceived the same invention. The society decided both were entitled to the honor and sent Godfrey household furniture valued at $1,000. He died in Philadelphia, December, 1749.

GODFREY, THOMAS, poet, was born in Philadelphia, December 4, 1736. He was the author of "The Prince of Parthia" (1759), a tragedy, considered to be the first drama published in the United States. In 1763, appeared "The Court of Fancy; a Poem," and in 1767, Nathaniel Evans, his friend, collected his poems in a volume. He died near Wilmington, N. C., August 3, 1763.

GODMAN, JOHN D., naturalist, was born in Annapolis, Md., in 1794. In 1813, he entered as a sailor in the flotilla then stationed in Chesapeake Bay, but in 1815 he left the service and commenced the study of medicine. After lecturing for some time at Baltimore in the room of the professor of anatomy in the University of Maryland, and holding a chair of anatomy for a short time in Cincinnati, he settled in Philadelphia as a physician and private teacher of anatomy. His chief work is his "American Natural History," 1828. He also wrote "Anatomical Investigations," and "Rambles of a Naturalist." He died in Germantown, April 17, 1830.

GODON, SYLVANUS WILLIAM, naval officer, was born in Philadelphia, June 18, 1809. He was appointed midshipman, was active in the Mexican War, and in the Civil War; in command of the Mohican, with the rank of captain, he took part in DuPont's attack on Port Royal (1861). In 1863, he was promoted commodore and in 1864-1865 commanded the fourth division of Porter's fleet in the attacks on Fort Fisher. Having commanded the South Atlantic squadron in 1866-1867 and the Brooklyn navy yard in 1868-1870, he was retired in 1871 with the rank of rear admiral. He died in Blois, France, May 10, 1879.

GOOD, JAMES ISAAC, clergyman, was born in York, December 31, 1850. He was graduated from Lafayette College, in 1872, and entered the ministry of the German Reformed Church. He was a successful pastor of churches in York, Philadelphia and Reading, from 1875-1893. From 1893 to 1907 he was dean of the school of theology, Ursinus College, and taught later in Central Seminary, Dayton, Ohio. He wrote much on Reformed Church History. He died January 22, 1924.

GOOKIN, CHARLES, deputy governor under the proprietor, Penn, arrived in Pennsylvania in February, 1709. Because of the eccentric conduct of his predecessor, John Evans, Gookin encountered many difficulties with the Assembly and people. For a time, however, Gookin and the assembly worked together in harmony, but eventually the peace was broken and the governor was removed from office in May, 1717.

GORDON, PATRICK, Colonial governor, was born in England, in 1644, and became governor of Pennsylvania in 1726. He was the author of "Two Indian Treaties at Conestogoe." He died in Philadelphia, August 5, 1736.

GORDON, THOMAS F., historian, was born in Philadelphia, in 1787, where he also practiced law. His publications include: "Digest of the Laws of the United States," "History of Pennsylvania from Its Discovery to 1776," "History of New Jersey from Its Discovery to 1789," "History of America," "Gazetteer of New Jersey," "Gazetteer of New York," and "Gazetteer of Pennsylvania." He died in Beverly, N. J., January 17, 1860.

GOUGE, WILLIAM M., author, was born in Philadelphia, November 10, 1796. He was connected with the United States Treasury Department for thirty years. He published "History of the American Banking System," "Fiscal History of Texas," etc. He died in Trenton, N. J., July 14, 1863.

GOUGH, JOHN BARTHOLOMEW, temperance lecturer, was born in Sandgate, County of Kent, England, August 22, 1817. He arrived in New York, August, 1829, and worked on a farm for two years, was later connected with a publishing house in New York, lost his position in 1833, and fell into dissipation. Drifting to Worcester, Mass., he became converted in 1842 and signed the pledge. He was the best known temperance lecturer of his time. February 15, 1886, while delivering a lecture in the First Presbyterian Church, in Frankford, Pa., he was stricken with paralysis, after speaking for about fifteen minutes, and died in the afternoon of February 18th.

GRAHAM, JOSEPH, military officer, was born in Chester County, October 13, 1759. At an early age he removed to North Carolina. In 1778, he joined the Continental army and served throughout the remainder of the war with gallantry. In 1814, he was commissioned major-general, when he led 1,000 men from North Carolina against the Creek Indians. He died in Lincoln County, N. C., November 12, 1836.

GRATZ, REBECCA, educator, was born in Philadelphia, March 4, 1782. In 1838, she founded the Hebrew Sunday-School in Philadelphia, the oldest of its kind in America and for thirty-two years she was at its head. She responded to the claims of charity without regard for creed and she was long regarded as Philadelphia's representative Jewess for her simple piety, personal, charm, and social standing. Her name will always be associated with Scott's "Ivanhoe," for when Washington Irving was visiting Sir Walter Scott and learned that a Jewess was to be introduced in the latter's novel, then in course of preparation, the American described Rebecca Gratz with so much warmth—she was a dear friend of his betrothed, Miss Hoffman, whose early death caused so much grief—that Scott was deeply impressed. When "Ivanhoe" was finished he sent the first copy to Irving with the inquiry whether the "Rebecca" of the romance compared favorably with the Rebecca of reality. Miss Gratz died in Philadelphia, August 27, 1869.

GRAY, GEORGE, patriot, was born in Philadelphia, October 26, 1725. He became a member of the board of war in 1777 and later was chairman of that body till the conclusion of peace. He wrote the celebrated "Treason Resolutions." He died near Philadelphia, in 1800.

GRAY, JOHN PURDUE, alienist, was born at Half Moon, in 1825. He was graduated from Dickinson College, in 1846, and took a medical degree at the University of Pennsylvania in 1848. He was successively assistant physician and medical superintendent of the New York State Asylum at Utica, N. Y. He introduced many improvements into the treatment of the insane, and was for many years editor of the "American Journal of Insanity." He died at Utica, N. Y., November 29, 1886.

GRAYDON, ALEXANDER, author, was born in Bristol, April 10, 1752. He studied law and entered the Continental Army in 1775. He was captured in the engagement on Harlem Heights and imprisoned in New York and later in Flatbush; he was paroled and in 1778 exchanged. He wrote "Memoirs of a Life, Chiefly Passed in Pennsylvania, within the Last Sixty Years, with Occasional Remarks upon the General Occurrences, Character, and Spirit of that Eventful Period." He died in Philadelphia, May 2, 1818.

GRAYDON, WILLIAM, lawyer, was born near Bristol, September 4, 1759, a brother of Alexander Graydon. He studied law and removed to Pittsburgh where he began his practice. In 1794-1795, he was a prominent leader in the "Mill-Dam Troubles." He published a "Digest of the Laws of the United States," "Forms of Conveyancing and of Practice in the Various Courts and Public Offices," etc. He died in Harrisburg, October 13, 1840.

GREAT COVE MASSACRE—On Saturday, November 1, 1755, a party of about 100 Indians, Shawnee and Delaware, among them Shingas, the Delaware king, entered the Great Cove in the Tuscarora Mountains, divided into two parties and attacked the inhabitants. Many of the settlers saved their lives by fleeing after having been warned. John Potter, sheriff of Cumberland County, Rev. John Steel, Adam Hoop, and others, went in quest of the Indians but failed to overtake them. On November 14th, Sheriff Potter reported to the Provincial authorities in Philadelphia that 27 plantations were burned and that of 93 families which were settled in the Great Cove and Little Cove and the Conolloways, 47 were either killed or taken and the rest had deserted.

GREAT MEADOWS—At the beginning of the French and Indian War, in May, 1754, George Washington, with 150 men, was advancing upon Fort Duquesne, which had been seized by the French the year before. While on his way, at Great Meadows, he surprised a body of French, and in the action, Jumonville, the French commander, was killed with some of his men.

GREAT TROUGH CREEK—Tributary to Raystown Branch. Sub-basin: Upper Juniata; source, in Wells Township, northwestern Fulton County; course, northeasterly into Huntingdon County; thence northwesterly, by a circuitous route, to Raystown Branch Juniata River; mouth, in Penn Township, Huntingdon County; length, thirty miles.

GREENE COUNTY, formed from part of Washington, February 9, 1796. Named for General Nathaniel Greene. Land area, 574 square miles. Population (1930), 41,767. County-seat, Waynesburg; laid out in 1796.

GREENER, RICHARD THEODORE, lawyer, was born in Philadelphia, January 30, 1844. He was the first negro graduate at Harvard College. He was United States consul at Vladivostok, Siberia, in 1898-1906, and represented British and Japanese interests in Siberia during the Russo-Japanese War, 1904-1905. His addresses include "Charles Sumner, the Idealist, Statesman, and Scholar," "William Lloyd Garrison," and "The Intellectual Position of the Negro."

GREENSBURG, city and county-seat of Westmoreland County, was originally called Newtown, but in August or September, 1786, the name was changed to Greensburg in honor of General Nathaniel Green. The settlement which was laid out in 1782 was incorporated as a borough in 1799 and chartered as a city in 1928. In 1785, Greensburg was selected as the county-seat of Westmoreland County. It is located in a coal and gas region and has manufactures of engines, glass, nuts, bolts and flour, etc. Population (1930), 16,508; (1920), 15, 033.

GREGG, DAVID, clergyman, was born in Pittsburgh, March 25, 1845. He was graduated from Washington and Jefferson College, in 1865; settled in Brooklyn, N. Y., in 1889, and became president of Western Theological Seminary in 1904-1909. He is the author of "Makers of the American Republic." He died October 11, 1919.

GREGG, DAVID McMURTIE, military officer, was born in Huntingdon, April 10, 1833, and was graduated from West Point in 1855. He was in expeditions against the Indians in Washington Territory and the State of Oregon (1858-1860). He was colonel of the 8th Pennsylvania Cavalry through the campaign in Virginia in 1862 and in November was brigadier-general of the volunteers. He commanded a division of the Army of the Potomac, 1862-1865, when he resigned. In August, 1864, he was brevetted major-general. He wrote "Second Cavalry Division of the Army of the Potomac in the Gettysburg Campaign." His death occurred August 7, 1916.

GREGORY, CASPAR RENE, scholar, was born in Philadelphia, in 1846. He was graduated from the Universities of Pennsylvania, Princeton, and Leipzig (1864-76), and has done important work in New Testament criticism and has been professor of New Testament exegesis in the theological faculty at Leipzig. In addition to translations of critical works from the German he has written "Les Cahiers des Manuscrits Grees" (1885), and the "Prolegomena to Tischendorf's Editio Octava Critica Major of the New Testament" (1893). He died April 9, 1917.

GRIER, ROBERT CASPER, jurist, was born in Cumberland County, March 5, 1794. He was graduated from Dickinson College in 1812, and became a justice of the United States Supreme Court from 1846 to his death. He died in Philadelphia, September 26, 1870.

GRIERSON, BENJAMIN HENRY, military officer, was born in Pittsburgh, July 8, 1826. He commanded the 6th Illinois Cavalry in the Civil War. In 1865, he was made major-general of volunteers and for his services in the war was brevetted major-general, United States Army, in March, 1867. He had been commissioned lieutenant-colonel of United States Cavalry in July, 1866. From 1868-1873, he was actively employed in campaigns against hostile Indians; and in 1873-1881 was similarly engaged in Western Texas and New Mexico. He was retired in 1890 and died in Omena, Mich., September 1, 1911.

GRIMSHAW, WILLIAM, author, was born in Greencastle, Ireland, in 1782, and came to the United States in 1815 settling in Philadelphia. He was the author of the "American Chesterfield," a school history of the United States, and the editor of a revised edition of Ramsay's "Life of Washington." He died in Philadelphia in 1852.

GROSS, SAMUEL D., physician, was born in Northampton County, July 8, 1805. He began the practice of medicine in Philadelphia, devoting his leisure to study and the translation of French and German medical works. In 1835, he became professor of pathological anatomy in the medical department of Cincinnati College, where he delivered the first systematic course of lectures on morbid anatomy that had ever been given in this country and composed the first systematic treatise upon the subject ever published in the United States. In 1840, he became professor of surgery in the University of Louisville. He wrote much on anatomy and surgery. He died May 6, 1884.

GROVE CITY, a borough in Mercer County, 58 miles north of Pittsburgh, originally called Pine Grove. The town was laid out in 1844 and 1845 and was incorporated as a borough in 1883. It is the seat of Grove City College. Its chief manufactures are brooms, gas engines and machinery. Population (1930), 6,156; (1920), 4,944.

GROVE CITY COLLEGE, a non-sectarian co-educational college, founded at Grove City, in 1876, as the Pine Grove Normal Academy. Enrollment (1930-1931), 790.

GROW, GALUSHA AARON, statesman, was born at Ashford (now Eastford), Windham County, Conn., August 31, 1822. He was graduated from Amherst College, in 1844, and was admitted to the bar of Susquehanna County, Pa., in 1847; was reelected to Congress in 1850, and was six times reelected, once unanimously, from the same district. During his first three terms he was a Free-Soil Democrat and during the last three a Republican. He introduced the Homestead Bill into the House, fought for it for ten years, finally obtained its enactment, and signed it as speaker. In 1879, he declined the mission to Russia; in 1894, he was elected from Pennsylvania as congressman-at-large, and was successfully reelected to the 54th, 55th, 56th, and 57th Congresses. He was also delegate to the National Republican Conventions of 1864, 1884, and 1892, and chairman of the Pennsylvania State Republican Committee in 1868. His long record of conspicuous service is almost unparalleled in the political annals of the United States. He died in 1907.

GRUBER, JACOB, itinerant Methodist minister, was born in Bucks County, February 3, 1778. At a conference of the Methodist Church, in 1800, he was appointed an itinerant minister subsequently serving circuits in northern Pennsylvania, western New York and Carlisle. From 1807-1810, he was presiding elder of the Greenbrier district, which included mountain sections of Virginia and North Carolina; in 1810, he became presiding elder of the Monongahela district which extended from Clarksburg, Va., to Armstrong County, Pa. The hardships which he endured on his trips through these wild and mountainous sections of the country were many and varied. Gruber served numerous other circuits until his death on May 25, 1850.

GUGGENHEIM, SIMON, legislator, was born in Philadelphia, December 30, 1867. He received a public school education, studied abroad, and engaged in the mining and smelting business in the United States and Mexico. In 1888, he removed to Colorado and was elected a Republican United States Senator for the term of 1907-1913. He became chairman of the Committee on the Philippines and a member of those on the Conservation of Natural Resources, Mines, and Mining, and Public Lands. The Guggenheim brothers were largely interested in the exploitation of the various mineral resources in Alaska. His home is in New York City.

GUNMAKERS—During the Revolution the Council of Safety had established a gun factory at Philadelphia. This factory was later moved to Allentown. Henry Derringer, an early settler at Easton, was the inventor of the Derringer pistol, in general use for duelling. Daniel Kleist conducted a gun shop in Bethlehem Township and made the rifles for the Moravian store at Bethlehem, which furnished many of them to troops passing through the town.

GUYASUTA, an Indian chief, generally called a chief of the Senecas, but probably of the mongrel Iroquois, known as the Mingoes, inhabiting the Allegheny Valley, and region to the west. He was one of the chiefs who accompanied Washington from Logstown to Fort LeBoeuf in 1753 and is referred to in Washington's Journal of that trip, as the Hunter. Some years later Wash-

GALUSHA A. GROW

ington with Guyasuta and two others made a journey down the Ohio Valley to examine the lands. Shortly after Braddock's defeat Guyasuta went over to the French, visited the governor of Canada, and remained near Montreal for an entire winter. He attended a Council at Fort Pitt, in July, 1759, another in 1768, and a third in 1776. In Pontiac's War and in the Revolution, Guyasuta figured prominently. After the war he lived in the neighborhood of Fort Pitt and became destitute. It is said that he died at Custaloga's Town, on French Creek, Mercer County. Guyasuta Station on the Pennsylvania Railroad near Sharpsburg, is named for him.

HAHNEMANN MEDICAL COLLEGE, at Philadelphia, was organized in 1867, an outgrowth of the Homeopathic Medical College of Philadelphia, with which it was later consolidated. It is probably the oldest college in the world which teaches the method of medical treatment originated by Samuel Hahnemann.

"HAIL COLUMBIA," a patriotic song, written in 1798, by Joseph Hopkinson, of Philadelphia, when war between the United States and France was impending. The song was first sung in a Philadelphia Theatre by Gilbert Fox, a young actor, and immediately gained universal popularity.

HALDEMAN, SAMUEL STEHMAN, naturalist, was born at Locust Grove, August 12, 1812. He attended a classical school at Harrisburg and Dickinson College. He was assistant to the state geologist of New Jersey, in 1836, and from 1837-1842 was a member of the Pennsylvania Survey. From 1851-1855, he was professor of Natural Sciences at the University of Pennsylvania and afterward held the same chair in Delaware College. He was professor of Comparative Philology at the University of Pennsylvania from 1869 to his death on September 10, 1880. Haldeman possessed an ear of such delicacy that he was enabled to determine forty varieties of vocal repertoire in the human voice. He is the author of "Fresh Water Univalve Molluska of the United States," "Analytical Orthography," "Zoological Contributions," "Elements of Latin Pronunciation," "Affixes in Their Origin and Application," "Rhymes of the Posts," "Pennsylvania Dutch," "Outlines of Etymology," etc.

HALE, CHARLES REUBEN, clergyman, was born in Lewistown, in 1837. He graduated from the University of Pennsylvania in 1858, and in 1892 became a bishop of the Protestant Episcopal Church. He wrote, among other things, "Universal Episcopate and the American Church and Methodism." His death occurred December 25, 1900, at Cairo, Ill.

HALE, SARAH JOSEPHA (BUELL), author and editor, was born in Newport, N. H., October 24, 1788. Following the death of her husband, David Hale, in 1822, she devoted her time to literature. She had charge of the Ladies' Magazine, published in Boston, from 1828-1837, and in the latter year when the publication merged with Godey's Lady's Book, in Philadelphia, Mrs. Hale became the editor. She was interested in the advancement of women's rights, particularly in greater educational advantages for women, and urged that Thanksgiving Day be made a national holiday, a suggestion that was carried out by President Lincoln in 1864. Among her writings are several poems: "The Light of Home"; "Mary's Lamb"; "It Snows," etc. She also wrote: "Woman's Record"; "Northwood"; "Sketches of American Character"; "Traits of American Life"; "Flora's Interpreter"; "The Ladies' Wreath"; "The Way to Live Well and to be Well While We Live"; "Dictionary of Poetical Quotations"; "The Judge, a Drama of American Life"; "The Bible Reading-Book," etc. Mrs. Hale died at Philadelphia, April 30, 1879.

HALKETT, SIR PETER, military officer, was born at Pitfirrane, Scotland. He commanded a regiment in the French and Indian War and with his son was killed at Braddock's Defeat, near Pittsburgh, July 9, 1755.

HALL, DAVID, printer, was born in Edinburgh, Scotland, in 1714. He came to America in 1747 and for a time was a partner of Benjamin Franklin in the printing business. Later he was a member of the firm of Hall and Sellers, which firm printed the colonial currency of Pennsylvania and the Continental money issued by Congress. He died in Philadelphia, December 24, 1772.

HALL, JAMES, military officer, was born at Carlisle, August 22, 1744. After graduation from Princeton in 1774, he became a minister in the Presbyterian Church. In 1778, he was appointed pastor of the Presbyterian Church at Bethany, N. C. During the Revolution he raised a troop of cavalry and served as commander and chaplain. He wrote "Report of a Missionary Tour Through the Mississippi and the Southwestern Country." He died at Bethany, N. C., July 25, 1826.

HALL, JAMES, lawyer, author, military officer, was born at Philadelphia, August 19, 1793. In 1812, he entered the army as a private and three years later received a commission. He served in the Battle of Chippewa at Fort Erie and in Decatur's expedition to Algiers on the United States brig Enterprise. He retired from the army in 1818 and was admitted to the bar. He moved to Illinois in 1820 and to Cincinnati in 1833. At different times he was editor of the "Illinois Gazette," the "Illinois Intelligencer," the "Illinois Monthly Magazine," and the "Western Monthly Magazine." He wrote the biographies of "Thomas Posey" and "Gen. W. H. Harrison;" "Notes in the Western States"; "History of the Indian Tribes"; "The Wilderness and the War Path," etc. He died July 5, 1868.

HALLOWELL, RICHARD PRICE, author and wool merchant, was born at Philadelphia, December 16, 1835. He was actively identified with the abolition movement and was appointed by Governor Andrew, of Massachusetts, to recruit negro regiments. He wrote "The Quaker Invasion of Massachusetts." He died at Medford, Mass., January 5, 1904.

HAMER, THOMAS LEWIS, military officer, was born in Pennsylvania about 1800. In 1821, he was admitted to the bar in Ohio and subsequently was a member of the Ohio Legislature and a representative in Congress. He participated in the Mexican War, rose to the rank of brigadier-general of volunteers and died December 2, 1846, of wounds received in the Battle of Monterey.

HAMILTON, ANDREW, lawyer, was born in Scotland about 1676. At one time he was known by the surname Trent. He opened a classical school in Accomac County, Virginia, about 1697; in 1716, he moved to Philadelphia and became attorney-general of Pennsylvania in 1717. He was a member of the provincial council from 1721-1724 and of the assembly from 1727-1739. In 1737, he was appointed judge of the Vice-Admiralty Court of Pennsylvania. He died at Philadelphia, August 4, 1741.

HAMILTON, ANDREW, deputy governor, under the proprietor William Penn, was formerly a proprietor of East Jersey and governor of East and West Jersey. On November 1, 1701, Penn finding it necessary to return to England because a bill for changing the proprietaryship to royal governors was before the British House of Lords, appointed Hamilton as his deputy and James Logan, Provincial Secretary and Clerk of the Council. Much opposition was made against Hamilton so Penn was compelled to remain near the court or have a representative there to explain charges brought to Queen Anne concerning the government of his colony. Hamilton attempted, without success, to unite the Territories and the Province. He also planned for the colony's defense by the organization of a military force. He died suddenly April 20, 1703.

HAMILTON, JOHN CHURCH, biographer and historian, was born at Philadelphia, in 1792, the son of Alexander Hamilton. He edited the works of his father and wrote: "Memoirs and Life of Alexander Hamilton," "History of the Republic," "The Prairie Province," "Sketches of Travel." He died in 1882.

HAMILTON, JOHN McLURE, painter, was born in Philadelphia, January 31, 1853. After studying in Philadelphia, Antwerp and Paris, he went to London, where he opened a studio. Hamilton attained greatest success in portraits and pastels. His principal works are: "Gladstone" (in Luxembourg Gallery); "Gladstone at Hawarden"; "Richard Vaux"; "Cardinal Manning"; "George Meredith," and "Henry Thonron" (in Pennsylvania Academy of Fine Arts); "Prof. Tyndall"; "Anslow Ford"; "Cosmo Monkhouse"; and "M. Ridley Corbet" (in National Portrait Gallery, London); "Prof. Lewis Campbell" (University of St. Andrews), and Portraits of Gen. Booth, Dr. Archibald Geikie,

Col. Edward House, Joseph Pennell, Charles M. Burnes, and Judge Alexander Simpson. His home is in Kingston-on-Thames, England.

HAMILTON, JOHN TAYLOR, Moravian clergyman, was born at Antigua, W. I., April 30, 1859. He graduated from Moravian College, Bethlehem, in 1875; from Moravian Theological Seminary, in 1877, and from 1881–1886 was pastor of the Second Moravian Church, Philadelphia. He was a member of the faculty at Moravian College and Theological Seminary from 1886–1903; president of Moravian College, 1918–1928, and president emeritus since 1928. In 1903, he became a member of the Moravian Mission Board, Herrnhut, Germany, and since 1905 has been missionary bishop of the Moravians. His writings include: "History of the Moravian Church in the United States" (American Church History Series); "A History of the Moravian Church During the Eighteenth and Nineteenth Centuries"; "A History of Moravian Missions"; "Twenty Years of Pioneer Missions in Nyasoland"; "The Recognition of the Episcopate of the Moravian Church by Act of Parliament in 1749." Hamilton resides at Bethlehem.

HANCOCK, WINFIELD SCOTT, soldier, was born at Montgomery Square, February 14, 1824. In 1844, he graduated from the United States Military Academy, after which he served with the Sixth Infantry on the frontier and participated in the Mexican War. During the Seminole War he was stationed at Fort Myers, Florida, and from 1859–1861 was chief quartermaster of the southern district of California. He was commissioned brigadier-general of volunteers at the opening of the Civil War and commanded a brigade in the Fourth Corps, Army of the Potomac. During the Battle of Antietam he was made commander of the First Division, Second Army Corps. In November, 1862, he was raised to the rank of major-general and with his division took part in the Battle of Fredericksburg and at Marye's Heights. After the Battle of Chancellorsville in which he distinguished himself, he became commander of the Second Corps. Gen. Meade ordered him to Gettysburg in July, 1863, to investigate it as a proper site for a battle. He commanded the left wing of the army and the left center in the ensuing battle, and on the second day was shot from his horse. Recovering from his wound he distinguished himself at the Battle of Spottsylvania where his command captured several thousand prisoners. In 1866, he was appointed major-general of the United States army; from 1866–1868, he commanded the departments of Missouri, Texas and Louisiana; 1868–1869, the military division of the Atlantic; 1869–1872, the department of Dakota and again in 1872 the division of the Atlantic. He was Democratic candidate for the presidency in 1880, but was defeated, by a narrow margin, by Garfield. He died at Governor's Island, New York Harbor, February 9, 1886.

HAND, EDWARD, soldier, was born at Clyduff, King's County, Ireland, December 31, 1744. He came to America in 1774 as surgeon's mate in the 18th

Royal Irish Regiment. Later he resigned and began the practice of medicine in Pennsylvania. He became a lieutenant-colonel at the opening of the Revolutionary War and took part in the siege of Boston. In 1777, he was made brigadier-general, in the following year commanded at Albany and took part in Sullivan's expedition. He was a member of Congress, 1784-1785, and was a signer of the Pennsylvania Constitution of 1790. He died at Rockford, Lancaster County, September 3, 1802.

HANOVER, borough in York County, about 32 miles south of Harrisburg, was settled about 1729 and incorporated in 1815. It is located near iron-ore mines in a rich farming section. Its manufactures are shoes, machine-shop products, cigars, gloves, flavin, auto truck bodies, furniture, etc. Population (1930), 11,805; (1920), 8,664.

HANOVER, BATTLE OF, an engagement of the Civil War; took place at Hanover, York County, June 30, 1863. Unknown to Gen. Meade, the Confederate cavalry, under Gen. Stuart, was encamped during the night of June 29th at Union Mills, a few miles south of Littlestown. Consequently, Gen. Kilpatrick, sent by Meade to Taneytown and Hanover to reconnoiter the position and determine the movements of Gen. Early, was surprised by a Confederate attack. The first conflict occurred a few miles west of Hanover, between Captain Freeland, with a small scouting party, and a small band of Confederates. On the morning of June 30th, a brigade of Confederates under Chambliss appeared on the hills on both sides of the Westminster Road and began an attack on the Eighteenth Pennsylvania Regiment passing through Pennville on its way to Hanover. Because of its position, the Pennsylvania Regiment was cut in two by the enemy, part of it being in the rear of Pennsville, the other part escaping through Hanover and out the Abbottstown Road, closely followed by the enemy. For a short time Hanover was in the possession of the Confederates. Upon learning of the proximity of Stuart's cavalry, Gen. Kilpatrick, riding at the head of his troops toward York, returned to Hanover. By that time the Confederates had been driven from the town, taking positions in the environs. A terrific artillery duel continued during the afternoon, after which the Confederates departed taking with them 1,000 York County horses, which they rode into the Battle of Gettysburg.

HARBAUGH, HENRY, clergyman, was born near Waynesboro, October 28, 1817. He attended Marshall College at Mercersburg and the Mercersburg Seminary. In 1843, he was ordained to the ministry of the German Reformed Church and subsequently held pastorates at Lewisburg, Lancaster and Lebanon. He was elected to the chair of theology at the Mercerburg Seminary in 1864. He edited the "Guardian" from 1850-1866, and the "Mercersburg Review," 1866-1867. He is the author of "Heaven," "Life of Michael Schlatter," "Christo-

WINFIELD SCOTT HANCOCK

logical Theology," and a collection of "Pennsylvania Dutch" poems. He died at Mercersburg, December 28, 1867.

HARE, JOHN INNES CLARK, jurist, was born in Philadelphia, October 17, 1817. He graduated from the University of Pennsylvania, in 1834; was admitted to the bar and eventually became an associate and presiding judge of the district court of Philadelphia and presiding judge of the Court of Common Pleas. He is the author of "American Constitutional Law," and edited "Smith's Leading Cases in Law," and "White and Tudor's Leading Cases in Equity." He died in 1905.

HARE, ROBERT, scientist, was born in Philadelphia, January 17, 1781. He engaged in private study of chemistry and in 1818 became professor of chemistry at William and Mary College. Later he was professor of the same subject at the University of Pennsylvania. Hare discovered the oxyhydrogen blowpipe which he called "hydrostatic blowpipe"; invented the valve-clock; the calorimeter demonstrated that foggy air is not a conductor of electricity, and built the first electric furnace. He was the Smithsonian Institute's first honorary member. He is the author of "Brief View of the Resources of the United States," "Chemical Apparatus and Manipulations," "Memoir on the Explosiveness of Nitre," etc. He died at Philadelphia, May 15, 1858.

HARK, JOSEPH MAXIMILIAN, clergyman, was born at Philadelphia, June 4, 1849. After graduation from Moravian College and Theological Seminary at Bethlehem he entered the ministry of the Moravian Church and held pastorates at Lebanon, Philadelphia and Lancaster. In 1893, he became principal of Moravian Seminary and College for Women at Bethlehem, which position he held until his retirement in 1909. Rev. Hark was one of the founders of the Pennsylvania-German Society and of the Pennsylvania Chatauqua. He wrote "The Unity of the Truth in Christianity and Evolution," and translated and edited "Chronicon Ephratense." His home is at Mt. Gretna.

HARLAN, JOHN, physician, was born at Philadelphia. In 1825, he sailed from Boston as surgeon apothecary of an East India merchant ship. He served throughout the British Burmese War and afterwards returned to India. He became a member of the court of Ranjit Singh, independent Sikh king of the Punjab and in 1827 was appointed governor of the province of Gujarat. Harlan was the only American to become a ruler in India and was the first to visit Afghanistan. Upon his return to the United States he made his home in New York. He died about 1850.

HARMONY, DAVID BUTTZ, naval officer, was born at Easton, September 3, 1832. He graduated from the United States Naval Academy and in 1889 became rear-admiral. During the Civil War as executive officer of the Iroquoisat he took part in the attacks on and passage of Forts Jackson and Saint Philip and in the capture of New Orleans, Vicksburg, Charleston and Mobile. He held various naval offices following the war and was retired June 26, 1893. He died at Washington, November 2, 1917.

HARMONISTS, a community, founded in 1787 by George Rapp, of Wurttemberg, Germany, on a religious and socialistic basis. In 1803, they were driven by persecution to America where they settled in the Connoquenessing Valley. Later they moved to Indiana and in 1825 returned to Pennsylvania and built Economy Township, Beaver County. The town of Beaver Falls, in Beaver County, owes its industrial prosperity to the Harmony Society. The organization held all property in common, believed in the second coming of Christ and practiced celibacy. Because of the latter practice the membership gradually dwindled until few members were left. The property is now in possession of the Pennsylvania Historical Commission.

HARRIS, JOHN, was the first permanent settler on the Susquehanna. He was a native of Yorkshire, England, but came to Philadelphia before 1698. In 1705, as an Indian trader, licensed by the province, he settled on the Susquehanna River, making a permanent residence on the present site of Harrisburg, where he purchased a large tract of land. He exerted a powerful influence over the Indians. His son, John, the founder of Harrisburg, figured prominently in Indian-Colonial affairs. John Harris, Sr., died in 1748, and is buried at the foot of a mulberry tree along Riverside Drive, where on one occasion he was about to be burned at the stake by drunken Indians whom he had refused rum, when friendly Indians intervened.

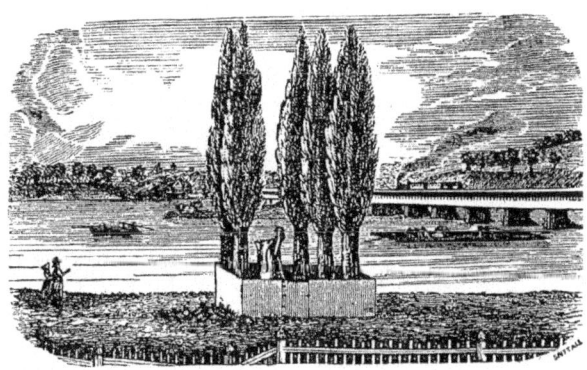

JOHN HARRIS' GRAVE, HARRISBURG (1843)

HARRIS, JOHN, founder of Harrisburg, was the son of John Harris, the first permanent white settler on the Susquehanna. In 1753, he received a grant from Thomas and Richard Penn, provincial proprietors, giving him the right to operate a ferry over the Susquehanna River. On December 17, 1733, the Proprietaries granted him three hundred acres of land on the site of which he founded a settlement early known as Harris' Ferry, now the city of Harrisburg.

HARRISBURG, city and county-seat of Dauphin County, and capitol of the state, is situated on the Susquehanna River, about 106 miles northwest of Philadelphia. The city is named for its founder, John Harris, whose father built the first house there in 1726. John Harris conducted a ferry in 1753 and for many years the settlement was known as Harris' Ferry. The town was laid out in 1785, incorporated as a borough in 1791, and chartered as a city in 1861. In 1812, Harrisburg became the capitol of the state. The capitol buildings stand upon an elevation and will include, when the present building project, inaugurated by ex-Governor Fisher, is completed, the main capitol building, dedicated in 1906, the museum (now used as library and museum), the North office building, South office building and Education building. The interior of the capitol building contains the mural paintings of Violet Oakley and other decorations depicting the development of cilivilization in America and the history of Pennsylvania.

Harrisburg's industries include the manufacture of iron and steel, machinery, boilers, castings, brooms, cars, lumber, cotton goods, beds, mattresses, coffins, silk goods, etc. Here also are located the repair shops of the Pennsylvania Railroad, nearby at Rutherford, those of the Reading Railroad, rolling mills, tin mills, nail works, blast furnaces, typewriter works and shoe factories. Population (1930), 80,339; (1920), 75,917.

HARRISBURG CONVENTION. On September 3, 1788, a meeting of anti-Federalists of Pennsylvania was held at Harrisburg to confer concerning the new Federal constitution. Resolutions were adopted that twelve amendments to the Federal constitution be presented in petition form to the Pennsylvania Legislature but the petition was never formally presented. In 1828, a second convention was held at Harrisburg, when the anti-protectionists of New England and Middle States met to consider the rejection of the high tariff "Woolen Bill" in the Senate.

HARRISBURG TELEGRAPH, THE, was founded as the *Pennsylvania Telegraph*, in September, 1831, by Theophilus Fenn, succeeding the *Statesman Anti-Masonic Republican*, founded in 1828, by John McCord. In November, 1853, it was sold to John J. Patterson, who consolidated it with the *Whig State Journal*, founded in 1850, by John J. Clyde. It was also consolidated with the *Harrisburg Daily American*, founded in December, 1850, by George Bergner and Company, and the *Daily Times*, founded in 1853, by William H. Egle, later

HARRISBURG FROM THE WEST SHORE OF THE SUSQUEHANNA RIVER (1843)

State Librarian, and Theodore F. Scheffner. The paper is now owned by the Telegraph Printing Company, of which E. J. Stackpole is president and editor-in-chief. It was originally issued weekly, and during the sessions of the Legislature, semi-weekly. Since 1856, it has appeared daily. The publication was known successively as *The Pennsylvania Telegraph*, *The Daily Telegraph*, and the *Pennsylvania Daily Telegraph*. It adopted the present name in 1860. During the Civil War period the *Telegraph* was loyal to the cause of the Union, and was issued twice daily. Originally adhering to the policies of the Whig Party, the publication later became a staunch supporter of the Republican Party. It has a circulation of 47,894, the largest home circulation of any daily paper in southern Pennsylvania.

HARRISBURG AND PRESQUE ISLE COMPANY, was organized in 1796 for "settling, improving and populating the country near and adjoining to Lake Erie."

HARRISON, GABRIEL, author and artist, was born at Philadelphia, March 25, 1825. At an early age he became a photographer and actor. Later he taught elocution and was a dramatic and art critic. He wrote "Life of Howard Payne" and a dramatization of "The Scarlet Letter." He exerted notable influence over art education in the public schools of Brooklyn, N. Y. He died December 15, 1902.

HARRISON, JOSEPH, engineer, was born at Philadelphia, September 20, 1810. He began the construction of locomotives in 1834 and in 1840 built an engine for the Reading Railroad Company that was eventually introduced into Russia, and received with such popularity there that Harrison was invited to Russia and with other American engineers contracted with the Russian government for the building of the rolling-stock and locomotives of the Saint Petersburg and Moscow Railroad. Following his return to America in 1852 he patented a safety-boiler. He published "The Locomotive Engine" and a work containing his autobiography, accounts of his experiences in Russia and a poem "The Ironworker and King Solomon." He died at Philadelphia, March 27, 1874.

HARRISON, LOVELL BERGE, artist, was born at Philadelphia, October 28, 1854. He studied in Paris under Alexander Cabanel and attained success as a landscape painter and in particular in the painting of snow scenes. Among his works are: "Friends or Foes "; "A Waif from the Sea"; "Calling Home the Cows;" "November" (purchased by the French government for the Marseilles Museum); "Fifth Avenue at Twilight."

HARRISON, THOMAS ALEXANDER, painter, was born at Philadelphia, January 17, 1853, a brother of Lovell Berge Harrison. He studied at the Ecole des Beaux Arts, Paris; was awarded the gold medal by the Pennsylvania Academy of Fine Arts, in 1894, and elected an associate of the National Academy in 1898. His works include "Coast of Brittany," "Little Slave," "The Sea-Shore."

HARRISON, THOMAS SKELTON, diplomat and manufacturer, was born at Philadelphia, September 19, 1837. He was educated at private schools and business colleges. From 1861 to 1864, he was acting paymaster of the United States Navy and from 1864-1897 was a member of the firm of Harrison Brothers and Company. He was influential in political reform movements in Philadelphia; was a member of the Committee of 100, and of many historical and antiquarian societies. In 1897, he received the appointment of diplomatic agent and consul-general to Egypt and was twice decorated by Khidive of Egypt. His death occurred May 3, 1919.

HART, ALBERT BUSHNELL, historian and educator, was born at Clarksville, July 1, 1854. He was educated at Harvard where he received the A.B. degree in 1880, and at the University of Freiburg, Baden, Germany, where he received the Ph.D. degree in 1883. Since that year he has been successively instructor of American history, instructor of history, assistant professor of history, professor of history, professor of government and professor emeritus at Harvard University. Among his writings are: "Guide to the Study of American History" (with Edward Channing and later with Channing and F. J. Turner); "Foundations of American Foreign Policy"; "Essentials of American History"; "Slavery and Abolition"; "New American History"; "Monroe Doctrine"; "School History of the United States"; "America at War." He edited "Epochs of American History" (4 vols.); "American History Told by Contemporaries" (5 vols.); "American Citizen Series" (7 vols.); "Source Book of American History"; "American Patriots and Statesmen" (5 vols.), etc. His home is in Cambridge, Mass.

HARTRANFT, CHESTER DAVID, educator, was born in Pennsylvania, October 15, 1839. He graduated from the University of Pennsylvania in 1861, and from New Brunswick Theological Seminary in 1864. Entering the ministry of the Dutch Reformed Church he became pastor of churches at South Bushwick, N. Y., and New Brunswick, N. J. In 1879, he became professor of Ecclesiastical History at Hartford Theological Seminary, was elected president of that institution in 1888 and at different times taught Biblical theology and ecclesiastical dogmatics there. He also served as president of the Conservatory of Music at New Brunswick, N. J. In 1903, he resigned the presidency of Hartford Theological Seminary. He died December 30, 1914.

HARTRANFT, JOHN FREDERICK, soldier and governor, was born at New Hanover, December 16, 1830. After graduating from Union College, in 1853, he was admitted to the bar. At the opening of the Civil War he became colonel of the 51st Pennsylvania Regiment which he organized, and took part in

Burnside's Expedition to North Carolina in 1862, and in the Battles at Antietam and Fredericksburg. He was in command of a division of the Ninth Corps in an attack on Fort Steadman and was subsequently brevetted major-general. In 1865, he was elected auditor-general of Pennsylvania and was reelected in 1868. In 1872, he was elected to the governorship of Pennsylvania and reorganized the state militia of which he became commander in 1879. He died at Norristown, October 17, 1889.

HARWOOD, ANDREW ALLEN, naval officer, was born at Settle, in 1802, a great-grandson of Benjamin Franklin. He entered the navy in 1818 and was successful in suppressing the slave trade and piracy in the West Indies. In 1855, he was promoted to captain and in 1862 was appointed chief of the Bureau of Ordnance and Hydrography. In 1862 with the rank of commodore, he was appointed to the command of the Washington Navy Yard and Potomac flotilla. He retired in 1869 with the rank of rear-admiral. Harwood wrote "Law and Practice of United States Navy Courts-Martial" and "Summary Courts-Martial." He died at Marion, Mass., August 28, 1884.

HASKINS, CHARLES HOMER, educator, was born at Meadville, December 21, 1870. He received the A.B. and Ph.D. degrees at Johns Hopkins University and subsequently was instructor of history there. In 1890, he joined the faculty of the University of Wisconsin, first as instructor of history, then as assistant professor of history and finally as professor of European history. From 1902-1912, he was professor of history at Harvard; from 1912 to date, Gurney professor of history and political science there and from 1908-1924, dean of the Graduate School of Arts and Sciences. He served in 1918-1919 as chief of the division of western Europe of the American Peace Commission and in 1919 as American member of the Commission on Belgian and Danish affairs and on a special commission on Alsace-Lorraine and the Saar Valley at the Paris Peace Conference. He is the author of: "The Normans in European History"; "Norman Institutions"; "Some Problems of the Peace Conference" (with R. H. Lord); "The Rise of Universities"; "Studies in the History of Medieval Science"; "The Renaissance of the Twelfth Century"; and is editor of the American Historical Series. His home is in Cambridge, Mass.

HASTINGS, DANIEL HARTMAN, governor, was born in Lamar Township, Clinton County, February 26, 1849. He began to teach school before he was fifteen and in 1867 took charge of the Bellefonte Academy. Later, he was for seven years principal of the public schools of Bellefonte and editor of the *Bellefonte Republican*. Subsequently he studied law and was admitted to the bar in 1875. His interests turning to coal mining he engaged in that business at Hastings, Cambria County. At the time of the Johnstown Flood he was Adjutant-General of the State and assumed the supervision of relief work. In 1895, he became governor of Pennsylvania having been elected in the previous

DANIEL H. HASTINGS (245)

year with the greatest majority in the history of gubernatorial elections. He died at Bellefonte, January 9, 1903.

HAUPT, HERMAN, engineer, was born at Philadelphia, March 26, 1817. In 1855, he graduated from West Point, became a civil engineer and was connected with the construction of the public works of Pennsylvania. Later he was professor of civil engineering and mathematics at Pennsylvania College and in 1847 was consulting engineer of the Philadelphia Railroad. He was chief engineer of the Hoosac Tunnel and served as chief of the United States Bureau of Military Railroads during the Civil War. He invented a drilling machine and discovered a method for the transportation and distribution of oil from the well. He wrote "Hints on Bridge Building," "General Theory of Bridge Construction," "A Consideration of the Plans Proposed for the Improvement of the Ohio River," and "Military Bridges." He died December 14, 1905.

HAUPT, LEWIS MUHLENBERG, engineer, was born at Gettysburg, March 21, 1844. He was educated at Harvard University and West Point; was professor of civil engineering at the University of Pennsylvania, 1872-1892, and edited the "Engineering Register." He served as a member of the Nicaraguan and Isthmian Canal Commission, 1897-1902. He is the author of "Engineering Specifications and Contracts," "Canals and Their Economic Relation to Transportation," "A Move for Better Roads," "The Transportation Crisis," "The Nation and the Waterways," "Mississippi River Problems," "The New York Entrance," etc. He invented the "Reaction Breakwater," for creating channels through ocean bars and has received awards from the American Philosophical Society, Paris Exposition of 1900, National Export Exposition, the Elliott Cresson gold medal from Franklin Institute, and gold and silver medals from the St. Louis Exposition, 1904. Haupt's home is at Bala-Cynwyd.

HAVERFORD COLLEGE, for men, was founded in 1833, at Haverford, It was the first institution of collegiate standing in this country, founded and controlled by the Society of Friends. After 1849 others than the sons of Friends were admitted. The college offers courses leading to the A.B., B.S., and M.A. degrees. Enrollment (1930-1931), 300.

HAWKINS, ALEXANDER LEROY, soldier, was born in Washington County, September 5, 1842. After attending George's Creek Academy and Waynesburg College, he taught for several years in the township schools. On August 30, 1862, he enlisted in Company K, 15th Regiment, Pennsylvania Cavalry, which regiment was active in the defense of Chambersburg. In 1864, he attained the rank of lieutenant and in 1865 was made captain of the colored troops at Nashville Barracks. Upon his return from the army, in 1865, he entered the drug business in Pittsburgh, subsequently returning to Washington where he became actively engaged in the reorganization of the 10th Regiment,

Pennsylvania National Guards, of which he became colonel. He led this regiment against the rioters in Pittsburgh, in 1877; in the strike at Homestead, in 1892; and in the Philippines during the Spanish-American War. He died on board the transport, Senator, en route from Tokohana to the United States, July 18, 1899.

HAYES, ISAAC, physician and editor, was born at Philadelphia, July 5, 1796. He graduated from the University of Pennsylvania, in 1816, and from the Medical School of that institution in 1820. He engaged in the practice of his profession in Philadelphia and for 52 years was a member of the staff of the "American Journal of the Medical Service." In 1843, he established the "Medical News," a monthly, and in 1874 the "Monthly Abstract of Medical Science." He edited "Wilson's American Ornithology," "Hoblyn's Dictionary of Medical Terms," "Lawrence on Diseases of the Eye," "Arnott's Elements of Physics." From 1865-1869, he was president of the Philadelphia Academy of Natural Sciences. He died at Philadelphia, April 12, 1879.

HAYES, ISAAC ISRAEL, arctic explorer, was born in Chester County, March 5, 1832. In 1852, he graduated from the Medical School of the University of Pennsylvania. He was surgeon in the second Grinnell expedition sent out under Captain Kane in 1853, in search of Franklin. In 1860, he sailed on a second expedition and reached the farthest point north ever recorded. He made a voyage to Greenland in 1869. The geographical societies of Paris and London presented him with gold medals. The accounts of his explorations are recorded in the following of his publications: "An Arctic Boat Journey," "The Open Polar Sea," "Cast Away in the Cold," "The Land of Desolation." Hayes died December 17, 1881.

HAZARD, EBENEZER, author, was born at Philadelphia, January 15, 1744. In 1762, he graduated from Princeton University. From 1782-1789, he was postmaster-general. In 1791, he engaged in business in Philadelphia and was instrumental in the establishment of the North American Insurance Company. His publications include: "Historical Collections" and "Remarks on a Report Concerning Western Indians." He died June 13, 1817, at Philadelphia.

HAZARD'S REGISTER OF PENNSYLVANIA, containing miscellaneous news of state wide interest, edited by Samuel Hazard, was established January 5, 1828, and continued until December 26, 1835. This periodical, published at Philadelphia, is historically valuable.

HAZLETON, city in Luzerne County, about 24 miles south of Wilkes-Barre, was laid out in 1820, incorporated as a borough in 1840 and received a city charter in 1890. Because of its location in a coal region, mining is the chief industry. Its manufactures are foundry and machine-shop products, paper boxes, shirts, underwear, cigars, coffins and caskets, knit goods, silk, etc. A state hospital for miners is located here. Population (1930), 36,765; (1920), 32,277.

HEATON, AUGUSTUS GOODYEAR, artist, was born at Philadelphia, April 28, 1844. He studied under Cabanel at the Paris Beaux Arts, and was the first pupil from the United States to study there. Some of his paintings are: "Washington at Fort Duquesne"; "The Recall of Columbus," engraved on the fifty cent World's Columbian Exposition stamp of 1893; "Hardships of Emigration," engraved on the ten cent Omaha Fair stamp; and portraits of Bishop Bowman and Paul Tulane. He wrote: "The Heart of David, the Psalmist King," "Fancies and Thoughts in Verse," and "Coinage of the United States Branch Mints." His home is at West Palm Beach, Fla.; his summer home at Black Mountain, N. C.

HEBRON MORAVIAN CHURCH—In the beginning of the eighteenth century leaders of the Moravian Church from Saxony and Moravia, Germany, learning of the religious needs of the German settlers in Pennsylvania, came to this country as missionaries. Their leaders were scholars and noblemen like Spangenberg, Boehler, Lembke, Cammerhof and Zinzendorf. After a time their influence centered about Bethlehem and the present city of Lebanon. Near Lebanon they surveyed and laid out a town which they called Hebron, and which is now a part of Lebanon. Here in 1751 they built a stone church which was used for worship until 1848. During the French and Indian War the Hebron Church was used by settlers as a place of refuge from Indian attack and during the Revolution as powder magazine, hospital and prison, where many Hessians were quartered.

HECKEWELDER, JOHN GOTTLIEB ERNEST, Moravian missionary, was born at Bedford, England, March 12, 1743. When he was twelve years old he came to Pennsylvania with his father. In 1762, he was with Post on his expedition to the Indians on the Ohio and in 1771 he became a missionary to them. After more than forty years of missionary service he joined the Moravian settlement at Bethlehem. He wrote: "Account of the History, etc., of the Indian Nations," and "Narrative of the Mission of the United Brethren." He died at Bethlehem, January 21, 1823.

HEILPRIN, ANGELO, naturalist, was born at Satoralja-Ujhely, Hungary, March 31, 1853. In 1856, he came to America with his parents. He was educated in Europe where he specialized in natural history. From 1880-1900, he was professor of invertebrate palaeontology and geology at the Academy of Natural Sciences, Philadelphia, and from 1883-1891 was executive curator there. He was professor of geology at Wagner Free Institute from 1885 to 1890 and president of the Geographical Society of Philadelphia for five years. In 1892, he was leader of the Peary Relief Foundation and in 1902 investigated the cause of the Mont Pelee disaster. He published among other works: "Contributions to the Tertiary Geology and Palaeontology of the United States," "The Lesson of the Philadelphian Rocks," "Geographical and Geological Distribution of Animals," "The Animal Life of Our Seashore," "The Arctic Problem and Narrative of the Peary Relief Expedition," "Mont Pelee and the Tragedy of Martinique." He died in New York City, July 17, 1907.

HEINTZELMAN, SAMUEL PETER, military officer, was born at Manheim, September 30, 1805. He graduated from the United States Military Academy, in 1826; served during the Mexican War and during the Civil War; was in the Battle of Bull Run, where he was wounded. Subsequently he rose to the rank of brigadier-general of volunteers and in March, 1862, commanded the 3rd army corps of the Army of the Potomac. He served in the second battle of Bull Run in August, 1862, and later was in command at Washington. In May and July, 1863, during the Battles of Chancellorsville and Gettysburg, he commanded the Department of Washington and the 22nd Army Corps. He retired in 1869 with rank of major-general, and died at Washington, D. C., May 1, 1880.

HELM, ISRAEL, a Swedish colonist in America, was born in 1615. In 1649, he settled along the Delaware River. He was collector of Customs at Philadelphia in 1659 and as an interpreter was of great assistance at the meeting of New Jersey Indians, Governor Andros and Swedish authorities in 1675. He died in 1695.

HELMUTH, WILLIAM TODD, physician, was born at Philadelphia, October 30, 1833. After graduating from Homeopathic Medical College, Philadelphia, and Hahnemann College, San Francisco, he became professor of surgery and dean of the New York Homeopathic College and Hospital. He published: "Treatise on Diphtheria," "Scratches of a Surgeon," "Suprapubic Lithotomy," and several volumes of poetry. He died in New York, May 15, 1902.

HENDERSON, CHARLES HANFORD, educator and author, was born at Philadelphia, December 30, 1861. He graduated from the University of Pennsylvania in 1882 and received the Ph.D. degree at the University of Zurich in 1892. He was a lecturer at the Franklin Institute, 1883-1885; lecturer on education at Harvard, 1897-1898; director of Pratt Institute H. S., Brooklyn, 1898-1900; headmaster, Marienfeld Summer School, Chesham, N. H., 1896-1912. He is the author of "Elements of Physics," "Education and the Larger Life," "What Is It To Be Educated?", etc. His home is at Chesham, N. H.

HENRI, ROBERT, painter, was born in Cincinnati, Ohio, in 1865. He became an instructor in the Philadelphia School of Design and later exhibited in Paris where he maintained a studio. He attained success as a landscape and portrait painter. Among his paintings are "The Equestrian," Carnegie Art Institute, Pittsburgh; "Girl with Fan," Pennsylvania Academy, Philadelphia; "Himself" and "Herself," studies of Irish types were exhibited at the Pennsylvania Academy in 1914. Henri died July 12, 1929.

HERING, CONSTANTIN, physician, was born at Oschatz, Germany, January 1, 1800. He studied at the University of Leipzig and at the University of Wurzburg, where he graduated in medicine in 1826. He became instructor in mathematics and natural sciences in Blochmann's Institute, Dresden, and was later appointed by the King of Saxony director of the zoological department of an expedition to Surinam. Hering advocated the homeopathic doctrines of medicine originated by Hahnemann. In 1833, he came to America going to Philadelphia where his former pupil Dr. George Bute had already introduced homeopathy. In 1835, Dr. Hering became president of a homeopathic academy at Allentown, known as the North American Academy of the Homeopathic Healing Art. Owing to financial difficulties the academy was not long in existence and Dr. Hering returned to Philadelphia and resumed his practice. He died July 23, 1880.

HERING, RUDOLPH, hydraulic and sanitary engineer, was born in Philadelphia, February 26, 1847. In 1867, he graduated from the Polytechnic School, Dresden, Germany. He became assistant engineer of Prospect Park, Brooklyn, N. Y., in 1868; from 1869-1871 was assistant engineer at Fairmount Park, Philadelphia, and in 1872 was astronomer at Yellowstone National Park. Later he engaged in private work and designed many plans for sewerage disposals and water supplies for many cities and towns in the United States, Canada and South America.

HERMITS OF THE WISSAHICKON, a group of German pietists, tending toward mysticism, came to Pennsylvania in 1694 and settled near the Wissahickon. Shortly before their embarkation their leader, Rev. John Jacob Zimmerman, died at Rotterdam. The remainder of the party, including Zimmerman's family, went to London, where they remained until February, 1694, when they began the journey to America under the leadership of John Kelpius.

HERON, MATILDA, actress, was born at Droperstown, near Londonderry, Ireland, December 1, 1830. She made her first appearance on the stage in Philadelphia in 1851 as Bianca in "Fazio." She was particularly successful as Camille in "La Dame aux Camelias," and as Ulah in "De Soto." She appeared in leading Canadian and United States cities and was in London in 1861. She died in New York, March 7, 1877.

HERR, HANS, religious leader, was born near Zurich, Switzerland, September 17, 1639, and died in Lancaster County, in 1725. He joined the Mennonite Church and became a preacher in that denomination. In 1709, he with

JOHANNES KELPIUS

the Mennonites bought 10,000 acres on the south side of Pequea Creek, and led the Mennonite migration to that place.

HERRON, FRANCIS JAY, soldier, was born at Pittsburgh, February 17, 1837. He graduated from Western University of Pennsylvania (now University of Pittsburgh), in 1854. At the opening of the Civil War he commanded the Governor's Grays in the First Iowa Regiment; he was commissioned lieutenant-colonel of the Ninth Iowa Regiment in 1861 and brigadier-general of volunteers in 1862. He was with Grant at Vicksburg in 1863 and later captured Yazoo City; commanded the Thirteenth Army Corps and received the surrender of the Confederates west of the Mississippi in June, 1865. From 1873 until his death on January 8, 1902, he practiced law in New York.

HERSHEY, MILTON SNAVELY, manufacturer, was born in Derry Township, Dauphin County, September 13, 1857. In 1893, he began the manufacture of chocolate at Lancaster. Later he moved to Derry Township, Dauphin County, where he established the Hershey Chocolate Company, and founded the town of Hershey. He is now chairman of the board of the company, which has fifteen subsidiary companies in the United States and Cuba, and is the owner of most of its stock. In 1905, he founded the Hershey Industrial School for orphan boys, to which institution in 1918 he donated his entire fortune as a trust for the school's maintenance. His home is at Hershey.

HERSHEY, a model industrial town, in Derry Township, Dauphin County, was founded in 1903 by M. S. Hershey, chocolate manufacturer. The town is carefully planned and contains a department store, hospital, banks, theatres, and a large amusement park, with swimming pool, dance floor, golf course, playgrounds, amusements and zoological gardens. The Hershey Chocolate factory, modern in every detail, employs about twenty-five hundred workers. The Hershey Industrial School, founded by Mr. Hershey and his wife, for orphan boys, is located a short distance south of the town.

HESSELIUS, GUSTAVUS, the first organ builder in America, was born in Sweden, but spent most of his life in Philadelphia. In 1746, he built a pipe organ for the Moravians at Bethlehem. John G. Klemm, a native of Dresden, Saxony, who was in his employ, continued to build organs after the death of Hesselius in May, 1755.

HESSIANS—During the American Revolution, the English, having insufficient troops, hired soldiers from German provinces. Most of them came from the province of Hesse and were accordingly called Hessians. They participated in the Battles of Long Island and White Plains, at Fort Washington, Trenton, in Burgoyne's expedition, at Philadelphia, Germantown, Guilford Court House and Yorktown. A great many of the 29,867 who came to America, never returned. Some were killed or died of wounds but the greatest number settled among the German people of Pennsylvania, and intermarried with those from other sections of their native country. The diary of the Hebron Moravian Church, where many Hessians were held prisoners, gives an interesting account of them, their characteristics, etc.

HIBERNIAN SOCIETY, organized in Philadelphia for the purpose of encouraging emigration from Ireland, received a charter April 27, 1792. The organization was actively engaged in the assistance of emigrants.

HICKS, THOMAS, painter, was born at Newtown, October 18, 1823. He studied at the Philadelphia Academy, at the National Academy at New York and under Conture in Paris. He opened a studio in New York and became popular as a portrait painter. He died in 1890.

HIESTER, JOSEPH, governor, was born in Bern Township, Berks County, November 18, 1752. After his marriage in 1771, he removed to Reading where he entered the mercantile business with his father-in-law. In June, 1776, he represented the Whig Party at the state conference which met in Philadelphia to frame a new constitution for Pennsylvania. As captain of militia, Hiester, in 1775, organized a volunteer company and marched to the assistance of Washington at Long Island. In the Battle of Long Island many of Hiester's men were killed or wounded. The remaining, and Hiester himself, were taken as prisoners. After several months of imprisonment, Hiester was exchanged and returned to Reading. Later, he returned to the army and participated in the Battle of Germantown, where he was wounded. He was a member of the convention which met at Philadelphia, in 1787, for the ratification of the Constitution of the United States and in 1789 was a member of the convention which framed the state constitution of 1790. He was a member of the Legislature for several years and in 1799 succeeded his uncle, Daniel Hiester, as representative in Congress, in which body he served for fourteen years. In December, 1820, he was elected governor of Pennsylvania and served the three-year term. He retired from public office at the expiration of his term and died June 10, 1832.

HIGBEE, ELNATHAN ELISHA, educator, was born at St. George, near Burlington, Vt., March 27, 1830. At fifteen years of age he entered the freshman class of the University of Vermont. After graduation he taught in an academy at South Woodstock, Vt. In 1851 or 1852, he entered the Theological Seminary of the Reformed Church at Mercersburg. After graduation he was assistant teacher in the high school at Lancaster, and in 1854 was licensed to preach by the Maryland Classis of the Reformed Church, accepting a call to the Congregational Church at Bethel, Vt. In 1858, he returned to Maryland and in 1859 became pastor of the First Reformed Church of Tiffin, Ohio. In connection with his work there he taught Latin and Greek in Heidelberg College. In 1862, he became pastor of Grace Church, Pittsburgh. May 3, 1864, he became professor of Church History and New Testament Exegesis in the Theological Seminary of the Reformed Church at Mercersburg. In 1881, he was appointed state superintendent of Public Instruction of Pennsylvania upon the recommendation of State Senator John Stewart, of Franklin County, entering upon his duties April 1st. He was reappointed by Governor Pattison in 1885, but was removed by the Governor the following year because of a controversy over the management of the Soldiers' Orphan Schools. The Supreme Court, however, decided that the Governor may not dismiss the Superintendent of Public Instruction, and he was reappointed by Governor Beaver in 1889. He died December 13, 1889. He introduced Arbor Day into Pennsylvania.

HIGH DUTCH PENNSYLVANIA HISTORIOGRAPHER, THE, or Collection of Important Intelligence from the Kingdom of Nature and the Church, was issued by Christopher Sauer, printer, of Germantown, on August 20, 1739. The journal contained foreign and domestic news, was issued quarterly, later monthly and eventually became a weekly under the name "Der Germantauner Zeitung." Sauer made his own printer's ink and it is said cast the type for this publication.

HILL, DAVID JAYNE, educator and diplomat, was born at Plainfield, N. J., June 10, 1850. He was professor of Rhetoric at Bucknell University from 1877–1879, and president of the institution from 1879–1888. From 1898–1903 he was first assistant secretary of State; 1903–1905, minister to Switzerland; 1905–1908, minister to the Netherlands; 1908–1911, minister to Germany. Among his publications are biographies of Washington Irving and William Cullen Bryant, "Elements of Rhetoric," "Elements of Psychology," "Principles and Fallacies of Socialism," "The Contemporary Development of Diplomacy," etc. Hill lives in Washington, D. C.

HILLEGAS, HOWARD CLEMENS, journalist and author, was born at Pennsburg, December 30, 1872. In 1894, he graduated from Franklin and Marshall College. He was war correspondent of the New York World in South Africa, 1899–1900, having previously been a member of the staffs of various Pennsylvania publications. He wrote: "Oom Paul's People," "The Boers in War," and "With the Boer Forces." He died January 29, 1918.

HILPRECHT, HERMAN VOLRATH, Assyriologist, was born at Hohenerxleben, Germany, July 28, 1859. After his graduation from the University of Leipzig, in 1883, he became curator of the Semitic section of the museum of the University of Pennsylvania. He presented the museum with most of the original cuneiform inscriptions in its possession. From 1886 to 1911, he was professor of Assyrian and comparative Semitic philology at the University of Pennsylvania. He was Assyriologist and scientific director of the University's expedition to Nippur, Babylonia, in 1888-1889. Later he traveled in Asia Minor, Syria, Ceylon, India, China, Japan and Korea. He studied Assyrian inscriptions in the British Museum and became an authority on cuneiform inscriptions. From 1893-1909, he was in Constantinople where he reorganized the Babylonian department of the Imperial Ottoman Museum. His publications include: "History of the Babylonian Expedition of the University of Pennsylvania to Nippur," "Old Babylonian Inscriptions Chiefly from Nippur," and "Explorations in Bible Lands During the 19th Century."

HIMMELSBRIEF, or letter of Jesus Christ, is an admonition to sinful man to repent, and is believed by the superstitious, to have been written by Christ or by the archangel Michael. Copies of Himmelsbrief have been found in Philadelphia, Lehigh, Berks, Montgomery, Carbon, Lebanon, Lancaster and York Counties. They are of different types and have been classified as the Meckelburg letter, printed in 1725, by Heinrich Kapp; the St. Germain letter, the letter of which is followed by 88 lines of exhortative and devotional poetry; the Magdeburg letter, elaborately ornamented with two flying angels, a standing Christ and two eyes with balances; the Holsteiner letter, and the Himmelsbrief of 1815. Dr. E. M. Fogel, of the University of Pennsylvania who has made a study of the Himmelsbrief, believes that all the letters bear relation to the old heathen Zauber or Segens-formel (pow-wowing formula). The difference between the two is that the pow-wowing formula is used to combat or cure disease or effect a charm while the Himmelsbrief is used to ward off hell, disease and disaster.

HISTORICAL SOCIETY OF PENNSYLVANIA—See PENNSYLVANIA HISTORICAL SOCIETY.

HITTELL, THEODORE HENRY, historian, was born at Marietta, April 5, 1830. He was admitted to the bar in Cincinnati, in 1852, and three years later moved to San Francisco where he was connected with the "Bulletin and Times" until 1862, after which he practiced law. From 1880-1882, he was a state senator. He is the author of "History of California," "The General Laws of California," "Review of Goethe's Faust," "Adventures of James Copen Adams—California Grizzly Bear Hunter."

HOBART, JOHN HENRY, Protestant Episcopal bishop, was born at Philadelphia, September 14, 1775. He attended the College of Philadelphia (now University of Pennsylvania) and the College of New Jersey (now Princeton). He was ordained deacon in 1798 and priest in 1801. After serving pastorates in Pennsylvania, New Jersey and Long Island, he became assistant in Trinity Parish, New York. In 1811, he was consecrated bishop-coadjutor of the diocese of New York and in 1816 became rector of Trinity Church. Hobart College, which he supported, is named for him. He also aided in establishing the General Theological Seminary and was at one time professor of pastoral theology there. Among his works are: "Companion for the Festivals and Fasts" and "Apology for Apostolic Order." He died at Auburn, N. Y., September 10, 1830.

HODGE, CHARLES, Presbyterian theologian, was born in Philadelphia, December 28, 1797. In 1815, he graduated from Princeton University where he later studied at the Theological Seminary. He became an instructor at Princeton, in 1820, and professor of Oriental and Biblical literature there in 1820. In 1840, he was made professor of didactic and exegetical theology in the seminary, and later he was appointed to the chair of polemical theology. He founded the Biblical Repertory which later merged in the Presbyterian Quarterly and American Theological Review. In 1872, the Charles Hodge professorship with an endowment of $50,000, was founded in his honor. His writings include: "Princeton Theological Essays" and "Essays and Reviews" (compilations of his contributions to the Review), "Commentary on the Epistle of the Romans," "Constitutional History of the Presbyterian Church in the United States," "The Way of Life," "Systematic Theology," and "What is Darwinism?" He died at Princeton, N. J., June 19, 1878.

HOFF, WILLIAM BAINBRIDGE, naval officer, was born at Philadelphia, in 1846. In 1863, he entered the naval service and during the Civil War served in several naval campaigns. He was marine commissioner to Great Britain for the World's Fair at Chicago in 1893 and was retired in 1897. He wrote: "Elementary Naval Tactics" and "Avoidance of Collisions at Sea." He died at Washington, D. C., May 23, 1903.

HOFFMAN, WALTER JACOB, physician, explorer and scientist, was born in Lowhill Township, Lehigh County, May 30, 1846. After his graduation from Jefferson Medical College he practiced his profession in Reading and at the beginning of the Franco-Prussian War joined the seventh corps of the German army as surgeon. Later as surgeon in the United States army he was sent with an expedition to Nevada and Arizona. He became interested in natural history, geology and anthropology and devoted much of his time to collecting natural history specimens for the Smithsonian Institution at Washington. Eventually he abandoned his profession to engage in the study of anthropology. In 1877, he joined the surveying corps of Prof. Frederic V. Hayden as anthropologist and naturalist; in 1881, he visited the Mandans, a people supposedly of Welsh descent, and the Hidatsa and Arikara Indians in North Dakota. He made a study of the sign language and hieroglyphics of the latter tribes. He did research work among the Mission Indians in Southern California and among the Washoes and Pah-Utes in Western Nevada and the Shoshones in Eastern Nevada in 1882. In 1883, he studied the hieroglyphics and artistry of the Ottawas in Northern Michigan and of the Sioux in Minnesota; in the following year he made a trip to the Indians in British Columbia, on Vancouver's Island, in Washington,

California and Oregon and during the next two years specialized in picture rocks, rock shelters, quarries, etc., in the valleys of the Susquehanna, Potomac, James, Kanawha, Tennessee, and French Broad River (N. C.). In the years following he visited the Ojibways in Northern Minnesota, and was the first white man who was admitted to membership in their Grand Medicine Society. Subsequently he visited the Menomonee Indians in Wisconsin, and made a study of their ceremonial customs. In 1897, Dr. Hoffman was appointed consul at Mannheim, Germany. He is the author of a memoir on the Menomonee Indians in the 14th annual report of the Bureau of Ethnology and "The Midewiwin, or Grand Medicine Society of the Ojibways," published in the seventh annual report of the Bureau. He died at Reading, November 8, 1899.

HOLLAND, WILLIAM JACOB, zoologist and palaeontologist, was born at Jamaica, W. I., August 16, 1848. He entered the ministry of the Moravian Church following his graduation from Amherst College and Princeton Theological Seminary, and held a pastorate at Pittsburgh from 1874-1891. From 1891-1901, he was chancellor of the Western University of Pennsylvania (University of Pittsburgh) and in 1898 became director of the Carnegie Museum at Pittsburgh, which position he held until 1922, when he became director emeritus. He is the author of "The Butterfly Book," "The Moth Book," "To the River Platte and Back," "The Butterfly Guide," and many scientific papers published by the United States government and the Zoological Society of London. His home is in Pittsburgh.

HOLLAND POPULATION COMPANY—In order to encourage purchasers to buy lands lying west of the Allegheny Mountains, land companies were organized. These companies advanced money to the provincial treasury enabling settlers to be brought to the western section of the province. The warrants of the Holland Population Company were taken out in 1792, 1793 and 1794 and in those years, with two other companies, paid about $200,000 to the Commonwealth, besides later patenting fees to the state. However, a group of speculators organized companies to seize the lands of the companies maintaining that they were held without title and that the warrants were forfeited because more than two years had elapsed without settlement being made. Riots resulted and a settler under the company might return to his home to find his family and household goods thrown out of doors and another in possession.

HOLLIDAYSBURG, borough and county-seat of Blair County, on the Juniata River, 82 miles east of Pittsburgh and five miles south of Altoona. It is the seat of Highland Hall, a boarding school for girls. The region surrounding Hollidaysburg is rich in deposits of coal, iron ore, ganister and limestone and the borough has manufactories of agricultural and mining implements, foundry products, nails, silks, cars, furniture and classification yards. Population (1930), 5,969; (1920), 4,071.

"HOLLOW SCHOOL, THE," in Philadelphia, was opened January 11, 1808, by the "Philadelphia Association for the Instruction of Poor Children," organized in 1807. The school built on the Lancaster system then in vogue in New York, was a two-roomed building, located on Pegg's Run. Six hundred pupils between the ages of five and fifteen could be accommodated. Four dollars a year was paid by subscribers and fifty dollars for a life membership.

HOLLS, GEORGE FREDERICK WILLIAM, lawyer and statesman, was born at Zelienople, July 1, 1857. He graduated from Columbia University, in 1878, and from Columbia Law School in 1880. He was admitted to the bar, practiced in New York City and became the senior member of the firm of Holls, Wagner and Burghard. Later he established a branch of the firm in Germany. He became well known for his philanthropic endeavors and as a member of the Republican party, was a prominent delegate-at-large to the New York Constitutional Convention in 1893. In 1899, he was secretary of the American delegation at the Hague Conference. He wrote: "Sancta Sophia and Troitza," "Compulsory Voting," "The Peace Conference at the Hague and Its Bearings on International Law and Policy." He died at Yonkers, N. Y., July 23, 1903.

HOLME, THOMAS, surveyor-general and provincial officer, was a member of the first Assembly of the Province of Pennsylvania. From 1683-1685, inclusive, he represented Philadelphia County in the Provincial Council, and was a member of commissions appointed by William Penn to treat with the Indians and with Lord Baltimore and the Governor and Council of West Jersey, concerning land difficulties. Holme also served as surveyor-general of Pennsylvania. He died in 1695.

HOMESTEAD, borough in Allegheny County, on the Monongahela River, about seven miles south of Pittsburgh, was settled in 1871 and incorporated in 1880. Chief among its industries are steel works which employ more than 7,000 men. Homestead was the scene of a strike in 1892 which resulted from reduced wages, refusal to recognize the Amalgamated Iron and Steel Association or to hold any conference with the men. H. C. Frick, the manager, was burned in effigy, and the works were closed on July 1st. The advisory committee of the union with armed companies controlled the town and permitted no one to enter mills without their consent. The company's efforts to protect their property and alleged rights were of no avail; 300 Pinkerton detectives, hired by the company, were mobbed and driven out of town. Seven of them were killed, twenty or thirty wounded and eleven strikers were killed. Governor Pattison refused to send state militia to quell the uprising until local authorities had thoroughly tested their powers of self-defense. However, on July 12th, the troops arrived and the town was placed under martial law. On July 21st, Mr. Frick was shot and stabbed in his office, but recovered. Finally new men were employed and

CHIMNEY ROCKS, HOLLIDAYSBURG (1856)

the mills reopened but the strike did not end officially until November 20, 1892. Population (1930), 20,141; (1920), 20,452.

HONESDALE, borough and county-seat of Wayne County, is located on the Lackawaxen River, 30 miles northeast of Scranton, in a coal mining and agricultural region. The town has manufactures of woolen goods, shoes, machine shops, foundries, axes, concrete blocks, paints, electric elevators, and glassware. Population (1930), 5,490; (1920), 2,756.

HOPKINSON, FRANCIS, jurist and writer, was born at Philadelphia, September 21, 1737. He was the first student to enter the College of Philadelphia (now the University of Pennsylvania) upon its opening, was graduated there, and later studied law. He represented New Jersey in Congress in 1776 and in 1779 became judge of the admiralty of Pennsylvania, which position he held until the inauguration of the Federal government when Washington made him United States District Judge for Pennsylvania. Hopkinson was one of the signers of the Declaration of Independece. His political and satirical writings during the period of the Revolution did much to prepare the people for political independence. Hopkinson was perhaps the most versatile man that Pennsylvania has ever produced. Besides being a clever writer he was a talented artist, musician and composer. His political writings include: "The Pretty Story," "The Prophecy" and "The Political Catechism." Among his poems are: "The Battle of the Kegs" and "The New Roof, a Song for Federal Mechanics." He died at Philadelphia, May 9, 1791.

HOPKINSON, JOSEPH, jurist and poet, was born at Philadelphia, November 12, 1770, a son of Francis Hopkinson. He attended the University of Pennsylvania, studied law and practiced at Easton. In 1791, he returned to Philadelphia and from 1815 to 1819 represented that city in the House of Representatives. Later he removed to Bordentown, N. J., and was elected a member of the New Jersey Legislature. He became judge of the United States Court for the eastern district of Pennsylvania in 1828 and in 1837 was chairman of the judiciary committee of the convention to revise Pennsylvania's constitution. He is the author of a national song, "Hail Columbia." His death occurred in Philadelphia, January 15, 1842.

HORSEFIELD, THOMAS, naturalist and explorer, was born at Bethlehem, May 12, 1773. He graduated from the Medical School, University of Pennsylvania, and from 1794-1799 was connected with the Pennsylvania Hospital. In the latter year he was commissioned regimental surgeon by the Dutch Colonial government and sailed for Java. He became interested in the natural and geologic features of the island and in 1824 published the results of his study, "Zoological Researches in Java and the Neighboring Islands." He also wrote: "Plantae Javanicae Rariores," "Catalogue of the Birds in the Museum of the East India

FRANCIS HOPKINSON

Company" and with Frederick Moore, "Catalogue of the Lepidopterous Insects in the Museum of the East Indian Company." He died in 1866 at London, England.

HORSTMANN, IGNATIUS F., Roman Catholic prelate, was born in Philadelphia, December 16, 1840. He was educated at Central High School and St. Joseph's College, Philadelphia. Later he studied at the American College in Rome and was ordained to the priesthood in 1865. In the following year he became professor of mental philosophy in the Seminary of Saint Charles Borromes, Philadelphia, later Overbrook Seminary. He became pastor of St. Mary's Church, Philadelphia, in 1877 and Chancellor of the Archdiocese in 1885. In 1892, he was consecrated bishop of the See of Cleveland, Ohio, which position he held at the time of his death, May 13, 1908.

HORTICULTURAL SOCIETY, THE PENNSYLVANIA, was founded at Philadelphia, December 21, 1827. Its aim was "The promotion of horticulture, that interesting and highly important branch of science." The first exhibition sponsored by the organization was held on June 6, 1829.

HOSENSACK ACADEMY, THE, a school under the control of the Schwenkfelders, was opened at Hosensack, Montgomery County, in 1790 or 1791.

HOUCK, HENRY, educator, was born near Palmyra, Lebanon County, March 6, 1836. He attended the Annville Academy and Arcadia Institute at Orwigsburg, and studied Greek and Latin privately. Later, Franklin and Marshall College conferred upon him the degree of Master of Arts. From the age of sixteen to his death Houck was identified with the field of education. At different times he served as country school teacher, superintendent of schools of Lebanon County and as deputy superintendent of education of Pennsylvania, which position he held for 38 years. In 1903, he was sent by the state to investigate educational conditions in Porto Rico. From 1906 until his death on March 13, 1917, he was state secretary of Internal Affairs. Houck was well known throughout the state as a public speaker.

HOUSE OF REPRESENTATIVES—See LEGISLATURE.

HOUSTON, EDWIN JAMES, electrical engineer, was born at Alexandria, Va., 1847. He attended Central High School, Philadelphia, and later taught there. Afterwards he became teacher of physics at Franklin Institute and at the Medico Chirurgical College. He was one of the inventors of the Thompson-Houston arc-lighting system, a member of the United States Electrical Commission and chief electrician of the International Exposition at Philadelphia in 1884. From 1893-1895, he was president of the American Institute of Electrical Engineers. Houston wrote: "Elements of Physical Geography," "Dictionary of

HENRY M. HOYT

Electrical Word Terms and Phrases," "Arc Lighting," "Electricity in Every Day Life," "Wonder Book of Magnetism," "The Land of Drought" and "Born an Electrician." He died in 1914.

HOVENDEN, THOMAS, artist, was born in Ireland. He attended the Cork School of Design and later came to America where he studied art in New York. Subsequently he studied in Paris and upon his return settled in Plymouth Township, Montgomery County. Notable among his paintings are: "Breaking Home Ties," "The Last Moments of John Brown," and "The Confederate in a Pennsylvania Farm House." He was killed in an attempt to rescue a child from beneath a locomotive near Norristown in 1895.

HOWE, FREDERIC CLEMSON, lawyer, was born at Meadville, November 21, 1867. He graduated from Allegheny College, Johns Hopkins University and studied at Halle University, Germany. After attending the University of Maryland and New York Law School, he practiced law at Cleveland, Ohio. In 1914, he became commissioner of immigration at the port of New York. He was a member of the Ohio Senate from 1906–1909; professor of law at the Cleveland College of Law, and lecturer at Western Reserve University and the University of Wisconsin. His publications are: "Taxation and Taxes in the United States under the Internal Revenue System, 1791–1895," "The City the Hope of Democracy," "Privilege and Democracy in America," "Wisconsin: An Experiment in Democracy," "European Cities at Work," "Socialized Germany," "Why War?", "The High Cost of Living," "The Only Possible Peace," "Denmark—a Cooperative Commonwealth," "Revolution and Democracy" and "The Confessions of a Reformer." His home is at Harmon-on-the-Hudson, N. Y.

HOYT, HENRY MARTYN, lawyer, soldier, and governor, was born at Kingston, June 8, 1830. He attended Wyoming Seminary, Lafayette College and Williams College, graduating from the latter institution in 1849. He taught school for three years thereafter, studied law, was admitted to the bar in 1853, and began the practice of his profession at Wilkes-Barre. At the outbreak of the Civil War he helped to raise the 52nd Pennsylvania Regiment of which he was commissioned lieutenant-colonel. He served throughout the Peninsula Campaign and was taken prisoner in a night attack on Fort Johnson. Following exchange of prisoners Hoyt was mustered out and given the rank of brigadier-general. He resumed his practice in Wilkes-Barre and in 1867 was appointed judge of the courts of Luzerne County. Subsequently he was the choice of the Republican party for the governorship of Pennsylvania which office he held from 1879–1883. During his administration the state debt was reduced to $10,000,000 and refunded at three per cent. Hoyt is the author of "The Controversy Between Connecticut and Pennsylvania" and "Protection versus Free Trade." He died at Wilkes-Barre, December 1, 1892.

HUGUENOTS, French Protestants arrived in Pennsylvania at an early period, but unlike the English, Germans and Scotch-Irish did not settle in compact communities. With the exception of Georgia, perhaps no other colony received so many French emigrants as did Pennsylvania. Their advent was due to political, economic and religious causes. Practically all of the Huguenots came to this country indirectly, having previously emigrated to other countries. Almost from its beginning Philadelphia had French settlers. At an early period a group of Huguenots settled in the Perkiomen Valley and along the lower Schuylkill in Montgomery County. In 1712, a Huguenot settlement was formed in Lancaster County by Madame Ferree, whose husband, a friend of Penn's, had been killed in France. Penn gave her two thousand acres in the Pequea Valley, Lancaster County, and after purchasing an additional two thousand acres Madame Ferree established a settlement for French refugees. Later a group of Huguenots, encouraged by Penn to raise grapes in Lancaster County and establish a wine industry, joined Mme. Ferree's colony. Between 1704 and 1710 a Huguenot community was established in Berks County, in the Oley Valley. Other early Huguenot settlements were made in the Lehigh Valley, on the Schuylkill in what is now Chester County, in Lebanon County, along the Tulpehocken and Swatara Creeks, in Westmoreland, Somerset and Fayette Counties. Because of the fact that many of the Huguenots translated their names into the German or English it is difficult to estimate how many of them emigrated to this country. The Huguenots did not apparently organize their own churches, but joined others, such as the Reformed.

HUMPHREYS, ANDREW ATKINSON, soldier, was born at Philadelphia, November 2, 1810, a grandson of Joshua Humphreys. He graduated from West Point in 1831 and afterwards participated in the Seminole War. He left the army in 1836 and engaged in government work as a civil engineer. In 1838, he entered the topographical engineering corps of the army and was connected with several government surveys. He served in the Civil War as chief topographical engineer of the Army of the Potomac and as brigadier-general participated in the Battles of Fredericksburg, Chancellorsville, Gettysburg and in the final campaign of the war. His services in the Battle of Gettysburg merited him a promotion to the rank of major-general of volunteers. Later he became chief of staff to General Meade. He retired from the army in 1879. Humphreys is the author of "Preliminary Report Concerning Explorations and Surveys Principally in Nevada and Arizona"; "Report upon the Physics and Hydraulics of the Mississippi River, etc." (with H. L. Abbott); "The Virginia Campaigns of 1864 and 1865"; "From Gettysburg to the Rapidan"; "Historical Sketch of the Corps of Engineers," in Occasional Papers, No. 16 (United States Army, Engineer School, Washington). He died at Washington, D. C., December 27, 1883.

HUMPHREYS, JOSHUA, shipbuilder, was born at Haverford, June 17, 1751, the grandson of Daniel Humphreys who settled near Philadelphia in

1682. At the age of fourteen he was apprenticed to a Philadelphia shipbuilder and a few years later opened his own ship yard. He is called the father of the American navy because he built the first American war ships. The best known of these was the Constitution. He also constructed the Chesapeake, Congress, United States, President and Constellation. He died at Haverford, January 12, 1838.

HUNEKER, JAMES GIBBONS, musical critic, was born at Philadelphia, January 31, 1860. He studied under Barili, Ritter and Dontreleau, in Paris, and afterwards taught piano at the National Conservatory of New York. From 1891-1895, he was musical and dramatic critic of the New York Recorder; musical and dramatic critic of the Morning Advertiser, 1895-1897, and later musical, dramatic and art critic of the New York Sun. His writings include: "Mezzotints in Modern Music"; "Chopin, as Man and Musician"; "Melomaniacs"; "Overtones"; "Iconoclasts"; "Visionaries"; "Egoists: A Book of Supermen"; "Franz Liszt"; "The Pathos of Distance"; "Ivory Apes and Peacocks"; "New Cosmopolis"; "Unicorns" and "Charles Baudelaire." He died February 9, 1921.

HUNTINGDON, borough and county-seat of Juniata County, located on the Juniata River, about 200 miles west of Philadelphia, was settled in 1760 and chartered in 1796. It is situated in a rich agricultural region and is the seat of Juniata College, an institution under the control of the Church of the Brethren and of a state reformatory. Industries of the town include the manufacture of boilers, machinery, radiators, sewer pipes, furniture, flour, stationery, knit goods and stoves. Population (1930), 7,558; (1920), 7,051.

HUNTINGDON COUNTY, formed from part of Bedford, September 20, 1787, named for Selina Hastings, Countess of Huntingdon. Land area, 918 square miles; population (1930), 39,021; county-seat, Huntingdon, laid out in 1767.

HUNTINGDON CREEK—Tributary to Fishing Creek. Sub-basin: Lower North Branch Susquehanna; source, in North Mountain, Lake Township, northwestern Luzerne County; course, southwesterly into Columbia County to Fishing Creek; mouth, at Forks; length, twenty-six and one-half miles.

IBACH, LAWRENCE J., astronomer, was born at Allentown, October 9, 1838; moved to Newmanstown, Lebanon County, where he followed the trade as a blacksmith; studied astronomy with Charles V. Engleman, who on his death in 1860 bequeathed his charts, books and instruments to Ibach, who made astronomical calculations for almanacs which had been promised by Engleman. He filled his first order in 1863, and from that year until his death, October 9, 1888, he made annual calculations for almanacs in the United States, Canada and South America.

ILLUSTRATED WORLD, THE, was first published April 14, 1683, in Philadelphia, by James Elverson. It was designed to show to its subscribers the best contemporary American and European art.

IMMIGRANTS, SOCIETY TO AID, was formed in Philadelphia in August, 1794, and was known as "Philadelphia Society for the Information and Assistance of Persons Emigrating from Foreign Countries."

INDEPENDENCE, DECLARATION OF—See DECLARATION OF INDEPENDENCE.

INDEPENDENCE HALL, in Chestnut Street, Philadelphia, was erected by the provincial assembly and was probably first used by them as a state house in October, 1735. In later years additions were made to the building. On July 4, 1776, the Declaration of Independence, by which the colonies renounced all allegiance to England, was signed here. The square surrounding the hall has also since this event acquired the prefix "Independence."

INDEPENDENCE JUBILEE. In 1876, the 100th anniversary of American independence was observed in Philadelphia by a centennial exhibition.

INDIAN CREEK—Tributary to Youghiogheny River. Sub-basin: Monongahela; source, in Donegal Township, southeastern Westmoreland County; course, southwesterly into Fayette County to Youghiogheny River; mouth, at Indian Creek; length, twenty-three miles.

"INDIAN LAND" AND ITS "FAIR PLAY" SETTLERS, was the part of the present county of Lycoming north of the west branch of the Susquehanna, the settlements being mainly along the river. The period during which this "Fair Play" code had full sway was from 1773 to May 1, 1785, when the land office was opened for applications within the purchase of October 23, 1784. These settlers were hardy adventurers, settling on this doubtful territory. They formed a mutual compact among themselves, annually electing a tribunal, in rotation, of three of the settlers who were to decide all controversies and settle disputed boundaries. No appeal could be made from their decision and there could be no resistance. Every new-comer was obliged to apply to this tribunal, and upon his solemn oath to submit in all respects to the law of this land, he was permitted to take possession of some vacant spot. Their decrees were usually just. The act passed December 21, 1784, allowed a right of preemption to settlers without the bounds of purchases theretofore made, and the right of preemption to their respective possessions was given specially to all and every person heretofore settled on the north side of the west branch of the river Susquehanna, between Lycoming Creek on the east and Pine Creek on the west. This ended the rule of Fair-Play men.

INDIANA, borough and county-seat of Indiana County, 45 miles northeast of Pittsburgh. It is located in a bituminous coal mining region and contains glass works, enamelling works, woolen mills, ladder and tile factories, etc. Indiana is the seat of a State Teachers College. Population (1930), 9,569; (1920), 7,043.

INDIANA COUNTY, formed from part of Westmoreland and Lycoming, March 30, 1803. Probably named for the territory of Indiana. Land area, 829 square miles; population (1930), 75,395; county-seat, Indiana, laid out in 1805.

INDIANA PROGRESS, THE, was established in 1814, by James McCahan. Since 1826, members of the Moorhead family have been editors and publishers of the paper. The circulation is 1,900, and A. Sand and A. R. Moorhead are the present editors and publishers.

INDIANA STATE TEACHERS COLLEGE, was opened May 17, 1875. The entire control and ownership of the school passed to the state of Pennsylvania in 1920.

Indiana, the location of the college, is the county-seat of Indiana County.

INDIANS OF PENNSYLVANIA. The many thousands of mute stone implements of family life, agriculture, chase and war found along every stream, at nearly every spring, are proof of Indian occupancy during a considerable prehistoric period. At the time of the arrival of the white man, the Atlantic Coast from the Carolinas north into Canada and in a triangle terminating on the Great Lakes, was occupied by numerous tribes belonging to the same linguistic stock called Algonquin. They were a powerful and numerous tribe and dreaded by bordering tribes who applied to them the name of father or grandfather. Their tradition is that they came from the West and upon arriving at the Mississippi River were joined by the Iroquois with whom they fought their way through the Mound builder country east of the great river. If this tradition is correct they moved eastward like a wave, reaching the Atlantic Coast after a period of many years. Observations of the writer after more than half a century of field work, a comparison of the artifacts found, and a study of the history of early and late writers, indicates that the entire state was not populated all over at any one time. When the first white settlements were made on the Delaware River, the greater part of the eastern half of Pennsylvania was occupied by a clan of the Algonquin stock who called themselves Lenni Lenape, meaning "original people," called by the English, Delawares. This clan was divided into three great tribes, Minsi or Wolf, Unalachtigo or Turkey, and Unami or Turtle. These tribes were again divided and received names from the places where they lived; each settlement had its petty chief who was subject to the head Sachem. Many of these Indians were Christianized by the Moravians. David Zeisberger was probably the most zealous missionary. On March 8,

1782, Col. Williamson and a company of militia committed one of the blackest crimes in our country's history. Ninety Christian Indians were murdered in cold blood at Gnadenhutten on the Muskingum River in Ohio. "The Romantic Story of Schoenbrum," published by the Ohio State Archaeological and Historical Society, is a well written history of the missions.

The Nanticokes belonged to the Algonquin group. They lived on the Susquehanna at various places, on the Juniata in 1747 at Nanticoke in the Wyoming Valley in 1751, and later moved to the West before the advance of civilization. These people had the unusual custom of exhuming the bones of their ancestors and carrying them to their new abode.

The Iroquois Indians were also a powerful tribe. Their main clans settled along the Finger Lakes in New York state. In prehistoric times they formed a confederacy called the Five Nations. They were not residents of Pennsylvania but they extended their hunting trips down the Delaware and Susquehanna Rivers for a considerable distance. Some of the Senecas camped on the head waters of the Allegheny River. They carried on a relentless warfare with southern tribes for a long period of years, and their war-paths extended across Pennsylvania, down the Susquehanna Valley and west of the Allegheny Mountains. Some of their enemies were subjugated and others exterminated. It is an unsolved problem, but apparently, if their tradition is correct, and there is evidence to this effect, the Iroquois divided after crossing the Mississippi. The Cherokee, Susquehannocks, Allegewi, Tuscaroras, Eries and Conoy, are all of the same linguistic stock. And all of these excepting the Eries, at sometime lived south and southwest of Pennsylvania and did not belong to the Five Nation Confederacy. Dr. George P. Donehoo believes that the Susquehannocks came into Pennsylvania by a southern route. It is known since historic times that the Shawnees, Tuscarora and Conoy and sub-tribes followed.

The Susquehannock Indians, after whom the great river is named, probably came about the year 1600 and settled on the Susquehanna, from near the southern boundary line, and a considerable distance eastward in Lancaster County, and north to the vicinity of Sunbury. They were conquered by the Five Nations who placed Shikellamy as resident chief at Sunbury. It is claimed that some of their chiefs were present at the Penn Treaty in 1682. It may also be noted that they were friendly with the Lenni Lenape, and did considerable trading with the whites in the vicinity of Philadelphia. This is evidence that the Lenape had moved eastward and were not driven out by the Susquehannocks on their arrival. It is reasonable to suppose that the Susquehannocks arrived on the river by their name, at a comparatively recent date. The excavation of Indian burials made under the direction of the Pennsylvania Historical Commission during 1930 and 1931, in Lancaster County, has proven beyond the question of a doubt that they had contact with white traders. All of over two hundred burials produced glass beads by the thousands, many iron axes and hoes, brass kettles, brass and copper ornaments, guns and a sword. The only articles made by the Indians were a few hundred artistic pots made of clay. These pots were put in the burials so profusely that apparently the brass kettles were much better adapted to their use for cooking.

Prehistoric burials were found on other sites nearby on more elevated ground, which presumably represents an earlier tribal occupation. The pictographs carved on the rocks on islands in the river are probably the work of prehistoric Indians. The exaggerated age of thousands of years for these carvings by newspaper writers has no foundation. The rock is soft mica—schist and designs can easily be pecked with any pointed hard stone. Weathering and ice flood would long ago have erased the figures as three-fourths of them were fully exposed. They have been known for generations by residents and not recently discovered as published, broadcast in newspapers. As to age, six to seven hundred years is a fair guess.

Stone implements found on the surface are the same types as in eastern Pennsylvania, hence it may be assumed that the prehistoric occupation was Algonquin.

The Susquehannock Indians got into trouble with the Five Nations and were almost exterminated during a period of years beginning in 1608. The remnant were murdered by the Paxton Boys from Dauphin County.

The Tuscarora tribe (Iroquoian), driven from the southern states, were permitted to live on the Susquehanna River for some time. About 1713, they joined the Confederacy, afterwards called Six Nations.

The Shawnee (Algonquin) were one of the most nomadic tribes in the country. A clan of these people, in 1698, were settled at Pequea, in Lancaster County, by permission of the provincial government and the Conestogas then removed west of the Susquehanna, between Yellow Breeches Creek and Conodoguinet, thence to western Pennsylvania about 1727 and later to Ohio, believed to have been their earlier abode. Another section lived on the Upper Delaware, later at Wyoming, thence to the West. Part of this tribe occupied southwestern Pennsylvania for some years. Cornplanter and Tecumseh were noted chiefs of this tribe.

The Conoy (Algonquin) were permitted to live near Conestoga, in Lancaster County, in 1704, then moved to the site of Washingtonboro. Later, they moved west of the Susquehanna to the mouth of the Conejohella Creek; in 1731 on the Conodoguinet in 1744; on the Juniata River; later at Catawissa; still later at Wyoming, subsequently moving to New York state.

The Eries (Iroquoian) lived in northwestern Pennsylvania. Due to stubbornness in refusing to join the Five Nation Confederacy they were exterminated between 1654 and 1656.

The Allegewi Indians lived west of the Allegheny Mountains, mostly on the Allegheny River, and were called Black Minquas by other tribes. Their origin is not so well known. Cyrus Thomas believed they were associated with the Cherokee as the original so-called Mound Builders. There is still a small Indian reservation in Warren County. Cornplanter, the great Seneca chief and friend of the whites, died here in 1836, aged about one hundred years. Commonly all Indians west of the Allegheny Range were erroneously called Allegewi.

The full history of their respective places of abode, their migrations, modes of living, religion, land purchases, treaties, wars, trails, trading, etc., is a long tale. For details refer to Colonial records, Pennsylvania Archives; Heckewelder's Narratives; Loskiel, "Handbook of American Indians"; "Frontier Forts of Pennsylvania"; "Indian Chiefs"; and "Indian Wars"; by Sipe. "Indian Villages and Place Names in Pennsylvania," by Dr. George P. Donehoo, is valuable for short sketches.

H. K. D.

INGERSOLL, CHARLES JARED, statesman, lawyer and author, was born at Philadelphia, October 3, 1782. After his admittance to the bar he traveled in Europe and became attached to the American Embassy in France. He was elected to Congress in 1812; was appointed United States District Attorney for Pennsylvania in 1815 and held office until 1829. Later he served as a member of the Pennsylvania Legislature and from 1841-1847 was a member of Congress from one of the districts of which Philadelphia County is composed. He is the author of "Chiomara," "Jesuit Letters on American Literature and Politics," "Historical Sketch of Second War Between United States and Great Britain." He died May 14, 1862.

INGERSOLL, JARED, lawyer, was born in Connecticut, in 1749; was graduated from Yale, in 1766; entered at the Middle Temple, London, and spent five years in the study of law. At the outbreak of the Revolution he went from London to Paris where he met Franklin. Returning to America he took up his residence in Philadelphia where he won distinction as a lawyer. In 1787, he represented Pennsylvania in the convention which framed the United States Constitution; was Attorney-General of Pennsylvania, August 20, 1791, to May 19, 1800; and again December 13, 1811, to December 21, 1816; candidate of the Federalist party for vice-presidency of the United States, 1812. He died at Philadelphia, October 21, 1822.

INGERSOLL, JOSEPH REED, lawyer, was born in Philadelphia, June 14 1786; graduated from Princeton, 1804, and practiced law in Philadelphia; member of Congress, elected by the Whig Party, 1835-1837, and from 1842-1849; Minister to England, 1852; wrote "Secession a Folly and a Crime," just before the Civil War, and a "Memoir of Samuel Breck," 1863. He died in Philadelphia, February 20, 1868.

INGHAM, SAMUEL DELUCENNA, politician, was born in Bucks, County, September 16, 1779; member of Pennsylvania Legislature for several years; U. S. House of Representatives, 1813-1818, and 1822-1829; Secretary of

Commonwealth of Pennsylvania, July 6, 1819, to December 19, 1820; Secretary of Treasury of New Jersey, 1829-1831, by appointment of President Jackson. Died June 5, 1860, at Trenton, N. J.

IRON INDUSTRY IN PENNSYLVANIA—Iron was not manufactured in Pennsylvania until after the arrival of William Penn in 1682. The first iron in Pennsylvania was made, experimentally, before 1692 but at what place is not known. The first historic iron works in the state were established by Thomas Rutter, an English Quaker, on the Manatawny Creek, in Berks County, in 1716. The second iron enterprise was Coventry Forge on French Creek, in Chester County, built by Samuel Nutt, an English Quaker. The third enterprise was the operation of Colebrookdale Furnace, in Berks County, about 1720. Durham Furnace, on Durham Creek, in Bucks County, was built in 1727. The iron industry in Pennsylvania was fairly well established by 1729, for in 1728 to 1729 the colony exported 274 tons of pig iron to England. In 1731, George Megee manufactured nails at the corner of Front and Arch Streets, Philadelphia. The Reading Furnace on French Creek was in operation in 1728. In 1742, Benjamin Franklin invented the Franklin stove. The Windsor Forge, Valley Forge, Charming Forge, Oley Furnace and the enterprise of William and Mark Bird indicate the progress of the iron industry in Lancaster and Berks Counties. Elizabeth Furnace, built in 1750 by John Hughes, was an early achievement in the present county of Lancaster. Baron Stiegel, James Old, Robert Coleman, Cyrus Jacobs and Peter Grubb were identified with the iron industry in Lancaster County. In 1750, Pennsylvania was the most advanced of all the colonies in the manufacture of iron. In the Lehigh Valley, William Henry's, near Nazareth, and Hampton Furnace, near Shimersville, were among the earliest. The Juniata Iron Company was organized in the Juniata Valley in 1767 and Bedford Furnace, at Orbisonia, built in 1788, was the first furnace in the Juniata Valley. Centre Furnace, in Centre County, was built in 1791 by Col. John Patton and Samuel Miles. The first manufactory of iron west of the Alleghenies was the building of a furnace and forge on Jacobs Creek, in Fayette County, built by William Turnbull, Peter Marmie and Col. John Holker, in 1789-1790 The Cambria Iron Works was begun in 1853. The iron industry at Pittsburgh began about 1792, when George Anshutz built a small blast furnace at Shady Side. The first iron foundry at Pittsburgh was built by Joseph McClurg about 1805. The first rolling mill at Pittsburgh was built by Christopher Cowan in 1811. In York County, William Bennett built a furnace and forge on Codorus Creek about 1765. In 1822, the Hanover Furnace and Forge was built in Fulton County, nine miles below McConnellsburg.

IRVINE, FRANK, lawyer, was born in Sharon, September 15, 1858. He studied at Cornell University and at the National University at Washington and was admitted to the bar in 1883. For about a year he was assistant United States Attorney. In 1884, he removed to Nebraska where he was judge of the

4th District of Nebraska and Supreme Court Commissioner. In 1901, he became a member of the faculty of the Law College at Cornell and dean of the faculty in 1907. From 1914-1921, he was a member of the Public Service Commission of the second district of New York. His home is in Ithaca, N. Y.

IRVINE, JAMES, military officer, was born at Philadelphia, August 4, 1735. He served in Bouquet's expedition and during the Revolution was successively captain and lieutenant-colonel of the 1st Pennsylvania Regiment. In 1776, he became colonel of the 9th Pennsylvania Regiment, was taken prisoner at Chestnut Hill, December 5, 1777, and held in New York until 1781. From 1785-1786, he was a member of the General Assembly of Pennsylvania and from 1795-1799 the State Senate. He died at Philadelphia, April 28, 1819.

IRVINE, WILLIAM, Revolutionary general, was born in Ireland, November 3, 1741; graduated from Dublin University; appointed surgeon on board a ship of war; served in part of war between Great Britain and France, 1756-1763; emigrated to America and in 1764 settled in Carlisle. Was member of Provincial Convention held in Philadelphia, July 15, 1774, until appointed by Congress, colonel of the 6th Battalion of the Pennsylvania line, January 9, 1776. At Three Rivers, in Canada, he was captured in an engagement, June, 1776; was exchanged April 21, 1778; promoted on May 12, 1779, to rank of brigadier-general and assigned to command of 2nd Brigade of Pennsylvania Line. In autumn of 1781 was ordered to Fort Pitt where he remained until the war closed. In 1785 was appointed Agent by the State under an "Act for directing the Mode of Distribution of Donation Lands, promised the troops of the Commonwealth." Was a member of Congress, 1787-1788, and of the 3rd Federal Congress, 1793-1795. During the Whiskey Insurrection was in command of Pennsylvania troops, taking an active part in all important movements. In 1797, was one of thirteen electors from Pennsylvania who elected John Adams president of the United States. In 1801, after Thomas Jefferson's election to the presidency, he had charge of arsenals, ordnance, army supplies and Indian affairs. Was president of the State Society of the Cincinnati at the time of his death in Philadelphia, July 29, 1804.

IRVING COLLEGE, for women, at Mechanicsburg, was founded in 1856 by Soloman Gorgas and was early known as Irving Female College. Washington Irving, for whom the college was named, was a member of the first board of trustees. In 1929, three years after the death of Dr. E. E. Campbell, president and owner of the college, the institution was closed by order of the executors of the estate.

JACK, CAPTAIN, was called the Black Hunter, the Black Rifle, the Wild Hunter of the Juniata, the Black Hunter of the Forest; a noted character in Cumberland County between 1750 and 1755. His real name is not known.

Finding his cabin burned and his wife and children murdered, he left civilization, lived in caves, protected the frontier inhabitants from the Indians to whom he was a terror.

JACOBS, CAPTAIN—See CAPTAIN JACOBS.

JACOBS, HENRY EYSTER, clergyman and theologian, was born at Gettysburg, November 10, 1844. He was graduated from Pennsylvania College (Gettysburg), 1862, and from the Lutheran Theological Seminary there in 1865. From 1870-1883, he was a professor in Pennsylvania College, and since 1883, he has been professor of systematic theology at the Lutheran Theological Seminary at Mt. Airy, Philadelphia. He was president of the Board of Foreign Missions of the Lutheran Church, of the American Society of Church History, and of the Pennsylvania German Society. He wrote several Bible Commentaries, translated and wrote various German Theological works; his publications include: "Elements of Religion," "Life of Martin Luther," "The German Emigration to America, 1709-1780," etc. His home is in Philadelphia.

JACOBS, MICHAEL, Lutheran clergyman, was born near Waynesboro, in 1808. He was graduated in 1828 at Jefferson College, Cannonsburg, and in the following year was appointed instructor at the Gettysburg Gymnasium. After 1832, he served as professor there and retired in 1865. In 1832, he entered the Lutheran ministry. He was a very versatile man; invented a method of preserving fruit and was a meterologist of note. He published "The Rebel Invasion of Pennsylvania and Maryland." He died in 1871.

JACOBS CREEK—Tributary to Youghiogheny River. Sub-basin: Monongahela; source, in Bullskin Township, northeastern Fayette County, near Westmoreland-Fayette County boundary; course, northeasterly into Westmoreland County; thence westerly to Youghiogheny River, forming Westmoreland-Fayette County boundary from Laurelville to mouth; mouth, at Jacobs Creek; Length, thirty-one miles. Named by the Indians for a famous Delaware chief, "Captain Jacobs."

JACOBUS, MELANCTHON WILLIAMS, Presbyterian clergyman and educator, was born at Allegheny, December 15, 1855. He was graduated from Princeton, in 1877; from Princeton Theological Seminary, in 1881, and after studying at Gottingen and Berlin was pastor of the Presbyterian Church at Oxford, 1884-1891. He became professor of New Testament exegesis and criticism in the Hartford (Conn.) Theological Seminary, in 1891, and held that position until 1928 when he became professor emeritus. Besides extensive editorial work his Stone Lectures at the Princeton Theological Seminary appeared as "A Problem in New Testament Criticism." His home is in Hartford, Conn.

JADWIN, EDGAR, military engineer, was born at Honesdale, August 7, 1865. He studied at Lafayette College; was graduated from West Point, in 1890; was an assistant in government engineering, in the Spanish-American War; was successively major and lieutenant-colonel of the 3rd United States Volunteer Engineers, and for a time commanded a battalion of this regiment in the sanitation of Matanzas, Cuba. He was promoted captain in the corps of engineers, U. S. A., 1900. From 1907-1911, he was engaged on the Panama Canal, becoming lieutenant-colonel in 1913. In 1924, he was appointed assistant chief of engineers with rank of brigadier-general and in 1926 chief of engineers with rank of major-general. He retired August 7, 1929, and makes his home in Honesdale.

"JAEGER, DER EWIGE" (The Eternal Hunter), a Pennsylvania-German legend, told for many generations. The eternal hunter, a boaster named Jacob Brewster, failing to carry out his boast to ride to New Amsterdam in five days or to ride through eternity, hunts endlessly. Also according to the legend, those born on Christmas night can sometimes see his spirit riding among his ghostly pack. When the baying of hounds and sounds of the hunter's horn would be heard in the summer evening the mother would say in awe inspiring tones to her children, "Es Ist Der Ewige Jaeger."

JAMES, BUSHROD WASHINGTON, oculist, was born in Philadelphia, August 25, 1836; was elected president of Homeopathic Medical Society, in 1883. In 1896, was vice-president of the Homeopathic Medical Congress held at London, England. He published "Manual of Chinatology," "Echoes of Battle," "Alaska—Its Neglected Past and Brilliant Future." He died in 1903.

JAMES, THOMAS POTTS, botanist, was born at Radnor, in 1803; lived in Philadelphia almost all his life; was interested in wholesale drug business in Philadelphia. Removed to Cambridge, Mass., 1867; carried on extensive research work in Botany. His papers appeared in Proceedings of Philadelphia Academy of Natural Sciences, also Proceedings in Philadelphia Academy of Arts and Sciences. He wrote "Musci," in Kings Exploration of 40th Parallel, also "Manual of American Mosses," in collaboration with Lesquereux. He died in 1882.

JANVIER, CATHARINE ANN, painter and author, was born in Philadelphia. She married A. Janvier, in 1878. Her paintings are: "Guitar Player," "Violinist," etc. She has written: "White Terror," "Keramics for Students" (translated from the "Provencal of Felix Gras), and "The Reds of Medi." She died July 17, 1923.

JANVIER, THOMAS ALLIBONE, author, was born in Philadelphia, July, 1849; was editorial writer for Philadelphia Bulletin, Press and Times, in 1870 and 1871; traveled in Colorado and New Mexico, finally making his residence in France and England. His works are: "The Dutch Founding of New York," "In Old New York," "Aztec Treasure House." He died June 18, 1913.

JASTROW, MORRIS, JR., orientalist, was born in Warsaw, Poland, August 13, 1861. Coming to Philadelphia with his parents in early childhood (1866), he was trained in the schools of that city, was graduated from the University of Pennsylvania in 1881, and from the University of Leipzig, 1884, receiving the degree Ph.D., after which he spent another year in the study of Semitic languages at the Sorbonne. On his return to the United States he was for a short time assistant to his father in Philadelphia. He was connected with the University of Pennsylvania after 1885, first as instructor in Semitic languages and afterward, in 1891, appointed to the chair of Semitic languages which chair he held till his death, June 22, 1921, in Jenkintown. He wrote papers on Assyriological, Biblical and Hebrew topics and contributed to periodicals.

JAYNE, HORACE, biologist, was born in Philadelphia, March 5, 1859. After graduation from the University of Pennsylvania, in 1879, and from the medical school of the University, in 1882, he attended the Universities of Leipzig and Jena. He became lecturer in biology at the University of Pennsylvania, later Professor of Vertebrate Morphology there, and in 1900 director of the Wistar Institute, University of Pennsylvania. He has written "Mammalian Anatomy," "Revision of the Dermestidae of North America," "Abnormities Observed in North American Coleoptera," etc. He died July 9, 1913.

JEANES, ANNA T., Quaker philanthropist, was born at Philadelphia, in 1822. She was greatly interested in charitable and educational institutions giving liberally to their support. She was also interested in the projects concerning the elevation of the Negro Race. She gave to Spring Garden Institute, Hicksite Friends, Quaker Schools of Philadelphia and to the Home of Aged Friends, to which she retired in her last years. She created a million dollar fund for schools for southern negroes and made a bequest to Swarthmore, providing the College abandon intercollegiate sports, which was refused by the trustees. She died in Philadelphia, September 25, 1907.

JEANES (ANNA T.) FOUNDATION, a fund of $1,000,000 placed under the trusteeship of Booker Washington and Hollis B. Frissell, April, 1907, by Miss Anna T. Jeanes, for the purpose of assisting in the southern United States community, country, and rural schools for negroes to whom the rural and community schools are alone available. This work is closely allied with that of the General Education Board. The fund is employed in stimulating effort rather than in actual payment of the cost of such extensions.

JEANNETTE, a borough in Westmoreland County, about 25 miles southeast of Pittsburgh. The natural gas which supplies the borough has contributed somewhat to its development. It is situated in a fertile agricultural region, which is also a coal mining section. It manufactures window and flint glass, lamps and shades, mine fans, rubber goods, etc. Jeannette was settled in 1888 and incorporated the following year. Population (1930), 15,126; (1920), 10,627.

JEFFERSON, JOSEPH, actor, was born at Philadelphia, February 20, 1829. From infancy he was on the stage, appearing in "Pizarro" at the age of three. In 1843, he became a member of a band of strolling players that traveled through Mexico and Texas, and followed the United States army into Mexico. Later he appeared in Philadelphia at the Arch Street Theatre and became famous as a stock actor. His prominence began with "Our American Cousin," which eliminated from the stage the traditional caricature of Yankee character. His other plays were: "The Cricket on the Hearth," "The Rivals" and "Rip Van Winkle." Jefferson had this play rewritten, and with slight changes, afterward acted it as rewritten. This play ran many weeks in London, and in the United States it was so successful that for many years Jefferson appeared in nothing else. Jefferson's "Rip" is established as a stage classic. He was a member of the American Academy of Letters. His publications include: "Twelve Americans," "Intimate Recollections of Joseph Jefferson," "Actors and Actresses of Great Britain and the United States." He died at Palm Beach, Florida, April 23, 1905.

JEFFERSON COUNTY, formed from part of Lycoming, March 26, 1804. Named for President Thomas Jefferson. Land area, 666 square miles; population (1930), 52,114; county-seat, Brookville, laid out in 1830.

BROOKVILLE (1843)

JEFFERSON MEDICAL COLLEGE, at Philadelphia, founded by Dr. George McClellan, was incorporated April 7, 1826. The school was opened in November of the previous year and in 1826 a class of twenty was graduated.

JEMISON, MARY, was born on shipboard as her parents sailed from Ireland to America, sometime between 1742–1743. Shortly after their arrival in Philadelphia the family removed to the frontier settlements of Pennsylvania and settled along Marsh Creek, in Adams County, about ten miles northwest of Gettysburg. In the spring of 1758, Mary was taken by a party of French and Indians and carried down the Ohio River. Until the time of her death, seventy-eight years later, she lived among her captors. She had two husbands, the first a Delaware Indian and the second a Seneca chief. Mary Jemison died in 1833 at the Seneca Reservation in New York, aged ninety years. Her burial took place according to the practices of the Christian Church at the Seneca Mission Church. Her body was later reinterred in a high location on the left bank of the Genessee River on the estate of Dr. William Pryor Letchworth, and in her memory Dr. Letchworth had erected a bronze statue.

JENKINS, JOHN, military officer, was born at New London, Conn., November 27, 1751. He served throughout the Revolution as a lieutenant and commanded Forty Fort at the time of the Wyoming Massacre. He died at Wyoming, March 19, 1827.

JENKINTOWN, a borough in Montgomery County, ten miles north of Philadelphia. It is situated in a well-to-do farming district and has railway supply works.

JERMYN, a borough in Lackawanna County, twelve miles northeast of Scranton, on the Lackawanna River. It is located in a rich coal-mining region, has powder mills and other manufacturing interests.

JERSEY SHORE, a borough in Lycoming County, on the Susquehanna River, fifteen miles southwest of Williamsport. It is situated in a fertile agricultural district and has machine shops, foundries, electric works, a silk mill and other industries. Population (1930), 5,781; (1920), 6,103.

JESSUP, HENRY HARRIS, Presbyterian missionary and author, was born in Montrose, April 19, 1832. He was graduated from Yale in 1851, from Union Theological Seminary in 1855 and was ordained in that year. He served as a missionary in Tripoli and Syria in 1856–1860 and from 1860 to his death was at Beirut. He was missionary editor of the Arabic journal, "El-Neshrah," and was professor of theology and homilitics in the Syrian Theological Seminary at Beirut. He was moderator of the General Assembly at Saratoga in 1879. Author of: "The Women of the Arabs," "The Greek Church and Protestant Missions" and "Fifty-Three Years in Syria." He died April 28, 1910.

JEWS IN PENNSYLVANIA—The first Jews of whom there is any record in Pennsylvania were two traders who carried on their business along the Delaware River. After June 14, 1656, when the Jews, through the directors of the West India Company, received permission to trade with the Indians and Swedes along the Delaware, many came to the province.

Jonas Aaron, who lived at Philadelphia in 1703, is the earliest Jewish resident of that city on record. One of the most prominent of the early Jews in Pennsylvania was Isaac Miranda who came to the province in the beginning of the eighteenth century, early resided in Philadelphia, was the first Jewish resident of Lancaster, and the first Jew to hold judicial office in this country, having been appointed deputy judge of the court of vice-admiralty on June 19, 1727. The earliest Jewish physician in Pennsylvania was Dr. Isaac Cohen, one of the first residents of Lancaster.

Jews settled at Easton at an early date. The first merchant there was Myer Hart de Shira, one of the founders of that city.

Prior to 1730, a Jewish settlement was made at Schaefferstown, Lebanon County, where a synagogue was built and a Jewish cemetery existed until the latter part of the nineteenth century. By 1750 the Jews had disappeared and no remnant of their settlement remains.

Although Jews had carried on trade in western Pennsylvania at the beginning of the settlement of that section of the state, it was not until the early part of the nineteenth century that they actually settled there. Pittsburgh had Jewish residents at the time of its incorporation in 1804. "Etz-Chayim," the first congregation in the city, was organized in 1846. Other Jewish congregations are at Harrisburg, Wilkes-Barre, Scranton, Reading, Allentown, Altoona, Beaver Falls, Braddock, Bradford, Butler, Carbondale, Chambersburg, Chester, Connellsville, Danville, Dunmore, Duquesne, Erie, Greensburg, Hazleton, Homestead, Honesdale, Johnstown, McKeesport, Newcastle, Oil City, Phoenixville, Pottsville, Shamokin, Sharon, Shenandoah, South Bethlehem, South Sharon, Titusville, Uniontown, Washington, Williamsport and York.

JOHNSON, ALBA BOARDMAN, manufacturer, was born at Pittsburgh, February, 1858. Graduated from Philadelphia Central High School, 1876, and entered Baldwin Locomotive Works. In 1878-1879, he was employed by Edge Moor Iron Works, Wilmington, Del. Later he returned to Baldwin Locomotive Works and was admitted as partner in 1896, was subsequently made vice-president and treasurer, and in 1911, president. He is a director of the Federal Reserve Bank, Standard Steel Works, New York Life Insurance Co., and is president of the American Manufactures Export Association, and others. His home is in Rosemont.

JOHNSON, HERMAN MERRILL, educator, was born at Butternuts, N. Y., November 15, 1815. He was graduated from Wesleyan University, Connecticut. He was professor at St. Charles College, Missouri; Augusta College, Kentucky, and Ohio Wesleyan University. In 1850, he became professor of philosophy and English literature at Dickinson College, and was called to the chair of moral science in 1860, accepting in the same year the presidency which he held until his death. He edited "Orientalia Antiquaria Herodoti," published an edition of the "Clio" of Herodotus, and was a regular contributor to the "Methodist Quarterly Review," and other religious periodicals. He died in Carlisle, April 5, 1868.

JOHNSTON, WILLIAM FREAME, governor, was born at Greensburg, Westmoreland County, in 1808, of Scotch-Irish ancestry. His educational advantages were limited; he was admitted to the bar at the age of twenty-one and began his practice in Armstrong County, where he was appointed district attorney. From 1836 to 1841, he represented his county in the Legislature and in 1847 was elected to the State Senate. Upon the resignation of Governor Shunk, he became, under the constitution, the temporary executive and was elected for a full term, which extended to January 20, 1852, at the ensuing election. He was a strong advocate of protective tariff. During his administration as governor, upon his recommendation, the "Colonial Records" and the first series of the "Pennsylvania Archives" were published under the editorship of Samuel Hazard. Upon the conclusion of his term as governor he became president of the Allegheny Valley Railroad and was interested in the mining and manufacturing of iron, salt and other products of the state. President Johnson appointed him collector for the port of Philadelphia, but his nomination was rejected by the Senate. He died at Pittsburgh, October 25, 1872.

JOHNSTOWN, city of Cambria County, eighty miles east of Pittsburgh, was settled in 1794. Owing to its location in a rich coal and iron ore region, combined with natural water power, it has become an important manufacturing city. Johnstown was the scene of one of the greatest disasters in the history of this country when on May 31, 1889, a dam in the hills above the city burst, flooding the entire city and almost destroying it. Six thousand persons were drowned and property loss was valued at $10,000,000. Population (1930), 66,993; (1920), 67,327.

JONES, HORATIO GATES, lawyer, was born in Philadelphia, January 9, 1822. After graduation from the University of Pennsylvania, in 1841, he was admitted to the bar. He became interested in history and is the author of: "History of Roxborough and Manayunk," "Report of the Committee of the Historical Society of Pennsylvania on the Bradford Bicentenary," "Andrew Bradford, Founder of the Newspaper Press in the Middle States of America," etc. He died in 1893.

JONES, WILLIAM, soldier and statesman, was born in Philadelphia, in 1760. During the Revolution he served in both army and navy; was subsequently a member of Congress and in 1813 was appointed Secretary of the Navy. He died at Bethlehem, September 5, 1831.

JORDAN, JOHN WOOLF, editor and librarian, was born in Philadelphia, September 14, 1840. He edited "Pennsylvania Magazine of History and Biography"; was librarian of Historical Society of Pennsylvania; vice-president of Colonial Society of Pennsylvania. In 1902, he received the LL.D. degree from Lafayette College. He is the author of: "Narrative of John Heckwelder's Journey to the Wabash in 1792," "Bethlehem During the Revolution," "Military Hospitals at Bethlehem and Lititz During the Revolution" and "Franklin as a Genealogist." He died at Wilmington, June 12, 1921.

JORDAN CREEK—Tributary to Little Lehigh Creek. Sub-basin: Middle Delaware; source, on southern slope of Blue Mountain, Heidelberg Township, Lehigh County; course, southeasterly to Little Lehigh Creek; mouth, at Allentown; length, thirty-two miles.

JUMONVILLE, ENSIGN M. DE, was a half-brother of M. Coulon de Villiers, the French commander. He was in the French military service at Fort Duquesne, in 1754, under Capt. M. de Contrecoeur, of His Majesty's troops on the Ohio. Under instructions at Fort Duquesne, May 23, 1754, he was sent out to scout the country along the headwaters of the Monongahela to the crest of the Allegheny Mountains and to deliver a summons to any English he might meet to depart from French territory. When Washington discovered de Jumonville's camp, a skirmish ensued at Great Meadows, May 28, 1754, when de Jumonville and ten of his men were killed and twenty-one taken prisoners.

JUNIATA COLLEGE, a co-educational institution, at Huntingdon, was founded in 1876 by the German Baptist Brethren. The college has art, music, normal and commercial departments and a preparatory school. Enrollment (1930–1931), 510.

JUNIATA COUNTY, formed from part of Mifflin, March 2, 1831; named for the Juniata River and an Indian tribe who once resided there; land area, 392 square miles; population (1930), 14,325; county-seat, Mifflintown, laid out in 1791.

JUNIATA (LITTLE) RIVER—Tributary to Frankstown Branch. Sub-basin: Upper Juniata; source, in Logan Township, western Blair County; course, southeasterly to Altoona; thence northeasterly to Tyrone; thence southeasterly into Huntingdon County to Frankstown Branch Juniata River, forming Blair-Huntingdon County boundary for five miles; mouth, one mile west of Petersburg; length, thirty-eight and one-half miles. Indian name, a corruption of Tyunayate, signifying "projecting rock."

JUNKIN, GEORGE, Presbyterian clergyman, was born near Carlisle, in 1790. An Old School Presbyterian, he was founder of Lafayette College at

Easton in 1832 and served as president until 1841. In 1848, he became president of Washington College (now Washington and Lee). He was an outspoken upholder of slavery, opposed to secession, and on account of sentiments, resigned the presidency of the college in 1861. He spent over $10,000 of his wife's and his own fortune to meet current expenses of Lafayette College. Junkin became the father-in-law of Gen. Stonewall Jackson. He published "Political Fallacies" and several religious works. He died in 1868.

JUNTO, THE, club formed in Philadelphia by Benjamin Franklin, in 1727, principally for mutual improvement. The main subjects discussed were morals, politics and natural philosophy. The club was continued for thirty years. During the reign of William III, the name was also applied to an English Whig Ministry, members of which were Admiral Russell, Somers, and Montague, the great financier. From "The Junto" originated The Library Company of Philadelphia, the first library of a public nature in America.

KAKOWATCHEKY, a Shawnee chief, lived at Pechoquealin, near Delaware Water Gap. In 1728, his name appears in the Colonial Records in connection with Indian troubles. Sometime in the latter part of that year he settled in the Wyoming Valley, below Plymouth, Luzerne County. Kakowatcheky, with other Shawnee chiefs, attended the conference with colonial authorities of Pennsylvania at Philadelphia in July, 1739, when the Conestoga-Shawnee agreement with William Penn, made on April 23, 1701, was confirmed. He moved from Wyoming to Logstown, on the Ohio River below Pittsburgh, in 1743. Here he attended a conference with Conrad Weiser in September, 1748, and earlier in that year met George Croghan at a council with Logstown Indians. When a band of Shawnees, under Peter Chartier, went over to the French, Kakowatcheky remained loyal to the English. He died about 1755.

KANE, ELISHA KENT, Arctic voyager, was born in Philadelphia, February 20, 1820. He was graduated with degree of M.D., from University of Pennsylvania, 1842. Shortly afterward he became surgeon to American Embassy in China. After much travel he returned to America, in 1846; was employed in the government survey of Gulf of Mexico; became senior medical officer of two vessels, Advance and Rescue, on May 22, 1850. He sailed in search of Sir John Franklin and upon his return published "The United States Grinnell Expedition in Search of Sir John Franklin," a personal narrative. On May 31, 1853, the Advance sailed again from New York under Kane's command proceeded to Baffin Bay, 78 degrees 43 min. north latitude, and remained frozen up for twenty-one months, when abandoned. They left for Danish settlements in Greenland, taking ten weeks and losing only one man by accident. "The Second Grinnell Expedition," published in 1856, was awarded gold medals from Congress, Royal Geographical Society and New York Legislature. He died in Havana, Cuba, February 16, 1857.

LIBRARY COMPANY OF PHILADELPHIA, FORMERLY FRANKLIN'S LIBRARY

KANE, JOHN KINTZING, jurist, was born in Albany, N. Y., May 16, 1795. He was graduated from Yale, in 1814, and admitted to the bar in 1817; practiced in Philadelphia; elected to the Pennsylvania Legislature as a Federalist, in 1823, later became a Democrat and supported Jackson in the campaign of 1828. In 1845, he became attorney-general of Pennsylvania; in 1846, United States district judge for Pennsylvania; in 1856, president of the American Philosophical Society. He won distinction by his legal attainments and his decisions in patent and admiralty law, but his commitment of Passmore Williamson for contempt of court in an action under the Fugitive Slave Law was attacked by the Abolitionists. He died in Philadelphia, February 21, 1858.

KANE, THOMAS L., commander of the famous Bucktail Regiment, and founder of the town of Kane, in McKean County, was born February 27, 1822, the son of John K. Kane, attorney-general of Pennsylvania and subsequently judge of the United States District Court, and Jane Leiper. Thomas and his brother, Elisha Kent Kane, differed from the rest of their family on the question of slavery, Thomas resigning from the United States commissionership and clerkship of the District Court to go on a special mission to avert the impending Mormon War. In 1856, he went to Elk County as agent of a land improvement company. He was the first man to offer his services to the Governor of Pennsylvania at the commencement of the rebellion. He raised in McKean, Elk and neighboring counties, the celebrated "Bucktails." In 1864, crippled by many wounds, he returned to McKean County. The state roads and railroads running through McKean, Elk, Forest and Clarion Counties are monuments to his legislative influence and engineering skill. He died in Philadelphia, December 26, 1883.

KAUFFMAN, DAVID S., politician, was born in Cumberland County, in 1813. Following his graduation from Princeton University, he studied law in Mississippi and later settled in Texas. He was twice elected to Congress from Texas and twice was speaker of the House. In 1843, he entered the State Senate of Texas and favored its annexation. He was one of the first members of the House of Representatives from Texas, serving from 1846-1851. He died in 1851 at Washington, D. C.

KAUFFMAN, REGINALD WRIGHT, author, was born in Columbia, September 8, 1877. He was educated at Harvard University, joined the Philadelphia Press and finally became associate editor of the Saturday Evening Post (1904-07). He held the same position on the Delineator, was dramatic critic on the North American and managing editor of Hampton's Magazine. He was active in war work in Europe, especially in Belgium, during the first year of the European War. He has contributed poems, essays and stories to newspapers, journals and magazines, written numerous photo plays and is the author of many books,

JUNCTION OF FRANKSTOWN AND LUCKAHOE BRANCHES OF
THE JUNIATA RIVER BELOW ALEXANDRIA (1856)

among which are: "The Book of Gratitude," "House of Bondage," "The Ranger of the Susquehannox," "A Man of Little Faith," etc. His home is in Geneva, Switzerland.

KEELY, JOHN ERNEST WORRELL, mechanic, was born in Philadelphia, September 3, 1837. Prior to 1872, he became interested in music and afterward claimed that the tuning fork had suggested to him a new motive of power. In 1874, a stock company was formed for the purpose of supplying funds for the perfection and promotion of the alleged discovery. Keely built and destroyed many models, gave exhibitions at which numerous remarkable and unexplained effects were produced, but never attained any important result. Upon his death it was found that the so-called Keely motor was operated by an invisible compressed air apparatus, and that the entire scheme was fraudulent. He died in Philadelphia, November 15, 1898.

KEEN, DORA, explorer, was born in Philadelphia, in 1871. She was educated at Bryn Mawr College; was an Alaskan explorer, a noted mountain climber and an extensive traveler.

KEEN, GREGORY BERNARD, librarian, was born in Philadelphia, March 3, 1844. He graduated from the University of Pennsylvania, in 1861, and from the Divinity School of the Protestant Episcopal Church, Philadelphia, in 1866. From 1887-1897, he was librarian of the University of Pennsylvania; from 1898-1903, librarian of the Historical Society of Pennsylvania, and later curator and editor of the Pennsylvania Magazine of History and Biography. His home is in Bryn Mawr.

KEEN, WILLIAM WILLIAMS, surgeon, was born in Philadelphia, January 19, 1837. He was graduated from Brown University, in 1859; Jefferson Medical College, in 1862, and became assistant surgeon in Federal Army during the Civil War. From 1864-1866, he studied in Europe; 1875-1890, was professor of Artistic Anatomy at Pennsylvania Academy of Fine Arts; 1884-1889, was professor of surgery at Womans Medical College, and on January 4, 1907, became professor emeritus of Jefferson Medical College. On the 50th anniversary of his graduation from Jefferson (1912), he received the honorary degree Sc.D.; later he received honorary degrees from Brown, Northwestern, Toronto, University of Edinburgh and University of St. Andrews. He was elected president of the American Surgical Association, 1898; the American Medical Association, 1899; College of Physicians of Philadelphia, 1900; was honorary fellow in Royal College of Surgeons of England; of Royal College of Surgeons of Edinburgh; of the German, the Italian, the Palermo Surgical Societies; the Berlin Medical Society and of the American Academy of Arts and Sciences. He is the author of: "First Baptist Church of Philadelphia," "Keen's System of Surgery," "Gray's Anatomy," "American Text-Book of Surgery," and "Surgical

Complications and Sequels of Typhoid Fever." He has contributed a large number of articles to various medical and other journals. He lives in Philadelphia.

KEGS, BATTLE OF THE—*See* BATTLE OF THE KEGS.

KEITH, GEORGE, Scottish Quaker, was born probably in Aberdeenshire, about 1639. He was educated at Marischal College, Aberdeen; became a Quaker in 1662 and in 1667 accompanied George Fox and William Penn to Holland on a missionary journey; came to Philadelphia, in 1689, was there accused of heresy and interdicted from preaching in 1692. He then held separate meetings of his followers, known first as Keithites and then as Christian Quakers. Disowned by the yearly meeting of 1694, he established a congregation in which the Quaker externals were observed but the Lord's Supper and Baptism were administered. In 1700, he conformed to the Anglican Church and was a missionary in America for the Society for the Propogation of the Gospel, and from 1705 till his death was rector of Edburton, Sussex. He died in England, March 27, 1716.

KEITH, SIR WILLIAM, governor, was born in England, in 1680. In 1717, he was appointed governor of Pennsylvania and Delaware by George I. He was the only pre-Revolutionary governor who sympathized with the colonists in their difficulties with the British government. In 1728, he returned to England and wrote a series of colonial histories of which only one, that of Virginia, was ever published. He died in London, November 18, 1749.

KELLEY, FLORENCE, social worker, was born in Philadelphia, September 12, 1859. She was graduated from Cornell University, in 1882; received degree LL.D., at Northwestern University, in 1894; was state factory inspector of Illinois, 1893-1897; American editor of "The Archives," Berlin. She later became general secretary of the National Consumers' League; associate editor of "The Survey"; trustee of National Child Labor Committee; lived at Hull House, Chicago, 1891-1899, and Henry Street Settlement, New York City, 1899-1924. She has written: "Some Ethical Gains through Legislation" and "Modern Industry in Relation to the Family." She edited Edmond Kelly's "Twentieth Century Socialism" and compiled "The Supreme Court and Minimum Wage Legislation," "Comment of the Legal Profession on the District of Columbia Minimum Wage Case."

KELLEY, WILLIAM DARRAGH, legislator, was born in Philadelphia, April 12, 1814. He studied law in Philadelphia and in 1841 was admitted to the bar there. In 1845-1846 was attorney-general of Pennsylvania and from 1846 1856 was judge of the Court of Common Pleas at Philadelphia. Previously a Democrat, he became a Republican in 1854 and in that year gave, at Philadelphia, a well-known address on "Slavery in the Territories." From 1860 until his death he was a member of the House of Representatives where he was chairman of the Committee on the Centennial Exposition and was known as "Pig Iron Kelley." He died in Washington, D. C., January 9, 1890.

KELLY, WILLIAM, inventor, was born in Pittsburgh, August 22, 1811. He early turned his attention to invention, engaged in the forwarding and commission business at Pittsburgh and from 1846 was engaged in the iron business in Kentucky. The "Kelly's air boiling process" was the same as that patented by Sir Henry Bessemer in England in 1856 or 1857, and Kelly asserted that Bessemer had gained knowledge of it through American workmen. He is said to have introduced Chinese labor into the United States. He died in Louisville, Ky., February 11, 1888.

KELPIUS, JOHN—See HERMITS OF THE WISSAHICKON.

KELTON, JOHN CUNNINGHAM, soldier, was born in Delaware County, in 1828. He was graduated from West Point, in 1851; received the commission of lieutenant in the infantry, and served for six years in the frontier garrisons of Minnesota, Kansas and Dakota. At the conclusion of that period he was appointed to West Point as instructor in the use of small arms. During the Civil War he returned to active service. After the war he was appointed a staff colonel and assistant adjutant-general of the Pacific department and later at Washington. He invented improvements in military firearms which met with the acceptance of the Ordnance Department. He retired from active service in 1892 and from then on till his death was governor of the Soldiers' Home, Washington, D. C., where he died July 15, 1893.

KENNEDY, JOSEPH CAMP GRIFFITH, statistician, was born in Meadville, in 1813. He practiced law, edited country newspapers, and in 1849 assumed charge of reorganizing the United States Census Bureau and in 1859 became head of the Bureau. He was instrumental in the holding of the Statisticians' Congress in Brussels in 1853, and to him is much of the early organization of United States statistical reports owed. He died in 1887.

KENT, JACOB FORD, general, was born in Philadelphia, September 14, 1835. He was graduated from West Point, in 1861; entered the army as a 2nd lieutenant, May 6, 1861; became captain in January, 1864, and was brevetted colonel of volunteers in October, 1864, for faithful and meritorious services in the field during the campaign before Richmond. After the war he was assistant instructor in tactics at West Point, and from 1869-1898 was on frontier and garrison duty. At the opening of the war with Spain he was colonel of the 24th infantry. He was made major-general of volunteers in 1898 and served with distinction in Cuba and afterward in the Philippines. He was retired in October, 1898, soon after attaining the rank of brigadier-general. He died December 22, 1918.

KENT, WILLIAM, engineer, was born in Philadelphia, March 5, 1851. Graduated from Stevens Institute of Technology and Syracuse University; became editor of "American Manufacturer and Iron World," 1877-1879; editor of "Engineering News," 1895-1903; chosen dean of L. C. Smith College of Applied Sciences (Syracuse University), 1903-1908. He held numerous patents on his own inventions; contributed to magazines and encyclopædias. Some of his published works are: "The Strength of Materials," "Strength of Wrought Iron and Chain Cables," and "Steam Boiler Economy." He died September 18, 1918.

KERR, MICHAEL CRAWFORD, statesman, was born in Titusville, March 15, 1827. He graduated from Louisville University, in 1851, and the following year began the practice of law in Indiana. He served in Congress from 1864-1872; was defeated for reelection in the latter year, but in 1874 was reelected and in 1875 became Speaker of the House. He died at Rockbridge, Va., August 19, 1876.

KERR, MINA, educator, was born at Saville, Saville Township, Perry County, September 25, 1878, the daughter of Lewis Barnett Kerr, one of the earliest county superintendents of schools of Perry County. She graduated from Smith College with the A. B. degree and Phi Beta Kappa honors in 1900, and in 1909 was granted the Ph. D. degree by the University of Pennsylvania. From 1900-1906, she was instructor and professor of English at Hood College, Frederick, Md.; in 1909-1910, was professor of English at Cornell College, Mt. Vernon, Iowa; from 1910-1921, was dean of Milwaukee-Downer College, Milwaukee, Wisconsin; and from 1921 to date has been dean of Wheaton College, Norton, Mass. In 1920-1922, Miss Kerr was president of the National Association of Deans of Women. She has traveled extensively in Europe, Alaska, Canada, and the United States; is well known as a lecturer; is the author of "The Influence of Ben Johnson on English Comedy," and a frequent contributor to educational and religious periodicals.

KETTLE CREEK—Tributary to West Branch Susquehanna River. Sub-basin: Middle West Branch Susquehanna; source, in Elk Township, southwestern Tioga County; course, southwesterly, through Potter County, into Clinton County; thence southerly, by a circuitous route, to West Branch Susquehanna River; mouth, at Westport; length, forty-one and one-half miles.

KEYSTONE STATE, the name popularly applied to Pennsylvania because of its central position among the thirteen original colonies. It is believed that the term was first used in an address given before the Philadelphia Democrats, in August, 1803, when the Speaker called Pennsylvania the "keystone of the Democratic arch."

KIASHUTHA, Iroquois Indian, lived near Sharpsburg, Allegheny County. He was a follower of Pontiac and an ally of the English during the Revolution. After the war, he became friendly to the Americans and encouraged western Indians to submit to the government.

KING, JAMES MARCUS, clergyman, was born at Girard, March 18, 1839. He graduated from Wesleyan University, in 1862; taught in the Fort Edward Collegiate Institute, and entered the Methodist Episcopal ministry in 1866. After serving various important charges in the Troy and New York Conferences, in 1899, became assistant corresponding secretary, and the following year secretary of the Board of Church Extension of the Methodist Episcopal Church. The work of the society was enlarged in 1907 and became the Board of Home Missions and Church Extension of the Methodist Episcopal Church; Dr. King was its first corresponding secretary and served until his death in 1907.

KING BEAVER, a chief of the Turkey Clan of Delawares, succeeded his brother, Shingas, as king of the Delaware tribe. He attended the meeting with George Croghan and Andrew Montour at Logstown, in May, 1751; the treaty between the Virginia Commissioners and western Indians at Logstown, June, 1752, and the conferences with Conrad Weiser, George Croghan, Tanacharison, and Scarouady, at Aughwick, in September, 1754. Without doubt he took an active part in the French and Indian War, leading many invasions upon the frontier of the province. He attended the great council at Fort Pitt, July 5, 1759, where he was the main speaker; the Indian Conference with General Monckton at Fort Pitt on August 12, 1760; the conference at Fort Pitt in May, 1765, held in the interests of resuming trade relations between Pennsylvania and western tribes after the close of Pontiac's War; and the great council at Fort Pitt in April and May, 1768, held between Pennsylvania, the western tribes, and the Six Nations, for the purpose of settling land difficulties. During the latter part of his life, King Beaver came under the influence of the Moravians and accepted Christianity. He died at King Beaver's Town, in Ohio, in 1771. Beaver River in western Pennsylvania is named for him.

KINZUA CREEK—Tributary to Allegheny River. Sub-basin: Upper Allegheny; source, in Keating Township, central McKean County; course, southwesterly to near Mt. Jewett; thence northwesterly into Warren County to Allegheny River; mouth, near Kinzua; length, thirty-four miles. Indian name, Kentschuak, "they gobble," having reference to the sound made by a wild turkey.

KIRKBRIDE, THOMAS STORY, physician, was born near Morrisville, Bucks County, July, 1809. His ancestors came to this country with Wm. Penn and were members of Society of Friends. Kirkbride graduated from University of Pennsylvania, in 1832, after which he became resident physician of Friends' Insane Hospital at Frankford. A year later he was elected resident physician of Pennsylvania Hospital, served for two years, then began general practice in Philadelphia. In 1841, he became superintendent and physician of the Pennsylvania Hospital for Insane and continued in that position until death, December 16, 1883. He wrote many valuable articles on care of the insane and on construction and general arrangements of hospitals for the insane. He was instrumental in bringing about more humane and rational treatment of insane persons and many of the fine conditions now existing in hospitals are due to his efforts. In Pennsylvania Hospital Report (1883), page 26, is found a Memorial of T. S. Kirkbride.

KISHACOQUILLAS, a chief of the Shawnees, lived at Ohesson, later Kishacoquillas' Town, on the Juniata River, near Lewistown, at the mouth of the creek which bears his name. In July, 1739, he attended a conference at Philadelphia with Kakowatcheky, Neucheconneh, Tamenbuck and other Shawnee chiefs, and the colonial authorities of Pennsylvania at which the Shawnees, for some time under strong French influence, agreed to abide by the Shawnee treaty of April 23, 1701. Kishacoquillas was a constant friend of the English. He died in 1754.

KISKIMINITAS RIVER (INCLUDING CONEMAUGH RIVER)—Tributary to Allegheny River. Sub-basin: Lower Allegheny; source, formed by junction of Little Conemaugh River and Stony Creek at Johnstown, southwestern Cambria County; course, northwesterly to Allegheny River, forming southern boundaries of Armstrong and Indiana Counties and northern boundary of Westmoreland County; mouth, opposite Freeport; length, total seventy-eight miles. Conemaugh River, fifty-one miles; Kiskiminitas River, twenty-seven miles. Indian name, Gieschgumanito, signifying "make daylight," or Kee-ak-kshee-man-nit-toos, signifying "cut spirit."

KITTANNING, borough and county-seat of Armstrong County; located on the Allegheny River, 45 miles north of Pittsburgh. Bituminous coal, oil and gas are the products of the region in which Kittanning is located. The borough is connected by trolley with Ford City, the largest plate glass manufactory in the world. Population (1930), 7,808; (1920), 7,153.

KITTANNING FREE PRESS, THE, originally known as the *Kittanning Gazette*, was established on August 17, 1825, by Josiah Copley and John Croll. It is issued each Friday and is Republican in politics. W. W. and M. B. Oswald are the editors and publishers. Circulation, 2,590.

KITTANNING, BURNING OF—Because of unjust treatment at the hands of the white people the Delaware Indians in revenge committed many outrages. Consequently in September, 1756, Col. John Armstrong marched against the Indian town of Kittanning, without warning attacked the savages, burned their wigwams, and killed their chief, Captain Jacobs, and his wife and son. About eleven Englishmen, held as prisoners, were released, and forty Indians killed.

KLINE, JACOB, military officer, was born in Pennsylvania, November 5, 1840. He served during the Civil War, distinguishing himself at Shiloh and in the Atlanta campaign, and was brevetted captain and major for his services. During the Spanish-American War he performed meritorious service at San Juan, Cuba, and in the Philippines. He was commissioned brigadier-general, United States Army, in 1904, and died at Baltimore, March 23, 1908.

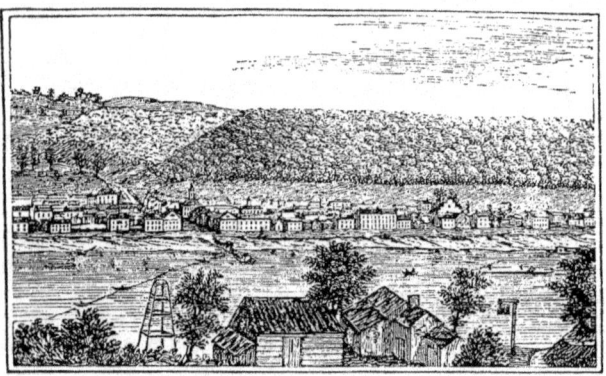

KITTANNING (1843)

KNIGHT, DANIEL RIDGWAY, painter, was born in Philadelphia, in 1850. In 1872, he studied in Paris and received honors from Paris, Munich and Antwerp, and in 1893 received medals at Chicago and Philadelphia Academy of Fine Arts. Among his paintings are: "Washerwoman," "Harvest Scene," and "Hailing the Ferry" (Pennsylvania Academy). He was made officer of the Legion of Honor in 1909 and received The Cross of St. Michael of Bavaria.

KNIGHT, JONATHAN, civil engineer, was born in Bucks County, November 22, 1787, and with his parents came to Washington County in 1801. In 1816, he was appointed by the governor of the State to make a map of Washington County in order to complete Milesh's map of Pennsylvania. He assisted in the survey of the Chesapeake and Ohio Canal and in the National or Cumberland Road between Cumberland, Md., and Wheeling, W. Va. In 1825, by order of the Federal Government he extended the road through the states of Ohio and Indiana to the eastern border of Illinois. He became a member of the State Legislature in 1822, resigning in 1828 to enter the service of the Baltimore and Ohio Railroad in the interests of which he visited many foreign countries. From 1830-1842, he was chief engineer of that company. He died December 5, 1858.

KNOX, PHILANDER CHASE, lawyer, was born at Brownsville, May 6, 1853. He graduated from Mt. Union College, 1872, studied law and was admitted to the bar in 1875; became assistant United States District Attorney, Western District of Pennsylvania, 1876-1877. He practiced law with J. H. Reed and was known as one of the most successful corporation lawyers in the United States; was counsel for Carnegie during Homestead strike; appointed Attorney-General of United States, in 1901, and held that office until June, 1904, when he became senator from Pennsylvania, filling out Senator Quay's term. He was prominent in Panama Canal debate, and as Attorney-General involved in "anti-trust" agitation, brought suit against Northern Securities Company and the so-called "beef-trust." Owing to violation of Federal statutes, in 1907, he received 68 votes for nomination for president in the Republican National Convention. In 1909, he was made secretary of State in President Taft's Cabinet; in 1912, made a tour of the Latin-American countries; was reelected to the United States Senate in 1916 for years 1917-1923. He died in Washington, D. C., October 12, 1921.

KUTZTOWN STATE TEACHERS' COLLEGE, was founded September 15, 1866, as the Keystone State Teachers' College, an outgrowth of Fairview Seminary, opened in the "Fairview Mansion" near the present site of the State Teachers' College. In December, 1926, the State Council of Education granted the institution the authority to confer the degree of Bachelor of Science in Education and in May, 1928, the name was officially changed to Kutztown State Teachers' College. In June, 1929, the institution was further authorized to grant the degree of B.S. in Public School Art.

The college is located on the William Penn Highway in the western end of Kutztown, Berks County.

KYN, JORAN (Keen, George), the founder of Uplands (now Chester), was born in Sweden about 1620. He came to America as aide to Governor Printz and lived at Tinicum. About 1644, Kyn or Keen received from the Swedish government a grant of land one and a half miles inland along the right bank of the Chester Creek and eastward along the Delaware to Ridley Creek. For more than twenty-five years he was the proprietor of Uplands, where a settlement was begun sometime between 1646 and 1648.

LABOR DAY, a legal holiday, observed in Pennsylvania and other manufacturing and industrial states, on the first Monday in September.

LACEY, JOHN, military officer, was born in Bucks County, February 4, 1755. During the Revolution he served as commander of a volunteer company and attained the rank of brigadier-general before he was twenty-three. Leaving military life he became a member of the Pennsylvania Assembly, in 1778, and of the Council, in 1779. Later he reentered the military service. Upon removing to New Jersey he served as a member of the legislature. He died at New Mills, N. J., February 17, 1814.

LACKAWANNA COUNTY, formed from part of Luzerne, April 13, 1878. Named from the Delaware Indian name, Lechanhannek, meaning "forks of the stream," that was applied to the Lackawanna River. Land area, 451 square miles; population (1930), 310,397; county-seat, Scranton, laid out in 1841.

LACKAWANNA RIVER—Tributary to North Branch Susquehanna River. Sub-basin: Lower North Branch Susquehanna; source, formed by junction of east and west branches, in Clifford Township, southeastern Susquehanna County; course, southeasterly into Wayne County; thence southwesterly, through Lackawanna County, into Luzerne County to North Branch Susquehanna River; mouth, near Pittston; length, forty miles. Indian name, a corruption of Lechau-hannek, "the forks of a stream."

LACKAWAXEN RIVER—Tributary to Delaware River. Sub-basin: Upper Delaware; source, formed by junction of West Branch and Waymart Branch at Prompton, central Wayne County; course, southeasterly to Hawley; thence easterly into Pike County to Delaware River; mouth, at Lackawaxen; length, twenty-seven miles. Indian name, Lechauwesink, "where the roads fork."

LADIES' UNION RELIEF ASSOCIATION and The Ladies' Aid Society were organizations established in Philadelphia during the Civil War period (1861), for the purpose of making clothing for the soldiers and for providing relief, by various means, for sick and wounded soldiers and sailors.

LAFAYETTE COLLEGE, a Presbyterian college for men at Easton, was founded in 1832 and named for the Marquis de Lafayette. It was originally chartered in 1826, but owing to the failure of the legislature to make any appropriation, the college was not opened until 1832. Enrollment (1930-1931), 1,000.

LAMBERT, LOUIS A., Roman Catholic clergyman, was born at Charleroi, April 13, 1835. He was educated at St. Vincent's College and the Archdiocesan Seminary, St. Louis, and was ordained to the priesthood in 1859. He was chaplain in an Illinois regiment during the Civil War; pastor at Cairo, Ill., 1863-1869, and subsequently at Seneca Falls and Waterloo, N. Y. He founded the Catholic Times in 1874 and was its editor until 1880. In 1894, he became editor-in-chief of the New York Freeman's Journal. He died in 1910.

NORTH QUEEN STREET, LANCASTER, ABOUT 1840

LAMBERTON, JOHN PORTER, editor and author, was born in Philadelphia, October 22, 1839. He was graduated from the University of Virginia, in 1858, and after teaching, 1859-1880, became an assistant in the library of the University of Pennsylvania. He was associate editor of the American Supplement to the Encyclopædia Britannica, 1881-1890; reviser to Webster's Dictionary, 1891-1899, and edited: "Historic Characters and Famous Events," "Literature of All Ages," and "Literature of the 19th Century." He died July 26, 1917.

LANCASTER, city and county-seat of Lancaster County, 68 miles west of Philadelphia and 37 miles east of Harrisburg. It is the manufacturing trade center for the county; is an important tobacco market; and is engaged in tobacco growing, cigar making, cattle raising, and manufacture of cotton goods, iron and steel goods, shoes and combs. It is the seat of Franklin and Marshall College.

The city was founded in 1718 by Mennonites and was called Hickory Town until 1730. In 1777, Congress sat here for a few days, and from 1799 to 1812 it was the capital of the state. It became a borough in 1742 and a city in March, 1818. Here was the birthplace of General John Fulton Reynolds and a monument has been erected to his memory. Population (1930), 59,949; (1920), 53,150.

LANCASTER COUNTY, formed from part of Chester, May 10, 1729. Named for the English Shire of Lancashire. Land area, 941 square miles; population (1930), 196,882; county-seat, Lancaster, laid out in 1730.

LANCASTER COUNTY COLONIZATION SOCIETY, was founded in 1837 in the interests of the colored race. Attempts were made to form a colony of free colored people on the coast of Africa, through which Africa might become civilized and Christianized.

LANCASTER INTELLIGENCER-JOURNAL, THE, is the result of a merger of the *Lancaster Intelligencer*, established in 1799, and the *Lancaster Journal*, established in 1794. The merger took place in 1839. The motto of the *Journal* was: "Not too rash, yet not too fearful." It is a daily morning paper with a Sunday edition and maintains independence in politics. J. H. Steinman is the editor. Circulation, 19,378.

LANCASTER NEW ERA, THE, appears daily in the evening except Sundays. It is Republican in politics and was established in 1830. Elmer Curry is the editor. Circulation, 32,071.

LANCASTER STAGE DISPATCH, THE—In 1792, Matthias Slough, Hunt Downing, and John Dunwoody entered into an agreement to run a line of stages, between Philadelphia and Lancaster, under the name of "The Lancaster Stage Dispatch." In 1796, Slough and William Geer extended the line from

Lancaster to Shippensburg. Stages had been run from Lancaster before 1777, but it was not until 1792 that a regular line was established. In 1799, when Lancaster became the capital of the state, stage travel increased and other lines were begun so that by 1823 no less than eleven stages ran daily from Philadelphia to Lancaster and points further west.

LANCASTER, TREATY OF—In 1744, deputies of the Six Nations met with commissioners from Maryland and Virginia at Lancaster where a treaty was made providing that the Indians cede all lands which they claimed in Virginia to the white men for about $2,000; by treaty the lands claimed by the Indians in Maryland were also given over to the proprietor of that province, Lord Baltimore.

LANDRETH, BURNET, agriculturist, was born in Philadelphia, December 30, 1842. He was educated at the Polytechnic College, Philadelphia; was captain of infantry during the Civil War, serving in the Army of the Potomac, and since the war period has devoted himself to the promotion of higher agricultural and allied interests in many important fields of service. He was chief of the Bureau of Agriculture at the Centennial Exhibition, director-in-chief of the American Exhibition in London and is a member of many American scientific societies; also holds honorary membership in similar bodies in European countries, in India, and in Japan. He founded and is president of the Association of Centenary Firms of the United States, and is head of the seed house of D. Landreth & Sons, established in 1784 in Philadelphia. He has published several works on agricultural subjects. His home is in Bristol.

LANSFORD, borough in Carbon County, on the Central Railroad of New Jersey, 44 miles north of Reading. It is the center of the anthracite coal fields. It was settled in 1845 and was incorporated in 1876. Population (1930), 9,632; (1920), 9,625.

LAPORTE, borough and county-seat of Sullivan County, was laid out in 1850. It was incorporated as a borough in 1853 and was named in honor of John LaPorte, surveyor-general of Pennsylvania and a descendant of one of the French families who settled at Asylum.

LARRY CREEK—Tributary to West Branch Susquehanna River. Sub-basin: Lower West Branch Susquehanna; source, in Cogan House Township, central Lycoming County; course, southwesterly to West Branch Susquehanna River; mouth, at Larry's Creek; length, twenty miles.

LA SALLE COLLEGE, for men, founded at Philadelphia, in 1863, is under the control of the Brothers of Christian Schools of the Roman Catholic Church.

LATROBE, JOHN HAZLEHURST BONEVAL, lawyer, was born in Philadelphia, May 4, 1803. He was admitted to the bar in 1825 and practiced law for more than sixty years. He was actively identified with the American Colonization Society in 1824 and assisted in drawing the first map of Liberia. Among his publications are: "History of Mason and Dixon's Line," "History of Maryland in Liberia," etc. He died September 11, 1891, at Baltimore, Md.

LATTER DAY SAINTS—See MORMONS.

LAUREL HILL CREEK—Tributary to Casselman River. Sub-basin: Upper Allegheny; source, in Summit Township, central Erie County; course, northeasterly and southeasterly to French Creek; mouth, two miles south of Waterford; length, fourteen miles.

LAWRENCE COUNTY, formed from part of Beaver and Mercer, March 20, 1849. Name taken from "Lawrence," Perry's Flagship, which was named in honor of Captain James Lawrence. Land area, 360 square miles; population (1930), 97,258; county-seat, New Castle, laid out in 1802.

LAY, BENJAMIN, one of the earliest advocates of the abolition of slavery, was born in Colchester, England, in 1681, emigrated to America and settled in Abington, Pa. He wrote: "All Slavekeepers, that Keep the Innocent in Bondage, Apostates." He died at Abington, in 1760.

LEA, HENRY CHARLES, author, was born in Philadelphia, September 19, 1825. He entered his father's publishing house, in 1843; became its head, in 1865, and retired from business in 1900. He was actively engaged in public undertakings for civil and social advancement and during the Civil War rendered conspicuous services in support of the Federal government. Between 1840 and 1860, he wrote many papers on chemistry and after 1857 devoted his attention to European medieval history. He died in 1909.

LEA, ISAAC, naturalist, was born at Wilmington, Del., March 4, 1792. In early life he engaged in commercial pursuits, and from 1821 to 1851 was partner in a large publishing business, but from boyhood he was devoted to the study of natural history and his various collections of minerals and fossils, and especially of shells were valuable contributions to science. He was a member of the Academy of Natural Sciences of Philadelphia and of the Philosophical Society of the same city, in whose "Transactions" many of his observations were published. He was also elected to membership in learned societies abroad. His work in the study of fresh water and land mollusks brought him special distinction. He died at Philadelphia in December, 1886.

LEA, MATTHEW CAREY, chemist, was born in Philadelphia, in 1823. His work in developing the chemistry of photography has served important purposes. Besides many articles treating on the chemical action of light, his publications include an authoritative "Manual of Photography." He was the eldest son of Isaac Lea. His death occurred March 15, 1897, at Philadelphia.

LEAGUE ISLAND, lying above the mouth of the Schuylkill, consisting of over nine hundred acres, was purchased by the city of Philadelphia during the Civil War and presented to the United States government for a navy yard.

LEAGUE, UNION—See UNION LEAGUE.

LEATHER APRON CLUB, THE, a union of tradesmen of Philadelphia, was formed in 1728 by Benjamin Franklin and ten others, for the protection of the tradesman's rights. An unsuccessful attempt on the part of this club to organize a library, resulted ultimately in the Philadelphia Library, the first in the city.

LEBANON, city and county-seat of Lebanon County, is located about 66 miles northwest of Philadelphia and 23 miles northeast of Harrisburg. Lebanon was settled as early as 1700 by German emigrants. The borough of Lebanon was laid out by George Steitz, in 1750, and was first called Steitztown. It was incorporated in 1820 and chartered as a city in 1885. It is situated in the Lebanon Valley, noted for the fertility of its soil, but the largest part of the wealth of the city comes from the quarries and mines of the vicinity. The Cornwall iron mines about five miles distant from the city, the limestone and brownstone at the base of the mountains, the brick clay, the iron ore, all contribute to the industrial wealth of Lebanon. Its chief industrial establishments are furnaces and foundries, rolling mills, steel plants, machine shops, a very large nut and bolt works, chain works, shirt, hosiery, paper box and shoe factories. Population (1930), 25,561; (1920), 24,643.

LEBANON COUNTY, formed from part of Dauphin and Lancaster, February 16, 1813. Named for the Hebrew word, Lebanon, meaning "white mountains." Land area, 360 square miles; population (1930), 67,103; county-seat, Lebanon, laid out in 1750.

LEBANON COURIER AND REPORT, THE, established as the *Courier* in 1819, is an independent paper which appears twice a week. William R. Mark is the editor.

LEBANON VALLEY COLLEGE, a co-educational institution, was founded in 1867, at Annville, by the United Brethren Church. Aside from the liberal arts course, the college has departments of education and business administration and a conservatory of music. Enrollment (1930-1931), 360.

LEE, GUY CARLETON, educator and author, was graduated from Dickinson College, Carlisle, where he was for a time professor of history. He has since filled other educational posts and was literary editor of the Baltimore Sun from 1901-1908; editor-in-chief, International Literary Syndicate, 1900-1916; managing director, National Society for Broader Education, New York, 1909 to date. His publications include: "Hincmar—An Introduction to the Study of the Church in the Ninth Century," "Historical Jurisprudence," "Source Book of English History," and "True History of the War between the States." His home is in Carlisle.

LEGISLATURE—Under Penn's Frame of Government, issued in 1682, which consisted of twenty-four articles and forty laws, the government was vested in the Governor and the Freemen of the province. The Freemen were to elect a Provincial Council and a General Assembly; the former to consist of seventy-two members and the latter of all the Freemen the first year, and of two hundred of them the next year, the members to be increased with the growth of population. The governor or his deputy was the president of the council and was to have a treble vote. The General Assembly had no power to initiate legislature and no privilege to debate. They could vote yes or no on legislation proposed by the council. They could also name persons for sheriffs and justices of the peace for the governor to select from, being obliged to name twice as many as were appointed. A vote of six-sevenths of the Freemen in both the Provincial Council and the General Assembly was required to amend the Frame with the consent of the governor. The first General Assembly met at Chester, in 1682. They accepted the Frame of Government and its accompanying laws, to which were added twenty-one others, making sixty-one laws on the statute books of the province. Under the Constitution of 1776, the General Assembly consisted of only one branch, the members being elected annually, and its acts were called Acts of Assembly. Members could serve only four years in seven. The Constitution of 1790 provided for a senate, the members of which were elected for a term of four years and their numbers could not be less than one-fourth nor greater than one-third of the number of representatives. Senators must have attained the age of twenty-five years. The representatives were chosen annually, and shall never be less than sixty nor more than one hundred. Under the Constitution of 1838, senators were elected for three years. Under the Constitution of 1873, members of the General Assembly are chosen at the general election every second year, and their term of service begins on the first day of December next after their election. Senators are elected for four years and representatives for two years. The General Assembly meets at 12 o'clock noon on the first Tuesday in January every second year but may be called into extra session by the governor. Under the Constitution of 1790 and 1838, the senate elected a presiding officer from its own membership and named the speaker. This office was abolished by the Constitution of 1873, which provided for a lieutenant-governor who presides over the senate. Provision is made, however, for a president protempore of the senate to preside in the absence of the lieutenant-governor. The House of Representatives is made up of approximately two hundred members and the Senate of fifty.

LEHIGH COUNTY, formed from part of Northampton, March 6, 1812. Named for the Indian word, Lecha, originally Lechauwekink. Land area, 344 square miles; population (1930), 172,893; county-seat, Allentown, laid out in 1751.

LEHIGH (LITTLE) CREEK—Tributary to Lehigh River. Sub-basin: Middle Delaware; source, in Topton Mountain, Longswamp Township, Berks County; course, northeasterly into Lehigh County to Lehigh River; mouth, at Allentown; length, twenty-four miles. The name Lehigh is an English corruption of the German shortening of the Indian name, which was Lechauweing, Lechauweeki, Lechauwiechink, which the German settlers contracted to Lecha, and the English to Lehi or Lehigh. The Indian names signified "at the forks."

LEHIGH RIVER—Tributary to Delaware River. Sub-basin: Middle Delaware; source, in Sterling Township, southwestern Wayne County; course, southwesterly to White Haven, being boundary of Lackawanna and Luzerne Counties to northwest and Monroe and Carbon Counties to southeast; mouth, at Easton; length, one hundred miles. The name Lehigh is an English corruption of the German shortening of the Indian name which was Lechauweing, Lechauweeki, Lechauwiechink, which the German settlers contracted to Lecha, and the English to Lehi or Lehigh. The Indian names signified "at the forks."

FORT AND VILLAGE OF LENNI LENAPE INDIANS

LEHIGH UNIVERSITY, a college for men, at South Bethlehem, was founded in 1866 by Asa Packer. Eight technical courses, civil engineering, mechanical engineering, metallurgical engineering, electrometallurgy, mining engineering, electrical engineering, chemical engineering and chemistry, are offered. There are also courses leading to the A.B. and B.S. degrees, a course in Business Administration and Graduate courses, leading to the Master's degree. Enrollment (1930-1931), 1,570.

LEIDY, JOSEPH, naturalist, was born in Philadelphia, September 9, 1823. He graduated from University of Pennsylvania in 1844 and was elected to the chair in Anatomy in 1853. In 1871 became professor of Natural History at Swarthmore College; in 1881, was made president of Academy of Natural Science at Philadelphia; and in 1885 became president of Wagner Institute of Science. He is the author of many valuable memoirs, among them: "Treatise on Human Anatomy," and "Ancient Fauna of Nebraska." He died in Philadelphia, April 30, 1891. (Consult the Memoir by Chapman in Proceedings of Natural Science Academy, 1891.)

LEISHMAN, JOHN G. A., diplomatist, was born in Pittsburgh, March 28, 1857. From 1897-1900 he was minister to Switzerland; 1900-1906, minister to Turkey; 1906-1909, Ambassador to Turkey; 1909-1911, Ambassador to Italy. He died March 27, 1924.

LE LAND, CHARLES GODFREY, author, was born in Philadelphia, August 15, 1824. He showed poetic talent in youthful contributions to newspapers and a growing genius, marked by unusual versatility, during his college days at Princeton, where he graduated in 1846. He studied afterward at Heidelberg, Munich and Paris, giving special attention to modern languages and philosophy. In 1848, he took part in the revolutionary uprising in Paris. The same year he returned to Philadelphia and studied law; was admitted to the bar in 1851 but gave up the legal profession and devoted himself to literary pursuits, becoming prominent in various fields of journalism and authorship. For a time he was editor of the New York Illustrated News; in 1861, established the Continental Magazine in Boston and two years later returned to Philadelphia, where for several years he edited the Press. During the Civil War he published "The Book of Copperheads," a political satire. From 1869 to 1880 he resided chiefly in London. In England and on the continent he studied gypsies and gypsy lore, in which he became one of the leading authorities of his time. In 1880, he returned to Philadelphia and was instrumental in establishing industrial teaching in the public schools, in furtherance of which he wrote a number of manuals and gave his supervision to the work. From 1886 he lived in Europe, mainly in Florence. Among his publications are: "Hans Breitmann's Ballads," "France, Alsace and Lorraine," "Life of Abraham Lincoln," "Industrial Work in Schools"

LENNI LENAPE INDIAN FAMILY
Drawing by Peter Lindestrom (1654-1655)

(U. S. Bureau of Education), "One Hundred Profitable Arts," "Algonquian Legends," and "Practical Education." He died in Florence, Italy, March 30, 1903.

LE MOYNE, FRANCIS JULIUS, physician, was born in Washington, Pa., September 24, 1798. He studied medicine in Philadelphia and began practice in his home town. In 1835, he allied himself with the abolitionists, was subsequently the Liberty Party's first nominee for Vice-President, which he declined and was several times that party's candidate for the governorship of Pennsylvania. In 1876, he built near Washington, the first crematory in the United States. He died in Washington, October 14, 1879.

LENNI-LENAPE, or Delaware Indians, occupied land in eastern Pennsylvania. They were one of many tribes belonging to the Algonquian nation.

LESLEY, J. PETER, geologist, was born in Philadelphia, September 17, 1819. He graduated from the University of Pennsylvania, in 1838; engaged as assistant in the first geological survey of Pennsylvania; graduated from Princeton Theological Seminary and licensed as a minister; traveled in Europe and studied at the University of Halle. From 1845 to 1848, he labored for the American Tract Society among people in the mountain districts of Pennsylvania and then served two years as a minister of a Congregational church at Milton, Mass., resigning on account of a change in his religious views. He returned to Philadelphia and resumed his geological researches in this country and in Canada. In 1855, he became secretary of the American Iron Association; in 1858, secretary and librarian of the American Philosophical Society. Was state geologist of Pennsylvania, in 1874; professor of geology at the University of Pennsylvania, 1872-1878; and in 1886, was appointed emeritus professor there. In 1863, he went to Europe to examine the Bessemer Iron Works for the Pennsylvania Railroad Company, and in 1867 was appointed by the United States Senate a commissioner to the Paris Exposition. He died at Milton, Mass., in June, 1903.

LETITIA HOUSE, was built in Philadelphia by William Penn and is said to have been erected for his daughter, for whom it was named. Penn, himself, occupied the residence for a time.

LETTERS FROM A PENNSYLVANIA FARMER. Political writings, entitled "Letters from a Farmer in Pennsylvania to the Inhabitants of the British Colonies," were written by John Dickinson, and published anonymously in a Philadelphia newspaper in 1767. In his "Letters," which are the literary masterpieces of all the political writings of the period, Dickinson advocated a conservative policy for the colonies in their dealings with England. He maintained that his object was "to convince the people of these colonies, that they are, at this moment, exposed to the most imminent dangers; and to persuade them, immediately, vigorously, and unanimously, to exert themselves, in the most firm but most peaceable manner, for obtaining relief."

The Letters were collected and published in pamphlet form, of which there were eight editions in America, two in London, one in Dublin and one in France. So popular were these writings that Dickinson ranked next to Franklin as the literary highlight of the day.

LETITIA HOUSE

LEVY, URIAH PHILLIPS, naval officer, was born in Pennsylvania about 1795. In 1812, he joined the navy and while on duty on the Argus was captured and held prisoner for two years. He was promoted to a captaincy in 1844. He is the author of a "Manual of Internal Rules and Regulations for Men-of-War." He died in New York City, March 22, 1862.

LEWIS, DAVID, an outlaw, who lived in central Pennsylvania, in the early nineteenth century. Tradition has made him a hero, and among the tales related of him is one concerning his escape from the Bedford jail. All the prisoners except one, who refused to go, were released by Lewis. All were finally recaptured, with the exception of Lewis and a man named Connelly, who while crossing Will's Mountain into Milliken's Cove by the Packer's Path were warned by a slight noise of the approach of their pursuers, stepped aside behind a huge rock which concealed them until the sheriff and his party went by.

Another traditional story is that Lewis once stayed over night at the house of a poor widow in an obscure section of the country. She was in great trouble for her cow and household goods were levied upon by a constable for a debt she could not pay. Lewis asked the amount of the debt, gave the widow the money and received her sincere thanks for his generosity. Soon after the constable arrived and the widow paid her debt. A mile or two away Lewis lay in wait for the constable and when he arrived relieved him of the money he had but a few hours before loaned the widow.

Tradition attributes to Lewis characteristics of Robin Hood, some of these being that he never robbed the poor, that he took from the rich to give the poor, and that he never shed human blood.

Lewis was born in Carlisle in March, 1790, but soon after his family removed to Northumberland County. He died from a gun-shot wound in the Bellefonte jail in 1820.

LEWIS, HENRY CARVILL, geologist, was born in Philadelphia, November 16, 1853. He was graduated from the University of Pennsylvania, in 1873; served as a volunteer in the state geological survey of Pennsylvania, in 1879–1884; was professor of mineralogy in the Academy of Natural Sciences of Philadelphia, in 1880–1888, and of geology at Haverford College, in 1883–1888. In 1886–1887, he studied at Heidelberg and in 1887–1888 made special investigations regarding the origin of the diamond. He prepared a chart of the various ancient ice-sheets and glaciers of England, Ireland, and Wales. He died July 21, 1888, in Manchester, England.

LEWIS, LAURENCE, lawyer, was born in Philadelphia, June 20, 1857. He graduated from the University of Pennsylvania, in 1876, and three years later was admitted to the bar. He is the author of: "Courts of Pennsylvania in the Seventeenth Century," "History of the Bank of North America," and "Memoir of Edward Shippen, Chief Justice of Pennsylvania."

LEWIS, WILLIAM DRAPER, lawyer, was born in Philadelphia, April 27, 1867. He was graduated at Haverford College, in 1888, and at the University of Pennsylvania, in 1891. In the latter year he was instructor in legal historical institutions in the Wharton School, University of Pennsylvania; in 1890–1896, was lecturer on economics at Haverford; and from 1896–1914, was dean of the law department, University of Pennsylvania. Since 1923 he has been director of the American Law Institute. Lewis is the author of: "Federal Power Over Commerce and Its Effect on State Action," "Our Sheep and the Tariff," "Restraint of Infringement of Incorporeal Rights," and "Life of Theodore Roosevelt." He has also edited several legal compilations. His home is in Germantown.

LEWISBURG, county-seat of Union County, situated on the Susquehanna River. It is in the center of anthracite coal fields and a fertile farming valley; is the seat of Bucknell University, founded by the Baptist Church in 1846.

LEWISBURG JOURNAL, THE, was established as an organ of the Democratic Party by Daniel Gotshall, in 1830. It took for its motto: "Civil liberty never can flourish on the same soil with ignorance." It is a weekly paper now independent in politics. Charles R. Smith is the editor and publisher. Circulation, 1,660.

LEWISTOWN, borough and county-seat of Mifflin County, is located on the Juniata River and on the Pennsylvania Railroad, about 60 miles northwest of Harrisburg. It is situated in a fertile agricultural region in which are valuable mineral deposits, especially iron and glass sand. Lewistown is a trade center for an extensive farming section and is also a manufacturing borough. The chief manufactures are steel, iron, flour, leather, lumber, foundry machine-shop products, and silk. Population (1930), 13,357; (1920), 9,849.

LEWISTOWN GAZETTE, THE, originally called *Juniata Gazette*, was founded in 1811, by James Dickson and William P. Elliott. It appears every Thursday; is Republican in politics; edited by W. W. Cunningham; published by Sentinel Company, Inc.

LIBERTY BELL—*See* BELL, LIBERTY.

LICK, JAMES, philanthropist, was born in Fredericksburg, Lebanon County, August 25, 1796. In 1821, he set up in the piano-forte business in New York and later was a manufacturer of musical instruments at Buenos Ayres, Philadelphia, Valparaiso and elsewhere. In 1847, he went to California where he gained wealth through investments in real estate and various enterprises. In 1874, he placed $3,000,000 at the disposal of seven trustees by whom it was to be applied to specified uses. The principal division of the funds were: To the University of California for the construction of an observatory and the placing therein of a telescope to be more powerful than any other in existence, $700,000; for the building and maintenance of free public baths in San Francisco, $150,000; to found and endow an institution of San Francisco to be known as the California School of Mechanic Arts, $540,000; for the erection of three appropriate groups of bronze statuary to represent three periods in Californian history and to be placed before the city hall of San Francisco, $100,000; to erect in Golden Gate Park, San Francisco, a memorial to F. S. Key, author of "The Star Spangled Banner," $60,000. Lick died at San Francisco, October 1, 1876.

LICKING CREEK—Tributary to Tuscarora Creek. Sub-basin: Lower Juniata; source, in Bratton Township, southern Mifflin County; course, northeasterly into Juniata; thence northeasterly and southeasterly to Tuscarora Creek; mouth, near Port Royal; length, twenty-two miles.

LICKING CREEK—Tributary to Potomac River. Basin: Potomac; source, in Todd Township, northeastern Fulton County; course, southwesterly to Knobsville; thence westerly and southerly into Franklin County; thence southeasterly into Maryland, returning to Pennsylvania and again crossing boundary into Maryland, thence southerly to Potomac River; mouth, near Ernstville, Md.; length, in Pennsylvania, thirty-five miles.

LIGHTON, WILLIAM RHEEM, prose writer, was born in Lycoming County, July 13, 1866. He was admitted to the Kansas and Nebraska bar in 1891 and has published "Sons of Strength, a Romance of the Kansas Border Wars."

LIMESTONE—An early reference to limestone is found in a deed from Lawrence Pearson to his brother, Enoch, in 1703, for a tract of land in Bucks County in which the grantor reserves and excepts "the privilege to get limestone from the within granted premium for the use of the said Lawrence and his children, their heirs and assigns forever."—See also PENNSYLVANIA RESOURCES.

LINCOLN, ABRAHAM, IN PENNSYLVANIA—Abraham Lincoln on his way to Washington to take the oath of office, in 1861, arrived in Pittsburgh from Columbus, on Thursday, February 14th, where he spent the night. On the morning of the 15th, he delivered an address. Both in the evening at the time of his arrival, and in the morning at his departure, the crowd was so dense as to become beyond control. From Pittsburgh, the President-elect went to Cleveland, thence to Buffalo, Albany, New York City and Trenton, arriving in Philadelphia, Thursday, February 21st. On the morning of Washington's Birthday, he raised a flag over Independence Hall. Rumors of plans to assassinate him on his way to Washington were brought to his attention here. From Philadelphia, he proceeded to Lancaster, where he spoke briefly from the balcony of the hotel. He arrived in Harrisburg where he was greeted by the Legislature, to whom he delivered his last address en route. While in Harrisburg, he was entertained by Governor Curtin. Because of the rumors regarding plans to assassinate him he left the special train and the presidential party and made a night journey to Washington, secretly, but not in disguise, accompanied only by Colonel Lamon and Allan Pinkerton. Lincoln arrived at Gettysburg, November 18, 1863, to dedicate the national cemetery. In the evening he was the guest of honor at a reception given by Judge Wills at whose home he was a guest. On the morning of the 19th, he mounted a horse but the crowd forced him to hold an informal reception. After delivering his famous address he never revisited Pennsylvania.

LINCOLN FAMILY IN PENNSYLVANIA—President Lincoln's immigrant ancestor was Samuel Lincoln, of Hingham, Mass., who arrived in this country in 1637 and died in 1690. He was the president's great-great-great-great-grandfather. Samuel's son, Mordecai, was born in Hingham, Mass., in 1657, and died in Scituate, Mass., in 1727; his son, also named Mordecai, was born in Scituate, Mass., April 24, 1686, and after residing in New Jersey died in Berks County, Pennsylvania, in 1736. His son, John Lincoln, known as

"Virginia John," was born in Berks County, Pennsylvania, in 1716, and died in Virginia, in 1788. Captain Abraham Lincoln, son of John, was born in Virginia, in 1744, and died in Kentucky, in 1786. He was the father of Thomas Lincoln and the grandfather of the president. Abraham Lincoln, son of Mordecai, was born January 13, 1688-89, and died in 1745, in Springfield, Pa. Two brothers of "Virginia John" Lincoln rose to prominence in Berks County: Thomas, who became sheriff of the county and posthumous Abraham who was a member of the Legislature of Pennsylvania and of the Pennsylvania Constitutional Convention of 1790, which document bears his signature.

ANCESTRAL HOME OF THE LINCOLNS,
EIGHT MILES SOUTH OF READING

LINDERMAN, HENRY RICHARD, financier, was born in Lehman, December 26, 1825. From 1855-1864, he was head clerk in the United States Mint in Philadelphia; became director of the Mint, in 1867, and held that position for two years. With John Jay Knox he framed the Coinage Act of 1873 and subsequently supervised all assay offices and mints in the United States. He wrote "Money and Legal Tender in the United States." He died in Washington, D. C., January 27, 1879.

LINDSAY, SAMUEL McCUNE, political economist and educator, was born in Pittsburgh, May 10, 1869. He was graduated from the University of Pennsylvania, in 1889, and took post-graduate courses there and abroad. After his return to the United States he was appointed assistant professor of sociology at the University of Pennsylvania. Later he became professor of social legislation at Columbia University, which position he holds to date. His home is in New York.

LINN, WILLIAM, clergyman, was born in Shippensburg, February 27, 1752. In 1772, he graduated from Princeton and in 1775 was ordained to the ministry of the Presbyterian Church. He was a chaplain in the Continental

Army in 1776 and wrote: "Signs of the Times," "A Funeral Eulogy on General Washington," etc. He died in Albany, N. Y., January 8, 1808.

LIPPARD, GEORGE, author, was born near Yellow Springs, April 10, 1822. He is the author of: "Legends of the Revolution," "New York— Its Upper Ten and Lower Million," "The Quaker City," "Washington and His Generals," etc. He died in Philadelphia, February 9, 1854.

LITERARY MAGAZINE AND AMERICAN REGISTER, THE, was founded in October, 1803, by Charles Brockden Brown, Philadelphia, and existed for about five years.

LITITZ, borough in Lancaster County, about 28 miles southeast of Harrisburg and 8 miles north of Lancaster. The first permanent settlement was made in 1757 by Moravians who named the place after their old home in Bohemia. Lititz is situated in a rich agricultural region. Its chief industries are in manufacturing; the principal products are knit goods, and food products. The mineral springs are noted and much frequented. The borough is the seat of Linden Hall Seminary, a girl's school, established in 1794.

LITTLE, CHARLES JOSEPH, theologian, was born in Philadelphia, September 21, 1840. He graduated from the University of Pennsylvania, in 1861; was professor of philosophy and history at Dickinson College, 1874-1885; professor of logic and history, Syracuse University, 1885-1891; professor of historical theology, Garrett Biblical Institute, 1891-1895, and later president of Garrett Biblical Institute. He died in 1911.

LITTLEHALES, GEORGE WASHINGTON, hydrographic engineer, was born in Schuylkill County, October 14, 1860. He was graduated from the United States Naval Academy, in 1883, and in 1900 became engineer in the United States Hydrographic Office. Among his publications are: "Submarine Cables," "The Azimuths of Celestial Bodies," and "Geographical Positions—Line Tables." He has done extensive research in hydrography, oceanography, and terrestrial magnetism, the results of which are given in more than 100 papers and has published about 3,000 charts used in the navigation of vessels. His home is in Washington, D. C.

LLOYD, NELSON McALLISTER, journalist and author, was born in Philadelphia, December 18, 1872. He was educated at the Germantown Academy and graduated in electrical engineering at Pennsylvania State College in 1892. From 1892-1909, he was engaged in newspaper work on the New York Evening Sun. In addition to numerous contributions of historical sketches and short stories to magazines he has written: "The Chronic Loafer," "A Drone and a Dreamer," "The Soldier of the Valley," "Mrs. Radigan," "The Robberies Company, Ltd.," "Six Stars," and "David Malcolm." He lives in Lawrenceville, N. J.

LOCK HAVEN, city and county-seat of Clinton County, was laid out in 1833, by Jeremiah Church, of New York. He named the town Lock Haven because of the lock in the canal at that point. It is the seat of the Lock Haven State Teachers College and among its industrial establishments are a paper mill, furniture factory, silk mill and planing mill. Population (1930), 9,668; (1920), 8,557.

LOCK HAVEN STATE TEACHERS' COLLEGE, was incorporated February 14, 1870, by a group of subscribers, as the Central Normal School. It is located at Lock Haven, Clinton County, on the West Branch of the Susquehanna.

LOG COLLEGE, one of the earliest classical schools in the province, founded before 1725, at Neshaminy, Bucks County, by Rev. William Tennent, for the education of young men for the ministry. Built of logs, and about twenty-five feet square, it was the only classical school within the bounds of the Presbyterian Church where young men could be fitted for the ministry, and many eminent men were educated there. In 1746, the College of New Jersey was established first at Elizabethtown, removed in 1748 to Newark and in 1756 again removed to Princeton, where it remained. Log College was the germ of Princeton College. After the doors of Log College were closed but a short time elapsed before Princeton College was permanently established to take its place.

THE LOG COLLEGE

LOGAN, a Cayuga chief whose Indian name was Ta-ga-jute, was born in Shamokin about 1725. In 1774, his family was massacred by a band of white people and he vowed vengeance against the race. He refused to accept an invitation to a conference with Lord Dunmore on the Scioto, sending Col. John

Gibson, who married his sister, with a message explaining that until the murder of his family he had been a friend of the white man. Afterwards he killed many, securing vengeance for the wrongs done him.

LOGAN, JAMES, statesman, was born in Lurgan, Ireland, October 20, 1674. He became Secretary of Pennsylvania under Penn in 1699 and later was Chief Justice of the province. After Governor Gordon died, Logan, the president of the Council, supervised governmental affairs for two years, and always maintained friendly relations with the Indians. His death occurred near Philadelphia, October 31, 1751.

LONG, CHESTER I., statesman, was born in Perry County, October 12, 1860. In 1879, he moved to Paola, Kansas; was a member of Congress, 1895-1897, and 1899-1903; United States Senator, 1903-1909. He is a member of the law firm of Long, Houston, Depew, Norton, and Stanley, with offices in Wichita, Kansas.

LORD DUNMORE'S WAR—See DUNMORE'S WAR.

LOSKIEL, GEORGE H., Moravian bishop, came to this country from Europe, July 23, 1802, and succeeded Bishop John Ettwein as head of the American General Board of the Moravian Church. New activities were awakened after his arrival. He labored under great difficulties until 1811, when, broken in health, he was relieved of his duties, and after some months received a call to return to Europe. When war with England broke out he was detained here, and in the meantime his physical infirmities increased and upon two occasions he was dissuaded from making the trip. He wrote "A History of the Missions of the Brethren." He died at Bethlehem, February 23, 1814.

LOTTERIES IN PENNSYLVANIA—With the settlement of the province came the need for internal improvements, and consequently for adequate finances. In order that the people need not be overburdened with taxes, lotteries, authorized by the State Legislature, came into general use for religious, charitable, public and speculative purposes. The Quaker element in Pennsylvania was from the beginning of the province opposed to this method of raising money. Various acts were passed by the legislature in attempts to suppress the practice, which had never been popular with the English government. In 1762, an act was passed making it illegal under penalty of 500 pounds to "publicly or privately set up, erect, make, exercise, keep open, show or expose to be played at, drawn or thrown at any such lottery, play or device or that shall cause or procure the same to be done after the publication of this act," and providing that any person convicted of buying or selling lotteries, or being in any way connected with them, be fined twenty pounds for every offense. This act was more effective than any previous one, although it did not prevent the sale of tickets for lotteries authorized by other states. Later legislatures, because of changed personnel, were not so opposed to the lottery, and consequently from 1796-1808, seventy-eight different lotteries, nearly half the entire number in the history of the state, were authorized. Lottery brokers resided in all the large cities. Philadelphia had sixty in 1827, one hundred and seventy-seven in 1831 and nearly two hundred in 1833. In the latter year an act was passed entirely abolishing lotteries.

LOWRY, ROBERT, hymn writer, was born in Philadelphia, March 12, 1826. After graduation from Lewisburg (now Bucknell) University, in 1854, he entered the ministry of the Baptist Church and held pastorates at West Chester, New York City, Brooklyn, N. Y., and Plainfield, N. J. From 1869-1875, he was professor of literature at his alma mater and from 1876-1882 was chancellor of the University. He served as president of the New Jersey Baptist Sunday-School Union, 1880-1886, and was a delegate to the Robert Raikes Centennial in London in 1880. Among the hymns which he composed are: "Shall We Gather at the River?", "One More Day's Work for Jesus," "I Need Thee Every Hour," "Where is My Wandering Boy Tonight?" He died in Plainfield, N. J., November 25, 1899.

LOYALHANNA CREEK Tributary to Kiskiminitas River. Sub-basin: Lower Allegheny; source, in Cook Township, southeastern Westmoreland County; course, northerly to Ligonier; thence northwesterly to Kiskiminitas River; mouth, opposite Saltsburg; length, forty-nine miles. Indian name, a corruption of Lawel-hanne, "middle stream."

LOYALSOCK CREEK—Tributary to West Branch Susquehanna River. Sub-basin: Lower West Branch Susquehanna; source, in Forkston Township, southwestern Lycoming County; course, westerly into Sullivan County to Forksville; thence southwesterly into Lycoming County to West Branch Susquehanna River; mouth, at Montoursville; length, fifty-nine and one-half miles. Indian name, a corruption of Lawisaquick, "middle creek."

LOYPARCOWAH, son of Opessah, chief of the Shawnees, remained constant to the English. He moved from the Susquehanna Valley to the Allegheny Valley, probably accompanying the first band of Shawnees to go to western Pennsylvania about 1727. Loyparcowah strongly opposed the sale of rum among the Indians and at a council with his people in 1738 instituted a pledge which was signed by ninety-eight Shawnees and Peter Chartier and George Miranda, traders.

LUDINGTON, MARSHALL INDEPENDENCE, military officer, was born in Smithfield, July 4, 1839. During the Civil War he served in the Union Army, becoming captain and quartermaster in 1862. He later attained rank of major and quartermaster and on March 13, 1865, was brevetted brigadier-general. After the war he served in the regular army and on February 8, 1898, was promoted to brigadier-general. He died July 29, 1919.

LUKENS, JOHN, surveyor-general, was born in 1720, son of Peter and (Gainor) Evans Lukens and grandson of Jan Lukens who came to this country in 1688. He was surveyor-general of Pennsylvania and Delaware, 1761-1776, and of Pennsylvania, 1781-1789. He married October 31, 1741, his first cousin, Sarah Lukens. He died October 21, 1789.

LUTHERAN CHURCH, THE, IN PENNSYLVANIA, had its inception in the Swedish treaties and purchases which extended west to the Great Falls of the Susquehanna, near York Haven. Swedish Lutherans, nearly fifty years before Penn's Treaty with the Indians under Shakamaxon Elm, laid the foundations for the friendly attitude of the savage toward William Penn, by teaching and practicing among the Indians righteous principles and brotherly love. Lutherans were the first missionaries in Pennsylvania. Luther's Small Catechism was the first Protestant book to be translated into a heathen tongue, the Delaware language. Campanius was the translator. The first Lutheran Church was a block-house at Wicacoa, a mile below the southern limits of Philadelphia, in 1669. Pastor Fabricius, a Dutch preacher, who had also mastered the Swedish language, was the pastor of the Swedish-Lutherans who worshipped there. This church was superseded by a new church which was erected on a site near the old church, and was dedicated on July 2, 1700, on the first Sunday after Trinity under the name of Gloria Dei. The first German-Lutheran congregation organized within the limits of the United States was undoubtedly that of Falckner's Swamp (New Hanover), on the Mataney Creek, in Montgomery County, of which Justus Falckner was pastor. He was the first Lutheran minister ordained in this country in the Swedish Church, at Wicacoa, on November 24, 1703. Swedish pastors ministered to the little German congregation in Philadelphia and to the numerous surrounding settlements. They preached in groves and barns. In Germantown and Lancaster they founded churches in 1730. A church was established in York in the year 1733. Cordial relations existed between the Swedes and the Germans. About this time deep anxiety for the spiritual needs of the Lutheran people drove them to action. They wrote appealing letters to the homeland, with ungratifying results. It was decided to send a delegation to Europe to endeavor to gain the attention of Lutheran divines to extend help to their brethren in America. The purpose, further, was to arouse sympathy, to solicit contributions toward the erection of church buildings and school-houses, and especially to seek for a proper and competent man for the pastoral office, and teachers for the instruction of the young. This action was taken in the year 1733 by the congregation of Philadelphia conjointly with the congregation at New Providence and the one at Falckner's Swamp.

"At Philadelphia, Pastor Fabricius while serving the Swedish churches preached in the years 1688-1691, also for the German-Lutherans, who appear, however, at that day to have had neither church building nor organization, and held their worship for a long time in the Swedish Church at an early hour. In 1734, Lutherans and Reformed conjointly rented for £4 'a weatherboarded house' for the use of divine worship * * * The first trace of Lutheran services at New Providence (The Trappe) is in 1732, when a certain Christian Schultz, officiated there and at New Hanover, and Philadelphia. There was no proof that he was an ordained clergyman, yet he proceeded to grant ordination in 1733 to John Caspar Stoever, the ceremony being conducted in a barn which served for many years as a Bethel. The organization of a congregation with constitution and officers dates doubtless from the year 1733."——— Wolf, "The Lutherans in America."

As an evident answer to the prayers and the petitions made by the American Lutherans to those in Germany, the lot of carrying on the work of the Lutheran Church in America fell to Heinrich Melchior Muhlenberg, a graduate of the University of Gottingen. He was brought under the influence of the Pietistic movement at Halle. Muhlenberg arrived at Philadelphia on the 25th of November, 1742. Mentally, physically, and in every other way he was well equipped for the abundant life before him. In 1745, Muhlenberg's labors were strengthened by the arrival from Halle of Peter Brunholtz, John N. Kurtz and John Helfrich Schaum. Muhlenberg and Brunholtz became known as "the united ministers." In 1748, the Rev. J. F. Handschuh arrived, an emissary from Francke. The first attempt at proper order of public worship in a Lutheran congregation was made by Muhlenberg and Brunholtz in conjunction with Handschuh; also the formulating of a common liturgy. The first proposal for Synodical organization came from a layman, Peter Kock, an officer in the Swedish congregation at Wicacoa, in 1748. After several attempts such an organization took place. At this first Synodical convention the first Synodical ordination was performed on J. N. Kurtz at the request of the congregations which he served as a catechist. J. H. Schaum was ordained at the second meeting of the Synod in Lancaster, in 1749. Before adjourning, the Synod resolved to meet annually, alternating between Lancaster and Philadelphia. The language question had to be met, and a choice made between German and English, which resulted in the organization of the first English Lutheran Church in Pennsylvania in the year 1806. The mother of all the other Synods in America was the Synod of Pennsylvania, also spoken of as the Reverend Ministerium. A resolution introduced at the meeting of the Synod at Harrisburg, in 1818, was the seed from which grew the General Synod organized at Hagerstown, Md., October 22, 1830. Missionary and educational activities of the church have grown tremendously. In addition to the purely secular institutions of the church in Pennsylvania, the following colleges have been established in the State: Pennsylvania College, Gettysburg; Susquehanna University, Selinsgrove; Muhlenberg College, Allentown; Thiel College, Greenville. There are colleges such as Franklin and Marshall founded by the joint activities of the Lutheran and Reformed churches. At present there are more than half a million adherents to the Lutheran faith in Pennsylvania.

T. R.

LUZERNE COUNTY, formed from part of Northumberland, September 25, 1786. Named for the French nobleman, Anne Cesar Chevalier de la Luzerne, a brother of Cardinal de la Luzerne. Land area, 892 square miles; population (1930), 444,409; county-seat, Wilkes-Barre, laid out in 1783.

LYCOMING COUNTY, formed from part of Northumberland, April 13, 1795. Delaware Indians named the creek running through this county, Lycoming, meaning "sandy or gravelly creek." Land area, 1,220 square miles; population (1930), 93,421; county-seat, Williamsport, laid out in 1796.

LYCOMING CREEK—Tributary to West Branch Susquehanna River. Sub-basin: Lower West Branch Susquehanna; source, in Canton Township, southwestern Bradford County; course, southwesterly into Lycoming County to West Branch Susquehanna River, being Tioga-Lycoming County boundary for six miles; mouth, at Williamsport; length, thirty-four and one-half miles. Indian name, a corruption of Legaui-hanne, "sandy stream "

MACCAULEY, CLAY, Unitarian clergyman and author, was born in Chambersburg, May 8, 1843, He was graduated at Princeton, in 1864, and at the Theological Seminary of the Northwest, Chicago, in 1867, and read philosophy and divinity at Heidelberg, 1873. He was active in the Civil War, first as a lieutenant in the 126th Pennsylvania Regiment, and in 1864–65 was a member of the Christian Commission in the U. S. Army. Entering the Unitarian ministry he was pastor of the First Church, Waltham, Mass., 1869–72, and of All Souls Church, Washington, D. C., 1876–81. After 1890, he was active in Japanese mission work. From 1891 to 1899, he was president of the College for Advanced Learning at Tokio. He has done much lecturing and writing on Japan. He died November 15, 1925.

MACLAY, ROBERT SAMUEL, Methodist Episcopal clergyman, was born at Concord, Franklin County, February 7, 1824. He was graduated at Dickinson College, in 1845, and entered the Methodist ministry, in 1846. He sailed as a missionary to Foochow, China, in 1847; was a member of the committee which translated the New Testament into the Foochow dialect; held high administrative offices in both the Chinese and Japanese missions: was instrumental in founding at Tokio, in 1883, the Anglo-Japanese College of which he was president to 1887; and the Philander Smith Biblical Institute, in 1884, as well as the Anglo-Chinese College at Foochow. He was dean of the Maclay College of Theology at San Fernando, Calif., from 1888 until his retirement in 1893. He died 1907.

MACLAY, WILLIAM, soldier and politician, was born at New Garden, Chester County, 1737. He was educated in his native place; was a lieutenant in the French and Indian War. He studied law, was admitted to the bar, went to England on behalf of militia officers serving in the French and Indian War, to confer upon their claims for land-grants with the proprietors of Pennsylvania, and on his return became attorney to the Penn family. In the Revolution he raised troops and equipped them, was assistant commissary of purchase and performed some field service. In 1781, he was elected to the Pennsylvania assembly, afterward held other offices in the State, and with Robert Morris was elected to the U. S. Senate, Pennsylvania's first representatives in that body. His service there ended in 1791, but in the Senate he had shown deep-seated hostility to Washington and his administration, which was the chief distinction of Maclay's senatorial career. In his later years he was a member of the Pennsylvania Legislature and his last public office was that of a county judge. He died 1804.

WILLIAM MACLAY

MACVEAGH, FRANKLIN, ex-cabinet officer, was born near Phoenixville, Chester County, 1837. He was graduated at Yale, in 1862, and took his LL. B. degree at Columbia University, in 1864. He was admitted to the bar in 1864; and in 1864–66 was engaged in practice in New York. His health failing he went to Chicago and there engaged in the wholesale grocery business. He also became connected with various banking and manufacturing interests. In 1894, he ran for U. S. Senator but was defeated. In 1909, he was appointed Secretary of the Treasury by President Taft, serving throughout the Taft administration. He also was active and held offices in several Civic and Municipal Associations. His home is in Chicago.

MACVEAGH, WAYNE, lawyer and diplomat, was born in Phoenixville, April 19, 1833. He was graduated from Yale, in 1853, and was admitted to the bar in 1856. He was district attorney of Chester County 1859-64, became prominent as a Republican leader, and in 1870-71, was Minister to Turkey. He was Chairman of the "MacVeagh Commission" sent by President Hayes to Louisiana, in 1877, to act as the President's unofficial representative and aid in adjusting political differences there. He was Attorney-General of the United States, in 1881, and was Ambassador to Italy, 1893-97. In 1903, he was chief counsel of the United States in the Venezuela arbitration before the Hague Tribunal. He died January 11, 1917.

MAHANOY CITY, borough, in Schuylkill County, on Mahanoy Creek, about fifty-five miles northeast of Harrisburg. The first settlement was made in 1859, and it was incorporated in 1863. It is in the anthracite region, and in the vicinity is fire-clay and an excellent building stone. Its chief manufactures are: pottery, foundry products, flour, hosiery, and lumber. Population (1930), 14,784; (1920), 15,599.

MAHANOY CREEK—Tributary to Susquehanna River. Sub-basin: Middle Main Susquehanna; source, in Delano Township, northern central Schuylkill County; course, westerly into Northumberland County to Susquehanna River; mouth, near Herndon; length, fifty-two miles. Indian name, a corruption of Mahoni, "a lick."

MAHANTANGO CREEK—Tributary to Susquehanna River. Sub-basin: Middle Main Susquehanna; source, in Eldred Township, western Schuylkill County; course, southwesterly to Susquehanna River, forming Northumberland-Dauphin County boundary for fifteen miles; mouth, one mile from Paxton; length, thirty-two miles. Indian name, a corruption of Mohantango, "where we had plenty of meat to eat."

MAHONING CREEK—Tributary to Allegheny River. Sub-basin: Middle Allegheny; source, in Brady Township, northwestern Clearfield County; course, southwesterly, through Jefferson County, into Indiana County to junction of Little Mahoning Creek; thence northwesterly into Armstrong County to Allegheny River; mouth, at Mahoning; length, seventy-four miles. Indian name, a corruption of Mahoni, "a lick."

MAHONING (LITTLE) CREEK—Tributary to Mahoning Creek. Sub-basin: Middle Allegheny; source, in Green Township, eastern Indiana County; course, northwesterly, by a circuitous route, to Mahoning Creek; mouth, two miles northwest of Smicksburg; length, thirty-four and one-half miles. Indian name, a corruption of Mahoni, "a lick."

MAIDEN CREEK—Tributary to Schuylkill River. Sub-basin: Lower Delaware; source, in Shochary Ridge, Lynn Township, western Lehigh County; course, westerly into Berks County; thence southerly to Schuylkill River; mouth, two miles southeast of Leesport; length, twenty-six miles.

MAIL ROUTES, were established in this country, in 1732, when Governor Spottswood, of Virginia, was postmaster-general. At that time Andrew Bradford was postmaster at Philadelphia and had the following schedule for mails: "Mail from New England, New York, etc., was received in Philadelphia each Wednesday; on Thursday morning it was forwarded to New Castle, arriving at eleven; departed at once for Susquehanna, reaching there at night and laying over until midnight Sunday, when it was forwarded to Joppa, arriving there at 6:00 P. M., Patapsco Ferry at noon; Annapolis, Monday night at 6:00 P. M.; lays over six hours and at midnight starts for Marlborough, arriving at 5:00 A. M. Tuesday. The mail is expected in Williamsburg, Thursday, 6:00 P. M., and to be back in Philadelphia by three o'clock Wednesday." All mail was carried by stage.

MAIL SERVICE. A postal system was established by Congress as soon as the Federal government began to operate. An act of September 22, 1789, provided for the appointment of a postmaster-general. An act of February 20, 1792, provided that post roads be opened so that mails could be carried more easily.

A central post-office was established at Philadelphia, then the capital of the United States.

Mails were carried by stage and horseback, and persons obstructing their passage were liable to a fine of one hundred dollars. Ferrymen delaying the passage of the mail might be fined ten dollars for each half-hour of delay.

For each single letter the following postage was charged: not exceeding 30 miles, 6 cents; over 30 and not exceeding 60 miles, 8 cents; over 60 and not exceeding 100 miles, 10 cents; over 100 miles and not exceeding 150 miles, 12½ cents; over 150 and not exceeding 200 miles, 15 cents; over 200 and not exceeding 250 miles, 17 cents; over 250 and not exceeding 350 miles, 20 cents; over 350 and not exceeding 450 miles, 22 cents; over 450 miles to any distance, 25 cents.

MAILLY, WILLIAM, Socialistic journalist, was born in Pittsburgh, November 22, 1871. He was educated in the common schools of Scotland and England, and in 1895-96 was editor of the Birmingham *Labor Advocate*. He returned to the United States and in 1898 organized the Social Democratic Party of New York. He edited several Socialist newspapers and was an active worker in the cause of that party. He died September 4, 1912.

MALLERY, GARRICK, ethnologist, was born in Wilkes-Barre, April 23, 1831. He was graduated from Yale College, in 1850, and was admitted to the bar, in 1853; he practiced law in Philadelphia until 1861, when he enlisted and served through the war in the Federal Army, attaining the rank of Lieutenant-Colonel. He was executive officer of the Signal Service Bureau until 1876, when he was engaged in a geological survey in Dakota, and in 1879 was returned from the army and appointed chief of the bureau of ethnology. Among his books are: "A Calendar of the Dakota Nation," and "Picture Writing of the American Indians." He died at Washington, D. C., October 24, 1894.

MANATAWNY CREEK—Tributary to Schuylkill River. Sub-basin: Lower Delaware; source, in District Township, eastern Berks County; course, southerly, by a circuitous route, into Montgomery County to Schuylkill River; mouth, at Pottstown; length, twenty-one and one-half miles. Indian name, a corruption of Menhaltanink, "where we drank liquor."

MANDERSON, CHARLES FREDERICK, lawyer and politician, was born in Philadelphia, February 9, 1837. He received his early education in Philadelphia; removed to Canton, Ohio, in 1856; studied law and was admitted to the bar, in 1859. He was chief attorney in Canton, 1860-61; at the outbreak of the Civil War he enlisted as a private in the Union Army, and rose to the rank of brigadier-general of volunteers until he was severely wounded and was forced to resign from the army, in 1865. He resumed his law practices, but removed to Omaha, Nebraska, in 1869. Here he became prominent in public and political affairs being elected to the U. S. Senate, 1883-95, and being chosen speaker pro tem in two Congresses, 1889-93. After 1895 he was solicitor for the Burlington system of railroads, west of the Mississippi; and was president of the American Bar Association, in 1900-01. He died 1911.

MANSFIELD, borough, in Tioga County, on the Tioga River, about twenty-five miles southwest of Elmira, N. Y. It is in the midst of an agricultural region and near the bituminous coal region.

MANSFIELD STATE TEACHERS COLLEGE. On January 7, 1857, the Mansfield Classical Seminary was formally opened. Because of financial difficulties the trustees in 1861 applied to the State to have the institution changed to a State Normal School. This petition was granted on December 12, 1862. Later the institution was authorized to grant the degree of B. S. in Education and the name was changed to Mansfield State Teachers College. The college offers special courses in home economics and music.

MARCH, PEYTON CONWAY, military officer, was born in Easton, December 27, 1864. He graduated from Lafayette College, in 1884, and determining upon a military career, graduated from the U. S. Military Academy, in

1888. He entered the army as a lieutenant of artillery and later graduated from the Fort Monroe Artillery School. He took a very active part in the Spanish War, and for a time afterwards was a military and later a civil governor in Ilocus. In 1911, he was commissary-general in the Philippines; in 1916, he was a lieutenant-colonel of field artillery; the next year he was made a brigadier-general, and in 1917 he was raised to the rank of major-general. He was appointed general and chief of staff, United States Army, in 1918, and in 1921 was retired. General March was decorated a number of times for gallantry in action in both the Spanish-American and World Wars. His home is in Great Neck, L. I.

MARKHAM, WILLIAM, English Colonial governor in America, was born in England, about 1635. When William Penn obtained a charter for Pennsylvania, he made Markham a first cousin of his, his deputy. Markham had all rights granted to Penn save that of convoking a legislative assembly. On August 3, 1681, he established a council, later chose the site for Philadelphia and conferred with Lord Baltimore as to the Maryland-Pennsylvania boundary. Penn himself arrived on October 27, 1682, and Markham, whose commission accordingly lapsed, was elected to the council. In 1684-99, he was secretary to the province; in 1686, became land commissioner, and in 1689, an auditor of accounts. When, in 1691, the territory now constituting the State of Delaware was detached from the province, he was appointed its deputy-governor, and in 1694-99, as lieutenant-governor, administered both this territory and the province. He died at Philadelphia, June 12, 1704.

MARKLE, JOHN, coal operator, was born in Hazleton, December 15, 1858. He was graduated in the mining engineering department of Lafayette College, in 1880, and in the same year was appointed general superintendent of mines of G. B. Markle and Co., his father's firm. Upon his father's death he succeeded him to the presidency of the company which was one of the largest of the "independent" companies in the anthracite coal industry. He was one of the leading figures and represented the independent operators in the negotiations with President Roosevelt and his commission in connection with the anthracite coal strike of 1902. Markle lives in New York.

MARKOE, THOMAS MASTERS, surgeon, was born in Philadelphia, 1819. In 1836, he was graduated at Princeton, and in 1841 at the New York College of Physicians and Surgeons. He was on the faculties of Castleton Medical College, Vermont; University of the City of New York; New York College of Physicians and Surgeons. He published "Treatise on Diseases of the Bone" (1872). He died in 1901.

MAROT, HELEN, labor leader, was born in Philadelphia, 1865. She became interested in labor problems in her native city and after a few years of activity in labor circles there removed to New York, where she made important investigations into Child Labor conditions. Her publications include: "Handbook of Labor Literature," "American Trade Unions," and "Creative Impulse in Industry." Her home is in New York.

MARSH CREEK—Tributary to Monocacy River. Basin: Potomac; source, in South Mountain, Franklin Township, western Adams County; course, southeasterly, by a circuitous route, into Maryland, returning to state boundary to join Rock Creek and form Monocacy River; mouth, on state boundary, eight miles south of Gettysburg; length, twenty-five and one-half miles (last mile in Maryland).

MARSH CREEK—Tributary to Pine Creek. Sub-basin: Middle West Branch Susquehanna; source, in Duncan Township, southern central Tioga County; course, northwesterly and southwesterly to Pine Creek; mouth, one mile southwest of Ansonia; length, twenty miles.

MARSHALL, HUMPHREY, botanist, was born in West Bradford (the present Marshallton), October 10, 1722. He followed the stonemason's trade, but devoted his leisure to astronomy, building a small private observatory, and to natural history. In 1773, he established the Marshallton botanical garden, where were assembled trees and herbaceous plants of the United States. For years he was treasurer of Chester County, and in 1786 he was elected to the American Philosophical Society. His "Arboretum Americanum" described as "an alphabetical Catalogue of Forest Trees and Shrubs, Natives of the American United States," was translated into several European languages. He died at West Bradford, November 5, 1801.

MARTIN, CHARLES CYRIL, civil engineer, was born in Springfield, August 30, 1831. He was educated at Rensselaer Polytechnic Institute, Troy, N. Y. He was engineer in the Brooklyn navy yard during the Civil War; and afterward chief engineer of Prospect Park, Brooklyn. He became John A. Roebling's second assistant in building the Brooklyn Bridge, of which he became chief engineer after Roebling's retirement. He died at Far Rockaway, N. Y., July 11, 1903.

MARTIN, HELEN REIMENSNYDER, author, was born in Lancaster, October 18, 1868. She made a special study of English subjects at Swarthmore College, and Radcliffe College, Cambridge, Mass. In 1889, she married Frederic C. Martin. Mrs. Martin is a contributor of short stories of Pennsylvania-German life to several periodicals. Among her books are: "Tillie, a Mennonite Maid"; "For a Mess of Pottage"; "Sabina, a Story of the Amish"; "Barnabetta" (dramatized as "Erstwhile Susan" and played by Mrs. Fiske); "The Church on the Avenue"; "The Snob"; "Ye That Judge," and "Sylvia of the Minute." Mrs. Martin lives in Harrisburg.

MASON AND DIXON'S LINE, the boundary between Pennsylvania and Maryland, was established in 1763, by Charles Mason and Jeremiah Dixon, surveyors from England, sent to America by an agreement between Lord Baltimore and Thomas and Richard Penn.

MAUCH CHUNK, a town and county-seat of Carbon County, on the Lehigh River, forty-six miles northwest of Easton. The town is picturesquely built on the side of a mountain rising 1,500 feet from the river, here winding through a narrow, deep ravine. It has a number of foundries, shoe factories, car shops, silk mills, etc., but it is best known as an important coal center, marking the extreme boundary of the anthracite coal region of Pennsylvania. The coal is now carried through a tunnel, but was formerly transported to Mauch Chunk by a gravity railroad known as the Switchback, which has become famous as an exciting pleasure route for tourists.

INCLINED RAILROAD, MAUCH CHUNK (1843)

MAUCH CHUNK GRAVITY RAILROAD, extending from Mauch Chunk to Summit Hill, was the first railroad in Carbon County. The railroad was constructed with a descending grade from Summit Hill to the Lehigh River. The cars, run by their own gravity, were brought back by mules which had been carried down the road in a small cattle car. In 1844, the use of mules was abandoned and a switchback with planes was adopted. By means of this railroad which is still in use, coal was also brought from the mines.

MAYFIELD, borough of Lackawanna County, fifteen miles northeast of Scranton. It has extensive interests in coal, the mining of which is the leading industry.

McADOO, a borough on the Lehigh Valley and Pennsylvania Railroads, five miles south of Hazleton and seventy-eight miles northwest of Philadelphia. There are rich deposits of anthracite coal in the vicinity, and, consequently, coal-mining is one of the chief industries. Shirts are also manufactured here. In this borough are situated the picturesque Silver Brook Hollow and Tresckow Water Falls. Population (1930), 5,239; (1920), 4,674.

McCALL, GEORGE ARCHIBALD, soldier, was born in Philadelphia, March 16, 1802. He was graduated at West Point, in 1822; in 1836, reached the rank of captain, and that of colonel, in 1850. Having served against the Seminoles in Florida, he won distinction in the Mexican War; in 1850, he became inspector-general, resigning from the army three years later. In 1861, he was given command of the Pennsylvania Reserves, with the rank of brigadier-general of volunteers. He participated in the Peninsular Campaign of 1862, was taken prisoner in June and exchanged in August. Impaired health prevented him from returning to the army, and in 1863 he resigned. He wrote "Letters from the Frontier" (1868). He died February 25, 1868.

McCALL, SAMUEL WALKER, public official, was born in East Providence, February 28, 1851. In 1874, he was graduated at Dartmouth College, studied law and was admitted to the bar in 1876, after which he practiced in Boston. He was editor-in-chief of the Boston *Daily Advertiser*, in 1888-89, and served as delegate at the Republic National Conventions of 1888, 1900 and 1916. He was a member of the Massachusetts House of Representatives in 1888, 1889 and 1892 and was a member of Congress from 1893 to 1913. He was an unsuccessful candidate for the governorship of Massachusetts in 1914. He was successful the following year and was re-elected for the terms of 1917 and 1918. He has published: "Life of Thaddeus Stevens," "Dartmouth Centennial Address on Daniel Webster," "The Business of Congress," "Life of Thomas B. Reed," and "The Liberty of Citizenship." He died November 4, 1923.

McCAMMON, JOSEPH KAY, lawyer, was born in Philadelphia, October 13, 1845. He graduated at Princeton, in 1865; studied law; became register in bankruptcy, in 1870; was special counsel of the United States in Washington, 1871; president of the board of investigation of the Indian service, 1877; assistant Attorney-General of the United States, 1880-85; and in 1881 was appointed United States Commissioner of Railroads. Under Presidents Garfield and Arthur, he conducted treaties with various Indian tribes. Among his writings are: "A Report on Indian Service," "Reports of Councils with Bannock and Shoshone Indians," "Reports of Councils with Flathead and Other Indians," and "Arguments in Cases Affecting Pacific and Other Railroads." He died January 2, 1907.

McCAUSLAND'S RAID, an incursion of the Confederate general, McCausland, into Maryland and Pennsylvania, the chief incident, of which was the burning of Chambersburg. The sum of $100,000 in gold or $500,000 in currency was demanded of the town. It could not immediately be raised; McCausland knew that General Averell was close upon him and setting fire to the place, laying a greater part of it in ashes, he hastily marched westward to McConnellsburg and encamped. Averell started in pursuit, went through the burning town and a few miles from McConnellsburg, struck McCausland's rear, forcing him back to the Potomac.

PART OF SUMMIT COAL MINE, MAUCH CHUNK (1843)

McCLELLAN, GEORGE BRINTON, soldier, was born in Philadelphia, December 3, 1826. He was educated at the University of Pennsylvania and at West Point where he was graduated in 1846. He saw action in the Mexican War and because of bravery rose to the rank of captain. Up to the time of the Civil War he was largely active in the management and growth of the railroads, especially the Illinois Central. In 1861, with the outbreak of the war, he received a commission as major-general from the governor of Ohio and proceeded to organize the volunteers of Ohio, Illinois, Indiana, the western parts of Pennsylvania and Virginia. This army did very creditable work under his command. On July 22nd, McClellan was summoned to Washington to take command of the Army of the Potomac, and was commissioned as major-general of the U. S. Army. On the retirement of General Scott from active service, McClellan was appointed general-in-chief of the armies of the U. S. The army did not move until March, 1862, and discontent having arisen over the delay he was removed from the chief command, leaving him the command of only the Army of the Potomac. He was engaged in the siege of Yorktown, and was victorious at Williamsburg and Hanover Court House. After the Seven Days' Battle dissatisfaction against him was so strong that he was relieved of his command. He was then put in command of the fortifications of Washington, till after the second battle of Bull Run, when he again took command of the Army of the Potomac. On Lee's invasion of Maryland, McClellan fought the Battle of Antietam and forced him back to the Potomac. Because of his failure to cross and follow up his victory he was deprived of his command and took no further part in the war. In 1864, he was Democratic nominee for President of the United States, and was defeated, the electoral vote being 212 for Lincoln against 21 for McClellan. In 1877, he was elected governor of New Jersey. He wrote several books concerning the Civil War, and died at Orange, N. J., October 29, 1885.

McCLINTOCK, EMORY, actuary, was born in Carlisle, September 19, 1840. He was graduated from Columbia University, in 1859. He was consular agent at Bradford, England, 1863-66. As actuary he held positions with the Asbury, the New York, and the Northwestern Mutual Life Insurance Companies. Besides being actuary of the Mutual Life Insurance Company New, York, he was also vice-president, trustee, and consulting actuary afte r1911. He was president of the American Mathematical Society, in 1890-94, and of the Actuarial Society of America, in 1895-97. He was a Fellow of the American Academy of Arts and Sciences and Fellow of the Institute of Actuaries, London. Mathematical journals also received his contributions. He died July 10, 1916.

McCLINTOCK, JOHN, scholar, was born in Philadelphia, October 27, 1814. He was graduated at the University of Pennsylvania, in 1835. He entered the ministry of the Methodist Episcopal Church and from 1836 to 1851 was professor of mathematics and of Greek and Latin in Dickinson College. From 1848 to 1856, he edited the "Methodist Quarterly Review." He held the pastorate of St. Paul's Church and of the American Chapel in Paris. Failing health caused his resignation in 1864. He removed to New Brunswick, N. J., in 1866, and became chairman of the Central Centenary Committee of the Methodist Episcopal Church. For the last three years of his life he was president of the Drew Theological Seminary. He was joint editor and compiler of the "Cyclopedia of Biblical, Theological and Ecclesiastical Literature," and wrote numerous other religious works. He died March 4, 1870.

McCLURE, ALEXANDER KELLEY, journalist, was born in Sherman's Valley, Perry County, January 9, 1828. He was reared on a farm, educated at home and apprenticed to a tanner in 1842, soon after began to write for the Perry "Freeman" and edited and published the *Juniata Sentinel* at Mifflin in the Whig interest, 1846-50. He then published (1850-56) the Chambersburg "Repository," which he made influential in the cause of anti-slavery. He was state superintendent of printing, in 1855; a member of the state convention of 1855, which met at Pittsburgh to organize the Republican Party; in 1856, was

COLONEL A. K. McCLURE

admitted to the bar and was a delegate to the first Republican National Convention in Philadelphia. He served in the state Senate and the House of Representatives. In a close election, in 1873, he was defeated as an independent candidate for mayor of Philadelphia. In 1875, he established the Philadelphia "Times," of which he was editor-in-chief till 1901. Among his best known works are: "Recollections of Half a Century," and "Old Time Notes of Pennsylvania." He died in 1909.

McCLURG, ALEXANDER CALDWELL, publisher, was born in Philadelphia, in 1834. He was graduated at Miami University, Oxford, Ohio, in 1853, engaged in business with S. C. Griggs and Co., publishers in Chicago, and in 1862 entered the Union Army. He rose to the rank of colonel and brevet brigadier-general, and served as chief of staff to the 14th Corps during the Atlanta campaign. Returning from the war he was admitted to partnership in the publishing house mentioned above, and some years later established the firm of Jansen, McClurg and Co., afterward A. C. McClurg and Co. He died at Saint Augustine, Fla., April 15, 1901.

McCONNELLSBURG, borough and county-seat of Fulton County, was laid out in 1786, by Daniel McConnell, for whom it was named. It was incorporated as a borough in 1814.

McCOOK, DANIEL, soldier, was born in Canonsburg, June 20, 1798. Having received a college education, he removed from Pennsylvania to Ohio and settled at Carrolton. Although 63 years old at the outbreak of the Civil War, he entered the Union Army, in which he served as major of volunteers. During one of the Morgan raids he received a wound from which he died shortly after. Eight sons of his served as officers in the Federal Army, three of whom were killed in battle. He died near Buffington's Island, Ohio, July 21, 1863.

McCOY, ISAAC, missionary and Indian agent, was born near Uniontown, June 13, 1784. His early life was spent in Kentucky. Reared on the frontier, his educational advantages were very limited, but he was of a studious disposition. He was ordained to the ministry of the Baptist Church at twenty-four, settling in Indiana about the same time. After serving eight years as pastor of a church, he entered the mission field among the Miami Indians in 1817. His subsequent life was devoted to the interests of the Indians and the procuring of government aid in their care and welfare. His last years were spent at Louisville, Ky., where he had charge of the work of the American Indian Mission Association. He died in this place, June 21, 1846.

McDONALD, borough of Washington County, eighteen miles southwest of Pittsburgh. It is situated in a coal and oil district and there are flour mills, bottle works, and tool factories.

McFARLAND, JOHN HORACE, master printer, was born in McAlisterville, Juniata County, September 24, 1859. He was privately educated, learned the printing business and in 1878 established his own business, which after several changes was incorporated as the J. Horace McFarland Co., in 1891. In 1890-93, he printed and contributed to *American Gardening*, and in 1901-04, he printed *Country Life in America*. He edited the "Beautiful America" department in *The Ladies' Home Journal*, in 1904-07, and also edited the *American Rose Annual*, 1916-18. McFarland is a popular lecturer on subjects concerning civic improvement and horticulture, particularly roses. He has served as president of the American League for Civic Improvement, American Civic Association, and as vice-president of the National Municipal League. Aside from his contributions to periodicals he has written: "Beginning to Know the Trees," "Laying Out the Home Grounds," "My Growing Garden," and "The Rose in America." His home is Breeze Hill, Bellevue Road, Harrisburg.

McGIFFIN, PHILO NORTON, naval officer, was born in Washington County, December 13, 1860. He was graduated in 1882 at the U. S. Naval Academy and was stationed in China, and at the outbreak of the war between China and France was permitted to resign from the U. S. Navy to enter the service of China. He established a naval academy at Wei-hai-wei, of which he had charge. When the China-Japan War broke out he was placed in command of the "Chen Yuen," and was the first American or European to command a modern warship in action. He was in command at the battle of Yalu River, in which action he was severely injured. Died February 11, 1897.

McGREADY, JAMES, Presbyterian clergyman, was born in Pennsylvania, about 1760. He studied for the ministry in the school of John McMillan, of Canonsburg, and in 1788 was licensed to preach. After some years of work in North Carolina, in 1796, he removed to southwestern Kentucky, and under his direction began the great revival of religion which culminated in 1800 and became memorable in the religious history of the country. He organized and conducted the first camp-meeting, and employed as preachers unordained young men without special theological training, thereby provoking dissension in the Presbyterian Church. Out of this disagreement arose the Cumberland Presbyterian Church, organized in 1810. McGready, however, afterward became reconciled to the older church and resumed his fellowship in it. He died in 1817.

McGUFFEY, WILLIAM HOLMES, educator, was born in Washington County, September 23, 1800. He was graduated at Washington College, in 1826, and was appointed to a professorship at Miami University in that year. He was president of Cincinnati College and of Ohio University and in addition was professor of moral philosophy at Woodward College, Cincinnati, in 1843-45, and thereafter until his death was professor at the University of Virginia. He prepared the series of school reading and spelling-books known under his name and for many years widely popular in the schools of the United States. He died at Charlottesville, Va., May 4, 1887.

McILHENNEY, CHARLES MORGAN, landscape painter, was born in Philadelphia, April 4, 1858. Having studied under Frank Briscoe, he continued his training at the Academy of Fine Arts in Philadelphia, and soon began to win recognition in his chosen field. Among his best known works are: "A Gray Summer Noon," and "Passing Storm." In 1893, he was awarded medals at the Columbian Exposition and won the first Hallgarten prize. He died 1904.

McKEAN, THOMAS, governor and jurist, signer of the Declaration of Independence, was born in New London, Chester County, March 19, 1734. He was privately educated at Newcastle, Del., having settled there, he studied law and was admitted to the bar in 1755. He assisted in a revision of the Delaware laws, in 1762, and in the same year was elected to the Delaware assembly, in which his membership continued till 1779. In 1765, he was elected to the Stamp Act Congress. About 1771, he began to practice law in Philadelphia, although retaining a Delaware residence, and from Delaware, in 1774, he was elected to the Continental Congress, in which he served nine years and of which he was president in 1781. He was not present at the signing of the Declaration of Independence, but added his signature some years afterward. He also helped in the drafting and signing of the Articles of Confederation. In Pennsylvania he was made chairman of the Committee of Safety, in 1776, and from 1777 to 1799 was chief justice of the state. He became a strong supporter of Jefferson, and a leader of the Republican Party of that day, and was governor of Pennsylvania from 1779 to 1808. With James Wilson he wrote "Commentaries on the Constitutions of the United States." He died at Philadelphia, June 24, 1817.

McKEAN, THOMAS, philanthropist, was born in Philadelphia, November 23, 1842. In 1862, he was graduated at the University of Pennsylvania and entered upon a successful business career, becoming an officer in many railroad and financial corporations. He acquired a large fortune, which he spent freely in endowing educational and charitable enterprises, his various gifts to the University of Pennsylvania alone amounting to $300,000. He died at Philadelphia, March 16, 1898.

McKEAN COUNTY, was formed from part of Lycoming, March 26, 1804. Named for Governor Thomas McKean. Land area, 987 square miles; population (1930), 55,167. County-seat, Smethport, laid out in 1807.

McKEESPORT, city, in Allegheny County, at the junction of the Monongahela and the Youghiogheny Rivers. The first permanent settlement was made in 1795 by David McKee, was incorporated as a borough, 1842, and chartered as a city, 1890. McKeesport is situated in a region noted for its extensive fields of bituminous coal and its natural gas. The chief industrial establishments are steel and iron works. The city has a large trade in its own manufacture and in coal and lumber. Population (1930), 54,632; (1920), 46,781.

McKEES ROCKS, borough in Allegheny County, on the south bank of the Ohio River, opposite Allegheny and three miles northwest of Pittsburgh. There is an abundance of bituminous coal and natural gas in the district, and there are large iron and steel industries with their kindred smaller manufactories. The town ships lumber and there are manufactures of wall plaster and concrete. The land was originally settled in 1830 and the town was incorporated in 1892. Population (1930), 18,116; (1920), 16,713.

McKENNA, JOSEPH, jurist, was born in Philadelphia, August 10, 1843. In 1855, he went to California and graduated from the Benicia Collegiate Institute, in 1865, and was admitted to the bar the same year. He held numerous judicial positions, was a member of the State Legislature and of the United States House of Representatives. He became Attorney-General in the Cabinet of President McKinley, in 1897. In 1897, he was also made an associate justice of the United States Supreme Court and 1898 he took his seat.

McKENNAN, THOMAS M. L., lawyer, was born in New Castle, Del., March 31, 1796. He removed with his parents to Washington, Pa., and was educated at Washington College. In 1815-1816, he was district attorney of Washington County, and in 1831-1832, was a member of the United States House of Representatives. In 1842, he was for a short time Secretary of the Interior under President Fillmore. He died July 9, 1852.

McKENNAN, WILLIAM, lawyer, was born in Washington, Washington County, September 2, 1816, the son of Thomas M. L. McKennan. After graduation from Washington College, in 1832, he entered the legal profession and served as district attorney of his county in 1837-1839. In 1861, he was a member of the Peace Congress at Washington, D. C., and in 1869, President Grant appointed him United States Circuit Judge for three circuits, a position which he held until his death in October, 1893.

McKIBBEN, CHAMBERS, soldier, was born in Pittsburgh, November 2, 1841. He enlisted as a private in the volunteer service, in 1862, was brevetted captain for gallant services, and in 1896, attained the rank of lieutenant-colonel of the 21st U. S. Infantry. At the beginning of the war with Spain he went to Cuba with Shafter's Army, fought at Santiago, and was made brigadier-general of volunteers and appointed military governor of Santiago. On May 12, 1899, he was mustered out of the volunteer service. In 1902, he retired with the rank of brigadier-general and died in May, 1919.

McKIM, CHARLES FOLLEN, architect, was born in Chester County, August 24, 1847. He studied at the Lawrence Scientific School, in 1866, at the Beaux-Arts of Paris, in 1867–70, and shortly afterward entered into partnership with Sanford White and William R. Meade. This firm achieved some of the finest triumphs of recent American architecture. Among notable examples of its work are the buildings of Columbia University, and the Public Library of Boston. In 1903, McKim received the royal gold medal from the Royal Institute of British Architecture, being the second American to obtain this honor. He also served as president of the American Institute of Architects. He died September 14, 1909.

McKIM, JAMES MILLER, abolitionist, was born near Carlisle, November 14, 1810. He was graduated from Dickinson College, in 1828, studied medicine at the University of Pennsylvania and theology at Princeton (1831) and Andover (1832) and in 1835 was ordained a Presbyterian pastor in Womelsdorf. An original member of the American Anti-Slavery Society he devoted his life to the interest of the negro and later became active in the Pennsylvania Freedman's Relief Association and the American Freedman's Commission. In 1865, he assisted in founding and became a proprietor of the New York Weekly *Nation*. He died at Llewellyn Park, West Orange, N. J., June 13, 1874.

McMICHAEL, MORTON, journalist, politician and orator, was born in Burlington, N. J., October 2, 1807. After education in the public schools, he studied law at the University of Pennsylvania and became a member of the Philadelphia bar in 1827. The year previously he became editor of the *Saturday Evening Post*, and as an active politician served for several years on the alderman's bench in Philadelphia. He was connected with the *Saturday News*, the *Saturday Gazette*, the *North American* and *United States Gazette*, in 1847, consolidating the last two in one journal, of which he was sole proprietor from 1854 until his death. He was mayor of Philadelphia from 1866 to 1869 and in 1873 was a delegate to the Fourth Constitutional Convention of Pennsylvania. His speeches were renowned as models of oratory and a bronze statue was erected to his memory in Fairmount Park. He died at Philadelphia, January 6, 1879.

McMICHAEL, WILLIAM, soldier and lawyer, was born in Philadelphia, March 4, 1841. The third son of Morton McMichael, he graduated at the University of Pennsylvania, in 1859, but left his law studies in April, 1861, to enlist as a private when President Lincoln issued his first call for troops. He attained rapid promotion to the grade of colonel and served under generals Thomas, Rosecrans and Grant. He resumed his law studies after the war and in 1865 became a member of the Philadelphia bar. He held various federal positions under Presidents Grant and Garfield and later became a member of the bar of New York City. Like his father, he was renowned for his oratorical gifts. He died in New York City, April 20, 1893.

McMICHAELS CREEK—Tributary to Brodheads Creek. Sub-basin: Upper Delaware; source, in Pocono Mountains, Jackson Township, southwestern Monroe County; course, southerly and northeasterly to Brodheads Creek; mouth, at Stroudsburg; length, twenty-one miles.

McMILLAN, JOHN, minister, was born at Fagg's Manor, Chester County, November 11, 1752. After graduation from Princeton, in 1772, he studied theology under the Rev. Dr. Robert Smith, at Pequea, and on October 26, 1774, was licensed by the Presbytery of Newcastle. Subsequently for two years he engaged in missionary work and during this period made two journeys to western Pennsylvania. In June, 1776, he was ordained by the Presbytery of Donegal and became pastor of churches at Pigeon Creek and Chartiers, Washington County. He severed his connections with the church at Pigeon Creek, in 1794, but remained pastor at Chartiers until his death. Rev. McMillan was one of the founders of Jefferson College of which institution he became professor of Divinity in 1802, and vice-principal in 1805. In 1791, he was Moderator of the Synod of Virginia and in 1803 and 1816 of the Synod of Pittsburgh. He died November 16, 1833.

JOHN McMILLAN

McNAIR, FREDERICK VALLETTE, naval officer, was born in Jenkintown, January 13, 1839. He was educated at the United States Naval Academy and served in the "Minnesota," 1857-59. Becoming lieutenant he took an active part in the Civil War and from 1867-68 was an instructor at the naval academy. He was also superintendent of the Naval Observatory, became an admiral in 1895 and a member of the lighthouse board in 1898. In this year he was appointed to take charge of Admiral Cervera and other Spanish prisoners of war. Upon their return to Spain he was appointed superintendent of the naval academy. He died in 1900.

McPHERSON, EDWARD, journalist, was born in Gettysburg, July 31, 1830. In 1848, he was graduated from the University of Pennsylvania, and although he studied law soon gave it up for journalism. He sat in Congress, 1858-66, was clerk of the House of Representatives, and in 1876 permanent president of the National Republican Convention, and was chief of the Bureau of Engraving and Printing in Washington, 1877-88. He edited the Philadelphia Press, 1877-80, was for some years the American editor of the "Almanach de Gotha;" edited from 1872 a biennial "Handbook of Politics," and the "New York Tribune Almanac" from 1877 till his death. He was the author of a "Political History of the United States During the Great Rebellion," and "The Political History of the United States During Reconstruction." He died at Gettysburg, December 14, 1895.

McQUILLEN, JOHN HUGH, dentist, was born in Philadelphia, February 12, 1826. He began the study of medicine and dentistry, in 1847, engaged in the practice of dentistry, in 1849, took his M. D. at Jefferson Medical College, in 1852, and his D. D. S. at the Philadelphia College of Dental Surgery, in 1853. He became professor of operative dentistry and dental physiology at the Pennsylvania College of Dental Surgery, in 1857. In 1863, he was instrumental in securing a charter for the Philadelphia Dental College and he was from that time until his death its dean and professor of physiology. He was president of the American Dental Association, the Pennsylvania Dental Society, the State Adontographic Society. He edited Dental Cosmos, in 1859-71. His death occurred at Philadelphia, March 3, 1879.

MEADE, GEORGE GORDON, soldier, was born in Cadiz, Spain, December 31, 1815. His father, Richard Worsam Meade, was a resident of that city engaged in mercantile pursuits and acting as naval agent of the United States. In 1817, Meade's family moved to Philadelphia, the husband and father following three years later. Subsequently he moved to Washington, where he died June 25, 1828. The son, George Gordon, attended a boarding school at Mt. Airy, near Philadelphia, and later a school in Washington, conducted by Salmon P. Chase, afterwards Secretary of the Treasury, and Chief Justice, and still later a boarding school at Mt. Hope, Baltimore. In 1831, he was appointed to a cadetship at West Point, graduating in 1835. He was assigned to the third artillery and in 1835-1836 served in the Seminole War in Florida. October 26, 1836, he resigned from the army and became assistant engineer in the construction of the Alabama, Florida and Georgia Railway. Later, he assisted in making surveys of the mouth of the Mississippi and of the northeast boundary between

GEORGE GORDON MEADE

the United States and British North America. May 19, 1842, he reentered the army as second lieutenant of topographical engineers. He served on the staff of General Scott in the Mexican War participating in the siege of Vera Cruz and in the battles of Palo Alto, Monterey, and Resaca de la Palma. In 1857-61, he assisted in the geodetic survey of the Great Lakes. In 1856, he became captain of a corps of engineers. August 31, 1861, he was commissioned brigadier-general of volunteers and assigned to the command of the 2nd Brigade of the Pennsylvania Reserve Corps of the Army of the Potomac. Serving in the Peninsular Campaign he took part in the actions at Mechanicsville, June 26th; Gaines Mill, June 27th, and Fraysers' Farm, June 30th. June 18th he was appointed major of engineers. At the second battle of Bull Run he commanded the 1st Brigade of Reynold's division. He distinguished himself at South Mountain, September 14th, and at Antietam, September 17th, he commanded the first corps after Hooker was wounded. November 29, 1862, he was promoted major-general of volunteers and at Fredericksburg, December 13th, commanded the 3rd Division of the First Corps, breaking through Lee's right but was compelled to fall back for want of support. At Chancellorsville, May 2-4, he commanded the Fifth Corps. Early on the morning of June 28, 1863, at Frederick City, Md., he was appointed to succeed Hooker in command of the Army of the Potomac, the Confederate advance having by this time penetrated Pennsylvania. Within six days from his assumption of command he had marched his army to Gettysburg and fought a three days' battle.—See GETTYSBURG, BATTLE OF. He received the thanks of Congress and was made brigadier-general, United States Army. He remained in command of the Army of the Potomac until the close of the war and participated in the battles of the Wilderness, Spottsylvania, and Cold Harbor, and in the siege of Petersburg and Richmond. August 18, 1864, he was made major-general in the regular army. From July 1, 1865, until his death he was commander of the Military Division of the Atlantic with the exception of the period from January, 1868, to March, 1869, when he commanded the Third Military District and the Department of the South. He died in Philadelphia, November 6, 1872.

MEADVILLE, city and county-seat of Crawford County, thirty miles south of Erie. The first settlement was made in 1788; it became a borough in 1823 and in 1866 was chartered as a city. It is in a fertile agricultural region in the vicinity of extensive oil fields and in the part of the state noted for its iron and steel industries. Meadville Theological School, opened in 1844 by the Unitarians, and Allegheny College, opened in 1815 by the Methodist Episcopals, are found here. Population (1930), 16,698; (1920), 14,568.

MECHANICSBURG, borough, in Cumberland County, eight miles southwest of Harrisburg. It was settled in 1806 and in 1828 was incorporated as a borough. It is situated in a rich agricultural region. Population (1930), 5,647; (1920), 4,688.

MEDARY, SAMUEL, editor and politician, was born in Montgomery Square, Montgomery County, February 25, 1801. In 1825, he settled at Batavia, Ohio, where he edited and established several newspapers among which were the *Ohio Sun*, the *Western Hemisphere*, the *Ohio Statesman*, and the *Crisis*. He held several state political positions and was governor of Minnesota Territory, 1857-58, and of Kansas Territory, 1858-59. He gave active aid to Morse in the promotion of the electric telegraph, was a firm supporter of the measures of Jackson and Douglas; is said to have originated the battle cry, "Fifty-four forty, or fight!" in connection with the Oregon boundary dispute, and was often called the "old wheel-horse of Democracy." He died at Columbus, Ohio, November 7, 1864.

PUBLIC SQUARE IN MEADVILLE (1843)

MEDIA, borough, county-seat of Delaware County, about fifteen miles west of Philadelphia. It is a well built residential suburb of Philadelphia, and is situated in a fertile agricultural region. It is the headquarters for the Delaware County Institute of Science, established in 1833. The borough was incorporated in 1850. Population (1930), 5,372; (1920), 4,109.

MEDICINE BUNDLE, one or more fetishes wrapped in buckskin or cloth. Said to have been the most highly valued material possession of the medicine men, warriors, and chiefs in former times. The medicine bundle is still used by certain conservative Oklahoma Delawares one of whom is Wi'tapano'xwe, "Walking at Daylight" (James Webber, Dewey, Oklahoma, 1931), an herbalist. This complex has evidently evolved from the wearing of personal talismen—a custom which has a widespread distribution among the North American Indians. The Delawares obtained these charms from their guardian spirits who made known their identity in dream-visions. The visionary was instructed to obtain a feather, claw, tooth, horn, portion of bone, or the root of some rare plant as a symbol of his guardian spirit which would act as a protective agent for its owner.

A man may have one or more bundles the contents of which are assembled in accordance with the rules governing his profession as prescribed by his guardian spirit. A warrior's bundle would contain medicine especially prepared for men of this class, and a medicine stone. Among other personal charms the hunters carried medicine with which they lured game. The herbalists bundle would contain rare medicinal roots. A man may transfer his bundle to one of his own class (healer, warrior, or chief) if he so desires. In case the transfer is not made the bundle is placed in charge of a member of his family or buried with him according to his wishes. These sacred objects are kept carefully wrapped and concealed from the contaminating influences of civilization lest the guardian spirits become offended and cease to afford communication with the supernatural realm.

Among the Central Algonkian and tribes of adjacent areas there is a highly developed ritual connected with the medicine bundle and its functions. (See Skinner, A. B., *Social Life and Ceremonial Bundles of the Menomini*, Bull., American Museum Natural History, No. 13, p. 91, N. Y., 1913; *Medicine Ceremony of the Menomini, Iowa, and Wahpeton*, Indian Notes and Publications, Museum of the American Indian, Heye Foundation, Vol. 4, pp. 168, 266, N. Y., 1920; Hoffman, W. J., *The Menomini Indians*, 14th Annual Report, Bureau of American Ethnology, Washington, 1893; Kroeber, A. L., *The Arapaho*, Bulletin American Museum of Natural History, Vol. 18, p. 418, N. Y., 1907; Densmore, Frances, *Chippewa Customs*, Bull. 86, Bureau of American Ethnology, p. 93, Washington, 1929; Wissler, Clark, *Ceremonial Bundles of the Blackfoot Indians*, Anthropological Papers American Museum of Natural History, Vol. 7, Part 2, N. Y., 1912; *Societies of the Plains Indians*, ibid, Vol. 11, N. Y., 1916; Lowie, R. H., *Minor Ceremonies of the Crow Indians*, ibid., Vol. 21, Part 5, N. Y., 1924.)

G. T.

MEDICINE STONE, a concretion found in the alimentary organs of certain ruminants and regarded as a sacred and invaluable medicine gift. Known in Delaware terminology as *mi·ku ci·'k n*, "emergency gift." It is comparable to the European and Oriental *bezoar* and used similarly—chiefly as an antidote to poison. According to Delaware tradition, the blacktailed deer (Odocoileus heminus) affords the more highly prized stone although it occurs occasionally in other animals. The stones are said to be of varying shapes and sizes and act as protective agents to their owners. Medicine is prepared by scraping the stone and pouring hot water over the powder. It is administered in case of severe illness when other remedies have failed. It is believed that if the stone is rubbed on the flesh it will heal wounds and cure mad dog and snake bite. The Delaware warriors also carried medicine stones as protective charms because of their supposed magical and medicinal properties. (See Bezoar, New International Encyclopedia, 2nd Ed., Vol. 3. *The Bezoar in Aboriginal*

CAPITOL, HARRISBURG

American Culture, Ms. Data compiled by Dr. John M. Cooper, Catholic University of America, Washington, D. C., read before the American Anthropological Association, A. A. A. S. Section H., Cleveland, Ohio, December 29, 1930.)

G. T.

MEEKER, ROYAL, statistician, was born in Silver Lake, Susquehanna County, February 23, 1873. In 1898, he was graduated at Iowa State College and in 1906 took the degree of Ph. D. at Columbia University. He also studied at Leipzig and was subsequently a member of the faculty of Ursinus College and of Princeton. In 1913, he was appointed commissioner of labor statistics by President Wilson and in 1918 became a member of the United States meat commission. He was chief of the Scientific division, International Labor Office of League of Nations, 1920–1923; Secretary of Labor and Industry, Pennsylvania, 1923–1924; member, commission on social research in China, 1924–1925; professor, economics, Carleton College, Northfield, Minn., 1926–1927. Meeker founded the International Labor Review and other publications of the International Labor Office, is a contributor to many magazines and the author of "History and Theory of Shipping Subsidies." He lives in New Haven, Conn.

MEHOOPANY CREEK—Tributary to North Branch Susquehanna. Subbasin: Upper North Branch Susquehanna; source, in Colley Township, southeastern Sullivan County; course, northeasterly into Wyoming County to North Branch Susquehanna River; mouth, near Mehoopany; length, twenty-three miles. Indian name, Hobbenisink, "place of wild potatoes."

MEIGS, WILLIAM MONTGOMERY, lawyer and biographer, was born in Philadelphia, August 12, 1852. He was graduated from the University of Pennsylvania, in 1872, studied law and was admitted to the bar, in 1879. In addition to his law practice he devoted much time to literary work and is author of: "Life of Joseph Meigs," "The Growth of the Constitution," etc. He died December 30, 1929.

MELLON, ANDREW WILLIAM, secretary of the treasury, was born in Pittsburgh, March 24, 1854, and was educated at the Western University of Pennsylvania (University of Pittsburgh). Engaging in business in his native city he attained eminence as a financier. He was president of the Mellon National Bank, Pittsburgh, held offices in numerous financial and industrial corporations and was connected with coal, coke, and iron industries. On March 4, 1921, he became secretary of the treasury in the cabinet of President Harding and has remained in that office during the administrations of Presidents Coolidge and Hoover.

MENNONITES, a body consisting of a dozen or more branches of followers of Menno Simons, a Dutch religious reformer who lived from 1492 to 1559. He was not the founder of this body, but was a convert to it several years after it

MENNONITE WOMEN, LANCASTER COUNTY

began, and became its chief leader and author. He early left the priesthood of the Roman Catholic Church, espousing the views of the Anabaptists, who were opposed to the baptism of infants, baptizing only on confession of faith. The followers of Menno Simons became numerous in Holland, Germany and Switzerland, and thousands were persecuted to death, particularly in Holland, because of their views in regard to the temporal power. Rising in the first half of the sixteenth century (they were first called Mennonites in 1550, though the name was never generally adopted in Europe as it was in America), they increased under persecution and emigrated to Russia and the United States to escape it— to the former country near the close of the eighteenth century and to the latter from 1640 on, coming from Holland and Germany to New York and New Jersey. They were drawn to Pennsylvania by William Penn's announcement that those settling in that colony would enjoy freedom in the practice of their religious faith. The Society of Friends in England assisted the Mennonites of Holland to emigrate. The first Mennonite colony was formed at Germantown, near Philadelphia, in 1683. Thence they spread to Lancaster, Bucks, Berks and other counties in Pennsylvania and other states and localities. Though Mennonites are widely divided among themselves on questions of practice and principle, they are in substantial agreement in holding doctrines of the evangelical type, as expressed in a declaration of faith adopted at Dort, Holland, in 1632. They adhere to the principles of autonomy of the churches, freedom of conscience, separation of church and state, adult baptism, non-resistance and practical piety. Baptism is administered on confession of faith not by immersion, but by pouring the candidate either kneeling or standing in water and the minister taking up water in both hands and pouring it upon the head, using the scriptural formula. Ministers are selected by members of the church, who go one by one to a private room for the purpose. If more than one are thus selected choice between them is made by lot. The Lord's Supper is observed twice a year in the spring and in the fall, preceded by an examination of each member in faith and standing, and followed by the ceremony of feet-washing and the kiss of peace, the sexes separating for this purpose. Mennonites are opposed to the judicial oath and many practice non-conformity to the world.

MERCER, HENRY CHAPMAN, anthropologist, was born in Doylestown, June 24, 1856. He was graduated from Harvard, in 1879; was curator from 1894 to 1897 of American and prehistoric archaeology at the University of Pennsylvania; honorary member of the United States Archaeological Commission, Madrid, 1893. He made extensive investigations and studies in anthropology in America, discovering several unknown extinct species and 1897 to 1917 made and presented to the Historical Society of Bucks County an extensive collection of objects illustrating the Colonial and early history of the United States by means of the implements and handiwork of the pioneer settlers. In 1916, he built and presented to the society a fireproof museum for preserving the above collection. He established a pottery at Doylestown, in 1898, experimented upon and developed the processes of the Pennsylvania-Germans for making and decorating pottery as well as a new method of manufacturing tiles for making mosaics. He has received several valuable awards and has made numerous writings concerning his work.

MERCER, borough and county-seat of Mercer County, was laid out in August, 1803, by William McMillan, John Findley and William Mortimer, trustees appointed for that purpose, on land donated by John Hoge. It was named in honor of General Hugh Mercer. There are coal mines and oil and gas wells in the neighborhood. Agriculture is a leading industry, and this section produces dairy products, fruit and truck crops and wool and cattle. The manufactured products are: iron, stoves, brooms, and silk.

MERCER COUNTY, formed from part of Allegheny, March 12, 1800. Named for General Hugh Mercer. Land area, 700 square miles; population (1930), 99,246. County-seat, Mercer, laid out in 1803.

MERCERSBURG, a borough in Franklin County, about seventy miles southwest of Harrisburg. It was settled in 1730 and was originally called Black Town. It was incorporated in 1831 and the borough was enlarged in 1901. It is in a farming section of the country but has some coal and iron industries. It was formerly noted for its educational institutions, which were under the auspices of the German Reformed Church in America. It is the seat of Mercersburg Academy and was the home of James Buchanan.

MERCERSBURG THEOLOGY, a school of religious philosophy founded by F. A. Rauch, of the German Reformed Church, in 1836, his work being taken up by John W. Nevin and Philip Schaff. The name comes from the Mercersburg (Pa.) Theological Seminary of the German Reformed Church whence the teaching of this system spread. It urged that the Church was not a voluntary society of believers but a historic and spiritual growth, that the sacraments are more than symbols; that church worship should be more orderly—hence the "Liturgy," 1858, and "Order of Worship," 1866, and that religious education is of prime importance. The Mercersburg theology infused new life into the German Reformed Church.

MERCUR, JAMES, soldier, was born in Towanda, November 25, 1842. He was graduated from West Point, in 1866, and commissioned in the engineering corps. From 1867-1872, he was assistant professor of natural and experimental philosophy at West Point, after which he was in command of an engineering corps and in 1876-81 assisted in clearing the New York harbor of the obstructions at Hell Gate. He was professor of civil and military engineering at West Point from 1884 until his death. He published: "Elements of the Art of War," and "Military Mines, Blasting and Demolitions." He died at West Point, N. Y., April 22, 1896.

MERCURY, AMERICAN WEEKLY, THE, was the first newspaper in Pennsylvania and the third in the colonies. Its initial appearance was made on December 22, 1719, with the imprint: "Philadelphia: Printed by Andrew Bradford, and sold by him and John Copson." Upon the death of Bradford, in 1742, his widow continued the publication as the "Pennsylvania Mercury," until 1746, when it was discontinued.

MEREDITH, SAMUEL, patriot and first treasurer of the United States, was born in Philadelphia, 1740. Meredith became a member of the Pennsylvania colonial legislature and when the American Revolution broke out he entered the Colonial Army as major, took part in several battles and was made brigadier-general for gallant services. He gave £10,000 in silver for carrying on the war, and was exiled from Philadelphia when the British occupied it. Meredith served in Congress, in 1787-1788, and in 1789 became the first treasurer of the United States, advancing to the government, on taking the office, $20,000 and later $120,000, for which he was never reimbursed. He remained in the office of treasurer till 1801. He died March 10, 1817, in Philadelphia.

MEREDITH, WILLIAM M., jurist and statesman, was born in Philadelphia where he entered the legal profession. He was chairman of the convention that framed the Constitution of 1873 and also assisted in framing the Constitution of 1838. From 1849 until the death of President Taylor, he was secretary of the treasury. During the administration of Curtin as governor of Pennsylvania he was attorney-general.

MERRILL, LEWIS, soldier, was born at New Berlin, October 28, 1834. He was graduated from West Point, in 1855, and at the outbreak of the Civil War was appointed colonel of a volunteer cavalry regiment and served with distinction through the war. He was active in warfare with the Indians and performed the notable service of breaking up the Ku Klux Klan, in 1868, which act was recognized by Congress after some delay by Merrill's promotion to the rank of lieutenant-colonel of cavalry. He retired from active service in 1891 and died February 27, 1896, in Philadelphia.

MESHOPPEN CREEK—Tributary to North Branch Susquehanna River. Sub-basin: Upper North Branch Susquehanna; source, in Bridgewater Township, central Susquehanna County; course, southwesterly into Wyoming County to North Branch Susquehanna River; mouth, at Meshoppen; length, twenty-four miles. Indian name, a corruption of Maschapi, "corals or beads."

METCALF, WILLIAM, steel manufacturer, was born in Pittsburgh, 1838. In 1858, he was graduated from Rensselaer Polytechnic Institute, Troy, N. Y., and from 1860-1865 supervised the manufacture of Rodman and Dahlgren guns at Fort Pitt, Pittsburgh. In 1868, he entered the steel manufacturing field and in 1898 organized the Braeburn Steel Company of which he was president for eleven years. It is said that Metcalf made the first steel crucible in America. He published: "Steel—A Manual for Steel Users." He died in Pittsburgh in 1909.

METHODIST EPISCOPAL CHURCH. The earliest Methodist preaching in Philadelphia was by Captain Webb, a British army officer, stationed at Albany, N. Y., who had been converted to Methodism in Bristol, England, by John Wesley, about 1765. The first regular itinerant preachers of the church in America were Joseph Pillmore, who was stationed at Philadelphia, and Richard Boardman, stationed at New York. They landed at Gloucester, about six miles below Philadelphia, October 24, 1769. The first conference of the church was held in Philadelphia, July 4, 1773. In 1926, there were 452,145 members of the Methodist Episcopal Church in Pennsylvania.

METHODIST EPISCOPAL CHURCH, AFRICAN— See AFRICAN METHODIST EPISCOPAL CHURCH.

MEYERSDALE, a borough in Somerset County, on the Casselman River, thirty-seven miles northwest of Cumberland, Md. The borough is located in a coal mining district, which forms its principal industry. There are also manufactories of bricks, machinery and cigars.

MIDDLE CREEK—Tributary to Penns Creek. Sub-basin: Middle Main Susquehanna; source, formed by junction of Ulsh Gap Run and Krepp Gap Run, in West Beaver Township, western Snyder County; course, easterly to Penns Creek; mouth, south of Selinsgrove; length, twenty-eight miles.

MIDDLE CREEK—Tributary to Lackawaxen River. Sub-basin: Upper Delaware; source, in Moosic Mountain, southeast of Carbondale, Lackawanna County; course, southeasterly into Wayne County; thence easterly to Lackawaxen River; mouth, at West Hawley; length, twenty-one miles.

MIDDLEBURG, borough and county-seat of Snyder County, was laid out in 1800. It was named Middleburg because of its location on Middle Creek, in Middle Creek Valley, but had originally been called Swinesfordstown for John Swineford on whose land the town was plotted. It is situated in an agricultural region and its manufactured products include shirts, silk, flour, etc.

MIDDLETOWN, a borough in Dauphin County, on the Susquehanna River, about ten miles southeast of Harrisburg. It was founded in 1756 and in 1828 was incorporated. It is in a farming region but has considerable manufacturing interests. The principal manufactures are shoes, foundry products, stoves, furniture and cars. Stone quarries in the vicinity contribute to the industrial wealth of the borough. Population (1930), 6,085; (1920), 5,920.

MIFFLIN, LLOYD, poet and artist, was born at Columbia, Lancaster County, September 15, 1846. He was educated at the Washington Classical Institute, Columbia, and by private tutors. At an early age he displayed great interest in art, and developed the talent inherited from his father, J. Houston Mifflin, under T. Moran and Isaac Williams, of Philadelphia. In 1869, he went to Europe where he studied under Henry Herzog, at Dusseldorf, Germany and traveled in Italy, France, England, and Scotland, painting and sketching. At an early age, too, he showed keen interest in literature. His first published work was a poem of sixteen verses entitled, "The Hills," which appeared in 1896 In the following year, "At the Gates of Song," a volume containing one hundred and fifty sonnets was published. His other collections include: "The Slopes of Helicon and Other Poems," "Echoes of Greek Idyls," "The Fields of Dawn and Later Sonnets," "Castailian Days," "The Fleeing Nymph and Other Verses," "Collected Sonnets of Lloyd Mifflin," "My Lady of Dreams," "Toward the Uplands," "Flower and Thorn," and "As Twilight Falls." He died at Norwood, Columbia, July 16, 1921.

MIFFLIN, THOMAS, soldier and governor, was born in Philadelphia, 1744. He was graduated from Philadelphia College, in 1760, and entered public life, in 1772, as a member of the Pennsylvania Assembly. In 1774, he was elected a delegate to the Continental Congress and in 1775 entered the army with the rank of major, and as colonel and first aide-de-camp to Washington accompanied him to Cambridge. He also fought in the battles of Long Island and Trenton. In 1777, he was made a major-general and in the same year became an active member of the faction organized for the purpose of placing Gates at the head of the Continental Army, known in history as the Conway Cabal. The project failed and he resigned his commission and in 1782 was elected to Congress of which body he became president during the following year. In 1785, he became speaker of the Pennsylvania Legislature and 1787 was a delegate to the Constitutional Convention. In October, 1788, he succeeded Franklin as president of the Supreme Executive Council of Pennsylvania and served two years. From 1790-1799, he was governor of Pennsylvania and in 1794 rendered important assistance to Washington in quelling the Whiskey Insurrection. He died in Lancaster, January 20, 1800.

MIFFLIN COUNTY, formed from part of Cumberland and Northumberland, September 19, 1789. Named for Governor Thomas Mifflin. Land area, 398 square miles; population (1930), 40,335. County-seat, Lewistown, laid out in 1790.

MIFFLINTOWN, borough and county-seat of Juniata County, was laid out in 1791. It was named in honor of Thomas Mifflin, governor of Pennsylvania. Among the manufactured products of Mifflintown are: automobile bodies, agricultural implements, overalls, silk, etc.

MILBURN, WILLIAM HENRY, clergyman, was born in Philadelphia, September 26, 1823. At the age of five through an accident he lost his sight completely. He was educated at Illinois College and in 1843 became a Methodist itinerant preacher, was active in the south and held charges in Alabama. In 1845, he was elected chaplain of the House of Representatives and served as such in 1853, 1885, and 1887. In 1893, he was made a chaplain of the Senate. He was widely known as the "blind preacher" and as such lectured in Great Britain and the United States. He wrote: "Pioneers and People of the Mississippi Valley," and others all based on his western experiences. He died in 1903.

MILFORD, town and county-seat of Pike County, on the Delaware River, about forty-five miles east of Scranton. It is situated in a portion of the Delaware Valley noted for its beautiful and picturesque scenery. The Sawkill Falls and the Cliffs are in the vicinity and south of the town are mountains. Milford is one of the pre-Revolutionary settlements but it was not made a separate township until 1832. The town of Milford was laid out in 1796. It is a favorite resort for hunting and fishing parties. Population is about 900, but in summer is over 6,000.

MILFORD (1843)

MILFORD DISPATCH-PRESS, THE, originally *The Eagle of the North*, was established in 1826 or 1827. It appears on Thursday, is independent in politics, and Josiah F. Terwilliger is editor and publisher. Circulation, 1,532.

MILL CREEK—Tributary to Conestoga Creek. Sub-basin: Lower Main Susquehanna; source, in Welsh Mountain, East Earl Township, eastern Lancaster County; course, southwesterly to Conestoga Creek; mouth, two miles south of Lancaster; length, twenty-six miles.

MILLER, GEORGE ABRAM, mathematician, was born at Lynnville, July 31, 1863. He studied at Muhlenberg College, Cumberland University, and at Paris and Leipzig. He was instructor in mathematics at the University of Michigan, Cornell, Leland Stanford, Jr., University, and since 1906 he has been professor of mathematics at the University of Illinois. He is editor of the "American Mathematical Monthly" and of "School Science and Mathematics." He wrote: "Determinents," "Historical Introductions to Mathematical Literature," and is co-author of "Mathematical Monographs" and "Theory and Application of Groups of Finite Order."

MILLER, JOHN PETER, minister of the Seventh-Day Baptist Church, was born in the upper Palatinate, Germany, December 25, 1709. He graduated from the University of Heidelburg and in August, 1730, came to America, landing at Philadelphia. He was ordained to the ministry of the Presbyterian Church and in 1731 was in charge of several congregations. One of these was on the Cocalico Creek, near the present town of Ephrata, and it was doubtless here that Miller came under the influence of John Conrad Beissel, founder of the community of the Seventh-Day Baptists. Eventually Miller was converted to Beissel's faith and became a leader in the Ephrata community. In 1745, he became prior of the convent and upon the death of Father Friedsam, Miller, known as Brother Jabez, succeeded him as superintendent and pastor of the community, which position he held until his death in 1769. Miller was widely known as a scholar, and was a friend of Benjamin Franklin and of George Ross, of Lancaster, one of the Signers of the Declaration of Independence. After the adoption of the Declaration of Independence by Congress, Thomas Jefferson deputized Miller to translate it into seven European languages.

MILLERITES, a religious group, followers of a Vermont farmer, William Miller, originated about the year 1844. Miller who maintained that the second coming of Christ was scheduled for a certain date, had many followers in Pennsylvania. Prior to the date set for the second advent they sold their properties, gave away many of their belongings and dressed in ascension robes, awaited the coming of Christ. Such groups stood in readiness for the great event on an island in the Susquehanna River near Middletown and in a field near Darby, Philadelphia. When the hour passed and nothing happened many lost faith altogether and returned to their homes.

MILLERSVILLE STATE TEACHERS COLLEGE, was organized in 1855. In 1927, the School was authorized to confer the degree of Bachelor of Science in education and the name was subsequently changed from Normal School to Teachers College.

The town of Millersville is in Lancaster County three miles southwest of Lancaster City.

MILLHEIM JOURNAL, THE, of Millheim, Centre County, established in 1827. It appears on Thursday; is Democratic in politics; J. C. Hosterman is editor and publisher.

MILLIGAN, ROBERT WILEY, rear-admiral, was born in Philadelphia, April 8, 1843. He entered the navy with rank as third assistant engineer and was attached to the United States steamship "Mackinaw" in the North Atlantic Blockading Squadron. He saw service at both battles of Fort Fisher and was present at the fall of Wilmington, N. C., and of Petersburg and Richmond, Va. Afterwards he served in the North and South Atlantic and Pacific Squadrons, and was on duty as instructor at the United States Naval Academy. He was promoted chief engineer in 1892 in which capacity he served on the United States battleship "Oregon" on her famous run from the Pacific to the Atlantic coast in the Spanish-American War, and also at the battle of Santiago. He was fleet engineer of the North Atlantic fleet in 1899 and chief engineer of the Norfolk navy yard in 1899–1905. He retired in 1905 with rank as rear-admiral. He died October 14, 1909.

MILLIKIN, JAMES, banker and philanthropist, was born in Pennsylvania, August 2, 1830. In 1860, he engaged in banking and later founded the firm of Millikin and Company, at Decatur, Ill., now the Millikin National Bank. He founded the Anna B. Millikin Home, an institution for the care of aged women and children, and named after his wife. He also founded the James Millikin University, dedicated in 1904 by President Roosevelt. He died March 2, 1909, at Orlando, Florida.

MILLSTONE GRIT, a hard siliceous conglomerate with quartz pebbles found at the base of the Pennsylvania coal measures series of the carboniferous system. The formation occurs as far north as New York and as far south as Alabama, throughout the Appalachian Range. In Pennsylvania the beds are coarse and over 1,200 feet thick. The rock in Pennsylvania is light in color and is called the Pottsville Conglomerate. It is interstratified with some sandstone, thin beds of carbonaceous shells and thin beds of coal. In the southern portion of the Appalachian Mountains the coal beds are richer and more plentiful.

MILLVALE, borough in Allegheny County, on the Allegheny River, opposite Pittsburgh. It is an industrial suburb of Pittsburgh, its chief manufactures are lumber, iron and steel products, saws and dressed stone. Population (1930), 8,166; (1920), 8,031.

MILTON, borough in Northumberland County, fifty miles north of Harrisburg, on the Susquehanna River. The scenery is picturesque and a fine bridge spans the river. Milton was settled in 1792 and incorporated in 1817. Its industries and manufactures are rolled iron, lumber, cars, wood-working, machinery, shops, nails, nuts, bolts, furniture, shot, fly-nets, bamboo novelties and paper boxes. It suffered from a severe fire in 1880. Population (1930), 8,552; (1920), 8,638.

MILTONIAN, THE, a weekly newspaper, was established at Milton, in 1816. It appears on Thursday and is Republican in politics. V. W. McHale is the editor; the Keystone Telegraph Press, Inc., are the publishers. Circulation, 1,620.

MINER, CHARLES, journalist, was born at Norwich, Conn., February 1, 1780. At the age of nineteen, he removed to the Wyoming Valley, Pennsylvania, where with his brother he established the "Luzerne Federalist," and afterward the "Gleaner," for which he wrote humorous sketches. Subsequently he became assistant editor of the "Political and Commercial Register" of Philadelphia and also established with his brother the West Chester "Village Record," to which he contributed under the name of "John Harwood." He was a member of Congress from Pennsylvania in 1825-1829, and was the first to bring to the notice of that body the possibilities of the culture and manufacture of silk in the United States. His "History of Wyoming" contains a vivid description of the Wyoming Massacre, obtained from an eye witness. He died in Wilkes-Barre, October 26, 1865.

MINERSVILLE, a borough in Schuylkill County, on the west branch of the Schuylkill River, about forty-five miles northeast of Harrisburg. Situated in the hard coal region, its chief industries are connected with mining and shipping coal. Industrial establishments include machine shops, foundries, underwear factories, lumber and brick yards. Population (1930), 9,392; (1920), 7,845.

MINT, a government establishment for the coining of lawful metallic money. Besides making the coined money of the country the United States mint makes metallic money for foreign nations, and also does considerable business in the line of supplying fine gold and silver in bars for industrial uses, and in making assays of bullion and ores of the precious metals for private owners. Pennsylvania is favored in having one of the three United States mints within its territory; viz., one at Philadelphia.

MIQUON, the name by which the Delaware Indians familiarly referred to William Penn.

MISCHIANZA, the entertainment given in Philadelphia, May 18, 1778, during the War of the Revolution, by officers of the British Army, in honor of Sir William Howe, about to return to England after he had been superseded by General Clinton. The entertainment was given at the country home of Thomas Wharton and comprised a dinner, dancing, a regatta, mock tournaments and various games. Major Andre was prominent in planning the entertainment.

MITCHELL, JOHN H., lawyer and senator, was born in Washington County, June 22, 1835. He was educated at Witherspoon Institute, Pa., was admitted to the bar of Pennsylvania and went to California where he established a law practice, but in 1860 removed to Oregon and engaged in practice there. He was state senator and president of the senate, professor at Willamette University (Salem, Oregon), and United States Senator. He acquired a considerable fortune as a lawyer to the great Western railroads. He died in 1905.

MITCHELL, JOHN KEARSHEY, physician, was born at Shepherdstown, Va., May 12, 1798. Returning from Ayr and Edinburgh, Scotland, where he had been sent at the age of eight, he studied medicine under Dr. Nathaniel Chapman and was graduated at the medical department of the University of Pennsylvania in 1819. After making three voyages to China and the East Indies as ship surgeon he settled in Philadelphia as general practitioner. In 1826, he became professor of chemistry at the Philadelphia Medical Institute. From 1841-1858, he was professor of theory and practice of medicine at Jefferson Medical College. Dr. Mitchell was visiting physician to the Pennsylvania and City Hospitals. In addition to numerous papers published in medical and scientific journals he wrote: "Saint Helena, a Poem by a Yankee"; "On the Wisdom, Goodness, and Power of God as Illustrated in the Properties of Water." His "Five Essays on Various Chemical and Medical Subjects" were not published until after his death by his son, Silas Weir Mitchell. He died in Philadelphia, April 4, 1858.

MITCHELL, LANGDON ELWYN, author and playwright, was born in Philadelphia, February 17, 1862, a son of Dr. Silas Weir Mitchell. He was educated at St. Paul's School, Concord, N. H., and in Europe. He studied law at Harvard and Columbia and in 1886 was admitted to the New York bar. After 1883, he devoted himself to literature and drama. His most successful plays are: "Becky Sharp" and "The New York Idea." His pen-name is "John Philip Varley."

MITCHELL, SAMUEL AUGUSTUS, geographer, was born at Bristol, Conn., March 30, 1792. He spent his early life in successful teaching, but the inadequate treatment of geography by the textbooks then in use induced him to turn his attention to the making of satisfactory ones and he spent forty years in Philadelphia in the preparation of textbooks on that subject. So general was their adoption that they reached a total sale of 400,000 annually. Besides his geographical textbooks of which there were twenty-four, he edited a new edition of John James Audubon's "Birds of America," and wrote "New Traveler's Guide Through the United States." He died in Philadelphia, December 20, 1868.

MITCHELL, SILAS WEIR, physician, inventor of "rest cure," poet, and novelist, was born in Philadelphia, February 15, 1829. He studied at the University of Pennsylvania, was graduated from Jefferson Medical College, in 1850, entered practice in Philadelphia, during the Civil War was in charge of the Turner's Lane United States Hospital (Philadelphia) for diseases and injuries of the nervous system and subsequently was president of the Philadelphia College of Physicians. To a wider degree, however, he is known through his literary work, composed principally of poetry and fiction. One of the best known is his novel "Hugh Wynne, Free Quaker." He was elected to the American Academy of Arts and Sciences and the National Academy of Sciences and was also made associate corresponding or honorary member of foreign scientific societies. He died January 4, 1914.

MOLLY MAGUIRES (an Irish secret society formed in 1843 at Farney, County Monaghan, to intimidate bailiffs or process-servers distraining for rent, or others impounding the cattle of those who were unable or unwilling to pay rent). A similar society, called by the same name, existed, 1854-1877, in the mining districts of Pennsylvania. The members dressed in "Molly Maguire" or women's dresses, sought to effect their purpose by intimidation, and in some cases by murder. Under perilous detective work, several at length were arrested, tried and executed, and the society finally disbanded.

MONEY, PAPER, the earliest known bill was dated August 10, 1723, and was printed by Benjamin Franklin. The general style of the notes is the same as used in Delaware, bearing the royal arms, or in 1756 those of William Penn with his motto: "Mercy Justice." In 1764, a curious notion was adopted of spelling the colony differently on each bill, thus on the series we find Pennsylvania, Pensylvania, Pennsilvania, and Pensilvania, perhaps a protection against counterfeiting. In 1777, the shape of the bill changed to the oblong form and the arms of Pennsylvania took the place formerly devoted to those of Great Britain. In 1785, the last of the series saw the light, the denominations running from three pence to £4, sixteen values in all. The varieties issued by the colony of Pennsylvania were over 250.

MONONGAHELA, BATTLE OF—*See* BRADDOCK'S DEFEAT.

MONONGAHELA CITY, a city in Washington County, on the Monongahela River, about thirty-two miles south of Pittsburgh; it is in a coal region, in which the chief industries are coal mining and manufacturing. It was settled in 1792 by Joseph Parkison, was incorporated as a borough, April 3, 1833, and chartered as a city, March 24, 1873. The chief manufactures are: glass, foundry and machine shop products, flour, lumber, chemicals, and paper. Population (1930), 8,675; (1920), 8,688.

MONONGAHELA RIVER—Tributary to Ohio River. Sub-basin: Monongahela; source, formed by junction of Tugart Valley River and West Fork River, near Fairmont, West Virginia; course, northeasterly into Pennsylvania; mouth, at Pittsburgh; length, total, 128.1 miles; in Pennsylvania, 91.6 miles. Indian name, a corruption of Menaungehilla, "high banks, breaking off and falling down at places."

MONROE COUNTY, formed from part of Northampton and Pike, April 1, 1836. Named for President James Monroe. Land area, 623 square miles; population (1930), 28,286. County-seat, Stroudsburg, laid out in 1806.

MONTGOMERY COUNTY, formed from part of Philadelphia, September 10, 1784. Named for General Richard Montgomery. Land area, 484 square miles; population (1930), 265,804. County-seat, Norristown, laid out in 1784.

MONTOUR, ANDREW, "the Half-Indian," whose Indian name was Sattelihn, was the oldest and most noted of the children of Madam Montour. He accompanied George Croghan on many missions in the Ohio and Allegheny Valleys. He received from Governor Dinwiddie a captain's commission to head a company of friendly Indians as scouts. Instead he headed a company of men and with Croghan joined Washington at Great Meadows. During the French and Indian War he acted as an interpreter in many councils. He was granted a three hundred acre tract of land in 1769. A town, county, mountain range, creek and island, all in Pennsylvania, are named for him and his mother.

MONTOUR, ESTHER (called Queen Esther), American half-breed Indian of the eighteenth century. She had French blood in her veins and was supposed to have been a descendant of Count de Frontenac, governor of New France. She was married to a chief of the village Sheshequin, and her keen intelligence enabled her to completely dominate the Senecas over whom she reigned as "Queen Esther." She was friendly to a Moravian mission which was located near her village for some years, and accompanied delegates to various congresses of the Six Nations in Philadelphia where she was well received among the best people owing to her pleasing manners and beautiful person. In the Wyoming Massacre in July, 1778, the savage in her nature, however, asserted itself and to avenge the death of her son she deliberately tomahawked fourteen prisoners.

MONTOUR, MADAM, was born in Canada, about 1684, the daughter of a French gentleman and a Huron Indian woman. When but ten years of age she was captured by warriors of the Five Nations, and brought up by them. She married a Seneca named Roland Montour, and upon his death, she married Carondowanen, or "Big Tree," who later took the name of Robert Hunter in honor of the Governor of New York. Madam Montour first appeared as an interpreter at Albany, in 1711. She lived for many years at the village, sometimes called French Town, at the mouth of the Loyalsock Creek, in Lycoming County. A creek, a river, a town, a county, and a mountain range, all in Pennsylvania, are named for her or members of her family. It is thought that she died at the home of her son, Andrew, about 1752. It is claimed that Madam Montour was a lady of education, of genteel manners, and handsome face and form, and that upon her visits to Philadelphia was entertained by ladies of the best society. Near the end of her life she became blind but was bodily able to go on horseback from Logstown to Venango, a distance of seventy miles, her son, Andrew, leading the horse. She and this son are among the most picturesque characters of Pennsylvania history.

MONTOUR COUNTY, formed from part of Columbia, May 3, 1850. Named for Madam Montour, famous Indian interpreter. Land area, 130 square miles; population (1930), 14,517. County-seat, Danville, laid out in 1790.

MONTROSE, a borough, county-seat of Susquehanna County, about forty miles northwest of Scranton. It is about 2,000 feet above the sea, and its cool climate in summer and the beauty of its scenery make it a favorite summer resort. The manufactures are: machine shops, lumber mills, and flour mills.

MONTROSE INDEPENDENT, THE, is an independent weekly newspaper, appearing on Thursday and was established in 1816. It is edited by B. R. Gardner, and is published by the Montrose Publishing Company, Inc. Circulation, 2,458.

MOORE, CHARLES LEONARD, poet and essayist, was born in Philadelphia, March 16, 1854. He was educated in the public schools of his native city. In 1878-1879, he was one of the managers of the Madeira and Mamore Railroad Construction Company and was United States Consular Agent at San Antonio, Brazil, the headquarters of that operation. He was afterward connected with railroad construction in Pennsylvania, and was later secretary of one of the Disston Florida Sand Companies for four years. For the last twenty years he has been occupied with literary work. During that time he has been a constant contributor to the "Dial." He published: "Atlas," "Poems Antique and Modern," "Odes," and "Incense and Iconoclasm."

MOORE, CLARENCE BLOOMFIELD, archaeologist, was born in Philadelphia, January 14, 1852. He was graduated from Harvard (1873), and then traveled through most of Europe, Asia, and Egypt. He crossed the Andes and traveled down the Amazon (1876), and made a journey around the world (1878-1879). Later he explored the Indian mounds of South Carolina, Georgia, Florida, Alabama, Mississippi, and Louisiana. His many scientific writings have been published by the Academy of Natural Sciences of Philadelphia.

MOORE, EDWARD CALDWELL, theologian, was born at West Chester, September 1, 1857. He was graduated from Marietta College, in 1877, then at Union Theological Seminary, in 1884. He studied at the universities of Berlin, Gottingen, and Giessen, and received in 1891 the degree, Ph. D., at Brown University. In 1884, he was ordained to the Presbyterian ministry and served as pastor at Yonkers, N. Y., and Providence, R. I. He then became Parkman professor of theology and Plummer professor of Christian morals at Harvard University (1901-1929). He lectured at many colleges. He wrote: "The New Testament in the Christian Church," "History of Christian Thought Since Kant," etc. He was a member of the American Board of Commissioners of Foreign Missions (1899-1914), and was elected its president, 1914. Dr. Moore is now professor emeritus at Harvard University.

MOORE, FRANK GARDNER, educator, was born in West Chester, September 25, 1865. He was graduated from Yale (1886), and received the Ph. D. degree in 1890. He studied at the University of Berlin and was tutor in Latin (1888-1893) at Yale. He was made assistant professor in Latin (1893-1900) at Dartmouth College, then associate professor of Latin and Roman archaeology (1900-1908). He was professor of Latin (1908-1910) at Trinity College, Hartford, Conn., and professor of classical philology at Columbia University from 1910-1919. In 1919, he became professor of Latin at Columbia University, which position he holds at present. He edited: Tacitus' "Histories," Vols. I and II, 1910; Cicero's "Cato Major," 1904, and "Transactions and Proceedings of the American Philological Association," of which society he was secretary (1904-1916), and president in 1917.

MOORE, GEORGE FOOT, orientalist, was born at West Chester, October 15, 1851. He was graduated from Yale, in 1872, and at Union Theological Seminary, in 1877. Entering the Presbyterian ministry, he was pastor of a church at Zanesville, Ohio, 1878-1883, and in the latter year became Hitchcock professor of Hebrew and the history of religions at Andover Theological Seminary, and from 1899-1901 was president of the faculty. In 1902, he was appointed professor of theology at Harvard and, in 1904, Frothingham professor of the history of religions. For some years he edited the "Journal of the American Oriental Society" of which he was president, 1911-1912. He has written: "A Commentary of Judges"; "The Book of Judges in Hebrew"; "The Literature of the Old Testament"; "History of Religions," Vol. I, 1913; and "Metempsychosis"; "Ingersoll Lecture at Harvard, 1914."

MOORE, ROBERT, civil engineer, was born at New Castle, June 19, 1838. He was graduated (1858) at Miami University, receiving A. M. degree in 1866. He has been engaged principally in the location and construction of railways such as the Illinois Central, the Illinois Southern, the Baltimore and Ohio, etc. He was sewer commissioner and a member of the board of public improvements at Saint Louis (1877-1881) and has been consulting engineer for a number of railway companies and reorganization commissions. From 1897-1913, he was a member of the St. Louis board of education. He was a member of the Brazos River Board and the Southwest Passboard of Engineers and is past-president of the American Society of Civil Engineers.

MOORE, WILLIS LUTHER, meteorologist, was born in Scranton, January 18, 1856. At eight years of age he joined his father, with Grant's Army, at City Point, Va., and sold papers to the troops in field; was educated in the Binghamton public schools; was student of natural sciences under scientific staff of the Weather Bureau for fifteen years and under private tutors six years. He served as printer and pressman and rose through successive grades to local forecast official in Milwaukee (1891-94); won professorship of meteorology in open competitive examination against twenty-three contestants, 1894, and was assigned to duty as district forecaster at Chicago; was chief United States Weather Bureau, 1895-1913; professor applied meteorology, George Washington University, 1914. He is popular as a lecturer on the Lyceum and Chautauqua circuits, and is a contributor to scientific journals.

MORAIS, SABATO, Rabbi and educator, was born in Leghorn, Italy, April 13, 1823. He was carefully trained in Hebrew lore, and taught first in Leghorn and then for a few years in London. In 1851, he came to Philadelphia and until his death was minister of the Mikve Israel Synagogue. In 1867, he was appointed professor of biblical exegesis in the short-lived Maimonides College of Philadelphia and was one of the founders and the first president of the Jewish Theological Seminary of New York. He was a representative of conservative Judaism, unremitting in his efforts in behalf of education and charity and an earnest and scholarly contributor to the Jewish press on historical, literary and theological themes. He died in Philadelphia, November 11, 1897.

MORAVIAN CHURCH, THE, the common name given to the renewed Unitas Fratrum or Church of the Brethren for a time styled also in English the Church of the United Brethren, which originally flourished in Bohemia, Moravia, and Poland, was disrupted in the seventeenth century, and resuscitated in Saxony in the eighteenth century and now exists in Europe and America with an extensive mission work in many parts of the world. The first Moravian evangelists came to Pennsylvania, in 1734. Political conditions in Savannah, Ga., their first settlement in America, caused its abandonment in 1740 and the removal of the colonists to Pennsylvania where a permanent settlement arose in the present Northampton County with organized activity in Philadelphia and New York and extensive itinerary among white settlers and Indians. On a tract of land at the confluence of the Monocacy Creek and the Lehigh River its chief settlement was founded in 1741, and on Christmas, when Count Zinzendorf was at the place it received the name of Bethlehem. In 1762, a cooperative union was maintained at Bethlehem, and Nazareth, another Moravian settlement, which was called the General Economy. All labored for a common cause and received sustenance from a common stock, but there was no surrender of private property and no obligation which prevented the individual from withdrawing when he chose. The material benefits of the settlement were appreciated by the authorities of Pennsylvania and the spiritual activities prosecuted by the Moravians, although misunderstood and opposed by some, were epoch-making in the religious growth of the country. Besides Bethlehem and Nazareth, Lititz was another Moravian settlement.

MORAVIAN COLLEGE AND THEOLOGICAL SEMINARY, for men, was founded at Bethlehem, in 1807. Enrollment (1930-1931), 120.

MORAVIAN SEMINARY AND COLLEGE FOR WOMEN, at Bethlehem, founded almost at the beginning of the Moravian settlement of Bethlehem (1741); it is the second oldest girl's boarding school in the United States. "Colonial Hall," built in 1748, is the oldest structure in the group of buildings owned by the seminary. From the roof of this building it was customary in pre-Revolutionary days to play the trombone on festal occasions or to announce the death of members. Tradition says that on one occasion during the French and Indian War a band of Indians had planned to attack the settlement, and at sunset as they lay waiting on Calypso Island, for the darkness, they heard a strange melody floating down from the sky. They had never heard anything like it before, and thinking it must be the voice of the Great Spirit warning them, they held a hurried council and silently stole away in the darkness. In 1776-78, "Colonial Hall" served as a military hospital for continental troops. After the Battle of Brandywine the place was crowded with wounded. Many of the distinguished women of the nation have been graduated from this institution. A preparatory school, music, art, and science departments are connected with the seminary and about twenty years ago a fully accredited college course leading to A. B. and B. S. degrees was added, and is recognized by the College and University Council of Pennsylvania. Enrollment (1930-1931), 100.

MORDECAI, ALFRED, engineer, was born in Warrenton, N. C., January 3, 1804. Graduating at the head of his class from West Point, in 1819, he became second lieutenant of engineers, and after work as instructor at West Point and assistant engineer was appointed captain of ordnance corps, May 30, 1832. Brevetted major (1848) for meritorious conduct in the Mexican War, he was sent to the Crimea (1855-57), his observations on military organization and ordnance being published by order of Congress, in 1860. He resigned from the service, in 1861, settling in Philadelphia where after acting as assistant engineer of the Mexican and Pacific Railroad (1863-1866) he became (1867-1887) treasurer and secretary of canal and coal companies controlled by the Pennsylvania Railroad. Among his works are: "Digest on Military Laws," "Reports of Experiments on Gunpowder," and "Ordnance Manual for the Use of Officers of the United States Army." He died in Philadelphia, October 23, 1887.

MORDECAI, ALFRED, engineer, son of Alfred Mordecai, was born in Philadelphia, June 30, 1840. He was graduated from West Point (1859) and brevetted second lieutenant, topographical engineers. After service in the field (June to August, 1861), he taught at West Point for nearly a year and then was promoted until he became chief of ordnance, Department of the South (1863-1864). Brevetted lieutenant-colonel for services in the war (March 13, 1865), he was instructor of ordnance and gunnery at West Point, 1865-1870, and again 1874-1881. He was commander, with rank of colonel, of the Benicia (Calif.) Arsenal, 1899-1902; promoted brigadier-general and retired, 1904. He died January 20, 1920.

MORE, NICHOLAS, English colonist, was born in England. He was a physician and left a promising career in England to come with William Penn to America, in 1682. He was from the first prominent in the affairs of the colony, was president of the first assembly, in 1682, and in that year, presiding judge of the courts of Philadelphia. In 1683, he was clerk of the provincial council and the next year was speaker of the assembly. He was appointed first chief justice of the Supreme Court of the province, in 1684, and in this position incurred the disapproval of the colony and was impeached for having wielded an unlimited and arbitrary power. He retained the confidence of Penn, however, who appointed him, in 1686, one of the five commissioners in control of the government. He died in Philadelphia, in 1689.

MORGAN, JOHN, physician, was born June 10, 1735. He was graduated (1751) at the College of Philadelphia (now the University of Pennsylvania). He entered the provincial army as surgeon and lieutenant, resigning his commission to continue (1760) his medical studies in London and Edinburgh, receiving the degree of M. D., 1763. Returning (1765) to Philadelphia he laid the plan for establishing a medical school in that city, which he had formulated at the request of the trustees of the College of Philadelphia. The plan adopted he became professor of the theory and practice of medicine. In 1775, he was appointed by Congress, director-general and physician-in-chief of the American Army and reorganized the hospitals of the army. He wrote on medical subjects and won a gold medal from England. He died October 15, 1789, in Philadelphia.

MORGAN, TALI ESEN, choral conductor, was born in Llangynwyd, South Wales, October 28, 1858. He studied music and came (1877) to Scranton. In 1879 was publisher of the "Cambro-American," and editor of "The People," the State Prohibition organ for six years. He was associated with Walter Damrosch in musical work and later with Anton Seidl; conducting the Ocean Grove (N. J.) Festivals since 1888, becoming manager and conductor of the Ocean Grove Summer Music Festivals, in 1898. Later he was conductor of the New York Festival Chorus. He is editor and publisher of "The American Musical Times," and founder and president of the International Correspondence School of Music, Asbury Park, N. J. Morgan is the author of a standard course of music instruction for teachers and public school supervisors.

MORMONS. Joseph Smith, the founder of the Mormons, or the Latter Day Saints, was a resident of Harmony, now Oakland, Susquehanna County, shortly before the "vision," responsible for the new religious organization appeared to him. It is claimed by students of the history of Mormonism that Smith was directly influenced by Solomon Spaulding, a native of Ashford, Conn., and graduate of Dartmouth College, who, in 1812, moved from Ohio to Pittsburgh and later to Amity, Washington County, Pa., where he died in 1816 and is buried. Spaulding was the author of a work entitled, "Manuscript Found," in which he gave a detailed history of the Indian occupants of America. Since the material of Spaulding's manuscript is identical with that written upon the gold plates, said to have been discovered by Smith, it is believed that Spaulding's work was known by Smith. The actual founding of the Mormon Church took place in Manchester, N. Y., on April 6, 1830. About 1845 members of the society purchased land between Mercersburg and Greencastle, and settlements numbering about two hundred were formed there and in Greencastle. Mormon residents of Greencastle issued a publication the "Conococheague Herald." In a graveyard near New Jerusalem, Pa., a number of followers of the Mormon faith are buried.

MORRIS, BENJAMIN WISTAR, Protestant Episcopal bishop, was born at Wellsboro, May 30, 1819. He was graduated from the General Theological Seminary, in 1846, and held successive rectorates at Sunbury, Manayunk, and Germantown. He was consecrated missionary bishop of Oregon and Washington in December, 1868, and on the division of the diocese in 1880 became bishop of Oregon. He published "Presbyterian, Baptist, and Methodist Testimony to Confirmation." He died in Portland, Oregon, April 8, 1906.

MORRIS, CHARLES, author, was born in Chester, October 1, 1833. He was educated in Chester, engaged for a short period in teaching; for a considerable time was manager in a manufacturing concern; and after 1878 devoted himself to literary work. His publications include: "A Manual of Classical Literature," "The War with Spain," "The Story of Mexico," "Heroes of America," and others. He also compiled dictionaries and encyclopedias. He died September 6, 1922.

MORRIS, EDWARD JOY, author, was born in Philadelphia, July 16, 1815. He was graduated from Harvard, in 1836, and was admitted to the bar, in 1842. He was a member of the Pennsylvania Legislature, 1841-1843, and of Congress, 1843-1845, and in 1850 was appointed to a mission in Naples where he remained four years. He was again in Congress from Pennsylvania in 1858-1861, and from 1861-1870 was Minister to Turkey. He published "Notes of a Tour Through Turkey," and numerous translations. He died in Philadelphia, December 31, 1881.

MORRIS, GEORGE POPE, journalist and poet, was born in Philadelphia, October 10, 1802. He removed to New York and devoted his entire life to the editorship of the "Mirror." He wrote "Briarcliff," a popular drama, and "Poems" in which are included "Woodman, Spare that Tree"; "A Long Time Ago"; "My Mother's Bible," etc. He died in New York City, July 6, 1864.

MORRIS, HARRISON SMITH, author, was born in Philadelphia, October 4, 1856. He was educated in the public and private schools and early began to do literary work. From 1899-1905, he was editor of "Lippincott's Magazine." He is versed in the history of art and was managing director of the Pennsylvania Academy of Fine Arts in Philadelphia, from 1893-1905. He has written: "A Duet in Lyrics"; a continuation of Lamb's "Tales from Shakespeare"; "Tales from Ten Poets"; "Madonna and Other Poems"; "Hannah Bye" (a novel); "The Landlord's Daughter" (a novel); "Walt Whitman" (a biography published in Italian), etc. He resides in Oak Lane, Philadelphia.

MORRIS, ROBERT, financier and statesman, a signer of the Declaration of Independence, was born in Liverpool, England, January 31, 1734. He came to the colonies about 1747 and entered at Philadelphia the counting-room of Charles Willing, merchant. Despite his strong loyalty to England, he opposed the Stamp Act and signed the non-importation agreement of 1765. In October, 1775, he was elected to the provincial assembly, and in 1776-1778 was a member of the Continental Congress. In July, 1776, he voted against the Declaration of Independence and on July 4th absented himself; but on 2nd of August he was one of the signers. Most of the business of the colonies was transacted by him. On February 20, 1781, he was elected superintendent of finance. The treasury was in a disordered state through a vastly depreciated paper currency, but he presented a plan of organization to Congress for the Bank of North America and he himself subscribed $39,200 worth of shares. He was a member of the Pennsylvania Assembly in 1776-1778, 1778-1779, 1780-1781, 1785-1787. In 1787, he was a member of the convention that framed the constitution of the United States. He declined the Secretaryship of the Treasury and was United States

ROBERT MORRIS

Senator from Pennsylvania in 1789-1795. Largely through the defaulting of his partner in land speculation he was compelled to make an assignment and was imprisoned for debt at Philadelphia, February 19, 1798, to August 26, 1801. The influence of his credit, his ability in raising loans and his financial skill were of utmost importance to the struggling cause of the Revolution. He is known as the Financier of the Revolution. He died May 8, 1806, in Philadelphia.

MORTON, HENRY, scientist, was born in New York, December 11, 1836. He was graduated from the University of Pennsylvania, in 1857, and became professor of physics and chemistry at the Episcopal Academy of Philadelphia in 1860. He was one of the founders of the Philadelphia Dental College, in 1863, and its professor of chemistry. In 1867, he was appointed professor of chemistry at the University of Pennsylvania, and in the same year became editor of the Franklin Institute "Journal." His reputation as a scientist became worldwide and his services as a chemical expert were eagerly sought for litigation. From 1876-81, he was president of the American Chemical Society. Besides writing numerous papers on electricity and fluorescence he assisted in the preparation of "The Student's Practical Chemistry." He died May 9, 1902, in Philadelphia.

MORTON, JAMES ST. CLAIR, soldier, was born in Philadelphia, September 24, 1829. He was graduated from West Point, in 1851, was appointed to the engineering corps and in 1855-1857 was assistant professor of engineering there. He was in charge of the Chiriqui expedition in Central America, in 1860, and later superintended the work on the Washington aqueduct. He built the entrenchments around Murfreesboro, Tenn., and was engaged in the battles of Chattanooga and Chickamauga. He was chief engineer of the 9th army corps in the Richmond Campaign of 1864, and was killed in the Battle of Petersburg (Va.), June 17, 1864. He published: "An Essay on Instruction in Engineering," "Memoir on Fortification," etc.

MORTON, JOHN, Signer of the Declaration of Independence, was born in Ridley, Delaware County, 1724. After working several years as a surveyor he began the practice of law. In 1764, he was elected to the General Assembly of Pennsylvania and was speaker from 1772-1775. In 1765, he was a member of the Stamp Act Congress; in 1766, he became sheriff of his county and shortly afterward was appointed one of the judges of the Supreme Court of Pennsylvania. In 1774, he was elected a delegate to the 1st Continental Congress and was a member of that body until his death. He gave the casting vote of Pennsylvania in favor of the Declaration of Independence, the four other delegates present being equally divided as to the measure, and affixed his signature to the Declaration. He died in April, 1777, in Delaware County.

MORTON, SAMUEL GEORGE, anatomist, was born in Philadelphia, January 26, 1799. He studied medicine at the University of Pennsylvania and in Edinburgh and began to practice in Philadelphia in 1824; was immediately prominent in the Academy of Natural Sciences being its secretary in 1825 and its president in 1850; became professor of anatomy in Pennsylvania College in 1839; and made special studies of ethnology, craniology, and plant physiology. His valuable collection of skulls numbering 1,500 specimens (900 human) led him to argue the diverse origin of the human race. He contributed to Silliman's "Journal" and published: "Crania Americana," "Crania Egypta," and "Illustrated System of Human Anatomy." He died in Philadelphia, May 15, 1851.

MOSHANNON CREEK—Tributary to West Branch Susquehanna River. Sub-basin: Upper West Branch Susquehanna; source, in Snyder Township, northern Blair County; course, northeasterly, forming Clearfield-Centre County boundary, to West Branch Susquehanna River; mouth, southwest of Pine Glen; length, forty-six miles. Indian name, a corruption of Moos-hanne, "elk stream."

HOME OF JOHN MORTON
Signer of the Declaration of Independence
House built, 1764

MOTT, LUCRETIA, abolitionist, was born in Massachusetts, in 1793. She married James Mott when she was eighteen, for a time afterwards taught school in Philadelphia, but later became a preacher in the Society of Friends, being a disciple of Elias Hicks. At an early period she became a strong exponent of the abolition of slavery and traveled about through New England and the Middle Atlantic states in its interest. She was one of the original members of the Anti-Slavery Society, founded in 1833, and was a representative to the world's Anti-Slavery Convention in Liverpool, in 1840. Mrs. Mott was also intensely interested in the advancement of woman's suffrage and was one of the leading spirits in calling the first Woman's Rights Convention which met at Seneca Falls and issued a declaration. She early became affiliated with the Peace Society in which organization she was active until her death on November 11, 1880. Her motto was: "Not authority for truth but truth for authority."

MOUNT CARMEL, a borough in Northumberland County, about forty-five miles northeast of Harrisburg. It is in a mountainous region in the midst of valuable coal fields and nearby are a large number of anthracite mines. The manufactures are: mining implements, miner's lamps, hats, caps, cement blocks, men's clothing, and cigars. Population (1930), 17,967; (1920), 17,469.

MUDDY CREEK—Tributary to Slippery Rock Creek. Sub-basin: Main Ohio; source, in Clay Township, northern central Butler County; course, westerly into Lawrence County to Slippery Rock Creek; mouth, one mile northeast of Rose Point; length, twenty-one and one-half miles.

MUHLENBERG, FREDERICK AUGUSTUS CONRAD, Lutheran clergyman and politician, son of H. M. Muhlenberg, was born at Trappe, January 1, 1750. He was educated in Halle, Germany, and returning in 1770 was ordained to the Lutheran ministry. From 1773-1776, he had charge of a Lutheran Church in New York and then removed to Pennsylvania where he served several charges. He was a hearty sympathizer with the cause of the colonies and though not participating in the war aided his countrymen politically and ultimately abandoned his pastoral work for a political life. He served in the Continental Congress, was speaker of the first House of Representatives under Washington and in 1795 his was the deciding vote which rescued the Jay Treaty from defeat. He died in Lancaster, June 4, 1801.

MUHLENBERG, GOTTHILF HENRY ERNST, Lutheran clergyman and botanist, was born at Trappe, November 17, 1753, a son of H. M. Muhlenberg. He was educated with his brother, F. A. C. Muhlenberg, in Halle, Germany. He returned to America, in 1770, was ordained to the ministry and became an assistant to his father who was in charge of a Lutheran Church in Philadelphia. In 1779, he accepted a call to Lancaster where he remained until his death. In addition to his pastoral duties he distinguished himself as a scientist and took first rank as a botanist. He published "Catalagous Plantarum Americae Septentrionalis" and "Descriptio Uberior Graminium." He died in Lancaster, May 23, 1815.

MUHLENBERG, HEINRICH MELCHIOR, German-American clergyman, organizer of the Evangelical Lutheran Church in America, was born in Eimbeck,

H. M. MUHLENBERG

Hanover, September 6, 1711. He was educated at the University of Gottingen (1735-37), studied theology there (1737-38) and at Halle (1738-39) and was ordained in 1739. On September 6, 1741, he was called as missionary to the Lutheran congregations of Pennsylvania located at Philadelphia, New Providence (now Trappe) and New Hanover. There were a large number of Lutherans in America, but they were unorganized and without pastors. Muhlenberg, who arrived at Philadelphia, November 25, 1742, was well qualified for the work of effecting union and order. Though his local pastorship was largely restricted to the three congregations which had summoned him his activities were really those of a bishop. He traveled over a wide extent of territory, preached at Lancaster, York, and other places in Pennsylvania, in New York, and also occasionally in New Jersey, Maryland, among the Salzburger Lutherans of Georgia. On August 14, 1748, the first Lutheran Synod in America was organized under the direction of Muhlenberg who became its first president. In 1754, he prepared the "Kirchen Agende," a directory for public worship, and in 1762 reorganized the Philadelphia congregation under a constitution which became the basis of most congregations later established. He identified himself with the American cause in the Revolution, and was subjected to many annoyances when Pennsylvania was the scene of the war (1777-78). He was versed in Hebrew, Greek, and Latin, and proficient in English, Dutch, French, Bohemian and Swedish. He died at Trappe, October 7, 1787.

MUHLENBERG, JOHN PETER GABRIEL, patriot, was born at Trappe, October 1, 1746, a son of H. M. Muhlenberg. He was educated for the ministry and was pastor of German Lutheran churches in New Germantown and Bedminster, N. J. In 1772, he went to Woodstock, Va., and was ordained to the Episcopal Church to enforce the payment of tithes. He was a colonel in the Continental Army. In his last sermon he said, "There is a time for all things— a time to preach and a time to fight—and now is the time to fight," and stripped off his gown after service, appeared in full uniform, called for recruits and enrolled about 300 of his parishioners. He was made brigadier-general, in 1777, and major-general at the close of the Revolution. After the war he returned to Pennsylvania where he served as a representative in Congress from 1789 to 1795 and from 1799 to 1801. In 1801, he was elected to the Senate but soon resigned and was appointed supervisor of the revenue for the district of Pennsylvania. He died near Philadelphia, October 1, 1807.

MUHLENBERG, WILLIAM AUGUSTUS, clergyman, was born in Philadelphia, September 16, 1796. He was graduated from the University of Pennsylvania and ordained deacon and priest of the Episcopal Church. In 1821, he became rector of St. James, Lancaster, and established there the first public school in the state outside of Philadelphia. In 1828, he went to New York where he founded a Christian High School (later Saint Paul's College). He collected funds for a hospital, out of which St. Luke's Hospital was built. His last very useful

JOHN PETER GABRIEL MUHLENBERG

work was in founding St. Johnland Christian Industrial Community, on the north shore of Long Island. He wrote several well-known hymns: "I Would Not Live Alway," "Like Noah's Weary Dove," and "Shout the Glad Tidings." He died in New York, April 8, 1877.

MUHLENBERG COLLEGE, a college for men in Allentown, founded in 1867 under the auspices of the Lutheran Church. The courses of study lead to the degrees of A. B., B. S., and Ph. B. Enrollment (1930-1931), 440.

MULFORD, ELISHA, Episcopal clergyman and philosophical writer, was born at Montrose, November 10, 1833. He was graduated from Yale, in 1855, and subsequently studied theology, law, and philosophy. He entered the Episcopal ministry and held several rectorates, but from 1881 till his death he taught at the Episcopal Theological School at Cambridge, Mass. He wrote: "The Nation," a treatise on the philosophy of the state, and "The Republic of God," relating to the philosophy of religion. He died at Cambridge, Mass., December 9, 1885.

MUNCY CREEK—Tributary to West Branch Susquehanna River. Sub-basin: Lower West Branch Susquehanna; source, in Davidson Township, southeastern Sullivan County; course, southwesterly into Lycoming County to West Branch Susquehanna River; mouth, near Muncy; length, thirty-three miles. Indian name, a corruption of Munsee (from Min-asin-ink, "where stones are gathered together").

MUNCY (LITTLE) CREEK—Tributary to Muncy Creek. Sub-basin: Lower West Branch Susquehanna; source, in Jordan Township, southeastern Lycoming County; course, southwesterly and northwesterly to Muncy Creek; mouth, one mile northwest of Clarkstown; length, twenty-two miles. Indian name, a corruption of Munsee (from Min-asin-ink, "where stones are gathered together").

MUNCY HILLS, BATTLE OF. In August, 1763, Colonel John Armstrong with 200 soldiers from Paxtang, Hanover and Cumberland County marched upon the Indian town at Great Island, now Lock Haven, to learn that the Conestoga Indians had warned their fellows of the expedition. Fighting ensued and several persons were killed in the Muncy Hills.

MURDOCH, JAMES EDWARD, actor, was born in Philadelphia, June 25, 1811. He made his debut as an actor in Philadelphia, in 1829, playing Frederick in "The Lover's Vow," and in 1833 acted with Fanny Kemble during her American tour. He appeared in New York, in 1845, as Hamlet and for fifteen years played with considerable success in the United States and England. During the Civil War he devoted himself to caring for the wounded soldiers and in giving entertainments for their benefit. His best roles were: Hamlet, Mercutio, Benedick and Claude Melnotte. He died in Cincinnati, Ohio, May 19, 1893.

MURRAY, LINDLEY, grammarian, son of M. L. Murray, was born at Swatara, Dauphin County, April 22, 1745. He studied law (1761-1765) and practiced as a barrister, but after the Revolution left his profession, entered commercial speculation, and having realized a fortune went, in 1784, to England and settled at Holgate near York. His "English Grammar" (1795) met with great success, being almost universally introduced as a textbook in England and United States, and for years was regarded as standard authority. It passed through fifty editions in its original form and the abridgment went through 150 editions. Murray was also a botanist. He died near York, England, February 12, 1826.

MURRAY, MARY LINDLEY, heroine, was born in Pennsylvania. She is known through an incident of the Revolution. On September 17, 1776, the British line of march passed by her residence "The Grange," a small country-seat at Murray Hill, New York. Putnam, having evacuated New York, was at the same time marching along the Bloomingdale Road near the North River intending to join Washington at Harlem Heights. Howe thought by marching across the island to cut off the American retreat. He was however invited with his officers to luncheon by Mrs. Murray, accepted and remained more than two hours during which time Putnam escaped. Mrs. Murray died December 25, 1782.

MUSICAL FESTIVALS, series of performances by large choruses and orchestras, usually held in large cities yearly or bi-yearly. In Pennsylvania the best-known entertainments of this kind are the Bache festival at Bethlehem and the Mozart festival at Harrisburg.

MUSSER, A. MILTON, Mormon historian, was a native of Marietta, Lancaster County. In 1847, he went to Salt Lake City with Brigham Young and became a prominent member of the Mormon Church. Musser had three wives and twelve sons and daughters. He died September 24, 1909.

NAAMAN, chief of the Delawares, one of the two leaders in Indian-Colonial affairs before the arrival of William Penn. Naaman attended a council of the Delawares at Printz Hall, Tinicum, on June 17, 1654, held in the interests of renewing the friendship between the Delawares and Swedes. Naaman's Creek, near the Delaware State line, is named for him.

NAGLEE, HENRY MORRIS, soldier, was born in Philadelphia, January 15, 1815. Entering the Union Army early in the Civil War he participated in the peninsular campaign of 1862, and in the following year was appointed to the command of the 7th Army Corps and of the District of Virginia. He retired from the army in 1864 and later went to California, where he cultivated a vineyard at San Jose, and gave his name to a well-known brandy. He died in San Francisco, March 5, 1886.

NANCREDE, CHARLES BEYLARD GUERARD DE, surgeon, was born in Philadelphia, December 30, 1847. He was educated at the University of Pennsylvania and Jefferson Medical College; he began practice in Philadelphia and after 1889 was professor of surgery and clinical surgery and surgeon of the university hospital at the University of Michigan, retiring in 1913. In the Spanish-American War he served as surgeon at the front and in 1908-09 was president of the American Surgical Association. He wrote: "Principles of Surgery," "Dennis System of Surgery," "American Practice of Surgery," etc. He died at Ann Arbor, Mich., April 13, 1921.

NANTICOKE, borough in Luzerne County, on the Susquehanna River, about eighty miles northeast of Harrisburg. The town was laid out in 1793. It is situated in an anthracite coal region and has extensive water power which is utilized in manufacturing. The industry contributing most to the wealth of the town is coal mining. This is the greatest coal deposit and the richest mining district in the world. The chief manufacturing establishments are: mining and agricultural implement works, hosiery mills, flour and grist mills, silk mills and cigar factories. Population (1930), 26,043; (1920), 22,614.

NATIONAL BOARD OF TRADE, THE, was organized at the annual conventions of the Boards of Trade, held at Philadelphia, June 31, 1869.

NATURALIZATION OF FOREIGNERS IN PENNSYLVANIA. Shortly after his arrival in Pennsylvania, Penn had a law passed at Chester to naturalize the Swedes and the Dutch, whom he found in the province. In 1700, an act was passed giving the Proprietary the power to naturalize all foreigners who came to the province. This was one of the thirty-six Acts of Assembly passed in 1700, which was disallowed and repealed by the Privy Council, in 1705, because, according to his charter the Proprietary had no such power. Acts were passed in 1708, 1729, 1730, 1734 and 1737 naturalizing by name prominent residents of the province. In 1742, a general act was passed providing for the naturalization of those foreigners who had lived in the province for seven years, who were Protestants, who were willing to take the Tests and subscribe the Declaration. This law, excluding all foreign born Catholics, Jews or Socinians, was effective until the Revolution.

NAZARETH, borough in Northampton County, about five miles northwest of Easton. It is near large anthracite coal fields and has considerable manufacturing. The chief industrial establishments are: cigar factories, cement works, paper and hosiery mills, machine shops and large brick and coal yards. It is the seat of the Nazareth Hall Military Academy, Gray Cottage and the historic Whitefield House. There is an Indian monument about 190 years old and the borough exhibits what is believed to be the oldest piece of fire apparatus in the United States—a fire engine imported from England in 1791. Population (1930), 5,505; (1920), 4,288.

NEGLEY, JAMES SCOTT, soldier, was born at Liberty, Tioga County, December 22, 1826. He was educated at the Western University of Pennsylvania and served in the ranks through the Mexican War. At the outbreak of the Civil War he organized a brigade, was commissioned brigadier-general and joined the Army of the Ohio. He defeated the Confederates at Lavergne, in 1862, and was promoted to the rank of major-general for gallant conduct at Stone River. He was a member of Congress in 1869–73, 1875–77, and 1885–87. He died August 8, 1901, in Plainfield, N. J.

NEILL, EDWARD DUFFIELD, historian and educator, was born in Philadelphia, August 9, 1823. He was graduated from Amherst, in 1842, and later studied at Andover Theological Seminary. In 1848, he entered the Presbyterian ministry and served as pastor of the First Protestant Church established in St. Paul, Minn. As army and hospital chaplain he served in the Civil War from 1861 to 1864, then till 1869 was assistant private secretary first to President Lincoln and then to President Johnson. In 1869, he was for a short time consul at Dublin. He was president of Macalester College, St. Paul, 1873–84, and professor of history and literature there until his death which occurred September 26, 1893. Among his books are: "History of Minnesota"; "Terra Mariae," a history of early Maryland; "Minnesota Explorers and Pioneers"; "Virginia Vetusta," etc.

NESCOPECK CREEK—Tributary to North Branch Susquehanna River. Sub-basin: Lower Branch Susquehanna; source, in Dennison Township, southeastern Luzerne County, one mile northwest of White Haven; course, southwesterly, by a circuitous route, to North Branch Susquehanna River; mouth, at Nescopeck; length, thirty-five miles. Indian name, probably a corruption of Neskchoppeek, "black," or "deep and still water."

NESHAMINY CREEK—Tributary to Delaware River. Sub-basin: Middle Delaware; source, formed by junction of north and west branches at Chalfont, New Britain Township, Bucks County; course, southeasterly to Delaware River, forming southwestern boundary of Buckingham, Wrightstown, Newtown, Middletown and Bristol Townships, and northeastern boundary of Warwick, Northampton, Southampton and Bensalem Townships; mouth, one and one-half miles southeast of Eddington, twelve miles above Philadelphia; length, thirty-eight miles. Indian name, a corruption of Nischam-hanne, "two streams or double stream."

NESHANNOCK CREEK—Tributary to Shenango River. Sub-basin: Main Ohio; source, formed by junction of Otter Creek and Cool Spring Creek, at Mercer, southern Mercer County; course, southwesterly into Lawrence County to Shenango River; mouth, at New Castle; length, twenty-four and one-half miles. Indian name, a corruption of Nischam-hanne, "two streams" or "double stream."

NEUCHECONNEH, Shawnee chief, was one of the leaders in Indian affairs. He corresponded with Thomas Penn, Secretary James Logan, and other Colonial authorities, regarding Indian troubles, and his opposition to the sale of rum by traders among the Indians. With Peter Chartier he founded Chartier's Town, on the Allegheny, near Tarentum; with Chartier deserted to the French, but afterwards returned to Logstown and in 1748 asked the colony to forgive him for his desertion.

NEUMANN, JOHN NEPOMUCENE, Roman Catholic bishop, was born in Prachatitz, Bohemia, March 28, 1811. He was educated at Budweis and Prague; took orders; came to America as a missionary in 1836. He was busy in mission work in Pennsylvania, Maryland, and Virginia; was appointed superior of the Redemptorist Convent in Pittsburgh where he built the church of St. Philomena. In 1852, he became bishop of Philadelphia. He went to Rome, in 1854, and assisted in the definition of the dogma of the Immaculate Conception. Bishop Neumann was a man of culture and administrative ability, and did much for Catholic education in America. He died in Philadelphia, June 5, 1860.

NEVILLE, JOHN, military officer, was born in Virginia, in 1731. He was with Washington in Braddock's expedition, took part in Lord Dunmore's War and was sent by Virginia to take possession of Fort Pitt in 1775. Throughout the Revolution he served as Colonel of the Fourth Virginia Line. He was a member of the Pennsylvania Supreme Executive Council from 1783-1786, and was a delegate to the Pennsylvania Convention which ratified the Federal Constitution, in 1787, and signed the ratification. At the time of the Whiskey Insurrection he was appointed Inspector of Revenue by President Washington and Secretary Hamilton. He died in 1803.

NEVILLE, PRESLEY, military officer, was born in Virginia, about 1756. After graduating from the University of Philadelphia, he entered the army as an ensign in the company commanded by his father, Gen. John Neville. Later he advanced to a captaincy and served as aide-de-camp to Marquis de La Fayette. Three years later he joined the Southern Army, was brevetted lieutenant-colonel, and taken prisoner at the surrender of Charleston. He served in the battles of Princeton, Trenton, Germantown, Brandywine and Monmouth. In 1792, he moved to Pittsburgh where he resided until 1816 when he moved to Ohio.

NEVIN, ETHELBERT WOODBRIDGE, composer, was born at Edgeworth, November 25, 1862. He obtained his musical education in Pittsburgh and in Berlin, and after three years spent in the latter city returned to the United States and opened a studio in Boston. His reputation rests upon his compositions which date from his twelfth year. "Narcissus" was written when he was thirteen, and "O That We Two Were Maying," a year later. His other compositions are: "A Day in Venice," "Cradle Song," "Milkmaid's Song," etc. He died at New Haven, Conn., February 17, 1901.

NEVIN, JOHN WILLIAMSON, Reformed (German) clergyman, was born at Shippensburg, February 20, 1803. He was graduated from Union College, Schenectady, N. Y., in 1821, and from Princeton Theological Seminary, in 1826. He was professor of Hebrew at the Presbyterian Theological Seminary at Allegheny City, 1829-1839, president of Mercersburg Theological Seminary, in 1840, and president of Marshall College, 1841-1853. His translation of Schaff's "The Principle of Protestantism" created the once famous controversy over "Mercersburg Theology," of which he was for the rest of his life the principal advocate. He edited the "Mercersburg Review," 1849-1853. In 1853, Marshall College was merged with Franklin College, at Lancaster. He served as president from 1866 to 1876. He published "The Mystical Presence." He died in Lancaster, June 7, 1886.

NEW BLOOMFIELD, borough and county-seat of Perry County, was settled as early as 1753, by David Mitchell, who later sold the warrant rights to Thomas Barnett. Barnett named the land he owned Bloom Field. In 1823, his son, George, sold a tract of land to the county commissioners as a nucleus for the county-seat. The village was incorporated as a borough in 1831. It is located in an agricultural region and is the seat of the Carson Long Institute, a preparatory school for boys.

NEW BRIGHTON, a borough in Beaver County, on the east bank of Beaver River, twenty-eight miles northwest of Pittsburgh. It was settled in 1799 by the laborers employed to build Wolf's Mill—a flouring mill laid out in 1818 and incorporated as a borough in 1838. It is in a section of the state in which manufacturing and industries connected with coal are prominent. The water power furnished by Beaver Creek is utilized in a number of manufactories, among which are: potteries, flour mills, wall paper, glass and nail factories, brick and brass-casting works. It has a public art gallery, a fine government building and library and a park. Population (1930), 9,950; (1920), 9,361.

NEW CASTLE, city and county-seat of Lawrence County, situated about fifty miles north of Pittsburgh, at the confluence of the Shenango, Neshannock, and Mahoning Rivers, which there form the Beaver River; it is situated in one of the richest and most charming valleys in the world. Aside from being the commercial center for a productive, agricultural region, the city is in the heart of rich deposits of iron ore, limestone, coal, and clay and is noted for its great variety of industries. New Castle was first settled in 1800 by Robert White; became a borough in 1869, and was chartered as a city in 1875. Population (1930), 48,674; (1920), 44,938.

NEW COMER, or Nettawatwees, was a chief of the Turtle Clan of Delawares. He attended numerous conferences with representatives of the colony and late in his life was influenced by Moravian missionaries, especially by Bishop Zeisberger, with whom he was extremely friendly. New Comer's death occurred while he was attending a conference between William Wilson, agent of George Morgan, in charge of Indian affairs at Fort Pitt, and chiefs of the Delawares, Shawnees and Wyandots of Ohio, at Fort Pitt, in the summer of 1776.

NEW JERUSALEM CHURCH—The New Jerusalem or Swedenborgian Church, was organized in Philadelphia, December 25, 1815, as the American Society for Disseminating the Doctrine of the New Jerusalem Church. As early as 1784 the doctrines of Swedenborg were advanced by means of lectures delivered in Philadelphia by James Glen, of Scotland. The Second Philadelphia Society of the New Church was formed in 1822.

NEW KENSINGTON, a triborough composed of New Kensington, Parnassus and Arnold, in Westmoreland County, on the Allegheny River, eighteen miles northeast of Pittsburgh. It is described as the "Queen City of Westmoreland County," "The Metropolis of the Allegheny Valley," and industrially is known as the home of aluminum, having the largest aluminum mill in the United States. Population (1930), 16,762; (1920), 11,987.

NEW WALES, the name originally chosen by William Penn, for the province, later named Pennsylvania. The name New Wales was considered for a time because the country was hilly like Wales. Because of the refusal of his secretary, a Welshman, to confirm the name, Penn suggested Sylvania, to which the prefix Penn was later added.

NEWJAHRSWUNSCHE, an old Pennsylvania-German custom of welcoming or "shooting-in" the New Year. A company of people would visit the homes of friends on New Year's eve and repeat verses of scripture, or special newjahrswunsche, and sing hymns beneath their windows. The newjahrswunsche were verses, some particularly adapted to a young unmarried girl, others for the heads of the family and others for the entire family. Sometimes the new year wishes were conveyed by shooting; the participants would meet in a blacksmith's shop, load the anvil with powder and fire the charge. Those to whom the new year's wishes were extended would return the favor by serving refreshments.

NEWTON, HENRY JOTHAM, manufacturer and chemist, inventor of the dry-plate photographic process, was born at Hartleton, Union County, February 23, 1823. At twenty, he was a partner in the firm of Wittlesey Brothers, piano-makers, Salem, Conn., and was later connected with the Bradbury's in the piano trade. His invention of a permanent collodion emulsion and of the other details of the dry-plate process in photography dates from 1875. Educated a Presbyterian, Newton joined the Methodist Church, then the Unitarian and finally allied himself with the Spiritualists. A society formed by him in 1875 for psychical research and of which he was president, was, he claimed, the first Theosophical Society from which Mme. Blavatsky and Henry S. Olcott took the ideas which they falsely proclaimed to be of Indian origin. He died from a street railroad accident, New York, December 23, 1895.

NEWTON, RICHARD HEBER, Episcopal clergyman, was born in Philadelphia, October 31, 1840. He studied at the Philadelphia Divinity School and was assistant to his father at St. Paul's, Philadelphia. He succeeded his father there and resigned in 1869 to go to All Soul's Church, New York. In 1903, he was appointed preacher to Leland Stanford, Jr., University, but soon resigned his position. He was a broad churchman and was several times threatened with trial for heresy. He took a prominent part in the Congress of Religions held at Chicago, in 1893, and was vice-president of the organization of this congress. He wrote: "The Morals of Trade," "Church and Creed," "Parsifal." He died December 19, 1914.

NIXON, JOHN, soldier, was born in Philadelphia, in 1733. He was early prominent in opposing the taxation demands of England and in 1774 became a member of the first committee of correspondence in Pennsylvania. In 1775, he became lieutenant-colonel of a battalion which he led at the Battle of Princeton, in 1777. In 1776, he was placed in command of the guard of the city of Philadelphia; he was the first to publicly proclaim the Declaration of Independence in the city on July 8th. He was one of the organizers of the Bank of North America and its president from 1792–1808. He died in Philadelphia, December 31, 1808.

NOAH, MORDECAI MANUEL, politician and journalist, was born in Philadelphia, July 19, 1785. In 1813, he was appointed United States consul at Tunis, with a special mission to Algiers. He settled in New York, in 1819, and in 1822 was elected high sheriff of the county and city of New York. He assisted in many newspapers. A project in which he engaged in 1820 was to re-establish the Jewish nation and form a place for Jewish emigrants on Grand Island in the Niagara River near Buffalo. In 1825, he laid the cornerstone of the proposed city of White Haven, but the new "Ararat" as it was termed came to naught. He died in New York, May 31, 1851.

NON-IMPORTATION RESOLUTIONS, THE, of October 25, 1765, drafted in Philadelphia, had a great influence upon the movement leading to American independence. The original manuscript was presented to the Historical Society of Pennsylvania by William Bradford, in 1854.

NORRIS, ISAAC, was born in Philadelphia, in 1701, the son of Isaac Norris who came to Philadelphia from Jamaica, in 1690. The younger Norris became a merchant, a leader of the Quaker Church, and in all matters of trade and finance. In 1742, he became a member of the provincial legislature and in 1751 was elected speaker of the assembly a position which his father at one time held. He represented the province of Pennsylvania at a conference with the Indians at Albany, in 1745. Norris married Sarah Logan, daughter of James Logan, in 1739. Their daughter, Mary, subsequently became the wife of John Dickinson. Norris died in 1766.

NORRISTOWN, borough, county-seat of Montgomery County, on the Schuylkill River, about fifteen miles northwest of Philadelphia. It was settled about 1688 by a colony from Wales, laid out in 1785, and incorporated as a borough in 1812. It was named in honor of Isaac Norris who owned a large tract of land in what is now Montgomery County. It is an agricultural and mining section and has extensive manufacturing interests. Granite, limestone and marble are mined nearby. It has a State Insane Hospital, St. Joseph's Protectory for Girls, Friends' Home, and the Ganes Stinson Home for Aged Ladies. The tomb of Winfield Scott Hancock is on Montgomery Cemetery, also a memorial shaft to John F. Hartranft. Population (1930), 35,853; (1920), 32,319.

NORRISTOWN TIMES-HERALD, THE, was established as the *Gazette*, in 1799. It is Republican in politics, and appears each evening except Sunday. Walter A. Wilson is the editor, and the Norristown Herald Printing and Publishing Company are the publishers. Circulation, 14,977.

NORTH BRADDOCK, a borough in Allegheny County, about six miles east of Pittsburgh. It was a part of Braddock until 1897 when it was incorporated as a separate township. It has extensive steel rail interests, but a portion of the borough is residential. Population (1930), 16,782; (1920), 14,928.

NORTH EAST, a borough in Erie County, fourteen miles northeast of Erie. St. Mary's (R. C.) College is situated here. Fruit-growing is the chief industry; but there are manufactures of grape juice, canned goods, wooden novelties, flour, foundry products and copper.

NORTHAMPTON COUNTY, formed from part of Bucks, March 11, 1752. Named for Northamptonshire, England. Land area, 372 square miles; population (1930), 169,304. County-seat, Easton, laid out in 1738.

NORTHUMBERLAND, a town in Northumberland County, fifty-four miles north of Harrisburg. The town is beautifully situated in picturesque mountain scenery and is a popular summer resort. In the vicinity are mineral springs and large deposits of iron ore and limestone. The town manufactures: nails, hats, caps, coffins, and silk and has iron and forge works and extensive freight yards with machine shops and other buildings constructed by the Pennsylvania Railroad Company.

NORTHUMBERLAND COUNTY, formed from part of Lancaster, Cumberland, Berks, Bedford and Northampton, March 21, 1772. Named for the county of Northumberland in England. Land area, 454 square miles; population (1930), 128,504. County-seat, Sunbury, laid out in 1772.

NUTIMUS, chief of the Munsee Clan of Delawares, lived near the forks of the Delaware River. He was actively identified with the "Walking Purchase" of 1737, having refused, with other Delaware chiefs, who had signed the treaty of 1737, to remove from the lands covered by the "Purchase." Eventually Canassatego, of the Iroquois tribe, ordered the removal of the Delawares, and Nutimus and his people settled on the site of the present city of Wilkes-Barre, and at Niskebeckon, on the North Branch of the Susquehanna. Near the mouth of the Nescopeck Creek, they established Nutimy's Town. Nutimus, as chief of his tribe, was a signer of the Purchase of 1749 by which the deputies of the Six Nations sold to Pennsylvania the land between the Susquehanna and the Delaware which includes all or part of the present counties of Northumberland, Dauphin, Lebanon, Schuylkill, Columbia, Carbon, Luzerne, Monroe, Pike and Wayne. Nutimus attended the conference at Easton on July, 1757. After that there is no record of him.

OAKLEY, VIOLET, mural painter, was born in New York, in 1874. She first devoted her talent to illustration but soon turned to mural painting and the designing of stained glass windows. Her first important commission was for thirteen panels depicting the "Founding of the State of Spiritual Liberty" for the governor's reception room of the State Capitol at Harrisburg and nine panels "Creation and Preservation of the Union" for the Senate Chamber. Miss Oakley has received medals from the St. Louis Exposition (1904), the Pennsylvania Academy of Fine Arts (1905), and also the San Francisco Exposition (1915). She resides in Philadelphia and is a member of many art societies.

OAKMONT, a borough in Allegheny County, ten miles northeast of Pittsburgh, situated on the Allegheny River. The industries are glass, iron, and powder works, tools, pipes and fittings, hot-water boilers and structural steel manufactories. Population (1930), 6,027; (1920), 4,512.

OBERHOLTZER, ELLIS PAXSON, historian, son of Mrs. S. L. Oberholtzer, was born in Philadelphia, in 1868. He was educated at the University of Pennsylvania, at Berlin, Heidelberg, and Paris. He also did some journalistic work from 1889 to 1908. He has published: "The Referendum in America," "Die Bezuluing Zursdun dem Staat und der Zeitungspresse," "Henry Clay," "Abraham Lincoln," etc.

OBERHOLTZER, SARA LOUISA (Vickers), poet, author, and philanthropist, was born in Uwchlan, Chester County, May 20, 1841. She was educated at Friends' Boarding School, Millersville Normal School and by private tutors. From 1890, Mrs. Oberholtzer spent most of her time in the introduction of the schools savings banks into the public schools of the United States and Canada, and is regarded as its leader. She published: "Violet Lee," "Come for Arbutus," "Daises of Verse," "Dialogues," "Letters of Travel," etc. Her songs and hymns set to music by different composers are in hymnals and many of them in sheet form.

OCOWELLOS, a Shawnee chief, who early came under French influence. In the minutes of a Council held at Philadelphia, May 20, 1723, when an address from the chief to the Provincial Council was read, Ocowellos is referred to as "King of the Upper Shawnees." Probably he lived along the West Branch of the Susquehanna, in Northumberland, and later moved to the Conemaugh Valley.

OCTORARO CREEK, EAST BRANCH—Tributary to Octoraro Creek. Sub-basin: Lower Main Susquehanna; source, in Highland Township, western Chester County, 1.5 miles south of Parkesburg; course, southwesterly to join West Branch and form Octoraro Creek, being Lancaster-Chester County boundary for last sixteen miles; mouth, four miles northwest of Oxford; length, twenty and one-half miles.

OGDEN, ROBERT CURTIS, merchant and philanthropist, was born in Philadelphia, June 20, 1836. From 1885, he was a retail merchant, a member of the John Wanamaker firm. He is best known by his work in behalf of the cause of education in the south. His efforts were directed chiefly toward providing education for both negroes and illiterate whites in the south through friendly cooperation between northerners and southerners. He received the degree of LL. D. from Tulane University. He published: "Pew Rents and the New Testament," and "Sunday-School Teaching." He died August 6, 1913.

O'HARA, JAMES, pioneer manufacturer, was born in Ireland, about 1753. Prior to emigrating to America, in 1772, he served as ensign in the Coldstream Guards of the British Army. After he arrived at Philadelphia he set out for western Pennsylvania and engaged in the Indian trade at Fort Pitt. Upon the opening of the Revolutionary War he raised and equipped, at his own expense, a company of volunteers for Virginia, and himself became captain of the Ninth Virginia Regiment, and later assistant quartermaster. After the war ended he served as purchasing agent for supplies for the armies engaged in the Indian campaigns in the Northwest Territory. In 1788, O'Hara was a presidential elector and at the first presidential election, voted for George Washington. He became the first Quartermaster-General of the United States, in 1792, and held this office during the Whiskey Insurrection and the Indian campaigns in the Northwest Territory. He was with General Anthony Wayne at the Battle of Fallen Timbers and the Treaty of Greenville. O'Hara was the pioneer in industry in Pittsburgh. In partnership with Major Isaac Craig he erected the first glass works there in 1797. He early engaged in foreign trade, sending glass, furs, and flour on ships which he built, to Liverpool, England, South America and the West Indies. By establishing a line of communication from Lake Erie, then by portage to the head of French Creek, and down the creek and the Allegheny to Pittsburgh, O'Hara greatly reduced the price of salt in Pittsburgh. He died at his Pittsburgh residence, December 21, 1819.

OHIO RIVER—Tributary to Mississippi River. Basin: Ohio; source, formed by junction of Allegheny and Monongahela Rivers at Pittsburgh, Allegheny County; course, northwesterly into Beaver County to junction of Beaver River at Rochester; mouth, at Cairo, Ill.; length, total, 967 miles; in Pennsylvania, 39.4 miles. Indian name, Kit-hanne, "great river," or "main stream," or Ohiopeek, "white with froth," Ohiopeekhanne, "a stream whitened by froth."

OIL CITY, city in Venango County, at the junction of Oil Creek and the Allegheny River, about 130 miles northeast of Pittsburgh. It was settled in 1825, but was only a small place until the oil wells of the vicinity were developed in 1860. It was incorporated as a borough in 1863 and chartered as a city in 1874. A terrible catastrophe occurred in 1892, when burning oil came down Oil Creek from Titusville, a distance of eighteen miles, and swept over the city. More than 100 persons were killed, $1,000,000 worth of property was destroyed. Population (1930), 22,075; (1920), 21,274.

OIL CREEK—Tributary to Allegheny River. Sub-basin: Upper Allegheny; source, Canadotha Lake, in Bloomfield Township, northeastern Crawford County; course, southeasterly to Titusville; mouth, at Oil City; length, thirty-five miles.

OLD FORGE, a borough in Lackawanna County, on the Lackawanna River, five miles southwest of Scranton. It was settled in 1830 and remained a part of the Old Forge Township until 1899 when it was incorporated as a borough. The chief industries besides mining and the shipping of coal are glass-blowing, manufacturing silk goods, and making chemicals and fertilizers. Population (1930), 22,661; (1920), 12,237.

OLMSTEAD CASE. In 1778, a number of prisoners were captured by the British ship, "Active," and were ordered to be taken to Jamaica. But Gideon Olmstead took command, confined the crew to the cabin, and sailed for the United States. They were captured by a Pennsylvania brig, brought into Philadelphia, and claimed as a prize. This was opposed by Olmstead who claimed that he had completed the capture, and the case was tried before Judge Ross in the Pennsylvania Court, where it was decided that Olmstead should have one-fourth and his captors three-fourths. Olmstead appealed, and the money, fifty thousand pounds continental money, was held by the treasurer of Pennsylvania, David Rittenhouse. A committee of the Continental Congress to whom the appeal was made reversed the decision, and awarded the entire prize to Olmstead. Pennsylvania denied the right of Congress to interfere and would not pay the award. When the United States Constitution was adopted Olmstead sued the executors of Judge Ross, who sued Rittenhouse, but the supreme court of the Commonwealth, Chief Justice McKean presiding, decided against Olmstead. In 1795, the supreme court of the United States declared the decisions of the Continental Congress valid, and Olmstead in 1803 received from a United States Court a decree entitling him to the prize money. McKean was governor and induced the General Assembly to pass a bill ordering the Rittenhouse heirs to pay the money to the State Treasurer. In 1808, Olmstead took his case to the supreme court of the United States and Chief Justice Marshall, speaking for the court, directed that the money be paid. The Pennsylvania Militia surrounded the home of the Rittenhouse daughters and prevented the United States Marshal from serving a warrant. The legislature finally appropriated eighteen thousand dollars to Governor Snyder to use as he saw fit, and in 1809, thirty-one years after the incident, Olmstead received the money for his prize.

OLYPHANT, a borough in Lackawanna County, on the Lackawanna River, about six miles above Scranton. It was settled in 1857 and incorporated in 1877. It is in the anthracite region and its chief industries are connected with mining and shipping coal. Population (1930), 10,743; (1920), 10,236.

OMISH—See AMISH.

ONAS, meaning quill or pen, was the name given to William Penn by the Indians. All his successors were called by the same name. By the Delawares he was called "Miquon."

OPESSAH, or Wopaththa, was chief of a band of Shawnees, who came from Cecil County, Maryland, and settled in Pequea, Lancaster County, about 1697 or 1698. Opessah as "King" of the Shawnees, with two other chiefs of the tribe, was present at Penn's Treaty with the Indians at Philadelphia, April 23, 1701, and at subsequent meetings with Colonial authorities in the interest of Indian affairs. In 1711, he left his chieftainship and lived with the Delawares under

Chief Sassoonan. About the year 1722, he went to Maryland where he settled along the Potomac at what was called for a long time Opessah's Town.

O'REILLY, ROBERT MAITLAND, army surgeon, was born in Philadelphia, January 14, 1845. He was appointed a medical cadet in the United States Army, January 7, 1864, and served through the remainder of the Civil War, taking his M. D. degree at the University of Pennsylvania in 1866. He was appointed assistant surgeon in the army in 1867, remained in the service and was regularly promoted reaching the rank of surgeon-general in 1902. He served in the Spanish War in the volunteer service as lieutenant-colonel and chief surgeon, and in 1909 was retired with the rank of major-general. He served for a time as personal medical advisor to President Cleveland. He died in 1912.

ORETYAGH, chief of the Conestogas, was one of the grantors of lands on the Susquehanna to William Penn. On July 6, 1694, he attended a council at Philadelphia at which Tamanend, of the Delawares, addressed Lieutenant-Governor Markham. At the time of Penn's final departure for England, in 1701, Oretyagh with several sachems of the Conestogas and Shawnees, came to Philadelphia to bid him farewell.

ORGAN BUILDING. David Tannenberg, one of the oldest organ builders in Pennsylvania, was born in Berthelsdorf, Saxony, came to Pennsylvania, in 1749, and was associated with John Klemm in building organs. Tannenberg continued the business at Lititz, Lancaster County, for about forty years after the death of Klemm. He built an organ for Zion Lutheran Church, Philadelphia, the largest in the United States. John Philip Bachman, his son-in-law, continued the business after Tannenberg's death in 1804. Among the earliest organ builders in Philadelphia was John Lowe, who entered the business in 1804. In 1809, John Shermer, of Philadelphia, built an organ with four stops for the Moravians.

ORMOND, ALEXANDER THOMAS, philosophical writer, was born in Punxsutawney, April 26, 1847. He was graduated from Princeton, in 1877; was professor of philosophy and history in the University of Minnesota, of mental science and logic at Princeton, and McCosh professor of philosophy at the latter institution. He was president of Grove City College from 1913 until his death in 1915.

ORTH, GODLOVE STONER, legislator, was born near Lebanon, April 22, 1817. He was graduated from Pennsylvania College at Gettysburg, admitted to the bar in 1839, and began his law practice in Lafayette, Ind., where he at once interested himself in politics. He served in the 39th, 40th, 41st, 46th and 47th Congresses. In 1875, he was appointed Minister to Vienna. He died at Lafayette, Ind., December 16, 1882.

OSWAYO CREEK—Tributary to Allegheny River. Sub-basin: Upper Allegheny; source, in Genesee Township, northern Potter County; course, southwesterly to Coneville; mouth, at Mill Grove, N. Y.; length, in Pennsylvania, twenty-three and one-half miles. Indian name, O-so-a-yeh, "pine forest."

OTIS, BASS, who introduced the art of lithography into the United States, for more than half a century was a portrait painter in Philadelphia, New York and Boston. He came to Philadelphia in 1811 or 1812, and displayed portraits of James Madison, Joseph Hopkinson, Thomas Jefferson, Gen. Arthur St. Clair, the Washington family, etc., in the Philadelphia Academy of Fine Arts.

OTTERBEIN, PHILIP WILLIAM, United Brethren clergyman, was born in Dillenburg, Germany, June 4, 1726. He was ordained in the Reformed ministry at Herborn, in 1749, and in 1752 was sent as a missionary to America, where he first settled at Lancaster, Pa.; thereafter having charge of the congregations at Tulpehocken and York, and of Frederick, Md. At Lancaster he experienced what he termed a change of heart and as a result introduced class meetings, open air meetings and prayer meetings and frequently made lengthy tours, founding what later became a new sect, the United Brethren in Christ. In 1800, he was elected bishop. He died November 17, 1813, and at the time of death the church had in its service 100 preachers and 20,000 members.

OVENSHINE, SAMUEL, military officer, was born in Pennsylvania, April 2, 1843. He entered the Union Army at the outbreak of the Civil War, in 1861, and was commissioned second lieutenant, rising to the rank of captain in 1864. He continued in the army after the close of the war; in 1898, was appointed brigadier-general of volunteers; in 1899, was made brigadier-general of regulars and in the same year commanded a brigade in the Philippine Islands. He retired after over thirty years of active service.

PACKARD, LEWIS RICHARD, classical scholar, was born in Philadelphia, in 1836. In 1856, he was graduated from Yale and subsequently engaged in graduate study at Berlin. He became assistant professor of Greek language and literature at Yale, in 1863, and after three years was made full professor. He was president of the American Philological Association, in 1881, and in 1883 was made second director of the American School of Classical Studies at Athens. He was joint author of the "College Series of Greek Authors." His death occurred in 1884.

PACKER, JOHN HOOKER, physician, was born in Philadelphia, August 15, 1832. He was graduated from the University of Pennsylvania, in 1850; was acting surgeon in the United States Army, 1861–1865, and surgeon to the Episcopal Hospital, Philadelphia, 1863–1884. He also served as surgeon to two other hospitals in Philadelphia, the Pennsylvania, 1884-1896, and the Woman's, 1876-1877. He published "Minor Surgery," "Lectures on Inflammation," etc. He died May 20, 1907.

PACKER, WILLIAM FISHER, governor, was born in Howard Township, Centre County, April 2, 1807. At the age of fifteen he learned the printing trade and afterwards studied law. Being more interested in journalism than in the practice of law, he bought an interest in the *Williamsport Gazette* and later assisted in establishing *The Keystone*, a Democratic paper, at Harrisburg. Before he was elected governor, in 1858, he was a member of the Board of Canal Commissioners, Auditor-General, and a member of the state House of Representatives and Senate. At the conclusion of his term of office, Packer retired to his home in Williamsport where he died September 27, 1870.

PAINE, THOMAS, political writer, came to Philadelphia from England at the beginning of the Revolution. In Philadelphia, he was editor of the *Pennsylvania Magazine*. During the war he published *Common Sense* and the *Crisis*, both of which were of great assistance to the American cause. Upon the organization of the Commonwealth of Pennsylvania, Paine became clerk of the Legislature. During the French Revolution he was in both England and France. Continuing his writings there he produced *Rights of Man* for which he was outlawed by England and his *Age of Reason* while imprisoned by the Jacobins in France. Eventually he returned to the United States and died in New York, in 1809.

PALMER, ANTHONY, colonial governor, was born in England about 1675. He was a merchant in Barbadoes for some time, but in 1707 purchased a large tract of land in Philadelphia, where he settled. In 1708, he was a member of the provincial council and served until his death. When Lieut. Governor Thomas resigned in 1747 the government devolved upon Palmer, who was president of the executive council and during the succeeding eighteen months he administered the affairs of the colony with much ability. He conciliated the Indians and took precautions for the military defense of the colony against Spain and France, though opposed by the Quaker members of the council. The Kensington District of Philadelphia was originally a portion of his farm. He died in Philadelphia, in May, 1749.

PALMER, FREDERICK, author and war correspondent, was born in Pleasantville, January 29, 1873. He was graduated from Allegheny College, in 1893; acted as correspondent during the Greco-Turkish War, 1897; Alaskan sledge journey, Philippines, 1898; march to Peking, 1900; Siberian travel, 1902; with Kuroke's army for Collier's and London Times, 1904-1905; cruise American battleship fleet, 1908-1909; Mexican and Central American travels, 1909; Balkan War, 1912, and Mexico, 1914. Chosen as an accredited correspondent to represent the American Press with the British Army, 1914-1916. Author of: "Going to War in Greece," "The Ways of the Service," "The Last Shot" (novel), "My Year of the Great War," etc. He lives in New York.

PANCOAST, HENRY SPACKMAN, author and educator, was born in Germantown, August 24, 1858. He was educated at Germantown Academy and by private tutors. Studied law; admitted to the bar in 1822, but retired from practice in 1887 to devote himself to writing and teaching. Received degrees of L. H. D., Trinity, 1912; A. M., University of Pennsylvania, 1913. Author of: "Representative English Literature" (1892), "Standard English Poems" (1900), "Standard English Prose" (1902), and "A Vista of English Verse" (1911).

PANCOAST, JOSEPH, surgeon, was born in Burlington, N. J., in 1805. In 1828, he was graduated from the University of Pennsylvania and began teaching surgery in 1831. For a long period he was connected with various hospitals in Philadelphia; was professor of surgery in the Jefferson Medical College from 1838 to 1847, and professor of anatomy from 1847 to 1874. He resigned in the latter year, becoming professor emeritus, and was succeeded by his son, William H. Pancoast. He was a remarkably skillful operator, devised many improved methods, and made some important discoveries. He contributed to medical journals, translated and edited various works and published "A Treatise on Operative Surgery," etc. He died March 7, 1882.

PANCOAST, WILLIAM HENRY, surgeon, was born in Philadelphia, in 1835. In 1856, he was graduated from Jefferson Medical College and subsequently studied in London, Paris, and Vienna. He established his practice in Philadelphia and during the Civil War was superintendent of a hospital there. He joined the faculty of Jefferson College in 1867 and in 1874 succeeded his father as professor of surgery. In 1887, he was one of the founders of the Medico-Chirurgical College of Philadelphia, where he became professor of anatomy and clinical anatomy. Dr. Pancoast published a report in 1884 concerning the anatomy of Siamese twins, which attracted wide attention. He died in 1897.

PARKE, JOHN GRUBB, soldier, was born near Coatesville, September 22, 1827. He was graduated from West Point, in 1849; assigned to the topographical engineering corps, and at the outbreak of the Civil War was appointed brigadier-general of volunteers. He served in North Carolina; was in command at the capture of Fort Macon, and in 1862 was promoted to major-general of volunteers. He was in service at Antietam and South Mountain; he accompanied Sherman on his march to Vicksburg. In 1866, he was retired from the volunteer service. In 1887, he was appointed superintendent at West Point. He retired at his own request, in 1889, and died in Washington, D. C., in 1900.

PARKER, GEORGE HOWARD, zoologist, was born in Philadelphia, December 23, 1864. He was graduated from Harvard, in 1887, pursued special courses there and at the universities of Leipzig, Berlin and Freiburg. He became assistant instructor in zoology at Harvard, in 1888, and occupied different positions there, becoming professor of zoology, in 1906, which position he still holds in addition to directorship of the Harvard Zoological Laboratory. In 1914, he was sent by the United States government to investigate the Pribilof seal herd. He is internationally known and holds membership in many professional and honorary scientific organizations throughout the world. He is the author of: "Biology and Social Problems," "The Elementary Nervous System," "Smell, Taste and Allied Senses," "What Evolution Is" etc.

PARKESBURG, a borough in Chester County, 44 miles west of Philadelphia. It is situated in a thriving agriculture region, and has iron and chemical works, and a flour mill.

PARRISH, EDWARD, pharmacist, was born in Philadelphia, May 31, 1822. He was graduated from the Philadelphia College of Pharmacy, in 1842, and engaged in practice in Philadelphia. In 1864, he became professor of materia medica at the College of Pharmacy and from 1867 until his death he occupied the chair of practical pharmacy. He was actively associated with the founding of Swarthmore College and was its first president in 1868 to 1870. He died of fever, September 9, 1872, at Fort Hill, Indian Territory, while acting as United States peace commissioner to the Indians.

PARRISH, STEPHEN, landscape painter and etcher, was born in Philadelphia, July 9, 1846. He first exhibited in the Pennsylvania Academy (1878) and in 1879 in the New York National Academy. Since then he has produced a series of landscapes, usually large canvases, showing much power of expression and poetic feeling. The subjects of his earlier work were mostly taken from the New England coast, and harbors, and the later years from the Connecticut Valley. His home is in Windsor, Vt.

PARSONS, a borough in Luzerne County, two miles northeast of Wilkes-Barre. It is situated in a coal and oil region, and manufactures tinware and silks.

PASSAVANT, WILLIAM ALFRED, Lutheran clergyman, was born October 9, 1821, at Zelienople. He was graduated from Jefferson College, in 1840, the Lutheran Theological Seminary, Gettysburg, in 1842. After serving in the ministry till 1855, he devoted himself entirely to editorial and philanthropic work. He founded numerous hospitals and orphanages in different cities, and cooperating with A. Lewis Thiel founded Thiel College at Greenville. He collected over $1,000,000 for these institutions. He introduced the Order of

Deaconesses into the United States; edited the "Missionary" at Pittsburgh till its merger with the "Lutheran"; founded the "Workmen" and edited it till his death, June 3, 1894.

PASTORIUS, FRANCIS DANIEL, was born in Germany, in 1651. In August, 1683, he came to Philadelphia and in October began the laying out of Germantown. For many years he taught school in Germantown and Philadelphia, was a member of the Assembly and a signer of the first protest against slavery made in America. He wrote a number of books, several of which were published. Whittier translated his Latin prologue to the Germantown book of records in an ode and wrote a poem, "The Pennsylvania Pilgrim," based on the signing of the protest against slavery by Pastorius. Pastorius died at Germantown, in 1719.

PATTERSON, JOSEPH, banker, was born near Norristown, September 25, 1808. He became a banker and during the Civil War, through his influence, the bankers of the country made a loan of $50,000,000 in gold to Secretary Chase at the famous conference of New York, and $100,000,000 the following year. Secretary Chase constantly sought his advice on the financial policy of the administration. He declined twice the offer of the office of comptroller of the United States treasury, also the post of assistant treasurer at Philadelphia. He was president of the Philadelphia Clearing-House Association from 1869 until his death in Philadelphia, September 25, 1887.

PATTERSON, ROBERT, soldier and educator, was born near Hillsborough, County Down, Ireland, May 30, 1743. He came to America, in 1768, and settled in Pennsylvania, where he engaged in teaching, and in 1774 was principal of the Academy at Wilmington, Del. He volunteered in the Federal Army at the outbreak of the Revolution, and rose to the rank of brigadier-major. In 1779, he was appointed professor of mathematics at the University of Pennsylvania, serving 35 years and acting as vice-provost in 1810–13. In 1799, he was chosen president of the select council of Philadelphia, and in 1805, President Jefferson appointed him director of the mint. He died in Philadelphia, July 22, 1824.

PATTERSON, ROBERT, pioneer, was born in Pennsylvania, 1753. In 1775, he removed to Kentucky; in 1776, he was one of seven men who made the daring expedition to Fort Pitt in quest of ammunition, receiving on the return trip a severe wound from a skirmish with the Indians, in which all the party were either killed or wounded. He fought under Daniel Boone at the Battle of Lower Blue Lick, being second in command. He built the first house in Lexington, Ky.; in 1779, owned one-third of the city of Cincinnati, Ohio, when laid out in 1788, and founded Kayton, Ohio, in 1804.

ROBERT E. PATTISON

PATTERSON, ROBERT, soldier, was born in Cappagh County, Tyrone, Ireland, 1792. He came to America with his parents when very young and settled in Philadelphia. He fought in the War of 1812 and was one of the five "Colonel Pattersons" who nominated Jackson for the presidency. He served with distinction in the Mexican War and at the outbreak of the Civil War he was mustered into service as major-general of volunteers and placed in command of the Department of Washington, where he rendered excellent service in training the raw recruits. He was retired in July, 1861. He died August 7, 1881, in Philadelphia.

PATTERSON, ROBERT MAYNE, Presbyterian clergyman, was born in Philadelphia, July 17, 1832. He was official reporter of the United States Senate (1850-1855), and was graduated from Princeton Theological Seminary in 1859. He held pastorates in Philadelphia and edited "The Presbyterian" (1870-80), and "The Presbyterian Journal" (1880-93). He was a member of thirteen general assemblies of the Presbyterian Church and of several Pan-Presbyterian Councils. Among his works are: "Character of Abraham Lincoln," "Revival Councils," "The Apostolic Church," "Pre-Millenialism," and "American Presbyterianism."

PATTISON, ROBERT EMORY, politician, and governor, was born at Quantico, Md., December 8, 1850. He was admitted to the bar in 1872, but soon turned his attention to politics and in 1877-82 was city comptroller of Philadelphia. Owing to a split in the Republican Party, in 1882, he was elected governor of Pennsylvania, although his party was in the minority, and served four years when he resumed his law practice. In 1891-95, he again served as governor of his state. He died in Philadelphia, August 1, 1904.

PATTON, JACOB HARRIS, historian, was born in Fayette County, May 20, 1812. He graduated from Jefferson College, in 1839, and from Union Theological Seminary in 1846. He is the author of: "A Concise History of the American People," "Yorktown, 1781-1881," "Natural Resources of the United States," and "Political Parties in the United States." He died in 1903.

PATTON, a borough in Cambria County, 65 miles northeast of Pittsburgh. It has agricultural, coal mining and coke interests and manufactures bricks and fire-clay products.

PAXINOSA, Shawnee chief, was friendly to the colonists. At the time of the councils of the Delawares at Nescopeck, in 1755, where outrages were planned, Paxinosa sent two of his sons to rescue the Moravian missionary, Keifer, who was living at Shamokin. They brought him to the Moravian Mission at Gnadenhuetten. He attended the third council with Teedyuscung at Easton in July, 1757.

PAXSON, FREDERICK LOGAN, historian, was born in Philadelphia, February 23, 1877. After graduation from the University of Pennsylvania, in 1898, he studied at Harvard. From 1906-1907, he was assistant professor of American history at the University of Michigan; from 1907-1910, junior professor there. In the latter year he became professor of American history at the University of Wisconsin, a position that he holds today. He has published: "The Independence of the South American Republics," "The Last American Frontier," "The Civil War," "The New Nation," "Recent History of the United States" (1912), revised edition (1928), "The United States in Recent Times." His "History of the American Frontier," published in 1924, was awarded the Pulitzer prize as the best work in American history for that year.

PEALE, CHARLES WILLSON, artist, was born at Chestertown, Md., April 16, 1741. He early engaged in the business of a saddler, but his interests turning to portrait painting he studied under J. S. Copley, at Boston, and under Benjamin West, in London. He was successful in portrait painting, mezzotinto engraving, modeling in wax and casting and molding in plaster. In 1776, he opened a studio in Philadelphia and in 1802 established Peale's Museum, where he displayed collections of portraits and natural history objects. In 1779, he was elected to the Pennsylvania Legislature. Peale was the most successful portrait painter of his time in this country. His work includes portraits of Washington, Robert Morris, Hancock, Gates, Franklin, Comte de Rochambeau, Jefferson, Hamilton, Monroe, Jackson, John Quincy Adams, Clay and Calhoun. He died in Philadelphia, February 22, 1827.

PEALE, REMBRANDT, artist and author, was born in Bucks County, February 22, 1778, a son of Charles Willson Peale. He studied in London as a pupil of Benjamin West and in 1810 opened a studio in Philadelphia. He achieved greatest success as a portrait painter, was technically more correct than his father, but lacked the latter's genius. Among his works are: "The Court of Death" (Detroit Art Gallery); "The Roman Daughter" (Boston Museum); "Portrait of Washington" (Independence Hall); "Thomas Jefferson"; "Mrs. Madison" (New York Historical Society). Peale also wrote: "Notes on Italy," "Graphics," "Reminiscences of Art and Artists," etc. He died in Philadelphia, October 3, 1860.

PEARY, ROBERT EDWIN, Arctic explorer, was born in Cresson, May 6, 1856. In 1881, after graduation from Bowdoin College, he entered the navy as a civil engineer. In 1886, he made his first northern trip and in 1891-1892, as chief of the Arctic expedition of the Philadelphia Academy of Natural Sciences, crossed Greenland from McCormick Bay to Independence Bay by polar sledge, a distance of 1,300 miles. He also discovered Melville Land and Heilprin Land and in another trip to Greenland, in 1893-1895, discovered the "Iron Mountain," a group of three large meteorites. His most important trip was made n 1898-1902, when he set out in search of the North Pole. After many unsuccessful attempts he reached the Pole on April 6, 1909. Subsequently he received degrees from universities and medals from learned societies in appreciation of his achievement. Congress, in March 3, 1911, promoted him to rear-admiral. He died in Washington, D. C., February 20, 1920.

PECKVILLE, a coal mining town in Lackawanna County, six miles northeast of Scranton.

PEFFER, WILLIAM ALFRED, statesman, journalist and author, was born in Cumberland County, September 10, 1831. He served in the Union Army during the Civil War; in 1865, entered the practice of law in Clarksville, Tenn.; moved to Kansas, in 1870, practiced law and established the Fredonia Journal and Coffeyville Journal. He was elected to the State Senate, in 1874; became editor of the Kansas Farmer, in 1881; was one of the founders of the People's Party, and elected its national president in 1891. In 1890, he was elected to the United States Senate. Peffer believed that the farmers should control our national politics. Later he joined the Prohibition Party and was that party's candidate for governor of Kansas in 1898. He is the author of: "Peffer's Tariff Manual," "The Way Out," "The Farmer's Side," "Americanism in the Philippines," and "Rise and Fall of Populism in the United States." He died in 1912.

PEMBERTON, JOHN CLIFFORD, soldier, was born in Philadelphia, August 10, 1818. He graduated from West Point, in 1837; was made first lieutenant, in 1842; served in the Mexican War and was brevetted captain for bravery at Monterey and major for his service at Molino del Rey. Entering the Confederate Army at the beginning of the Civil War, he organized the artillery and cavalry of Virginia and was made lieutenant-colonel, from which rank he rose successively to colonel, brigadier-general, major-general in command of the department of South Carolina, Georgia and Florida; and lieutenant-colonel. He commanded the department of Mississippi, Tennessee, and eastern Louisiana, in 1863; was defeated by Grant at Champion's Hill and Big Black Bridge, as a result of affairs for which Pemberton was criticised. Subsequently he resigned his commission, but in 1864, with rank of lieutenant-colonel, commanded the artillery defenses of Richmond. He died in Penllyn, July 13, 1881.

PEN ARGYL, borough of Northampton County, 20 miles north of Easton.

PENN, JOHN, Colonial governor, was born in London, England, July 14, 1729, the grandson of William Penn. After attending the University of Geneva, he came to Philadelphia, in 1753. Here he served as first member of the provincial council, returning to England after Braddock's defeat. In 1763, he again came to America, became lieutenant governor of Pennsylvania and settled difficulties with the Indians by the treaty of Fort Stanwix, in 1768. During the Revolution, because of disloyalty to the Colonial cause, he was imprisoned for several months. At the conclusion of the war he, with the remainder of the Penn family, lost all proprietary rights. He died in Philadelphia, February 10, 1795.

PENN, RICHARD, Colonial governor, was born in England, in 1735, the grandson of William Penn. He accompanied his brother, John, on his return to Pennsylvania, in 1763, and the following year became a member of the provincial congress. In 1769, he returned to England but during his brother's absence in that country, in 1771-1773, he served as deputy governor of the province. He spent the remainder of his life in England and was a member of Parliament from 1784-1808. He visited America, in 1808, and during the Revolution sympathized with the colonists, with whom he was extremely popular. He died in Richmond, Surrey, England, May 27, 1811.

OLD ASSEMBLY HOUSE AND PENN'S LANDING PLACE

PENN, THOMAS, colonial proprietor, was born in London, England, March 8, 1702, the son of William Penn. In 1732, having been authorized by his brothers, John and Richard, to look after their interests in the province, he came to Pennsylvania, where he was a member of the provincial council. He remained in the province until 1741. In 1775, when the estates of the Penn family were seized by the state, Thomas Penn received three-fourths of the £130,000 awarded by the state for the lands. He died March 21, 1775.

PENN, WILLIAM, founder of Pennsylvania, was born in London, October 14, 1644, of Dutch and English ancestry. In 1660 at the age of sixteen, he attended Christ Church College, Oxford. When he was yet but a boy he came under Quaker influence. Tradition says that his hatred for outward form became so great that upon one occasion he and Robert Spencer, who afterward became

Lord Sunderland, tore the surplices from the heads of the students who wore them. Whether this affair actually took place or not is questionable. Nevertheless, Penn must have been guilty of some such misdemeanor for he was expelled from college for some affair relating to his religious opinions. Subsequently he traveled in France and Italy and upon his return to England entered Lincoln's Inn as a law student. Because of the plague which broke out in London shortly afterwards, Penn abandoned his law studies and went to Ireland where his father placed him in a military position under the Duke of Armond, Lord Lieutenant of Ireland. In September, 1667, the Quaker faith which had always strongly influenced him, fully recognized him as one of her number, and in the following year he was accepted as a preacher. Because of his religious affiliations and his defense of the Quaker Society, Penn was twice imprisoned. His second sentence was imposed after the appearance of his "Sandy Foundation," a pamphlet in which he explained his rejection of the doctrines of the Trinity and of the atonement. While in prison he produced the best known of his writings, "No Cross, No Crown," in which he argued for primitive Christianity, protested against the balls, masks, pride, avarice and luxury of the times, and held that the faith of the Quaker could mitigate all these things. However, it is not this argument which makes the book popular with all ages but rather the general appeal which it makes to man's religious nature, regardless of creed. Later, in order to show that he had not denied the divinity of Christ, Penn wrote a pamphlet, "Innocency with Her Open Face." After his release from prison he again went to Ireland, this time to take charge of the family estate. In 1670, he was arrested for holding a silent meeting with other Quakers at the doors of the meeting-house in Gracechurch Street. Upon his father's death, September 16, 1670, Penn fell heir to a large estate. At the close of that year when Penn had begun to preach at a meeting in Wheeler Street, London, a group of soldiers rushed up and carried him to prison where he was forced to remain for six months. In 1680, Penn petitioned the crown for a grant of land in America where he might found a Quaker colony. The king signed the charter granting him the land, which was to be called Pennsylvania, on March 4, 1681. By the charter he was the perpetual governor of the colony, but he usually remained in England and appointed a deputy to exercise his authority. About a month after securing the charter he sent his cousin, William Markham, to Pennsylvania, to nominally take possession of it and to rule temporarily over the Swedish, English and Dutch settlers along the Delaware. Markham arrived in Pennsylvania in the beginning of July, 1681, and made his headquarters at Upland (Chester). For more than a year he took charge of the affairs of the colony. Penn, in the meantime, secured from the Duke of York the land now included in the state of Delaware. Before leaving for Pennsylvania, Penn advertised for settlers. To George Fox he gave twelve hundred and fifty acres of land. He also planned the details of his government of the colony and prepared a paper called "Conditions or Concessions," which provided for the laying out of a city, and of roads, and attempted to regulate relations with the Indians. On October 29, 1682, Penn arrived at Upland. He visited Tinicum Island where the Swedish governor had lived, the site of the proposed city of Philadelphia, New Jersey, and Long Island, everywhere preaching to any Quakers he found. The first winter was spent in Upland (Chester) and it was probably in the spring of 1683 that Letitia House was built. Penn made several treaties with the Indians, one in June 23, 1683, one on June 25th, and a third on July 14th. The one he made on June 23rd is that known as the Great Treaty and took place under a large elm at Kensington along the shore of the river just above Philadelphia. During Penn's lifetime and for almost seventy-five years Pennsylvania was at peace with the Indians. On August 16, 1684, he returned to England where he became a courtier, issued an anonymous pamphlet in support of James II and supported James' Declaration of Indulgence. In December, 1688, soon after the accession of William III and James II's flight to France, Penn who did not like William was arrested, but shortly afterward discharged because no witnesses appeared against him. Later because of his political affiliations he fled to France. During this period King William deprived him of the government of Pennsylvania. Near the end of 1693, however, he was no longer considered dangerous by England and in August, 1694, the king returned to him the government of the province. In September, 1699, Penn sailed for Pennsylvania, where for the next two years he lived at Pennsbury, his country seat. He traveled about on horseback, visiting sections of the country thirty or forty miles from Philadelphia, and the neighboring provinces of New York, New Jersey and Maryland. He governed the province with apparent ease in spite of the difficulties which had arisen during the fifteen years of his absence and before returning to England in 1701 granted a new constitution, which was effective until the outbreak of the American Revolution. After Penn's return to England, his debts, which had rapidly been growing, became so onerous that Penn suggested that he sell his government to the crown. Because of his careless business methods, he became involved in serious financial difficulties with Philip Ford, a Quaker, who had charge of his estates in England and Ireland. While he was attending a meeting in Gracechurch Street he was arrested and confined to Fleet prison for nine months. Upon his release he attended to the affairs connected with the government of his province until several paralytic strokes rendered him helpless. He died July 30, 1718. Penn was twice married. By his first wife, Gule Springett, he had three children: Springett, who died shortly after his father's second marriage; Letitia, who married William Aubrey, and William. By his second wife, Hannah Callowhill, he had six children: John, Thomas, Hannah, Margaret, Richard and Dennis. John, Thomas, Margaret and Richard survived their mother and became proprietors of Pennsylvania.

PENNELL, JOSEPH, etcher and illustrator, was born in Philadelphia, July 4, 1860. He studied at the Pennsylvania School of Industrial Art, and the Pennsylvania Academy of Fine Arts, and has been a lecturer on illustration at the Slade School of Art, University College, London, and at the Royal College of Art, South Kensington. His work includes illustrations for the Century Magazine and other periodicals; etchings for M. D. Howell's paper on Italian life; English cathedrals published with Mrs. Schuyler Van Rensselaer's book on that subject; "A Canterbury Pilgrimage"; "The Alhambra"; "Life of James McNeill Whistler" (with Mrs. Pennell); "Pictures of the Panama Canal," etc.

PENNS CREEK—Tributary to Susquehanna River. Sub-basin: Middle Main Susquehanna; source, in Gregg Township, southeastern Centre County; course, easterly, through Mifflin and Union Counties, into Snyder County, forming Union-Snyder County boundary for six miles; mouth, three miles south of Selinsgrove; length, fifty-nine miles. Indian name, Kayarondinhagh.

PENN'S OLD BREWHOUSE

[PENNSYLVANIA ACADEMY OF FINE ARTS, was founded in 1805, as the Philadelphia Academy of Fine Arts, at a meeting held in Independence Hall in the interest of art. George Clymer, a signer of the Declaration of Independence, was the first president of the association, and Benjamin West, whose paintings were among the first exhibited at the academy, was elected an honorary member. The organization was incorporated in 1806 as the Pennsylvania Academy of Fine Arts, and in that year a building was erected on Chestnut Street. Upon the opening of the academy to the public in 1806, it was deemed prudent, because of the character of some of the exhibits, to admit the sexes separately. This custom was followed as late as 1830. The academy is now located on North Broad Street.

PENNSYLVANIA COLLEGE OF GETTYSBURG—See GETTYSBURG COLLEGE.

PENNSYLVANIA COLLEGE FOR WOMEN, at Pittsburgh, was founded in 1869 by the Presbyterian Church. A classical and literary course leading to the A. B. degree is offered and there are departments of art, music, and social service. Enrollment (1930–1931), 125.

PENNSYLVANIA DUTCH, a dialect, spoken by the descendants of German settlers, in Pennsylvania.

PENNSYLVANIA GERMAN SOCIETY, was organized April 15, 1891, at Lancaster. Its aim is the preservation of documentary material, papers, and letters pertaining to the history of the Pennsylvania-Germans in America. The Society publishes accounts of its proceedings. Its members must be direct descendants of early German and Swiss emigrants to Pennsylvania.

PENNSYLVANIA HISTORICAL SOCIETY, was organized in Philadelphia, December 2, 1824, and incorporated June 2, 1826. The Society has valuable collections of historical and genealogical material, relating to Pennsylvania, among which are records and papers of the Penn family, the Charlemagne Tower collection of American-Colonial laws, first editions of books printed by Bradford, Christopher Sauer, and Franklin, etc. The Pennsylvania Magazine of History and Biography has been issued quarterly since 1877. Other publications are Memoirs of the Society in fourteen volumes; a volume of Bulletins, one of Collections, one on Pennsylvania and the Federal Constitution and a historical map of Pennsylvania. The library contains over 5,000 volumes of manuscripts, about 260,000 pamphlets and more than 152,000 bound books.

PENNSYLVANIA HOSPITAL, THE, at Philadelphia, chartered in 1751, was the first hospital in America.

PENNSYLVANIA MILITARY COLLEGE, for men, is a non-sectarian institution, founded in 1821, at Chester. Courses include civil engineering, chemistry, commerce and finance. Enrollment (1924), 157.

PENNSYLVANIA RAILROAD COMPANY, THE, was incorporated by an act of the State Legislature, on April 13, 1846, and was given the authority to build a road to Pittsburgh or any place in Allegheny County, or to Erie. The privilege of building a road to connect with the Harrisburg, Portsmouth, Mount Joy and Lancaster Railroad was also granted. The first division of the road, extending from Harrisburg to Lewistown, was opened on September 1, 1849. Cars ran through from Philadelphia to Pittsburgh, on February 15, 1854. On July 31, 1857, the Commonwealth of Pennsylvania sold to the Pennsylvania Railroad Company the line between Philadelphia and Columbia (the Philadelphia and Columbia Railroad). The Pennsylvania Company, in 1861, leased the Harrisburg, Portsmouth, Mount Joy and Lancaster Railroad for 999 years. During the Civil War period the Pennsylvania line was opened from Philadelphia to Washington and points north and east for the transportation of troops. Colonel Thomas A. Scott, general superintendent of the road in 1858, and vice-president in 1860, was appointed in charge of government railroads and telegraphs at the outbreak of the war. In 1862, the Pennsylvania Company leased the Philadelphia and Erie Railroad. Western expansion was begun by leasing the Pittsburgh, Fort Wayne, and Chicago Railroad, on June 7, 1869. Numerous other companies and their branches were leased in that year and at later periods, until the line extended from the Atlantic Coast to the valley of the Mississippi, and connected lines in Ohio, Indiana, Illinois, Michigan, Kentucky, West Virginia, Missouri, and other states. As in the west, the eastern lines developed rapidly after the Civil War. Railroads connecting Pennsylvania with points in New Jersey, New York and Maryland were acquired between 1868 and 1872, and many branch lines were built in mining and lumber regions. The Hudson River Tunnel, which has a terminal in New York City, and an extension to Long Island, was opened September 8, 1910.

PENNSYLVANIA RESOURCES—In 1830, of all the coal mined in the United States, Pennsylvania mined 99.03%, and of all the iron, 50%. At the present time Pennsylvania produces about one-seventh of the world's coal supply, and more pig iron than any other state or nation. The area of the anthracite coal fields is 484 square miles, and that of the bituminous fields, 14,200 square miles. The total anthracite produced in 1807-1925 was 3,478,458,909 short tons; the total bituminous produced, 1840-1925, 4,549,147,753 short tons. In 1926, 84,437,452 short tons of anthracite were produced in the state. In the same year the production of bituminous coal totaled 153,041,638 short tons.

The production of iron in Pennsylvania began in the Colonial period. At present, iron ore mining is confined to magnetite, found at Cornwall, Lebanon County. Iron production in the state in 1926 included 1,088,634 long tons, sold to furnaces; 2,215 long tons sold for paint, and 13,142,528 long tons of pig iron.

The production of oil and gas is confined to the western counties. The total producing area in Pennsylvania is 380,000 acres. The industry began in 1859, and from that time to 1925 the total production of oil was 788,366,000 barrels. After 1891, when the maximum production (31,424,000 barrels) was reached, the industry declined. Since 1921 the production has increased noticeably and in 1929, 11,805,000 barrels of oil were brought from the wells. Natural gas has been used extensively since 1882. In 1926, its total production was 107,089,000 cubic feet.

About one-eighth of the clay products of the United States are produced in Pennsylvania. Clay is found chiefly in the coal regions. In 1926, 855,832 short tons of raw clay were produced in the state.

The state leads in the total production of sand, gravel and sandstone. The latter product is quarried for building, paving, curbing, etc., and for roads, concrete and railroad ballast. The total production of sand and gravel in 1926 was 12,873,953 short tons.

Limestone produced in Pennsylvania is used for building, for ballast, lime, fluxing and cement. Seven hundred ninety-four thousand one hundred and ninety-six short tons were produced in Pennsylvania in 1926.

Granite occurs only locally and is found in the South Mountains of Berks and Lehigh Counties. Its production in 1925 was 308,930 tons.

Slate is extensively quarried in Lehigh and Northampton Counties, and to a lesser extent in York and Lancaster Counties. Pennsylvania leads in the production of this commodity, which in 1926 was valued at $5,413,177.

Although copper is found in the South Mountains and at other places in the state it is not mined. It is found with the iron ore in the Cornwall mines and 500 tons recovered annually.

Among other resources of Pennsylvania are: pyrite, found locally in coal mining; lead and zinc; aluminum minerals; manganese, mined locally; chromite, formerly mined in southern Lancaster County; nickel, formerly mined in Lancaster County; cobalt, found in Chester and other counties; gold and silver, mined as second minerals from the Cornwall mine; radium; mineral paints; serpentine, used for building stone and interior decoration; talc, found with serpentine, production in 1924, 8,281 tons; salt, bromide and iodine, formerly obtained from wells along the Allegheny River; graphite, formerly mined in southeastern counties; phosphate mineral, found in Cumberland and Juniata Counties; asbestos, found in Delaware and other counties; magnesia, valued in 1921 at $2,294,700; barite; feldspar, in Delaware and Chester Counties, production (1920), 8,562 tons; mica; vein quartz, produced in southeastern counties.

PENNSYLVANIA SOCIETY FOR THE PROMOTION OF THE CULTURE OF THE MULBERRY AND THE RAISING OF SILK WORMS.

At a meeting April 2, 1828, in which year the society was organized, offered a premium of $60.00 for the greatest quantity of sewing silk of the best quality produced in Pennsylvania from cocoons raised in the state and produced by one family, to be not less than twenty pounds. A premium of $50.00 was offered for the greatest quantity of good cocoons raised within the state, and a premium of $50.00 for the largest number of the best white mulberry trees raised within twelve miles of Philadelphia. Benjamin R. Morgan was president and M. Carey, secretary of the organization. This organization continued in existence until 1835, when the Philadelphia Silk Culture and Manufacturing Company and similar organizations in several counties were formed. In 1838, the Pennsylvania Legislature offered a premium of twenty cents a pound for silk produced in the state. In Lancaster County, in 1839, the Lancaster County Silk Growing Society was organized and in June of that year the Lancaster Union stated that a number of very beautiful handkerchiefs of Lancaster County silk had been made, having been reeled and spun in that city.

PENNSYLVANIA SOCIETY FOR THE PROMOTION OF PUBLIC SCHOOLS. This society was organized in 1828 for the purpose of promoting education throughout Pennsylvania by encouraging the establishment of public schools in which the elementary branches of education should be taught. The officers of the society were: President, Roberts Vaux; Vice-Presidents, John Sergeant, John Wurts; Corresponding Secretaries, George W. Smith, George M. Stroud; Treasurer, William B. Davidson; Recording Secretary, Augustus Richards. (See Hazard's "Register of Pennsylvania," Vol. I, 1828.)

PENNSYLVANIA STATE COLLEGE, at State College, Centre County, was established in 1863 by the act of 1862, under which the State and Federal government made grants of land for educational purposes. In 1855, it first received a charter as a Farmer's High School. The college includes the Schools of Agriculture, Engineering, Home Economics, Liberal Arts, Mining and Natural Science. The A. B., and B. S. degrees are offered as well as degrees in engineering and the master's degree. Experimental stations in agriculture, engineering and mining are conducted by the college. Through the agricultural extension division, farm agents are stationed in practically all the counties of the state, boy's and girl's agricultural clubs are organized and correspondence courses are offered. Apprentice schools in manufacturing plants and industrial centers are conducted by the engineering extension division. The liberal arts extension, among other activities, organizes public school debating leagues. The college occupies an attractive site in the Allegheny Mountains, 1,200 feet above sea level. Enrollment (1930-1931), 4,325.

PENNSYLVANIA STATE TEMPERANCE SOCIETY. This society was organized in 1826. In its annual report of 1833, submitted by Job R. Tyson, Esq., the statement was made that both in England and this country three-fourths of the pauperism, four-fifths of the crimes, nine-tenths of the suicides and nearly all cases of murder arose from the use of ardent spirits. The report further stated that in Pennsylvania alone there were, in 1810, 3,334 distilleries which manufactured 6,553,284 gallons of ardent spirits, being a little more than one-fifth of the supply of the whole United States. Auxiliary societies had been organized in the counties of Philadelphia, Montgomery, Chester, Lancaster, Northampton, Washington, Centre, Cambria, Bradford, Susquehanna, Bucks, Allegheny, Erie, Westmoreland, Franklin, Luzerne, Indiana, Juniata, York, Fayette, Union, Dauphin, Mifflin and Butler. In Erie County there were fifteen subordinate associations comprising 1,400 members. In Washington County there were twenty-two auxiliary bodies, giving the county about 3,000 members. The society in the Tuscarora Valley, Juniata County, reported that within that district eight distilleries were discontinued and four stores have ceased to retail spirituous liquors. In Mifflin County, six distilleries had been discontinued and the consumption of alcohol in this county was estimated to be less than one-fifth of its amount before the establishment of the Pennsylvania State Temperance

Society. Fayette County reported eleven auxiliaries with 1,500 members. A weekly paper sponsored by the association, called "The Pennsylvania Advocate" created sentiment against the use of ardent spirits.

PENNSYLVANIA, UNIVERSITY OF, at Philadelphia, owes its existence to Benjamin Franklin, who with other Philadelphians established the Philadelphia Academy, in 1751. Two years later the proprietors of Pennsylvania granted the institution a charter and it became a college and academy. The college was closed for a year and a half during the Revolutionary period and in 1779 the Legislature, claiming that the institution was not being conducted according to original plans, seized the property and rights and organized the "Trustees of the University of the State of Pennsylvania." The property was restored in 1789 and two years later the original college and university united under the corporate name of the University of Pennsylvania. From 1802-1829, the University was conducted in the home built for the president of the United States when it was believed that Philadelphia was to become the national capital, and later a new building was erected on that site. In 1872, the university was moved to its present location in West Philadelphia. The first medical school in the United States was founded in 1765 as a department of the University. The law department was organized in 1850 although lectures had been given since 1790. As a result of the gift of John Henry Towne, a trustee, who made the university the residuary legatee of his estate, the Towne Scientific School was organized in 1874. The University Museum, organized in 1889, became a part of the university in 1891. At present the university includes the College, the Graduate School, the Law School, School of Medicine, University Hospital, Wistar Institute of Anatomy and Biology, the Laboratory of Hygiene, the School of Dentistry, the School of Veterinary Medicine, the Veterinary Hospital, the University Library, the University Museum, Flower Astronomical Observatory, the Department of Physical Education, the Wharton School of Finance and Commerce, Towne Scientific School, the School of Education, the Henry Phipps Institute, Graduate School of Medicine and the Evans Institute. Enrollment (1930-1931), 6,770.

PENNSYLVANIA WAR HISTORY COMMISSION, was appointed by the Pennsylvania Council of National Defense and Committee of Public Safety to preserve a permanent record of Pennsylvania's part in the World War.

PENNYPACK CREEK—Tributary to Delaware River. Sub-basin: Lower Delaware; source, near Mapleglen, in Upper Dublin Township, Montgomery County; course, southeasterly into Philadelphia County to Delaware River; mouth, one and one-half miles southeast of Holmesburg; length, twenty-two miles. Indian name, "Pemecacka."

PENNYPACKER, SAMUEL WHITAKER, governor, jurist and author, was born in Phoenixville, April 9, 1843. He was educated at the Grovemont Seminary, Phoenixville, and at the West Philadelphia Institute. After the Civil War, in which he served with the 26th Emergency Pennsylvania Regiment at the first Gettysburg engagement, in 1863, he studied law at the University of Pennsylvania, was admitted to the bar and elected president of the Law Academy of Philadelphia, in 1868. In 1889, he became judge of the Court of Common Pleas, No. 2, served for twenty years during five of which he was president judge of that court. He became governor of Pennsylvania, in 1902, and during his administration a new capitol building was erected, the health and highway departments and the State Constabulary organized. Afterwards he served as president of the Historical Society of Pennsylvania. He is the author of: "Pennsylvania in American History"; "Pennsylvania, the Keystone"; "Settlement of Germantown"; "Supreme Court Reports" (four vols.); "Colonial Cases"; "Digest of the English Common Law Reports," etc. He died September 2, 1917, in Schwenksville.

PENROSE, BOIES, lawyer and politician, was born in Philadelphia, November 1, 1860. After his graduation from Harvard, in 1881, he studied law and was admitted to the bar in 1883. Subsequently he practiced his profession in Philadelphia; was a member of the State House of Representatives, 1884-1886; a member of the State Senate, 1887-1897, and president pro tem of the Senate, 1889-1891. As a delegate to the Republican National Conventions of 1900, 1904, 1908 and 1916, as chairman of the Republican State Committee, 1903-1905, and as a member of the Republican National Committee, he exerted a powerful influence in national political affairs. He succeeded J. Donald Cameron as United States Senator from Pennsylvania, in 1897, and was reelected in 1903, 1909, 1914 and 1920. He died in Washington, D. C., December 31, 1921.

PEPPER, GEORGE WHARTON, lawyer and author, was born in Philadelphia, March 16, 1867. He graduated from the University of Pennsylvania, in 1887, later studied law there and in 1889 was admitted to the bar. He practiced his profession in Philadelphia as a member of the firm of Pepper, Bodine, Stokes, and Schoch. In January, 1922, he was appointed United States Senator to fill the vacancy caused by the death of Boies Penrose, and was subsequently elected to serve during the 1923-1927 term. His publications include: "The Borderland of Federal and State Decisions"; "Pleading at Common Law and Under the Codes"; "Digest of the Laws of Pennsylvania, 1700-1901"; "Digest of Decisions and Encyclopedia of Pennsylvania Law, 1754-1898" (with William Draper Lewis); "The Way"; "A Voice from the Crowd," and "Men and Issues." He lives in Philadelphia.

PEPPER, WILLIAM, physician, was born in Philadelphia, August 21, 1843. He graduated from the University of Pennsylvania, in 1862; from the Medical

SAMUEL W. PENNYPACKER

School, in 1864, and began the practice of his profession in Philadelphia. In 1868, he became a lecturer in the University; from 1876-1887, was professor of clinical medicine there and later professor of theory and practice of medicine. He was provost of the University from 1881-1894 and during his administration the university hospital was established, new departments were added and the institutions in general made marked progress. He was one of the founders of the Pennsylvania Museum and School of Industrial Art and the founder, and editor for a year, of the Philadelphia Medical Times. He wrote: "Trephining in Cerebral Disease," "Local Treatment in Pulmonary Cavities," "Higher Medical Education," "Phthisis in Pennsylvania," "A Text-Book on the Theory and Practice of Medicine"; edited the "System of Medicine by American Authors," and made numerous contributions to medical journals. He died in Pleasanton, Calif., July 28, 1898.

PEQUEA CREEK—Tributary to Susquehanna River. Sub-basin: Lower Main Susquehanna; source, in Welsh Mountain, Salisbury Township, eastern Lancaster County; course, southwesterly by a circuitous route, to Susquehanna River; mouth, at Pequea Creek; length, forty-five miles. Named after the Piqua tribe of the Shawnee. The name means "dust" or "ashes."

PERKASIE, borough of Bucks County, 35 miles north of Philadelphia. Its industries include: brick yards, tile works, silk mills, cigar factories, iron, tag, label works, etc.

PERKIOMEN CREEK—Tributary to Schuylkill River. Sub-basin: Lower Delaware; source, near Seisholtzville, in Longswamp Township, Berks County; course, southeasterly into Montgomery County; mouth, near Perkiomen Junction; length, thirty-seven and one-half miles. Indian name, a corruption of Pakihmomink, "where there are cranberries."

PERKIOMEN CREEK, NORTHEAST BRANCH—Tributary to Perkiomen Creek. Sub-basin: Lower Delaware; source, in Bedminster Township, northern Bucks County; course, southwesterly into Montgomery County to Perkiomen Creek; mouth, near Schwenksville; length, twenty-four miles. Indian name, a corruption of Pakihmomink, "where there are cranberries."

PERRY COUNTY, was formed March 22, 1820, from part of Cumberland. Named for Commodore Oliver Hazard Perry. Land area, 564 square miles; population (1930), 21,744. County-seat, New Bloomfield, laid out in 1822.

PERSHING, CYRUS J., jurist, was born in Youngstown, Westmoreland County, February 3, 1825. After graduation from Jefferson College, in 1848, and admittance to the bar, in 1850, he practiced in Johnstown. He was elected to the State Legislature in 1861, 1862, 1863, 1864 and 1865, and in October,

1872 was elected president judge of Schuylkill County in which capacity he presided at the trial of the Molly Maguires. In 1875, Pershing was the Democratic nominee for governor of Pennsylvania. He died at Pottsville, June 29, 1903.

PERSONAL LIBERTY LAWS, were passed in Pennsylvania, about 1840, for the protection of negroes within the borders of the state.

PETERS, MADISON CLINTON, Baptist clergyman, was born in Lehigh County, November 6, 1859. After studying at Muhlenberg and Franklin and Marshall Colleges and Heidelberg Theological Seminary, Tiffin, Ohio, he entered the ministry of the Reformed Church. So successful was he that at the age of twenty-four, he was appointed to the pastorate of the First Presbyterian Church, Philadelphia. In 1889, he became pastor of the Bloomingdale Church, Broadway, New York, and after remaining there for eleven years joined the Baptist Church. He was pastor of Sumner Avenue Baptist Church, Brooklyn, until 1906 after which he was pastor of the Church of the Epiphany, New York, for two years. In addition to numerous contributions to newspaper syndicates he has written: "Justice to the Jew," "The Man Who Wins," "After Death—What?", "All for America," etc. He died October 12, 1918.

PETERS, RICHARD, jurist, was born near Philadelphia, August 22, 1744. He studied law in Philadelphia and in 1763 was admitted to the bar. From 1771 to the outbreak of the Revolutionary War, he was register of the admiralty; when the war began he joined a volunteer company and attained a captaincy; from 1776-1781, he was secretary of the board of war; he served in Congress from 1782-1783; was a member of the state assembly, in 1787, and speaker of the assembly from 1788-1790; in 1791, he was speaker of the state senate. In 1792, he became judge of the United States District Court for Pennsylvania, which position he held for the remainder of his life. He died at Philadelphia, August 21, 1828.

PETROLEUM. For many years Pennsylvania produced practically all of the petroleum used in the world. At an early period the oil was collected from oil springs and streams and was obtained in great quantities from the salt wells at Tarentum and the lower Allegheny Valley. The product began to find a market in Pittsburgh and New York and on March 4, 1858, nine barrels of oil from Tarentum were shipped to the Kerosene Oil Company, New York, where they sold for $275.19. In 1858, Colonel E. L. Drake was sent by the Seneca Oil Company to Titusville, where after persistent effort, on August 28, 1859, the first oil well in the United States was drilled, the well was equipped for pumping and soon produced about forty barrels of oil a day. Subsequently many other wells were produced along the Allegheny River in Venango, Clarion, Butler, Armstrong, Bradford and McKean Counties. Until 1895, Pennsylvania lead in the production of this product. In 1926, 8,961,000 barrels of petroleum, valued at $31,930,000 were produced in the state.

PHELAN, RICHARD, Roman Catholic Bishop, was born near Ballyragget, County Kilkenny, Ireland, January 1, 1828. He studied at the College of Saint Kieran, Kilkenny, before coming to this country in 1850. Subsequently he attended Saint Michael's Seminary and Saint Mary's Theological Seminary, at Baltimore, and in 1855 was ordained to the priesthood. He was successively curate at St. Paul's Cathedral, Pittsburgh, pastor at Freeport, Pa., and pastor of St. Peter's Church, Allegheny City. He was appointed vicar-general of the diocese in 1883 and was consecrated coadjutor bishop of the Sees of Allegheny and Pittsburgh, in 1885, and bishop in 1889. He died at Idlewood, Pa., December 20, 1904.

PHILADELPHIA, the largest city in Pennsylvania, and the third in size in the United States, lies at the junction of the Delaware and Schuylkill Rivers. It was founded by William Penn, who became proprietor of Pennsylvania in 1681. At that time the site of the city was occupied by more than 800 Quakers and some 300 Swedes and Dutch. The city which was the first whose plan was prepared for a particular site, was laid out, in 1682, by Captain Thomas Holme, surveyor-general of the province. It was chartered a city in 1701. From the beginning of the province the provincial council met in Philadelphia at the Letitia House, built by Penn for his town house, and later in the State House, erected in what later became Independence Square. Until 1799, when it was removed to Lancaster, Philadelphia was capital of the state. The first Continental Congress met in Carpenter's Hall, September 4, 1774, and the State House bell (the liberty bell) proclaimed America's independence on July 4, 1776. From 1790 to 1800, Philadelphia was the national capital. The leading educational institutions of the city are the University of Pennsylvania founded by Benjamin Franklin, in 1753, Temple University, founded in 1884, by Russell Conwell, and Drexel Institute, founded by Anthony J. Drexel. The Medical School of the University of Pennsylvania, the first in the United States, was established in 1765. Other well-known medical schools in the city are: Jefferson, Medico-Chirurgical, Woman's and Hahnemann. There are four dental schools in the city, and a College of Pharmacy. The Pennsylvania Academy of Fine Arts, the Philadelphia School of Industrial Art, the Pennsylvania Museum and the Woman's School of Design (Spring Garden Institute) give instruction in applied and high art. Dependent boys receive industrial training at Girard College and Williamson Trade School. The oldest circulating library in the United States is the Philadelphia Library Association, an outgrowth of Franklin's Junto, founded in 1731. Other libraries in the city are: the Mercantile, University of Pennsylvania and Free Library of Philadelphia, established in 1891. Industrially, Philadelphia has had a rapid growth. The American International Shipbuilding Corporation yard at Hog Island is the largest in the world. Other industrial establishments include foundries, machine shops, mills, Baldwin locomotive works (the largest in the country), manufactories of brass, bronze, copper, tin and sheet iron wares, cutlery, files, electrical machinery, saws, textiles, tanned leather, cordage and twine, dyeing and finishing, felt hats, chemicals, medical compounds, soap, paint and varnish, lumber and planing mill products, confectionery, fertilizer, millinery and lace. Philadelphia annually refines one-sixth of all the raw sugar in the United States. Population (1930), 1,950,961; (1920), 1,823,779.

INTERIOR OF WICACO BLOCK HOUSE
Showing altar, with rail, candles, and, as a reredos, the Swedish flag used at dedication of the House

PHILADELPHIA, ACADEMY OF NATURAL SCIENCES, OF, was founded in 1812, for the promotion of learning in the natural sciences. The institution includes a library of about 80,000 volumes, and thousands of pamphlets, a museum, publication office and department of instruction and lectures. The museum has more than 130,000 specimens of vertebrate animals of which 12,000 are mammals, 60,000 birds, 20,000 reptiles and 40,000 fish. Of insect specimens there are over 400,000. The academy possesses the largest collection of shells in the world, over 1,500,000; about 50,000 fossils, 30,000 minerals, 20,000 archaeological objects and more than 900,000 specimens of dried plants. Since 1814, lectures have been given at the academy. The institution financed Chaillu's African expeditions and sponsored several others. It publishes periodically its Proceedings and Journal.

406   ENCYCLOPEDIA OF PENNSYLVANIA

PHILADELPHIA, THE COLLEGE OF PHYSICIANS OF, was organized in 1786 and chartered March 26, 1789. It is the oldest medical society in Philadelphia and in the United States.

PHILADELPHIA COUNTY, one of the three original counties established at the settlement of the province in 1682. Named from the Biblical city in Asia Minor. Land area, 128 square miles; population (1930), 1,950,961. County-seat, Philadelphia, laid out in 1682.

PHILADELPHIA COUNTY SOCIETY FOR THE ENCOURAGEMENT OF AGRICULTURE AND DOMESTIC MANUFACTURES, was established August 4, 1789, in opposition to the Philadelphia Society for Promoting Agriculture. Only farmers were admitted to membership in the organization.

INTERIOR OF WICACO BLOCK HOUSE
Showing, steps at side cut, Swedish fashion, from a solid log

PHILADELPHIA INQUIRER, THE, a daily newspaper, appears every morning. It was established June 29, 1829, by John Norvell and John R. Walker. Its aim has been "Protection to Industry," and its political affiliation, Republican. The paper is edited by Charles Heustis and published by the Philadelphia Inquirer Company. Circulation, every morning, 271,580; Sunday, 489,974.

PHILADELPHIA SOCIETY FOR PROMOTING AGRICULTURE, founded in 1785, was the first agricultural organization in America.

PHILADELPHIA AND READING RAILWAY COMPANY, was incorporated in Pennsylvania, November 17, 1896, after it had leased the railroad lines of the old Philadelphia and Reading Railroad, sold under foreclosure on September 23, 1896. The main line extends from Philadelphia to Reading with branches from Reading to Harrisburg, Lebanon to Pine Grove and Auburn, Pine Grove to Rockville, Reading to Shenandoah, Mahanoy Plane to Port Trevorton, etc. Much coal is transported over the Reading lines from the anthracite mines of Pennsylvania to Port Reading, N. J., and Port Richmond, Philadelphia.

PHILIPSBURG, borough in Centre County, forty miles northeast of Altoona. It is located in a region in which there are large bituminous coal mines and deposits of clay. The industries of the town include the manufacture of hardware and tools, foundries, planing mills and machine shops.

PHILLIPS, ADELAIDE, singer, was born in Stratford-on-Avon, England, October 26, 1833. When she was seven, she moved to Boston with her family and on September 25, 1843, appeared as Little Pickle in "The Spoiled Child," at the Boston Museum. In 1846, she appeared at the Walnut Street Theatre, Philadelphia, as Rosa in "John of Paris." Later she made her debut as a concert singer, sang in the largest cities of the world, and for many years was the leading contralto singer in America. She died at Carlsbad, October 3, 1882.

PHILLIPS, HENRY, archaeologist, was born in Philadelphia, September 6, 1838. Although a lawyer, he was more particularly interested in numismatics, archaeology, etc. He is the author of: "History of American Colonial Paper Currency," "History of American Paper Money," "Pleasures of Numismatic Science," "Poems from the Spanish and German," a translation of Chamisso's "Faust," and four volumes of translations from the Spanish, Hungarian and German. He died at Philadelphia, June 6, 1895.

PHILLIPS, HENRY MYER, lawyer and politician, was born at Philadelphia, June 30, 1811. In 1832, he was admitted to the bar in Philadelphia and was particularly successful in the criminal and civil branch of the practice. He was Democratic representative in Congress, in 1856, and subsequently was commissioner of the Board of City Trusts, in charge of the Stephen Girard Estate, president of that board and president of the board of directors of the Academy of Music and of the Fairmont Park Commission. He died August 3, 1884.

PHILLIPS, THOMAS W., capitalist and legislator, was born at Mount Jackson, 1835. He became owner of large oil well interests and was one of the largest individual oil producers in the country. He served as a member of Congress, from 1893–1897, and introduced the bill which created the Industrial Commission. As a member of that commission he was responsible for the establishment of the Bureau of Corporations. He died in 1912.

PHILOSOPHICAL SOCIETY, AMERICAN, was founded in Philadelphia, in 1743, the first institution in America devoted to science and learning. On January 2, 1769 this organization and "The American Society for Promoting and Propagating Useful Knowledge, held in Philadelphia," an outgrowth of Franklin's "Junto," united under the name of American Philosophical Society.

PHIPPS, HENRY, manufacturer, was born at Philadelphia, September 27, 1839. Until 1861, he was engaged in business in Pittsburgh. Then he became a member of the firm of Bidwell and Phipps, powder dealers. Afterwards he entered the steel business in which he made a fortune. Both Philadelphia and Pittsburgh benefited by his philanthropic enterprises. He built the Phipps Conservatory and established a botanical garden in Schenley Park, Pittsburgh, endowed the Henry Phipps Institute, at Philadelphia, for the treatment of tuberculosis, and built a psychiatric clinic for Johns Hopkins Hospital, Baltimore. His home is in Great Neck, L. I.

PHIPPS INSTITUTE, THE HENRY, was founded at Philadelphia by Henry Phipps for "the study, treatment and prevention of tuberculosis." The institute opened February 1, 1903. Patients are treated both at the institute hospital and in the dispensary. Homes of outside patients are regularly visited by inspectors.

PHOENIXVILLE, borough in Chester County, located at the junction of the Schuylkill River and French Creek, was settled in 1792 and incorporated as a borough in 1849. Its principal industries are the manufacture of iron, cotton goods, hosiery, silk, steel, etc. Population (1930), 12,029; (1920), 10,484.

PHYSICK, PHILIP SYNG, surgeon, was born in Philadelphia, July 7, 1768, the son of Edmund Physick, an Englishman, who before the Revolution was keeper of the Great Seal of Pennsylvania. His son, Philip, graduated from the University of Pennsylvania, in 1785, and afterward studied medicine under Dr. Adam Kuhn, of Philadelphia, at the Medical School of the University of Pennsylvania, in England where he received a diploma from the Royal College of Surgeon's, London, and in Edinburgh, receiving the M. D. degree from the University of Edinburgh, in 1792. Returning to Philadelphia, in 1792, he entered upon the practice of his profession. He attained success as a surgeon; performed operations hitherto unknown and invented surgical instruments which were in use for many years. He performed notable service during the yellow fever epidemics of 1793, 1797, 1798 and 1799. In 1794, he became one of the surgeons of the Pennsylvania Hospital. He was professor of surgery at the University of Pennsylvania from 1805-1819 and professor of anatomy there from 1819-1831. From 1824 to his death he was president of the Philadelphia Medical Society; in 1825, he was elected to membership in the Royal Academy of Medicine of France and in 1836 he was made an honorary fellow of the Royal Medical and Chirurgical Society of London. Dr. Physick, a pioneer in the field of American Surgery, is often called "The father of American Surgery.". He died at Philadelphia, December 15, 1837.

PHOENIXVILLE (1843)

PICKENS, ANDREW, soldier, was born at Paxton, September 19, 1739. In 1752, he moved with his family to South Carolina. He took part in the Cherokee War in 1761 and became captain of militia at the opening of the Revolutionary War. He performed distinguished service during the war and rose to the rank of brigadier-general. In 1779, he defeated General Boyd at Kettle Creek, and participated in the Battle of Stone Ferry; in 1781, Congress voted him a sword for his services at the Battle of Cowpens. During 1783-1794, he was a member of the South Carolina Legislature and again in 1801 and 1812. He served as a member of Congress, 1793-1795, and was a member of the State Constitutional Convention. He died at Tomassee, S. C., August 17, 1817.

PICKERING, CHARLES, naturalist and physician, was born at Starucca Creek, November 10, 1805, a grandson of Timothy Pickering. After graduation from Harvard, in 1823, and from the Medical School there, in 1826, he began practice in Philadelphia. He was naturalist in the United States Exploring Expedition under Lieut. Charles Wilkes, 1838-1842, and in 1843-1845 he engaged in scientific research in Egypt, Arabia, East Africa and India. His publications include: "The Races of Man and Their Geographical Distribution"; "Chronological History of Plants"; "Man's Record of His Own Existence Illustrated Through Names, Uses and Companionship." He died at Boston, March 17, 1878.

PICKETT, GEORGE EDWARD, military officer at the Battle of Gettysburg, in July, 1863, made the famous assault on Cemetery Ridge, known as "Pickett's Charge." See also GETTYSBURG, BATTLE OF.

PICKING, HENRY FORRY, naval officer, was born in Somerset County, January, 1840. After his graduation from the United States Naval Academy, in 1861, he became a member of the North Atlantic Blockading Squadron. He took part in the sinking of the Confederate ship, Petrel, in the engagement between the Monitor and Merrimac, and with the East Gulf and South Atlantic Blockading Squadron. In 1862, he was raised to rank of lieutenant and in 1865 was put in command of the Nahant. In 1898, he became rear-admiral and died September 8, 1899, while in command of the navy yard at Charlestown.

PIER, ARTHUR STANWOOD, novelist, was born at Pittsburgh, April 21, 1874. In 1895, he was graduated from Harvard and in the following year became an assistant editor of the Youth's Companion. He has written: "The Pedagogues," "The Sentimentalists," "The Triumph," "Boys of Saint Timothy's," "The Ancient Grudge," "Harding of St. Timothy's," "The Young in Heart," "The New Boy," "The Crashaw Brothers," "The Jester of Saint Timothy's," "The Story of Harvard," "The Women We Marry," "Grannis of the Fifth," "The Plattsburgers," "Jerry," "The Son Decides," "Dormitory Days," "The Hilltop Troop," "David Ives," "Confident Morning," "Friends and Rivals," "The Coach," "The Captain," and "The Rigor of the Game." His home is in Concord, N. H.

PIKE COUNTY, was formed March 26, 1814, from part of Wayne. Named for General Zebulon Montgomery Pike. Land area, 544 square miles; population (1930), 7,483. County-seat, Milford, laid out in 1800.

PILMOOR, JOSEPH, clergyman, was born at Tadmouth, England, October 31, 1739. He attended John Wesley's School, at Kingswood, and in 1765 became a minister in the Methodist Church. He came to America, in 1769, where he introduced Methodism and founded the first Methodist Church in Philadelphia. He returned to England, in 1774, because he considered Wesley unjust for having omitted him from the "legal hundred." Upon his return to America, in 1785, he was ordained to the ministry of the Episcopal Church, and from 1804 to 1824 was rector of Saint Paul's, Philadelphia. He died July 24, 1825.

PINCHOT, GIFFORD, governor, was born in Simsbury, Conn., August 11, 1865. He was graduated from Yale University with the A. B. degree in 1889, and afterwards studied forestry in France, Germany, Switzerland and Austria. In January, 1892, he began the first systematic forest work in the United States at Biltmore, N. C. He has since served on many forestry commissions becoming president of the National Conservatism Association, in 1910;

professor of forestry at Yale, in 1903; forester and chief of division of forestry, U. S. Department of Agriculture, 1898-1910; and commissioner of forestry of Pennsylvania, 1920-1923. In 1923-1927, he was governor of Pennsylvania instituting a regime of strict economy, and reorganizing the departments. In 1930, he was elected to serve a second term. He is a member of many local and foreign scientific societies, and the author of: "The White Pine" (with H. S. Graves); "The Adirondack Spruce"; "A Primer of Forestry"; and "The Fight for Conservatism," etc.

PINE CREEK—Tributary to West Branch Susquehanna River. Sub-basin: Middle West Branch Susquehanna; source, formed by junction of Cushing Creek and Genesee Fork at West Pike, Pike Township, eastern central Potter County; course, easterly into Tioga County to junction of Marsh Creek; mouth, southwest of Jersey Shore; length, seventy-two miles. Indian name, Cuwenhanne, "pine stream."

PINE CREEK—Tributary to Allegheny River. Sub-basin: Lower Allegheny; source, in Marshall Township, northwestern Allegheny County; course, southeasterly to Allegheny River; mouth, at Etna; length, twenty-three miles. Indian name, Cuwenhanne, "pine stream."

PINE CREEK—Tributary to Mahantango Creek. Sub-basin: Middle Main Susquehanna; source, in Hegins Township, western Schuylkill County; course, westerly into Dauphin County; mouth, at Klingerstown; length, twenty and one-half miles. Indian name, Cuwenhanne, "pine stream."

PINEY CREEK—Tributary to Clarion River. Sub-basin: Middle Allegheny; source, in Limestone Township, eastern Clarion County; course, westerly to Clarion River; mouth, at Piney; length, twenty and one-half miles.

PIPE, CAPTAIN, chief of the Wolf Clan of Delawares, represented his tribe at the treaty of alliance with the Delawares, held by order of Congress, at Fort Pitt, in September, 1778. His defense of the Moravian missionaries on trial at Detroit in November, 1781, on charges of rendering assistance to the Americans, resulted in their acquittal. Captain Pipe ordered that Col. William Crawford be burned at the stake, and the torture was performed on June 11, 1782, in the valley of Tymoochee Creek, about five miles west of the present town of Upper Sandusky, Ohio. On July 4, 1783, the chief accompanied Major Ephraim Douglass, of Pittsburgh, to Detroit for the purpose of treating with all the Indian chiefs and the British commander.

PISQUETOMEN, a Delaware chief, brother of King Beaver and Shingas. In July, 1758, he accompanied the Moravian missionary, Christian Frederick Post, on a peace mission to the Indians on the Ohio.

PITCAIRN, borough in Allegheny County, fifteen miles east of Pittsburgh. Its industries are coal mining, railroad shops and yards, foundries, machine shops and electrical supply works. Population (1930), 6,317; (1920), 5,738.

PITCHER, MOLLY, heroine, who at the Battle of Monmouth, after her husband had been wounded, took his place behind the cannon. On the following morning General Greene presented her to Washington, who commissioned her sergeant and had her name placed upon a list of half-pay officers for life. She died at Carlisle, January 22, 1832, and was buried in the cemetery there, with military honors. On July 4, 1876, the citizens of Cumberland County erected a monument to her memory.

PITTSBURGH, second largest city of Pennsylvania and county-seat of Allegheny County, is located at the point where the Monongahela and Allegheny Rivers unite to form the Ohio. Here, in 1754, Captain Contrecoeur, a French officer, erected a fort, which he called Duquesne, after the governor of Canada, the Marquis Du Quesne de Menneville. Being unequal to meet Gen. Forbes, the French, on November 24, 1758, destroyed their stores at Fort Duquesne, burned the structure and evacuated. During the winter of 1758-1759, the first Fort Pitt was erected on the site of the French fort. In 1758, the settlement which included traders who lived under the protection of the fort, was first called Pittsburgh. By order of the proprietors of the province the "Manor of Pittsburgh," containing 5,766 acres, was surveyed in 1769. On April 22, 1794, Pittsburgh was incorporated as a borough and on March 8, 1816, was chartered as a city. In 1787, the Pittsburgh Academy which eventually became the University of Pittsburgh was incorporated. The Carnegie Institute of Technology, named for its founder, Andrew Carnegie, was opened in 1905. These are the leading educational institutions of Pittsburgh, today. Because of its location in the heart of the largest and most productive coal field in America, Pittsburgh and vicinity produces ten per cent of all the bituminous coal mined in the world, and one-half of all the coke manufactured in the United States. The city is located in one of the largest fields of natural gas in the world and lies in the center of great and productive oil fields. Leading manufactures are: pig-iron, steel, aluminum, bronze, brassware, copper, tin-plate, white lead, plate glass, window glass, etc. The Heintz Company, the largest of its kind, preserves and manufactures numerous food products. Meat packing, salt manufactures, oil refining, gasoline and fire-brick manufacture are important industries. The Westinghouse Electrical Company is internationally known. Population (1930), 669,817; (1920), 588,343.

PITTSBURGH POST-GAZETTE, which appears every morning except Sunday, was established by adherents to the Federalist Party, John Scull and Joseph Hall, as the *Pittsburgh Gazette*, July 29, 1786. It is Independent-Repub-

POST-OFFICE AT PITTSBURGH

lican in politics, and is edited by Oliver J. Keller, and published by the Post-Gazette Publishing Company. Circulation, 238,569.

PITTSBURGH, UNIVERSITY OF, a co-educational institution, at Pittsburgh. In 1787, the Pittsburgh Academy, the second institution of learning, west of the Allegheny Mountains, was chartered. By the Pennsylvania Constitution of 1790 provision was made for institutions of learning and the College of Philadelphia, in 1791, was rechartered as the University of Pennsylvania. In 1819, in order to provide proper educational facilities in the western part of the state, Pittsburgh Academy was rechartered as the Western University of Pennsylvania. In 1908, the name was changed to the University of Pittsburgh. Since 1895, all departments of the University have been open to women. The schools and departments of the University are: the college, school of economics, school of education, school of engineering, school of mines, school of chemistry, Mellon Institute, graduate school, observatory, school of medicine, school of law, school of dentistry, school of pharmacy, university extension department, department of physical education, department of health, department of military science and tactics. Enrollment (1930–1931), 13,670.

PITTSBURGH-AFRICAN EDUCATION SOCIETY, was organized at a meeting of the colored people of Pittsburgh and vicinity, January 16, 1832. The preamble adopted was in part: ". . . . . We . . . the people of colour, of the city and vicinity of Pittsburgh, and state of Pennsylvania, for the purpose of dispersing the moral gloom, that has long hung around us; have, under Almighty God, associated ourselves together, which association shall be known by the name of the Pittsburgh-African Education Society."

PITTSTON, city in Luzerne County, located in the Wyoming Valley, nine miles northwest of Wilkes-Barre. The city which was named for William Pitt, was laid out in 1768, incorporated as a borough in 1853 and chartered as a city in 1894. Due to its location in the center of an anthracite coal region, the chief industry is the mining of coal. Other industries are the manufacture of knit goods, stoves and engines, silk, underwear, etc. There are also foundries, machine shops, car shops, steel range works, etc. Population (1930), 18,246; (1920), 18,497.

PLYMOUTH, borough in Luzerne County, on the Susquehanna River, four miles west of Wilkes-Barre. It was settled in 1768 and was claimed by both Pennsylvania and Connecticut during the difficulties of those states regarding boundaries in 1799. The town is located in an anthracite coal region. The industries are the mining and shipping of coal, and the manufacture of drills, mining machinery and hosiery. Population (1930), 16,543; (1920), 16,500.

POE, EDGAR ALLAN, lived in Philadelphia when he was editor of Graham's Magazine, in which "The Murder of the Rue Morgue" was published. In November, 1849, in a magazine edited by John Sartain, of Philadelphia, appeared Poe's poem, "The Bells."

POHOPOCO CREEK (OR BIG CREEK)—Tributary to Lehigh River. Subbasin: Middle Delaware; source, in Chestnut Hill Township, southwestern Monroe County; course, southwesterly into Carbon County to Lehigh River; mouth, at Parryville; length, twenty-three miles. Indian name, a corruption of Pochpochka, or Buchkabuchka, "two mountains bearing down on each other," or "rock beside rock."

POLITICAL PARTIES IN PENNSYLVANIA—AMERICAN PARTY. One of three political parties in the United States to bear this name. It was organized at a Philadelphia Convention in September 1887 The platform adopted by this party consisted of the following: 14 years, residence in the United States before naturalization; exclusion of anarchists, socialists, etc.; free schools; building of strong navy, coast fortifications; internal improvements; prohibition of alien proprietorship; permanent separation of church and state; adherence to and enforcement of the Monroe Doctrine.

POLITICAL PARTIES IN PENNSYLVANIA—ANTI-CONSTITUTIONALISTS, a political group made up of elements opposed to the extremely Democratic Constitution of 1776. Among them were representatives of the Old Proprietary Party, the Quakers and moderate conservatives like Dickinson, Morris and Thomas Mifflin. Further difficulties arose as the result of the Act of Assembly, requiring every one to take an oath or affirmation of allegiance to the New Constitution and against the authority of George III. The German sectarians opposed this as did also the Quakers. The former were required after 1727 to take an oath of allegiance or affirmation of allegiance to the King of Great Britain, on their arrival in Pennsylvania and they could not take a contradictory oath. The forces opposed to the Constitution of 1776 finally triumphed and in 1790 a new constitution was framed in which the governor was given much power. The anti-constitutionalists became for the most part Federalists when the national government was organized and they were therefore favorable to the adoption of the constitution framed in Philadelphia in 1787.

POLITICAL PARTIES IN PENNSYLVANIA—ANTI-FEDERALISTS, a political party that succeeded the Constitutionalists (q. v.) and fought against the adoption of the constitution of the United States. It was made up largely of radicals who had supported the constitution of 1776. The bicameral legislative body provided by the national constitution seemed a rebuke to the Pennsylvania radicals whose constitution provided for a single chambered legislative body. The Federalists residing in Philadelphia and the southeastern counties were anxious to end the period of disorder and anarchy, and George Clymer offered a resolution calling for a convention in November. The Anti-Federalists could muster only nineteen negative votes against forty-three. Thereupon the nineteen resolved to break a quorum by absenting themselves, leaving the Federalists two short of a quorum. A crowd, however, forced two of the Anti-Federalists into the assembly and to remain until the vote was taken. The Anti-Federalists then engaged in a pamphleteer war to elect delegates, but the friends of the constitution won, Philadelphia electing James Wilson, Federalist, against David Rittenhouse, by a ten to one vote. On the other hand the Anti-Federalists carried the western counties. When the convention met, the vote for ratification on December 12th was forty-six to twenty-three. With the election of Mifflin to the governorship in 1790 a new alignment of parties took place, and Mifflin was supported by many elements hitherto composing the Anti-Federalist Party, but now becoming known as the Democratic Republican Party

POLITICAL PARTIES IN PENNSYLVANIA—CONSTITUTIONALISTS, a political party made up of the more radical and extremely Democratic leaders of the Revolutionary movement in Pennsylvania who succeeded in framing the constitution of 1776. Among their number were George Ryan, Timothy Matlack, and Thomas Paine. They attacked the college which was controlled by conservatives and in 1779 the charter was annulled and the University of the State of Pennsylvania was incorporated. They became divided at the close of the war and were defeated in the Pennsylvania Constitutional Convention of 1789 which framed the constitution of 1790. As Anti-Federalists they opposed unsuccessfully the Federal constitution.

POLITICAL PARTIES IN PENNSYLVANIA—CONSTITUTIONAL REPUBLICANS, a party opposed to the election of Simon Snyder as governor in 1805; also called the Quids (q. v.).

POLITICAL PARTIES—DEMOCRATIC PARTY (a) In national affairs., In his "Administration of Thomas Jefferson," Henry Adams says that in the issue of 1800 the Democratic Party could have better spared all the other states than to have lost Pennsylvania. The only true Democratic community then existing in the eastern states, Pennsylvania was neither picturesque nor troublesome. From the election of Jefferson, in 1800, to the election of Lincoln, in 1860, it was a common statement that "As Pennsylvania goes so goes the Union". Albert Gallatin, as Secretary of the Treasury, and diplomat during the administrations of Jefferson and Madison, was the most influential member of his party from Pennsylvania. He was succeeded in the Treasury department by Alexander James Dallas, who had been Secretary of the Commonwealth under Governor Mifflin. Later, James Buchanan became Secretary of State serving during the Mexican War, during which time George Mifflin Dallas was Vice-President. Buchanan served as President from 1857 to 1861 and named Jeremiah

S. Black, Attorney-General and later Secretary of State. During the closing months of his administration, Edwin M. Stanton was Secretary of War. Pennsylvania gave its vote to Democratic candidates for the Presidency as follows: Jefferson, in 1796, 1800, and 1804; Madison, in 1808, and 1812; Monroe, in 1816, and 1820; Jackson, in 1824, 1828, and 1832; Van Buren, in 1836; Polk, in 1844; Pierce, in 1852; and Buchanan, in 1856. From 1856 to 1928, the Democratic Party has been in a minority in Presidential elections in Pennsylvania. However, the party was influential in national politics, having furnished Samuel J. Randall as Speaker of the House of Representatives and General Winfield Scott Hancock as its candidate for President, in 1880. William F. Harrity was chairman of the Democratic National Committee in the campaign which resulted in the election of Cleveland, in 1892. During the Wilson administration, A. Mitchell Palmer was Attorney-General; William B. Wilson was Secretary of Labor, and Vance C. McCormick was chairman of the national committee in the campaign of 1916.

DEMOCRATIC PARTY (b) In state affairs. Although dominant in state affairs from 1800 to 1860, it was less powerful relatively than in national affairs. Nevertheless, the following candidates of the Democratic Party were successful in gubernatorial elections: Mifflin, McKean, Snyder, Findlay, Schulze, Wolf, Porter, Shunk, Bigler, and Packer, and later Robert E. Pattison, in 1882, and again in 1890.

POLITICAL PARTIES IN PENNSYLVANIA—FEDERALISTS. The Federalist Party in Pennsylvania began with a successful attempt to ratify the Federal Constitution and had among its leaders such able men as James Wilson and Robert Morris, followed later by Timothy Pickering. It was made up largely of eastern conservatives and supported the Federalist in national affairs in the early days of the Washington administration. All Pennsylvania's electoral votes were cast for Washington for president and Frederick A. Muhlenberg, a Federalist, was elected the first speaker of the National House of Representatives. In the election for governor in 1790, however, General Arthur St. Clair, who had been indorsed by Robert Morris, Dr. Benjamin Rush, Frederick A. Muhlenberg and James Wilson, was defeated, receiving only 2,802 votes against 27,725 for Mifflin. In 1793 and 1796, Muhlenberg was defeated by Mifflin and in a bitter contest in 1799, James Ross, Federalist, was defeated by Thomas McKean. In 1802, the Federalist forces made a poor showing against McKean and in 1805 they were practically eliminated from the contest, McKean having been supported by the Quids (q. v.) and Simon Snyder by the Democratic Party (q. v.). In 1808, the Federalist James Ross carried only six counties: Delaware, Chester, Bucks, Lancaster, Luzerne and Adams, and in 1811, Tilghman, Federalist, received less than four thousand votes. In 1814, Isaac Wayne, Federalist, received a large vote but could not overcome Snyder's popularity. In 1817, Joseph Heister, Federalist, was defeated by William Findley, Democrat, but in the election three years later, he won over Findley by a plurality of 1,605. A cause for this victory was the charge made against the governors for the misuse of patronage, for under the constitution of 1790 the governor appointed all the county officials. The last serious contest of the Federalist Party in state affairs took place in 1823 when Andrew Gregg was defeated by J. Andrew Shulze in a bitter campaign. The Federalist Party had become so unpopular that Gregg's supporters found it a liability to be identified with that party, and from this time on no Federalist Party existed in Pennsylvania, and in 1826 only 1,175 votes were cast for John Sergeant, candidate of the Federalist Party. During the period from 1790 to 1826 the Federalists succeeded in electing Robert Morris to the United States Senate, his colleague being William MacClay, the well known Democrat. In national elections the popular vote was uniformly cast against the Federalist candidates: Adams, in 1796; Pinckney, in 1804 and 1808; DeWitt Clinton, in 1812; and King, in 1816, having been defeated by the Democratic-Republican opposition. In 1800, the General Assembly having failed to provide for the election of electors, the General Assembly, as the result of a compromise on the method of election selected seven Adams electors and eight supporters of Jefferson.

LIBERTY PARTY, a political party, which originated in 1840, an outgrowth of abolition organizations. All strong advocates of the abolition of African slavery, regardless of political creed, were admitted to membership. The party opposed the annexation of Texas, believing it to be a plan of slave holders to extend their power; refused to vote for Polk for the presidency of the United States because he favored the annexation; refused to vote for Clay because he was a slave holder, so nominated James G. Birney for the office. Birney received a large number of votes. The party was merged into the Free-Soil Party in 1848 and supported Van Buren for the presidency.

NATIVE AMERICAN PARTY, THE, was organized in Philadelphia. The first meeting was held in Germantown, in 1837, when a preamble and constitution were adopted. The party incurred the enmity of non-members classed as foreigners, and riots in the neighborhood in which meetings were held, frequently resulted.

POLITICAL PARTIES IN PENNSYLVANIA—THE QUIDS, a political party, or more properly a faction, calling themselves the Tertium Quids, who were alarmed at the prospect of the election of Simon Snyder as governor in 1805. The movement was led by Alexander James Dallas, Governor Mifflin's Secretary of the Commonwealth, and supported by the Muhlenbergs and a majority of Federalists. Their cause was supported by those opposed to a revision of the constitution of 1790. McKean defeated Snyder by about five thousand majority. By 1808 the Quids had disappeared and Snyder defeated the Federalist, Ross, by twenty-eight thousand majority.

POLITICAL PARTIES—REPUBLICAN PARTY (a) In National Affairs. A preliminary Republican Convention was held at Pittsburgh, on Washington's Birthday, February 22, 1856, on the call of the chairmen of the Republican State committees of Maine, Vermont, Massachusetts, New York, Pennsylvania, Ohio, Indiana, Michigan, and Wisconsin. Twenty-three states were represented. A lengthy address, "to the people of the United States," written by Lieutenant-Governor Henry J. Raymond, of New York, was adopted. In this address "ardent and unshaken attachment to the Union of the American states was declared, and it was decided to call a national convention for the nomination of candidates for President and Vice-President of the United States to meet in Philadelphia, June 17th, the anniversary of the Battle of Bunker Hill. The convention met at the time and place designated. All the northern states were represented and also Maryland, Delaware, Virginia, Kentucky, the Territories of Minnesota, Nebraska, and Kansas and the District of Columbia. General John C. Fremont was nominated, notwithstanding strong objection on the ground that he could not carry Pennsylvania. In the election that November, the Republicans were defeated by a substantial majority by the Democratic candidate, James Buchanan. In the Republican National Convention which nominated Lincoln, in 1860, and in the election of that year Pennsylvania Republicans were very influential. David Wilmot was temporary chairman of the convention, and Senator Cameron had the endorsement for the presidency by the state convention. The Pennsylvania leaders, convinced that Seward could not carry the state, threw their support to Lincoln after the first ballot. The election of Andrew G. Curtin as Governor in October foreshadowed Lincoln's election in November and during this campaign the advocacy of a protective tariff by Pennsylvania Republicans was a decisive factor. Influential Republicans of this period in Pennsylvania were: Senator Cameron, who became Secretary of War; Governor Curtin; Alexander K. McClure, who was chairman of the state committee and Thaddeus Stevens, who became the leader of the Republican Party in the House of Representatives, a position which he held until the time of his death. From the election of 1860, Republican presidential electors have been successful with the single exception of the campaign of 1912, in which Roosevelt carried the state as Progressive candidate, running on the Progressive, Roosevelt Progressive, Washington and Bull Moose Parties. In the campaign of 1884, B. F. Jones, of Pittsburgh, was chairman of the National Committee and in 1888 the campaign was managed by Senator Quay. Among the influential national and state leaders were successively Simon Cameron, J. Donald Cameron, Matthew Stanley Quay, and Boise Penrose, State Senators. Galusha A. Grow was Speaker of the House of Representatives, 1861-1863; while J. Donald Cameron was Secretary of War under President Grant; Wayne MacVeagh, Attorney-General under President Garfield; B. Harris Brewster, Attorney-General under President Arthur; and Philander C. Knox, Attorney-General under President McKinley, and Secretary of State under President Taft; John Wanamaker was Post Master General under President Harrison, and

Charles Emory Smith under President McKinley. Adolph E. Borie was Secretary of the Navy, in 1869; James J. Davis, Secretary of Labor under Presidents Harding, Coolidge and Hoover, while Andrew Mellon has been Secretary of the Treasury from 1921 to date.

REPUBLICAN PARTY (b) In state affairs. The Republican Party has been successful in elections for governor since Curtin's election in October, 1860, with the exception of 1882, when Pattison, Democrat, defeated Beaver, Republican, and in 1890, when Pattison defeated Delamater, Republican. Earlier victories were won by narrow margins. Curtin in 1863 defeated Woodward by less than 16,000 and in 1869, Geary defeated Asa Packer by less than 15,000. In 1910, the Keystone Party nominated William H. Berry who was defeated by John K. Tener by a plurality slightly over 33,000. From these narrow margins Republican majorities ranged upward to the high water mark reached in 1926, when John S. Fisher defeated Eugene C. Bonniwell by a plurality of 737,543. In 1906, the Republican candidate for State Treasurer was defeated by William H. Berry, Democrat. In the Lieutenant-Governorship the only defeat suffered by the Republicans was in 1882, when Chauncey Forward Black, Democrat, was elected.

POLITICAL PARTIES—WHIG PARTY—The Whig Party was represented by many able men including the eminent lawyers, Binney and Sergeant, of Philadelphia; Thaddeus Stevens, of Adams, and later of Lancaster Counties, but was a minority party succeeding only when the opposition was divided or under unusual circumstances when it effected a combination with the Anti-Masonic Party. In 1835, Ritner defeated Wolf, Independent Democrat, and Muhlenberg, regular Democrat. In 1848, William F. Johnston, Whig, defeated Morris Longstreth, Democrat, by a plurality of 297 votes; in 1854, by combining with the American or Know Nothing Party, James Pollock defeated William Bigler for reelection by a plurality of 36,831. In the presidential vote, Pennsylvania gave Harrison a plurality of 334 votes over Van Buren, in 1840; and in 1848 gave General Taylor a plurality of 13,537.

POLLOCK, JAMES, governor, was born in Milton, Northumberland County, September 11, 1810. He attended the Milton Classical Academy and the College of New Jersey (Princeton), where he graduated in 1831. Afterwards he studied law in the office of Samuel Hepburn, in Milton, and was admitted to the bar in 1833. In the following year he entered upon the practice of his profession in his native town and in 1835 was appointed District Attorney of Northumberland County, which office he held for three years. In 1844, he was elected a member of Congress serving in this position for six years. He was appointed president-judge of the eighth judicial district, in 1850, and held this office until the amendment to the Constitution required the election of judges by the people. He was elected governor of Pennsylvania, in 1854. During his administration a policy was introduced by which the reduction of the public debt was begun. The main line of public works (Portage Railroad) was sold to the Pennsylvania Central Railroad for $7,500,000 and the money applied to the payment of the state's debt. Through the acts passed during Pollock's term of office the efficient development of the public school system was assured. In 1860, he represented Pennsylvania at the Peace Conference at Washington. As director of the Mint of Philadelphia, to which position he was appointed by President Lincoln, in 1861, he was responsible for having the motto: "In God We Trust," placed upon the coins. He was reappointed to the office during the administration of President Grant. His death occurred in Lock Haven, April 19, 1890.

POLOCK, MOSES, publisher and bookseller, was born in Philadelphia, May 14, 1817. At the age of fourteen, he entered the book business, published many books of fiction, drama, etc., and dealt in old and rare books. He possessed an excellent collection of books published by Benjamin Franklin and was greatly interested in the history of Pennsylvania. He died in Philadelphia, August 16, 1903.

PONTIAC'S WAR, a Colonial war, took place in 1763-1764. Pontiac, chief of the Ottawas, pretending to be friendly to the English, after their victories, was actually plotting against them with the Algonquins, Wyandots, Senecas and other tribes. Major Gladwin, commander at Detroit, hearing of Pontiac's plans to attack western forts in the spring of 1763, made due preparations, so that upon the arrival of Pontiac and sixty chiefs on May 6th, the post was well fortified. Fort Pitt, under Captain Ecuyder, was also prepared for the attack, so that at both places the Indians were repulsed. Colonel Bouquet and his men on their way to aid Fort Pitt, drove back an Indian attack at Bushy Run, twenty-five miles east of the fort. On June 17, 1763, the Indians took Fort Presqu' Isle, on the site of the present city of Erie, and on the following day Forts Le Boeuf, Erie County; Venango, Venango County. The war ended after a treaty held by Sir William Johnson and Bradstreet with two thousand representatives of the Ottawas, Ojibways, Iroquois and Wyandots at Fort Niagara.

POOR RICHARD'S ALMANAC, an almanac published in Philadelphia by Benjamin Franklin from 1732 to 1757. The maxims which it contained are still widely quoted.

PORT CARBON, borough in Schuylkill County, on the Schuylkill River, about two miles northeast of Pottsville. Coal mining is the leading industry.

PORTAGE, borough of Cambria County, six miles southeast of Ebensburg. The chief industry is coal mining.

PORTAGE RAILROAD, a section of the rail-water route from Philadelphia to Pittsburgh, was opened March 18, 1834. The entire line known as the main line of Public Works consisted of a double track railroad from Philadelphia to Columbia, a distance of eighty-one miles; the Eastern and Juniata divisions of the Pennsylvania Canal, from Columbia to Hollidaysburg, 173 miles; the double track Allegheny Portage Railroad from Hollidaysburg to Johnstown, 36 miles, and the western division of the Pennsylvania Canal, from Johnstown to Pittsburgh, 105 miles. Of the 395 miles which this route covered, 117 were by rail and 278 by canal. The Portage Railroad extending from Hollidaysburg to Johnstown, had at the point where it crossed the mountains, five levels and five inclined planes on both slopes, with a level, about $1\frac{1}{2}$ miles long, on the crest of the slope. On the levels the cars were drawn by horses and locomotives. They were drawn up and lowered down the planes by cables operated by stationary engines. Two pieces of engineering skill were performed in order that the route might be established. The Staple Bend Tunnel, at West Portal, four miles east of Johnstown, is one of these. This tunnel, the first railroad tunnel in America, is still standing. The Conemaugh Viaduct, which at the time of its erection was considered the most perfectly constructed arch in the United States, crossed the Conemaugh River, at Horseshoe Bend, about eight miles east of Johnstown. It was destroyed on May 31, 1889, during the Johnstown flood. Passengers were transported from Philadelphia to Pittsburgh by train and canal boat in three and a half days and freight in five or six days. The main line of Public Works operated for twenty-three years, and ultimately failed. Never was it self-supporting. On June 15, 1857, the entire Main Line of Public Works was sold at public auction to the Pennsylvania Railroad Company who operated it for three months, and closed it November 1, 1857, for the purpose of dismantling it.

PORTER, CHARLOTTE, author, was born in Towanda, about 1853. She graduated from Wells College, in 1875; in 1886-1888, edited "Shakespeareana," and in 1888 edited the "Ethical Record." Later she became editor of "Poet Lore" which she and Helen A. Clarke founded. With Helen Clarke she edited "Poems of Robert Browning"; "The Ring and the Book"; "Clever Tales"; "Robert Browning's Complete Poetical Works" (12 vols.); "Mrs. Browning's Complete Works" (6 vols.); and "Poet's Parleys." She is the author of "Browning's Study Programmes"; "Maeterlinck's Monna Vanna"; "Shakespeare Studies—Macbeth"; "The Tragedies"; "The Comedies"; "The Histories"; "Poetic Translation of D'Annunzio's Daughter of Jorio"; "Lips of Music" (poems); "Revels of Father Christmas and the Bishop," etc.

PORTER, DAVID DIXON, naval officer, was born at Chester, June 8, 1813, the son of David Porter. At the age of thirteen, he joined the Mexican Navy as midshipman and while serving on a ship engaged in destroying Spanish commerce was captured and held prisoner at Havana. After he was released he entered the service of the United States Navy as midshipman. During the

Mexican War he served as lieutenant and later as commander of the Spitfire. He served with distinction throughout the Civil War. By his bombardment of the Confederate Forts Jackson and Saint Philip, on April 18-24, 1862, Farragut's fleet was able to pass them and capture New Orleans and the forts were finally forced to surrender. He later bombarded the fort at Vicksburg and enabled the fleet to pass. As acting rear-admiral of the Mississippi Squadron he assisted Sherman in capturing Arkansas Post, and later aided General Grant in the siege of Vicksburg, for which he received the commission as rear-admiral and the thanks of Congress. In 1864, he commanded the North Atlantic Blockading Squadron and with Gen. A. H. Terry, captured Fort Fisher, January 15, 1865. In 1865-1869, he was superintendent of the United States Naval Academy. He became vice-admiral in 1866 and admiral in 1870. His writings include: "Life of Commodore David Porter"; a romance, "Allan Dare and Robert le Diable"; "Incidents and Anecdotes of the Civil War"; "History of the Navy in the War of the Rebellion," etc. He died February 13, 1891.

PORTER, DAVID RITTENHOUSE, governor was born near Norristown, October 31, 1788. He was educated at Princeton and became assistant to his father, upon the latter's appointment as surveyor-general. At the same time he studied law. His health failing he abandoned plans for entering the legal profession and engaged in iron manufacture in Huntingdon County. For a time he was employed in a clerical capacity but eventually entered into partnership with Edward Patton, in which because of the depression superinduced by the approaching War of 1812, he was not successful. In 1819, he was elected to the House of Representatives from Huntingdon County and was returned the following year. Afterwards, he served several county offices and in 1836 was elected to the state senate. In 1838, he was elected governor of the state and in 1841 was reelected. Porter was especially interested in the development of canals and railroads and in the success of the public school system. He died August 6, 1868.

PORTER, HORACE, diplomat, was born at Huntingdon, April 15, 1837. After graduating from West Point, in 1860, he was an instructor there, but at the outbreak of the Civil War served in the Department of the East. Later he was transferred to the Army of the Ohio and still later to the Army of the Cumberland. He took part in the battles at Chattanooga, Chickamauga, the Wilderness and New Market Heights. As aide-de-camp to Gen. Grant, he was present at the surrender at Appomattox Court House. He was brevetted brigadier-general for his services during the war. When Grant was Secretary of War, in 1867, Porter was his assistant, and upon the election of Grant to the presidency of the United States, Porter became his private secretary. He resigned from the army in 1873. In 1897, President McKinley appointed him United States Ambassador to France which position he held until 1905. He discovered the burial place of John Paul Jones, recovered the body and sent it to the United States for burial at Annapolis. He wrote: "West Point Life" and "Campaigning with Grant." He died in New York, May 28, 1921.

PORTER, THOMAS CONRAD, botanist, was born at Alexandria, in 1822. He graduated from Lafayette College, in 1840, and from Princeton Theological Seminary in 1843. For five years he was engaged in the ministry. Afterwards he was professor of natural science at Marshall College (now Franklin and Marshall), and in 1866 became professor of botany at Lafayette College. In 1897, he resigned the position to become curator of the botanical collection of the college and dean of the Pardee School. He wrote: "Sketch of the Flora of Pennsylvania"; "Sketch of the Botany of the United States"; "Synoptical Flora of Colorado" (with J. M. Coulter); "The Carices of Pennsylvania"; and "The Grasses of Pennsylvania." He died in 1901.

POSTAL SERVICE—See MAIL SERVICE.

POT HOLE, a large hole cut in hard sandstone rock was discovered at Archbald, Lackawanna County, in 1884, during mining operations. This geologic formation, filled with water and smoothly ground stones, is probably a result of the glacial period. According to this theory as the glacier moved, crevices formed, and the heat of the sun melted the surface of the ice, causing the water to fall through the crevices from a great height forming a whirlpool at the bottom and cutting through the hard sandstone rock until a whirling mass of stone cut through the solid strata to the bottom of the vein of coal. The pot hole at Archbald is approximately twenty-five feet in diameter and forty-five feet in depth, and is the largest in the world.

POTTER, ALONZO, Protestant Episcopal bishop, was born in Beekman, N. Y., July 6, 1800. In 1824, he was ordained to the ministry of the Episcopal Church. He was consecrated bishop of Pennsylvania, September 23, 1845, and through his plans for church extension the Episcopal Hospital and Philadelphia Divinity School were established. He died in San Francisco, Calif., July 4, 1865.

POTTER COUNTY, formed March 26, 1804, was formed from part of Lycoming. Named for General James Potter. Land area, 1,071 square miles; population (1930), 17,489. County-seat, Coudersport, laid out in 1807.

POTTSTOWN, borough of Montgomery County, on the Schuylkill River, forty miles northwest of Philadelphia. The town was laid out in 1752 and was originally called Pottsgrove for its founder John Potts. In 1815, it was incorporated as a borough and the name changed to Pottstown. The manufactories include rolling mills, blast furnaces, steel mills, boiler works, bridge works, nail factories, agricultural implement factories, cigar factories, planing mills, etc.

The Hill School, a non-sectarian, secondary school for boys, is located in the borough. Population (1930), 19,430; (1920), 17,431.

POTTSVILLE, borough and county-seat of Schuylkill County, on the Schuylkill River, ninety-five miles northwest of Philadelphia. The town was laid out in 1800, incorporated as a borough in 1828 and was made the county-seat in 1851. Because of its location in the midst of anthracite coal fields it has become an important coal mining and shipping center. Other industries are: steel mills, blast furnaces, rolling mills, foundries, planing mills, cotton-velvet and silk mills. Population (1930), 24,300; (1920), 21,876.

POWDERLY, TERENCE VINCENT, labor leader and lawyer, was born at Carbondale, January 22, 1849. In 1862, after attending the public schools, he became a railroad switch-tender and in 1866 went to Scranton where he worked as a machinist until 1877. In that year he was elected mayor of Scranton on the labor ticket and was reelected in 1880 and 1882. In 1893, he began to study law and was admitted to the Lackawanna County Bar in 1894 and to the bar of the Supreme Court of the United States in 1901. In 1892–1902, he was United States commissioner-general of immigration and in 1906 was special representative of the Department of Commerce and Labor to study causes of emigration from Europe. He became a chief in the Bureau of Immigration to distribute immigrants throughout the United States, in 1907. He is the author of: "Thirty Years of Labor, 1858-1889"; "History of Labor Day," etc.

POW-WOWING, the art of effecting a bodily cure by means of a charm, was practiced by the Indian medicine men, and it is with the Indian that the term "pow-wow" originated. The Pennsylvania-German still practices "pow-wowing" by using certain words as a ritual in the working of a charm or an incantation. These charms are valued highly and it was at one time believed that their secret could be transmitted only to a person of the opposite sex, but in 1820, Holman's "Brauch Bichly," a German book dealing with "pow-wowing," and teaching any one who owned the book, made its appearance. Pow-wow doctors still reside in urban and rural communities throughout Pennsylvania, particularly in the counties of York, Berks, Lancaster, Lebanon, Lehigh, and Northampton.

PRENDERGAST, EDMOND FRANCIS, Roman Catholic prelate, was born at Clonmel, Ireland, May 3, 1843. In 1859, he came to America, studied at the ecclesiastical Seminary Saint Charles Borromeo, Philadelphia, and in 1865 was ordained to the priesthood. He served as rector of Saint Paul's, Philadelphia, Susquehanna Depot, Saint Mark's, Bristol, at Allentown and Saint Malachy's, Philadelphia. He was consecrated auxiliary bishop of Philadelphia, in February, 1897, and in May, 1911, succeeded Dr. Ryan as archbishop. He died at Philadelphia, February, 1918.

PRESBYTERIAN CHURCH. The first Presbyterian Church in the United States was organized in Philadelphia in the beginning of the eighteenth century. By 1720 a Presbyterian Church known as Donegal Church was erected by Scotch-Irish settlers in Donegal Township, Lancaster County. The minister at Donegal was also in charge of congregations at Derry, Dauphin County, and at Paxtang, adjacent to Harrisburg. The Scotch-Irish settlers were driven to this country by both religious and economic oppression. With the accession of William and Mary to the English throne the Presbyterians began to emigrate to Scotland and northern Ireland. In 1718, many of these found their way to Pennsylvania. In 1706, the American Presbyterians united to form the Presbytery of Philadelphia, but because of increasing membership a larger body, the synod of Philadelphia was organized in 1716. In 1926, there were in Pennsylvania 370,394 members of the Presbyterian Church in the United States of America and 79,166 members of the United Presbyterian Church.

PRESTON, ANN, physician and educator, was born at West Grove, December 1, 1813. She graduated from the Woman's Medical College, Philadelphia, in 1852, and afterwards conducted a successful practice in Philadelphia. In 1854, she became professor of physiology and hygiene at the Woman's Medical College and in 1866 became dean of the college. She strongly advocated the rights of woman as a medical practitioner and wrote several articles on that subject. She died at Philadelphia, April 18, 1872.

PRESTON, MARGARET JUNKIN, author, was born at Milton, May 19, 1820, the daughter of George Junkin, the first president of Lafayette College. When her father became president of Washington College (now Washington and Lee University), at Lexington, Va., the family moved to that place. In 1857, Margaret Junkin married John T. L. Preston, a founder and member of the faculty of Virginia Military Institute. Her writing which is almost exclusively in verse, includes: "Beechenbrook," a Rhyme of the War; "Old Songs and New"; "For Love's Sake"; "A Handful of Monographs, Continental and English"; "Colonial Ballads, Sonnets and Other Verse"; "Chimes for Church Children"; "Aunt Dorothy"; "An Old Virginia Plantation Story," etc. She died in Baltimore, March 28, 1897.

PRESTON, WILLIAM CAMPBELL, legislator and educator, was born in Philadelphia, December 27, 1794. In 1812, he graduated from the South Carolina College, after which he studied law, was admitted to the bar and practiced in Columbia, S. C. He rapidly attained success in his profession and became known for his ability as an orator. In 1828 and in 1830-32, he was a member of the state legislature, where he advocated nullification. He was elected to the United States Senate, in 1833, but resigned in 1842 after refusing to aid Calhoun in the support of Van Buren. From 1845-1851, he was president of South Carolina College. He died at Columbia, S. C., May 22, 1860.

PRIESTLY, JOSEPH, clergyman, scientist and author, was born in Fieldhead, England, March 13, 1733, and became a minister in the Unitarian Church. Because of his sympathies with the French Revolution his church and home were destroyed by a mob and in 1794 he came to America. He settled in Northumberland where he continued his scientific research, begun in England, and made valuable discoveries. Because of his discovery of oxygen he ranks among the founders of modern chemistry. He died at Northumberland, in 1804.

PRIGG vs. PENNSYLVANIA. The question of returning fugitive slaves to their owners gave rise to serious difficulties between Maryland and Pennsylvania. The United States law of 1793 was of little effect. In 1822, the governor of Maryland transmitted to the Legislature of Pennsylvania a resolution of the Legislature of Maryland which declared that the encouragement given to runaways by the citizens of Delaware and Pennsylvania had become a serious matter with slave owners of that state. A committee of the Pennsylvania House admitted that it did not consider the laws adequate. In 1823, the Maryland authorities stated that Pennsylvania was being looked upon as a hostile commonwealth. Three years later a joint conference of legislative committees of Pennsylvania and Maryland was held and a bill was signed by Governor Shulze, of Pennsylvania, permitting a claimant to place an alleged runaway in the Pennsylvania jails awaiting trial. One provision of the law was designed to prevent kidnapping of negroes. In 1837, Edward Prigg and his associates, agents for a Maryland owner whose slave had escaped into Pennsylvania in 1832, took out a negress who was an alleged fugitive together with her children, one of whom had been born in Pennsylvania. They were indicted for kidnapping in the York County court and found guilty. The case finally reached the Supreme Court of the United States on Prigg's appeal and the Act of 1826 was declared unconstitutional. An important effect of this decision was that state magistrates were not bound to carry into effect the Law of 1793 and it became a dead letter. In this decision Chief Justice Taney and three associate judges dissented.

PRINTZ, JOHAN, Colonial governor, was born in Bottneryd, Sweden, about 1600. In 1641, he was made the third governor of the Swedish colony on the Delaware River. He came to America, in 1643, landing at Fort Christina, and during his residence here the settlement prospered. On Tinicum Island he built a rudely constructed mansion known as "Printz Hall." He built forts at Tinicum, and at Wilmington and New Castle, was influential with the Indians and protected his trade with them. In 1653, he returned to Sweden where he died in 1663.

PROTESTANT EPISCOPAL CHURCH. The first clergyman of the Church of England arrived in Pennsylvania, in 1685, three years after William Penn's first visit and in 1695 Christ Church, Philadelphia, the first in Pennsylvania, was organized. The Swedes who settled in the province, in 1636, built the first church, Lutheran in doctrine, and Episcopal in government, in 1646, but a few years after the establishment of the Episcopal Church, the Swedish Congregations joined it. The Rev. Evan Evans, the first missionary of the church to the province of Pennsylvania, arrived in 1700 and within two years, due to his efforts, five hundred Quakers joined the church. In 1742, there were fifteen Episcopal parishes in Pennsylvania; in 1752, nine clergy and twenty-seven parishes; immediately after the Revolution six clergy and fifteen parishes and in 1844 one hundred and nine parishes and one hundred and twenty-one clergy. There were 191,261 members of the Protestant Episcopal Church in Pennsylvania in 1926.

PROTHONOTARY, in Pennsylvania, the name given the clerk of the Orphan's Court.

PROUD, ROBERT, historian, was born near Yarm, Yorkshire, England, May 10, 1728. He came to America, in 1759, and settled in Pennsylvania, where he taught Latin and Greek in the Philadelphia Friends' Academy. He remained loyal to England during the Revolutionary War and during that period wrote his "History of Pennsylvania," published in two volumes, a valuable work because of the original material which it contains. He died in Philadelphia, July 7, 1813.

PUNXSUTAWNEY, borough in Jefferson County, on the Mahoning Creek, about ninety miles northeast of Pittsburgh, is located on the site of an Indian Village called Ponksutenink meaning, "sand fly place," the Indian word for sand fly being Ponkis. One of the earliest settlers of Punxsutawney was Dr. John Jenks who came there in 1818. The town was laid out in 1821 by Rev. David Barclay, and became a borough in 1849. Punxsutawney is the commercial center of a large bituminous coal and coke region, and of a large agricultural region. Its chief manufactures are iron and steel products, and glass. Population (1930), 9,266; (1920), 10,311.

PURVES, GEORGE TYBOUT, clergyman, was born in Philadelphia, September 27, 1852. He graduated from the University of Pennsylvania, in 1872, and from Princeton Theological Seminary, in 1876. In 1877–1880, he was pastor of the Presbyterian Church, at Wayne; in 1892-1900, he was professor of New Testament literature and exegesis at Princeton Theological Seminary; in 1900, he became pastor of Fifth Avenue Presbyterian Church, New York. Among his writings are: "The Testimony of Justin Martyr to Early Christianity," "The Apostolic Age," etc. He died in New York, September 24, 1901.

PUSEY, CALEB, Quaker colonist, was born in Berkshire, England, about 1650. In 1682, he came with Penn to America and built Chester Mills, the first mills in Pennsylvania. He served as sheriff of Chester County; as justice of the

GOVERNORS OF PENNSYLVANIA UNDER THE CONSTITUTION OF 1790
Thomas Mifflin
Thomas McKean   Simon Snyder
William Findlay

peace; as an associate justice of the supreme court, and as a member of the provincial assembly for ten years. He wrote: "A Serious and Seasonable Warning," "A Modest Account from Pennsylvania of the Principal Differences in Point of Doctrine between George Keith and Those of the People called Quakers," "Saturn's Harbingers Encountered," etc. He died in Chester County, February 25, 1727.

PUTZ. The Christmas Putz was a custom brought to Pennsylvania by the Moravians. One of the essential features of every Moravian household is the Christmas Putz, which in German means an embellishment or an ornament. It is generally a miniature representation of a beautiful scene in nature, some made on a grand scale, and smaller ones in abundance, every humble home having one. Christmas Eve is the time for showing them, and during the Christmas holidays the people make the rounds visiting them. This is a Moravian custom still carried on by many.

QUAKER BLUES, a military company organized in Philadelphia by young men of Quaker faith, prior to the Battle of Lexington. This light infantry company under Joseph Cowperthwait, competed with "the Greens" or the "silk stockings," under John Cadwalader, who afterwards became brigadier and commander of Pennsylvania militia.

QUAKERTOWN, borough in Bucks County, thirty-eight miles north of Philadelphia. It was early settled by Friends and was probably originally called Quaker's Town. The Friends erected the first school in the upper end of the county here, and in 1795 a public library was established. The town was incorporated in 1854. Chief among its industries are the manufacture of cigars, stoves and silk.

QUARRYING. The leading products procured in Pennsylvania by quarrying are: limestone, lime, cement rock, clay, fire brick, sand, gravel, sandstone, granite and slate. Limestone is found in the Chester, York, Lancaster, Lebanon, Lehigh and Cumberland Valleys and in the Allegheny Plateaus. In 1926, Pennsylvania's total production of limestone was 3,830,210 tons for concrete and roads and 8,694,810 tons for fluxing. Pennsylvania produces about one-eighth of the clay products of the United States. Clay is found principally in the coal regions. The state leads in the total production of sand, gravel and sandstone. These products are used for building, paving, curbing, etc. Their value in 1927 was $12,040,406; the total value of sandstone in that year was $2,625,730. Granite is found in the Piedmont upland, and in the South Mountains of Berks and Lehigh Counties. Its production in 1925 totaled 308,930 tons, valued at $812,810. Pennsylvania leads in the production of slate which is quarried extensively in Lehigh and Northampton Counties and to a lesser extent in York and Lancaster Counties.

MATTHEW STANLEY QUAY

QUAY, MATTHEW STANLEY, senator, was born in Dillsburg, York County, September 30, 1833. Subsequent to his graduation from Jefferson College, in 1850, he studied law and was admitted to the bar in 1854. He served as colonel of the 134th Pennsylvania Regiment during the Civil War, and also as assistant commissary general of Pennsylvania, state military agent at Washington and military secretary to the governor. In 1865-1867, he was a member of the Pennsylvania Legislature; in 1872-1878 and 1879-1882, state secretary and in 1885, state treasurer. After 1869 when he became secretary of the executive committee of the Republican State Committee, he was the Republican leader of Pennsylvania. In 1888 was chairman of the Republican national committee; in 1887-1899, he was a United States Senator, failing of re-election in the latter year because of the failure of the People's Bank where state funds were deposited. Quay was accused of having part in a conspiracy for the misappropriation of public funds, was tried in April, 1899, and acquitted. The governor then appointed him senator ad interim and in 1901 he was again elected to the senate where he strongly opposed the Panama Canal. He died at Beaver, May 28, 1904.

QUIETISTS, THE, called "die Stillen im Lande," by the Rev. Dr. Muhlenberg, were persons who had imbibed the principles of Michael Molinos, a Spanish ecclesiast, born at Patacina, December 21, 1627. They said that good works, the sacraments, prayer are not necessary and hardly even compatible with repose of the soul. They said, "The apostle tells us the spirit makes intercession for us. Now if the spirit pray in us, we must resign ourselves to his impulses, by remaining in a state of absolute quiet or rest till we attain the perfection of the unitive life." In 1749, Quietists were very numerous in Pennsylvania. Dr. Muhlenberg wrote, "There are many who separate themselves from visible things, feign to worship God in spirit and truth calling themselves quietists. They expound the doctrine of the Bible in their own way, obscuring the plainest truths."

QUIT-RENTS, a small rent paid by tenants to the Proprietors of Pennsylvania to be "quit and free" from all feudal service. The proceeds were used to pay the expenses of the government. The survival of feudal practices is shown in the type and value of payment. The requirement might be a red rose, a pepper corn, an Indian arrow, a buck's foot, a bear skin, a bushel of wheat or several shillings per hundred acres. The payment of a red rose by each of several churches has come down to recent times as an interesting ceremony. There was much difficulty in collecting the early quit-rents and many persons settled without any title to their lands.

RACCOON CREEK—Tributary to Ohio River. Sub-basin: Main Ohio; source, in Mount Pleasant Township, northern Washington County; course, northerly into Beaver County to Ohio River; mouth, opposite Merrill; length, forty-five miles. Indian name, Nachenum-hanne, "raccoon stream."

RACES. At an early period horse races were held in Philadelphia. Race Street in that city was so named because it lead directly to the racing grounds. Racing on the city streets continued long after the Revolution and eventually became so dangerous that on March 22, 1817, the Legislature passed an act prohibiting horse-racing on any of the streets of Philadelphia. For violation of the law the offender forfeited his horse and was liable to a fine of fifty dollars.

RAFINESQUE, CONSTANTINE SAMUEL, scientist, was born in a suburb of Constantinople, October 22, 1783. His father, G. F. Rafinesque, was a native of Marseilles, and his mother, Mme. Schmaltz, was born in Greece of German parentage. His father died in 1793. Later his mother fled to Leghorn, Italy, to escape the Reign of Terror. At the age of eleven he began making plant collections. In March, 1802, he sailed for America, landing in Philadelphia where he accepted a position in the counting house of the Clifford Bros. He soon relinquished this position and went to Germantown to live with Col. Forrest a horticulturist. Later he became acquainted with the botanists of his day, including Muhlenberg, Bartram, Marshall and the French traveler, Michaux. At twenty years of age he had traveled widely in Pennsylvania, New Jersey, Delaware, Maryland and Virginia. Returning to Europe he spent ten years in Sicily, after which he became a private tutor in the family of Mr. Livingston in New York. In 1818, he set out for the west, finally reaching the Illinois country and the Kentucky region. In 1818, he was elected to a professorship in Transylvania University, Lexington, Kentucky, where he taught Natural History, Botany and Modern Languages. During vacations he traveled widely, largely on foot, studying botany and natural history. In September, 1826, he returned to Philadelphia and became a lecturer in the Franklin Institute. He died in reduced circumstances September 18, 1840.

His writings cover a wide range, and show great versatility. He founded the *Atlantic Journal* and *Friend of Knowledge* (1832), and published: "Notes on the Apennines" (1793), "Analyse de la Nature" (1815), "Antikon Botanikon" (1815-1840), "Ancient History and Annals of Kentucky" (1824), "Medical Flora of the United States" (1828-1830), "The Ancient Monuments of North and South America" (1838), and "Celestial Wonders and Philosophy" (1838).

RAGNET, CONDY, political economist, was born at Philadelphia, January 28, 1784. He attended the University of Pennsylvania and then studied law. He entered upon a commercial career, amassing a huge fortune during his business activities He was active in providing for the defense of Philadelphia against the expected attack of the British fleet during the War of 1812. He was elected to the state legislature in 1815, serving in both houses. In 1822, he was appointed United States consul at Rio de Janeiro, and later became charge'd' affaires to Brazil. He edited several journals among them being: "The Free Trade Advocate," the "Examiner," "The Financial Register," and two small volumes: "The Principles of Free Trade," and "On Currency and Banking." He died at Philadelphia on March 22, 1842.

RALPH, JAMES, author, was born at Philadelphia, about 1698. In 1724, he accompanied to England, Benjamin Franklin. Having failed as an actor, editor, and newspaper writer, he became a teacher in Berkshire. He supported the Prince of Wales' Party by pamphlet, poem and newspaper contributions. His most valuable contribution to literature is: "History of England During the Reigns of King William, Queen Anne, and George I." He died at Chiswick, Surrey, England, on January 24, 1762.

RAMSAY, DAVID, physician and historian, was born in Lancaster County, on April 2, 1749. He studied medicine and practiced in Charleston; later becoming a field surgeon in the Continental Army. In 1776, he was elected to the state legislature, was a British prisoner from 1780-1781, and served in the Continental Congress from 1772-76; acting as President in 1775-76. He was a member of South Carolina's Legislature in 1801-1815, and was president of the State Senate when he was killed by a lunatic. He wrote many publications to further the cause of American independence, among which are: "History of the American Revolution," "The Life of Washington," and "The History of South Carolina." He died at Charleston, South Carolina, May 8, 1815.

RAMSAY, NATHANIEL, soldier, was born in Lancaster County, 1751. He graduated from Princeton in 1767, studied law and was admitted to the bar in 1771. He entered the Continental Army in 1776 with the rank of lieutenant-colonel. In the Battle of Monmouth, in 1778, he distinguished himself by aiding Colonel Stewart in checking the advance of the British. He was severely wounded and taken prisoner. His only other public service was as a member of Congress from Maryland in 1786-87. He died October 25, 1817.

RAMSEY, ALEXANDER, politician and cabinet officer, was born near Harrisburg, September 8, 1815. He studied at Lafayette College and Dickinson College, being admitted to the bar in 1839. In 1843-47, he was a Whig representative in Congress. He became a member of the Whig State Committee in 1848, and on April 2, 1849, was appointed governor of the Minnesota Territory. In 1855, he became mayor of St. Paul; in 1859, was elected first governor of the state of Minnesota, which office he held by re-election until he resigned on July 10, 1863. He then served two terms in the United States Senate ending in 1875, during which period visited France in the effort to obtain a cheaper rate of international postage. In 1879-81, he was President Hayes' Secretary of War. During his administration as governor of Minnesota Territory he concluded several important treaties with the Indians. He was the first president of Minnesota Historical Society and was the first Civil War governor to offer volunteers to Lincoln. He died at St. Paul, Minn., April 22, 1903.

SAMUEL J. RANDALL

RANDALL, SAMUEL JACKSON, statesman, was born at Philadelphia, on October 10, 1828. Having received only a common school education, he became a store clerk and later entered the wholesale iron business. He was drawn into politics serving four years as a member of the city council and was elected to the state senate in 1858. He enlisted in the cavalry at the beginning of the Civil War and rose to the rank of a captain. During the Battle of Gettysburg he was advanced to provost-marshal. He was elected to Congress in 1862, and continued as a member of that body for twenty-eigh years. During the 43rd Congress he secured for himself the leadership of the Democratic Party of that body and was elected speaker of the House and subsequently re-elected by the 45th and 46th Congresses. Thus he presided during the dispute over the Presidential election of 1876 and did not favor the electoral commission suggested. He took views opposite to those of his party on the tariff question. He was an indefatigable worker, always willing to expend the last ounce of his energy in the performance of his numerous duties and was a staunch believer and supporter of honesty and economy in the management of public affairs. He died at Washington, D. C., April 12, 1890.

RAPP, (JOHANN), GEORGE, a German secretary and founder of the communistic society called the Harmonists, was born at Iptingen, Wurtemberg, November 1, 1757. He had peculiar religious ideas which leaned so much towards political socialism that his followers were persecuted by the German government causing him to emigrate to America in 1803. The next year at Harmony, Pa., he founded a communistic colony where work, equality, celibacy, and unity were the rule. He founded a new colony on the Wabash River, in Posey County, Indiana, in 1815. This was later sold to Robert Owen. In 1824, Rapp and his followers returned to Pennsylvania and founded on the Ohio River the town of Economy, where he died August 7, 1847.

RAWLE, WILLIAM, lawyer, was born at Philadelphia, April 28, 1759. He studied law in New York and London, and was appointed by Washington as district attorney of Pennsylvania, assisting in 1794 in the prosecution of the offenders in the Whiskey Rebellion. He acted as counsel for the United States Bank for many years; was active in many legal societies and also was a trustee of the University of Pennsylvania, from 1796 until his death. He was one of the founders of the Historical Society of Pennsylvania in 1824, serving as its first president and also as president of the Abolition Society. He aided in revising his states' civil code in 1830, and published numerous works of a legal nature. He died in Philadelphia, April 12, 1836.

RAWLE, WILLIAM HENRY, lawyer, was born in Philadelphia, August 31, 1823. He was graduated at the University of Pennsylvania, in 1841, and three years later was admitted to the bar, where he rapidly attained prominence. In 1861, he enlisted in the Union Army serving in the capacity of quartermaster.

He was vice-provost of the Law Academy (1865-73), and vice-chancellor of the Law Association from 1880 to the time of his death which occurred at Philadelphia, April 19, 1889.

RAYSTOWN BRANCH—Tributary to Juniata River. Sub-basin: Upper Juniata; source, formed by junction of Deeters Run and Spicer Brook, in Juniata Township, Bedford County; course, easterly to Rays Hill; mouth, near Ardenheim; length, one hundred and eight miles.

READ, JOHN ELLIOT, journalist, was born at Philadelphia. He was educated in the public schools and has written much for agricultural, religious, and literary periodicals. He was associate editor of the "Working Farmer," in New York for ten years, and was corresponding editor of the "Practical Farmer," Philadelphia, for twelve years.

READ, JOHN MEREDITH, jurist, was born at Philadelphia, July 21, 1797, son of George Read, a signer of the Declaration of Independence. He was a graduate of the University of Pennsylvania and was admitted to the bar in 1818. He was a member of the state legislature, and was city solicitor for Philadelphia. He was the United States attorney-general for the eastern district of Pennsylvania, in 1837-44, and also served as judge of the supreme court, in 1858, and chief justice of that state from 1860 until his death. In the Chicago Convention of 1860 his name was mentioned as the Republican candidate for President, and although he polled several votes he threw all his personal influence and support in favor of Lincoln. His views on the suspension of the Writ of Habeas Corpus was the basis of the act of March 3, 1863, authorizing the President to suspend the Habeas Corpus Act. His legal opinions extend through forty-one volumes of reports. He died at Philadelphia, November 29, 1874.

READ, JOHN MEREDITH, diplomat, was born at Philadelphia, February 21, 1837, a member of the illustrious Read family of Philadelphia. He was a graduate of Brown University and the Albany Law School. He settled at Albany and from 1860-66 he was adjutant-general of New York State. In 1869, he was appointed United States consul for France and Algeria; and during the Franco-Prussian War he acted as consul-general for the German government, for which he gained great recognition and distinction. He also served from 1873-79 as United States minister to Greece. He rendered important services during this tenure of office, securing the free sale of the Bible in Greece, and the despatch of a grain fleet to a Russian port during the Turkish War. He continued to reside in Europe, engaging in archaeological, historical and art studies until his death at Paris on December 27, 1896.

READ, THOMAS BUCHANAN, poet and painter, was born in Chester County, March 12, 1822. He had only a meagre education, and during his youth he lived at various times in Philadelphia, Cincinnati, Boston and New York, occupying himself in ways which suited his fancy. He made his living by writing verses, painting signs, making cigars and acting in plays. In 1850, he went to Europe, joining the circle of American artists in Rome. Here he lived studying art and painting for the rest of his life, except for occasional visits to America. He painted portraits of Henry W. Longfellow, some of his children and the ex-Queen of Naples. His most famous work in poetry is: "Sheridan's Ride." He died in New York, May 11, 1872.

READER, FRANCIS SMITH, journalist, was born at Coal Centre, Washington County, November 17, 1842. He was connected with the United States Civil Service for ten years and served with the Union Army throughout the Civil War. He later became editor of the *Beaver Valley News*. Some of his published works are: "Life of Moody and Sankey," "History of the 5th West Virginia Cavalry," and "History of New Brighton, Pennsylvania."

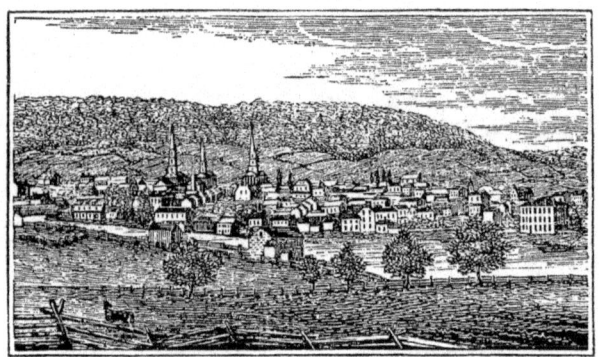

READING (1843)

READING, city, county-seat of Berks County, on the Schuylkill River, about fifty-eight miles northeast of Philadelphia and fifty-three miles east of Harrisburg. It was first settled by German immigrants, and later a number of English colonists located there and named it after the city, Reading in England. It was laid out in 1748, and was incorporated as a borough in 1783, receiving a city charter in 1847. It is located in a flourishing agricultural region, and is in close proximity to great mineral resources. Near it are coal mines, limestone quarries and small iron ore deposits. Among its chief industries are iron and steel foundries and machine shops, cigar factories and great textile mills. Some of the educational institutions located there are: Albright College, formerly Schuylkill Seminary; Mount Saint Michael's Academy, and Reading Business College. Reading at present is one of the strongholds of the Socialist Party,

From the "Wagoner of the Alleghenies"
by Thomas Buchanan Read

and for some time previous to this date, its government has been controlled by the Socialist Party. Population (1930), 111,171; (1920), 107,784.

RED STONE, OLD FORT, a Pennsylvania structure which held a prominent place in the English-French struggle for the mastery of the Ohio Valley. It was first used as a storehouse of the Ohio Company, and became the assembling point for the English in their advance against the French in 1754. At its ruins the leaders of the Whiskey Rebellion held a meeting in August, 1794, to plan opposition to the Whiskey tax.

REDBANK CREEK—Tributary to Allegheny River. Sub-basin: Middle Allegheny; source, formed by junction of North Fork and Sandy Lick Creek at Brookville, Jefferson County; course, southwesterly to Allegheny River, forming Clarion-Armstrong County boundary for last thirty miles; mouth, at Redbank; length, forty-seven and one-half miles.

REDBANK CREEK, NORTH FORK—Tributary to Redbank Creek. Sub-basin: Middle Allegheny; source, in Polk Township, northern Jefferson County; course, southwesterly, by a circuitous route, to Sandy Lick Creek and forms Redbank Creek; mouth, at Brookville; length, twenty and one-half miles.

REDSTONE CREEK—Tributary to Monongahela River. Sub-basin: Monongahela; source, on western slope of Chestnut Ridge, in South Union Township, southern central Fayette County; course, northwesterly to Monongahela River; mouth, one mile north of Brownsville; length, twenty-six miles. Indian name, Machkachsen-hanne, "redstone stream."

REED, DAVID AIKEN, lawyer and statesman, was born at Pittsburgh, December 21, 1880. He received instruction at the Shadyside Academy, Pittsburgh, in 1896, and was graduated from Princeton in 1900. He started practicing law in Pittsburgh, in 1903; was appointed a member of the United States Senate by the governor of Pennsylvania, in 1922, to succeed William E. Crow, and was subsequently elected to succeed himself in 1923 and again in 1929. He was a delegate to the London Naval Conference of 1930, was a major in the World War, being awarded the Distinguished Service Medal and the Chevalier Legion of Honor. He is a trustee of the University of Pittsburgh, a member of the American Battle Monuments Commission and is one of the leaders of the Republican Party. He lives at Pittsburgh.

REED, JOSEPH, soldier and statesman, was born at Trenton, N. J., August 22, 1742. He was graduated from Princeton and spent two years studying law in London. In 1767, he was appointed deputy secretary of New Jersey. In 1774, he became a member of the committee of correspondence for Philadelphia, and in 1775 was president of the second provincial convention held in Pennsylvania. Reed became Washington's military secretary. He was made adjutant-general in 1776 but refused to become the first chief justice of Pennsylvania preferring to remain Washington's volunteer aid, without rank or pay. He held various other public positions during the remainder of his life among which were: member of the Continental Congress, President of the Supreme Executive Council of Pennsylvania. He was one of the founders of the University of Pennsylvania and in 1780 he successfully quelled the dissatisfaction among the Pennsylvania troops in the army. He died March 5, 1785, at Philadelphia.

REED, WILLIAM BRADFORD, lawyer, was born at Philadelphia, June 30, 1806. He was graduated from the University of Pennsylvania in 1825. Having taken up the practice of law, he became attorney-general of Pennsylvania in 1838. In 1850, he was appointed professor of American history at the University of Pennsylvania and became United States minister to China in 1857. He negotiated treaties with China regulating the commercial relations between it and our country. Returning to America, in 1860, he settled in New York where he contributed articles to a number of periodicals. He died February 18, 1876, at New York.

REEDER, ANDREW HORATIO, politician, was born at Easton, August 6, 1807. He was practicing law at Easton and was a prominent Democratic politician when, in 1854, he was appointed by President Pierce the first governor of the Kansas Territory. He there brought order out of chaos in respect to the slavery question, and re-established order following the fraudulent election of 1855 in that territory. He was dismissed from office by the President and was then nominated by the Free Soil Party as a territorial delegate to Congress. He was elected to the United States Senate, in 1856, but the election was declared not genuine by Congress. He was offered rank of brigadier-general by President Lincoln, at the outbreak of the Civil War, but declined on account of his advanced age. On July 5, 1864, he died at Easton.

REFORMED CHURCH IN THE UNITED STATES, known for many years as the German Reformed Church, originated chiefly with the German, Swiss, and French people who settled in America early in the eighteenth century. In 1683, Pastorius, with a little group of Mystics, came to Pennsylvania, and founded Germantown. However, it was not until 1709 that the majority of immigrants of this faith came to America. About that year more than 30,000 immigrants from the German Palatinate came to the Schoharie in New York and later to Pennsylvania. Almost immediately they began to establish churches. The first German Reformed minister in this country was Samuel Guldin, who preached at Germantown in 1718. John Philip Boehm held the first communion service of which there is any record, at Falckner Swamp, October 15, 1725. In August, 1746, after the authorities in the Palatinate had petitioned the classis of Amsterdam for regularly ordained ministers for the colony, Michael Schlatter, was sent as a missionary evangelist. The first synod of the German Reformed Church was held April 27, 1793, at Lancaster. There were then in this country according to report, 178 congregations and 15,000 members. The largest churches were at Philadelphia, Lancaster, and Germantown, Pa., and at Frederick, Md. In 1840, the synod established a printing company at Chambersburg, which was removed to Philadelphia after the destruction of Chambersburg, during the Civil War. In 1926, there were 215,751 members of the Reformed Church in the United States in Pennsylvania.

REINHART, BENJAMIN FRANKLIN, artist, was born at Waynesburg, August 29, 1829. He began to study art at the age of fifteen, and then took a three-year course at the National Academy in New York. In 1850, he went to Europe and studied art in Paris and Dusseldorf. He returned to the United States in 1868 and engaged in painting and engraving. Included among his numerous engravings are: "Evangeline," "Washington Receiving the News of Arnold's Treason," and "Pocahontas." He died in Philadelphia, May 3, 1885.

REINHART, CHARLES STANLEY, artist, was born at Pittsburgh, May 16, 1844. He studied at the various art centers in Europe, returning to the United States in 1870. He made noteworthy illustrations for magazines; produced works in black and white, water color, and oil. He received high recognition of his works of art in Europe and became a member of the Society of American Artists, New York. He died at Philadelphia, August 30, 1896.

RENOVO, a borough in Clinton County, is situated on a division of the Pennsylvania Railroad about 125 miles northeast of Pittsburgh and 25 miles northwest of Lock Haven. It is in the heart of the Allegheny Mountains noted for its beautiful scenery, and is becoming increasingly popular as a summer resort. It is a busy railroad town, has brick works, and coal yards, being situated in a bituminous coal field region and near fire-clay deposits.

REPPLIER, AGNES, author, was born in Philadelphia, April 1, 1858, of French parentage. She was educated at the Sacred Heart Convent, Torresdale, and during recent years has spent much time in Europe. She has attained prominence as an essayist and is the author of: "Books and Men," "Essays in Miniature," "Philadelphia—The Place and the People," "Americans and Others," "Counter Currents," "Life of Pere Marquette," etc. Her home is in Philadelphia.

REYNOLDS, JOHN FULTON, military officer, was born at Lancaster, September 20, 1820. He was graduated from West Point, in 1841, served in the Mexican War as first lieutenant and became a captain in 1855. He commanded West Point from 1859-1861 and was appointed lieutenant-colonel of volunteers at the outbreak of the Civil War, being promoted to the rank of brigadier-general of volunteers shortly afterwards. He lead a brigade in the Seven Days' Battle, in June, 1862, and was brevetted colonel and brigadier-general in the regular army for gallant service. He was placed in command of the First Army Corps, in 1863, and promoted major-general of volunteers. He participated in the Battle of Fredericksburg and commanded on the field of Gettysburg on July 1st, until killed by a Confederate sharpshooter July 1, 1863.

REYNOLDS, WILLIAM, naval officer, was born at Lancaster, December 18, 1815. He entered the navy in 1831 and in 1851 was retired in consequence of failing health. He was later assigned to duty in Hawaii where he negotiated a reciprocity treaty. At the beginning of the Civil War he was again assigned to active duty. In 1862, he received command of the Asiatic station and through successive promotions became a rear admiral in 1873. He was chief of bureau and acting secretary of navy in 1873-74. In 1877, he was again retired on account of continued ill health. He died at Washington, D. C., November 5, 1879.

RHEES, WILLIAM JONES, bibliographer, was born at Philadelphia, March 13, 1830. He was in charge of the social statistics of the 7th Census in 1850-52. In 1852, he became chief clerk of the Smithsonian Institution. He died in 1907.

RHODES, MOSHEIM, Lutheran clergyman, was born at Williamsburg, April 14, 1837. He was graduated from Susquehanna University in 1861, ordained to the ministry that same year. He held numerous charges in Pennsylvania and Ohio at various times, and was an active promoter of religious educational movements. He was president of the General Synod of the Evangelical Lutheran Church in 1885-86, and is the author of several religious works.

RICHARDS, WILLIAM TROST, artist, was born at Philadelphia, November 14, 1833. He first studied under Paul Weber and in 1855 went abroad for observation and study in Paris and Italy returning in 1856 and establishing a studio in Philadelphia. He specialized in landscape artistry. His greatest success, however, was in marines where he carefully studied the motion of waves in storm and calm. He was a member of the National Academy of Design. A series of his water-color marines hang in the Metropolitan Museum, New York. He died at Newport, R. I., November 8, 1905.

RIDDLE, MATTHEW BROWN, theologian, was born at Pittsburgh, October 17, 1836. He was graduated from Jefferson College, in 1852, and from the New Brunswick Theological Seminary, in 1859. He held charges in Hoboken and Newark, N. J., at different times, and was also on the faculty of several theological schools at various times. He was a member of the American committee for New Testament Revision, editor of the Standard Edition of the Revised Version, and was a revising editor on the Standard American Revised

Version of the New Testament (1901). He was also an associate editor of several other religious publications. He died September 1, 1916.

RIDGWAY, borough, county-seat of Elk County, is situated on the Clarion River, about 150 miles northeast of Pittsburgh and 115 miles southeast of Erie. It is in a region devoted mainly to lumbering and agriculture. Among its chief industries are: lumber mills, flour and grist mills, machine, engine and boiler works, and dry kilns. Population (1930), 6,313; (1920), 6,037.

RIDLEY CREEK—Tributary to Delaware River. Sub-basin: Lower Delaware; source, near Frazer, East Whiteland Township, Chester County; course, southeasterly into Delaware County to Delaware River; mouth, at Chester; length, twenty-one miles.

RIFLES, MANUFACTURE OF. It is not known who was the first manufacturer of rifles in Pennsylvania. Letters to General Edward Hand indicate that he was engaged in the manufacture of rifles at Lancaster in 1792.

RIGDON, SIDNEY, a Mormon leader, was born in Allegheny County, February 19, 1793. He was employed in a printing office in Pittsburgh, in 1812, where he became so impressed, upon reading Mormon literature, that he became an adherent of that faith. In 1819, he became a Baptist preacher, meeting Joseph Smith, in 1829, with whom (according to a story denied by the Mormons) he published the "Book of Mormon," a new bible intended as the foundation of a new sect. He accompanied Smith to the west, assisted him in founding the Mormon Church and became one of its presidents. He was one of the originators of the "New revelation" authorizing polygamy, and in 1844, on the death of Smith, Rigdon aspired to the leadership. He refused to acknowledge the authority of Brigham Young, was excommunicated, and returned to the east, where he lived until his death at Friendship, N. Y., July 14, 1876.

RIGGS, JOHN DAVIS SEATON, educator, was born at Washington, Pa., January 29, 1851. He was graduated from the University of Chicago, in 1878, and was principal of various academies during the next twelve years. In 1887, he organized the Granville (now Doane) Academy, of Denison University, Ohio, and was its principal until 1896; from 1896-1905, he was president of Ottawa University, Kansas, and from 1905-1910, president of Shurtleff College. In 1913-1920, he was principal of the Wolcott School, Denver, Colorado. He is the author of: "In Latinum" (Caesar), "In Latinum" (Cicero), and various articles, addresses and lectures. He lives in Denver, Colorado.

RIOTS. Early riots in Pennsylvania were as follows: Bucks County (Doan family,) 1781; Allegheny County, 1877; Washington, Allegheney, Fayette, Westmoreland, Bedford and Somerset Counties (Whiskey Insurrection), 1794; Lycoming

GOVERNORS OF PENNSYLVANIA UNDER THE CONSTITUTION OF 1790
Joseph Hiester
George Wolf
J. Andrew Schulze
Joseph Ritner

County and Williamsport, 1872; Myerstown, Lebanon County, 1793; Philadelphia, 1844.

RITNER, JOSEPH, governor, was born in Berks County, March 25, 1780. His early years were spent on his father's farm. Educational advantages were meager; for six months, at the age of six, he attended a primary school. In 1800, he moved to Westmoreland County and later to Washington County, where he engaged in farming. In 1820, he was elected a member of the House of Representatives of Pennsylvania, in which capacity he served for six years. In 1824 and 1825, he was speaker of the House. After being twice defeated for the office of governor of Pennsylvania, Ritner was elected in 1835. During his administration the common school law of 1836 was passed. Throughout his entire life Ritner fostered the cause of the public school system. At the close of his term of office he retired to a farm near Mt. Rock, Cumberland County. In 1848, President Taylor appointed him Director of the Mint, at Philadelphia, which position he held for only a short time. He died October 16, 1869.

RITTENHOUSE, BENJAMIN, surveyor, was born in Norriton Township, now Montgomery County, about 1740. From 1776 to 1778, he was superintendent of a gun factory, maintained by the State of Pennsylvania. He sat in the assembly of Pennsylvania from 1784-88 and was appointed commissioner to survey the Schuylkill River in 1789. In 1792, he became associate judge of the common pleas court of Montgomery County. His surveyor's chain, made by order of Congress in 1796, was the standard of the United States land office until his death. He was a brother of David Rittenhouse. He died at Philadelphia, August 31, 1825.

RITTENHOUSE, DAVID, astronomer and mathematician, was born at Germantown, April 2, 1732. He early displayed his interest and skill in science and mechanical inventions. All his delving into the intricacies of mathematics and astronomy was accomplished by his own initiative and persistence. His first public employment was in 1763, the laying out of the boundary line of Delaware and Pennsylvania with which later the Mason and Dixon line coincided. In 1769, he located the point where the 41st parallel of latitude, the boundary between New York and Pennsylvania, strikes the Delaware River. In 1769 occurred the transit of Venus, and Rittenhouse publicly read his computations of the time of ingress and egress. He was appropriated £200 by the Pennsylvania Legislature for his observations; his results were the best then in the world and his computations the most accurate then known. In 1770, he completed his famous orrery based on computations of his own. This showed the movements of the planets and their satellites, their relative positions in the solar system, and the time of eclipses for a period of 5,000 years preceding and following that time. He made surveys for public waterways, improvement projects in and about the Delaware River, receiving many honors at home and abroad for his scholarly work.

DAVID RITTENHOUSE

During the Revolutionary War he gave his services to war problems. In 1776, he was made a member of the Assembly of Pennsylvania, and was active in the creation of the new state constitution. For twelve years including and following 1777 he was state treasurer; he was also trustee of the Loan office, and was engaged in determining the boundaries of his state and in 1787 was appointed by Congress to determine the boundary lines between New York and Massachusetts. From 1779-82, he was professor of astronomy at the University of Pennsylvania and afterwards trustee and vice-provost of that institution. In 1792, he was made director of the United States Mint, serving in that capacity for three years. He succeeded Franklin as president of the American Philosophical Society in 1790. Many honorary degrees from various educational institutions both in this country and abroad were conferred upon him. He was an ardent Republican. He became an anti-Federalist after the war being a member of the Jeffersonian party. He was also president of a radical society organized to sympathize with the French Revolution. His publications, about twenty in number, appeared in the Transactions of the American Philosophical Society. He died at Philadelphia, June 26, 1796.

RIVER BRETHREN—*See* BRETHREN IN CHRIST, CHURCH OF.

ROACH, JOHN, shipbuilder, was born at Mitchelstown, Ireland, in 1815. He came to the United States in 1829, obtained employment in various machine works and iron foundries. He later established the Aetna Iron Works, where he constructed the first compound engines built in the United States, and also built the largest engines which had been made in the country, at that time. In 1871, he purchased the Rainer shipyards at Chester, enlarged the establishment until its value was estimated at $2,000,000 and under the name of the Delaware River Iron Shipbuilding and Engine Works, built a large number of merchantmen and also constructed the first ships for the new United States Navy, among them the cruisers Atlanta, Boston, and Chicago. He died at New York, January 10, 1887.

ROBERDEAU, DANIEL, military officer, was born on the island of St. Christopher, British West Indies, in 1727. He was a son of Isaac Roberdeau, a native of Rochelle, France, and following the death of his father was brought by his mother to Philadelphia. He became a successful merchant and strongly advocated colonial independence. On July 4, 1776, he was elected first brigadier-general of the Pennsylvania Associators and participated in the campaign in New Jersey. In 1777-1779, he was a member of Congress, and signed the Articles of Confederation. He removed to Alexandria, Va., after the war and died there January 5, 1795. Fort Roberdeau or Lead Mines Fort in Blair County was named for him.

ROBERTS, HOWARD, sculptor, was born at Philadelphia, 1843. He studied at the Pennsylvania Academy of Fine Arts, and in 1866 went to Paris to study art. In 1875, he established a studio in Philadelphia and exhibited at the Centennial Exhibition a statue, "La Premiere Pose," that created a sensation on account of its superior technical qualities. He received one of the three medals awarded to American sculptors. Most of his works can be found at the Pennsylvania Academy. He died in Paris, April 19, 1900.

ROBERTS, JOHN BINGHAM, surgeon, was born at Philadelphia, February 29, 1852. He was graduated at the University of Pennsylvania, in 1871, and at the Jefferson Medical College, in 1874. He was president of the Philadelphia County Medical Society, Medical Society of the State of Pennsylvania, and vice-president of the American Surgical Society. He was a contributor to several medical and scientific papers and has published numerous medical treatises. He died November 28, 1924.

ROBERTS, WILLIAM MILNOR, civil engineer, was born at Philadelphia, February 12, 1810. In 1835, he planned and built across the Susquehanna River at Harrisburg the first combined railroad and highway bridge in the country. During the next twenty years he was engineer or contractor on many American railroads and canals. He went to Brazil in 1857 and undertook the construction of the Dom Pedro II Railroad. During 1866-68, he was U. S. civil engineer in charge of improvements of the Ohio River; from 1868-70, was associate contractor in building the bridge across the Missouri at Saint Louis. He became chief engineer of the Northern Pacific Railroad, in 1870, and went to Europe to observe the construction of jetties as a member of a commission of civil and military engineers to report on plans of the improvement of the mouth of the Mississippi River. In 1879, the Emperor of Brazil appointed him to work on the improvement of rivers and harbors in that country; he contracted fever and died there July 14, 1881. He was president of the American Society of Civil Engineers in 1879.

ROBINS, EDWARD, author, was born at Pau, France, March 2, 1862. He was educated at the military academy in Philadelphia, and in 1883 engaged in newspaper work. He was on the editorial staff of the Philadelphia *Public Ledger*, in 1884-88, 1895-97, and has since devoted himself to authorship. He has written: "Echoes of the Play House," "Benjamin Franklin," "Twelve Great Actors," "Twelve Great Actresses," "Romances of Early America," "Life of General Sherman"; and the following books for juveniles: "A Boy in Early Virginia," "Chasing an Iron Horse," "With Thomas in Tennessee," and "With Washington in Braddock's Campaign." He has also contributed to newspapers and magazines on dramatic and historical subjects. His home is in Philadelphia.

ROCHESTER, a borough in Beaver County, at the junction of the Ohio and Beaver Rivers, about 25 miles northwest of Pittsburgh. It is splendidly brought into close proximity to the neighboring towns and cities by electric lines and bridges spanning the rivers. It is in the coal and oil region, and in the vicinity are deposits of fire-clay and building-stone quarries. The chief manufactures are: flour, lumber, brick, glassware, oil well supplies, and iron products. Population (1930), 7,726; (1920), 6,957.

ROCKHILL, WILLIAM WOODVILLE, diplomat, was born at Philadelphia, April 1, 1854. He attended academic and military schools in France, serving with a French regiment in Algeria. In 1884, he entered the diplomatic service as second secretary of the legation at Peking, China. He was charge'd' affaires at Seoul, Korea, 1887-88; visited China, Mongolia and Tibet during 1888-92, on exploring tours; was appointed chief clerk of the State Department in 1893; was made third assistant secretary of state a year later; and first assistant in 1896. He was minister to Greece, Rumania, and Servia; commissioner to China where, in 1901, he signed the final peace negotiations. In October, 1901, he resumed his duties as director of the Bureau of American Republics to which he was appointed in 1890. He has published several books mostly of oriental interest. He died December 8, 1914.

RODENBOUGH, THEOPHILUS FRANCIS, army officer, was born at Easton, November 5, 1838. He was educated at Lafayette College, and in 1861 was appointed second lieutenant in the United States Army. In 1862, he was captured at Manassas, but was soon exchanged and at the Battle of Gettysburg commanded a regiment. He lost an arm in the Battle at Winchester, and was brevetted major for his bravery. In 1865, he was appointed major in the regular army, retiring in 1870 with full rank as a colonel. He was secretary of the Military Service Institution, in 1879; its vice-president, in 1890-91; assistant inspector-general of New York, in 1880-83, and in 1890-1901, chief of the bureau of elections in New York. He has written several novels dealing with military life. He died December 19, 1912.

ROEBLING, JOHN AUGUSTUS, civil engineer, was born at Muhlhausen, Prussia, June 12, 1806. He was educated in Berlin, coming to America, in 1831, and settling in Pittsburgh. He was engaged in surveying the lines of the Pennsylvania Railroad across the Allegheny Mountains from Harrisburg to Pittsburgh. There he started the manufacture of iron and steel wire, using his new product to build an aqueduct across the Allegheny River at Pittsburgh. In 1846, he built a suspension bridge over the Monongahela River at Pittsburgh, and after building several other bridges, removed his business to Trenton, N. J., beginning in 1851 the construction of the suspension bridge across the Niagara River, which connected the New York Central and Canadian Railway systems. He also built other bridges across the Allegheny and Ohio Rivers. He was chosen chief engineer for the construction of the Brooklyn Bridge, in 1868, but died the following year on the 22nd of July, leaving the completion of the structure to his son.

ROEBLING, WASHINGTON AUGUSTUS, civil engineer, was born at Saxonburg, Butler County, May 26, 1837. He was graduated at the Rensselaer Polytechnic Institute, Troy, N. Y., in 1857, and joined his father in the construction of suspension bridges. He served with distinction in the Union Army during the Civil War, being cited for bravery and receiving meritorious promotions. He became assistant engineer in the construction of the Brooklyn Bridge, and upon the death of his father, assumed full direction of operations, the bridge being completed in 1883. He was vice-president of the iron and steel wire and wire rope manufacturers concern of John A. Roebling and Sons Co., of Trenton, N. J.

ROGERS, FAIRMAN, civil engineer, was born at Philadelphia, November 15, 1833. He was graduated from the University of Pennsylvania, in 1853; was professor of civil engineering and trustee of that institution; was also a lecturer on mechanics at the Franklin Institute. He served in the Union Army, in 1861, and completed the survey of the Potomac River, northward from Blakiston Island, in 1862. He spent a large part of his life abroad, dying at Vienna, Austria, August 23, 1900.

ROGERS, HENRY DARWIN, geologist, was born at Philadelphia, August 1, 1808. He held professorships at several educational institutions in Pennsylvania in geology and physical science from 1830-46. He made geological surveys of the states of New Jersey and Pennsylvania, respectively, in 1835-36. He was also engaged as an expert for various coal companies. From 1857 until his death on May 29, 1866, he was professor of geology and natural history at the University of Glasgow. He has published numerous geological reports.

ROGERS, WILLIAM BARTON, geologist and physicist, was born at Philadelphia, December 7, 1804. He was educated at William and Mary College and later became one of its faculty members. From 1835 until his resignation in 1853, he was professor of natural philosophy in the University of Virginia, where he conducted individual study and research. In 1853, he removed to Boston where he continued his researches, and made voluminous contributions to scientific publications. In 1859, he became one of the founders of the Massachusetts Institute of Technology, becoming its first president. He was also made professor of physics and geology and instituted the educational plan of laboratory work with all science courses. He was chosen the first president of the American Association for the Advancement of Science, in 1875, and was a founder and the first president of the American Social Science Association. His gifts of expression as speaker and writer were excellent. Many of his researches added materially to scientific knowledge. He died at Boston, Massachusetts, May 30, 1882.

RORER, SARAH TYSON, teacher of domestic science, was born at Richboro, Bucks County, October 18, 1849. She was graduated from the academy at East Aurora, N. Y., and was married in 1871 to W. A. Rorer. She was for many years principal of the Philadelphia School of Domestic Science, was editor and part owner of "Table Talk," in 1886–92; edited "Household News," in 1893–97, and served on the editorial staff of the *Ladies' Home Journal*, 1897–1911. She published several books on the preparation and selection of food, and is now editor of the domestic department of the *Post-Gazette*, Pittsburgh. Her home is at Colebrook, Lebanon County.

ROSE, THOMAS ELLWOOD, military officer, was born in Bucks County, March 12, 1830. He served in the Union Army during the Civil War, being taken prisoner at Chickamauga and was sent to Libby prison. He escaped through a tunnel, was recaptured and confined until his exchange in 1864. He was brevetted brigadier-general of volunteers and colonel in the United States Army. He died in Washington, D. C., November 6, 1907.

ROSENGARTEN, JOSEPH GEORGE, lawyer, was born at Philadelphia, July 14, 1835. He was graduated from the University of Pennsylvania, in 1852, and served through the Civil War on the staff of General John F. Reynolds. He is the author of: "The German Soldier in the Wars of the United States," "French Colonists and Exiles in the United States," etc.

ROSS, CHARLIE, four-year-old son of Christian K. Ross, of Germantown, was kidnapped July 1, 1874. Playing with his older brother, Walter, on the afternoon of that day in a lane in the rear of the home, the boys were invited to take a ride in a carriage with two men. Later Walter was given money to buy fire-crackers and went into a store for that purpose. In the meantime the men had driven off with Charlie. The kidnappers advertised in the *Public Ledger*, offering to return the child for a ransom of $20,000. The father announced through the newspapers his readiness to comply with the demand, but with no results. Mayor Stokely accepted the offer made by wealthy citizens for a reward of $20,000 for the arrest of the kidnappers and the return of the child, but without result. For many years in all sections of the country came reports of the finding of the boy or of a confession by some person, but the mystery has never been solved. *Harper's Weekly* of August 8, 1874, expresses the opinion that it was the first case of kidnapping for the express purpose of exacting a ransom that has occurred in this country.

JAMES ROSS
Leader of Allegheny County bar for half a century;
United States Senator, 1794-1803

ROSS, ELIZABETH, familiarly called Betsy, patriot, was born in Philadelphia, January 1, 1752. She was the daughter of Samuel Griscom, a noted builder of pre-Revolutionary days, who constructed the greater part of the old State House—now Independence Hall—in that city. She married John Ross, in 1773, and after his death, in 1776, she engaged in making flags at her little home on Arch Street. Tradition says that in the latter part of May, 1776, Washington accompanied by Col. George Ross and Robert Morris, called on Betsy and engaged her to make the first American flag, the stars and stripes.

ROSS, GEORGE, patriot, was born at Newcastle, Delaware, 1730. On being admitted to the bar in 1751 he settled in Lancaster. As a member of the Pennsylvania Assembly, 1768-70, he drew up the declaration of rights which was presented by the assembly to the proprietary government. He was a member of the Continental Congress from 1774-77, and as such was one of the signers of the Declaration of Independence. In 1779, shortly before his death, he was made judge of the admiralty court of Pennsylvania. He died in July, 1779.

ROSS, JOHN, patriot, was born at Ross-shire, Scotland, January 29, 1726. He emigrated to America at the beginning of the rebellion of its colonies and at once became a staunch defender of the cause of independence. He with other Philadelphia merchants resisted British importations and unjust taxation. He died at Philadelphia, March, 1800.

ROTHERMEL, PETER FREDERICK, painter, was born in Luzerne County, July 8, 1817. He opened a studio as a portrait painter at Philadelphia, in 1840, and eventually turned his attention to historical subjects. His pictures reveal a fine sense of color, but he has a tendency to exaggeration. Among his paintings are: "De Soto Discovering the Mississippi," and "The Battle of Gettysburg" (in Pennsylvania State Museum). He died near Pottstown, August 15, 1895.

ROTHROCK, JOSEPH TRIMBLE, scientist, was born in Mac Veytown April 9, 1839. He graduated at Harvard, in 1869; took part in the Civil War, and was wounded in the Battle of Fredericksburg. He was a professor of botany in the University of Pennsylvania, in 1877, and a member of the Pennsylvania Commission of Forestry, in 1893-1905. Among his publications are: "Flora of Alaska," "Pennsylvania Forestry Reports," etc. He died June 2, 1922.

ROWLAND, HENRY AUGUSTUS, scientist, was born at Honesdale, November 27, 1848. He was graduated from Rensselaer Polytechnic Institute, in 1870, and later taught physics there. In 1876, he accepted the chair of physics at Johns Hopkins University which he occupied until his death. He was a member of the Electrical Commission in Paris, in 1881, and was elected to the National Academy of Science in that year. He was the inventor of a greatly

BENJAMIN RUSH

improved process of ruling large diffraction gratings directly on concave mirrors. He made valuable experiments and investigations in electricity, among them an extremely accurate determination of the ohm. He was the author of more than 100 scientific papers and monographs. He died at Baltimore, Md., April 16, 1901.

RUPP, ISRAEL DANIEL, historian, was born in Cumberland County, July 10, 1803. He was the author of: "History of Religious Denominations of United States," "Events in Indian History," and of many Pennsylvania County histories. He died in Philadelphia, May 31, 1878.

RUSH, BENJAMIN, physician, was born at Byberry, near Philadelphia, December 24, 1745. He was graduated from Princeton, in 1760; from the University of Edinburgh, in 1768, and became a professor of chemistry at the College of Philadelphia, in 1769. He was a member of the provincial conference of 1776 and as such made a motion that independence be declared, of which he was a signer the following month. He was a surgeon to the Pennsylvania Navy, in 1775-76, and in 1777 was appointed surgeon-general and later physician-general of the hospitals of the middle section. He was a member of the convention which formed the constitution of 1780 and of that which ratified the Federal Constitution. He established the first dispensary in the United States, in 1785, and was one of the founders of Dickinson College. He was connected with various religious and scientific societies, and was treasurer of the United States Mint from 1799 until his death, which occurred at Philadelphia, April 19, 1813.

RUSH, RICHARD, diplomat, was born at Philadelphia, August 29, 1780. He started practicing law in 1800 at Philadelphia. In 1811, he was appointed attorney-general of Pennsylvania, and in 1814-17 was attorney-general of the United States. He was temporary secretary of state under President Monroe. in 1817, and was then appointed minister to England, being recalled in 1825 to become secretary of the treasury under President Adams. He was a candidate for the vice-presidency on the ticket with Adams in 1828 and was appointed by President Jackson, in 1836, as commissioner to obtain the legacy for the founding of the Smithsonian Institute then pending in an English Court. From 1847-51, he was minister to France being recalled at his own request and spending the remainder of his life in retirement. He is the author of several volumes pertaining to law and government. He died at Philadelphia, July 3, 1859.

RUSH, WILLIAM, sculptor, was born at Philadelphia, July 4, 1756. He never worked in marble, confining himself to wood and clay, gaining a high reputation for his busts, statues and figure heads. He served in the American Revolution and was a member of the city councils of Philadelphia for more than a quarter of a century. He died at Philadelphia, January 17, 1833.

SADTLER, SAMUEL PHILLIP, chemist, was born at Pine Grove, July 18, 1847. He graduated from Lehigh University, in 1867, and later studied at the

Universities of Berlin and Gottingen. He was professor of natural science at Pennsylvania College, 1871-1874; assistant professor of chemistry at the University of Pennsylvania, 1874-1886; professor there, 1887-1891; professor of chemistry at Philadelphia College of Pharmacy, 1878-1916; chemical editor of the "United States Despensatory" (15th to 19th editions); from 1900 a member of the committee on revision of the "United States Pharmacopoeia"; author of "Handbook of Chemical Experimentation"; "Industrial Organic Chemistry"; joint author of "Pharmaceutical Chemistry." He died December 20, 1923.

ST. CLAIR, ARTHUR, soldier, was born in Edinburgh, Scotland, in 1734. He served under General Wolfe at Louisburg and Quebec; established a home and manufacturing industry in Westmoreland County; took the side of the colonists in the Revolution; served through the entire war and rose to the rank of major-general; represented Pennsylvania in the Continental Congress from 1785-1787, and was president of that body when it passed the famous ordinance of 1787 by which the northwest territory was organized; was governor of that territory from 1789 to 1802. He commanded the expedition against the Miami Indians which ended disastrously, and although sick at the time, and giving his orders from a litter, public opinion obliged him to resign his command. After his long and distinguished public service he lived poor and neglected on Chestnut Ridge, Westmoreland County, until his death, August 31, 1818. He published: "A Narrative of the Manner in Which the Campaign Against the Indians was Conducted under the Command of Major-General St. Clair."

ST. CLAIR, borough in Schuylkill County, five miles north of Pottsville. It is located in the anthracite coal region and its chief industries are connected with mining and shipping coal. There are large mining implement works and large coal shipping yards. Population (1930), 7,296; (1920), 6,495.

SAINT MARY'S, borough in Elk County, one hundred miles northeast of Pittsburgh. The town is located in a region rich in deposits of bituminous coal, fire clay and natural gas. It is the seat of the Roman Catholic Convent School of the Sisters of Saint Benedict. Population (1930), 7,433; (1920), 6,967.

SALOMON, HAYM, patriot and financier, was born in Lissa, Poland, in 1740. In 1778, he came to Philadelphia, where he acquired wealth as a banker, loaned Robert Morris over $350,000; negotiated all the war subsidies from France and Holland, and when the Continental money was withdrawn, causing suffering among the poor of Philadelphia, he distributed $2,000 in specie to relieve the distress. The large indebtedness of the government to Salomon was never repaid to him nor to his heirs, but has been the subject of some discussion and was favorably reported to the United States Senate in 1850. The amount of public securities and Revolutionary papers filed in the register's office, Philadelphia, 1785, reached $353,744, but the inroads of the British Army in 1814 destroyed all records in relation to vouchers. Salomon died in Philadelphia, January 6, 1785.

SALT INDUSTRY, THE, was established in the Conemaugh Valley early in the nineteenth century. In 1812, salt was discovered near the present site of Saltsburg, in Indiana County, and later in Armstrong, Erie and Westmoreland Counties. The industry, in Pennsylvania, has since declined.

SANDERSON, JOHN, author, was born near Carlisle, in 1783. He was professor of Latin and Greek in the Philadelphia High School, 1836–1844, and is co-author with his brother of "The Signers of the Declaration of Independence." He also wrote: "Sketches of Paris," and London edition, "The Americans in Paris." He died in Philadelphia, April 5, 1844.

SANDY CREEK—Tributary to Allegheny River. Sub-basin: Upper Allegheny; source, in East Fallowfield Township, southwestern Crawford County; course, southeasterly into Mercer County; mouth, five miles south of Franklin; length, thirty-eight miles.

SANDY (EAST) CREEK—Tributary to Allegheny River. Sub-basin: Upper Allegheny; source, in Washington Township, northern Clarion County; course, westerly into Venango County; mouth, five miles southeast of Franklin; length, twenty-two and one-half miles.

SANDY LICK CREEK—Tributary to Redbank Creek. Sub-basin: Middle Allegheny; source, in Sandy Township, northwestern Clearfield County; course, southwesterly, by a circuitous route, into Jefferson County; mouth, at Brookville; length, thirty-six miles. Formerly Lycomick Creek, a corruption of Legauwimahoni, "sandy lick."

SARGENT, WINTHROP, lawyer and author, was born in Philadelphia, September 23, 1825. He graduated from the University of Pennsylvania, in 1845, and from Harvard Law School, in 1847. For a short time he engaged in the practice of law in Philadelphia but eventually settled in New York where he became well known as a writer on history and genealogy. He is the author of: "History of an Expedition Against Fort Duquesne, in 1775, under Major-General Braddock"; "The Loyalist Party of the Revolution"; "Life and Career of Major John Andre"; and "Les Etats Confederes et de l'esclavage." He died in Paris, France, May 18, 1870.

SARTAIN, EMILY, artist, was born March 17, 1841. She studied under her father, John Sartain, at the Pennsylvania Academy of Fine Arts and later in Italy and Paris. She excelled in mezzotint engraving, in etching and in portrait painting; has accomplished much in book illustration, the etching of framing prints, and in genre work; received a medal at the Centennial Exhibition in 1876, and the Mary Smith prize at the Pennsylvania Academy in 1881 and 1883; exhibited oil paintings at the Paris Salon, 1875 and 1883; editor of *Our Continent*, 1881-1883; principal of the Philadelphia School of Design for Women, 1886-1919; official delegate from the United States government to International Congress on Instruction in Engraving, 1900. She died June 18, 1927.

SARTAIN, JOHN, engraver and editor, was born in London, England, October 24, 1808. He came to the United States in 1830 and settled at Philadelphia. He introduced mezzotint into this country; added to engraving miniature-painting on vellum and ivory and portrait painting in oil; designed public monuments of which the best known is that to Washington and Lafayette in Philadelphia. He was the editor of the *Foreign Semi-Monthly Magazine* and of the *Union Magazine* which he renamed *Sartain's Union Magazine*. Among his more important engravings are: "Christ Rejected," after Benjamin West; "The Ironworker and King Solomon," after Christian Schussele and the "Battle of Gettysburg," after Rothermel. He engraved many other historical paintings, and portraits of famous Americans, after well-known artists; accomplished important results in the development of art in this country by his long career of varied and productive work, his services as chief administrator of fine arts at the Centennial Exhibition in 1876, and through the many positions which he held in connection with prominent societies and institutions. He wrote: "Reminiscences of a Very Old Man." His death occurred at Philadelphia, October 25, 1897.

SARTAIN, WILLIAM, landscape, genre, and portrait painter, was born in Philadelphia, November 21, 1843, the son of John Sartain. He studied under Schussele, at the Pennsylvania Academy of Fine Arts, under Bonnat in Paris and at L'Ecole des Beaux Arts. He exhibited in London, in 1875, and in the New York Academy, in 1876, in which year he settled in New York. He was one of the founders of the Society of American Artists and for some years was professor of the life class of the Art Students' League, New York. His oil paintings include: "Italian Head," "Narcissus," "Near Algiers," "Young Musician," "Nubian Schiek," "Chapter from the Koran," "In the Basilicate," "Portrait of His Mother," and others. He died October 25, 1924.

SASSOONAN, Delaware Indian chief, became the head of his tribe, about 1715. As a little boy he was present at the "Great Treaty," made by the Delawares with William Penn, and later joined his father and brothers in conveying to Penn certain lands between the Pennypack and Mahoning Creeks. After attaining the chieftainship of his tribe he became the representative of the Indians in many councils with the provincial authorities, and always in the interests of peace. In 1718, Sassoonan with other chiefs, visited Philadelphia and executed a release, by the terms of which they acknowledged that a large tract of land between the Delaware and Susquehanna Rivers had been conveyed to William Penn. He was living at Paxtang at this time but later removed to Sunbury. While living at Sunbury he secured, through negotiations with Governor Gordon, the payment for lands in the Tulpehocken Valley, upon which the German Palatines had settled in 1727. Sassoonan continued his good offices between the Indians and whites until his death in 1747.

SATURDAY EVENING POST, THE, a weekly periodical, was founded by Samuel Keimer on December 24, 1728, in Philadelphia. It was originally called *The Universal Instructor in All the Arts and Sciences and Pennsylvania Gazette.* Benjamin Franklin assumed its editorship less than a year after its establishment and called it the *Pennsylvania Gazette.* It received its present name on August 4, 1821. George Horace Lorimer is the editor, and the Curtis Publishing Company are the publishers. Circulation, 2,924,363.

SAXTON, JOSEPH, inventor, was born in Huntingdon, March 22, 1799. He was employed for a time as watchmaker and engraver in Philadelphia, and constructed an astronomical clock, with a compensating pendulum and original escapement. Later he went to England where, in 1833, he exhibited before the British Association a magneto-electric machine, and won a reputation as a maker of instruments of precision, constructing, among various apparatus, that by which Wheatstone measured the velocity of electricity in its passage through a long wire. Returning to the United States he was made constructor and curator of the standard weighing apparatus in the mint at Philadelphia, and in 1843 began the construction of the standard balances, weights, and measures to be presented to each state for securing uniformity. Saxton was admitted to membership in Franklin Institute, Philadelphia. He died at Washington, D. C., October 26, 1873.

SAY, THOMAS, naturalist, was born in Philadelphia, July 27, 1787. He was one of the earliest entomologists and is said to have discovered more species of the genus Insectivora than any naturalist before him. His contributions to natural science were contained in his reports upon his expedition to the coast of Georgia and Florida in 1818, and that as chief geologist to the United States Survey of the Rocky Mountain region in 1819-1820. He was one of the founders of the Academy of Natural Sciences in 1812. He died at New Harmony, Ind., October 10, 1834.

SAYRE, borough in Bradford County, on the north branch of the Susquehanna River. The leading industrial establishments are: machine shops, stove fixture works, metal works and lumber and coal yards. Population (1930), 7,902; (1920), 8,078.

SCAIFE, WALTER BELL, author, was born in Pittsburgh, September 10, 1858. He was educated at the University of Michigan, Johns Hopkins Univer-

GOVERNORS OF PENNSYLVANIA UNDER THE CONSTITUTION OF 1838
DAVID R. PORTER   FRANCIS R. SHUNK
WILLIAM F. JOHNSTON
WILLIAM BIGLER   JAMES POLLOCK

sity and the University of Vienna and has lectured widely throughout eastern United States on historical and other subjects. He has published: "American Geographical History, 1492-1892"; "Florentine Life During the Renaissance"; "The Boundary Dispute Between Maryland and Pennsylvania"; "A Century's Labor Legislation in France"; "From Energy to Wisdom," etc.

SCAROUADY, a noted Oneida Indian chieftain, was active in the negotiation of treaties between the Shawnee Indians of the Ohio Valley, over whom he became vice-gerent about 1747. Later he represented the Delawares and Ottawas, and during his negotiations he met with the Colonial authorities at Carlisle, Lancaster and Philadelphia. He assisted Washington in his campaign in western Pennsylvania in 1754, and later joined Braddock in his expedition against Fort Duquesne. Following the massacre at Penn's Creek, Snyder County, Scarouady used his influence to the utmost to effect a reconciliation on the part of the Shawnees, Delawares, and Ottawas toward the whites. He remained an unfailing friend of the colonist until his death in 1758.

SCHADDLE, GEORGE HENRY, scholar, was born in Allegheny City, April 15, 1854. He graduated from Capital University, in 1872, and from Leipzig, in 1877; was professor of Greek and Theology at Capital University, Columbus, Ohio, 1880-1917; editor, *Lutheran Standard*, 1880-1917; editor, *The Theological Magazine*, 1897-1917; published: "The Protestant Church in Germany"; translated the "Book of Enoch and the Book of Jubilees from the Ethiopic and Day in Capernaum from the German of Deletzsch," and Weiss' "Religion of the New Testament." He died September 15, 1917.

SCHAEFFER, NATHAN C., Reformed clergyman and educator, was born at Maxatawny, February 3, 1849. After graduation from Franklin and Marshall College he continued his education at the theological seminary of the Reformed Church and at the Universities of Berlin, Tubingen and Leipzig. He was professor at Franklin and Marshall College, 1875-1877; principal of Keystone State Normal School, now Kutztown State Teachers College, 1877-1893; Pennsylvania State Superintendent of Public Instruction, 1893-1919. He was a prolific writer on educational and religious subjects, his chief works including: "Thinking and Learning to Think"; "History of Education in Pennsylvania"; Riddle's "Nicholas Comenius"; "Life of Henry Harbaugh." From 1893-1919, he was editor of the *Pennsylvania School Journal*. He died March 14, 1919.

SCHAFF, DAVID SCHLEY, Presbyterian clergyman and educator, was born in Mercersburg, October 17, 1852, the son of Philip Schaff. He was graduated from Yale, in 1873; was ordained to the ministry of the Presbyterian Church, 1877; served as pastor, 1877-1907; professor of Church History at Lane Theological Seminary, 1897-1903; professor of ecclesiastical and doctrinal history, Western Theological Seminary, 1903-1925; lecturer on American Church History, Union Theological Seminary, 1925 to date; delegate to celebration of 400th anniversary of John Calvin's birth in Prague and Geneva, 1909. He was one of the editors of the Schaff-Herzog Encyclopedia and of a History of the Christian Church and is the author of: "Commentary on Acts," "Life of Philip Schaff," and "John Huss."

SCHAFF, PHILIP, clergyman and scholar, was born at Coire, Switzerland, January 1, 1819. He was educated at Tubingen, Halle and Berlin and lectured at the latter university, 1842-1844; came to this country as professor in the theological seminary of the German Reformed Church at Mercersburg, in which position he served during 1844-1863. In 1864-1869, he was lecturer in several other theological seminaries; professor in Union Theological Seminary, 1870-1893; president of American Bible revision committee, which he organized, 1871. His writings include: "History of Apostolic Church," "History of Christian Church," "Creeds of Christendom," "Schaff-Herzog Encyclopedia of Religious Knowledge," "Church and State in the United States," and "Literature and Poetry." He died in New York, October 20, 1893.

SCHELLING, FELIX EMANUEL, educator and scholar, was born in New Albany, Ind., September 3, 1858. He graduated from the University of Pennsylvania where, since 1893, he has been John Welsh Centennial professor of English literature. Dr. Schelling is a recognized authority on Shakespeare and the Elizabethan period. His publications include: "Literary and Verse Criticism of the Reign of Elizabeth," "Life and Works of George Gascoigne," "A Book of Elizabethan Lyrics," "A Book of 17th Century Lyrics," "The English Chronicle Play," "The Queen's Progress and Other Elizabethan Sketches," "History of Elizabethan Drama," "English Literature During the Lifetime of Shakespeare," "The Restoration Drama" (Cambridge History of Literature), "The English Lyric," and "A History of English Drama."

SCHLATTER, MICHAEL, German Reformed clergyman, was born at Saint Gall, Switzerland, July 14, 1716. He was educated at the University of Helmsted; came to America as missionary to the German Reformed emigrants at Philadelphia; served as pastor of the united churches of Germantown and Philadelphia, 1746-1751; organized a synod, which met in Philadelphia, in 1747; made extended missionary tours through Pennsylvania, Maryland, Virginia, New Jersey and New York; raised £20,000 in England and Holland for the establishment of schools among the Germans in America, and in 1755 became superintendent of the enterprise, but resigned in 1757 because of opposition among the Germans to the teaching of the English language in the schools; preached at Chestnut Hill and its environs; died near Philadelphia, November, 1790.

SCHMAUCK, THEODORE EMANUEL, Lutheran clergyman, was born in Lancaster, in 1860. He graduated from the University of Pennsylvania in

1880, and in 1883 was ordained to the ministry. He became editor-in-chief of the *Lutheran Church Review*, in 1895; literary editor of *The Lutheran*, in 1889; professor of Christian Faith in Mt. Airy Theological Seminary, Philadelphia, 1911; president of the General Council of Evangelical Lutheran Churches in North America, 1903. He published: "The Negative Criticism of the Old Testament"; "History of Old Salem, Lebanon"; "The Early Churches of the Lebanon Valley"; "The History of the Lutheran Church," and "Christianity and Christian Union." He died March 23, 1920.

SCHMUCKER, SAMUEL MOSHEIM, historical writer, was born at New Market, Va., January 12, 1813. He graduated from Washington College, in 1840, and was licensed to preach in the Lutheran Church. Subsequently he studied law and was admitted to practice in Philadelphia but gave up the profession in 1855 and devoted his time almost entirely to literature. He is the author of: "Errors of Modern Infidelity"; "Court and Reign of Catherine II, Empress of Russia"; "Life of John C. Fremont"; "Life of Alexander Hamilton"; "Life of Thomas Jefferson"; "Arctic Explorations and Discoveries"; "Life of Dr. Elisha Kane and Other American Discoverers"; "Life of Daniel Webster," and "History of Modern Jews." He died in Philadelphia, May 12, 1863.

SCHMUCKER, SAMUEL SIMON, Lutheran clergyman and educator, was born in Hagerstown, Md., February 28, 1799. He was educated at the University of Pennsylvania and Princeton Theological Seminary; served as pastor of Lutheran congregations, 1821-1826; chairman of faculty of Lutheran Theological Seminary at Gettysburg, 1826-1864; author of: "Elements of Popular Theology," "Fraternal Appeal to the American Churches on Christian Union," "Lutheran Manual," "Evangelical Lutheran Catechism," and "Unity of Christ's Church." He died at Gettysburg, July 26, 1873.

SCHOFIELD, WALTER ELMER, artist, was born in Philadelphia, September 9, 1867. He studied at the Academy of Fine Arts, Philadelphia, and in Paris. He specialized in landscape work, notable examples being: "Morning" and "Midwinter Thaw" (in Cincinnati Museum); "Across the River" (in Carnegie Institute); "Morning After Snow" (in Corcoran Art Gallery); and "Sand Dunes Near Lelant" (in the Metropolitan Museum). He has received many medals and honor awards for his work and in 1907 was elected National Academician. He has a studio in New York, but maintains his residence in Suffolk, England.

SCHOOLMASTER BROWN AND HIS PUPILS, MASSACRE OF. One of the most shocking atrocities committed by the Delaware Indians within the bounds of Pennsylvania, was the massacre of schoolmaster Brown and his pupils on July 26, 1764. The school building was located three miles northwest of Greencastle, in Franklin County. When the marauding party of young Indians entered the school building with murderous intent, the schoolmaster, Enoch Brown, offered his life and scalp, if the savages would spare the lives of his ten pupils, two girls and eight boys. His offer was unheeded, and all were scalped and murdered excepting one boy, Archie McCullough, who was only stunned by the blow he received, and survived the effects of scalping, but was somewhat demented for life.

SCHUYLKILL COUNTY, was formed March 1, 1811, from parts of Berks and Northampton. Named for the Schuylkill River. Land area, 177 square miles; population (1930), 235,505. County-seat, Pottsville, laid out in 1816.

SCHUYLKILL HAVEN, borough in Schuylkill County, located in the coal mining region. It is an important coal shipping point and its chief manufacturing establishments are rolling mills, railroad car shops, pipe mills, and manufactures of underwear, hosiery, shoes, soap, paper boxes, and flour. Population (1930), 6,514; (1920), 5,437.

SCHUYLKILL RIVER—Tributary to Delaware River. Sub-basin: Lower Delaware; source, in Locust Mountain, near Tuscarora, Schuylkill County; course, southeasterly, through Berks, between Chester and Montgomery, and through Montgomery and Philadelphia Counties, to Delaware River; mouth, at League Island Navy Yard, below Philadelphia; length, one hundred and thirty-one miles.

SCHUYLKILL (LITTLE) RIVER—Tributary to Schuylkill River. Sub-basin: Lower Delaware; source, formed by junction of east and west branches, in Rush Township, Schuylkill County; course, southerly to Schuylkill River; mouth, at Port Clinton; length, twenty-seven miles.

SCHWAB, CHARLES M., financier, was born in Williamsburg, April 18, 1862. He was educated at Saint Francis College, Loretto, Pa., and subsequently entered the service of the Carnegie Steel Company as stake driver in the engineering corps of the Edgar Thompson Steel Works; became chief engineer and assistant manager, 1881; superintendent of Homestead Steel Works, 1887-1889; president of Carnegie Steel Company, 1897-1901; president of United Steel Corporation, 1901-1903; is at present chairman of the board of the Bethlehem Steel Company and of the Bethlehem Steel Corporation; director in many trust and manufacturing companies; appointed director-general of shipbuilding of United States Shipping Board Emergency Fleet Corporation, April 28, 1918, and earned high approbation for the energy and ability with which he handled its affairs. He has residences in New York and Bethlehem and a summer home in Loretto.

SCHWEINITZ, EDMUND ALEXANDER DE, bishop of the Unity of the Brethren Church, son of L. D. von Schweinitz, was born in Bethlehem, March 20, 1825. He graduated from the Moravian Theological Seminary at Bethlehem, in 1844; studied at Berlin, 1845; held pastorates, 1850-1880; consecrated bishop, 1870; president of theological seminary at Bethlehem, 1867-1884; founder of the *Moravian* and editor, 1856-1866. De Schweinitz's family was continuously represented in the American branch of the Moravian ministry for more than one hundred years. He wrote: "Moravian Manual," "Some of the Fathers of the Moravian Church," and "History of the Unitas Fratrum." He died at South Bethlehem, December 18, 1887.

SCHWEINITZ, GEORGE EDMUND DE, opthalmologist, son of Edmund A. de Schweinitz, was born in Philadelphia, October 26, 1858. After graduation from Moravian College, in 1876, he studied at the medical school of the University of Pennsylvania where he received the M. D. degree in 1881. In 1902, he became professor of opthalmology at the University of Pennsylvania, and later was consulting opthalmologist at the Philadelphia Hospital and the Philadelphia Polyclinic. In 1924, he became professor of opthalmology in the University of Pennsylvania Graduate School of Medicine which position he still holds. For many years he was first lieutenant in the United States Army Medical Reserve Corps. He was lieutenant-colonel, medical corps, United States Army in France, 1917-1919. He was joint editor of *Ophthalmic Year Book* (1905-1907), and is the author of: "Diseases of the Ear"; "Toxic Amblyopias," and "Diseases of the Eye, Ear, Nose and Throat."

SCHWEINITZ, LOUIS DAVID VON, Moravian clergyman and botanist, was born in Bethlehem, February 13, 1770. He was educated in Germany; became agent of the Moravian Church in United States, 1812. As a botanist he added 1,400 new specimens to the catalogue of American flora; specialized in American fungi; at his death he possessed the largest collection of plants in America which he willed to the American Academy of Natural Science. He died at Bethlehem, February 8, 1834.

SCHWENKFELDERS, a religious organization, formed by the followers of Kaspar von Schwenkfeld, a strong advocate of the Reformation, through whom the principles of Luther gained a stronghold in Silesia. Being an independent thinker, he differed from the followers of Luther in many of his beliefs and consequently he and his followers fled from place to place to avoid persecution. After von Schwenkfeld's death, in 1561, his followers held meetings in Silesia, Switzerland and Italy. In September, 1734, about two hundred Schwenkfelders landed at Philadelphia and settled in Bucks, Berks and Lehigh Counties, where their descendants still reside. In 1764, they adopted a school system and in 1774 established a charity fund. Like the Quakers and Mennonites they opposed war, secret societies and the taking of oaths. Later the opposition to secret

GOVERNORS OF PENNSYLVANIA UNDER THE CONSTITUTION OF 1838
WILLIAM F. PACKER
ANDREW G. CURTIN   JOHN W. GEARY
JOHN F. HARTRANFT

societies was dropped and the attitude toward war left to the individual. Perkiomen School for boys at Pennsburg is under the control of the Schwenkfelders.

SCOTT, EBEN GREENOUGH, author, was born in Wilkes-Barre, June 15, 1836. He graduated from Yale, in 1858, and is the author of: "Interstate Law of Pennsylvania," "Development of Constitutional Liberty," and "Reconstruction During the Civil War."

SCOTT, ROBERT KINGSTON, soldier and governor, was born in Armstrong County, July 8, 1826. He studied medicine and practiced in Ohio, 1851-1857; was commissioned lieutenant-colonel in 68th Ohio Regiment, 1861; took part in campaigns in Mississippi and Tennessee; was commissioned brigadier-general of volunteers, 1865; assistant commissioner Freedman's Bureau in South Carolina, 1865-1868; governor of South Carolina, 1868-1870, charged with complicity in fraudulent overissue of state bonds, but cleared. He died in Ohio, August 13, 1900.

SCOTT, THOMAS ALEXANDER, railway manager, was born in London, December 28, 1824. He entered the Pennsylvania Railroad service, in 1850; became its general superintendent, 1858, and vice-president, 1859. As superintendent of all railroads and telegraphic lines at the beginning of the Civil War he rendered outstanding service. He was appointed assistant secretary of war, in 1861; resigned the post in the following June, but re-entered government service and won distinction as rapid builder of emergency railroad lines. Re-entering the service of the Pennsylvania Railroad he was president of the system in 1874-1880. He died at Darby, May 21, 1881.

SCOTTDALE, borough of Westmoreland County, about thirty miles southeast of Pittsburgh. It is located in a coal mining region. Its manufacturing interests are large pipe works, rolling mills, foundry, machine shops and steel works. Population (1930), 6,714; (1920), 5,768.

SCOVEL, SYLVESTER, journalist and engineer, was born at Denny Station, July 29, 1869. He was educated at the University of Michigan; was war correspondent in Cuba before and during the Spanish-American War, 1897-1898; correspondent in the Turco-Greek War; consulting engineer for the United States Military Government, Cuban Customs Service, 1899-1902. He died at Havana, Cuba, February 11, 1905.

SCRANTON, GEORGE WHITEFIELD, manufacturer, was born in Madison, Conn., May 11, 1811. With his brother he engaged in the manufacture of iron at Oxford, N. J., in 1839, and in the following year established smelters at Slocum, Pa. (now named in their honor, Scranton). He became interested in railroad transportation and was finally president of the Lackawanna and Western and of the Cayuga and Susquehanna Railroads. In 1859-1861, he was a member of Congress. He died at Scranton, March 24, 1861.

SCRANTON, third city in population in the state and county-seat of Lackawanna County, is located in the center of the anthracite coal mining industry. It has large and varied industrial establishments in iron and textile manufactures. Among the products manufactured are: silk and silk goods, clothing, buttons, lace curtains, pianos, pumps, etc. Scranton was settled about 1788-1800 and was originally called Slocum Hollow, for the Slocum family, then prominent residents of the locality. Through the interest of Col. George W. and Seldon T. Scranton the settlement grew and was named in honor of Col. Scranton. It was incorporated as a borough in 1854 and chartered as a city in 1866. Population (1930), 143,433; (1920), 137,783.

SEIDEL, EMIL, Socialist politician, was born in Ashland, December 13, 1864. He learned the wood carvers' trade in Germany, and was one of the founders of the Wood Carvers' Union and Socialist Party in the United States. In 1902, he was candidate for governor of Wisconsin. He became mayor of Milwaukee in 1910.

SELINSGROVE TIMES, THE, a Democratic weekly newspaper, which appears every Thursday, was established in 1822. Marion S. Schoch is the editor, and the Selinsgrove Times, Inc., the publishers. Circulation, 1,775,

SELLERS, COLEMAN, engineer, was born in Philadelphia, January 28, 1827. He was educated at Stevens Technological Institute and became professor of engineering practice there in 1886. He was chief engineer of the Niagara Falls Power Company, and chief mechanical engineer of Canadian Niagara Power Company. He was the inventor of numerous mechanical appliances, a member of many American and foreign societies and was widely known as a consulting engineer. He died in Philadelphia, December 28, 1907.

SERVITUDE, WHITE. The development of Pennsylvania as of all the colonies was influenced largely by the supply of labor which came from Europe. In Pennsylvania there were three kinds of laborers: free laborers, indentured servants, and slaves, the latter limited to negroes. Until the middle of the eighteenth century the mother country sent thousands of persons convicted of misdemeanors and crimes to the colonies where they were indentured for a number of years.

Annually thousands of men and women from the British Isles voluntarily came to Pennsylvania as indentured servants. This practice was continued until the Revolutionary War. Germans from the Palatinate came by shiploads annually, many of them entered as indentured servants. Children without parents and children of parents too poor to support them were legally indentured until they attained the age of twenty-one years. (See Cheeseman Herrick's "White Servitude in Pennsylvania.")

SEVENTH-DAY BAPTISTS—See BAPTISTS, SEVENTH-DAY.

SEWICKLEY, borough in Allegheny County, fourteen miles northwest of Pittsburgh, is a residential suburb of that city. An abundance of natural gas and petroleum are found in the neighborhood. Population (1930), 5,599; (1920), 4,955.

SEWICKLEY CREEK—Tributary to Youghiogheny River. Sub-basin: Monongahela; source, in Unity Township, southern Westmoreland County; course, westerly to Youghiogheny River; mouth, at Gratztown, one mile northwest of West Newton; length, thirty-one and one-half miles. Indian name, a corruption of Asswekales, the common name given to the Hathawekela division of the Shawnee by the English traders.

SHAMOKIN, borough in Northumberland County, about forty-five miles northeast of Harrisburg. It is the center of an anthracite coal mining region and has an extensive trade in coal, and manufactures of iron products, silk and knit goods. It was settled in 1835 by promoters of the mining industry and was incorporated as a borough in 1864. Population (1930), 20,274; (1920), 21,204.

SHAMOKIN CREEK—Tributary to Susquehanna River. Sub-basin: Middle Main Susquehanna; source, in Conyngham Township, southern Columbia County; course, westerly into Northumberland County to Shamokin; mouth, at Sunbury; length, thirty-five miles. Indian name, a corruption of Schamoki, or Schahamokink, "the place of eels."

SHARON, borough in Mercer County, located in a bituminous coal mining area. Other industries are the manufacture of iron and steel. Hall Institute (under the Baptist Church) founded in 1888 and Saint Scholastica (Roman Catholic) are located here. Population (1930), 25,908; (1920), 21,747.

SHARPLESS, ISAAC, educator, was born in Chester County, December 16, 1848. He attended Lawrence Scientific School, Harvard; was professor of mathematics and astronomy at Haverford College, 1879-1885, and afterwards president of the college. He is the author of textbooks on astronomy and geometry; published: "English Education," "A Quaker Experiment in Government," and "Two Centuries of Pennsylvania History." He died in New York, January 16, 1920.

SHARPSBURG, borough in Allegheny County, six miles northeast of Pittsburgh. It is located in the bituminous coal mining region, and has large iron, steel, planing and brick-making industries. Population (1930), 8,642; (1920), 8,921.

SHARSWOOD, GEORGE, jurist, was born in Philadelphia, July 7, 1810. He was educated at the University of Pennsylvania, was admitted to the bar, in 1831; served in the state legislature, 1837-1838, and in 1842-1843; was appointed judge of the district court of Philadelphia, 1845; was appointed to the Supreme Court of Pennsylvania, 1848, of which he was chief justice from 1878 to 1882; professor of law at the University of Pennsylvania, 1850-1867. Sharswood ranked as one of the most eminent jurists of the state. He wrote: "Professional Ethics," and "Popular Lectures on Common Law." His death occurred in Philadelphia, May 28, 1883.

SHAVERS CREEK—Tributary to Raystown Branch. Sub-basin: Upper Juniata; source, in Monroe Township, southeastern Bedford County; course, northeasterly to Raystown Branch Juniata River; mouth, three miles east of Everett; length, twenty-five miles.

SHENANDOAH, borough in Schuylkill County, about one hundred miles northwest of Philadelphia. Coal mining is the leading industry there being six large collieries within the limits of the borough. Other industrial establishments are: machine shops, mining tool works, and hat and cap factories. The town was settled in 1850 by William Kelley, was laid out in 1862, and incorporated in 1866. Population (1930), 21,782; (1920), 24,726.

SHENANGO RIVER—Tributary to Beaver River. Sub-basin: Main Ohio; source, in East Fallowfield Township, southwestern Crawford County; course, northwesterly to a point three miles west of Linesville; mouth, two and one-half miles southwest of New Castle; length, eighty-seven and one-half miles. Indian name, Ochenango, "large bull thistles."

SHENANGO (LITTLE) RIVER—Tributary to Shenango River. Sub-basin: Main Ohio; source, in Lake Township, eastern Mercer County; course, northwesterly to junction of Crooked Creek; mouth, at Greenville; length, twenty-two and one-half miles. Indian name, Ochenango, "large bull thistles."

SHERMAN CREEK—Tributary to Susquehanna River. Sub-basin: Lower Main Susquehanna; source, in Toboyne Township, southwestern Perry County; course, northeasterly to Susquehanna River; mouth, at Duncannon; length, fifty-one miles.

SHIKELLAMY, vice-gerent, or deputy of the Iroquois, in 1727 or 1728 was sent by the Great Council of Onondaga to rule over the Delawares, Shawnees and other tribes in the Susquehanna Valley. He resided near Milton and later at Shamokin (Sunbury). In 1731, Governor Gordon sent him to Onondaga to arrange for a treaty that would bring the Six Nations into closer touch with Pennsylvania. He attended numerous treaties and conferences, accompanied Conrad Weiser to Onondaga in 1736 to attempt to arrange peace between the Iroquois, the Catawbas, the Cherokees and other southern tribes, and again to Onondaga in 1743 to arrange for a conference between the Six Nations and Virginia. The Lancaster Treaty of 1744 which Shikellamy attended, resulted from this mission. On Weiser's third trip to Onondaga in 1745, Shikellamy again accompanied him. The Iroquois chief died on December 17, 1748, at Sunbury. Christian funeral services were held in charge of David Zeisberger, of the Moravian Church, and burial was made in the Indian burying ground at Sunbury. After Shikellamy's death, Sunbury gradually ceased to be the center of Indian affairs.

SHIMMELL, LEWIS S., educator, lecturer and historian, was born in Bucks County, September 14, 1852; educated at public schools, Millersville State Normal School, Wadsworth Boarding School, Ohio, and University of Pennslyvania; studied medicine for a time; superintendent of schools of Huntingdon, 1893; teacher of German and Civil Government in Central High School, Harrisburg, 1893-1906; supervisor of schools, Harrisburg, 1906-1919; editor of *School Gazette*, published at Harrisburg, 1892-1905; author of: "The Border Warfare of Pennsylvania During the Revolution," "The Pennsylvania Citizen," "The History of Pennsylvania," "The American Government," "The Government of Pennsylvania," and "The United States"; died March 9, 1919, at Harrisburg.

SHINGAS, sachem of the Delawares, called "King Shingas," was a brother of King Beaver and Pisquetomen. He was the leader of numerous invasions against the settlers, one of the most dastardly of which took place on October 31, 1755, when one hundred Delawares and Shawnees from the Ohio and Allegheny invaded the Scotch-Irish settlements in the Big Cove and along the Big and Little Conolloway Creeks, in Fulton County, and the Little Cove, in Franklin County. On April 1, 1756, he attacked and burned Fort McCord, near Fort Loudon, and either killed or captured the twenty-seven inmates of the fort. Shingas attended councils with the Moravian missionary, Post, in 1758, and was present at various councils with Pennsylvania authorities at Fort Pitt.

SHIPPENSBURG, borough in Cumberland County, forty-one miles southwest of Harrisburg, is the seat of Shippensburg State Teachers College.

SHIPPENSBURG STATE TEACHERS COLLEGE, was opened as the Cumberland Valley State Normal School, on April 15, 1873. In 1926, it was authorized by the state council of education to prepare students for teaching in junior high schools and for supervisory positions in addition to the regular two-year courses which prepared for teaching in elementary schools. In August, 1927, the official name of the institution was changed to State Teachers College. The town of Shippensburg, where the college is located, lies in the Cumberland Valley, forty-one miles south of Harrisburg.

SHIRAS, GEORGE, JR., jurist, was born in Pittsburgh, January 26, 1832. He graduated from Yale University and law school and from 1856-1892 practiced law in his native city. From 1892 until his retirement in 1903, he was associate justice of the United States Supreme Court. He died August 2, 1924.

SHIRAS, GEORGE, III, son of George Shiras, Jr., was born in Allegheny, January 1, 1859. He graduated from Cornell University and from the law school of Yale University, and in 1883 began the practice of law in his native city. In 1889-1890, he was a member of the Pennsylvania House of Representatives and in 1903-1905 a member of Congress. After 1905 he devoted his time to writing upon biological subjects and legal questions connected with federal jurisprudence. He became widely known as an amateur photographer of wild animals, as a student of natural history, and as a promoter of legislation for the protection of wild animals and birds. His home is in Washington, D. C.

SHOHOLA CREEK—Tributary to Delaware River. Sub-basin: Upper Delaware; source, in Pocono Mountains, Palmyra Township, western Pike County; course, northeasterly to Delaware River; mouth, at Shohola; length, twenty-five miles. Indian name, a corruption of Schauwihilla, "weak."

SHRADER BRANCH (OR SCHRADER RUN)—Tributary to Towanda Creek. Sub-basin: Upper North Branch Susquehanna; source, in McNett Township, northeastern Lycoming County; course, northeasterly, through Sullivan County, into Bradford County to Towanda Creek; mouth, opposite Powell; length, twenty-three and one-half miles.

SHULZE, JOHN ANDREW, governor, was born in Tulpehocken Township, Berks County, July 19, 1775. He received his early education from his father, a minister in the German Lutheran Church. Later, he studied under his uncle, Dr. Henry Muhlenberg, in Lancaster, and still later attended school in New York, afterwards studying theology there with another uncle, Dr. Kunze. In 1796, he was ordained to the ministry of the German Lutheran Church and for six years served as minister to congregations in Berks County. Because of ill health he retired from his profession and entered the mercantile business at Myerstown, Lebanon County. He was elected a member of the House of

Representatives of Pennsylvania in 1806, and was reelected for the two succeeding years. In October, 1821, he was elected to represent Lebanon County in the House of Representatives and in the next year was elected state senator for Dauphin and Lebanon Counties. Less than a year after he had taken his seat in the Senate he was nominated by the Republican Party for the office of governor. He was elected by a large majority, was nominated for a second term in 1826, and elected with the largest majority in the history of the state. At the end of his second term as governor he retired from public life. However, in 1839, he was a senatorial delegate to the National Convention at Harrisburg, and in 1840 was president of the Electoral College. He died at Lancaster, November 18, 1852.

SHUNK, FRANCIS RAWN, governor, was born at Trappe, Montgomery County, August 7, 1788. His early life was spent in farming and teaching. In 1812, he became a clerk in the surveyor-general's department while at the same time he studied law under Thomas Elder, at Harrisburg. In 1814, he marched to the defense of Baltimore, and shortly afterwards became clerk of the House of Representatives. Governor Porter appointed him Secretary of State, in 1838, and after his retirement from the office he engaged in the practice of law at Pittsburgh. He was elected governor of Pennsylvania in 1844, and three years later was reelected but because of ill health was forced to resign. His death occurred at Harrisburg, July 30, 1848.

SIMON, JOSEPH, pioneer, was born in 1712 and emigrated to Lancaster about 1740. He engaged in trade with the Indians, and became one of the largest landholders in Pennsylvania, with interests extending to the Mississippi River. During the Revolution he supplied the Continental Army with rifles, ammunition, drums, blankets, etc. A deed, still preserved in Independence Hall, Philadelphia, records the treaty of Fort Stanwix, whereby a tract of land comprising the present state of West Virginia was granted to Simon and eleven other traders, November 8, 1768, but the state's resistance prevented the grant from passing into the hands of the purchasers.

SIMS, WILLIAM SNOWDEN, naval officer, was born in Port Hope, Canada, October 15, 1858. He was appointed from Pennsylvania to the United States Naval Academy and graduated there in 1880. On January 5, 1917, he was promoted to rear admiral, on May 28th of that year to vice-admiral, and on December 4, 1918, to admiral. He attained the permanent rank of rear admiral on March 31, 1919. At different times he was naval attache at American embassies in Paris and St. Petersburg and at several Chinese stations. He served as president of the Naval War College from February, 1917, until America's entrance into the World War, when he became commander of American naval operations in European waters. He served in this capacity from April 28, 1917, until the end of the war and resumed the presidency of the Naval War College on April 7, 1919. His services during the war merited him medals from England, France, Japan, Belgium, and Italy and the United States Distinguished Service Medal which he declined. He retired from the navy, October 15, 1922, and lives at Newport, R. I.

SINNEMAHONING CREEK, FIRST FORK—Tributary to Sinnemahoning Creek. Sub-basin: Upper West Branch Susquehanna; source, formed by junction of Prouty Branch and Ayer Hill Branch, in Summit Township, central Potter County; course, southwesterly into Cameron County to Sinnemahoning Creek; mouth, at Sinnemahoning; length, thirty-one miles. Indian name, a corruption of Achsinni-mahoni, "stony lick."

SLATINGTON, borough in Lehigh County, fifty-eight miles northwest of Philadelphia. Its industries are the quarrying of slate, the manufacture of slate roofing, as well as of machinery, rolling mill products, knit goods and silks. The borough was settled in 1738 and incorporated in 1864.

SLIPPERY ROCK CREEK—Tributary to Connoquenessing Creek. Sub-basin: Main Ohio; source, in Venango Township, northern Butler County; course, southwesterly into Lawrence County to Connoquenessing Creek; mouth, one mile east of Ellwood City; length, forty-seven miles. Indian name, Weschachapochka, "slippery rock."

SLIPPERY ROCK STATE TEACHERS COLLEGE, was opened March 26, 1889, with an enrollment of 168. In June, 1926, the institution was authorized to grant degrees of Bachelor of Science, in Health Education, Elementary Education and in Junior High School Education. In August, 1927, the name was officially changed from State Normal School to the State Teachers College at Slippery Rock. The college is located in Butler County, between Pittsburgh and Erie.

SLOCUM, FRANCES. On November 2, 1778, the home of Jonathan Slocum, in the Wyoming Valley, was attacked by a band of Indians. Among those carried away were a small boy by the name of Kingsley, visiting in the home at the time, and Frances Slocum, then five years old. The Kingsley child was never afterward heard of, but Frances was given to an Indian family living in Ontario, Canada. They later moved to the present site of Fort Wayne, Indiana, where Frances grew to womanhood, and became the wife of a Delaware chief, who deserted her in 1794. Later she married a chief of the Miamis in Indiana, and reared a family. After years of search she was finally discovered by one of her brothers in 1835, but declined to return with him to his home in Wilkes-Barre. She said, "I have always lived with the Indians; they have always used me kindly, and I am used to them. The Great Spirit has allowed me to live with them, and I wish to live and die with them."

SMALL, JOHN KUNKLE, botanist, was born in Harrisburg, January 31, 1869. He was educated at Franklin and Marshall College and received the Ph. D. degree at Columbia University in 1895. He was curator of herbarium at Columbia, 1895-1899, and assistant at New York Botanical Garden after 1899. He is the author of: "Shrubs of Florida," "Flora of the Florida Keys," "Flora of the Southeastern United States," etc. Since 1906 he has been head curator of herbarium, New York Botanical Garden.

SMEDLEY, WILLIAM THOMAS, painter, was born in Chester County, March 26, 1858. He studied engraving and painting at the Pennsylvania Academy of Fine Arts and in New York and Paris. He won distinction as an illustrator of books and periodicals; traveled through western and northwestern Canada for drawings to illustrate "Picturesque Canada," and in 1890 made a sketching tour around the world. Among his paintings are: "An Indiscreet Question," "A Thanksgiving Dinner," and "A Summer Occupation." He died March 26, 1920.

SMETHPORT, borough and county-seat of McKean County, was laid out in 1807. It was named for Raymond and Baron Theodore de Smeth, two Amsterdam bankers, in charge of the financial interests of the Ceres Land Company which contributed much to the development of McKean and Cameron Counties. The town is located in the vicinity of natural gas and oil wells, silica mines, and stone and brick shale quarries. It has chemical, glass, toy and novelty factories.

SMITH, ANDREW JACKSON, army officer, was born in Bucks County, April 28, 1815. He graduated from the United States Military Academy and prior to the Civil War served on the western frontier. He was promoted to rank of colonel in 1861, and to brigadier-general of volunteers and chief of cavalry, Department of Missouri, 1862; he was in active service throughout the Civil War. In 1876, he was appointed postmaster of St. Louis. He died January 30, 1897.

SMITH, CHARLES FERGUSON, soldier, was born in Philadelphia, April 24, 1807. He graduated from West Point, in 1825, and later served there as instructor of tactics, and as adjutant and commandant, 1829-1845. He won distinction for his services during the Mexican War and at the beginning of the Civil War was made brigadier-general of volunteers in the Union Army. He was active in the attack on Fort Donelson and was subsequently promoted to major-general. He died at Savannah, Tennessee, April 25, 1862.

SMITH, CLEMENT LAWRENCE, scholar and educator, was born in Upper Darby, April 13, 1844. He graduated from Haverford College, in 1860, from Harvard, in 1863, and afterwards studied at Göttingen. He was professor of Latin and Greek at Swarthmore College, 1869-1870; professor of Latin at

Harvard, 1883-1904, and dean of the faculty of arts and sciences, 1898-1902. He edited "Odes and Epodes of Horace." His death occurred on July 1, 1909.

SMITH, EDGAR FAHS, chemist and educator, was born in York, May 23, 1856. He graduated from Pennsylvania College, in 1874, and secured his Ph. D. degree at Göttingen, in 1876. He was professor of chemistry at the University of Pennsylvania, 1888-1911; vice-provost there, 1899-1911, and provost, 1911-1926. He was a member of numerous scientific societies and served as president of the American Chemical Society, in 1898, and of the American Philosophical Society, 1902-1906. He is the author of: "Electro-Chemical Analysis," and "Chemistry in America." He died May 3, 1928.

SMITH, HANNAH WHITALL, Quaker philanthropist, was born in Philadelphia, in 1832. She was educated at a Quaker school and in 1851 married Robert P. Smith, also of Quaker faith. She conducted Bible classes for women at her home and in 1888 removed to England where she conducted meetings of a similar nature. She was well known as a speaker on religion, temperance and woman's suffrage. Among her writings are: "The Unselfishness of God," and "The Christian's Secret of a Happy Life." She died in England, May 1, 1911.

SMITH, HENRY HOLLINGSWORTH, surgeon, was born in Philadelphia, December 10, 1815. He was educated at the University of Pennsylvania and in Europe; practiced at Philadelphia, and was surgeon in several hospitals there; was professor of surgery at the University of Pennsylvania, 1855-1871; was appointed surgeon-general of Pennsylvania at the outbreak of the Civil War; originated the plan of removing the wounded to hospitals in Philadelphia, Harrisburg and Reading. He is the author of: "System of Operative Surgery," and "Practice of Surgery." He died in Philadelphia, April 11, 1890.

SMITH, JAMES, legislator and signer of the Declaration of Independence, was born in Ireland about 1720, and came to America with his father in 1829. He was educated at the College of Philadelphia (now the University of Pennsylvania) and subsequently engaged in the practice of law and in surveying at Shippensburg. Later he moved to York where for some time he was the only lawyer. He raised the first volunteer company in Pennsylvania to resist British authority, and hastened the patriotic movement through his essay "On the Constitutional Power of Great Britain over the Colonies in America." He was a member of the Continental Congress, a signer of the Declaration of Independence, served in the state assembly, in 1779, was judge of the High Court of Appeals, ardently supported Washington and sacrificed his personal fortune in the cause of the Revolution. He died in York, July 11, 1806.

SMITH, JAMES, pioneer, was born in Franklin County, in 1737. At the age of eighteen he was captured by the Indians and was adopted by one of their tribes, but escaped four years later. He became leader of the "Black Boys," a company formed for Indian warfare in 1763. He served as lieutenant under General Bouquet in the expedition against the Ohio Indians, in 1764; was a member of the Pennsylvania Convention of 1776, and served in the Pennsylvania Assembly, 1776-1777; was commissioned colonel in command of warfare on the frontier. He is the author of: "Remarkable Adventures in the Life and Travels of Col. James Smith," and "A Treatise on the Mode and Manner of Indian Warfare." He died in Washington County, Ky., in 1812.

SMITH, JESSIE WILCOX, artist, was born in Philadelphia. She studied at the Philadelphia Academy of Fine Arts and under Howard Pyle at Drexel Institute. She specialized in the painting of childrens' portraits and is the illustrator of magazines. Her work has appeared in many books some of which are: *The Five Senses, Seven Ages of Childhood* and in connection with the Mother Goose Rhymes. She also illustrated Stevenson's "Child's Garden of Verses"; Kingsley's "Water Babies," and "At the Back of the North Wind." She lives in Philadelphia.

SMITH, RICHARD PENN, dramatist, was born in Philadelphia, March 13, 1799. He is the author of numerous plays, fifteen of which were produced on the Philadelphia stage. The most notable of these are the following: "Caius Marius," a tragedy (acted by Edwin Forrest, 1831); "The Disowned," and the "Deformed," both presented abroad. He died at Schuylkill Falls, August 12, 1854.

SMITH, RICHARD SOMERS, educator, was born in Philadelphia, October 30, 1813. He was graduated from West Point, in 1834, and was instructor of mathematics there in 1840-1855. He later served as professor of the same subject at Brooklyn Institute of Technology. During the Civil War he served as major of infantry until 1864, when he became president of Girard College, Philadelphia. Relinquishing this position in 1867, he became professor of mathematics in the United States Naval Academy. He published a "Manual of Topographical Drawing" and "Linear Perspective." He died at Annapolis, Md., January 23, 1877.

SMITH, SAMUEL, soldier, was born in Lancaster, July 27, 1752. At the outbreak of the American Revolution he became captain of a Maryland Regiment and served until 1779. He represented Maryland in Congress for two terms and was a United States Senator from that state in 1803-1815 and 1822-1833. He died at Baltimore, April 22, 1839.

SMITH, SAMUEL STANHOPE, Presbyterian clergyman and educator, was born in Pequea, March 16, 1750. After graduation from Princeton University he was ordained to the ministry of the Presbyterian Church. He was the first president of Hampden-Sidney College serving in that capacity from

1775-1779; was professor of moral philosophy at Princeton, 1779; became professor of theology there in 1783; was vice-president of Princeton, 1786-1795, and president, 1795-1812. He is the author of "Lectures of Moral and Political Philosophy and View of Natural and Revealed Religion." He died at Princeton, N. J., August 21, 1819.

SMITH, WILLIAM, educator, was born in Scotland and was educated at the University of Aberdeen. When he was twenty-four years old he came to America and settled in Philadelphia. He became the first provost of the College of Philadelphia and held that position until the institution became the University of Pennsylvania. Because of his sympathy with the provincial proprietors, the Assembly imprisoned him. During that period his classes met in the jail. Although he sympathized with the colonies at the time of the Revolution and made many speeches in their behalf he was arrested in 1777 for disloyalty, went to Maryland on parole and remained there until 1789 when he returned to Philadelphia.

SNYDER, SIMON, governor, was born at Lancaster, November 15, 1759. At the age of seventeen he removed to York where he learned the business of a tanner and currier, and where he also attended a night school conducted by a member of the Society of Friends. In 1784, he removed to Selinsgrove, where he conducted a store and mill, and became a justice of the peace. He was elected a member of the convention which framed the State Constitution of 1789, and in 1797 was elected a member of the House of Representatives, of which body he was chosen speaker in 1802. In 1805, Snyder was nominated for governor, but at the election was defeated by McKean. He continued as speaker of the House until 1808 when he was again nominated for governor and received the election. He was reelected in 1811 and in 1814. The War of 1812 was fought during his administration and the governor did his utmost to encourage enlistments. The Olmstead Case (q. v.), growing out of a Revolutionary claim, was settled during his term of office. In 1817, Snyder retired to his home in Selinsgrove. Afterwards, he was elected to the State Senate and served during one session. He died November 9, 1819.

SNYDER COUNTY, was formed March 2, 1855, from part of Union. Named for Governor Simon Snyder. Land area, 311 square miles; population (1930), 18,836. County-seat, Middleburg, laid out in 1800.

SOMERSET, borough and county-seat of Somerset County, was organized in 1795. It was formerly called Brunerstown, but later was named Somerset for Somersetshire, England. It is located in a region rich in coal and limestone.

SOMERSET COUNTY, was formed April 17, 1795, from part of Bedford. Named for English shire. Land area, 1,034 square miles; population (1930), 80,764. County-seat, Somerset, laid out in 1795.

SOUTH BETHLEHEM, borough of Northampton County, about forty miles north of Philadelphia. It was settled in 1741. The industries of the town include: iron and steel works, machine shops, foundries, zinc and brass works, wood-working factories, knitting and silk mills, coke works and cigar factories. Lehigh University is located here, as is Bishopthorpe Manor, a school for girls.

SOWER (or SAUER), CHRISTOPHER, was born in Germany, in 1693. He graduated from Marburg University, studied medicine, and in 1724 came to Philadelphia. He settled as a farmer in Lancaster County but later removed to Germantown. Feeling the want of books among his countrymen, especially in the line of religion, he imported Bibles and other works from Germany; established a printing house and published an almanac in the German language, long continued as a magazine by his descendants, and among the first published in America. In 1843, he published Luther's translation of the Bible, the largest work yet published in the colonies, and, with the exception of Eliot's Indian Bible, the first Bible printed in America. He introduced cast iron stoves into general use, made eight-day "grandfather clocks," and practiced his profession as a physician. His son, Christopher, likewise a prominent man in the province, continued the printing business, now known as the Christopher Sower Printing Company. Sower died at Germantown, September 25, 1758.

SPARKS, EDWIN ERLE, educator and author, was born in Licking County, Ohio, July 16, 1860. He graduated from Ohio State University, 1884, from the University of Chicago, in 1900, receiving the Ph. D. degree in that year. In 1884–1885, he was instructor in Ohio State University; 1890–1895, professor at Pennsylvania State College; lecturer before the American Society of University Extension, 1892–1895; professor of American history, University of Chicago, 1895–1908; president of Pennsylvania State College, 1908–1920. He wrote: "Expansion of the American People"; "The Men Who Made the Nation"; "Formative Incidents in American Diplomacy"; "The United States, in the Story of the Nation Series"; "Foundations of National Development," and "The Lincoln-Douglas Debates." He died June 15, 1924.

SPIVAK, CHARLES D., physician, was born in Russia, December 25, 1861. On account of his political views he came to America, worked as a mill hand in Maine, as a laborer in New York and as a farmer in New Jersey until he was finally enabled to graduate from the Jefferson Medical College, Philadelphia, in 1890. In 1891–1892, he studied at the University of Berlin; was chief of gastrointestinal diseases at Philadelphia Polyclinic, 1894–1895; in 1896, became lecturer in Denver School of Medicine, Denver, Col. He died October 16, 1927.

SPRING CREEK—Tributary to Bald Eagle Creek. Sub-basin: Middle West Branch Susquehanna; source, in Tussey Mountain, Potter Township, middle southern Center County; course, northwesterly and northeasterly to Bald Eagle Creek; mouth, at Milesburg; length, twenty-four miles.

SPROUL, WILLIAM CAMERON, governor, was born in Octoraro, Lancaster County, September 16, 1870. He was graduated from Swarthmore College, in 1891, and subsequently engaged in business. He was the organizer and president, for a time, of the Seaboard Steel Casting Company now owned by the American Locomotive Company. He was also the organizer of the General Refractories Company, the Lebanon Iron Company, Lackawanna and Wyoming Valley Railroad and many railroads, mining, traction and power enterprises in West Virginia. At one time he was president of the *Chester Daily Times* and the *Morning Republican*, of Chester. In 1896, he was elected to the Pennsylvania Senate serving as a member of that body for twenty-two consecutive years. In 1919-1923, he was governor of the state, during which period he inaugurated and carried out a campaign for better roads throughout the state. He built and endowed the Sproul Observatory, at Swarthmore College, and at his own expense restored the Chester Court House, the oldest public building in Pennsylvania. He died March 21, 1928.

SQUAW CAMPAIGN, THE—Indian outrages on the western frontier, at the instigation of the British military authorities, led the Continental Congress, early in the Revolutionary War, to assume the responsibility of offensive operations against these persistent marauders. Brigadier-General Edward Hand was placed in command of Fort Pitt, with authority to call upon the militia officers of the frontier counties of Pennsylvania and Virginia for assistance. After considerable delay a force of five hundred horsemen were assembled at Fort Pitt, February 15, 1778, with which a foray was made against Indian villages in Lawrence County. The warriors were away from the villages at the time, the only persons found being an old man, some squaws and children. In the attack upon the villages the old man, a boy and four squaws were killed and two squaws captured and brought back as trophies. The expedition was generally derided by the frontiersmen and dubbed the "squaw campaign."

STANDING STONE CREEK—Tributary to Frankstown Branch. Sub-basin: Upper Juniata; source, in Jackson Township, northeastern Huntingdon County; course, southwesterly to Frankstown Branch Juniata River; mouth, at Huntingdon; length, twenty-eight and one-half miles. Indian name, Achsinnink, "where there is a large stone," or "the place of the large stone."

STAR-GAZERS STONE, THE, a stone planted in 1764, by Charles Mason and Jeremiah Dixon, while they were in the process of establishing the boundary between the provinces of Pennsylvania and Maryland. The stone is known as the Star-Gazers Stone because it was the site of astronomical observations made by the two English scientists. It is of flint, six inches square at the top, without any markings, and is located in Newlin Township, Chester County. At this place Mason and Dixon, in January, 1764, set up an observatory for the purpose of determining the exact latitude of this point. The Star-Gazers Stone was planted to indicate the exact distance from the point at which their observations began. In 1908, the stone was enclosed in a wall by the Chester County Historical Society.

STEELTON, borough in Dauphin County, suburban to Harrisburg. The settlement was laid out in 1866 under the name Baldwin, was later called Steelworks P. O., and in 1880 was incorporated under its present name. The great industry of the town is the Bethlehem Steel Works which has bridge and construction works, blast furnaces, and rail and blooming mills. Population (1930), 13,291; (1920), 13,248.

STERNE, SIMON, lawyer and economist, was born in Philadelphia, July 23, 1839. He studied at the University of Heidelberg and at the law school of the University of Pennsylvania and became a specialist in real estate and constitutional law. He was active in social and civic reform, lectured on political science at Cooper Institute, 1861-1863; secretary of the committee of seventy for the overthrow of the Tweed ring, 1870; was appointed by President Cleveland on 1896 to report on relations of western European governments to railways. His publications include: "Representative Government," "Suffrage in Cities," "Hindrances to Prosperity," and "Constitutional History and Political Development of the United States." He died in New York, September 22, 1901.

STERRETT, JAMES MACBRIDE, clergyman and educator, was born in Howard, Centre County, January 13, 1847. He was educated at Harvard University and at the Episcopal Theological School, Cambridge, Mass.; was ordained to the ministry in the Protestant Episcopal Church, 1872; served a pastorate in Bedford, 1872-1882; was professor of ethics and apologetics in Seabury Divinity School, Faribault, Minn., 1882-1892; professor of philosophy in George Washington University, 1892-1909; president emeritus, Carnegie Foundation, 1909; president, Society for Philosophical Inquiry, 1893-1910. He is the author of: "Studies in Hegel's Philosophy of Religion," "Reason and Authority in Religion," and "The Freedom of Authority." He died March 15, 1923.

STEVENS, THADDEUS, statesman, was born in Danville, Vt., April 4, 1792. After his graduation from Dartmouth College, in 1814, he came to York, where he taught school and studied law. He began the practice of the legal profession in Gettysburg. In 1828, he joined the Whig Party and became active in politics. He served as a member of the Pennsylvania House of Representatives, 1833-1835; 1838-1839, and 1841-1842; and on April 11, 1835, made an eloquent address in defense of free public education. A partner's venture in the iron business having involved him in a debt of $217,000, he retired from public life and practiced law with such success that he reduced the debt in six years to $30,000. He became widely known through his opposition to slavery and his defense of fugitive slaves. He was representative in Congress, in 1849-1853, and in 1859-1868, where he opposed all concessions to the southern states. He became the leader of his party in the House of Representatives, served throughout the Civil War as chairman of the committee on Ways and Means, and later as chairman of the Committee on Reconstruction, and chairman of the House Committee which had charge of the impeachment of Andrew Johnson. Stevens was a man of boundless energy and tenacity of will, intensely radical in his opposition to the south, and in his support of legislation favoring the freed slaves. He died in Washington, D. C., August 11, 1868.

THADDEUS STEVENS

STEVENSON, JOSEPH ROSS, clergyman and educator, was born in Ligonier, March 1, 1866. He was graduated from Washington and Jefferson College, in 1886, and from McCormick Theological Seminary, in 1889, and later studied at Berlin. He served as pastor, 1890-1894; occupied the chair of ecclesiastical history in McCormick Theological Seminary, 1897-1902; was pastor of Fifth Avenue Presbyterian Church, New York, 1902-1909, and of Brown Memorial Church, Baltimore, 1909-1914; president of Princeton Theological Seminary, 1914 to date.

STEWART, CHARLES, naval officer, was born in Philadelphia, July 28, 1778. At the age of thirteen he shipped on a merchant vessel. He became lieutenant in the United States Navy, 1798; commanded privateers and captured several French vessels preying on English commerce; took part in operations against Tripoli; commanded the "Constitution," in 1813, in a cruise during which two large British ships were captured; commanded a squadron on the Mediterranean, a Pacific squadron and finally, 1842-1843, the home squadron; in 1859-1862, was in charge of the Philadelphia navy yard, until he was retired as rear-admiral. He died in Bordentown, N. J., November 7, 1869.

STEWART, GEORGE BLACK, Presbyterian clergyman and educator, was born in Columbus, Ohio, February 28, 1854. Subsequent to his graduation from Princeton University, in 1876, and from Auburn Theological Seminary, in 1879, he held several pastorates. In 1899-1926, he was president of Auburn Seminary. He was one of the founders of the Pennsylvania Chautauqua of which he was president for five years, and is the author of: "Life of Jesus for Juniors," and "A Study of the Life of Jesus." He is now president emeritus of Auburn Theological Seminary, and professor of practical theology there.

STEWART, JULIUS, artist, was born in Philadelphia, September 6, 1855. He studied in Paris where he spent the greater part of his life. His work merited him gold medals from numerous local and foreign art societies.

STIEGEL, HENRY WILLIAM (BARON STIEGEL), was born in or near Mannheim, Germany, in 1730. In 1750, he came to Philadelphia where he probably settled for a time. In 1757, he purchased from Jacob Huber, whose daughter he had married in 1752, a furnace and land in Lancaster County. With Charles and Alexander Stedman, from whom he purchased a tract of 714 acres in Lancaster County, and John Barr Stiegel, he formed an iron works firm. The furnace, named Elizabeth, for Stiegel's wife, was located on the east side of the Blue Mountains, about one and a half miles northeast of Brickerville. The first six-plate wood stoves in Pennsylvania were made by Stiegel, who also improved the Benjamin Franklin stove. About 1763, Stiegel laid out the town of Manheim, where he erected a residence commonly called Stiegel Castle, and a glass factory, where the finest quality of glass was manufactured. In 1769, he built on a hill near Schaefferstown a tower, which was to be used as a place of refuge in times of danger and as a place where he might entertain his friends. About 1769, Stiegel reached the height of his financial success. From that year his projects gradually declined until his properties were sold by the sheriff and he was left utterly destitute. In the latter part of his life he engaged in surveying and school teaching at Brickerville and Womelsdorf. He died in his mansion at Charming Forge, in August, 1783.

STILL, WILLIAM, philanthropist, was born, of African descent, at Shamony, N. J., October 7, 1821. He was chairman and corresponding secretary of the Philadelphia branch of the Underground Railroad, 1851-1861; post sutler at

Camp William Penn for colored troops, during the Civil War. He wrote: "The Underground Railroad," "Voting and Laboring," and "Struggle for the Rights of the Colored People of Philadelphia." He died in 1902.

STILLE, ALFRED, physician, was born in Philadelphia, October 30, 1813. He attended Yale University and graduated from the University of Pennsylvania, in 1832, and from the medical school there, in 1836. Later he studied at Paris and Vienna; was resident physician at the Pennsylvania Hospital, 1839-1841; professor of the theory and practice of medicine at the Pennsylvania Medical College, 1854-1859, and at the University of Pennsylvania, 1864-1884. He was one of the founders of the American Medical Association, serving as its first secretary and as president in 1867. He is the author of: "Medical Instruction in the United States," "Therapeutics and Materia Medica," etc. He died in Philadelphia, September 24, 1900.

STILLE, CHARLES JANEWAY, educator and historian, was born in Philadelphia, September 23, 1819. After graduation from Yale, in 1839, he was admitted to the bar but abandoned law for literature. During the Civil War he was a member of the United States Sanitary Commission. In 1866, he became professor of history and English literature at the University of Pennsylvania and in 1868-1880 was provost of that institution. He is the author of: "Historical Development of American Civilization," "Studies in Mediaeval History," and "Beaumarchias and the Lost Milton." He died in Philadelphia, August 11, 1890.

STILLMAN, SAMUEL, Baptist clergyman, was born in Philadelphia, March 18, 1738. He was ordained to the Baptist ministry, in 1765; served as pastor of the First Baptist Church, Boston, 1765-1805, and was among the most influential of New England clergymen of his day. He was a member of the convention that ratified the United States Constitution of 1788. His writings include: "A Sermon on the Repeal of the Stamp Act," and "A Sermon Occasioned by the Death of George Washington." He died at Boston, March 12, 1807.

STOCKTON, CHARLES HERBERT, rear-admiral, was born in Philadelphia, October 13, 1845. During the Civil War he served on the *Macedonian* and in 1865 was graduated from the United States Naval Academy. He was promoted to commander in 1892, captain, 1899, and rear-admiral, 1906. He was president of the Naval War College, 1898-1900, naval attache at the American Embassy, London, 1903-1905, president of George Washington University, 1911-1913, and first United States delegate to the London Naval Conference, 1908-1909. He has written extensively on international law. His death occurred May 31, 1923.

STOEVER, MARTIN LUTHER, educator and author, was born in Germantown, Philadelphia, February 17, 1820. He graduated from Gettysburg College, in 1838, and was principal of the preparatory school there, 1840-1870, during which time he was also professor of Latin, history and political economy. For several years he was secretary of the General Synod of the Lutheran Church, and editor of the *Evangelical Quarterly Review*. He published biographies of Dr. Henry M. Muhlenberg, and Dr. Philip F. Mayer, and "A Brief Sketch of the Lutheran Church in the United States." He died at Gettysburg, July 22, 1870.

STONE, WILLIAM ALEXIS, soldier and governor, was born in Delmar Township, Tioga County, April 18, 1846. He was educated at the Mansfield State Normal School and at the age of eighteen joined the army as a private and took part in the siege of Petersburg. In 1865, he was promoted to the rank of lieutenant-colonel. After the war he studied law and was admitted to the bar, beginning his practice at Wellsboro and continuing it at Pittsburgh. He was United States District Attorney for the western district of Pennsylvania and for eight years was a member of Congress. In 1898, he was the candidate of the Republican Party for the office of governor. He was elected and served from 1899-1903. He died March 1, 1920.

STONE, WITMER, naturalist, was born in Philadelphia, September 22, 1866. He was educated at the University of Pennsylvania; was assistant curator of the Academy of Natural Sciences, Philadelphia, 1891-1908; curator, 1908-1924; director, museum, 1925-1928; vice-president, 1927; director emeritus since 1929. He is a member of many American and foreign ornithological societies. His publications include: "Birds of Eastern Pennsylvania and New Jersey," "Mammals of New Jersey," "Flora of Southern New Jersey," "Birds of Yucatan and Southern Mexico," "The Phylogenetic Value of Color Characters in Birds," etc.

STONY CREEK—Tributary to Conemaugh River. Sub-basin: Lower Allegheny; source, in Brothers Valley Township, central Somerset County, on the divide between Allegheny, Youghiogheny, Juniata and Potomac watersheds; course, northerly into Cambria County, forming Cambria-Somerset County boundary for three miles, to join Little Conemaugh River and form Conemaugh River; mouth, at Johnstown; length, forty and one-half miles. Indian name, Sinne-hanna, or Achsinne-hanne, "stony stream."

STONY CREEK—Tributary to Susquehanna River. Sub-basin: Lower Main Susquehanna; source, in Cold Spring Township, northwestern Lebanon County; course, southwesterly into Dauphin County to Susquehanna River; mouth, at Dauphin; length, twenty-two and one-half miles. Indian name, Sinne-hanna, or Achsinne—hanne, "stony stream."

STOYSTOWN TEMPERANCE SOCIETY, an organization meeting at Stoystown, Somerset County, October 1, 1835, decided to learn how many farmers in Quemahoning and adjoining townships had harvested their grain without the aid of spirituous liquors. The report made October 24, 1835, indicated that the greater number of farmers house their grain without the use of any liquor and the unanimous conclusion was that the grain was cut in less time with less waste than formerly and with greater peace and quiet.

STRAIN, ISAAC G., naval officer, was born in Roxbury, Pa., March 4, 1821. He was appointed midshipman in the United States Navy, in 1837; led explorations to the interior of Brazil, 1849; raised to rank of lieutenant, 1850, and was engaged that year with the commission that laid out the boundary between the United States and Mexico. He was in charge of the expedition for the survey of the Isthmus of Darien, in 1854, and attracted public attention through his skill and daring in this work. In 1856, he was assigned to the Arctic, and supervised the making of soundings in the north Atlantic Ocean for the purpose of ascertaining the possibilities of laying a submarine cable between United States and Great Britain. He wrote: "The Cordillera and Pampa," "The History and Prospects of Interoceanic Communication," etc. He died May 14, 1857.

STROUDSBURG, borough and county-seat of Monroe County, a popular summer resort, lies between the Delaware Water Gap and Mount Pocono. Population (1930), 5,961; (1920), 5,278.

STUART, EDWIN SYDNEY, governor, was born in Philadelphia, December 28, 1853, and was educated in the public schools of his native city. In 1868, he engaged in the bookselling and publishing business. He was a Republican presidential elector in 1884 and 1900; delegate to the Republican National Conventions of 1888, 1896, and 1908; mayor of Philadelphia, 1891-1895; president of the Electoral College of Pennsylvania, 1901. As governor of Pennsylvania, 1907-1911, he conducted an investigation in the capital scandal. He is president of the board of directors of the City Trusts of Philadelphia, and has charge of all trusts managed by the city, including the Girard Estate and Girard College. He is also one of the managers of the Western Saving Fund Society of Philadelphia.

STUART'S RAID AT CHAMBERSBURG—Early in October, 1862, General Lee, commander-in-chief of the Confederate Army, ordered General J. E. B. Stuart to invade Pennsylvania, in the direction of Chambersburg, for the purpose of securing information concerning General McClellan's plans, and disarranging them, if possible. Stuart crossed the Potomac on October 10th, and marched northward by way of Mercersburg, and advanced to Chambersburg. On the morning of the 11th, he destroyed the railroad depots and such military supplies as could be found; seized five hundred good cavalry horses in the surrounding country and moved southward through Cashtown, passing to the west of Gettysburg, through Emmitsburg and on to the Potomac. Forces from various sources were sent to intercept him, but he avoided them, dislodged a force of Pennsylvania infantry guarding White's Ford, and recrossed the Potomac into Maryland, taking with him 1,200 horses from the farms of Pennsylvania, and thirty prominent citizens of the state to be held as hostages for citizens of the confederacy who had been arrested and imprisoned. Stuart succeeded in securing valuable information, and in delaying McClellan.

SUGAR CREEK—Tributary to North Branch Susquehanna River. Sub-basin: Upper North Branch Susquehanna; source, in Armenia Township, western Bradford County; course, easterly to North Branch Susquehanna River; mouth, at North Towanda; length, twenty-eight miles.

SULLIVAN, JOHN, patriot, soldier, and statesman, was born in Berwick, Maine, February 18, 1740. He received his education from his father who was a teacher, studied law and was admitted to the bar in Durham, N. H. He became major of a New Hampshire Regiment, in 1772; delegate to the Continental Congress, by which he was appointed brigadier-general, 1775, and major-general, 1776; was appointed by Washington to conduct an expedition against the Iroquois Indians of central New York in defense of frontier settlers in northern Pennsylvania and in New York, which resulted in the conquest of these allies of the British and the devastation of their country; served his state with distinction in various positions, closing his career as judge of the United States District Court of New Hampshire, 1789-1795. He died at Durham, N. H., January 23, 1795.

SULLIVAN COUNTY, was formed March 15, 1847, from part of Lycoming. Named for General John Sullivan. Land area, 458 square miles; population 1930, 7,499. County-seat, Laporte, laid out in 1850.

SULLIVAN'S EXPEDITION—The incursions of the Iroquois Indians of central New York upon the frontier settlements of New York and Pennsylvania, culminating in the massacres of Wyoming and Cherry Valleys, led the Continental Congress to authorize General Washington to send an expedition into their country with orders for a destructive campaign. Major-General John Sullivan who had won distinction in the battles of Brandywine and Germantown, and in his association with the Continental Army during its winter at Valley Forge, was appointed to the command of this expedition in March, 1779. Delay in securing enlistments, and difficulties in furnishing and transporting supplies and equipment, prevented a forward movement until July 31st, when the army broke camp at its concentration point at Wyoming. From this point the line of march over mountains and across morasses, through a country without roads, rendered progress slow and exceedingly fatiguing. The Indians kept themselves well informed of Sullivan's movements, but offered little resistance to the advance of his forces, with the exception of ambushing some reconnoitering parties, at slight loss to the invaders, and sending out marauding parties to draw Sullivan from his purpose, or divide his forces. Sullivan refused to allow himself to be diverted from his main purpose of penetrating into the heart of the Indian territory, and continued his movements, finding many deserted Indian villages along the way. These villages, with their surrounding fields of corn and potatoes, were destroyed, excepting such as could be used by his troops. Finally, in approaching the more populous regions of the Six Nations, returning scouts informed Sullivan that a considerable force of Tories and Indians had fortified a strategic position at Newtown, now Elmira, N. Y. The Tories were under the command of Colonel John Butler and his son, Captain Walter N. Butler, while the Indians were commanded by the great Mohawk warrior, Joseph Brandt. Their entire force was estimated at about 1,500. A skillful flanking movement drove Tories and Indians from their position with considerable loss in killed and wounded, and with complete destruction in morale, from which they did not sufficiently recover to make another decided stand.

The greatest Indian confederation on this continent, at this time, occupied central New York. No other Indians in North America possessed the genius for organization, or developed as high a type of civilization as was found among the Six Nations, comprising the Senecas, Mohawks, Oneidas, Cayugas, Onondagas, and Tuscaroras. Among their chieftains were statesmen, orators, and warriors of a high order. In the Genesee Valley and about the lakes in central New York, there were many villages of well, and even elegantly built houses. There were well-cultivated fields planted in corn, and all the vegetables common today. There were fine orchards of peach, pear and apple trees, laden with fruit at the time of this invasion. The tribes of this confederation were not entirely united in their opposition to the colonies, and the Oneidas and Onondagas took no part in this campaign; indeed sixty of the Onondagas were in the field on the American side.

Following the battle of Newtown (Elmira), and a slight stand at Narrows, a few miles beyond, General Sullivan's Army marched to and fro through the Genesee Valley, burning the villages and laying waste corn fields and orchards for 280 miles. Forty Indian towns were reported completely destroyed. The Tories and hostile Indians, following this wide spread destruction of their homes and food supplies, were obliged to retreat to Fort Niagara under the protection and care of Great Britain. Such was the durable quality of this Indian confederation, however, and the type of civilization that they here developed that they later returned to their country, rebuilt their homes, and have continued to be a growing and developing people in New York to this day. Nevertheless Sullivan's campaign broke their power. Their depredations by small squads continued during the war, but there were no repetitions of Wyoming and Cherry Valleys.

SULLY, ALFRED, military officer, was born in Philadelphia, in 1821. He graduated from the United States Military Academy, in 1841; took part in the

Seminole War and served in the war with Mexico, 1846-1848; was promoted brigadier-general, in 1862, and in 1863 was given command of the Department of Dakota, where he distinguished himself in his campaigns against hostile Indians. At the close of the Civil War he was brevetted major-general of volunteers, and brigadier-general in the United States Army. He died at Fort Vancouver, Washington, April 17, 1879.

SULZBERGER, MAYER, jurist, was born in Heidelsheim, Germany, June 22, 1843. He came to America with his family during the Revolution of 1848 and settled in Philadelphia. In 1859, he graduated from the Central High School in that city and subsequently engaged in the study of Hebrew language and literature. He was admitted to the bar, September 16, 1865, became successful in his profession and in 1895-1915 was judge of the Court of Common Pleas and in 1902-1915 presiding judge. During President Harrison's administration he was offered the position of United States Minister to Turkey, but declined. He wrote: "Am-ha-Aretz" (the ancient Hebrew Parliament); "The Polity of the Ancient Hebrews," and "The Ancient Hebrew Law of Homicide." He died April 20, 1923.

SUMNER, SAMUEL STORROW, military officer, was born in Pennsylvania, February 6, 1842. He served in the Civil War; was brevetted first lieutenant, June 1, 1862, for battle of Fair Oaks, Va.; captain, September 17, 1862, for Antietam; major, March 13, 1865, for campaign against Vicksburg; lieutenant-colonel, February 27, 1890, for action against Indians at Summit Springs, Colo., July 11, 1869. He served in the campaign against the Indians, 1869-1878; was appointed brigadier-general of volunteers, May, 1898; served in Cuba during the Spanish-American War; joined the United States troops in China, 1900; later was sent to the Philippines where he was promoted brigadier-general, United States Army, 1901, and major-general, 1903. He retired from the army, February 6, 1906, and lives at Brookline, Mass.

SUNBURY, borough and county-seat of Northumberland County, on the Susquehanna River, 157 miles north of Philadelphia. It is located on the site of the Indian village, Shamokin, an important center of Indian affairs. Fort Augusta was erected here in 1756 as a means of protection against the French and Indians. The present settlement was begun in June, 1772, by Surveyor-General Lukens and William Maclay. It was incorporated as a borough, March 24, 1797. Sunbury is located in a coal region and is a center for coal shipping. Its industrial establishments are: railroad shops, planing mills, silk mills, sash and door factories, nail factories and coffin and casket works. Population (1930), 15,626; (1920), 15,721.

SUNDAY SCHOOLS, EARLY. A Sabbath School was established at Ephrata about 1740. The Schwenkfelders had them from the time of their first settlement in 1738.

SUSQUEHANNA, borough of Susquehanna County, on the Susquehanna River, twenty-three miles east of Binghampton, N. Y. Its industrial establishments are machine shops, washing machine and metal ware factories.

SUSQUEHANNA COUNTY, was formed February 21, 1810, from part of Luzerne. Named for the Susquehanna River. Land area, 824 square miles; population (1930), 33,806. County-seat, Montrose, laid out in 1811.

SUSQUEHANNA INDIANS, were one of the smaller independent tribes of American Indians. They lived in central Pennsylvania.

SUSQUEHANNA RIVER—Tributary to Chesapeake Bay. Basin: Susquehanna; source, formed by junction of north and west branches at Northumberland, Northumberland County; course, southerly to junction of Juniata River, then southeasterly to Chesapeake Bay, crossing Pennsylvania-Maryland boundary at elevation 71. The stream forms the western boundary of Northumberland, Dauphin and Lancaster Counties, and the eastern boundary of Union, Juniata, Perry, Cumberland and York Counties. Indian name, Quenischachachgek-hanne, "the long reach river" (a name first applied to the West Branch).

SUSQUEHANNA RIVER, NORTH BRANCH—Tributary to Susquehanna River. Basin: Susquehanna; source, in Otsego Lake, Catskill Mountains, southeastern New York; course, southwesterly, entering Pennsylvania in Susquehanna County, returning to New York after forming a loop sixteen miles long, and flowing westerly, re-entering Pennsylvania near Sayre, Bradford County; mouth, at Northumberland; length, total, three hundred and sixteen miles. Indian name, Quenischach-achgek-hanne, "the long reach river" (a name first applied to the West Branch). The name first given to the North Branch was M'chewamisipu, "the river on which are extensive clear flats."

SUSQUEHANNA RIVER, WEST BRANCH—Tributary to Susquehanna River. Basin: Susquehanna; source, in Carroll Township, northwestern Cambria County; course, northerly into Clearfield County; mouth, at Northumberland; length, two hundred and twenty-eight miles. Indian name, Quenischachachgek-hanne, "the long reach river" (a name first applied to the West Branch).

SUSQUEHANNA UNIVERSITY, co-educational institution at Selinsgrove, was founded in 1858 by the Lutheran Church. Enrollment (1930-1931), 375.

SUTPHEN, WILLIAM GILBERT VAN TASSEL, author, was born in Philadelphia, May 11, 1861. He was graduated from Princeton, in 1882, and afterward pursued a literary career. In 1923, he was ordained priest of the Protestant Episcopal Church. His writings include: "The Golficide," "The Cardinal's Rose," "The Golfer's Alphabet," "The Nineteenth Hole," "The

Doomsman," "The Gates of Chance," "In Jeopardy," "The Sermon on the Cross," and "Kings Champion." His home is in Morristown, N. J.

SWANK, JAMES MOORE, economist, was born in Westmoreland County, July 12, 1832. He founded the Johnstown *Tribune*, in 1853, and was secretary of the American Iron and Steel Association, 1873-1885. He wrote: "History of Iron in All Ages," "Iron Making and Coal Mining in Pennsylvania," and many tracts on the tariff question. He died June 21, 1914.

SWARTHMORE COLLEGE, founded by the liberal or Hicksite body of the Society of Friends at Swarthmore, was opened in 1869. But one baccalaureate degree, that of Bachelor of Arts, is conferred. The degrees of master of arts and civil engineer are conferred for graduate work. From the beginning Swarthmore was co-educational, being the second institution east of the Alleghney Mountains to admit women as students. Enrollment (1930-1931), 575.

SWATARA CREEK—Tributary to Susquehanna River. Sub-basin: Lower Main Susquehanna; source, in Broad Mountain, Foster Township, western central Schuylkill County; course, southwesterly, through Lebanon and Dauphin Counties, to Susquehanna River; mouth, at Middletown; length, sixty-nine miles. Written in old deeds, Esutara and Suatara; Swahadowry, corrupted from Schaha-dawa, "where we fed on eels."

SWATARA (LITTLE) CREEK—Tributary to Swatara Creek. Sub-basin: Lower Main Susquehanna; source, on Bethel-Upper Tulpehocken Township boundary, northwestern Berks County; course, southwesterly into Lebanon County to Swatara Creek; mouth, at Jonestown; length, twenty-three and one-half miles. Esutara and Suatara; Swahadowry, corrupted from Schaha-dawa, "where we fed on eels."

SWENSSON, CARL AARON, Lutheran theologian, was born at Sugar Grove, Warren County, June 25, 1857. After his graduation from Augustana College, Rock Island, 1877, and from the Augustana Theological Seminary, in 1879, he became secretary to the General Council of the Lutheran Church of North America, and was its president in 1893-1894. In 1889, he was a member of the Kansas Legislature. He founded Bethany College, in 1881, and served as president of the institution until his death February 16, 1904.

SWINGLE, WALTER TENNYSON, botanist and agriculturist, was born at Canaan, January 8, 1871. He graduated from the Kansas State Agricultural College in 1890 and in 1895-1896, and 1898 engaged in study in Europe. He has been connected with the United States Department of Agriculture since 1891 when he became special agent, division of vegetable physiology and pathology. In 1898, he became agricultural explorer for the department during which period he investigated agricultural conditions in southern Europe, Asia Minor, China, Japan and the Philippines. In 1902, he took charge of crop physiology and plant breeding investigations.

SWISSHELM, JANE GREY, reformer and author, was born in Pittsburgh, September 6, 1815. She was a pioneer advocate of woman's rights, strongly opposed slavery and expressed her feelings on the subject so forcefully that the office and press of the Saint Cloud, Minn., *Visitor* which she was editing, was destroyed by a mob. Upon the outbreak of the Civil War she joined the Union Army as a nurse. She has written: "Letters to Country Girls," and "Half of a Century" (an autobiography). She died at Swissdale, July 22, 1884.

SWITCHBACK, MAUCH CHUNK—See MAUCH CHUNK GRAVITY RAILROAD.

TABARD INN LIBRARY, founded in Philadelphia, in 1900 and 1902, respectively, as a traveling library on a commercial basis.

TACONY CHEMICAL WORKS, established in 1831 by Nicholas Lennig & Co. These works were formerly at Port Richmond, but were later removed to the village of Bridesburg, now a part of the city of Philadelphia.

TAGGART, COL. JOHN H., editor of the Sunday Times, in Philadelphia, raised a company of volunteers called "The Wayne Guards," and marched them from Philadelphia to Harrisburg. They arrived at Camp Curtin, June 7, 1861.

TAMANEND (TAMMANY, ETC.), was the chief of the Unami or Turtle clan of Delaware Indians. Lived in what is now Bucks County. Penn's treaty under the great elm at Shakamaxon, within the limits of Philadelphia, was made with Tamanend and other Delaware chiefs. Tamanend is supposed to have died before July, 1701, and his grave is believed to be in "Tammany Burial Ground" near Chalfonte, Bucks County.

TAMAQUA, borough in Schuylkill County, on the Little Schuylkill River. It is in a region noted for the quantity and quality of coal deposits. It was settled in 1799 and became a borough in 1833. Population (1930), 12,936; (1920), 12,368.

TAMMANY SOCIETY OF PHILADELPHIA, organized at the close of the Revolution, and the Tammany Society of New York, organized in 1789, were named for the Indian chief, Tammany.

TANGRAM OR FASHIONABLE TRIFLER, THE, had its origin in 1810. Had three authors, one not known, the others, Alexander Coxe, son of Tench Coxe, and Mordecai Manassas Noah.

494   ENCYCLOPEDIA OF PENNSYLVANIA

TANNENBERG, DAVID, organ builder, was born in Berthelsdorf, Saxony, March 21, 1728. He came to Pennsylvania, in 1749, and assisted John Klemm in building organs. After the death of his employer, in 1762, Tannenberg continued the business at Lititz, Lancaster County, for about forty years. Among the organs which he built was one for Zion Lutheran Church, Philadelphia, the dedication of which on January 8, 1791, was attended by President and Mrs. Washington, members of Congress and of the Pennsylvania Assembly. This organ, the largest in the United States, was destroyed by fire in 1794. Tannenberg, who also built pianos, was an excellent musician. Upon his death on May 19, 1804, he was succeeded by his son-in-law and partner, John Philip Bachman.

TANNER, BENJAMIN TUCKER, African Methodist bishop, was born in Pittsburgh, December 25, 1835. Educated at Avery College, Allegheny, and at Western Theological Seminary. Editor of the Christian Recorder for sixteen years, founded and was editor for four years of the A. M. E. Church Review, and in 1888 was appointed bishop. He was a delegate to the Third Ecumenical Methodist Conference held in London in 1901. He wrote several books on the Negro. Died in Philadelphia, January 15, 1923.

TANNER, HENRY OSSAWA, artist, son of B. T. Tanner, was born in Pittsburgh, June 21, 1859. Studied under Thomas Eakins at the Pennsylvania Academy of Fine Arts, later moving to Paris where he became a pupil of Jean Paul Laurens and Benjamin Constant. Was awarded the Walter Lippincott Prize, Philadelphia, in 1900; Second Medal Paris Exposition in the same year. He also won medals at the Buffalo, St. Louis and San Francisco expositions.

TANNERY, EARLY. Penn and the Free Society of Traders established a tannery in Philadelphia, in 1683.

TARASCON, LOUIS ANASTASIUS, a French gentleman, emigrated in 1794 from France, and established himself in Philadelphia. He was an importer of silks, and all kinds of French and German goods. In 1799, he sent two of his clerks, Charles Brugiere and James Berthoud, to examine the course of the Ohio and Mississippi Rivers from Pittsburgh to New Orleans, and ascertain the practicability of sending ships, and clearing them from Pittsburgh, ready rigged, to the West Indies and Europe. These two men returned with a favorable report and Mr. Tarascon associated them and his brother, John Anthony, with himself, under the firm of John A. Tarascon, Brothers, James Berthoud & Co., and immediately established in Pittsburgh a large wholesale and retail store and warehouse, a shipyard, a rigging and sail-loft, an anchor-smith shop, a block manufactory, and in short, everything necessary to complete vessels for sea. In 1801, they built the schooner Amity and the ship Pittsburgh, sending the former, loaded with flour, to St. Thomas, and the latter to Philadelphia, from whence they sent them to Bordeaux, and brought back a cargo of wine, brandy, and other French goods, part of which they sent here in wagons at a cost of six to eight cents per pound for transportation.

TARBELL, IDA MINERVA, biographer, was born in Erie County, November 5, 1857. She was graduated from Allegheny College, Meadville; from 1883 to 1891 was associate editor of The Chautauquan; studied at the Sorbonne and College de France, 1891 to 1894; was on the editorial staff of McClure's Magazine from 1894 to 1906; associate editor of The American Magazine, 1906 to 1915. Her publications include: "A Short Life of Napoleon Bonaparte" (1895); "Early Life of Abraham Lincoln" (1900); "History of the Standard Oil Company" (1904); "Father Abraham" (1909); "The Business of Being a Woman" (1913); "Making Men at Ford's" (1916); "In the Footsteps of the Lincolns" (1924); and "Life of Elbert H. Gary" (1925).

TARENTUM, town in Allegheny County, laid out by Judge Henry M. Brackenridge and his wife, Caroline, who owned the land on which the town was built. Population (1930), 9,551; (1920), 8,925.

TASKER, THOMAS T., SR., iron master, was born at Nottingly, Yorkshire, England, May 12, 1799; came to American in 1819. In 1820, he opened a stove manufacturing business at West Chester, removing again to Philadelphia, in 1824, where he obtained employment with Stephen P. Morris, a manufacturer of grates for the burning of anthracite coal. In 1831, he entered into partnership with Morris, and continued in that business until his death in 1871.

TAWNEY, JAMES A., congressman, was born near Gettysburg, January 3, 1855. He was educated in the common schools and learned the blacksmith's and machinist's trade. He went to Winona, Minn., in 1877, and was admitted to the bar there in 1882, practicing law until 1890, when he was elected to the State Senate of Minnesota. Was elected to Congress, in 1893, and served continuously until 1911; was appointed by President Taft to the International Joint Commission created by treaty with Great Britain for the settlement of disputes between the United States and Canada, and was chairman of the United States part of the Commission until his death at Excelsior Springs, Mo., June 12, 1919.

TAYLOR, BAYARD, writer, was born at Kennett Square, Chester County, in 1825. After attending the academies at West Chester and Unionville, he resolved to learn the printer's trade and accordingly entered the office of the Village Record. As he did not care for his apprentice-work he took to sketching and making cartoons, and also to writing verse. In Graham's Magazine of May, 1843, there appeared one of his poems, "Modern Greece." He later became a contributor to the Saturday Evening Post. In 1844, he sent to the press "Ximena and Other Poems." Young as he was he made up his mind to visit Europe, which he did, and what he saw during his first tour and his experiences are related in "Views Afoot or Europe Seen with Knapsack and Staff," published in 1846, upon his return. His great literary work was his translation of "Faust." He was made Secretary of the Legation at St. Petersburg by President Lincoln, in 1861, and Minister to Berlin by President Hayes, in 1877. He died in Berlin, Prussia, on December 19, 1878, and his remains were brought to this country and consigned to their last resting-place at Longwood Cemetery, East Marlborough Township, Chester County.

TAYLOR, FREDERICK WINSLOW, efficiency engineer, was born in Germantown, Philadelphia, March 20, 1856. Educated at Phillips Exeter Academy, but left on account of trouble with his eyes, and was later graduated from Stevens Institute of Technology. In 1878, he entered service at the Midvale Steel Co., Philadelphia, first as a gang-boss, and by continued promotion became chief engineer, in 1889, the same year he commenced his notable career of efficiency expert reorganizing manufacturing plants. He was inventor of the Taylor-White process of treating modern high-speed tools for which he received a personal gold medal at the Paris Exposition in 1900. He was president of the American Society of Mechanical Engineers, 1905-06. He died March 21, 1915.

TAYLOR, GEORGE, statesman, one of the signers of the Declaration of Independence, was born in Ireland, in 1716. He came to America as a redemptioner, and on arriving bound himself out for a term of years to an iron manufacturer at Durham, Pa. When his employer discovered his intelligence he made him his clerk, and after he died Taylor married his widow. He was a member of the Provincial Assembly, 1764-70; judge of the county court and colonel of militia, and in 1775 he was again elected to the Provincial Assembly. On July 20, 1776, he was elected a member of the Continental Congress, and in March, 1777, retired from Congress to private life. He died at Easton, February 23, 1781.

TAYLOR, ISAAC EBENEZER, physician, was born in Philadelphia, April 25, 1812. He was graduated from Rutgers College, in 1830, and in medicine from the University of Pennsylvania, in 1834. He later studied in Europe and then settled in New York, where he was connected with various dispensaries. In 1851, he was elected physician to Bellevue Hospital, where he secured the foundation of the hospital college and in 1861 became its head. He died in New York, October 30, 1889.

TAYLOR, town in Lackawanna County, named for the late Moses Taylor, a prominent New York merchant and capitalist. Population (1930), 10,428; (1920), 9,876.

TAYLOR'S ALMANAC, published in Philadelphia, by Jacob Taylor, before 1706.

TEEDYUSCONG, one of the famous chiefs of the Delawares, was a son of the Delaware chief, Captain John Harris, of the Turtle Clan, and was born in New Jersey, about 1705. When about fifty years of age, he was chosen chief of the Delawares on the Susquehanna and until his tragic death, April 16, 1763, he was one of the chief figures in the history of the Indians in Pennsylvania. He founded the Delaware town of Wyoming in 1742 or 1743. He was called Honest John by the Moravians after he was baptized by them. In March, 1756, he and the Delawares under him left the town of Wyoming and removed to Tioga (now Athens, Bradford County). After the death of Shikellamy, in 1749, Teedyuscong was chosen "King of the Delawares" by some of the Shamokin Delawares and the Delawares of the Munsee Clan.

TELEGRAPH. The first telegraph of any kind by which intelligence was brought to Philadelphia was established in 1809, according to the plan of Jonathan Gront who set it up. Gront, a native of Mass., received a patent from Congress in 1800.

TEMPLE UNIVERSITY, an institution of higher learning, founded in Philadelphia in 1884, by Russell H. Conwell, pastor of the Baptist Temple. It was designed to give instruction to young men who were employed during the day. In 1891, a day school was added. There are all departments to the highest university courses; it is non-sectarian and co-educational. Enrollment (1930–1931), 8,600.

TENER, JOHN KINLEY, governor (1911–1915), was born in County Tyrone, Ireland, July 25, 1863; came to America at the age of nine years. He was educated in the public schools of Pittsburgh. In 1891, he located in Charleroi, where he became interested in several business concerns. He was a member of the 61st Congress (1909–11), from the 24th Pennsylvania District, and Governor of Pennsylvania (1911–15). He was president of the National Baseball League, resigning in 1918. He lives at Charleroi.

TENMILE CREEK—Tributary to Monongahela River. Sub-basin: Monongahela; source, in South Franklin Township, southern central Washington County; course, southeasterly to Monongahela River, forming Washington-Greene County boundary for last 7.5 miles; mouth, at Millsboro; length, thirty-four and one-half miles.

TENMILE CREEK, SOUTH FORK. Tributary to Tenmile Creek. Sub-basin: Monongahela; Source, in Richhill Township, western Greene County; Course, easterly to Waynesburg; Mouth, at Clarksville; Length, thirty-four miles.

TENNENT, WILLIAM, Presbyterian minister, was born in Ireland, about 1673. He was educated for the Episcopal Church, and ordained in 1704. In 1702, he married the daughter of Mr. Kennedy, a Presbyterian minister; came to America, in 1718; was licensed by the Philadelphia Presbytery; called to East Chester first; in 1721, he was called to Bensalem, Bucks County, and in 1726 to Neshaminy, Bucks County. He built the Log College in Neshaminy for the education of men for the ministry, and this college prepared for the pulpit some of the ablest divines of the last century. The college, built of logs, was one of the earliest classical schools in the province. William Tennent was the father of four sons who all became distinguished ministers in the Presbyterian Church. He died in 1746.

TEUTONIA, town built by the Society of Industry, in 1843, on a tract of land containing 4,000 acres, in McKean County, five miles southwest of Smethport. The Society of Industry was organized on a communistic basis with community of property, money and furniture accepted. The leader was Henry Ginal, a German.

THATCHER, HENRY CALVIN, first chief justice of Colorado, was born in Perry County, April 21, 1842, the son of Henry and Lydia Ann (Albert) Thatcher. He was educated at Franklin and Marshall College, at Lancaster, later read law at Altoona and at the same time edited the educational columns of the Hollidaysburg Standard. In the spring of 1866, he was graduated from the law department of Albany University, N. Y., and in the fall of that year went to Colorado, locating at Pueblo, and began the practice of law. In 1869, President Grant appointed him U. S. Attorney for the state of Colorado. When Colorado gained statehood he was a member of the Constitutional Convention. In 1876, he was elected to the Supreme Court. In drawing lots for terms, Judge Thatcher drew the short term of three years and by the law's provision thus became the Chief Justice. At the time of his retirement he resumed the practice of law in Pueblo, becoming senior partner in the firm of Thatcher and Gast. Justice Thatcher died March 20, 1884.

THATCHER, JOHN A., brother of Chief Justice Henry C. Thatcher, was born August 25, 1836, in Perry County; attended school in New Buffalo and Newport, the Tuscarora Academy and Prof. Wilson's Airy View Academy. In 1857, he went to Holt County, Missouri, where he clerked for five years. In 1862, he went to Denver, Colorado, and in 1862 started a business of his own, establishing the first general store in Pueblo, Colorado. In 1866, his brother, Mahlon D., joined him in the business. He died August 14, 1913.

THATCHER, MAHLON D., brother of Chief Justice Thatcher and John A. Thatcher, was born in Perry County. He was educated in the schools of Newport and attended Tuscarora Academy. He joined his father in business and in 1865 dissolved partnership and went to Pueblo, Colorado, to join his brother, John A., in the mercantile business, conducting it under "Thatcher Brothers, Merchants." They were very successful, later starting a bank as "Thatcher Brothers, Bankers." They later obtained the charter for the First National Bank of Pueblo. When Mahlon D. Thatcher died, in 1916, he was president of the bank and actively interested in thirty-six other banking institutions.

THEOPHILUS, THE BATTLE—AXE. Theophilus Gates, the founder of the religious sect known as the Battle-Axe, was born in Hartland, Connecticut, January 12, 1787. Having settled in Philadelphia, he published in June 1837, "Battle-Axe and Weapons of War." In it he advocated free love, and prophesied that all things would be in common in the new order; that no wife would lack a husband nor husband a wife. For a short time he had a few followers in Chester and adjoining counties. He died October 30, 1846.

THIEL COLLEGE, a co-educational college, was founded at Greenville, Mercer County, in 1870, and named for A. L. Thiel, of Pittsburgh, who made a number of liberal bequests to the institution. The college is under the control of the Lutheran Church. Enrollment (1930-1931), 250.

THOMAS, GEORGE, lt.-gov., (1738-1747), son of a West Indian planter, and at the time of his appointment, a member of the council of Antigua, his native isle. Gov. Thomas was a brilliant and powerful representative of the proprietary for nine years. During this period the remarkable religious movement led by George Whitefield occurred, but the operations necessitated by the hostile attitude of the French and their Indian allies were the most conspicuous features of his administration, which extended from August, 1738, until his resignation on account of ill health in May, 1747.

THOMPSON, DENMAN, actor, was born near Girard, in 1833; spent his youth in Swanzy, N. H., and made his debut in 1852, in Lowell, Mass., in the "French Spy." His most famous character was "Joshua Whitcomb," in the play by that name. He later introduced the character in the "Old Homestead." He died in 1911.

THOMPSON, JAMES, Judge of the Venango County District Court from May, 1839, to May, 1845, was one of the most distinguished jurists of Pennsylvania. He was born in Butler County, in 1805. In early life he learned the printer's trade, later preparing for the legal profession; was admitted to the bar in Franklin, Venango County, February 23, 1829. He was elected to the State Legislature, in 1832, and twice reelected. In 1834, he was chosen speaker of the house and subsequently served in Congress. In 1858, was elected Judge of the Supreme Court, in which capacity he served fifteen years; during the last five he was Chief Justice of the State.

THOMPSON, ROBERT ELLIS, educator, was born in Ireland, April 5, 1844; graduated from the University of Pennsylvania, in 1865, and held successively, from 1868 to 1892, professorships there in Latin and mathematics, Social Science, History and English literature. He also held lectureships at Harvard, Yale and Princeton Theological Seminary. In 1874, he was ordained to the Presbyterian ministry. In 1894, was elected principal of the Central High School of Philadelphia, continuing after 1921, as principal emeritus. He died in Philadelphia, October 19, 1924.

THOMPSON, WILLIAM, Revolutionary soldier, was born in Ireland, about 1725; served as a captain of militia in the French and Indian War (1759-60), and as a colonel in the War of the Revolution, later becoming brigadier-general. He died near Carlisle, September 4, 1781.

THOMSON, CHARLES, Secretary of the Continental Congress, from 1775, was a man of literary tastes, who when he had long served his country, and become one of the best known and most respected personages of our early political annals, occupied the remainder of his life in composition, publishing a translation of the Old and New Testament. He was born in Ireland, in 1729, and came to America at the age of eleven. He lived till 1824, dying at the venerable age of ninety-five years.

THOMSON, ELIHU, inventor and electrician, was born in Manchester, England, March 29, 1853. He came to America, in 1858; was educated in the Philadelphia public schools; from 1870-1880, was professor of chemistry and mechanics in Central High School, Philadelphia; became interested in lighting by electricity and his experiments resulted in patents secured in 1878 and 1879. In 1880, he became electrician to the American Electric Company, afterward known as the Thomson-Houston Electric Company, and later the General Electric Company. Thomson was the first recipient of the Edison medal.

THOMSON, FRANK, engineer and railroad president, was born in Chambersburg, July 5, 1841. As chief assistant to the Assistant Secretary of War, he constructed roads and bridges and superintended the transportation of troops during the Civil War. He was later appointed superintendent of the eastern division of the Philadelphia and Erie Railroad. In 1873, he entered the service of the Pennsylvania Railroad, and from 1897 until his death, June 5, 1899, he was president of the company.

THREE SPRINGS, a town in Huntingdon County, named for the three springs that form the creek of the same name. The "Three Spring Tract" was purchased by Col. Geo. Ashman, in 1779.

TICKLER, THE, edited by George Helmbold, first published by him September 16, 1807, under the nom de plume of "Toby Scratch'em." It was issued every Wednesday morning. Helmbold enlisted in the War of 1812, and was soon promoted to a lieutenancy. After the war he became editor of The Independent Balance. He died in 1821.

TILGHMAN, EDWARD, an eminent lawyer of Philadelphia, was a native of Maryland, born on the Eastern Shore of that state, December 11, 1750. His academic education was obtained at the best schools of Philadelphia. He studied law in the Middle Temple, London, of which he was a student in the year 1772. On the completion of his legal education he returned to Philadelphia, and was admitted to the bar of that city, where he was for a long time a successful practitioner. On the death of Chief Justice Shippen, of the Supreme Court of Pennsylvania, Governor McKean tendered him the office; but he declined it, and recommended his kinsman, William Tilghman, for the appointment. Edward Tilghman died November 1, 1815, in the sixty-fifth year of his age.

TILGHMAN, TENCH, soldier, was born in Talbot County, Md., December 25, 1744. He started his career as a merchant in Philadelphia. Appointed aide-de-camp to Washington, and in that capacity bore the news of the surrender of Cornwallis to Congress then sitting in Philadelphia, October 19, 1781. He died in Baltimore, Md., April 18, 1786.

TILGHMAN, WILLIAM, was born on the 12th of August, 1756, upon the estate of his father, on the Eastern Shore of Maryland. In 1762, his family removed from Maryland to Philadelphia. In 1772, William Tilghman began the study of law, in Philadelphia, under the direction of Benjamin Chew. In the spring of 1783, he was admitted to the courts of Maryland. In 1788, and for some successive years, he was elected a representative to the Legislature of Maryland. In 1793, he returned to Philadelphia and commenced the practice of law, which he continued until his appointment by President Adams, on the 3rd of March, 1801, as Chief Justice of the Circuit Court of the United States for this circuit. After the abolition of the Circuit Court, Mr. Tilghman resumed the practice of his profession, and continued it until July 31, 1805, when he was appointed President of the Court of Common Pleas, in the first district. On February 25, 1806, Mr. Tilghman was commissioned Chief Justice of the Supreme Court by Governor McKean, after the death of Chief Justice Shippen.

TINICUM CHURCH, established by the Swedes on Tinicum Island, was consecrated September 4, 1646, and was the first edifice of any denomination in Pennsylvania dedicated to the worship of God. When the new church was built at Wicaco (1700), Tinicum Church was torn down. In the graveyard adjoining was buried on October 28, 1646, the body of Catherine, daughter of Andrew Hanson, the first burial in a regularly established graveyard in Penna.

TINICUM ISLAND, where Pennsylvania history began. In the year 1642, Colonel Johan Printz, a soldier schooled in the Thirty Years' War, was appointed by the Royal Chancellor to Queen Christina, as the third governor of the colony in America called New Sweden. Invested with supreme authority he entered the Capes of the Delaware with two ships and landed on Great Tinicum Island the first white man's settlement within the present bounds of Pennsylvania. This was the seat of Swedish authority in America for twelve years.

TIOGA COUNTY, formed March 26, 1804, from Tioga Township, which had been organized in 1797 as a part of Lycoming County. The township and county both took their names from the Tioga River. Land area, 1,142 square miles. Population (1930), 31,871; county-seat, Wellsboro, founded in 1806.

BLOSSBURG (1843)

TIOGA POINT—See ATHENS.

TIOGA RIVER—Tributary to Chemung River. Sub-basin: Upper North Branch Susquehanna; source, in Armenia Township, western Bradford County; course, southwesterly into Tioga County to near Blossburg; mouth, in New York; length, in Pennsylvania, forty-five miles.

TIONESTA, borough and county-seat of Forest County, originally called Goshgoskunk and Saqualinget, and later named for the Tionesta Creek. A settlement was formed here prior to 1826. In the vicinity are petroleum wells. Agriculture is an important industry and the town has lumber and saw-mills, and coal boat and barge yards.

TIONESTA CREEK—Tributary to Allegheny River. Sub-basin: Upper Allegheny; source, in Watson Township, southern Warren County; course, northeasterly to Clarendon; mouth, at Tionesta; length, fifty-eight miles.

TITUSVILLE, town in Venango County, where the world's first oil well was struck, August 28, 1859, by Colonel Edwin L. Drake. The most important natural production of Pennsylvania, after iron and coal. Population (1930), 8,055; (1920), 8,432.

TOBACCO TRADE, THE, association organized by people interested in the tobacco business in Philadelphia, April 26, 1878, for the purpose of preserving good feeling between members and branches of the trade.

TOBY (LITTLE) CREEK— Tributary to Clarion River. Sub-basin: Middle Allegheny; source, in Fox Township, southern Elk County; course, southwesterly into Jefferson County; mouth, at Carman Siding, five miles southwest of Ridgway; length, twenty-five and one-half miles.

TOBYHANNA CREEK—Tributary to Lehigh River. Sub-basin: Middle Delaware; source, in Coolbaugh Township, northern Monroe County; course, southwesterly to Carbon-Monroe County boundary; mouth, opposite Stoddartsville; length, twenty-three miles.

TOHICKON CREEK—Tributary to Delaware River. Sub-basin: Middle Delaware; source, in Springfield Township, northwestern Bucks County; course, southeasterly to Delaware River; mouth, at Point Pleasant; length, twenty-eight miles.

TOME, JACOB, philanthropist, was born in York County, August 13, 1810. He settled in Port Deposit, Md., in 1833, and in 1864 became a State Senator. Among other public benefactions was a large gift to Dickinson College, and the establishment of a technical school, the Jacob Tome Institute at Port Deposit. He died March 16, 1898.

TOMJACK, an Indian of the Mingo tribe, who resided near what is now Burlington Township, Bradford County, and for whom Tomjack Creek in that township is named. Prior to 1790, Tomjack was the only resident of that section of the county. He was born at Logan's Gap, near the Juniata, and with the advent of the whites to the valley he moved to the Susquehanna, above Forty Fort. Tomjack refused to participate in the Wyoming Massacre and subsequently removed to Wysox, Bradford County, and eventually to Burlington Township, where he lived until 1793, when he removed to the Allegheny where he died in 1809.—*See also* WHITE FAUN.

TONER, JOSEPH MEREDITH, physician, was born in Pittsburgh, April 30, 1825. He was graduated at the Jefferson Medical College, in 1853, and began the practice of medicine in Washington, D. C., in 1855. He originated the plan for the American Medical Association Library established in 1868, and made a part of the Smithsonian Institute. He died in Washington, D. C., August 1, 1896.

TOWANDA, borough, county-seat of Bradford County. An agricultural and stock-raising region. Susquehanna Collegiate Institute (Presbyterian), founded in 1850, is located here.

TOWANDA CREEK—Tributary to North Branch Susquehanna River. Sub-basin: Upper North Branch Susquehanna; source, in Union Township, southeastern Tioga County; course, northeasterly into Bradford County to North Branch Susquehanna River; mouth, near Towanda; length, thirty-one miles.

TOW-BOAT OWNERS' ASSOCIATION, organized in Philadelphia, April 1, 1874, by a number of captains of vessels, for the purpose of establishing uniform rates of towage, and advancing the interests of tow-boat owners.

TOWER, CHARLEMAGNE, diplomatist, was born in Philadelphia, April 17, 1848. Graduated at Harvard, in 1872, and studied in Europe. Was attache to the American legation at Madrid under Daniel E. Sickles, minister to Spain. Admitted to the bar, in 1878, removed to Duluth, Minn., in 1882. In 1887, he settled in Philadelphia. In 1897, he was appointed United States Minister to Austria-Hungary, during 1899–1902, he was Ambassador to Russia, in the latter year becoming Ambassador to Germany, retiring in 1908. He died February 24, 1923.

TOWNE, HENRY ROBINSON, maufacturer, was born in Philadelphia, August 28, 1844. Attended the University of Pennsylvania and left school to become a draftsman in the Port Richmond Iron Works. Was placed in charge of the government work in these shops in 1863. He later took a course in physics at the Sorbonne, Paris, and in 1866 became associated with Linus Yale in making the famous locks. He died in New York, October 15, 1924.

TOWNSEND, CHARLES HASKINS, zoologist, was born in Parnassus, September 29, 1859. He was educated in public and private schools. In 1883, he became Assistant United States Fish Commissioner in charge of salmon propagation in California. Became director of the New York Aquarium, in 1902.

TOWNSEND, LAWRENCE, diplomat, was born in Philadelphia, August 13, 1860. He was educated at the University of Pennsylvania and studied international law and the history of diplomacy in Europe. He was first Secretary of the American Legation at Vienna, 1893–97; Minister to Portugal, 1897–99, and Minister to Belgium, 1899–1905.

TRAPPE, one of the oldest villages in Montgomery County. First called Landau. Many men of considerable importance were born and bred there. Among others, General Peter Gabriel Muhlenberg, eldest son of Rev. Henry Melchior Muhlenberg, born October 1, 1746, and Francis R. Shunk, who was elected Governor of the Commonwealth of Pennsylvania in 1844 and again in 1847.

TRAPPE CHURCH, the oldest Lutheran Church in America, now standing, was erected in 1743, by the Rev. Henry Melchior Muhlenberg, who has since become widely known as the founder of the Lutheran Church in America. This church is situated at Trappe, Montgomery County.

TRAPPE LUTHERAN CHURCH

TREATY ELM, a tree under which William Penn made his famous treaty with the Indians, near Philadelphia. A monument marks the place where it stood.

TRENTON DECREE, the decision given by a court composed of five commissioners—Messrs. Whipple, Arnold, Houston, Griffin and Brearly, settling the dispute between Pennsylvania and the State of Connecticut, respecting certain lands lying on the east branch of the Susquehanna. This court convened at Trenton, New Jersey, November 12, 1782. After sitting forty-one judicial days they gave their decision in these few words:

"We are unanimously of the opinion that Connecticut has no right to the lands in controversy."

"We are also unanimously of the opinion that the jurisdiction and preemption of all the territory lying within the charter of Pennsylvania and now claimed by the State of Connecticut, do of right belong to the State of Pennsylvania."

TREZIYULING, CHARLES, came from Poland in 1791. Was identified with the early settlement of Philipsburg, Centre County. He was an engineer of ability, and one of the first canal commissioners of the state (in 1824). He was a staunch advocate of river improvement, in preference to canals. Was Justice of the Peace in Centre County; was made postmaster of Bellefonte, June 18, 1833. Died in Bellefonte, July 9, 1851; ninety years of age.

TROMBONE CHOIR, belongs to the Moravian Church at Bethlehem. It is not known when music in an organized manner was first performed in Bethlehem in connection with the Moravian Church, however, it is recorded that musical instruments were used by the Moravians in Bethlehem in their religious services in 1743, and that the noted Indian chief, Tschoop, was buried amidst strains of music in 1746. In 1755, the probable destruction of the town by the Indians was averted by playing a dirge on the trombones. Benjamin Franklin, in a letter to his wife, in 1756, says he heard very fine music in the church; that flutes, oboes, french-horns and trumpets accompanied the organ. The Moravians believe music is suited to every occasion in life. After death the departure is made known to the congregation by a trombone quartette from the church spire. At the funeral the choir heads the procession and leads the singing at the grave. Trombones are also used on festal occasions, suiting the tunes to the occasion.

TROTTER, NEWBOLD HOUGH, artist, was born in Philadelphia, January 4, 1827. Graduated at Haverford College. At the beginning of the Civil War he joined the Germantown Home Guards. After the war he was appointed by the United States Government to paint all the mammalia of North America in a series of volumes to be issued by the government. His four paintings: "Grizzly Bears," "Wounded Buffaloes," "The Last Stand," and "Indian Encampment" were his best known. He also made three paintings representing the progress of the means of travel in Pennsylvania during fifty years. He died at Atlantic City, N. J., February 21, 1898.

TRUXTON, COMMODORE THOMAS, an officer in the American Navy, was born on Long Island, in 1755. In 1775, he obtained the command of a vessel, and distinguished himself by his depredations on British commerce during the Revolution. He engaged in commerce till the year 1794, when he was appointed commander of the frigate L'Insurgente; and in the year following obtained a victory over the La Vengeance. At the termination of the difficulties with France, he retired from the navy, and settled in Philadelphia, where he died, in 1822, honored and highly respected. October 8, 1816, he was elected High Sheriff of the City and County of Philadelphia.

TULPEHOCKEN CREEK—Tributary to Schuylkill River. Sub-basin: Lower Delaware; source, about two miles northeast of Lebanon, North Lebanon Township, Lebanon County; course, easterly into Berks County to Schuylkill River; mouth, opposite Reading; length, thirty-seven and one-half miles.

TUNKHANNOCK, county-seat of Wyoming County, on the Susquehanna River, thirty miles northwest of Wilkes-Barre.

TUNKHANNOCK CREEK—Tributary to North Branch Susquehanna River. Sub-basin: Upper North Branch Susquehanna; source, in Jackson Township, eastern Susquehanna County; course, southwesterly into Wyoming County to North Branch Susquehanna River; mouth, at Tunkhannock; length, thirty-seven miles.

TUNKHANNOCK CREEK, SOUTH BRANCH—Tributary to Tunkhannock Creek. Sub-basin: Upper North Branch Susquehanna; source, in Scott Township, northern Lackawanna County; course, westerly, by a circuitous route, into Wyoming County to Tunkhannock Creek; mouth, four miles northeast of Tunkhannock; length, twenty and one-half miles.

TURNER, ELIZA SPROAT, one of the outstanding leaders in progressive movements in Philadelphia. In 1875, she organized the Children's Country Week Association, which has extended to every large city in the United States. The New Century Club, the New Century Guild, Drexel Institute and the Consumers' League were organized through the efforts of this honored woman. Mrs. Turner identified herself with the Woman's Suffrage Movement, in 1870, when the Pennsylvania Society was formed. She died June 20, 1903.

TURNER, ROBERT, one of the most prominent of the early colonists of Pennsylvania, was an Irish gentleman of property, who had embraced the doctrines of the Society of Friends. He was an intimate friend and confidential adviser of William Penn. In 1683, Turner was one of the first jury empanelled in Philadelphia. When Penn returned to England, in 1684, Robert Turner and four others were appointed judges by him, receiving a commission to govern the colony in his absence. In 1689, he was again appointed one of five commissioners to administer the government. Turner, together with Thomas Lloyd and James Claypoole, was empowered by Penn to sign patents and grant warrants for land. He died intestate, about 1700, leaving no son, but two married daughters, who inherited his large estate.

TURNER, THOMAS, naval officer, was born in Washington, D. C., December 23, 1808. Entered navy in 1825. In 1838-1841, served on the Columbia, flagship of the East India squadron. He was commander of the Fredonia in the Gulf squadron in 1847. In 1858–60, he was in command of the Saratoga in the Home squadron, and in the latter years he captured the ships Miramon and Marquis de Habana, which were being used by the Mexican revolutionary party to blockade the port of Vera Cruz. He was assigned to command New Ironsides in the South Atlantic squadron, was promoted commodore, in 1862, became rear-admiral, in 1868, commanded the Pacific squadron, in 1868–70. Retired in 1870; died at Glen Mills, 1883.

TURNPIKES OF PENNSYLVANIA. The first turnpike company organized in America came into existence as the result of a long agitation for the improvement of the road leading from Philadelphia westward to Lancaster, sixty-two miles distant. A company was formed early in 1792, and on April 9th of that year the assembly incorporated the petitioners as the President and Managers of the Philadelphia and Lancaster Turnpike Road. Stock was offered for subscription on June 4th and by noon of the day following the 1,000 shares, valued at $300 each, had been oversubscribed. Construction was started in the early autumn of 1792, and finished two years later. The total cost was $465,000, averaging $7,500 a mile. The road was praised as "a masterpiece of its kind * * * paved with stone the whole way, and overlaid with gravel, so that it is never obstructed during the most severe season."

In spite of the temporary hostility shown toward corporate road building other companies were chartered before the close of the century. In 1794, a company was chartered to build a road from Lancaster to the Susquehanna at or near Wrights Ferry (Columbia). Like the Lancaster Turnpike, this road was a link in one of the routes from Philadelphia to the West, but due to financial difficulties, construction was not started until 1801. The road, only ten miles long, was finally completed in 1803. The year 1796 witnessed the chartering of two turnpike companies, the Lancaster, Elizabethtown, Middletown and Harrisburg, and the Gap, Newport and Wilmington, neither of which was begun until after the companies were organized. The first was divided into two companies, the Lancaster, Elizabethtown and Middletown, and the Middletown and Harrisburg which started construction in 1805 and 1815, respectively. The roads built by these two companies carried the main "Pittsburgh Pike" westward to the Susquehanna at Harrisburg. The Gap, Newport and Wilmington Turnpike was dependent on a similar act being passed by Delaware. When this was not forthcoming the company was rechartered as the Gap and Newport which began, in 1809, the construction of a road from the Gap Tavern on the Lancaster Turnpike to the Delaware line. In 1798, the Germantown and Reading Turnpike Company was incorporated to build a road from Philadelphia, through Germantown, by the route of Chestnut Hill to Reading. Work was not begun until 1801 when a rechartered company, the Germantown and Perkiomen, undertook the building of a stone surfaced road from Third and Vine Streets, Philadelphia, through Germantown, to the ten mile stone on Chestnut Hill, and then to the stone bridge over Perkiomen Creek, in Montgomery County, a distance of twenty-five miles. The road was opened to traffic in 1804, thus making it the third turnpike in Pennsylvania. The Cheltenham Willowgrove, and the Chestnut Hill and Springhouse branches of the Germantown Pike were opened in 1804 and 1805, respectively, making for the three roads a total distance of forty-three and one-half miles. No turnpike companies were chartered in 1802 but the next year brought important developments. Philadelphia was connected with Trenton, New Jersey, by the Frankford and Bristol Turnpike which ran from the intersection of Front Street and the Germantown Road, in the northern part of Philadelphia, to the ferry at Morrisville, on the Delaware, opposite Trenton, New Jersey. The Easton and Wilkes-Barre Turnpike Company was chartered to open a road between those two boroughs, by the best and nearest route. Construction was started in 1805 and during the next ten years forty-seven and one-half miles of road were improved. The other important turnpike chartered in 1803 was the Downingtown, Ephrata and Harrisburg, sometimes spoken of as the Horseshoe Pike. Work was commenced in 1803, and completed in 1819. It was one of Pennsylvania's longest and best roads; its total length of sixty-seven and three-fourths miles was surfaced with crushed limestone to the depth of from twelve to eighteen inches.

From 1803 afterward the turnpike movement grew with the assurance that comes with success. All the toll roads thus far authorized were in the region east of the Susquehanna, chiefly along routes leading out of Philadelphia. Beginning with 1804, the mania for turnpikes spread throughout the state. In that year a company was chartered to build a road from the village of Erie on Lake Erie to Waterford, fourteen miles southward; the Union and Cumberland Turnpike Company was authorized to build a road from near Uniontown to the state line, in the direction of Cumberland, Maryland; and the southern route to the West was further extended by the Susquehanna and York which, during 1809-10, built a stone road from Wrights Ferry (Wrightsville) to York. Five other companies were chartered in 1804, of which the most important were the Susquehanna and Lehigh, and the Coshecton and Great Bend. The former built a gravel and earth road, thirty miles in length, from Lausanne (Mauch Chunk) on the Lehigh to the Susquehanna opposite Berwick; the road of the latter company was the Pennsylvania link of a turnpike which ran from Newburg on the Hudson to Bath in western New York. The next year brought further turnpikes to the region east of the Susquehanna. The Berks and Dauphin was chartered to improve the road from Reading on the Schuylkill to the Downingtown, Ephrata and Harrisburg Turnpike at Hummelstown in Dauphin County; the Centre Turnpike was to open a road by the nearest and best route from

Sunbury to Reading, a distance of seventy-five miles. The Springhouse branch of the Germantown Turnpike was extended from the Springhouse Tavern in Montgomery County to Bethlehem.

This brief sketch of the early turnpikes of Pennsylvania shows that an effort was being made to improve the roads in the more populous regions east of the Susquehanna. In 1806, the state embarked on a policy of aiding turnpikes by subscribing to their stock. This assistance made it possible for the sparsely settled regions to raise the capital necessary for turnpike construction. Appropriations for this purpose remained rather limited until 1811 when "an act to encourage the construction of certain great leading roads, within this commonwealth, and the erection of bridges over the Susquehanna," etc., was passed. Eight hundred and twenty-five thousand dollars were appropriated to carry the objects of the act into effect. Companies were soon organized and an era of trunk line turnpike building was started. Liberal subscriptions on the part of the state caused the work to be pushed with zeal.

By the end of the year 1821, 146 turnpike companies had been authorized by law, of which 84 had received letters patent. Many of those that had been authorized, had failed in their endeavors to raise subscriptions to the amount required by their acts of incorporation, or had been rendered unnecessary by subsequent acts authorizing the incorporation of other companies for smaller sections of the same route. The mileage contemplated by the various companies that had received letters patent was 2,521 of which 1,807 miles had been completed. The corporate method of road construction was then in its most active period. By the end of another decade, the number of companies authorized had increased to 220, and the projected mileage was in excess of 3,000 miles. About this time, however, canals and railways so conclusively demonstrated their superiority over roads that both public and private capital was diverted to these newer forms of transportation. New turnpike companies continued to be chartered, but they were, almost without exception, for the building of short feeders to existing turnpikes or, as was more frequently the case, to the newly constructed canals and railroads. From about 1832 forward abandonment more than offset new construction, therefore, it may be said that the approximate 2,400 miles of toll roads then in operation in Pennsylvania represented the peak of the turnpike movement in this state.

When other systems of transportation came into being to challenge the supremacy of the road, Pennsylvania had turnpikes extending into every part of the state. A continuous line of turnpike road then connected Trenton on the Delaware with Steubenville on the Ohio, a distance of 353 miles. Two stone surfaced roads ran from Harrisburg to Pittsburgh, one by the southern route of Chambersburg, Bedford and Greensburg, the other by the northern route of Millerstown, Lewistown, Huntington, Hollidaysburg and New Alexandria. From Pittsburgh a turnpike route ran northward to the town of Erie, on the lake by that name, passing through Butler, Mercer, Meadville and Waterford. This extreme northwestern corner of the state was connected with

Philadelphia by a continuous turnpiked road which passed through Franklin, Philipsburg, Bellefonte, Sunbury and Reading. Two roads ran northward from Philadelphia to the New York State line. The most western of these passed through Lausanne, crossed the Susquehanna at Berwick and thence by the Susquehanna and Tioga Turnpike, passed through Lycoming and Bradford Counties to join at the state line a road leading to Newtown (Elmira), New York. The other great highway from Philadelphia passed through Bethlehem and Wind Gap, at which place the road branched. The western branch passed through Wilkes-Barre, Tunkhannock and Montrose to meet at the New York line a road leading to Binghamton. The eastern branch intersected at Rix's Gap and Belmont two important turnpikes running from the Delaware at Milford and Damascus, respectively. The road from Damascus was the Pennsylvania link of a turnpike route from Newburg on the Hudson to the Susquehanna region of central New York; while the turnpike from Milford connected important New Jersey routes with main highways in New York. The latter road followed a northwest course to pass through Montrose and thence through the extreme northeastern corner of Bradford County to the New York line. From this point it was continued by a New York company through Owego to Ithaca, where it intersected one of New York's principal turnpike routes to the West. At Easton other important connections were made with trunk line routes from New Jersey as they converged in Phillipsburg, on the opposite bank of the Delaware. Other important turnpikes were those in the southwestern and southern portions of Pennsylvania. It was in this region that turnpikes continued in service many years after road transportation had been rendered obsolete in other parts of the state. This condition can be explained in part by the country's physical features which were unfavorable for the construction of the newer forms of transportation. It will be noted also that Baltimore was more accessible to the southern counties of Pennsylvania than was Philadelphia. As long as the state was concerned in the financing of canals and railways, it assumed a hostile attitude toward those projects that tended to divert the western trade to Baltimore, Philadelphia's greatest rival.

Undoubtedly the most important turnpike in the southwestern part of the state was the eighty miles of the National Road which lay within Pennsylvania. It entered the state, from Cumberland, Maryland, at Smythfield and thence passed through Uniontown, Brownsville, Washington and West Alexandria before it crossed the Virginia line in the direction of Wheeling. From Washington a turnpike ran northward to Pittsburgh, twenty-five miles distant, while another pursued an eastward course through Williamsport, Mount Pleasant and Somerset to join the main Philadelphia-Pittsburgh Turnpike a few miles west of Bedford. An important turnpike branched from the "Pittsburgh Pike" at McConnellstown (McConnellsburg) to pass through Mercersburg, Greencastle, and Waynesburg in the direction of Emmetsburg, Maryland. Three other turnpikes connected southern Pennsylvania with Maryland routes leading to Baltimore. The Gettysburg and Petersburg Turnpike ran to the state line in the direction of Westminster, Maryland. Two small companies, the Hanover and Carlisle, and the Hanover and Maryland Line, operated a turnpike which connected Carlisle, Pennsylvania, with a road leading to Reisterstown, Maryland. The third of these roads, also operated by two companies, ran from York Haven on the Susquehanna, by the way of York to the Maryland line where it joined a turnpike leading directly to Baltimore.

TURTLE CREEK, borough in Allegheny County, twelve miles southeast of Pittsburgh. Large plant of Westinghouse Electric and Manufacturing Co., situated here. Population (1930), 10,690; (1920), 8,138.

TUSCARORA CREEK—Tributary to Juniata River. Sub-basin: Lower Juniata; source, in Tell Township, southeastern Huntingdon County; course, northeasterly into Juniata County to Juniata River; mouth, at Port Royal; length, forty-four miles.

TUSCARORA MOUNTAIN, divides Franklin and Perry Counties from Huntingdon and Juniata Counties.

TUSCARORA PATH VALLEY (now Path Valley), is in the western part of Franklin County at the eastern base of Tuscarora Mountain.

TUSCARORAS—This tribe of Indians were expelled from North Carolina and Virginia, and later sought refuge with the Five Nations. In 1722, they were added to the Iroquois Confederacy, making the Six Nations. The places of residence of the Tuscaroras in Pennsylvania during their migration to New York were those where their name has been preserved ever since.

TUTELO, a tribe of Indians entering Pennsylvania soon after 1722, who had been living prior to that in North Carolina and Virginia. They were first mentioned by Captain John Smith, of Virginia, in 1609, described by him as being very barbarous. They first settled, in Pennsylvania, at Shamokin (Sunbury), where they resided under Iroquois protection. The Rev. David Brainerd found them here in 1745. Later they moved up the Susquehanna to Skogari, and in 1771, the Tutelo were settled on the east side of Cayuga inlet about three miles from the south end of the lake of that name in New York.

TWOLICK CREEK—Tributary to Blacklick Creek. Sub-basin: Lower Allegheny; source, formed by junction of North and South Branches, in Cherryhill Township, eastern Indiana County; course, southwesterly to Blacklick Creek; mouth, near Black Lick; length, twenty-six and one-half miles.

TYPE FOUNDRY, established 1735, in Germantown, by Germans, was the first in America.

TYRON, GEORGE WASHINGTON, conchologist, was born in Philadelphia, May 20, 1838. He was educated at the Friends' School of Philadelphia and in 1865 originated the movement to construct the present edifice of the Philadelphia Academy of Natural Sciences. From 1865 to 1871, he edited the American Journal of Conchology. His publications were, among others, "Manual of Conchology" (12 vols., 1879-85); "American Marine Conchology" (1873); and "Structural and Systematic Conchology" (3 vols., 1882). Died in Philadelphia, February 5, 1888.

TYRONE, borough in Blair County, on a tributary of the Juniata River, settled in 1840 and incorporated as a borough in 1857. Population (1930), 9,042; (1920), 9,084.

TYSON, JAMES, pathologist, was born in Philadelphia, October 26, 1841. Graduated at Harvard, 1860; took his M. D. at University of Pennsylvania, in 1863. Professor of pathology and morbid anatomy (1876-89); professor of the practice of medicine (1899-1910), and thereafter professor emeritus of the University of Pennsylvania. He served as president of the College of Physicians of Philadelphia (1907-10). Died February 26, 1919, at Philadelphia.

UNDERGROUND RAILROAD—During the period prior to the Civil War in the United States, sympathizers of the slave organized methods by which he might safely escape to the north and eventually to Canada. This system came to be called the underground railroad. Its center in Pennsylvania was at Columbia, Lancaster County, on the Susquehanna River, where many colored people had settled. William Wright, a grandson of the founder of the town, was active in assisting fugitives. He established stations along the line of the railroad in eastern Pennsylvania, about ten miles apart. At times when closely pursued fugitives arrived at his house he dressed them as women and sent them to Daniel Gibbons, about six miles east of Lancaster. The stations in Pennsylvania nearest the Maryland line were Gettysburg and York. When large groups of fugitives arrived at Gettysburg they were divided and half sent to Columbia and half to Harrisburg. On the line running northward and eastward the principal agents were: Daniel Gibbons, Thomas Peart, Thomas Whitson, Lindley Coates, Dr. Eshleman, James Moore, Caleb C. Hood, of Lancaster County; James Fulton, Gideon Pierce, Joseph Haines, Thomas Bonsall, Gravner Marsh, Zebulon Thomas, Thomas Vickers, John Vickers, Micajah and William A. Speakman, Esther Lewis, Dr. Edwin Fussell, William Fussell, Norris Maris, Emmor Kimber, Elijah F. Pennypacker, of Chester County; Rev. Samuel Aaron, Isaac Roberts, John Roberts, Dr. William Corson, Dr. Jacob L. Paxson, Daniel Ross (colored), of Norristown. This was called the northern route through Chester County. Another route through southern Lancaster and Chester Counties, with its branches, was known as the southern and middle route. Sometimes the two routes intersected. The two formed the main lines of the underground railroad in Pennsylvania.

UNION CITY, a borough in Erie County, about twenty-five miles southeast of Erie, in an agricultural and oil region. Among its industrial establishments are: flour mills, barrel factories, a powdered milk plant, and an oil refinery. The town was founded by William Miles, a native of Ireland, and was originally called Miles' Mills. When it was incorporated as a borough in 1863 the name was changed to Union Mills and on July 4, 1871, to Union City.

UNION COUNTY, was formed from part of Northumberland, March 22, 1813. Named for unity "the sentiment which actuates the American people." Land area, 305 square miles; population (1930), 17,468. County-seat, Lewisburg, laid out in 1785.

UNION LEAGUE, THE, was organized in Philadelphia during the period of the Civil War. It was originally called the Union Club, but at a meeting held at the home of Dr. John F. Meigs, December 27, 1862, the name was changed to Union League. The membership of the organization soon grew to a thousand, thirty-six of whom equipped Union League regiments for the war. Nine regiments, a battalion known as Fell's, Chasseur's and five companies of cavalry were sent out. The League spent $33,000 on the equipment of the colored troops at Camp William Penn, under General Louis Wagner. On May 11, 1865, the League moved to its present quarters on Broad Street.

UNIONTOWN, borough, county-seat of Fayette County, about seventy miles south of Pittsburgh, in the southwestern part of the state. It was settled in 1768 by Henry Beeson and was first called Beesontown. It was incorporated in 1796. Uniontown is in an agricultural region, but the county is noted for its, annual output of coke. In the vicinity are coal fields, deposits of iron ore, glass, sand and natural gas. The chief manufacturing establishments are glass plants, brick yards, planing mills, and coke plants. Population (1930), 19,544; (1920), 15,692.

UNIONTOWN NEWS STANDARD, THE, a weekly newspaper, was established in 1827. It is Democratic in politics; appears every Thursday; is edited by O'Neil Kennedy, and published by the News Publishing Company. Circulation, 640.

UNITED BRETHREN, called also Moravians, a religious sect or society, the "Unitas Fratrum," the membership of which was made up of Moravians or Bohemians, the followers of John Huss. In 1740, the first colonies of the United Brethren were established in Pennsylvania, where they founded towns at Bethlehem, Nazareth, and Lititz, and exerted an influence on the early history of Pennsylvania.

UNITED BRETHREN IN CHRIST, CHURCH OF THE, a religious denomination, originated in 1767, during a religious revival among the German settlers in Pennsylvania and northern Maryland. The founders of the church were Philip William Otterbein, a native of Nassau, Germany, who came to America in 1752 as a missionary of the German Reformed Church, and Martin Boehm, a preacher in the Mennonite Church. The two met at services held at Isaac Long's barn, near Lancaster, in 1767. Boehm preached at the meeting, and Otterbein, feeling, upon hearing him speak, that their religious experiences were similar, at the conclusion of the sermon, rushed up to Boehm, embraced him, and exclaimed, "We are Brethren." Thus the name "United Brethren" originated. For the next fifteen years, Otterbein and Boehm conducted evangelistic services among the German-speaking communities. The new church was organized at a meeting at the home of Peter Kemp, near Frederick, Md., in 1800. Otterbein and Boehm were two of the first bishops of the church. The first general conference was held near Mt. Pleasant in 1815. The Church of the United Brethren in Christ is not related to the Unitas Fratrum or Moravians, nor to the Methodist. The importance of evangelism is emphasized. In 1926 there were 81,729 members of the United Brethren Church in Pennsylvania.

UNITED STATES INDIAN TRAINING AND INDUSTRIAL SCHOOL, at Carlisle, was founded in 1879, when Capt. R. H. Pratt, of the United States Army, brought a number of Indians from the Hampton Institute to the abandoned army post at Carlisle, in October of that year.

UNIVERSALISM—George De Benneville was the founder of Universalism in America. In 1741, he came to America and settled in Germantown, where he was successful in promulgating his doctrine among the descendants of the original German settlers of the mystic belief. In 1743, he visited Oley, Berks County, and preached in a Moravian schoolhouse, three miles away. Because of his interpretation of some of the scriptural passages, the doors were closed to him. In 1745, he purchased a tract of land in Oley Township, where he built a stone mansion for worship and lecture purposes. In 1755, he removed to Green Lane on account of the depradation of the savage Indians in Berks County. The hall of worship and teaching in the mansion of Dr. De Benneville was the first place of Universalist worship in America. In 1926, there were in Pennsylvania 1,591 members of the Universalist Church.

UPSON, ANSON JUDD, educator, was born at Philadelphia, November 7, 1823. He was graduated from Hamilton College, Clinton, N. Y., in 1843, and taught there until 1870. He was ordained to the Presbyterian ministry in 1868. He taught at Auburn Theological Seminary from 1880-1887 and from 1887 until his death he was vice-chancellor and chancellor, respectively, of the University of the State of New York. He published "Inquiry into the Nature and Character of Our Federal Government." He died June 15, 1902.

URSINUS COLLEGE, co-educational institution at Collegeville. It was incorporated in 1869 and was first opened to students in 1870. The college is non-sectarian in its control; it is, however, affiliated with the Reformed Church in the United States. Enrollment (1930-1931), 480.

VALLEY FORGE, a village in Chester County, on the Schuylkill River, twenty-four miles west of Philadelphia. It is noted as the place where Washington and his army of about 11,000 men went into winter quarters December 17, 1777, after the British occupied Philadelphia. The army suffered cold and hunger on account of the poverty of the country, but perhaps more from the incompetency of the commissary department. In June, 1778, Washington abandoned the camp and again took possession of Philadelphia. In 1893, the Pennsylvania Legislature took steps to acquire and preserve Valley Forge as a public park and historic landmark. The entire field is practically the same today as when Washington evacuated it.

VAN AMRINGE, JOHN HOWARD, educator, was born in Philadelphia. He was graduated from Columbia University, in 1860; and received from Columbia and other colleges the honorary degrees of Ph. D., L. H. D., and L. L. D. He was connected with Columbia University as tutor, professor of mathematics, becoming emeritus professor in 1910. He was the first president of the American Mathematical Society. He died in 1915.

VAN BUREN, WILLIAM HOLME, surgeon, was born in Philadelphia, April 5, 1819. He studied medicine at the University of Pennsylvania and in Paris, where he received his degree from the University in 1840. He was appointed assistant surgeon in the United States Army. From 1845-1866, he was at the University of the City of New York, and from 1866 to his death he was surgeon of Bellevue Hospital. He died in New York City, March 25, 1883.

VAN DYKE, HENRY, writer, was born at Germantown, November 10, 1852. He graduated from Brooklyn Polytechnic Institute, Princeton University and Princeton Theological Seminary. In 1879, he became pastor of the United Congregational Church, at Newport, R. I., and in 1883, 1900, 1902 and 1911 served in the Brick Presbyterian Church, New York. In 1900-1923, he was professor of English literature at Princeton. From 1913-1917, he was U. S. minister to the Netherlands. He was American lecturer at the University of Paris, 1908-1909. Among his writings are: "The Reality of Religion," "The Story of the Psalms," "The Poetry of Tennyson," "The Christ Child in Art," "The Other Wise Man," "The First Christmas Tree," "The Blue Flower," "Essays in Application," and "Even Unto Bethlehem." His home is in Princeton, New Jersey.

VAN INGEN, WILLIAM BRANTLEY, mural painter, was born in Philadelphia, 1858. He became widely known from his work at the capitol at Washington, at the U. S. Mint at Philadelphia, and the State Capitol at Harrisburg, the State Capitol at Trenton, N. J., and the United States Court House and post-office in Indianapolis and Chicago. Van Ingen is a lecturer on art and landscape architecture. His home is in New York.

VANUXEM, LARDNER, geologist and chemist, was born in Philadelphia, July 23, 1792. He was graduated from the Ecole des Mines at Paris in 1819. From 1820-26, he taught at the South Carolina College and at various times he was connected with the state department of geology. He died at Bristol, January 25, 1848.

VAUX, RICHARD, lawyer, was born at Philadelphia, December 19, 1816. He was admitted to the bar in 1836, and soon after became secretary of the American legation at London. In 1855, he was elected mayor of Philadelphia and in 1890 was elected to Congress. He died in Philadelphia, March 22, 1895.

VAUX, ROBERTS, jurist, was born in Philadelphia, on January 25, 1786. He was admitted to the bar there in 1808 and became judge of the court in 1835. He was active in penal reform and was one of the founders of the Deaf and Dumb Society. He favored public education and used his influence to bring about its adoption in Pennsylvania. He was an ardent supporter of charitable institutions and helped to institute the Philadelphia Savings Funds. He died in his native city, January 7, 1836.

VENANGO COUNTY, was formed March 12, 1800, from parts of Allegheny and Lycoming. Named for Venango River, now French Creek. Land area, 661 square miles; population (1930), 63,226. County-seat, Franklin, laid out in 1795.

VILLANOVA COLLEGE, a college for men, under the auspices of the Roman Catholic Church, was founded in 1842 at Villanova, near Philadelphia. Enrollment (1930-1931), 1,000.

WAGNER, SAMUEL, lawyer, was born in Philadelphia, December 28, 1842. He graduated from the University of Pennsylvania, studied law and was admitted to the bar in 1865. He was a founder of the Pennsylvania Museum and School of Industrial Art, Philadelphia; was president of the Wagner Institute of Science, 1884-1921, and president emeritus since 1921.

WAHL, WILLIAM HENRY, scientist, was born in Philadelphia, December 14, 1848. After graduation from Dickinson College he studied at the University of Heidelberg, afterwards engaging in special study in mineralogy, geology, and chemistry. In 1873-1874, he was professor of physics and physical geography at Central High School, Philadelphia; 1870-1874, resident secretary of Franklin Institute and editor of the institute journal; 1876, editor of the Philadelphia *Polytechnic*; 1878-1880, editor of the *Engineering and Mining Journal*; 1880-1882, editor of the New York *Manufacturer and Builder*; 1882, secretary of Franklin Institute.

WALKER, JAMES BARR, clergyman, was born in Philadelphia, July 29, 1805. After graduating from Western Reserve College, in 1831, he edited religious publications, but deciding to enter the ministry he was licensed to preach by the Chicago Presbytery in 1841. Subsequently he served a pastorate at Sandusky, Ohio, and lectured at Oberlin College and the Chicago Theological Seminary. He has written: "The Philosophy of Skepticism and Ultraism," "Philosophy of the Divine Operation in Human Redemption," "The Luring Question of the Age," and "The Doctrine of the Holy Spirit." He died at Wheaton, Ill., March 6, 1887.

WALKER, ROBERT JAMES, financier, was born at Northumberland, July 23, 1801, and graduated from the University of Pennsylvania in 1819. He moved to Natchez, Mississippi, in 1826 and from 1837 to 1845 was a Democratic leader in the United States Senate. He was a close friend of Presidents Van Buren, Tyler, and Polk. Under the latter he served as secretary of the Treasury. From 1857 to 1858 he served as governor of the Kansas Territory. During the Civil War he was active in raising finances for the United States and went to Europe in 1863 and 1864 in its interests. He was an advocate of free trade and was instrumental in establishing railroads to the Pacific. He married Mary Bache, daughter of Richard Bache and granddaughter of Benjamin Franklin. He died in Washington, D. C., November 11, 1869.

WALKER, WILLIAM HULTZ, industrial chemist, was born in Pittsburgh, April 7, 1869. He was graduated from Pennsylvania State College in 1890 and from Gottingen in 1892. In 1905-1908, he was professor of industrial chemistry at Harvard and later was connected with the production of art glass. He became an authority on industrial chemistry in the United States. His death occurred July 15, 1923.

WALKING PURCHASE, THE—In an agreement between William Penn and Delaware Indians the former was to gain title to as much land bounded on the east by the Delaware River, as a man could cover by walking to the interior for three days. Penn walked to a point forty miles inland in a day and a half and received a deed for the lands covered in 1686. After Penn's death in 1718 much controversy arose among Indians and white settlers over the country beyond the limit of Penn's walk. In 1737, Thomas and William Penn, his sons and heirs decided to have three expert walkers follow Penn's course for the stipulated time to decide the boundaries. They covered seventy miles instead of the original forty and upon their return took a northeasterly route to the colony. By these fraudulent means, 1,200 square miles of territory of the best Delaware and Minisink lands came into the possession of the Penns. The Delaware Indians became incensed about the matter and joined the French against the English in 1755.

WALLACE, HENRY, clergyman and agriculturist, was born in West Newton, March 19, 1836. He graduated from Jefferson College (now Washington and Jefferson) in 1859 and subsequently prepared for the ministry at the Allegheny Theological Seminary and at the United Presbyterian Seminary, Monmouth, Ill. After serving pastorates at Rock Island, Illinois; Davenport, Iowa; and Morning Sun, Iowa, he retired from the ministry because of ill health and moved to a farm at Winterset, Iowa. He edited a farm page of the local paper; in 1883 became editor of the *Iowa Homestead* and in 1895 founded *Wallace's Farmer*, at Des Moines, Iowa, to the editing of which he devoted his life. President Roosevelt appointed him a member of the Country Life Commission in 1908 and Governor Clarke of Iowa appointed him to investigate agricultural conditions in Great Britain in 1913. He wrote: "Clover Farming," "The Skim-milk Calf," "Trusts and How to Control Them," and "Uncle Henry's Talks with a Farm Boy." He died February 22, 1916, while attending a meeting of the Interdenominational Laymen's Missionary Convention in the First Methodist Church, Des Moines.

WALLACE, HORACE BINNEY, scholar, was born in Philadelphia, February 26, 1817. He graduated from Princeton, in 1835; studied law, medicine and chemistry, and devoted his life to literature. With J. S. Clarke Hare he edited: "American Leading Cases in Law," "Smith's Leading Cases," and White and Tudor's "Leading Cases in Equity"; he assisted Griswold in "Napoleon and the Marshals of the Empire," and himself wrote: "Stanley, or the Recollections of a Man of the World"; and "Art, Scenery and Philosophy in Europe." He died in Paris, France, December 16, 1856.

WALLACE, JOHN WILLIAM, lawyer, was born in Philadelphia, on February 17, 1815. In 1833, he graduated from the University of Pennsylvania and was admitted to the bar afterwards. For twenty-four years after 1860 he was president of the Pennsylvania Historical Society. He published, among other things, "Reporters"; "Cases Argued in the United States Supreme Court"; and "An Old Philadelphian, Col. William Bradford of 1776." He died in Philadelphia, on January 13, 1884.

WALLENPAUPACK CREEK—Tributary to Lackawaxen River. Subbasin: Upper Delaware; source, in Pocono Plateau, Coolbaugh Township, northwestern Monroe County; course, northeasterly to Lackawaxen River, being Wayne-Pike County boundary from two miles below source to mouth; mouth, at Hawley; length, twenty-eight miles. Indian name, a corruption of Walinkpapeek, "deep, still water," or "a deep spring."

WALNUT CREEK—Tributary to Lake Erie. Basin: Erie; source, in Greene Township, northern central Erie County; course, westerly to Lake Erie; mouth, eight miles southwest of Erie; length, twenty miles.

WALSH, JAMES JOSEPH, physician, lecturer and author, was born in Archbald, April 12, 1865. After completing his studies at St. John's College, Fordham, N. Y., and the Universities of Pennsylvania, Paris, Vienna and Berlin, he entered the practice of medicine in New York. Since 1906 he has been a member of the faculty of Cathedral College, New York. He has lectured widely on scientific, literary and historical subjects and is the author of: "Makers of Modern Medicine"; "The Thirteenth the Greatest of Centuries"; "The Popes and Science"; "Education, How Old the New"; "Modern Progress and History"; "The Century of Columbus"; "Medieval Medicine"; "Religion and Health"; "Psychotherapy"; "Eating and Health"; "The Church and Healing," etc.

WALTER, THOMAS USTICK, architect, was born in Philadelphia, on September 4, 1804. He drew plans for the federal patent office, treasury and post-office buildings, extensions to the capitol, including the dome, the government hospital for the insane, Moyamensing Penitentiary and Girard College. He died in Philadelphia on October 30, 1887.

WALTERS, WILLIAM THOMPSON, merchant and art collector, was born in Pennsylvania, May 23, 1820. He engaged in the coal and iron industry, conducted a smelting establishment in Pennsylvania and produced the first iron manufactured from mineral coal in the United States. In 1841, he moved to Baltimore where he became a wine merchant and in 1861-1865 traveled in Europe, gathering a remarkable art collection of French and Chinese work and Greek, Roman and Italian sculpture, which is housed in a building in Baltimore, open to the public. Walters was United States commissioner at the Paris expositions of 1867 and 1878, and at the Vienna exposition, 1873. He died at Baltimore, November 22, 1894.

WANAMAKER, JOHN, merchant, was born in Philadelphia, July 11, 1838, and received a common school education there. He served in minor positions in book and clothing stores before 1861 when he entered into partnership with Nathan Brown in the clothing business. In 1869, Wanamaker and Brown became the firm of John Wanamaker and Company. The business grew rapidly and soon became the largest department store in Philadelphia. In 1896, the business was extended to New York. Wanamaker was the first Philadelphia business man to advertise extensively and systematically. President Harrison appointed him Postmaster-General for his administration in 1889. Wanamaker

JOHN WANAMAKER

was a leader in the religious education of Philadelphia and the country. He organized and served as superintendent of the Bethany Presbyterian Sunday School (now one of the largest in the United States) in 1858, and was for several years president of the Y. M. C. A., of Philadelphia. He died in Philadelphia, December 12, 1922.

GREENSBURG (1843)

WAPWALLOPEN CREEK—Tributary to North Branch Susquehanna River. Sub-basin: Lower North Branch Susquehanna; source, Crystal Lake, in Bear Creek Township, eastern central Luzerne County; course, southwesterly to North Branch Susquehanna River; mouth, at Wapwallopen; length, twenty and one-half miles. Indian name, a corruption of Woaphallack-pink, "white hemp place," or "where the white hemp grows."

WARFIELD, ETHELBERT DUDLEY, educator, was born in Lexington, Ky., March 16, 1861. After graduating from Princeton in 1882 and Columbia Law School in 1885, he practiced law for two years in Lexington. In 1888–1891, he was professor of history and president of Miami University, Oxford, Ohio; 1891–1915, president and professor of history at Lafayette College, and 1915 to date, president of Wilson College, Chambersburg. He is the author of: "The Kentucky Resolutions of 1798," "At the Evening Hour," and "Memoir of Joseph Cabell Breckenridge, U. S. N."

WARREN, borough, and county-seat of Warren County, about 120 miles northeast of Pittsburgh. The town was laid out in 1795 by Daniel McQuay, and was incorporated as a borough in 1832. As the town is located in an oil region the leading industries are the manufacture of oil and gas engines, wood alcohol and oil and its by-products. Other manufactured products are iron and steel machinery, boilers, pianos and furniture. Population (1930), 14,863; (1920), 14,272.

WARREN COUNTY, was formed March 12, 1800, from parts of Allegheny and Lycoming. Named for General Joseph Warren. Land area, 902 square miles, population (1930), 41,453. County-seat, Warren, laid out in 1795.

WASHINGTON, GEORGE, IN PENNSYLVANIA—A large part of Washington's public life was spent in Pennsylvania. November 15, 1753, he left Virginia under orders from Governor Dinwiddie to Fort Le Boeuf, fifteen miles south of Erie, to protest to the French commander against the encroachments of the French on territory claimed by Virginia. On this journey he traversed the present site of Pittsburgh. April 2, 1754, Washington, appointed a lieutenant-colonel because of his success in his first mission, left Virginia in command of one hundred and fifty men, with Jacob Van Braam, a Dutchman, as interpreter, to resist the French who had built Fort Duquesne. On April 25th he had reached the Great Meadows near the present site of Uniontown, in Fayette County. The next morning he attacked a French force with great success, their leader, Jumonville, being among the slain. Learning of the presence of a large force of French and Indians he threw up entrenchments and built a palisade which he called "Fort Necessity." Finding his advance toward Fort Duquesne too hazardous, he retired to Fort Necessity, where he fought all through July 3rd, and surrendered July 4th, being permitted to march out his troops. The next year General Braddock was directed to proceed against the French in western Pennsylvania. Washington offered his services and at Frederick City, Md., met Benjamin Franklin for the first time. The part of Washington in this campaign is well known. In 1758, he became an important figure in the successful campaign of General John Forbes. Washington favored the old Braddock Road, but Forbes finally decided to cut a new road north of that taken by Braddock. In September, 1774, Washington arrived in Philadelphia as a delegate from Virginia to the First Continental Congress which met in Carpenter's Hall, Philadelphia, and June 13, 1776, he met with the delegates from the other colonies in the Second Continental Congress, which body unanimously elected him commander-in-chief of the armies. In this capacity he fought a majority of the battles of his career in defense of Philadelphia, or in relation to it; Trenton, Princeton, Brandywine, Germantown, White Marsh and Monmouth, and his winter at Valley Forge has made that place one of the most famous shrines of the Revolution. May 25, 1787, while attending the Constitutional Convention in the State House in Philadelphia, he was elected to preside over its deliberations. Washington spent his entire term as president, with the exception of the first year, in Philadelphia, which furnished him a home. He lived in a large double brick building on the south side of Market Street, sixty feet east of Sixth Street. In 1794, he accompanied the army as far west as Bedford, against the Insurrectionists of western Pennsylvania. Thus his military career which had begun in 1754 in western Pennsylvania ended forty years later in the same section. Washington had a pew in Christ Church, Philadelphia; became a member of the American Philosophical Society. He saw the Frenchman

Blanchard make the first balloon ascension in America, January 9, 1793. He and Mrs. Washington were present, December 15, 1790, when James Wilson, of the Supreme Court opened the Law School of the University of Pennsylvania. He left Philadelphia, March 9, 1797, less than three years before his death.

WASHINGTON, THE FATHER OF HIS COUNTRY—In a German Almanac, printed in Lancaster, in the year 1778, Washington was first called "The Father of His Country."

WASHINGTON, borough and county-seat of Washington County, about thirty-two miles southwest of Pittsburgh. It was settled by Irish in 1768; was laid out as a town in 1781, and incorporated as a borough in 1810. In 1910, the boroughs of Washington and North and South Washington were consolidated. Washington and Jefferson College is located here as are Washington and Jefferson Academy, Trinity Hall Military School, Washington Ladies' Seminary and two business colleges. The borough is located in a coal mining and agricultural region and the industrial establishments include steel works, tube and pipe works, glass factories, tin plate and iron works, petroleum works. Population (1930), 24,545; (1920), 21,480.

WASHINGTON AND JEFFERSON COLLEGE, for the education of men, is located at Washington. Originally two colleges, the preparatory and scientific departments were located at Washington while the sophomore, junior and senior classes met at Canonsburg, the seat of Jefferson College. In 1865, an act of legislature united the institutions under their present name and in 1869 the whole institution was centered at Washington. Enrollment (1930-1931), 450.

WASHINGTON BENEVOLENT SOCIETY OF PENNSYLVANIA, originated in Philadelphia on February 22, 1813, as a political club. Members signed the constitution and declared themselves to be adherents of the principles of George Washington, to support a free republican government and to preserve the rights of the United States against foreign and domestic disturbances. The funds of the society were used for charitable purposes among members and anniversary dinners were held on Washington's birthday. Washington Hall, on Third Street in Philadelphia, was built by the organization. Similar groups sprang up throughout the country during the remainder of the War of 1812, but disappeared with the Federal Party during Monroe's administration.

WASHINGTON COUNTY, was formed from part of Westmoreland, March 28, 1781. It was the first county in the United States to be named for George Washington. Land area, 862 square miles; population (1930), 204,802. County-seat, Washington, laid out in 1781.

WASHINGTON REPORTER, THE, a daily newspaper, which appears every evening except Sunday, was established in 1808. It is Independent-Republican in politics; is edited by John L. Stewart, and published by the Observer Publishing Company, Inc. Circulation, 6,528.

WATMOUGH, JAMES, naval officer, was born in Whitemarsh, July 30, 1822. He was educated at the University of Pennsylvania and from 1843-44 was acting midshipman. He served in the Mexican and Civil Wars. From 1873-1877, he was paymaster-general of the navy. In 1884, he was retired and in 1906 was created rear admiral. He died in Washington, D. C., January 18, 1917.

WATSON, DAVID THOMPSON, jurist, was born in Washington, Pa., January 2, 1844. He was educated in the public schools of Washington and was a student in Washington and Jefferson College at the outbreak of the Civil War. He enlisted for ninety days in the 59th Regiment, Pennsylvania Volunteers, and a year later was mustered in as a lieutenant in Knapp's Battalion, serving with credit until the close of the war. After the war he entered Harvard Law School where he graduated in 1866. For a time subsequent to his graduation he was associated with his father in Washington, but afterwards went to Pittsburgh where he entered the firm of Hopkins and Lezear. Later, he was associated with James Veech and at the time of his death had as his partner John Freeman. He was the recognized leader of the Allegheny bar and was frequently called to other states to settle legal questions. He was retained by the government in the Northern Securities Case, argued in 1903, before the Circuit Court of Appeals in St. Louis, a case which involved the legality of the Sherman Trust Case. Watson's greatest triumph was achieved in September, 1903, when he made his argument on the Alaskan Boundary dispute, in London. By his arguments he won the suit for the United States and the entire American Bar. He died February 24, 1916, at Atlantic City, N. J., leaving his entire fortune for the establishment of a home for crippled children at Sewickley Hills.

WATSON, JOHN FANNING, historian, who was born in Burlington County, New Jersey, June 13, 1779, came to Philadelphia as a book-seller after serving in the War Department as a clerk, and at New Orleans as a purveyor for the United States troops in 1804. He was cashier of a Germantown bank from 1814 to 1847 and later was treasurer for a railroad company. He was interested in historical and antiquarian information and published: "Annals of Philadelphia," in 1830, and "Historic Tales of the Olden Times in Philadelphia," in 1833. He made other valuable contributions including manuscripts to the Philadelphia Library and died at Germantown, December 23, 1860.

WAYNE, ANTHONY, soldier, was born at Easton, January 1, 1745. In 1767, he was elected to the Pennsylvania convention and legislature; in 1774 and in 1775 raised a regiment with which he took part in the campaign against

Canada. He fought in the Revolutionary War and on the night of July 15, 1779, achieved the most brilliant of American victories in the storming of Stony Point, for which he received a gold medal and the thanks of Congress. He became the popular hero, "Mad Anthony." In 1784, he retired from the army and became a member of the Pennsylvania Legislature. In 1792, he was made commander-in-chief of the United States Army. In 1793, he took to the field against the Indians in Ohio, whom he finally defeated at Fallen Timbers and forced them to conclude the treaty of Greenville (1795) which gave a large tract of territory to the United States. He died December 15, 1796, while he was engaged in completing this service, and is buried in Old Saint David's Churchyard, Wayne. Wayne County and the towns of Wayne, Waynesboro and Waynesburg in Pennsylvania are named for him as are numerous other places throughout the United States.

RESIDENCE OF ANTHONY WAYNE, NEAR PAOLI (1843)

WAYNE COUNTY, was formed from part of Northampton, March 21, 1798. Named for General Anthony Wayne. Land area, 739 square miles; population (1930), 28,420. County-seat, Honesdale, laid out in 1826.

WAYNESBORO, borough in Franklin County, about forty-eight miles southwest of Harrisburg. It was settled about 1750 by John Wallace and was originally called Wallacetown. Later the name was changed to Waynesburg and finally to Waynesboro, in honor of General Anthony Wayne. The village was incorporated December 21, 1818. About two miles north of Waynesboro are the ruins of the settlement made by the Seventh Day Baptists at Snow Hill, established in 1814 on plans similar to the cloistered settlement at Ephrata. The confederate army passed through Waynesboro on its way to and from Gettysburg. The manufactured products of the town are ice refrigerating machinery, stationery, portable and traction engines, machinery, iron and steel products, underwear, men's clothing, etc. Population (1930), 10,167; (1920), 9,720.

ANTHONY WAYNE

WAYNESBURG, borough and county-seat of Greene County, on Ten Mile Creek. It is located in an agricultural and stock-raising region, and in the natural gas and oil belt. The first settler on the site of the town was Thomas Slater who came there in 1771 and purchased 395 acres of land in 1787. In 1796, he sold this land, which he called Eden, to the trustees of Greene County. The borough of Waynesburg was incorporated in 1849. It is the seat of Waynesburg College established in 1850.

WAYNESBURG COLLEGE, located at Waynesburg, was chartered in 1850 and first opened to students in 1851. It was established by and is under the control of the Pennsylvania Synod of the Cumberland Presbyterian Church, and the trustees are elected by this synod. The college for many years labored under serious difficulties and it was not until 1898 that an adequate endowment was obtained. Since that time the curriculum has been extended, especially in the study of sciences, and the equipment greatly improved. Enrollment (1930-1931), 310.

WAYNESBURG DEMOCRAT-MESSENGER, THE, was established in 1813. It appears every Tuesday and Friday; is devoted to the principles of the Democratic Party; is edited by M. R. Travis; and published by the Democrat Printing Company, Inc. Circulation, 4,320.

WEATHERLY, a borough in Carbon County, eighteen miles southeast of Scranton. The manufactures include silks, machinery, woodwork, cigars and candy. The town which was formerly called Black Creek, owes its beginnings to the operations of the Beaver Meadow Railroad Company and its growth to the Lehigh Valley Railroad Company. In 1863, it was incorporated as a borough.

WEBSTER, PELATIAH, political economist, was born in Lebanon, Conn., 1725. He was graduated from Yale in 1746, and in 1748-1749 was engaged as a preacher. Afterward he entered upon a business career in Philadelphia and gained a considerable fortune. He was a student of the problems of the currency, finance, and national resources and during the Revolution aided the cause with his purse and pen. He was imprisoned by the British for more than four months in 1778 and had property to the value of £500 confiscated. He died in Philadelphia, in September, 1795.

WEIDNER, REVERE FRANKLIN, Lutheran theologian, was born in Centre Valley, November 22, 1851. After graduation from Muhlenberg College in 1869 and from the Lutheran Theological Seminary, Philadelphia, in 1873, he was ordained to the ministry and served pastorates at Phillipsburg, N. J., and at Philadelphia. In 1875-1877, he was professor of English, history, and logic at Muhlenberg, and 1882-1891 was professor of dogmatics and exegisis at Augustana Theological Seminary, Rock Island, Ill. Afterwards he became president and professor of dogmatic theology at the Chicago Lutheran Theological Seminary. He is the author of: "Commentary on the Gospel of Mark"; "Biblical Theology of the Old Testament"; "Theologia; or the Doctrine of Good," etc. He died January 5, 1915.

WEISER, CONRAD, pioneer diplomat, was born at Afsteadt, Herrenberg, near Wurtemberg, Germany, November 2, 1696. When he was thirteen, he came with his father to America, where he lived with different Indian chiefs and learned the Indian language. In 1729, Weiser led a band of German Palatines from the Schoharie, in New York, to the valley of the Tulpehocken, in Pennsylvania, where they formed a permanent settlement. Rapidly he gained prominence in his dealings with the Indians attending many conferences between them and the colonial authorities. In February, 1737, he was sent to treat with the Iroquois at Onondaga, to persuade them to send peace commissioners to Williamsburg, Va. The journey was made in midwinter with the added discomforts of an exceedingly meagre food supply. As a result of this mission the Indians were persuaded to sign an armistice pledging peace between their tribe and the southern Indians, but they refused to send commissioners to Williamsburg. During the next few years Weiser became extremely interested in religious affairs. He met Conrad Beissel, founder of the Seventh Day Baptist settlement at Ephrata who influenced him so strongly that he left the Lutheran Church at Tulpehocken and joined Beissel's settlement, where he was at once recognized as a leader. However, his interest in the settlement shortly afterward declined and he left the Brethren, only to become interested in the work of the Moravian missionaries. Spangenberg, Zeisberger and Zinzendorf enlisted his aid in 1737 and he became their guide and interpreter. About the year 1740 Weiser's interests again centered in the affairs of the province. For the next twenty years, until the time of his death, he was constantly in the employ of the government as Indian interpreter, agent and diplomat. Because of his influence over the Indians the Six Nations became allies of the English, and the French and Indian War in Pennsylvania ended in 1757, two years earlier than in other sections of the country. In order to accomplish this, Weiser was required to undertake many difficult journeys in order to attend numerous councils with the Indians. According to his official reports he attended, at the governor's order, conferences with the Indians at Shamokin, in 1742 and 1743; at Onondaga, N. Y., in 1743; at Shamokin, May 2, 1744; at Onondaga, May 19, 1745; in Ohio, August 11-September 29, 1748; in Onondaga, 1750, 1751 and 1753; in Aughwick, 1754; Carlisle, 1756; Fort Allen, 1756, and Easton, 1756 and 1757. In 1748, Weiser assisted in laying out the city of Reading, established a second home there, and built the first store in the town at what is now Fifth and Penn Streets, where he traded with both the settlers and the Indians. It was through his efforts that Berks County was formed, March 11, 1752, from parts of Lancaster, Chester and Philadelphia Counties. He became the first judge of the new county. Weiser's service to the province of Pennsylvania and to the nation cannot be estimated. At the beginning of the

French and Indian War he was commissioned colonel and led the volunteer militia of the Tulpehocken region in the defense of the colony. He died at his home near Womelsdorf, Berks County, July 13, 1760.

Weiser Park, surrounding the Weiser home, erected in 1730, near Womelsdorf, is a memorial to the great pioneer.

WELLSBORO, borough and county-seat of Tioga County, about thirty-five miles north of Williamsport. In 1931, it came into prominence as a result of the discovery of oil in the immediate vicinity. Agriculture and coal mining are carried on in the region and the industrial establishments of Wellsboro are chemical works, marble works, cut glass works, lumber mills and machine shops. Wellsboro was founded by Benjamin Wistar Morris who came there in the interests of the Pine Creek Land Company in 1799. He laid out the town in 1806.

WELSH, HERBERT, publicist and artist, was born in Philadelphia, December 4, 1851. He graduated from the University of Pennsylvania in 1871 after which he studied art in Philadelphia and under Bonnat in Paris. Believing that the Indian would become civilized if he received just treatment and came under the influence of Christianity, he was instrumental in the organization of the Indian Rights Association in 1882, which organization was the agency by which a bill, providing for the individual ownership of land and the application of the civil service law, to the Indian service, was passed. He was a leader in the reform movement in Pennsylvania state politics in 1890, and in 1895 published *City and State*, a weekly periodical, in the interests of good government. He is the author of: "Four Weeks Among Some of the Sioux Tribes"; "A Visit to the Navajo, Pueblo, and Tualpais Indians," and "The Other Man's Country." He lives in Germantown.

WELSH, JOHN, merchant, was born in Philadelphia, November 9, 1805. He became a prominent business man in his native city, with extensive railroad interests. He was active in relief work during the Civil War, serving as president in 1864 of the Philadelphia Sanitary Fair, which raised more than $1,000,000 for army hospitals. With $50,000 received from the citizens of Philadelphia for his work as president of the Board of Finance of the Centennial Exhibition, in 1873, he endowed the John Welsh Chair of English literature at the University of Pennsylvania. He was minister to England in 1878. His death occurred in Philadelphia, April 10, 1886.

WEST, ANDREW FLEMING, philologist, was born in Allegheny, May 17, 1853. He was graduated from Princeton University where he became professor of Latin in 1883 and was dean of the graduate school in 1901–1928. He edited "Terence," and "The Philobiblon of Richard de Bury," and is the author of: ""Alcuin and the Rise of the Christian Schools," "Latin Grammar," "American Liberal Education," and "Education and the War." His home is in Princeton, New Jersey.

BENJAMIN WEST (531)

WEST, BENJAMIN, painter, was born in Springfield, Delaware County, October 10, 1738. At an early period he showed remarkable genius for painting. When he was nine years old he painted a picture in water colors, which in some points, he said in later years, he never surpassed. Members of the Society of Friends did not encourage painting but since young West could not be kept from the art, a public meeting was called and the following decision reached: "To John West and Sarah Pierson a man-child has been born on whom God has conferred some remarkable gifts; something amounting to inspiration, and the youth has been induced to study painting. Such rare gifts cannot but be for a wise and good purpose. The Divine Hand is in this. We shall do well to encourage this youth." Afterward West painted in Philadelphia and New York. In 1760, he went to Italy to study—the first American artist to study in that country. He was elected member of the academies of Florence, Bologna and Parma and in 1763 went to England where he was so well received that he decided to make his home there. After the death of Sir Joshua Reynolds he was rated the best painter of his time in England. He worked with both quickness and ease, and excelled in his composition and drawing. The king, George III, became his patron; in 1772, he was made historical painter to the king, and in 1790 surveyor of the royal pictures. He was one of the four selected to draw up a plan of the Royal Academy and was one of the original members. His "Death of General Wolfe" was exhibited there in 1771. West planned a series of paintings illustrating the progress of revealed religion, for the Chapel of Windsor Castle, but only twenty-eight of them were finished, for when the king became insane the Prince Regent cancelled the order for the remainder of the series. Afterwards West began a new series of religious works of which "Christ Healing the Sick" was bought by the British Institute. Others are: "Death on the Pale Horse" (Pennsylvania Academy); "Christ Rejected"; the "Crucifixion," and the "Ascension." The "Battle of La Hague" is one of his greatest historical paintings. West died in London, England, March 11, 1820.

BIRTHPLACE OF BENJAMIN WEST (1843)

WESTMINSTER COLLEGE, at New Wilmington, was chartered in 1852 as Westminster Collegiate Institute, under the control of the United Presbyterian Church. In 1892, the name was changed to Westminster College. The degrees of A. B. and B. S. are conferred and there are departments of music and art and a preparatory course. Enrollment (1930–1931), 525.

WESTMORELAND COUNTY, was formed February 26, 1773, from part of Bedford and in 1785 part of the purchase of 1784 was added. Named for the English county of Westmoreland. Land area, 1,039 square miles; population (1930), 295,795. County-seat, Greensburg, laid out in 1782.

WESTMORELAND DEMOCRAT, THE, was established as *The Farmers' Register*, by John M. Snowden, in 1798. It is a weekly paper, appears each Wednesday, and maintains the political principles of the Democratic Party. E. Arthur Sweeny is the editor and the circulation is 930.

WEST CHESTER, borough and county-seat of Chester County, about twenty-seven miles west of Philadelphia. Until 1786 when Chester County was divided to form the counties of Delaware and Chester, the town was called Turk's Head. Then Chester became the county-seat of Delaware County, and Turk's Head, lying west of Chester, was renamed West Chester, and became the county-seat of Chester County. The manufactured products of West Chester are: gas engines, doors and sashes, hosiery, umbrellas, tags and wood products. West Chester is the seat of several educational institutions, viz., West Chester State Teachers College, Friends Select School, The Darlington Seminary, Villa Maria Academy and West Chester Business College. Population (1930), 12,325; (1920), 11,717.

WEST CHESTER STATE TEACHERS COLLEGE—In 1869, the properties of the West Chester Academy and Chester County Cabinet of Natural Science were sold and the proceeds made the basis of a fund for the erection of buildings for a State Normal School. The school was opened in 1871. In addition to two and four-year courses in elementary and junior high school education, special courses are offered in health education and music.

WEST HAZLETON, borough in Luzerne County, suburban to Hazleton, twenty-two miles southwest of Wilkes-Barre, is located in a coal mining region. It was made a separate municipality in 1889. Population (1930), 7,310; (1920), 5,854.

WEST PITTSTON, borough in Luzerne County, on the Susquehanna River, opposite Pittston, with which it is connected by bridges. It is a residential town. The settlement which was early known as Fort Jenkins for the fort which was within what is now the borough, was incorporated in 1857. Population (1930), 7,940; (1920), 6,968.

WHARTON, ANNE HOLLINGSWORTH, author, was born in Southampton Furnace, December 15, 1845. Her writings include: "Through Colonial Doorways"; "A Last Century Maid"; "Martha Washington: A Biography"; "Heirlooms in Miniature"; "Salons Colonial and Republican"; "An English Honeymoon"; "In Chateau Land," and "English Ancestral Homes of Noted Americans." She died July 29, 1928.

WHARTON, FRANCIS, jurist, was born in Philadelphia, March 7, 1820. After graduation from Yale in 1839, he studied law and was admitted to the bar in 1843. In 1856-1863, he was professor of logic and rhetoric at Kenyon College, Ohio; in 1863, entered the ministry of the Episcopal Church and became pastor of Saint Paul's, Brooklyn, Mass.; 1866, professor, Episcopal Divinity School, Cambridge, Mass.; and professor of international law, Boston Law School; in 1885, was appointed counsel for the State Department at Washington and in 1888 became editor of the Revolutionary diplomatic correspondence of the United States. His "Treatise on the Criminal Law of the United States" is recognized as a standard. Among the remainder of his writings are: "Precedents of Indictments and Pleas," "The Conflict of Laws," "Commentary on the Law of Contracts," and "Treatise in the Law of Evidence and Criminal Issues." He died at Washington, D. C., February 21, 1889.

WHARTON, THOMAS, journalist, was born in Philadelphia, August 1, 1859. In 1879, he graduated from the University of Pennsylvania. From 1888 until his death, when he was Sunday editor, he was a member of the editorial staff of the Philadelphia *Times*. He wrote: "A Latter Day Saint," "Hannibal of New York," and "Bobbo" (a short story). He died in Philadelphia, April 6, 1896.

WHEATLAND, residence of President James Buchanan, near Lancaster; purchased by him from William M. Meredith. Many notables were here entertained when Buchanan was at the height of his career and here a student of Franklin and Marshall College, William A. Duncan, afterwards a member of Congress, successful in a race of college students, was the first to inform him of his nomination for the presidency at Cincinnati in 1856.

WHISKEY INSURRECTION, THE—The counties of Washington, Allegheny, Westmoreland, and Fayette, in western Pennsylvania, were the scenes of active opposition to the Federal excise law passed by Congress on March 3, 1791. This law placed a duty or excise of four cents per gallon on distilled spirits, and was part of Secretary Hamilton's plan for raising funds to discharge the debts assumed by the national government. Objections to the excise were raised in Congress by Representative Smiley, of Fayette, and Findley, of Westmoreland, but they were in the minority and the law became effective. Western Pennsylvania objected to it because they felt that it was levied on a commodity and was not based upon the value of the product. Distilling was common at that time and the western farmer found it to be the most practical means for converting grain into a marketable product. Money was a rarity, too, and many grievances, remaining from Revolutionary and pre-Revolutionary days, gained momentum and expressed themselves in open opposition to the tax. General John Neville, who had been active in the service of the Colonists during the Revolution, was appointed chief inspector for the western counties, and it was his duty to appoint collectors to inspect stills, evaluate the products, collect the excise and report the condition and number of them regularly. The collectors were unpopular from the first, and many of them or their deputies were attacked by residents of the communities, tarred and feathered and ill-treated generally. Few names of men who participated in the attacks upon these collectors have come down to us. More information is available concerning the personnel of representatives who met at different towns throughout the affected counties. Albert Gallatin, Hugh Henry Breckenridge, William Findley, Edward Cook, and David Bradford were among the most outstanding opponents of the law. All of them but Bradford desired to support constitutional means to express opposition to the law. They advocated petitions and congressional action to bring about a repeal of the law, but in an extreme moment they gave sanction to the policy adopted at a meeting in Washington, on August 23, 1791, when under Bradford's influence the citizens who met there drew up the following resolutions: That "any person who had accepted or might accept an office under Congress, in order to carry the law into effect, should be considered inimical to the interests of the country; and recommending to the citizens of Washington County to treat every person accepting such office with contempt, and absolutely to refuse all kind of communication or intercourse with him, and withhold from him all aid, support, or comfort." The sanction of this resolution that was later adopted by a meeting of influential citizens at Pittsburgh, was later referred to by Gallatin as his "only political sin." The fires of opposition smouldered, although Congress made revisions in the law, with respect to length of time for payment of the excise. One of the principle objections remained. That was the fact that citizens guilty of non-payment of the tax had to go to Philadelphia for trial before the Federal court there. The journey was long and expensive, and not in proportion to the offences committed. In the summer of 1794, when Congress again made revisions in the law, a marshal was sent to the western counties to serve writs for appearance at court upon men who failed to comply with the conditions of the act before its last revision. The writs were served without direct opposition until the home of a farmer named Miller, who lived at Peter's Creek, south of Pittsburgh, was reached on July 15, 1794. Miller and his men were in the harvest field, and were so incensed at the appearance of the marshal, who was with General Neville at the time, that some of them fired upon the representatives of the law who then returned to Neville's home. Neville's house was destroyed two days later, after parties of men had appeared on the premises on two occasions, and in some manner, not absolutely clear, became engaged in gunfire with occupants of the house and servant's quarters. Major McFarland, who led the party of visitors, was killed. Citizens of Pittsburgh became excited when the events were reported, and a meeting at Braddock's Field did not serve to ameliorate matters. Many people met at the famous rendezvous but only a few of them, proportionally, marched into Pittsburgh, and aside from the burning of a barn nothing serious resulted. The more legal minded citizens realized that it was time to consider the consequences of any rash actions that might result in the destruction of lives and property. Meanwhile Neville and the marshal escaped to Philadelphia, fearing for their lives, and their report of the events connected with the burning of Neville's house were responsible for Hamilton's action in urging President Washington to send troops to the affected sections. In western Pennsylvania, Gallatin and Breckenridge gained control of the situation and through meetings at Mingo Creek and at Parkinson's Ferry urged the people to consider the situation and the consequences that would follow upon destruction of property and preparations for war. On the contrary, Bradford urged open opposition, encouraged tampering with the mails and hinted the desirability of forming a new government, independent of the United States. Gallatin and Breckenridge, each in his own way, sparred for time and eventually gained the allegiance of most of the citizens. The federal and state governments dispatched commissioners to Parkinson's Ferry and they arrived there late in August, and although popular feeling had become subdued, troops were sent from eastern counties and from adjoining states to the western counties. There was no violence after the arrival of troops, and only a few persons were arraigned before the federal court in Philadelphia as participants in the insurrection. Eventually all of them were pardoned. Bradford who was not apprehended fled down the Ohio River.

L. S.

WHITE, JAMES WILLIAM, surgeon, was born in Philadelphia, November 2, 1850. He was graduated from the University of Pennsylvania with the degrees of M. D. and Ph. D. In 1871–1872, he was a member of Prof. Agassiz's staff in the Hassler Expedition to the West Indies, the coasts of South America and the Straits of Magellan. Subsequently he engaged in the practice of his profession in Philadelphia, at the same time being a member of the faculty of the Medical School of the University of Pennsylvania where he was successively professor of genito-urino surgery, of clinical surgery and John Rhea Barton professor of surgery. In 1915, he was connected with the American Ambulance Hospital, Neuilly, France. He is the author of: "Text-Book of the War for Americans," and joint author of: "American Text-Book of Surgery," "Genito-Urinal Surgery," and "Human Anatomy." He died in Philadelphia, April 24, 1916.

WHITE, WILLIAM, Protestant Episcopal bishop, was born in Philadelphia, April 4, 1748. After graduating from the College of Philadelphia (University of Pennsylvania) in 1765 he studied theology and spent several years in England where he was admitted to the priesthood. Upon his return to Philadelphia he

WAYNE BLOCK HOUSE, ERIE

became assistant minister and later rector of Christ Church and Saint Peter's Church. In 1777, he was chaplain to Congress. The University of Pennsylvania conferred upon him the first honorary degree of that institution, that of D. D., in 1782. He was elected bishop of Pennsylvania in 1786. He is the author of: "Memoirs of the Protestant Episcopal Church," and "Lectures on the Catechism." He died in Philadelphia, July 17, 1836.

WHITE EYES, Delaware chief, was active in Indian-Colonial affairs. During Lord Dunmore's War he endeavored to prevent an Indian War and succeeded in influencing nearly all the Delawares from taking up arms against Virginia, in spite of the wrongs which the whites had committed against the Indians. Upon returning to his home after this treaty had been made, White Eyes found that the Virginians had entered his home and had taken a good deal of his property. At a conference at Fort Pitt, in June, 1778, White Eyes signed a treaty of alliance with the whites. The Delaware chief died of small-pox on November 10, 1778.

WHITE FAUN, daughter of the Indian, Tomjack, who lived in Bradford County. She became a teacher and missionary to the Indians along the Allegheny, and was instrumental in bringing about friendly relations between the Indians and whites. She never married, contending that the Great Spirit made her a mother of a nation rather than of a family. She died in 1823 and in 1836 the Moravian Church, of which she and her parents had been members, erected a monument to her memory.—*See also* TOMJACK.

WHITELEY CREEK—Tributary to Monongahela River. Sub-basin: Monongahela; source, in Whiteley Township, southern central Greene County; course, easterly, by a circuitous route, to Monongahela River; mouth, two miles west of Masontown; length, twenty-three miles.

WHITNEY, ASA, inventor and manufacturer, was born in Townsend, Mass., December 1, 1791. In 1842, after having served as state canal commissioner in New York, he moved to Philadelphia where he became a partner of Matthew Baldwin in the building of locomotives. He made extensive improvements in car wheels, which he manufactured. His $50,000 bequest to the University of Pennsylvania was for the founding of a chair of dynamical engineering. He died at Philadelphia, June 4, 1874.

WHITNEY, HENRY HOWARD, military officer, was born in Glen Hope, December 25, 1866. In 1892, he graduated from West Point; 1896-1898, was engaged on special duty for the War Department; in 1898, upon receiving orders from the Secretary of War, he disguised himself as an English sailor and made a military reconnoissance of Porto Rico, obtaining information which aided General Miles in his Porto Rican campaign; served throughout the Spanish-American War as captain and assistant adjutant-general on General Miles' staff. In 1902-1903, he was with General Miles in his tour around the world; in 1918–

1919, he was chief of staff, District of Paris. He retired June 30, 1920, at his own request, after thirty-two years of service and lives at Long Beach, California.

WICKERSHAM, GEORGE WOODWARD, lawyer and cabinet officer, was born in Pittsburgh, September 19, 1858. He was educated at Lehigh University and at the law school of the University of Pennsylvania where he graduated in 1880. After practicing for a time in Philadelphia he went to New York in 1882 where he became a member of the law firm of Strong and Cadwalader. He was counsel for numerous large corporations and companies and during President Taft's administration was attorney-general of the United States. He is the author of: "Changing Order" (essays and addresses); "Spring in Morocco," and of articles in The Covenanter, written with President Taft and others. He lives in New York.

WICONISCO CREEK—Tributary to Susquehanna River. Sub-basin: Middle Main Susquehanna; source, in Porter Township, southwestern Schuylkill County; course, southwesterly into Dauphin County to Susquehanna River; mouth, at Millersburg; length, thirty-eight miles. Indian name, Wikenkniskeu, "muddy house," or "muddy camp."

WIDENER, PETER A. BROWN, capitalist, was born in Philadelphia, November 13, 1834. He made a fortune in the meat business and had large interests in street railways, tobacco and Standard Oil. He presented the city of Philadelphia with his residence in 1897 to be used as a branch of the Philadelphia Free Library, and in 1898 gave to the library a collection of rare books. In 1899, he endowed the Widener Memorial Training School for Crippled Children at Logan, Philadelphia. He died November 6, 1915.

WIGGIN, KATE DOUGLAS SMITH, author, was born in Philadelphia, September 28, 1859. She attended Abbott Academy, Andover, Mass., and organized the first free kindergarten in the west at San Francisco. After her marriage to S. B. Wiggin in 1880, she moved to New York. Her husband died in 1889 and she married George C. Riggs in 1895. She wrote: "The Bird's Christmas Carol," "Penelope's Progress," "Penelope's Experience in Ireland," "Rebecca of Sunnybrook Farm," "New Chronicles of Rebecca," and "Mother Carey's Chickens." She died August 24, 1923.

WILKES-BARRE, city and county-seat of Luzerne County, on the north branch of the Susquehanna River, 110 miles northwest of Philadelphia and 110 miles west of New York. The first settlers came from Connecticut and other sections of New England under the Susquehanna Company in 1769. The settlement was named for two members of the British Parliament, John Wilkes and Isaac Barre. On July 3, 1778, male inhabitants of the Wyoming Valley were attacked at Forty Fort by British rangers and Indians, and many of them killed.

Forty Fort surrendered on July 4th, and the enemy practically destroyed Wilkes-Barre. From the time of its settlement to 1784, Wilkes-Barre was the center of dispute between Pennsylvania and Connecticut concerning the ownership of the Wyoming Valley. Wilkes-Barre was incorporated as a borough in 1806 and as a city in 1871. Anthracite coal was discovered here and was first used here for fires in blacksmith's shops and for domestic purposes. The mining of coal is still the leading industry. Other industrial establishments are silk and lace mills, wire-rope works, axle works, foundries and machine shops. Population (1930), 86,626; (1920), 73,833.

WILKES-BARRE RECORD, THE, a daily newspaper, appears every morning except Sunday, under the editorship of E. T. Giering. It was established in 1832; is Republican in politics; and is published by the Wilkes-Barre Record Company, Inc. Circulation, 28,480.

WILKINSBURG, borough of Allegheny County, seven miles east of Pittsburgh, is largely residential. It was originally named McNairville, then Rippeyville and finally Wilkinsburg in honor of William Wilkins, secretary of war in 1843-1845. In 1887, it was incorporated as a borough. Population (1930), 29,539; (1920), 24,403.

WILLIAM PENN CHARTER SCHOOL, a secondary day school for boys, is located at Philadelphia. The governor and council in 1683 employed Enoch Flower as teacher of the youth of Philadelphia. Charter School, founded in 1689, and incorporated in 1698, was a result of this. It was supported by the Quakers, but was a public school, the only school of its kind in Pennsylvania for many years. In 1701, the school was chartered by Penn who issued other charters in 1708 and 1711.

WILLIAMS, FRANCIS CHURCHILL, editor, was born in Philadelphia, April 23, 1869. From the time of his graduation from the University of Pennsylvania in 1891 until 1900 he was engaged in journalism; in 1902-1906, he was literary advisor to J. B. Lippincott Co.; in 1907-1927, associate editor of the *Saturday Evening Post.* He is the author of: "J. Devlin, Boss"; "The Captain," and contributes articles on various subjects to magazines. His home is in Chestnut Hill.

WILLIAMS, GEORGE WASHINGTON, author, was born in Bedford Springs, October 16, 1849, of African descent. He served in the Civil War, subsequently attended school, and was for a short time engaged as a preacher and later as a journalist. He was graduated from the Cincinnati Law School in 1877 and in 1879-1881 served in the Ohio Legislature. He was United States minister to Haiti in 1885-1886 and in 1888 was a delegate to the World's Conference of Foreign Missions at London. He was editor of the Cincinnati *South-*

western Review and of the Washington *Commoner*. He wrote a "History of the Negro Race in America from 1619-1880," and a "History of the Negro Troops in the War of the Rebellion." He died in 1891.

WILLIAMS, JONATHAN, soldier, was born in Boston, May 20, 1750. He was secretary to his grand uncle, Benjamin Franklin, while the latter was ambassador to France, and while abroad read widely concerning fortification, making a special study of military science. Returning in 1785, he was for some years a judge of Common Pleas at Philadelphia. In 1801, he entered the army and resigned in 1812. He died in Philadelphia, May 16, 1815. As the first person in the United States to apply the principles of scientific engineering, he has often been called "the father of the corps of engineers."

WILLIAMSITE, an ornamental and semi-precious variety of serpentine of apple-green color obtained in Lancaster County.

WILLIAMSON FREE SCHOOL OF MECHANICAL TRADES, an educational institution for boys dependent upon their own resources, founded in 1888 at Williamson School Station, near Philadelphia, by I. V. Williamson. It is non-sectarian. Boys between the ages of fifteen and eighteen are admitted, and are bound for three years as apprentices to the trustees. There is an academic course for general education and each student is taught one trade.

WILLIAMSPORT, city and county-seat of Lycoming County, on the west branch of the Susquehanna River, about seventy-five miles north of Harrisburg. It is on the Allegheny Plateau, covering an area of seven square miles, in an agricultural and mining region. The city originally had an extensive trade in lumber products and coal, but as the forests were cut away the trade disappeared, and many foundry and machine shops were located here. The manufactured products of the city are gasoline engines, rubber, woolen, and silk goods, furniture, shoes, etc. Williamsport was settled in 1779, and set off as a town in 1795. In 1806, it was incorporated as a borough and in 1866 was chartered as a city. Population (1930), 45,729; (1920), 36,198.

WILLIAMSPORT GAZETTE AND BULLETIN, THE, was established in 1801; is published every morning except Sunday. Elmer L. Schuyler is the editor, and the Sun Gazette Company, publishers. Circulation, 8,618,

WILLIAMSTOWN, a borough in Dauphin County, twenty-six miles northeast of Harrisburg. It is situated in an anthracite coal mining region, and the industries of the town are coal mining and the manufacture of hosiery. The borough was settled in 1865 and incorporated in 1888.

WILLING, THOMAS, jurist, merchant, and financier, was born in Philadelphia, December 19, 1731. He was educated at Bath, England, and studied law at the Temple, London. He returned to Philadelphia where he and Robert Morris established the mercantile firm of Willing and Morris, which became the largest in the country. Willing was mayor of Philadelphia in 1763, and in 1767-1774 was an associate judge of the Supreme Court of Pennsylvania. He was a member of the Continental Congress in 1774-1775, and voted against the Declaration of Independence. However, when in 1780 the Continental Army was hard pressed for funds, he himself contributed £5,000. In 1781, he was one of the founders of the Bank of North America, and was first president of the United States Bank, founded in 1791. He died in Philadelphia, January 19, 1821.

WILLS CREEK—Tributary to Potomac River. Basin: Potomac; source, in Larimer Township, southeastern Somerset County; course, northwesterly and easterly into Bedford County to Hyndman; mouth, at Cumberland, Md.; length, in Pennsylvania, twenty-seven miles. Named in honor of an Indian named Will, who lived near the site of Cumberland, before 1755.

WILMOT, DAVID, jurist and politician, was born at Bethany, January 20, 1814. He was admitted to the bar in 1834 and practiced at Towanda. He was a member of Congress in 1845-1851; was elected as a Democrat but was opposed to the extension of slavery into prospective new territory of the United States and in 1846 offered the famous amendment known as the Wilmot Proviso. He supported Van Buren for the presidency in 1848, but later joined the Republican Party. In 1857, he was an unsuccessful candidate for governor of Pennsylvania; from 1861-1863 was a member of the United States Senate and from 1863 to his death was judge of the United States Court of Claims. He died March 16, 1868.

WILSON, FRANCIS, actor, was born in Philadelphia, February 7, 1854. He made his first appearance on the stage in a minstrel company at the Chestnut Street Threatre, Philadelphia, in 1877. He later became leading comedian in different New York theatres, and afterward organized his own company, himself playing the leading comedy roles He published: "The Eugene Field I Knew," "Recollections of a Player," "Joseph Jefferson," "Francis Wilson's Life of Himself," "John Wilkes Booth"; and the dramas: "The Magic Ring," "The Bachelor's Baby," "The Spiritualist," and "The Dancing Master." He lives in New York.

WILSON, RUFUS ROCKWELL, author, was born in Troy, March 15, 1865. In 1883-1891, he was engaged in journalism in Pittsburgh, Washington and New York; in 1891-1906, he was a magazine writer and newspaper editor, for a time managing a newspaper syndicate. He entered political reform work in 1910 and the following year organized and superintended certain Chinese famine relief work. He has published: "Rambles in Colonial Byways," "Wash-

DAVID WILMOT

ington—The Capital City," and "Literary Landmarks in America." He is now associated with raising a $1,000,000 endowment fund for Oneida (Kentucky) Institute.

WILSON COLLEGE, a college for women, located at Chambersburg. It was established under the auspices of the Presbyterian Church and it is under the special care of the Synod of Pennsylvania. It was incorporated in 1869 as Wilson Female College. Enrollment (1930-1931), 445.

WINEBRENNER, JOHN, clergyman, founder of the denomination known as the Church of God, was born in Frederick County, Md., March 24, 1797. He was ordained a minister of the German Reformed Church in 1820 and was called the same year to the Salem Church, Harrisburg. He retained that charge until 1827, when his outspoken attitude against slavery and the liquor traffic led to his being asked to withdraw and in 1828 he ceased to be connected with the Reformed Church. In October, 1830, he established the denomination called the Church of God (Winebrennerians). He published a treatise on "Regeneration," a church hymn book, etc. He died September 12, 1860.

WINES, FREDERICK HOWARD, statistician, was born in Philadelphia, April 9, 1838. He was graduated from Washington College in 1857 and studied at Princeton Theological Seminary; was chaplain in the Union Army, 1862-1864. He devoted much of his time to the interests of the work carried on by the National Conference of Charities and Correction; the National Prison Association, and the International Prison Congress. He published: "Crime, Pauperism, and Benevolence in the United States"; "Punishment and Reformation," etc. He died in 1912.

WINTON, a borough in Lackawanna County, on the Lackawanna River, eight miles northeast of Scranton. It is chiefly occupied in coal mining. The settlement was originally called Mount Vernon and was incorporated as a borough in 1877. Population (1930), 8,508; (1920), 7,583.

WISSAHICKON CREEK—Tributary to Schuylkill River. Sub-basin: Lower Delaware; source, one mile east of Lansdale, Montgomery Township, Montgomery County; course, southerly, by a circuitous route, into Philadelphia County to Schuylkill River; mouth, at Wissahickon; length, twenty-three miles. Indian name, a corruption of Wisameckhan, "cat-fish stream."

WISTAR, CASPAR, physician, was born in Philadelphia, September 13, 1761. He attended the medical school of the University of Pennsylvania in 1782 and was graduated in medicine from the University of Edinburgh in 1786. From 1789 until his death he was a member of the faculty of the University of Pennsylvania. He opened his house once a week for meetings of students, travelers, scientists and citizens, and these symposiums continued long after his death, and were known as the Wistar parties. The wistaria vine was named in his honor as was also the Wistar Institute of Anatomy and Biology at the University of Pennsylvania. He died January 22, 1818.

WISTAR, ISAAC JONES, penologist, was born at Philadelphia, November 14, 1827. He was educated at Haverford College and served in the Civil War as brigadier-general of volunteers, United States Army, 1862-1865. He was president of the Academy of Natural Sciences of Philadelphia, 1892-1896; was inspector of the Eastern Penitentiary of Pennsylvania; was president of the state board of charities and founded the Wistar Institute of Anatomy and Biology, named in honor of Caspar Wistar. He died in Claymont, Del., September 18, 1905.

WISTER, ANNIS LEE FURNESS, translator, was born in Philadelphia, October 9, 1830. She was married to Dr. Caspar Wister in 1854. She made many translations of note, among them: Von Auer's "It is the Fashion," and Volkhausen's "Why Did He Not Die?" Her translations were issued in a uniform edition of thirty volumes in 1888. She died November 15, 1908.

WISTER, OWEN, author, was born in Philadelphia, July 14, 1860. He was graduated from Harvard in 1882, and was admitted to the bar in Philadelphia in 1889, but from 1891 he devoted his attention to literature. He has been especially successful in his delineation of western life and character and has published: "Red Men and White"; "The Virginian"; "Mother"; "U. S. Grant, a Biography"; "The Seven Ages of Washington"; "When West was West," etc. He is also a contributor of much verse and prose to magazines. His home is in Bryn Mawr.

WITMER, LIGHTNER, psychologist and educator, was born in Philadelphia, June 28, 1867. He was graduated from the University of Pennsylvania in 1888 and received the degree of Ph. D. at Leipzig in 1892. He has been connected with the faculty of the University of Pennsylvania since 1892, and since 1909 has been director of the psychological laboratory and clinic there, which he organized as a department of the university. He has lectured at Bryn Mawr College and at Lehigh University. In 1907, he founded the *Psychological Clinic* of which he is the editor. He is the author of: "Analytical Psychology," and the editor of "Experimental Studies in Psychology," and "The Special Class for Backward Children."

WOLF, GEORGE, governor, was born in Allen Township, Northampton County, August 12, 1777. He attended a classical school in Northampton County and subsequently engaged in farming and was principal of an academy. Later, he entered the office of the Prothonotary of Northampton County and at the same time studied law under Hon. John Ross. In 1814, after he had served successively as postmaster at Easton, and Clerk of the Orphan's Court of Northampton County, he was elected a member of the House of Representatives. In 1824, he was elected a member of the United States House of Representatives and was reelected for the two succeeding terms. In 1829, he was nominated as candidate for governor and was elected. As governor he advocated a system of public education, securing the passage of the free school law, and recommended the adoption of a system of taxation whereby the financial condition of the state, then in a bad condition, could be improved. Wolf was reelected governor and was a candidate for a third term but was defeated. After the expiration of his second term he was appointed First Comptroller of the Treasury of the United States which position he held for two years when President Van Buren appointed him Collector of the Port of Philadelphia. He died March 11, 1840.

WHITEFIELD HOUSE OR NAZARETH STOCKADE

WOLLE, JOHN FREDERICK, musician, was born in Bethlehem, April 4, 1863. He studied at Philadelphia, Munich, and New York; was organist at the Moravian Church at Bethlehem in 1885-1905, and of the Packer Memorial Church at Lehigh University in 1887-1905. In 1905-1911, he was professor of music at the University of California and in 1912 resumed his former positions at Bethlehem. He established the annual Bethlehem Bach festivals in 1898, the Choral Society of Harrisburg in 1914, the Oratorio Society at York in 1914, and a similar society at Lancaster in 1916. He received the degree, Mus. Doc., from Moravian College in 1904. He is one of the leading organists in America; is one of the founders of American Guild of Organists and a member of the International Music Society. He has composed hymn tunes, anthems for chorus and orchestra, and has transcribed for the organ, compositions of Bach and Wagner. He lives in Bethlehem.

WOOD, FERNANDO, politician, was born in Philadelphia, June 14, 1812. In 1820, he removed to New York where he became known as a politician. He was mayor of New York City for several terms and also served in Congress. He died in Washington, D. C., February 14, 1881.

WOOD, HORATIO CURTIS, physician, was born in Philadelphia, January 13, 1841. He was graduated from the University of Pennsylvania in 1862 and was professor there from 1866-1907 and thereafter emeritus professor of therapeutics. He is the author of: "Thermic Fever," "A Study of Fever," and "Nervous Diseases and Their Diagnosis."

WOOD, JAMES FREDERICK, Roman Catholic Prelate, was born in Philadelphia, April 27, 1813. He was educated in England and on returning to the United States entered the banking business. In 1836, he went to Rome to study for the priesthood and after his ordination in 1844 became assistant rector of the Cathedral in Cincinnati and afterward pastor of St. Patrick's Church. In 1857, he became bishop of Philadelphia where he completed the magnificent cathedral in Logan Square. He also established the Seminary of St. Charles Borromeo at Overbrook. He was created archbishop in 1875. He died in Philadelphia, June 20, 1883.

WOODRUFF, CHARLES EDWARD, army surgeon and ethnologist, was born in Philadelphia, October 2, 1860. He was graduated from the high school in Philadelphia in 1879, studied at the United States Naval Academy in 1879-1883, and was graduated from Jefferson Medical College in 1886. In 1887, he joined the army and was on duty in the Philippines in 1898, 1902-1904, and in 1909-1910, and attained the rank of lieutenant-colonel. In 1913, he was retired. He died June 13, 1915.

WOODRUFF, CLINTON ROGERS, lawyer, was born in Philadelphia, December 17, 1868. He was graduated from the University of Pennsylvania in 1889 and received the degree of LL. B. there in 1892. He served in the Pennsylvania Legislature two terms and was the author of the "personal registration" amendment to the constitution of Pennsylvania. In 1906, he was appointed president of the board of personal registration commissioners for Philadelphia. He is the editor of the "National Municipal Review," and has published "City Government by Commission." He is a frequent contributor to reviews and magazines and is a member of various religious and civic organizations.

WOODS, ROBERT ARCHEY, university settlement worker, was born in Pittsburgh, December 9, 1865. He was graduated from Amherst in 1886, and from Andover Theological Seminary in 1890, and made a European tour for the purpose of investigating social problems, spending six months at Toynbee Hall, London, and became head of the South End House, a university settlement in Boston, in 1891. He was active in investigating social problems in New England. He died February 18, 1925.

WRIGHT, J. J., jurist, was born in Luzerne County. When he was six years old his parents removed to Montrose, Susquehanna County, where for several years he attended the district school during the winter months, working for the neighboring farmers the rest of the year. Having saved a small sum of money he entered the Lancasterian University at Ithaca, N. Y., where he studied for a time, afterwards returning to the village where his parents resided. There he entered the office of a law firm, where he read law for two years and supported himself by teaching school Subsequently he entered the office of Judge Collins, in Wilkes-Barre, and read law there for a year. Afterwards he applied for admission to the bar; but because of the existing prejudice against the colored race he was refused an examination. In April, 1865, he was sent by the American Missionary Society to Beaufort, S. C., as a teacher and worker among the freedmen. He remained in Beaufort until after the Civil Rights Bill had been passed, when he returned to Montrose and demanded an examination. He was permitted to take the examination which he passed successfully. He was admitted to the bar, August 13, 1865, and was the first colored man ever admitted to the practice of law in Pennsylvania. In April, 1866, he was appointed by General O. O. Howard, legal advisor for the freedmen in Beaufort, and acted in that capacity until he was elected to the Constitutional Convention of South Carolina. He was soon after elected state senator which position he held until February 1, 1870, when he was elected to the Supreme Court of the state. He was judge of the Supreme Court of South Carolina until 1877, and took nonpartisan ground in the decision on the South Carolina election of 1876. His opinions show legal ability of a high order.

WRIGHTSVILLE, York County, on the Susquehanna River, thirty-one miles southeast of Harrisburg, was the farthest point east reached by the Confederates during the Civil War. In the campaign preceding Gettysburg, General Early was ordered to seize the bridge across the Susquehanna at this point, a wooden structure over a mile long, resting on stone piers. Included in the structure was a railroad bridge, a passway for wagons, and a towpath for the canal which crossed the Susquehanna here. The bridge was, however, totally destroyed by Union troops and the flames communicated to Wrightsville, consuming several buildings. The destruction of the bridge destroyed the plan for attack on Harrisburg from the east side of the river.

WURTS, JOHN, educator and writer, was born at Carbondale, July 10, 1855. He was educated at Yale and after traveling in Polynesia as a newspaper correspondent, in 1876-1877, was graduated from the Yale Law School in 1884, and practiced his profession in Jacksonville, Fla., in 1884-1896. He was a member of the faculty at Yale after 1897, lecturer at West Point in 1916, and exchange professor at the University of California in 1914-1915.

WURTZ, HENRY, chemist, was born at Easton, June 5, 1828. He was graduated at Princeton in 1848, studied at the Lawrence Scientific School at Harvard, was state chemist of New Jersey, 1854-1856, chemical examiner in the United States Patent Office, 1859-1861, and from 1871-1875 edited the *American Gas Light Journal.* In 1888, he entered the employ of T. A. Edison as chemist and afterwards made several important chemical discoveries, chief of which is that of the geometrical laws of condensation of chemical modules. He published "Geometrical Chemistry." He died November 10, 1910.

WYOMING, a borough in Luzerne County, on the Susquehanna River, five miles north of Wilkes-Barre. It is situated in an iron and coal mining district and there are manufactures of paints, shovels, and flour. A settlement was begun here in 1780 or 1781 by Benjamin Carpenter, of Connecticut, who erected a grist mill, and the place was early known as Carpenter's Mill and Carpenter Town. In June, 1885, it was incorporated as a borough.

WYOMING COUNTY, was formed April 4, 1842, from part of Luzerne. Named for the Wyoming Valley. Land area, 397 square miles; population (1930), 15,517. County-seat, Tunkhannock, laid out in 1790.

WYOMING MASSACRE—The Wyoming Valley, in colonial history, included a large part of the present counties of Lackawanna, Luzerne, Wyoming, and Bradford. Families from Connecticut had made a home for themselves in this beautiful and fertile region. The military forces of the valley were mustered during the Revolutionary War to repel Indian attacks and to assist the American cause against Great Britain. In January, 1777, acting under orders from the Continental Congress, two regular companies, comprising half the military strength of the territory, joined Washington's army. The defeat of Burgoyne in 1777 encouraged the Six Nations and their British allies and on July 4, 1778, they fell upon the defenceless inhabitants, who under the leadership of Zebulon Butler had hastily assembled. Butler's force, made up of old men and boys, three hundred in number, were overwhelmed by five hundred British and seven hundred Indians. The few survivors of the massacre of men, women and children, entrenched themselves in Forty Fort, but finally surrendered, only to be murdered. The few who fled to the woods alone escaped. Every home and barn in the valley was burned. The ultimate result was, however, unfavorable to the allies, for it stimulated the patriots to activity, and as the horrible incidents were told in Europe the attacks of Chatham on the British policy in America created much opposition to the war. Sullivan's expedition the next year avenged the massacre. The poet Campbell told the dreadful story of the massacre in his "Gertrude of Wyoming."

YARROW, HARRY CRECY, surgeon, was born in Philadelphia, November 19, 1840. He was a surgeon in the Union Army during the Civil War and in 1878 was assigned to duty in the Army Medical Museum at Washington. Subsequently he was honorary curator of the Department of Herpetology in the National Museum at Washington, and for twenty years was a member of the faculty of George Washington University. He is the author of "Study of Mortuary Customs Among the North American Indians."

YELLOW CREEK—Tributary to Twolick Creek. Sub-basin: Lower Allegheny; source, in Green Township, eastern Indiana County; course, southwesterly, to Twolick Creek; mouth, at Homer City; length, twenty-five miles.

YELLOW BREECHES CREEK—Tributary to Susquehanna River. Sub-basin: Lower Main Susquehanna; source, in South Mountain, Southampton Township, southwestern Cumberland County; course, northeasterly to Susquehanna River, forming Cumberland-York County boundary for twenty-one miles; mouth, at New Cumberland; length, fifty-four miles. Indian name, Callapat-scink, "where it returns."

YERKES, CHARLES TYSON, capitalist, was born in Philadelphia, June 25, 1837. He engaged in the flour and grain business and in 1859 became a stock broker. Later he was connected with the Philadelphia street railway system, but was convicted of misappropriating funds, sentenced to imprisonment, and later pardoned. He acquired a controlling position in the street railway system in Chicago, was a member of the board of directors of the World's Columbian Exposition at Chicago, and was connected with the London system of underground railways. He furnished the University of Chicago with funds for the buildings and instruments of the Yerkes Observatory with its famous telescope. He died December 29, 1905.

YERKES, ROBERT MEARNS, psychobiologist, was born in Breadysville, May 26, 1876. He was graduated from Ursinus College, and from Harvard where he received the degree of Ph. D. He was professor of comparative psychology at Harvard, 1908-1917, and in 1917-1919 professor of psychology and director of the psychological laboratory at the University of Minnesota. In 1917, he was commissioned major in the Sanitary Corps of the American Army and head of the section of psychology in the surgeon-general's office. Since 1929 he has been professor of psychobiology, Institute of Human Relation at Yale. He is a member of many scientific societies and the author of: "Introduction to Psychology," "Almost Human," "The Mind of a Gorilla," etc.

WYOMING VALLEY (1843)

YODER, JACOB, flat boatman, was born in Reading, August 11, 1758. He was a soldier during the War of the Revolution, 1777 and 1778; moved West in 1780, and in May, 1782, from Fort Redstone, on the Monongahela River, took the first flat boat that ever descended the Mississippi to New Orleans with a cargo of produce. He died in Spencer County, Kentucky, April 7, 1832.

YORK, city and county-seat of York County, on the Codorus Creek, about twenty-eight miles southeast of Harrisburg. A permanent settlement was made in 1735 by a German colony, but in 1741 the town was laid out by John, Thomas, and Richard Penn, and incorporated as a borough in 1787. In 1887, it was chartered as a city. In 1777, the Continental Congress left Philadelphia, fearing capture by Howe's army and convened in York, September 30th. Congress continued to hold sessions in York until June 27, 1778. York is in a productive farming section and has considerable manufacturing interests. The vast power generated at York Haven, eleven miles north of York, has greatly increased the manufacturing interests of the city. Population (1930), 55,254; (1920), 47,512.

YORK COUNTY, formed from part of Lancaster, August 19, 1749. Named for James Stuart, Duke of York, King James II, or County of York. Land area, 903 square miles; population (1930), 167,135. County-seat, York, laid out in 1741.

FORTY FORT

YORK GAZETTE AND DAILY, THE, was established in 1795. It is issued every morning except Sunday, and is Independent-Democratic in principle. The editor is J. W. Gitt, and the publishers the York Gazette Company. Circulation, 20,413.

YOUGHIOGHENY RIVER—Tributary to Monongahela River. Sub-basin: Monongahela; source, in Preston County, West Virginia, near Maryland-West Virginia boundary; course, northerly, through Maryland, into Pennsylvania to junction of Casselman River at Confluence; mouth, at McKeesport; length, total, 123 miles; in Pennsylvania, 83 miles. Indian name, Juh-wiah-hanne, "a stream flowing in a contrary direction."

YOUNG, HIRAM, publisher, was born May 14, 1830, in Schaefferstown Lebanon County, a village founded by his great-great grandfather. He learned the saddler's trade but later engaged in the publishing business at Lancaster. He founded the *True Democrat* at York on June 7, 1864, and the *York Dispatch* in 1876. In 1901, the Dispatch Publishing Company was incorporated under the management of Hiram Young and his four sons. This company bought the York *Daily*, the oldest newspaper of the city.

YOUNG, JAMES THOMAS, educator, was born in Philadelphia, September 23, 1873. He was graduated from the University of Pennsylvania and received the Ph. D. degree from Halle in 1896. In 1904–1912, he was director of the Wharton School of Finance and Commerce, University of Pennsylvania, and is now professor of public administration at the same institution. He is the author of "The New American Government and Its Work," and of articles on political science, etc., for various journals and proceedings.

YOUNG, JESSE BOWMAN, soldier and minister, was born in Berwick, July 5, 1844. He was graduated from Dickinson College in 1868 and served in the Union Army during the Civil War, attaining the rank of captain. He served pastorates in Pennsylvania and Missouri and was the editor of the *Central Christian Advocate*. He died July 30, 1914.

YOUNG, JOHN RUSSELL, journalist, was born in Downingtown, November 20, 1841. He was news editor of the Philadelphia *Press* eventually becoming managing editor. During the Civil War he was war correspondent with the Army of the Potomac, acting in that capacity from the Battle of Bull Run to the end of the Chickahominy campaign. In 1865, he joined the editorial staff of the New York *Tribune*; in 1869, he established the Philadelphia *Morning Post* and the New York *Standard*. He accompanied General Grant in his journey around the world in 1877 as the correspondent of the New York *Herald*. From 1882–1885, he was minister to China and in 1897 was appointed Librarian of Congress. He wrote "Around the World with General Grant." His death occurred at Washington, January 17, 1899.

YOUNG, SAMUEL BALDWIN MARKS, military officer, was born in Pittsburgh, in 1840. He volunteered to serve in the Union Army in 1861, and entered the service as a private but by the end of the war had attained the rank of colonel. Subsequently he was brevetted brigadier-general of volunteers and at the close of the war joined the regular army. He took part in the Indian Wars and during the Spanish-American War served in the Philippines. He was made military governor of northwest Luzon and was later appointed commander of the Department of California. In 1902, he became first president of the Army War College Board; later he was chief of staff and lieutenant-general of the army; in 1902, he was president of the Brownsville Court of Inquiry and from 1910-1917 was governor of the Soldiers' Home at Washington, D. C. He died September 1, 1924.

YOUNG, SAMUEL HALL, minister, was born in Butler, September 17, 1847. In 1878, after graduating from Wooster College, Wooster, Ohio, and from the Western Theological Seminary, Allegheny, he was ordained to the ministry of the Presbyterian Church, and went to Alaska as a missionary. He organized the first Protestant Church in Alaska in 1879 and the first Presbyterian Church in Dawson in 1898. In 1901, he was appointed superintendent of all the Presbyterian missions in Alaska, and in 1913 became special representative for Alaska of the Presbyterian Board of Home Missions with headquarters in New York.

ZECH, FREDERICK, pianist and composer, was born in Philadelphia, May 10, 1858. Taken to San Francisco when quite young, he began to study music there and afterward continued his studies at Berlin. Since 1882 he has resided in San Francisco where he has been conductor of the symphony orchestra and has given many piano recitals.

ZEISBERGER, DAVID, Moravian missionary, was born April 11, 1721, in a small village in Moravia. His parents emigrated to Georgia in 1736. At the age of fifteen he met Count Zinzendorf who took him to Holland. Two years later he followed his parents to Georgia. In 1740, the young man accompanied George Whitefield to Pennsylvania where the latter purchased a five thousand acre tract of land at the "Forks of the Delaware." In 1741, the Moravians settled Bethlehem. Zeisberger cast his lot with his old friend Count Zinzendorf and became part of the Moravian settlement. His first missionary journey was in company with Frederick Post to the Mohawk Valley where he went to learn the language of the Iroquois. Zeisberger had a part in the conversion of the great Chief Shikellamy and was with him at his death. Zeisberger's entire life was devoted to missionary work among the Indians. He did more than any other man of his century to develop both the Delaware and the Onondaga dialect of the Iroquois. A number of his works in Indian language have been published. No one except the Jesuit Fathers is his equal in the frequency of his journeys among the Indians and the privations which he endured in his efforts to convert them. He died November 17, 1808, at Goshen, Ohio.

NICHOLAS LOUIS ZINZENDORF

ZIEGLER, WILLIAM, capitalist, was born in Beaver County, September 1, 1843. In 1868, he entered the bakers' and confectioners' supplies business. In 1870, he organized the Royal Chemical Company which developed into the Royal Baking Powder Company. He retired from active business in 1886. He fitted an expedition to explore the Arctic, but it was never heard of after it left Norway, July 10, 1903. He died in Stamford, Conn., May 24, 1905.

ZIHLMAN, FREDERICK NICHOLAS, labor leader, was born at Carnegie, October 2, 1879. At the age of eleven he began work in a glass factory. He became a labor leader serving as president of the Allegheny Trade Council, 1904-1909, and as president of the Maryland State Federation of Labor, 1906-1907. He was a state senator of Maryland and was a member of Congress in 1917-1931. He is the author of the first workman's compensation law in operation in the United States. He lives in Cumberland, Md.

ZINZENDORF, COUNT NICHOLAS LEWIS VON, Moravian missionary, was born in Dresden, May 26, 1700. His father was premier of the court of Saxony and was a member of the Lutheran Church. In 1734, Count Zinzendorf was ordained a minister of the Moravian Church. He came to New York in November of 1741. On his arrival in Philadelphia soon afterward he hired a house in which he held regular religious services. The Lutherans who were without a pastor invited him to preach to them. When a group of Moravian emigrants came to Philadelphia he accompanied them to Bethlehem where a Moravian Church was organized. Zinzendorf accompanied by his daughter and Conrad Weiser journeyed among the Indian settlements trying to convert the natives to Christianity. On his third journey Count Zinzendorf went as far as Shamokin where he was fortunate in meeting the powerful Shikellamy. Count Zinzendorf wrote many books. Many of his hymns are still sung by the Brethren. He died at Herrenhut, which he founded, May 9, 1760.

APPENDIX I

Townships in Pennsylvania

The following is a list of the Townships in Pennsylvania with the names of the counties in which they are located

Township	County
A	
Abbott	Potter
Abington	Lackawanna
	Montgomery
Adams	Butler
	Cambria
	Snyder
Addison	Somerset
Albany	Berks
	Bradford
Aleppo	Allegheny
	Greene
Allegheny	Blair
	Butler
	Cambria
	Potter
	Somerset
	Venango
	Westmoreland
Allen	Northampton
	Washington
Allison	Clinton
Alsace	Berks
Amity	Berks
	Erie
Amwell	Washington
Annin	McKean
Annville	Lebanon
Anthony	Lycoming
	Montour
Antis	Blair
Antrim	Franklin
Apolacon	Susquehanna
Ararat	Susquehanna
Armagh	Mifflin
Armenia	Bradford
Armstrong	Indiana
	Lycoming
Ashland	Clarion
Aston	Delaware
Asylum	Bradford
Athens	Bradford
	Crawford
Auburn	Susquehanna
Ayr	Fulton

Township	County
B	
Bald Eagle	Clinton
Baldwin	Allegheny
Banks	Carbon
	Indiana
Barclay	Bradford
Barnett	Forest
	Jefferson
Barr	Cambria
Barree	Huntingdon
Barrett	Monroe
Barry	Schuylkill
Bart	Lancaster
Bastress	Lycoming
Beale	Juniata
Bear Creek	Luzerne
Beaver	Clarion
	Columbia
	Crawford
	Jefferson
	Snyder
Beccaria	Clearfield
Bedford	Bedford
Bedminster	Bucks
Beech Creek	Clinton
Belfast	Fulton
Bell	Clearfield
	Jefferson
	Westmoreland
Benezette	Elk
Benner	Centre
Bensalem	Bucks
Benton	Columbia
	Lackawanna
Benzinger	Elk
Berlin	Wayne
Bern	Berks
Berwick	Adams
Bethel	Allegheny
	Armstrong
	Berks
	Delaware
	Fulton
	Lebanon
Bethlehem	Northampton

(557)

TOWNSHIPS IN PENNSYLVANIA

Township	County
Big Beaver	Beaver
	Lawrence
Bigler	Clearfield
Bingham	Potter
Birmingham	Chester
	Delaware
Black	Somerset
Black Creek	Luzerne
Blacklick	Cambria
	Indiana
Blain	Washington
Blair	Blair
Bloom	Clearfield
Bloomfield	Bedford
	Crawford
Blooming Grove	Pike
Bloss	Tioga
Blythe	Schuylkill
Boggs	Armstrong
	Centre
	Clearfield
Borough	Beaver
Braddock	Allegheny
Bradford	Clearfield
	McKean
Brady	Butler
	Clarion
	Clearfield
	Huntingdon
	Lycoming
Bradys Bend	Armstrong
Braintrim	Wyoming
Branch	Schuylkill
Bratton	Mifflin
Brecknock	Berks
	Lancaster
Briar Creek	Columbia
Bridgeton	Bucks
Bridgewater	Susquehanna
Brighton	Beaver
Bristol	Bucks
Broad Top	Bedford
Brokenstraw	Warren
Brookfield	Tioga
Brooklyn	Susquehanna
Brothersvalley	Somerset
Brown	Lycoming
	Mifflin
Brownsville	Fayette
Brush Creek	Fulton
Brushvalley	Indiana

Township	County
Buck	Luzerne
Buckingham	Bucks
	Wayne
Buffalo	Butler
	Perry
	Union
	Washington
Buffington	Indiana
Bullskin	Fayette
Burlington	Bradford
Burnside	Centre
	Clearfield
Burrell	Armstrong
	Indiana
Bushkill	Northampton
Butler	Adams
	Butler
	Luzerne
	Schuylkill

C

Caernarvon	Berks
	Lancaster
Caln	Chester
Cambria	Cambria
Cambridge	Crawford
Canaan	Wayne
Canal	Venango
Canoe	Indiana
Canton	Bradford
	Washington
Carbon	Huntingdon
Carbondale	Lackawanna
Carroll	Perry
	Washington
	York
Cascade	Lycoming
Cass	Huntingdon
	Schuylkill
Castanea	Clinton
Catawissa	Columbia
Catharine	Blair
Cecil	Washington
Centre	Beaver
	Berks
	Butler
	Columbia
	Greene
	Indiana
	Perry
	Snyder

Township	County	Township	County
Ceres	McKean	Concord	Butler
Chanceford	York		Delaware
Chapman	Clinton		Erie
	Snyder	Conemaugh	Cambria
Charleston	Tioga	Conestoga	Lancaster
Charlestown	Chester		Indiana
Chartiers	Allegheny		Somerset
	Washington	Conewago	Adams
Chatham	Tioga		Dauphin
Cheltenham	Montgomery		York
Cherry	Butler	Conewango	Warren
	Sullivan	Conneaut	Crawford
Cherry Ridge	Wayne		Erie
Cherryhill	Indiana	Connellsville	Fayette
Cherrytree	Venango	Connoquenessing	Butler
Chest	Cambria	Conoy	Lancaster
	Clearfield	Conyngham	Columbia
Chester	Delaware		Luzerne
Chestnuthill	Monroe	Cook	Westmoreland
Chippewa	Beaver	Cooke	Cumberland
Choconut	Susquehanna	Coolbaugh	Monroe
Clara	Potter	Coolspring	Mercer
Clarion	Clarion	Cooper	Clearfield
Clay	Butler	Cooper	Montour
	Huntingdon	Cornplanter	Venango
	Lancaster	Cornwall	Lebanon
Clearfield	Butler	Corydon	McKean
	Cambria		Warren
Cleveland	Columbia	Covington	Clearfield
Clifford	Susquehanna		Lackawanna
Clifton	Lackawanna		Tioga
Clinton	Butler	Cowanshannock	Armstrong
	Lycoming	Cranberry	Butler
	Venango		Venango
	Wayne	Crawford	Clinton
	Wyoming	Crescent	Allegheny
Clover	Jefferson	Cresson	Cambria
Clymer	Tioga	Cromwell	Huntingdon
Coal	Northumberland	Cross Creek	Washington
Coalbrookdale	Berks	Croyle	Cambria
Codorus	York	Cumberland	Adams
Cogan House	Lycoming		Greene
Cold Spring	Lebanon	Cumberland Valley	Bedford
Colebrook	Clinton	Cummings	Lycoming
Colerain	Bedford	Cumru	Berks
	Lancaster	Curtin	Centre
College	Centre	Cussewago	Crawford
Colley	Sullivan		
Collier	Allegheny	D	
Columbia	Bradford	Dallas	Luzerne
Columbus	Warren	Damascus	Wayne

TOWNSHIPS IN PENNSYLVANIA

Township	County
Darby	Delaware
Darlington	Beaver
Daugherty	Beaver
Davidson	Sullivan
Dean	Cambria
Decatur	Clearfield
	Mifflin
Deer Creek	Mercer
Deerfield	Tioga
	Warren
Delano	Schuylkill
Delaware	Juniata
	Mercer
	Northumberland
	Pike
Delmar	Tioga
Denison	Luzerne
Derry	Dauphin
	Mifflin
	Montour
	Westmoreland
Dickinson	Cumberland
Dimock	Susquehanna
Dingman	Pike
District	Berks
Donegal	Butler
	Washington
	Westmoreland
Dorrance	Luzerne
Douglass	Berks
	Montgomery
Dover	York
Doylestown	Bucks
Dreher	Wayne
Drumore	Lancaster
Dublin	Fulton
	Huntingdon
Dunbar	Fayette
Duncan	Tioga
Dunkard	Greene
Dunnstable	Clinton
Durham	Bucks
Dyberry	Wayne

E

Township	County
Earl	Berks
	Lancaster
East Allen	Northampton
East Bethlehem	Washington
East Bradford	Chester
East Brandywine	Chester
East Brunswick	Schuylkill
East Buffalo	Union
East Caln	Chester
East Cameron	Northumberland
East Carroll	Cambria
East Chillisquaque	Northumberland
East Cocalico	Lancaster
East Coventry	Chester
East Deer	Allegheny
East Donegal	Lancaster
East Drumore	Lancaster
East Earl	Lancaster
East Fairfield	Crawford
East Fallowfield	Chester
	Crawford
East Finley	Washington
East Franklin	Armstrong
East Goshen	Chester
East Hanover	Dauphin
	Lebanon
East Hempfield	Lancaster
East Hopewell	York
East Huntingdon	Westmoreland
East Keating	Clinton
East Lackawannock	Mercer
East Lampeter	Lancaster
East Mahoning	Indiana
East Manchester	York
East Marlboro	Chester
East Mead	Crawford
East Nantmeal	Chester
East Norriton	Montgomery
East Norwegian	Schuylkill
East Nottingham	Chester
East Penn	Carbon
East Pennsboro	Cumberland
East Pike Run	Washington
East Pikeland	Chester
East Providence	Bedford
East Rockhill	Bucks
East St. Clair	Bedford
East Taylor	Cambria
East Union	Schuylkill
East Vincent	Chester
East Wheatfield	Indiana
East Whiteland	Chester
Easttown	Chester
Eaton	Wyoming
Economy	Beaver

TOWNSHIPS IN PENNSYLVANIA

Township	County	Township	County
Eden	Lancaster	Fishingcreek	Columbia
Edgemont	Delaware	Forest Lake	Susquehanna
Elder	Cambria	Forks	Northampton
Eldred	Jefferson		Sullivan
	Lycoming	Forkston	Wyoming
	McKean	Forward	Allegheny
	Monroe		Butler
	Schuylkill	Foster	Luzerne
Elizabeth	Allegheny		McKean
	Lancaster		Schuylkill
Elk	Chester	Fox	Elk
	Clarion		Sullivan
	Tioga	Frailey	Schuylkill
	Warren	Franconia	Montgomery
Elk Creek	Erie	Frankford	Cumberland
Elk Lick	Somerset	Franklin	Adams
Elkland	Sullivan		Allegheny
	Tioga		Beaver
Ephrata	Lancaster		Bradford
Eulalia	Potter		Butler
Exeter	Berks		Greene
	Luzerne		Carbon
	Wyoming		Chester
			Columbia
F			Erie
			Fayette
Fairfield	Crawford		Huntingdon
	Lycoming		Luzerne
	Westmoreland		Lycoming
Fairhope	Somerset		Snyder
Fairmount	Luzerne		Susquehanna
Fairview	Butler		Westmoreland
	Erie		York
	Luzerne	Frankstown	Blair
	Mercer	Frazer	Allegheny
	York	Frederick	Montgomery
Fallowfield	Washington	Freedom	Adams
Falls	Bucks		Blair
	Wyoming	Freehold	Warren
Fannett	Franklin	Frenchcreek	Venango
Farmington	Clarion	French Creek	Mercer
	Tioga	Fulton	Lancaster
	Warren		
Fawn	Allegheny	**G**	
	York		
Fayette	Juniata	Gaines	Tioga
Fell	Lackawanna	Gallagher	Clinton
Ferguson	Centre	Gallitzin	Cambria
	Clearfield	Gamble	Lycoming
Fermanagh	Juniata	Gaskill	Jefferson
Findley	Allegheny	Gearhart	Northumberland
	Mercer	Genesee	Potter

Township	County	Township	County
Georges	Fayette	Hamiltonban	Adams
German	Fayette	Hamlin	McKean
Germany	Adams	Hampden	Cumberland
Gibson	Cameron	Hampton	Allegheny
	Susquehanna	Hanover	Beaver
Gilmore	Greene		Lehigh
Gilpin	Armstrong		Luzerne
Girard	Clearfield		Northampton
	Erie		Washington
Glade	Warren	Harborcreek	Erie
Goshen	Clearfield	Harford	Susquehanna
Graham	Clearfield	Harmar	Allegheny
Grant	Indiana	Harmony	Beaver
Granville	Bradford		Forest
	Mifflin		Susquehanna
Great Bend	Susquehanna	Harris	Centre
Green	Clinton	Harrison	Allegheny
	Indiana		Bedford
Greene	Beaver		Potter
	Erie	Hartley	Union
	Forest	Hatfield	Montgomery
	Franklin	Haverford	Delaware
	Greene	Haycock	Bucks
	Mercer	Hayfield	Crawford
	Pike	Hazel	Luzerne
Greenfield	Blair	Heath	Jefferson
	Erie	Hebron	Potter
	Lackawanna	Hector	Potter
Greenville	Somerset	Hegins	Schuylkill
Greenwich	Berks	Heidelberg	Berks
Greenwood	Clearfield		Lebanon
	Columbia		Lehigh
	Crawford		York
	Juniata	Hellam	York
	Perry	Hemlock	Columbia
Gregg	Centre	Hempfield	Mercer
	Union		Westmoreland
Grove	Cameron	Henderson	Huntingdon
Grugan	Clinton		Jefferson
Guilford	Franklin	Henry Clay	Fayette
Gulich	Clearfield	Hepburn	Lycoming
H		Hereford	Berks
Haines	Centre	Herrick	Bradford
Halfmoon	Centre		Susquehanna
Halifax	Dauphin	Hickory	Forest
Hamilton	Adams		Lawrence
	Franklin		Mercer
	McKean	Highland	Adams
	Monroe		Chester
	Tioga		Clarion
			Elk

Township	County	Township	County
Hillsgrove	Sullivan	Jay	Elk
Hilltown	Bucks	Jefferson	Allegheny
Hollenback	Luzerne		Berks
Homer	Potter		Butler
Honeybrook	Chester		Dauphin
Hopewell	Beaver		Fayette
	Bedford		Greene
	Cumberland		Lackawanna
	Huntingdon		Mercer
	Washington		Somerset
	York		Washington
Horsham	Montgomery	Jenkins	Luzerne
Horton	Elk	Jenks	Forest
Hovey	Armstrong	Jenner	Somerset
Howard	Centre	Jessup	Susquehanna
Howe	Forest	Jones	Elk
	Perry	Jordan	Clearfield
Hubley	Schuylkill		Lycoming
Hunlock	Luzerne		Northumberland
Huntingdon	Adams	Juniata	Bedford
Huntington	Luzerne		Blair
Huston	Blair		Huntingdon
	Centre		Perry
	Clearfield	K	
I		Karthaus	Clearfield
Independence	Beaver	Keating	McKean
	Washington		Potter
Indiana	Allegheny	Kelly	Union
Industry	Beaver	Kennedy	Allegheny
Irwin	Venango	Kennett	Chester
J		Kidder	Carbon
Jackson	Butler	Kilbuck	Allegheny
	Cambria	Kimmell	Bedford
	Columbia	King	Bedford
	Dauphin	Kingsley	Forest
	Greene	Kingston	Luzerne
	Huntingdon	Kinzua	Warren
	Lebanon	Kiskiminetas	Armstrong
	Luzerne	Kittanning	Armstrong
	Lycoming	Kline	Schuylkill
	Mercer	Knox	Clarion
	Monroe		Clearfield
	Northumberland		Jefferson
	Perry	L	
	Snyder	Lack	Juniata
	Susquehanna	Lackawanna	Lackawanna
	Tioga	Lackawannock	Mercer
	Venango	Lackawaxen	Pike
	York	Lafayette	McKean

TOWNSHIPS IN PENNSYLVANIA

Township	County
Lake	Luzerne
	Mercer
	Wayne
Lamar	Clinton
Lancaster	Butler
	Lancaster
Laporte	Sullivan
Larimer	Somerset
Lathrop	Susquehanna
Latimore	Adams
Lausanne	Carbon
Lawrence	Clearfield
	Tioga
Lawrence Park	Erie
Leacock	Lancaster
Lebanon	Wayne
Le Boeuf	Erie
Leet	Allegheny
Lehigh	Carbon
	Lackawanna
	Northampton
	Wayne
Lehman	Luzerne
	Pike
Leidy	Clinton
Lemon	Wyoming
Lenox	Susquehanna
Leroy	Bradford
Letterkenny	Franklin
Lewis	Lycoming
	Union
	Northumberland
Liberty	Adams
	Bedford
	Centre
	McKean
	Mercer
	Susquehanna
	Tioga
	Montour
Licking	Clarion
Licking Creek	Fulton
Ligonier	Westmoreland
Limerick	Montgomery
Limestone	Clarion
	Lycoming
	Union
	Warren
	Montour

Township	County
Lincoln	Allegheny
	Bedford
	Huntingdon
	Somerset
Litchfield	Bradford
Little Beaver	Lawrence
Little Britain	Lancaster
Little Mahanoy	Northumberland
Liverpool	Perry
Locust	Columbia
Logan	Blair
	Clinton
	Huntingdon
London Britain	Chester
Londonderry	Bedford
	Chester
	Dauphin
London Grove	Chester
Longswamp	Berks
Lower Allen	Cumberland
Lower Alsace	Berks
Lower Augusta	Northumberland
Lower Burrell	Westmoreland
Lower Chanceford	York
Lower Chichester	Delaware
Lower Gwynedd	Montgomery
Lower Heidelberg	Berks
Lower Macungie	Lehigh
Lower Mahony	Northumberland
Lower Makefield	Bucks
Lower Merion	Montgomery
Lower Mifflin	Cumberland
Lower Milford	Lehigh
Lower Moreland	Montgomery
Lower Mt. Bethel	Northampton
Lower Nazareth	Northampton
Lower Oxford	Chester
Lower Paxton	Dauphin
Lower Pottsgrove	Montgomery
Lower Providence	Montgomery
Lower St. Clair	Allegheny
Lower Salford	Montgomery
Lower Saucann	Northampton
Lower Swatara	Dauphin
Lower Towamensing	Carbon
Lower Turkey Foot	Somerset
Lower Tyrone	Fayette
Lower Windsor	York
Lower Yoder	Cambria
Lowhill	Lehigh
Loyalhanna	Westmoreland

TOWNSHIPS IN PENNSYLVANIA

Township	County
Loyalsock	Lycoming
Lumber	Cameron
Lurgan	Franklin
Luzerne	Fayette
Lycoming	Lycoming
Lykens	Dauphin
Lynn	Lehigh

M

Township	County
Madison	Armstrong
	Clarion
	Columbia
	Lackawanna
	Perry
Mahoning	Armstrong
	Carbon
	Lawrence
	Montour
Mahony	Schuylkill
Maidencreek	Berks
Main	Columbia
Manchester	Wayne
	York
Manheim	Lancaster
	York
Mann	Bedford
Manor	Armstrong
	Lancaster
Marion	Beaver
	Berks
	Butler
	Centre
Marlboro	Montgomery
Marple	Delaware
Marshall	Allegheny
Martic	Lancaster
Mauch Chunk	Carbon
Maxatawny	Berks
Mayberry	Montour
McCalmont	Jefferson
McCandless	Allegheny
McHenry	Lycoming
McIntyre	Lycoming
McKean	Erie
McNett	Lycoming
Mead	Warren
Mehoopany	Wyoming
Menallen	Adams
	Fayette
Menno	Mifflin

Township	County
Mercer	Butler
Meshoppen	Wyoming
Metal	Franklin
Middle Paxton	Dauphin
Middle Smithfield	Monroe
Middle Taylor	Cambria
Middlebury	Tioga
Middlecreek	Somerset
	Snyder
Middlesex	Butler
	Cumberland
Middletown	Bucks
	Delaware
	Susquehanna
Mifflin	Allegheny
	Columbia
	Dauphin
	Lycoming
Miles	Centre
Milford	Bucks
	Juniata
	Pike
	Somerset
Millcreek	Clarion
	Erie
	Lebanon
	Lycoming
	Mercer
Miller	Huntingdon
	Perry
Millstone	Elk
Mineral	Venango
Monaghan	York
Monongehela	Greene
Monroe	Bedford
	Bradford
	Clarion
	Cumberland
	Juniata
	Snyder
	Wyoming
Montgomery	Franklin
	Indiana
	Montgomery
Montour	Columbia
Moon	Allegheny
	Beaver
Moore	Northampton
Morgan	Green

Township	County	Township	County
Morris	Clearfield	North Codorus	York
	Greene	North Cornwall	Lebanon
	Huntingdon	North Coventry	Chester
	Tioga	North East	Erie
	Washington	North Fayette	Allegheny
Mount Carmel	Northumberland	North Franklin	Washington
Mount Joy	Adams	North Heidelberg	Berks
	Lancaster	North Huntingdon	Westmoreland
Mount Lebanon	Allegheny	North Hopewell	York
Mount Pleasant	Adams	North Lebanon	Lebanon
	Columbia	North Londonderry	Lebanon
	Washington	North Mahoning	Indiana
	Wayne	North Manheim	Schuylkill
	Westmoreland	North Middletown	Cumberland
Muddycreek	Butler	North Sewickley	Beaver
Muhlenberg	Berks	North Shenango	Crawford
Munster	Cambria	North Strabane	Washington
		North Towanda	Bradford
N		North Union	Fayette
			Schuylkill
Napier	Bedford		
Nelson	Tioga	North Versailles	Allegheny
Nescopeck	Luzerne	North Whitehall	Lehigh
Neshannock	Lawrence	North Woodbury	Blair
Nether Providence	Delaware	Northampton	Bucks
New Britain	Bucks		Somerset
New Garden	Chester	Northmoreland	Wyoming
New Hanover	Montgomery	Norwegian	Schuylkill
New London	Chester	Norwich	McKean
New Milford	Susquehanna	Nottingham	Washington
New Sewickley	Beaver	Noxen	Wyoming
New Vernon	Mercer	Noyes	Clinton
Newberry	York		
Newcastle	Schuylkill	**O**	
Newlin	Chester	Oakland	Butler
Newport	Luzerne		Susquehanna
Newton	Cumberland		Venango
	Lackawanna	Ogle	Somerset
Newtown	Bucks	O'Hara	Allegheny
	Delaware	Ohio	Allegheny
Newville	Allegheny		Beaver
Nicholson	Fayette	Oil Creek	Crawford
	Wyoming		Venango
Nippenose	Lycoming	Old Lycoming	Lycoming
Nockamixon	Bucks	Oley	Berks
North Abington	Lackawanna	Oliver	Jefferson
North Annville	Lebanon		Mifflin
North Beaver	Lawrence		Perry
North Branch	Wyoming	Oneida	Huntingdon
North Buffalo	Armstrong	Ontelaunee	Berks
North Center	Columbia	Orange	Columbia
North Charleroi	Washington	Oregon	Wayne

TOWNSHIPS IN PENNSYLVANIA 567

Township	County	Township	County
Orwell	Bradford	Peters	Franklin
Osceola	Tioga		Washington
Oswayo	Potter	Piatt	Lycoming
Otter Creek	Mercer	Pike	Berks
Otto	McKean		Bradford
Overfield	Wyoming		Clearfield
Overton	Bradford		Potter
Oxford	Adams	Pine	Allegheny
P			Armstrong
			Clearfield
Packer	Carbon		Columbia
Paint	Clarion		Crawford
	Somerset		Indiana
Palmer	Northampton		Lycoming
Palmyra	Pike		Mercer
	Wayne	Pine Creek	Clinton
Paradise	Lancaster		Jefferson
	Monroe	Pine Grove	Schuylkill
	York		Venango
Parks	Armstrong		Warren
Patterson	Beaver	Piney	Clarion
Patton	Allegheny	Pittsfield	Warren
	Centre	Pittston	Luzerne
Paupack	Wayne	Plain Grove	Lawrence
Peach Bottom	York	Plains	Luzerne
Penn	Allegheny	Plainfield	Northampton
	Berks	Pleasant	Warren
	Centre	Pleasant Valley	Pike
	Chester	Plum	Allegheny
	Clearfield		Venango
	Cumberland	Plumcreek	Armstrong
	Huntingdon	Plumstead	Bucks
	Lancaster	Plunketts Creek	Lycoming
	Lycoming	Plymouth	Luzerne
	Snyder		Montgomery
	Westmoreland	Pocono	Monroe
	York	Pocopson	Chester
	Perry	Point	Northumberland
Penn Forest	Carbon	Polk	Jefferson
Pennsbury	Chester		Monroe
Pequea	Lancaster		
Perkiomen	Montgomery	Portage	Cambria
Perry	Armstrong		Cameron
	Berks		Potter
	Clarion	Porter	Clarion
	Fayette		Clinton
	Greene		Huntingdon
	Jefferson		Jefferson
	Lawrence		Lycoming
	Mercer		Pike
	Snyder		Schuylkill

TOWNSHIPS IN PENNSYLVANIA

Township	County
Potter	Beaver
	Centre
President	Venango
Preston	Wayne
Price	Monroe
Providence	Lancaster
Pulaski	Beaver
	Lawrence
Putnam	Tioga
Pymatuning	Mercer

Q

Township	County
Quemahoning	Somerset
Quincy	Franklin

R

Township	County
Raccoon	Beaver
Radnor	Delaware
Rahn	Schuylkill
Ralpho	Northumberland
Randolph	Crawford
Ransom	Lackawanna
Rapho	Lancaster
Rayburn	Armstrong
Rayne	Indiana
Reade	Cambria
Reading	Adams
Redbank	Armstrong
	Clarion
Redstone	Fayette
Reed	Dauphin
Reilly	Schuylkill
Reserve	Allegheny
Richhill	Greene
Richland	Bucks
	Cambria
	Clarion
	Allegheny
	Venango
Richmond	Berks
	Crawford
	Tioga
Ridgebury	Bradford
Ridgway	Elk
Ridley	Delaware
Ringgold	Jefferson
Roaring Brook	Lackawanna
Roaring Creek	Columbia
Robeson	Berks
Robinson	Allegheny
	Washington

Township	County
Rochester	Beaver
Rockdale	Crawford
Rockefeller	Northumberland
Rockland	Berks
	Venango
Rome	Bradford
	Crawford
Rose	Jefferson
Ross	Allegheny
	Luzerne
	Monroe
Rostraver	Westmoreland
Roulette	Potter
Ruscombmanor	Berks
Rush	Centre
	Dauphin
	Northumberland
	Schuylkill
	Susquehanna
Rutland	Tioga
Ryan	Schuylkill
Rye	Perry

S

Township	County
St. Clair	Westmoreland
St. Thomas	Franklin
Sadsbury	Chester
	Crawford
	Lancaster
Salem	Clarion
	Mercer
	Luzerne
	Wayne
	Westmoreland
Salford	Montgomery
Salisbury	Lancaster
	Lehigh
Saltlick	Fayette
Sandy	Clearfield
Sandy Creek	Mercer
	Venango
Sandy Lake	Mercer
Saville	Perry
Schuylkill	Chester
	Schuylkill
Scott	Allegheny
	Columbia
	Lackawanna
	Lawrence
	Wayne
Scrubgrass	Venango

TOWNSHIPS IN PENNSYLVANIA 569

Township	County
Sergeant	McKean
Sewickley	Allegheny
	Westmoreland
Sewickley Heights	Allegheny
Shade	Somerset
Shaler	Allegheny
Shamokin	Northumberland
Sharon	Potter
Sheffield	Warren
Shenango	Lawrence
	Mercer
Sheshequin	Bradford
Shippen	Cameron
	Tioga
Shippensburg	Cumberland
Shirley	Huntingdon
Shohola	Pike
Shrewsbury	Lycoming
	Sullivan
	York
Silver Lake	Susquehanna
Silver Spring	Cumberland
Skippack	Montgomery
Slippery Rock	Butler
	Lawrence
Slocum	Luzerne
Smith	Washington
Smithfield	Bradford
	Huntingdon
	Monroe
Snake Spring	Bedford
Snow Shoe	Centre
Snowden	Allegheny
Snyder	Blair
	Jefferson
Solesbury	Bucks
Somerset	Somerset
	Washington
South Abington	Lackawanna
South Annville	Lebanon
South Beaver	Beaver
South Bend	Armstrong
South Buffalo	Armstrong
South Canaan	Wayne
South Center	Columbia
South Coventry	Chester
South Creek	Bradford
South Fayette	Allegheny
South Franklin	Washington
South Hanover	Dauphin
South Heidelberg	Berks

Township	County
South Huntingdon	Westmoreland
South Lebanon	Lebanon
South Londonderry	Lebanon
South Mahoning	Indiana
South Manheim	Schuylkill
South Middleton	Cumberland
South Pymatuning	Mercer
South Shenango	Crawford
South Strabane	Washington
South Union	Fayette
South Versailles	Allegheny
South West	Warren
South Whitehall	Lehigh
South Woodbury	Bedford
Southampton	Bedford
	Bucks
	Cumberland
	Franklin
	Somerset
Sparta	Crawford
Spring	Berks
	Centre
	Perry
	Snyder
	Crawford
Spring Brook	Lackawanna
Spring Creek	Warren
Springhill	Fayette
	Greene
Springdale	Allegheny
Springfield	Bradford
	Bucks
	Delaware
	Erie
	Fayette
	Huntingdon
	Mercer
	Montgomery
	York
Springetsbury	York
Springgarden	York
Springville	Susquehanna
Spruce Creek	Huntingdon
Spruce Hill	Juniata
Standing Stone	Bradford
Sterling	Wayne
Steuben	Crawford
Stewardson	Potter
Stewart	Fayette
Stony Creek	Cambria
	Somerset

570   TOWNSHIPS IN PENNSYLVANIA

Township	County	Township	County
Stowe	Allegheny	Towanda	Bradford
Straban	Adams	Tredyffrin	Chester
Strasburg	Lancaster	Tremont	Schuylkill
Stroud	Monroe	Triumph	Warren
Sugar Creek	Armstrong	Troy	Bradford
	Venango		Crawford
Sugar Grove	Mercer	Tulpehocken	Berks
	Warren	Tunkhannock	Monroe
Sugar Loaf	Columbia		Wyoming
	Luzerne	Turbett	Juniata
Sullivan	Tioga	Turbut	Northumberland
Summer Hill	Cambria	Tuscarora	Bradford
	Crawford		Juniata
Summit	Butler		Perry
	Crawford	Tyrone	Adams
	Erie		Blair
	Potter		Perry
	Somerset		
Susquehanna	Cambria	U	
	Dauphin	Ulster	Bradford
	Juniata	Ulysses	Potter
	Lycoming	Union	Adams
Swatara	Dauphin		Allegheny
	Lebanon		Bedford
Sweden	Potter		Berks
Sylvania	Potter		Centre
T			Clearfield
			Crawford
Taylor	Blair		Erie
	Centre		Fulton
	Fulton		Huntingdon
	Lawrence		Jefferson
Tell	Huntingdon		Lawrence
Terry	Bradford		Lebanon
Texas	Wayne		Luzerne
Thompson	Fulton		Mifflin
	Susquehanna		Schuylkill
Thornbury	Chester		Snyder
	Delaware		Tioga
Tilden	Berks		Union
Tinicum	Bucks		Washington
	Delaware	Unity	Westmoreland
Tioga	Tioga	Upper Allen	Cumberland
Tionesta	Forest	Upper Augusta	Northumberland
Toboyne	Perry	Upper Bern	Berks
Toby	Clarion	Upper Burrell	Westmoreland
Tobyhanna	Monroe	Upper Chichester	Delaware
Tod	Huntingdon	Upper Darby	Delaware
Todd	Fulton	Upper Dublin	Montgomery
Towamencin	Montgomery	Upper Fairfield	Lycoming
Towamensing	Carbon	Upper Gwynedd	Montgomery

TOWNSHIPS IN PENNSYLVANIA

Township	County
Upper Hanover	Montgomery
Upper Leacock	Lancaster
Upper Macungie	Lehigh
Upper Mahanoy	Northumberland
Upper Mahantango	Schuylkill
Upper Makefield	Bucks
Upper Merion	Montgomery
Upper Mifflin	Cumberland
Upper Milford	Lehigh
Upper Moreland	Montgomery
Upper Mt. Bethel	Northampton
Upper Nazareth	Northampton
Upper Oxford	Chester
Upper Paxton	Dauphin
Upper Pottsgrove	Montgomery
Upper Providence	Delaware
	Montgomery
Upper St. Clair	Allegheny
Upper Salford	Montgomery
Upper Saucon	Lehigh
Upper Turkeyfoot	Somerset
Upper Tulpehocken	Berks
Upper Tyrone	Fayette
Upper Uwchlan	Chester
Upper Yoder	Cambria
Uwchlan	Chester

V

Valley	Armstrong
	Chester
	Montour
Venango	Butler
	Crawford
	Erie
Vernon	Crawford
Versailles	Allegheny
Victory	Venango

W

Walker	Centre
	Huntingdon
	Juniata
	Schuylkill
Wallace	Chester
Ward	Tioga
Warminster	Bucks
Warren	Bradford
	Franklin
Warrington	Bucks
	York
Warriors Mark	Huntingdon

Township	County
Warsaw	Jefferson
Warwick	Bucks
	Chester
	Lancaster
Washington	Armstrong
	Berks
	Butler
	Cambria
	Clarion
	Dauphin
	Erie
	Fayette
	Franklin
	Greene
	Indiana
	Jefferson
	Lawrence
	Lehigh
	Lycoming
	Northampton
	Northumberland
	Schuylkill
	Snyder
	Westmoreland
	Wyoming
	York
Waterford	Erie
Watson	Lycoming
	Warren
Watts	Perry
Wayne	Armstrong
	Clinton
	Crawford
	Dauphin
	Erie
	Greene
	Mifflin
	Lawrence
	Schuylkill
Weisenberg	Lehigh
Wells	Bradford
	Fulton
West	Huntingdon
West Abington	Lackawanna
West Beaver	Snyder
West Bethlehem	Washington
West Bradford	Chester
West Branch	Potter
West Brandywine	Chester
West Brunswick	Schuylkill
West Buffalo	Union

Township	County	Township	County
West Burlington	Bradford	Wharton	Fayette
West Caln	Chester		Potter
West Cameron	Northumberland	Wheatfield	Perry
West Carroll	Cambria	White	Beaver
West Chillisquaque	Northumberland		Cambria
West Cocalico	Lancaster		Indiana
West Cornwall	Lebanon	White Deer	Union
West Deer	Allegheny	Whitehall	Lehigh
West Donegal	Lancaster	Whitely	Greene
West Earl	Lancaster	White Marsh	Montgomery
West Fallowfield	Chester	Whitpain	Montgomery
	Crawford	Wiconisco	Dauphin
West Finley	Washington	Wilkes-Barre	Luzerne
West Franklin	Armstrong	Wilkins	Allegheny
Westfall	Pike	Williams	Dauphin
Westfield	Tioga		Northampton
West Goshen	Chester	Willistown	Chester
West Hanover	Dauphin	Wilmington	Mercer
West Hemlock	Montour		Lawrence
West Hempfield	Lancaster	Wilmot	Bradford
West Keating	Clinton	Wilson	Northampton
West Lampeter	Lancaster	Windham	Bradford
West Lebanon	Lebanon		Wyoming
West Mahoning	Indiana	Windsor	Berks
	Schuylkill		York
West Manchester	York	Winfield	Butler
West Manheim	York	Winslow	Jefferson
West Marlboro	Chester	Wolf	Lycoming
West Mead	Crawford	Wolf Creek	Mercer
West Nantmeal	Chester	Wood	Huntingdon
West Norriton	Montgomery	Woodbury	Bedford
West Nottingham	Chester		Blair
West Penn	Schuylkill	Woodcock	Crawford
West Pennsboro	Cumberland	Woodward	Clearfield
West Perry	Snyder		Clinton
West Pike Run	Washington		Lycoming
West Pikeland	Chester	Worcester	Montgomery
West Pottsgrove	Montgomery	Worth	Butler
West Providence	Bedford		Centre
West Rockhill	Bucks		Mercer
West St. Clair	Bedford	Wright	Luzerne
West Sadsbury	Chester	Wrightstown	Bucks
West Salem	Mercer	Wyalusing	Bradford
West Shenango	Crawford	Wysox	Bradford
West Taylor	Cambria	Y	
Westtown	Chester	York	York
West Vincent	Chester	Young	Indiana
West Whitefield	Indiana		Jefferson
West Whiteland	Chester	Z	
Wetmore	McKean	Zerbe	Northumberland

APPENDIX II

Finding it impossible to give correct Pennsylvania biography in full, a list of the names of Pennsylvanians appearing in "Who's Who in America" 1929-1930 is given here by the permission of the A. N. Marquis Company, Chicago.

ALLENTOWN
Buchman, Rev. Frank N. D.
Bernheim, Oscar F.
Butz, Reuben J., Lawyer
Dery, D. George, Silk Manufacturer
Ettinger, George T., College Dean
Fehr, Harrison R., Engineer
Gernerd, Fred B., Congressman
Haas, John A. W., College President
Horn, Robert C., Professor of Greek
Ruhe, Percy B., Editor
Rupp, Lawrence H., Lawyer
Sandt, Rev. George W.
Sanford, Chester M., Author, Lecturer
Smith, C. J., Newspaperman
Snelling, Walter O., Chemist, Inventor
Stickle, John W., Publisher
Trexler, Frank M., Judge
Trexler, Harry C.
Weiler, Royal W., Publisher
Wright, Isaac M., Educator

ALTOONA
Kline, Rev. Marion J.
Kurtz, Jacob B., Congressman
McCort, John J., Bishop
Sheedy, Rev. Morgan M.

AMBLER
Mattison, Richard V., Manufacturer
Lewis, Morris J., M. D.

ANNVILLE
Gossard, George D., College President
Shenk, Hiram H., Historian

ARDMORE
Anspach, Brooke M., Gynecologist
Collins, Alfred M., Manufacturer
Faris, Rev. John T., Editor
Harris, C. Addison, Jr., Banker
Kent, A. Atwater, Manufacturer, Inventor
Leisenring, E. B., Coal Operator
McHenry, Edwin H., Civil Engineer
Morris, Effingham B., Lawyer
Owen, Ralph D., Educator
Pennypacker, Isaac R., Editor
Reath, Theodore W., Lawyer
Rose, Philip S., Editor
Sellers, Horace W., Architect
Skillern, Ross H., M. D.
Skillman, Thomas J., Civil Engineer
Watkins, John E., Journalist

ASPINWALL
Bishop, Frederic L., Physicist

ATHENS
Keefe, David A., Engineer

BALA-CYNWYD
Brown, Samuel H., Jr., M. D.
Chubb, Lewis W., Electrical Engineer
Cooke, James F., Editor
Currie, Barton W., Editor
Haupt, Lewis M., Civil Engineer
Kolmer, John A., Pathologist
Littleton, William G., Banker
Logan, James A., Jr., Banker
Quinn, Arthur H., University Professor
Schoff, Wilfred H.
Sykes, Charles H., Cartoonist
Tily, Herbert J., Merchant
Witmer, Francis P., Civil Engineer

BANGOR
Kent, Everett, Congressman

BEAVER
Graham, Louis E., Lawyer
McGranahan, Ralph W., Missionary Secretary
Raymer, Albert R., Railway Official

BEAVER FALLS
Coleman, John, Theologian
Martin, James S., Reformer
Martin, Renwick H., Educator
Pearce, McLeod M., College President
Swick, J. Howard, Congressman

BEDFORD
Fitch, William E., M. D.

BELLEFONTE
Bogle, Sarah C. N., Librarian

BELLEVUE
Grier, Rev. James H.
McGill, Rev. David F.
Smith, Sion B.
Starr, Lee A., Minister

BEN AVON
Lesher, Carl E.
Wilson, William R.

BERWYN
Coates, Joseph H., Author
Donnelly, Harold I., Educator
Mason, J. Alden, Anthropologist
Newton, Alfred E.
Sagebeer, Joseph E., Lawyer
Stout, George C., M. D.
Woodruff, George W., Lawyer

(573)

BETHAYRES

Lippincott, Joseph W., Author
McClellan, William, Engineer

BETHLEHEM

Blakeley, George H., Engineer
Coyle, Wm. R., de Schweinitz, Paul, Congressman
Eckfeldt, Howard, Mining Engineer
Emery, Natt M., Educator
Estes, Wm. L., Surgeon
Fogg, Ralph J., Civil Engineer
Fort, Tomlinson, Mathematician
Fox, Charles S., University Professor
Gipson, Lawrence H., College Professor
Goodwin, Charles J., Professor of Greek
Grace, Eugene G., Manufacturer
Hall, Robert W., Biologist
Hamilton, J. Taylor, Bishop
Heath, Rev. Edwin J.
Hughes, Percy, University Professor
Johnston, Archibald, Manufacturer
Larkin, Fred., Mechanical Engineering
Leach, Howard S., Librarian
Mathews, James E.
Miller, Benjamin L., Geologist
Rau, Albert G., Educator
Reynolds, Joseph B., Mathematician
Richards, Charles R., University President
Roush, Gar A., Metallurgist
Sawyer, Paul B., Public Utilities
Schwab, Charles M., Capitalist
Schwarze, Rev. William N.
Smith, R. M., Professor of English
Snyder, Henry S., Steel Manufacturer
Sterrett, Frank W., Bishop
Stoughton, Bradley, Metallurgical Engineer
Thornburg, Charles L., Mathematician
Tower, W. S., Trade Advisor
Wolle, John F., Organist Conductor

BIRMINGHAM

Grier, Alvan R., School President

BLACK GAP

McKibben, F. P., Civil Engineer

BLAWNOX

Lehman, A. C., President, Blaw-Knox Co.

BLOOMSBURG

Haas, Francis B., Educator

BLOSSBURG

Wilson, W. B., ex-Secretary of Labor

BOALSBURG

Ham, William R., Physicist
Kliefoth, Alfred W., Foreign Service

BRADFORD

Jones, Evan J., ex-Congressman, Lawyer
Newell, Frederick H., Engineer
Schoonmaker, Frederic P., Judge

BRISTOL

Grundy, Joseph R., Senator

BROOKLYN

Lee, Alice L., Author

BROOKVILLE

Strong, Nathan L., Congressman

BRYN ATHYN

Pendleton, Louis, Author
Pendleton, N. D., Bishop

BRYN MAWR

Baker, Franklin, Jr., Manufacturer
Barnes, James, Physicist
Beck, Jean-Baptiste, Professor of Romantic Languages and History of Music
Bond, Earl D., Psychiatrist
Chew, Samuel C., College Professor
Deeter, Paxson, Lawyer
Drexel, George W. C.
Farr, Clifford B., M. D.
Fenwick, C. G., Political Scientist
Harcum, Edith H., Educator
Johnson, Elizabeth F., Educator
Keen, Gregory B., Curator
King, Helen D., Zoologist
King, Wyncie, Illustrator
Kingsbury, Susan M., Economist
Laguna, Theodore de L.College Professor
Leuba, James H., Psychologist
Mutch, Andrew, Clergyman
Norris, Henry, Surgeon
Park, Marion E., College President
Rhoads, Charles J., Banker
Richards, Alfred N., Pharmacology
Rogers, Agnes L., Professor of Education
Schenck, Eunice M., Educator
Schlacks, Chas. H., Corporation Official
Shumway, Rev. Walter B., Educator
Smith, W. Hinckle, Capitalist
Tatnall, Henry, Railway Official
Taylor, Lily R., College Professor
Tennent, David H., Biologist
Thomas, M. Carey, Educator
Van Harlingen, Arthur, M. D.
Wister, Owen, Author

BUCKINGHAM

Heyler, Mary P. G., Artist, Author

BUTLER

Baldinger, Rev. Albert H.
Phillips, B. D., Vice-President, T. W. Phillips Gas & Oil Co.
Phillips, Thomas W., Jr., ex-Congressman

CALIFORNIA

Steele, Robert McC., Educator

CAMBRIDGE SPRINGS

Rose, W. P., Writer, Publisher

CANTON

McFadden, Louis T., Congressman

CARLISLE

Biddle, Edward W.

Biddle, Gertrude B.
Filler, Mervin G., Educator
Landis, Wm. W., College Professor
Lee, Guy C., Publicist
McKeehan, Joseph P., Lawyer
Morgan, James H., College President
Patterson, Gaylard H., College Professor
Prince, Leon C., College Professor
Sadler, S. B., Judge, Author
Vulleumier, E. A., Professor of Chemistry

CARRICK
Phillips, John McF., Manufacturer

CATASAUQUA
Dery, D. George, Silk Manufacturer

CENTER VALLEY
Gipson, Lawrence H., College Professor

CHADDS FORD
Rogers, Robert W., Orientalist
Wyeth, Newell C., Artist

CHAMBERSBURG
Anstadt, Rev. Henry
Magill, Frank S., Teacher
Warfield, Ethelbert D., College President

CHARLEROI
Macbeth, George D., Glass Manufacturer
Tener, John K., ex-Governor

CHARMAIN
Allen, Henry T., Army Officer

CHELTENHAM
Edmunds, Albert J., Librarian
Foster, Major B., Economist

CHESTER
Brazer, Clarence W., Architect
Dickinson, Oliver B., Judge
Evans, Milton G., Theologian
Lewis, Frank G., Librarian
Matthews, Rev. Isaac G.
Price, Wm. G., Jr., Major-General
Taitt, Rev. Francis M.
Vedder, Henry C., Professor of Chemical History
Wyman, Levi P., Professor of Chemistry

CHESTNUT HILL—(See Philadelphia)

CHEYNEY
Calvert, Phillip P., Entomologist

CLARION
Riemer, Guido C. L., Educator

CLARKS GREEN
Fellows, Eugene H., Editor

CLEARFIELD
Chase, James M., Congressman
Kerr, Albert B., Lawyer
Swoope, William I., Congressman

COATESVILLE
Harris, Francis W., Electrical Engineer
Huston, Charles L., Manufacturer
Ridgway, Wm. H., Writer, Manufacturer

COLEBROOK
Rorer, Sarah T., Domestic Science

COLLEGEVILLE
Barnard, J. Lynn, Educator
Kline, Whorten A., Educator
Omwake, George L., College President
Smith, Homer, Professor of English
White, Elizabeth B., Professor of History

CONSHOHOCKEN
Jones, Horace C., Manufacturer, Banker

CORAOPOLIS
Bakewell, Donald C., Steel Manufacturer
Ladd, George T., Mechanical Engineer

CRAFTON
Burgess, Rev. Ellis B.
Campbell, Guy E., Congressman
Wentzel, Wm. F. H., Director of Humane Education

CYNWYD—(See Bala-Cynwyd)

DAYLESFORD
Schelling, Felix E., Educator

DEVON
Hayward, Harry
Lowell, Francis R., Educator
Master, Henry B., Denominational Secretary
Witmer, Lightner, Psychologist
Yarnall, Charlton, Banker

DOYLESTOWN
Hodges, Leigh M., Writer
Jaekel, Frederic B., Author

DU BOIS
Dubois, John E., Capitalist
Free, Spencer M., Surgeon

DUNMORE
Davis, Reuben N., Musical Director

DUQUESNE
Crawford, Edwin R., Banker, Manufacturer
Wright, Charles E., Librarian

EASTON
Anthony, Luther B., Editor
Bailey, Ervin G., Mechanical Engineer
Bingham, Eugene C., Chemist
Bowen, Ezra, Economics
Brown, Gabriel S., Manufacturer
Drake, Fred R.
Field, B. Rush, M. D.
Fox, Edward J., Lawyer
Fretz, Rev. Franklin K., Educator
Gordan, Clarence McC., Physicist

Hall, William S., Mathematics
Hart, Edward, Chemist
Kirkpatrick, Wm. H., U. S. District Judge
Kirkpatrick, Wm. S., ex-Congressman
Kunkel, Beverly W., Biologist
Lewis, William M.
Nevin, George B., Composer
Plank, William B., Mining Engineer
Prentice, Donald B., Engineer, Educator
Raul, Harry L., Sculptor
Rockwell, Edward H., Civil Engineer
Shimer, Porter W., Chemist
Tupper, James W., College Professor
Ward, Freeman, Geologist
Yarnelle, Edward R., Manufacturer

EAST PITTSBURGH
Davis, Harry P.
Merrick, Frank A., President, Westinghouse Elec. & Mfg. Co.
Skinner, Charles E., Electrical Engineer
Wilson, Robert L., Electrical Engineer

EAST STROUDSBURG
La Rue, Daniel W., Professor of Psychology

EBENSBURG
Kephart, John W., Judge
Leech, J. Russell, Congressman

EDGEWOOD
Koenig, Adolph, M. D.
Meyer, John D., Lawyer
Miller, Joseph T., Utility Executive
Prather, Thomas J., Lawyer

EDINBORO
Wheatley, William A., Educator

ELIZABETHTOWN
Ober, Rev. Henry K., Educator

ELKINS PARK
Billikopf, Jacob, Social Worker
Douty, Nicholas, Tenor
Elkins, William McI., Banking
Griffith, Ivor, Chemist
Rowland, Albert L., Educator
Stetson, John B., Jr., Diplomat

ERIE
Behrend, Ernst R., Paper Manufacturer
Benjamin, Louis, Publisher
Blodgett, Francis B., Theologian
Davis, Rev. Ralph M.
Gannon, John M., Bishop
Gearhart, Rev. Ephraim M.
Reed, Sarah A., Philanthropist
Shreve, Milton W., Congressman
Vincent, Henry B., Musical Director
Walling, Emory A., Judge
Wright, Ross P., Manufacturer

FALLSINGTON
Coghill, George E., Anatomist

FLOURTOWN
Ueland, Elsa, Educator

FOGELSVILLE
Fogel, Edwin M., Educator

FORT WASHINGTON
Breckenridge, Hugh H., Artist
McLean, Robert, Newspaper Executive

FRANKFORD—(See Philadelphia)

FRANKLIN
Lamberton, Chess, Banker
Rickards, George C., Chief of Militia Bureau

FULLERTON
Bailey, Ervin G., Mechanical Engineer

GEORGE SCHOOL
Walton, George A., Educator

GERMANTOWN—(See Philadelphia)

GETTYSBURG
Aberly, Rev. John
Alleman, Herbert C., Theologian
Bikle, Phillip M., College Dean
Hanson, Rev. Henry W. A.
Hoover, Harvey D., Theology
Huber, Charles H., Educator
Sanders, Rev. C. F., Educator
Singmaster, Elsie, Author
Valentine, Rev. Milton H.
Wentz, Rev. Abdel R., Educator

GIBSONIA
Thompson Alexander M., Lawyer
Trees, Joe C., Oil and Gas

GLENFIELD
Parsons, Rev. William, Editor

GLENOLDEN
Bonsall, Edward H.

GLENSHAW
Coleman, Rev. William J.
Meller, H. B., Combustion Engineer

GLENSIDE
Kuehner, Quincy A., Professor of Education
Smith, Thomas B., ex-Mayor

GREENCASTLE
Fletcher, Henry P.

GREENSBURG
Donohoe, J. P., Coal Operator
March, Thomas S., Educator
Shero, William F., College President
Woods, Cyrus E., Diplomat
Wyant, Adam M., Congressman

PENNSYLVANIANS IN "WHO'S WHO IN AMERICA" 577

GREENVILLE
Xander, Rev. Enos C., Educator

GROVE CITY
Daugherty, Harry K., Lawyer
Ketler, Weir C., Educator
Purvis, Rev. William E.

GWYNEDD VALLEY
Norris, G. W., Lawyer; Banker
Strassburger, R. B., Publisher; Diplomat

HANOVER
Brodbeck, Andrew R., ex-Congressman

HARFORD
Jones, Edward E.

HARRISBURG
Ainey, William D. B., Chairman, Public Service Commission
Ashley, George H., Geologist
Bagnell, Rev. Robert
Batdorf, Rev. Grant D.
Bliss, Robert P., Librarian
Brown, Arthur E., Educator
Darlington, James H., Bishop
Dennis, Lindley H., Educator
Donehoo, Rev. George P., Author
Doutrich, Isaac H., Congressman
Driver, Leeotis L., Educator
Fisher, John S., Governor
Foss, G. E., Commercial Secretary
Funk, J. C., Author; Lawyer
Ginter, Robert McN.
Godcharles, Frederic A., Librarian
Keith, J. A. H., State Superintendent of Schools
Kelley, J. Herbert, Educator
Kirby, C. Valentine, Art Educator
Kirk, Ralph G., Author
MacDonald, Anna A., Librarian
Martin, Helen R., Author
Maurer, James H., Labor Official
Maze, Mathew T., Bishop
McAlister, John B., M. D.
McCormick, Henry B., Trustee
McCormick, Vance C., Publisher
McDevitt, Rev. Phillip R.
McFarland, J. Horace, Master Printer
Myers, Myrl S., Consul
Ogelsby, Warwick M., Banker
Prugh, Byron E. P., Prohibitionist
Rasmussen, Frederik, Agriculturist
Schlegel, Rev. H. Franklin
Shenk, Hiram H., Historian
Stackpole, Edward J., Editor
Stephens, Ward, Musician
Stone, Ralph W., Geologist
Swartz, Joshua W., Congressman
Tait, Edgar W., Lawyer
Taylor, Elmer B., Banker
Tucker, W. L., Editor; Evangelist
Van Sickle, Frederick L., M. D.
Woods, Cyrus E., Diplomat

HARTSVILLE
Gemmill, Rev. Benjamin

HAVERFORD
Barringer, Daniel M., Mining Engineer
Bencker, Ralph B., Architect
Bigelow, Frederick S., Editor
Boyd, James
Brown, Paul G., Engineer
Cadbury, Henry J., Educator
Clement, Martin W., Railway Executive
Comfort, Wm. W., College President
Felton, Edgar C., Steel Manufacturer
Fernald, Robert H., Engineer
Fox, Herbert, Pathologist
Grant, Elihu, College Professor
Gummere, Amelia M., Author
Gummere, Richard M., Headmaster
Heiserman, Clarence B., Lawyer
Hoag, Clarence G., Civic Secretary
Jones, Rufus M., College Professor
Kelsey, R. W., Professor of History
Lesley, Robert W., Manufacturer
Lloyd, Horatio G., Banker
Lockwood, Dean P., Educator
Lunt, William E., College Professor
Meldrum, William B., Chemistry
Palmer, Frederic, Jr., Physics
Pancoast, Henry K., Medical Doctor
Peirce, Harold, Insurance
Post, Levi A., Professor of Greek
Pratt, Henry S., Zoologist
Rea, Paul M., Museum Administrator
Schaffer, William I., Judge
Schuler, Loring A., Editor
Scoville, Samuel, Jr., Lawyer; Lecturer
Watson, Frank D., Sociologist
Wilson, Edwin M., Educator

HAZLETON
Markle, Alvan, Corporation Official
Pardee, Israel P., Banker
Wilmot, George W., Manufacturer

HENRYVILLE
Hulbert, Rev. Gustavus A.
Willing, John T., Artist

HEREFORD
Johnson, Elmer E. S., Educator

HERSHEY
Hershey, Milton S., Manufacturer

HOLICONG
Sotter, George W., Artist

HOLLIDAYSBURG
Baldrige, Thomas J., Judge
Kemp, Rev. Matthew S.
Scheeline, Julia S., Social Worker

HONESDALE
Greene, Homer, Author; Lawyer
Jadwin, Edgar, Army Officer

HONEY BROOK
Bowman, Rev. John C.

HUNLOCK CREEK
Santee, Ellis M., Medical Doctor

HUNTINGDON
Brumbaugh, I. Harvey, College Professor
Brumbaugh, Martin G., ex-Governor
Ellis, Rev. Charles C., Educator
Hill, Wm. F., Farmer; Banker
McKeehan, Rev. Hobart D.
McKenzie, Fayette A., Educator

HUNTINGDON VALLEY
Johnson, Herbert, Cartoonist
Pearson, Joseph T., Jr., Artist

IMMACULATA
Raber, Oran L., Botanist

INDIANA
Fisher, John S., Governor; Lawyer
Robinson, L. W., Coal and Iron Mining

IVYLAND
Garver, Francis M., College Professor

JENKINTOWN
Greenway, Rev. Walter B., Educator
Jenkins, Arthur H., Editor
Laessle, Albert, Sculptor
Morrison, Charles M., Editor
Reaser, Matthew H., College President

JOHNSONBURG
Bixler, Harris J., Congressman

JOHNSTOWN
Camp, Irving L.
Cosgrove, John C., Banker; Coal Operator
Hays, Rev. Calvin C.
Nevin, Gordon B., Organist; Composer
Robinson, G. T., Coal Operator

KENNETT SQUARE
Whitney, Harry

KINGSTON
Laycock, Charles W., Banker
Sprague, Levi L., Educator

KIRKLAND
Rush, Benjamin, Underwriter

KUSHEQUA
Kane, Elisha K.

KUTZTOWN
Rothermel, Amos C., School Principal

LACKAWAXEN
Price, Frank J., Editor

LANCASTER
Appel, Theodore B., Medical Doctor
Apple, Henry H., College President
Atlee, John L., Surgeon

Bausman, J. W. B., Lawyer; Banker
Brinkman, William A., Merchant
Bromer, Edward S., Theologian
Cramer, Rev. W. Stuart
DeLong, Irvin H., Orientalist
Farmer, Clarence R., Surgeon
Frantz, Rev. Oswin S., Educator
Hartman, Edwin M., Educator
Herman, Theodore F., Theologian
Keller, William H., Judge
Klein, Harry M. J., College Professor
Kresge, Rev. E. E., Educator
Meminger, Rev. James W.
Mull, George F., College Professor
Omwake, Howard R., College Dean
Richards, Rev. George W.
Schiedt, Richard C. F., College Professor
Steinman, James H., Newspaper Publisher
Steinman, John F., Newspaper Publisher
Wenrich, Calvin N., Physicist
Wolf, Wm. A., Music School Director

LANGHORNE
Watson, Henry W., Congressman

LANSDOWNE
Brazer, Clarence W., Architect
Brown, Rev. Owen C., Editor
Bye, Frank P., Educator
Darby, Edwin T., Dentist
Glenn, Oliver E., Mathematician
Ivy, Robert H., Medical Doctor
Lewis, Wm. D., Educator; Author
Morse, Withrow, Biochemist
Prinz, Hermann, Dental Educator
Stevens, Rev. Daniel G., Editor
Thomas, Wilbur K., Humanitarian
Votaw, Albert H.
Webb, Walter L., Engineer
Williams, G. P., Missionary Secretary

LATROBE
Stehle, Rev. Aurelius, Educator

LEBANON
Moyer, Gabriel H., Lawyer
Grumbine, Harvey C., College Professor
Richards, Henry M. M., Manufacturer

LEWISBURG
Bartol, Wm. C., Mathematician
Davis, Nelson F., Biologist
Eyster, William H., Botanist
Focht, Benj. K., Editor; Publisher
Hunt, Emory W., Educator
Johnson, Albert W., Judge
Lawson, George B., Educator
Rivenburg, Romeyn H., Educator
Theiss, Lewis E., Journalist
West, Rev. Raymond M.
Whyte, James P., Educator

LEWISTOWN
McCoy, Frank R., Army Officer

LINCOLN UNIVERSITY
Carter, Rev. James

Johnson, George, University Professor
Johnson, William H., Educator

LITITZ
Cuppy, Hazlitt A., Editor
Stengel, Rev. Frederick W., Educator

LOCK HAVEN
Armstrong, Dallas W.

LUDLOW
Olmsted, Geo. W., Public Utilities

LUMBERVILLE
Garber, Daniel, Painter

MALVERN
Rosengarten, George D., Chemist

MANSFIELD
Straughn, William R., Educator

MARS
Davis, Sturgiss B., Professor of Education

MAST HOPE
Dyer, F. L., Mechanical and Electrical Expert

McELHATTAN
Shoemaker, H. W., Newspaperman

McKEESPORT
Crawford, E. R., Banker; Manufacturer
Hammitt, Jackson L., Banker

MEADOWBROOK
Kinter, William L., Lawyer

MEADVILLE
Akers, Oscar P., Mathematician
Bates, A. L., Lawyer; ex-Congressman
Bates, Walter I., Editor; Publisher
Beebe, Rev. James A.
Beiler, I. R., Professor of English Bible
Church, Henry W., College Professor
Crawford, Wm. H., Educator
Darling, Chester A., Biologist
Elliott, William A., College Professor
Gamble, Robert B., Surgeon
Henke, Frederick G., College Professor
Lee, Richard E., Chemist
Ling, Charles J., College Professor
Ross, Clarence F., College Dean
Schultz, John R., College Professor
Singley, B. L., Visual Educator
Swartley, Stanley S., College Professor

MECHANICSBURG
Stine, Wilbur M., Author; Engineer
Strong, William W., Physicist

MEDIA
Hare, Amory, Author

Hess, Henry L., Engineer
Jacobs, Merkel H., Physiologist
Martin, Edward, Surgeon
Sherlock, C. C., Writer; Editor
Stokes, Henry W.
Wanger, Irving P., ex-Congressman

MELROSE PARK
Ewing, Chas. H., Railway Official
Wolsey, Louis, Rabbi

MENDENHALL
Kelsey, Carl, College Professor

MERCER
Cochran, Thos. C., Congressman

MERCERSBURG
Edwards, Rev. Boyd, Educator
Rutledge, Archibald, Author

MERION STATION
Bartlett, Clarence, Medical Doctor
Benoliel, S. D., Electrochemist
Bok, Mary L. C.
Braum, John F., Manufacturer
Child, Clarence G., University Professor
Drinker, Henry S., Educator
Gest, William P., Banker
Hofmann, Josef, Pianist
Holloway, Thos. B., M. D.
Holton, J. S. W., Coal Producer
Kirk, Edward C., Dentist
Laird, Warren P., Architect
McClelland, G. W., Vice-Provost, University of Pennsylvania
Mitchell, Howard H., Mathematician
Pender, Harold, Electrical Engineer
Ritter, Verus T., Architect
Schwarz, William T., Artist
Turner, Chas. R., Dental Educator
Ward, Thomas J., Banker; Broker

MEYERSDALE
Kendall, Samuel A., Congressman

MIFFLINTOWN
Robison, S. S., Naval Officer

MIFFLINBURG
Lybarger, Lee F., Lawyer

MILFORD
Pinchot, Gifford, ex-Governor

MILTON
Godcharles, F. A., Librarian
Slocum, George W.

MINERSVILLE
Brumm, George F., Congressman

MORRISVILLE
Reich, Rev. Max I.

MORSTEIN
Lewis, John F., Lawyer

MORTON
Thompson, Charles S., Librarian

MOUNT AIRY—(See Philadelphia)

MOUNT CARMEL
Magrady, F. W., Congressman

MOUNT GRETNA
Sullivan, Rev. Wm. L., Author

MT. HOLLY SPRINGS
Steese, James G., Civil Engineer

MOUNT POCONO
Taggart, Marion A., Author
Weir, Hugh C., Author; Editor

MOUNT UNION
Beers, Edward M., Congressman

MOYLAN
Bilgram, Hugo, Machinist
Brewer, Franklin N., General Manager
Myers, Albert C., Historian
Shay, Howell L., Architect
Stephens, Alice B., Illustrator

MYERSTOWN
Bowman, Clellan A., College President

NARBERTH
Bolton, Thaddeus L., Psychologist
Chalfant, Harry M., Editor
Hipsher, E. E., Musician; Editor
King, LeRoy A., Educator
Neff, Joseph S., Medical Doctor
Pearson, Wm. A., Medical Doctor; Educator
Roberts, Percival, Jr., Capitalist
Stites, Fletcher W., Lawyer
Young, Louis A., Football Coach
Zentmayer, William, Medical Doctor

NAZARETH
Kreider, Charles D., Educator
Thaeler, Rev. Arthur D.

NEW BETHELEHEM
Andrews, Chas. E., Jr., Banker

NEW BRIGHTON
Wendt, Edwin F., Construction Engineer

NEW CASTLE
Marlin, Rev. Harry H., Writer
Randles, Rev. Andrew J.

NEW HOPE
Bredin, R. Sloan, Artist
Carson, John R., Research Engineer
Cooke, Morris L., Construction Engineer
Erskine, Laurie Y., Author
Folinsbee, John F., Painter
Lowell, Joan, Author; Actress
Miller, F. J., Industrial Engineer
Redfield, Edward W., Artist
Snell, Henry B., Artist
Spencer, Robert, Painter
Turnbull, Margaret, Author

NEW WILMINGTON
Anderson, Wm. T., Missionary
Wallace, Rev. William C., Educator

NORRISTOWN
Frees, Harry W., Author
Heysham, Rev. Theodore
McAvoy, Charles D., Lawyer

OAK LANE—(See Philadelphia)

OAKMONT
Frary, Francis C., Chemist
Hamor, William A., Chemist

OGONTZ SCHOOL
Madeira, Percy C., Coal Mining
Sutherland-Brown, Abby, Educator

OIL CITY
McCormick, Rev. Arthur B.
Rickards, G. C., Chief, Militia Bureau
Welker, George E., Gas Engineer

OLYPHANT
Hathaway, Charles M., Jr., Consul

OVERBROOK—(See Philadelphia)

PAOLI
Cilley, Gordan H., Editor
Pemberton, Ralph, Medical Doctor
Weisenburg, Theodore, Neurologist

PENNLLYN
Chambers, Francis T., Lawyer
Rankin, John H., Architect

PENNSBURG
Johnson, Elmer E. S., Educator
Kriebel, Rev. Oscar S., Educator

PHILADELPHIA
Abbott, Alexander C., Medical Doctor
Abbott, Edwin M., Lawyer
Addison, Wm. H. F., Anatomist
Adler, Cyrus, College President
Adolphe, Albert J., Artist
Alden, Ezra H., Railway Official
Allen, Perry S.
Allis, Oswald T., Theologian
Almond, Linda S., Author
Ames, Herman V., University Professor
Anders, James M., Medical Doctor
Anderson, Rev. William B.
Anspach, Brooke M., Gynecologist

Archambault, A. Margaretta, Artist
Arnstein, Henry, Chemical and Mechanical Engineer
Ash, William C., Educator
Ashcraft, Leon T., Surgeon
Ashhurst, Astley P. C., Surgeon
Ashhurst, John, Librarian
Ashton, William E., Gynecologist
Atterbury, Wm. W., Railway Official
Atwood, Albert W., Writer
Austin, Richard L., Banker
Austin, William L., Locomotive Manufacturer
Ayer, Rev. Joseph C.
Babcock, William W., Surgeon
Bachmann, Rev. Ernest F.
Baker, Rev. Arthur M., Editor
Baker, Franklin, Jr., Manufacturer
Baldwin, Rev. Arthur C.
Ball, Rev. Charles T., Educator
Ballagh, James C., University Professor
Ballard, Ellis A., Lawyer
Bane, Juliet L., Educator
Barnes, Rev. George E.
Barnhouse, Rev. Donald G.
Barrett, Michael T., Dentist
Barringer, D. M., Mining Engineer; Geologist
Bartholomew, A. R., Missionary Secretary
Bartlett, Clarence, Medical Doctor
Bartlett, Rev. George G.
Barton, George, Author
Barton, George A., University Professor
Bates, William N., University Professor
Bayliss, Chas. W., Vice-President, General Asphalt
Beamish, R. J., Lawyer; Writer
Beardwood, Matthew, Medical Doctor; Chemist
Beck, James M., Congressman
Beeber, Dimner, Lawyer
Belcher, W. E., Structural Engineer
Bell, John C., Lawyer
Bencker, Ralph B., Architect
Benoliel, S. D., Electrochemist
Benson, Rev. Louis F.
Benton, Rev. Herbert E.
Benze, C. Theodore, Theologian
Bergey, D. H., Bacteriologist
Beury, Charles E., University President
Biddle, A. J. D., Author; Explorer
Biddle, Gertrude B.
Bigelow, Frederick S., Editor
Bikle, Henry W., Lawyer
Bilbro, Anne M., Author; Composer
Bilgram, Hugo, Machinist
Billikoph, Jacob, Social Worker
Blankenburg, Lucretia L.
Blythe, Stuart O., Editor; Writer
Bodine, Samuel T., Business
Bohlen, F. H., Lawyer; Educator
Bolton, Rev. J. Gray
Bond, Earl D., Psychiatrist
Bonner, James B.
Bonsall, Edward H.
Borie, Adolphe, Artist
Bossard, J. H. S., Sociologist
Boston, L. Napoleon, Medical Doctor
Boswell, Rev. Charles M.

Boyd, D. K., Architect
Boyd, Rev. Harry B.
Bradbury, Robert H., Chemist
Bradbury, Samuel, Medical Doctor
Brakeley, George A., Educator
Braun, John F., Manufacturer
Bregy, Katherine M. C., Author; Lecturer
Brengle, Henry G., Banker
Brewer, Franklin N., General Manager
Brinton, Jasper Y., Judge
Brodhead, Rev. George M.
Bronk, Rev. Mitchell, Editor
Broome, Edwin C., School Superintendent
Broomell, I. Norman, Dentist
Brown, Francis S., Lawyer
Brown, Rev. Owen C., Editor
Brown, Paul G., Engineer
Brown, Reynolds D., Lawyer
Brown, Samuel H., Jr., Medical Doctor
Brown, W. Norman, Orientalist
Brownson, Mary W., College Professor
Brubaker, Albert P., Medical Doctor
Bryant, Henry G., Explorer
Buchanan, Mary, Oculist
Buckley, A. C., Neuropsychiatrist
Buffington, Joseph, Judge
Bullitt, William C.
Burch, Henry R., Economist
Burr, Anna R., Author
Burr, Charles W., Medical Doctor
Butler, Mary, Artist
Caldwell, Josiah S., Bishop
Caley, Rev. Llewelyn N.
Calhoun, Rev. John
Callender, Romaine, Musician
Calvin, Henrietta W., Home Economist
Carmichael, Thomas H., Medical Doctor
Carson, Norma B., Author
Casselman, Arthur V., Church Official
Cattell, H. W., Medical Editor
Chalfant, Harry M., Editor
Chambers, Francis T., Lawyer
Champion, Rev. John B., Educator
Chance, H. M., Mining Engineer
Chapman, Francis, Lawyer
Chesnutt, Nelson A., Musician
Cheyney, Edward P., University Professor
Church, Arthur L., Mechanical Engineer
Clark, Clarence M. Banker
Clark, Eliot R., Anatomist
Clark, Walton, Engineer
Clarke, Chas. W. E., Construction Engineer
Clarke, Walter I., Editor
Cleland, Rev. Charles S.
Clement, Martin W., Railway Executive
Clothier, Morris L., Merchant
Clothier Wm. J., Coal Merchant
Coates, George M., Surgeon
Coates, Joseph H., Author
Coghill, George E., Anatomist
Cohen, Solomon S., Medical Director
Collier, David C.
Collings, H. T., Professor of Commerce
Collins, H. LeR., Newspaperman
Collins, Philip S., Publisher
Combs, Gilbert R., Musician

Connell, Horatio, Bass-Baritone
Connell, Wm. H., Civil Engineer
Connolly, James J., Congressman
Connor, Rev. Charles F.
Cooke, James F., Editor
Cooke, Morris L., Construction Engineer
Copp, Owen, Medical Doctor
Coppedge, Mrs. Fern I., Artist
County, Albert J., Railway Official
Covert, Rev. William C.
Coyle, Robert M. C., Insurance Broker
Crampton, G. S., Ophthalmologist
Crawford, J. P. W., College Professor
Crawley, Edwin S., University Professor
Cret, Paul P., Architect
Crocker, W. J., Veterinarian
Cromie, Wm. J., Physical Instructor
Crosby, Henry L., Professor of Greek
Croskey, J. W., Ophthalmologist
Cunningham, Wilfred H., Banker
Curry, Rev. William M.
Curtis, Cyrus H. K., Publisher
Da Costa, Chalmers, Surgeon
Dager, Rev. Forrest E.
Daland, Judson, Medical Doctor
Daly, Thomas A., Writer
Darrow, George P., Congressman
D'Asenzo, Nicola, Artist
Davis, George T. B., Author
Davis, Paul A., III, Architect
Dawson, G. W., Artist; Teacher
Day, Charles, Mechanical Engineer
De Blois, Austen K., Educator
Deeter, Paxson, Lawyer
De Land, Clyde O., Artist
Delk, Rev. Edwin H.
Dercum, Francis X., Neurologist
Dice, Agnew T., Railway Official
Dickinson, John, Professor of Law
Dickinson, Oliver B., Judge
Dillon, John I., Writer
Dinkey, Alva C., Steel Manufacturer
Doane, Joseph C., Medical Doctor
Donaldson, Henry H., Neurologist
Donato, Giuseppe, Sculptor
Donnelly, Harold I., Educator
Donner, William H., Manufacturer
Dorrance, George M., Surgeon
Dorrance, Gordon, Publisher, Author
Dougherty, Denis J., Cardinal
Douglas, George W., Editor
Douty, Nicholas, Tenor
Downs, Wm. F., Public Utility Executive
Doyle, Michael F., Lawyer
Drexel, George W. C.
Duane, Russell, Lawyer
Duffy, James O. G., Editor
Duke, Charles W., Editor
Dunbar, W. C., President, Philadelphia Rapid Transit Co.
Dunham, Rev. James H., Educator
Durham, Edward, Manufacturer; Insurance Manager
Edmonds, Franklin S., Lawyer
Edmonds, G. W., ex-Congressman
Egbert, Seneca, Medical Doctor

Elkins, William McI., Banker
Emhardt, Rev. William C.
Eshner, Augustus A., Medical Doctor
Eveland, Samuel S., Capitalist
Everett, Herbert E., University Professor
Ewing, Chas. H., Railway Official
Eyre, Wilson, Architect
Eysmans, J. L., Railway Official
Faris, Rev. John T., Editor
Farley, Richard B., Artist
Farnham, Robert, Chief Engineer
Farr, Clifford B., Medical Doctor
Felton, Edgar C., Steel Manufacturer
Fenton, Beatrice, Sculptor
Ferguson, M. F., Editor; Author
Fernald, Robert H., Engineer
Ferris, Jean L. G., Painter
Fielding, Mantle, Architect
Fineman, Hayim, Professor of English
Finney, William P., Church Official
Fischer, Rev. Emil E., Educator
Fitzgerald, Harrington, Editor; Artist
Fleisher, Samuel S., Manufacturer
Flick, Lawrence F., Medical Doctor
Foley, George C., Theologian
Fonaroff, Vera, Violinist
Forbes, Rev. Roger S.
Fox, Rev. Francis M.
Fox, L. W., Ophthalmologist
Fox, William J., Librarian
Francis, Vida H., Illustrator
Franklin, Melvin M., Medical Doctor
Frazer, John, Chemist
Frazier, Charles H., Surgeon
Frazier, George H., Financier
Frost, Rev. Henry W., Author
Fry, Wilfred W., Advertiser
Fryer, Eugenie M., Author
Fuller, Edward, Newspaperman
Fulton, Rev. William P.
Gadsden, P. H., Public Utility Executive
Garber, John P., Educator
Garland, Thomas J., Bishop
Garrett, Erwin C., Author
Garrey, George H., Geologist
Garrison, F. L., Mining Engineer
Gates, Thomas S., Banker
Geibel, Adam, Composer; Organist
Gerson, Felix N., Editor
Gest, John M., Judge
Gest, William P., Banker
Gibbon, John H., Surgeon
Gibbs, George, Author; Illustrator
Giesecke, Albert A., Educator
Gill, Wilson L., Educator
Gillingham, Rev. C. H., Educator
Gimbel, Charles, Merchant
Gittings, J. Claxton, Pediatrist
Glasgow, William A., Jr., Lawyer
Gleason, Edward B., Medical Doctor
Gleaves, Albert, Naval Officer
Glendinning, Robert, Banker
Glover, Rev. Robert H.
Goepp, Philip H., Musician
Golder, Benjamin M., Congressman
Goodrich, Herbert F., Law Educator

Goodspeed, Arthur W., Physicist
Goodwin, Harold, Lawyer
Gordon, Alfred, Neurologist
Gordon, Irwin L., Journalist
Grafly, Dorothy, Writer
Graham, Edwin E., Pediatrist
Graham, George S., Congressman
Grammer, Rev. Carl E., Clergyman
Grant, Albert W., Naval Officer
Grayson, Charles P., Medical Doctor
Greenbaum, Max, Dentist
Greenfield, A. M., Banker; Realtor
Greenman, Milton J., Anatomist
Greenstone, Julius H., Author
Greenwalt, Mary H., Pianist
Gribbel, John, Manufacturer
Griffin, Rev. Frederick R.
Griffith, Helen S., Author
Griffith, Ivor, Chemist
Griffith, J. P., Crozer, M. D.
Griscom, Rodman E., Banker
Gummere, Richard M., Headmaster
Gummey, Henry R., Jr., Theologian
Hadzsits, George D., College Professor
Hahn, Conrad V., Construction Engineer
Hamill, Samuel McC., Pediatrician
Hammond, Frank C., Medical Doctor
Haney, John L., Educator
Hansell, H. F., Ophthalmologist
Harbeson, John F., Architect
Harding, George, Artist
Hare, Hobart A., Medical Doctor
Harms, Rev. John H.
Harris, Rev. Arthur E., Educator
Harris, C. Addison, Jr., Banker
Harris, J. Andrews, Jr., Banker
Hart, John F., Cartoonist
Hatfield, Charles J., Medical Doctor
Hathaway, Harle W.
Hauser, Conrad A., Church Official
Hawes, Rev. George E.
Hayward, Harry
Heber, Carl A., Sculptor
Heckel, George B., Editor
Hedley, Evalena, Writer
Heebner, Charles, Lawyer
Heffner, E. H., Professor of Latin
Heilner, Samuel
Heiserman, Clarence B., Lawyer
Heisler, John C., Medical Doctor
Henderson, Joseph W., Lawyer
Henry, J. Norman, Medical Doctor
Herr, Herbert T., Mechanical Engineer
Herrick, Cheesman A., College President
Hess, Henry L., Engineer
Heustis, Charles H., Editor
Hewson, Addinell, Surgeon
Heyler, Mary P. G., Artist; Author
Hill, Rev. Edward Y.
Hill, Francis, Author
Hill, Rev. Owen A.
Hilleary, E. D., Railway Official
Hipsher, E. E., Musician; Editor
Hires, Charles E., Jr.
Hirst, Barton C., Medical Doctor
Hoag, Clarence G., Civic Secretary

Hodgkinson, Francis, Mechanical Engineer
Hofmann, Josef, Pianist
Holland, Charles H., Insurance Executive
Holland, L. B., Professor of Fine Arts
Holloway, Thomas B., Medical Doctor
Holloway, E. S., Artist; Author
Holmes, Arthur, College President
Holton, John S. W., Coal Producer
Hopewell-Smith, Arthur, Author
House, Jay E., Writer
Houston, George H. Manager
Houston Samuel F.
Howard, Philip E., Publisher
Howe, George, Architect
Howland, Anne W., Librarian
Heubner, S. S., College Professor
Huff, William K., Editor
Hulme, Thomas W., Railway Official
Hunter, Chas. W., Construction Engineer
Huntingdon-Wilson, F. M., Musical Director
Hunton, Rev. William L., Editor
Husik, Isaac
Hyde, Theophilus R., Educator
Hyde, Walter W., University Professor
Ingersoll, Charles E., Lawyer
Ingram, E. L., Professor of Railway Engineering
Ives, Frederic E., Inventor
Ivy, Robert H., Medical Doctor
Jackson, Albert A., Banker
Jackson, Chevalier, Laryngologist
Jacobs, Rev. Charles M., Educator
Jacobs, Henry, Theologian
James, D. Bushrod, Gynecologist
James, Joseph H., Chemist
Jayne, Horace H. F., Archaeologist
Jefferys, Rev. Edward M.
Jenkins, Arthur H., Editor
Jenkins, Charles F., Publisher
Jenks, John S., Banker
Jennings, Rev. W. Beatty
Johnson, Alba B.
Johnson, Amandus, Educator; Explorer
Johnson, Emory R., University Dean
Johnson, Virgil L., Architect; Engineer
Jones, Lawrence E., Builder
Jones, Livingston E., Banker
Jopson, John H., Surgeon
Kaemmerling, Gustav, Naval Officer
Kane, Francis S., Lawyer
Kavanaugh, William H.
Keedy, Edwin R., Professor of Law
Keen, Gregory B., Curator
Keen, William W., Surgeon
Keene, Floyd E., Surgeon
Keith, Charles P., Author
Kellogg, Thomas M., Architect
Kelly, George, Dramatist
Kelsey, Albert, Architect
Kendrick, W. Freeland, Mayor
Kennedy, David S., Editor
Kennedy, Moorhead C., Railway Official
Kent, A. Atwater, Manufacturer; Inventor
Kent, Roland G., Philologist
Killian, John C., Church Official
Kimball, Fiske, Architect; Museum Director
King, Caroline B., Editor; Author

PENNSYLVANIANS IN "WHO'S WHO IN AMERICA"

King, Clyde L., Author
Kinnard, Leonard H., Telephone Official
Kinter, William L., Lawyer
Klauder, Charles Z., Architect
Klein, Louis A., Veterinarian
Knowles, Rev. Archibald C.
Kohlstedt, Rev. Edward D., Educator
Kolb, Louis J., Manufacturer
Krick, Charles S., Railway Official
Krumbhaar, E. B., Pathologist
Krusen, Wilmer, Director of Public Health
Kynett, Rev. Alpha G.
Laird, Rev. John B.
Lampe, William E., Church Official
Landis, Henry R. M., Medical Doctor
Lansdale, Maria H., Author
Laufer, Rev. Calvin W.
Law, William A., Insurance; Banker
La Wall, Charles H., Pharmacist
Ledoux, John W., Hydraulic Engineer
Lee, Elisha, Railway Official
Leeds, Morris E., Manufacturer
Leffmann, Henry, Chemist
Leidy, Joseph, Medical Doctor
Leinbach, Rev. Paul S., Editor
Leisenring, E. B., Coal Operator
Lesh, John A., University Professor
Lesher, Carl E., Engineer; Economist
Lesley, Robert W., Manufacturer
Levinthal, Bernard L., Rabbi
Lewis, John F., Lawyer
Lewis, Morris J., Medical Doctor
Lewis, William D., Lawyer
Lichtenberger, J. P., Sociologist
Lillie, Samuel M., Inventor; Manufacturer
Lingelbach, Anna L.
Lingelbach, William E., University Professor
Linnard, Joseph H., Naval Officer
Linthicum, Frank H.
Linton, Edwin, College Professor
Linton, M. A., Life Insurance Executive
Lippincott, Horace M., Author
Lippincott, J. W., Author; Publisher
Lippincott, Joshua B., Publisher
Lippincott, Martha S., Writer
Little, Nat, Illustrator
Littleton, William G., Banker
Lloyd, Horatio G., Banker
Lloyd, William H., Professor of Law
Lorimer, George H., Editor
MacCallum, Rev. John A.
MacColl, Rev. Alexander
Macfarlane, John M., Botanist
Machen, J. Gresham, Theologian
Mackey, Harry A., Mayor
Maclennan, Rev. Alexander G.
Madeira, Louis C., Coal Operator
Madeira, Percy C., Coal Mining
Mahany, Rowland B., ex-Congressman
Mahoney, John D., Lecturer
Main, Rev. William H.
Mallery, Otto T.
Margolis, Max L., Philologist
Marshall, C. J., Veterinarian
Martin, Carl N., Banker
Martin, J. C., Newspaper Publisher

Martin, Warren F., Lawyer
Mason, J. Alden, Anthropologist
Master, Henry B., Denominational Secretary
Matheson, Kenneth G., College President
Matthews, H. A., Organist; Composer
McCain, George N., Journalist
McCarter, Henry, Artist
McCarthy, Daniel J., Neurologist
McClelland, George W., Vice-Provost, University of Pennsylvania
McClenahan, Howard, Scientist
McConaughy, James, Editor
McCrae, Thomas, Physician
McDaniel, Walton B., College Professor
McFadden, George, Merchant
McFarland, Joseph, Pathologist
McGarrah, Rev. Albert F.
McIntyre, John T., Dramatist
McIver, Joseph, Neuro-Psychiatrist
McKenzie, Robert T., Medical Doctor; Sculptor
McKinley, Albert E., College Professor
McLean, Robert, Newspaper Executive
McLean, Wm. L., Newspaper Publisher
McMaster, John B., University Professor
Mead, Edward S., Educator
Meeker, George H., Chemist
Meigs, Arthur I., Architect
Meigs John, Civil Engineer
Meisenhelter, L. R., Mechanical Engineer
Meisle, Kathryn, Contralto
Melhorn, Rev. Nathan R., Educator
Mellor, Walter, Architect
Merrick, J. Hartley
Meyers, Milton K., Neurologist
Mikell, William E., Professor of Law
Miller, James C., University Professor
Miller, Park H., Editor
Miller, R. K., Composer; Organist
Mills, Charles K., Neurologist
Milne, Caleb J., Jr.
Minnick, John H., Teacher
Mitchell, Charles F., Surgeon
Mitten, Arthur A., Transportation; Banking
Mockridge, Rev. John C. H.
Moffett, Louis B., School Director
Moffett, Rev. Thomas C.
Monaghan, James, Lawyer
Montgomery, Rev. James A.
Moody, Lewis F., Mechanical Engineer
Moore, Clarence B., Archaeologist
Moore, J. H., ex-Congressman
Moore, John P., Zoologist
Moore, William G., Banker
Morgan, Charles E., III, Lawyer
Morgan, George, Author; Editor
Morgan, Rev. G. Campbell
Morris, Effingham B., Lawyer
Morris, Harrison S., Author
Morris, Roland S., Lawyer
Morrison, Charles M., Editor
Morton, Samuel W., Medical Doctor
Moyer, James A., Educator; Engineer
Mudge, Lewis S., Church Official
Mueller, Fred W., Church Official
Mull, J. Harry, Shipbuilder
Mullan, James McE., Denominational Secretary

Muller, George P., Surgeon
Munhall, Leander W., Evangelist
Murphy, William R., Journalist
Murray, Samuel, Sculptor
Myers, Albert C., Historian
Nason, Harry B., Jr., Editor
Neilson, Lewis, Railway Official
Newman, Rev. John G.
Newton, Alfred E.
Newton, Rev. Joseph F.
Nichols, Henry S. P., Lawyer
Nichols, Isabel McI.
Nitzsche, Elsa K., Painter
Nitzsche, G. E., Recorder, University of Pennsylvania
Nones, Robert H., Dentist
Norden, N. L., Organist; Conductor
Norris, George W., Medical Doctor
Norris, G. W., Lawyer
Oakley, Imogen B., Writer
Oakley, Violet, Painter
Oberholtzer, Ellis P., Author
Offermann, Henry F. Theologian
O'Harra, Margaret T., Social Worker
Ohl, Rev. Jeremiah F.
O'Malley, Austin, Oculist
Opie, Eugene L., Pathologist
Packard, Charles S. W., Capitalist
Packard, Francis R., Medical Doctor
Packard, George R., Insurance Executive
Pancoast, Henry K., Medical Doctor
Parker, Edward W., Statistician
Parks, Wythe M., Naval Officer
Passmore, Lincoln K., Insurance
Patenotre, Eleanor E., Publisher
Patterson, Catherine N., Artist
Patterson, Ernest M., Economist
Patterson, George S., Lawyer
Patterson, Ross V., Medical Doctor
Patton, Katharine, Artist
Paul, John R., Lawyer
Peach, Robert W., Bishop
Peck, S. B., Civil and Mechanical Engineer
Peirce, Harold, Insurance
Pemberton, Ralph, Medical Doctor
Penniman, James H., Author
Penniman, J. H., Provost, University of Pennsylvania
Penrose, Charles, Electrical Engineer
Penrose, R. A. F., Jr., Geologist
Pepper, George W., Lawyer
Pepper, William, Medical Doctor; Educator
Perot, T. Morris, Jr., Malt Manufacturer
Peter, Luther C., Ophthalmologist
Petty, Orlando H., Medical Doctor
Pfatteicher, Rev. Ernst P., Author
Philbrick, Francis S., Professor of Law
Piersol, George M., Medical Doctor
Pike, Clayton W., Construction Electrical Engineer
Pilcher, Lewis F., Architect
Pilsbry, Henry A., Zoologist
Plack, William L., Architect
Pollock, Rev. Thomas C.
Price, W. J., Writer; Lecturer
Raditz, Lazar, Artist

Raiguel, G. E., Medical Doctor; Lecturer
Ranck Rev. Clayton H.
Randall, Burton A., Medical Doctor
Rankin, John H., Architect
Ransley, Harry C., Congressman
Rau, Otto M., Construction Engineer
Reath, Theodore W., Lawyer
Reed, Rev. Luther D., Teacher
Reichert, Edward T., University Professor
Remak, Gustavus, Jr., Insurance Executive
Repplier, Agnes, Author
Rice, Joseph M., Author
Rice, Stuart A., Sociologist
Richardson, Ernest G., Bishop
Riesman, David, Medical Doctor
Riter, Frank M., Lawyer
Ritter, Verus T., Architect
Roberts, Kenneth L., Writer
Roberts, Seldon L., Church Official
Robertson, William E., Medical Doctor
Robinette, Edward B., Banker
Robins, Edward, Author
Robinson, Dwight P., Engineer
Robinson, Rev. H. McA., Educator
Robinson, William D., Medical Doctor
Rolfe, John C., University Professor
Romig, Rev. John S.
Roper, Wm. W., Football Coach
Rose, Philip S., Editor
Rosenbach, A. S. W., Writer; Bibliographer
Rosenthal, Albert, Artist
Rosewater, Victor, Journalist
Rowland, Albert L., Educator
Rudolph, Robert L., Bishop
Rue, Levi L., Banker
Rush, Benjamin, Underwriter
Ryan, M. J., Lawyer; Banker
Sagebeer, Joseph E., Lawyer
Samuel, Bunford, Librarian
Sartain, Paul J., Medical Doctor
Sayward, S. Janet, Educator
Scattergood, Alfred G.
Schaeffer, Charles E., General Secretary
Schaeffer, J. Parsons, Anatomist
Schaffer, William I., Judge
Schamberg, Jay F., Dermatologist
Schell, Frank C., Artist; Editor
Schinz, Albert, University Professor
Schoff, Hannah K., Philanthropist
Schoff, Wilfred H., Museum Secretary
Schramm, Jacob R., Botanist
Schuler, Loring A., Editor
Schweinitz, George E. de, Medical Doctor
Schweinitz, Karl de, Social Worker
Schweizer, J. Otto, Sculptor
Scott, Henri, Basso
Scoville, Samuel, Jr., Lawyer; Lecturer
Seal, Ethel D., Interior Decorator
Seegers, Rev. John C.
Sellers, Horace W., Architect
Seneff, Edward H., Lawyer
Sewall, A. W., President, General Asphalt Co.
Shay, Howell L., Architect
Shedd, Fred F., Newspaper Editor
Sherlock, C. C. Writer; Editor
Shields, John F., Lawyer

Simon, Edward P., Architect
Simpson, Alex, Jr., Judge
Sims, Charles A., Railway Contractor
Singer, Edgar A., Jr., Philosopher
Sinkler, John P. B., Architect
Sioussat, St. G. L., University Professor
Skillern, Ross H., Medical Doctor
Skillman, Thomas J., Civil Engineer
Sloan, Marianna, Artist
Smith, Harriet L., Writer
Smith, Henry B., Philosopher
Smith, James W., Banker
Smith, Jessie W., Artist
Smith, Thomas B., ex-Mayor
Smith, W. Hinckle, Capitalist
Smithers, William W., Lawyer
Spiller, William G., Neurologist
Squires, Rev. Walter A.
Stead, Robert, Architect
Steele, Rev. David McC.
Stein, Rev. James R.
Stengel, Alfred, Medical Doctor
Sterling, Sara H., Author
Stern, Horace, Judge
Stern, Julius D., Editor, Publisher
Stevens, Rev. Daniel G., Editor
Stevens, J. Franklin, Construction Engineer
Stevenson, John A., Life Insurance
Stewardson, Emlyn L., Architect
Stewart, Rowe, Newspaper Publisher
Stilwell, Rev. Herbert F.
Stimpson, William G., Public Health
Stine, Wilbur M., Author; Engineer
Stites, Fletcher W., Lawyer
Stockwell, F. E., Church Official
Stockwell, Rev. John W., Jr.
Stoddard, Alice K., Artist
Stokes, Henry W.
Stokes, John H., Dermatologist
Stokowski, Leopold, Conductor
Stone, John H., Lawyer
Stone, Witmer, Naturalist
Stork, Charles W., Critic
Stotesbury, Edward T., Capitalist
Stout, George C., Medical Doctor
Strecker, Edward A., Medical Doctor
Strodach, Rev. Paul Z., Editor
Stroud, M. W., President, American Gas Co.
Stuart, Edwin S., Governor
Styri, Haakon, Metallurgist
Sullivan, John J., Lawyer
Swift, Archie D., Banker
Sykes, Charles H., Cartoonist
Synnott, Thomas W.
Taggart, Walter T., Chemist
Taitt, Rev. Francis M.
Talbot, Walter LeM., Life Insurance
Tatnall, Henry, Railway Official
Taylor, A. M., Transit Official
Taylor, Earl H., Writer; Editor
Taylor, Emily D., Painter
Taylor, H. Birchard, Engineer
Taylor, J. Madison, Medical Doctor
Taylor, Mills J., Church Official
Taylor, William J., Surgeon
Taylor, Rev. William R.

Teall, Edward N., Editor; Author
Thomas, Rev. John S. L.
Thomas, Walter H., Architect
Thompson, Arthur W., Capitalist
Thompson, J. Whitaker, Judge
Thompson, Ruth P., Author
Thorington, James, Medical Doctor
Thornton, E. Quin, Medical Doctor
Thwing, Charles B., Physicist
Tilden, William T., Jr., Tennis
Tily, Herbert J., Merchant
Tomkins, Rev. Floyd W.
Toothaker, Charles R., Curator
Tope, Homer W., Temperance Worker
Towne, Robert D., Editor; Publisher
Tracy, Martha, College Professor
Trigg, Ernest T., Manufacturer
Triplett, Rev. John E., Educator
True, Rodney H., Botanist
Trumbull, Charles G., Editor
Tubbs, Arthur L., Playwright
Urdahl, Thomas K., University Professor
Van Baun, William W., Medical Doctor
Vanderkleed, Charles E., Chemist
Vare, William S.
Vauclain, Samuel M., Manufacturer
Von Moschzisker, Robert, Judge
Wagner, Samuel, Lawyer
Wagner, Samuel T., Civil Engineer
Wailes, Rev. George H., Educator
Walk, George E., Educator
Ward, Perley E., Publisher
Ward, T. J., Banker; Broker
Warren, George W., Dentist
Warriner, S. D., Corporation Officer
Warwick, Edward, Artist
Washburn, Rev. Louis C.
Watkins, John E., Journalist
Watson, B. M., Educator, Author
Watson, Charles R., Educator
Watson, Frank R., Architect
Wayne, Joseph, Jr., Banker
Weber, Samuel E., Superintendent of Schools
Webster, George S., Civil Engineer
Weimer, Albert B., Lawyer
Weisenburg, Theodore, Neurologist
Wells, George H., Medical Doctor
Welsh, George A., Congressman
Welsh, Herbert, Publicist; Artist
Weston, S. Burns, Editor; Publisher
Weygandt, Cornelius, College Professor
Wheeler, Janet, Painter
Wheelwright, Robert, Landscape Architect
Whetstone, Walter, Utilities Executive
White, Beaver, Engineer
White, Rev. Herbert J.
White, Thomas R., Lawyer
Whitfield, J. Edward, Chemist
Whitlock-Rose, Elise, Author
Widener, Joseph E., Capitalist
Wiggins, H. L., Hotel Operator
Wilbur, Rev. John M., Educator
Wilbur, Rollin H., Railway Official
Wiles, Rev. Charles P., Editor
Willcox, James M.
Willet, Anne L., Artist

Williams, Francis C., Editor
Williams, G. P., Missionary Secretary
Williams, Ira J., Lawyer
Williams, R. C., Jr., Entomologist
Williams, Sidney C., Editor
Williamson, Oliver R., Publisher
Willing, John T., Artist
Wilmeth, James L.
Wilson, James C., Medical Doctor
Wilson, Joseph R., Lawyer
Wilson, Lucy L. W., Educator
Wing, Asa S., Insurance Official
Wister, Owen, Author
Witherstine, Christopher S., Medical Doctor
Wolsey, Louis, Rabbi
Wood, Horatio C., Medical Doctor
Wood, Walter, Iron Manufacturer
Woodruff, Clinton R., Lawyer
Woodward, George, Medical Doctor
Worden, Charles B., Medical Director
Work, Milton C., Author
Wright, Austin T., Professor of Law
Wright, R. R., Educator; Banker
Wright, Rev. Richard R., Jr., Editor
Wunder, C. E., Architect; Engineer
Yarnall, Charlton, Banker
Yarnall, D. R., Mechanical Engineer
Yarnall, Stanley R., Educator
Yeatman, Pope, Mining Engineer
Yelling, Samuel, Metal Worker
Young, James T., College Professor
Young, Louis A., Football Coach
Zantzinger, C. C., Architect
Zentmayer, William, Medical Doctor
Zimmermann, John E., Mechanical Engineer

PHOENIXVILLE

Walker, Wm. K., Neurologist

PINE GROVE

Silliman, H. I., Editor; Publisher

PITTSBURGH

Aaron, Marcus, Manufacturer
Acheson, Marcus W., Jr., Lawyer
Ahrens, Theodore, Manufacturer
Alderman, Grover H., Educator
Alexander, Rev. Maitland
Alter, George E., Lawyer
Arbuthnot, Thomas S., Medical Doctor
Arensberg, Walter C., Author
Armstrong, C. D., Cork Products
Avinoff, Audrey, Director, Carnegie Museum
Babcock, Edward V.
Bain, Jarvis J., Army Officer
Baker, Horace F., Lawyer
Baker, Thomas S., Educator
Baldwin, Rev. Harmon A., Author
Barton, Olive R., Writer
Bayard, E. S., Agricultural Editor
Beach, William M., Surgeon
Beal, George D., Chemist
Beane, Rev. John G.
Behan, Richard J., Surgeon
Bell, Frank B., Steel Manufacturer
Bigger, Frederick, Architect

Bitner, Harry M., Editor
Blair, Wm. W., Ophthalmologist
Blough, Elijah R., Medical Doctor
Bowman, John G., Educator
Boyle, Hugh C., Bishop
Braun, Arthur E., Banker
Breed, Rev. David R.
Brooks, Frank F., Banker
Buchanan, James I., Business Manager
Buchanan, John J., Surgeon
Burns, Keivin, Physicist
Burrell, George A., Chemical Engineer
Callery, J. D., Street Railway President; Manufacturer
Carver, George, University Professor; Author
Chidester, John Y., Editor
Church, S. H., President, Carnegie Institute
Clause, William L., Manufacturer
Clopper, E. N., Social Worker
Clyde, Wm. G., President, Carnegie Steel Co.
Colbert, Chas. F., Jr., Coal Operator
Connelley, Clifford B.
Coolidge, Cora H., College President
Cooper, Chas. C., Social Worker
Crane, Judson A., Professor of Law
Crawford, George G., Engineer; Metallurgist
Crutchfield, James S.
Culley, David E., Professor of Hebrew and Old Testament Literature
Curtis, Heber D., Astronomer
Dalzell, William S., Lawyer
Danner, Peter C., Vicar General and Chancellor
Davidson, Wm. M., Superintendent of Schools
Davis, A. V., Corporation Officer
Davis, Harry P.
Davis, Herman S., Astronomer
Davis, James J., Secretary of Labor
Davison, George S., Civil Engineer
Day, Rev. Albert E.
Day, Ewing W., Medical Doctor
Dempster, Rev. William J.
Dickey, Charles E., Educator
Diller, Theodore, Medical Doctor
Dodds, Robert J., Lawyer
Donohoe, John P., Coal Operator
Drake, James F., Manufacturer
Du Puy, Herbert, Manufacturer
Dyche, Howard E., Electrical Engineer
Eavenson, H. N., Mining Engineer
Eckhardt, E. A., Physicist
Edwards, Ogden M., Jr., Medical Doctor
Elliott, Wm. S., Engineer; Manufacturer
Elmer, Manuel C., Sociologist
Ely, Sumner B., Educator
Eppley, Eugene C., Hotelman
Estep, Harry A., Congressman
Farmer, William R., Teacher
Fetterman, J. C., Bacteriologist
Finlay, Walter S., Jr., Engineer
Finley, W. S., Jr., President, West Penn Electric Co.
Fitzgerald, Thomas, Street Railway Executive
Flannery, John R., Manufacturer
Foote, Paul D., Physicist
Forsyth, Rev. Henry H.
Frank, Isaac W., Machinery Manufacturer

Frary, Francis C., Chemist
Frazer, Robert S., Judge
Friesell, H. E., Dental Education
Garland, Robert, Manufacturer
Garner, James B., Chemical Engineer
Garnett, Porter, Writer; Printer
Gaston, John M.
Gaul, H. B., Organist; Composer
Gaylord, Truman P., Electrical Engineer
Gerwig, George W.
Gibson, Robert M., Judge
Goodale, S. L., University Professor
Gow, J. Steele, Educator
Graham, Louis E., Lawyer
Grayson, Thomas W., Medical Doctor
Gregory, Thomas B., Oil and Gas
Guffey, J. F., Oil Producer
Guthrie, Chas. C., Physiologist
Guthrie, W. J., Oil Operator
Hall, Louis D.
Hamor, William A., Chemist
Harbison, Ralph W., Manufacturer
Hawkesworth, Rev. Alan S.
Hayes, Stephen Q., Electrical Engineer
Heald, Kenneth C., Geologist
Heard, James D., Physician
Heckel, Edward B., Ophthalmologist
Hehir, Rev. Martin A.
Heinroth, Charles, Organist
Heinz, Howard, Manufacturer
Hershman, O. S., Editor; Publisher
Hirsch, Isaac E., Editor; Publisher
Holbrook, Elmer A., Educator
Holland, William J., Zoologist; Paleontologist
Hornbostel, Henry, Architect
Hughes, Ray O., Educational Author
Hulley, Elkanah B.
Huggins, R. R., Gynecologist
Humes, E. Lowry, Lawyer
Humphrey, Arthur L., Manufacturer
Hunt, Percival, Professor of English
Hutchison, Rev. Robert A.
Hutchison, Rev. Stuart N.
Ihlder, John, Civic Worker
Ingham, Charles T., Architect
Jacobs, Harold D., Editor
Jennings, Otto E., Botanist
Johnson, Harry M., Psychologist
Johnson, Roswell H., Geologist
Johnston, Stewart, Steel Manufacturer
Jones, B. F., III, Steel Manufacturer
Jordan, Frank C., Astronomer
Kammerer, Rev. Percy G.
Kelly, M. Clyde, Congressman
Kelso, James A., Theologian
Kennedy, Julian, Mechanical Engineer
Kerr, Rev. Hugh T.
King, Willis L., Steel Manufacturer
Kistler, John C., Church Official
Kline, Charles H., Mayor
Knowles, Morris, Construction Engineer
Koch, Julius A., Chemist
Krumreig, Rev. Edward L.
Ladd, George T., Mechanical Engineer
Laporte, Ewing, ex-Assistant Secretary, U. S. Treasury

Laughlin, George, Jr., Steel Manufacturer
Laughlin, Irwin, Diplomat
Lehman, A. C., President, Blaw-Knox Co.
Lehman, George M., Construction Engineer
Leonard, John W., Oil Producer
Levin, Leonard S., Lawyer
Lewis, Charles F., Director, Buhl Foundation
Lincoln, Wm. E., Manufacturer
Linhart, Samuel B., University Professor
Lippincott, James, Steel Manufacturer
Logan, Albert J., Manufacturer
Love, Frank S., Coal Operator
Lyne, Wickliffe C., Insurance Manager
Lyon, John D., Banker
Macbeth, George D., Glass Manufacturer
MacGilvary, Norwood, Painter
Madden, Joseph W., Lawyer
Magee, James M., ex-Congressman
Magee, William A., ex-Mayor
Manley, Louis K., University Dean
Mann, Alexander, Bishop
Marsh, Joseph W., Banker; Manufacturer
Martin, R. H., Educator; Lecturer
May, Herbert L.
McCahill, David I. B., Railway Official
Macartney, Rev. Clarence E. N.
McClintock, Norman, Lecturer
McClintock, Walter, Ethnologist
McCown, Rev. Edward C.
McCready, Robert T. M., Lawyer
McCreary, Rev. George B., Educator
McCurdy, Stewart L., Surgeon
McEldowney, Henry C., Banker
McEwan, Rev. William L.
McGiffin, Malcolm, Banker
McGranahan, R. W., Missionary Secretary
McKay, Marion O., Economist
McKennan, Thomas McK. T., Neurologist
McNaugher, John, Theologian
McVicar, Nelson, Judge
Meller, H. B., Combustion Engineer
Mellon, Andrew W., Secretary of Treasury
Mellon, James R., Banker
Mellon, Richard B., Banker
Mellon, T. A., Corporation Official
Mellon, William L., Banker
Meloy, Luella P., College Professor
Messler, Eugene L., Engineer
Metzger, I. D., Ophthalmologist
Meyer, John D., Lawyer
Meyerholz, Charles H., Educator
Miller, Charles L., Manufacturer
Miller, John F.
Miller, Rev. Robert J., Editor
Milligan, Ezra McL., Author
Mitchell, Howard W., Lawyer
Mitchell, Walter S., Banker
Moorhead, William S., Lawyer
Morrison, Thomas, Steel Manufacturer
Morrow, J. D. A., Coal Producer
Morse, Edwin K., Engineer
Moses, E. R., Lecturer; Educator
Mott, William E., Civil Engineer
Mudge, Edmund W., Manufacturer
Munn, Ralph, Librarian
Nesbit, Harrison, Banker

PENNSYLVANIANS IN "WHO'S WHO IN AMERICA" 589

Nomer, Harold A., Educator
Oliver, Augustus K.
Oliver, George S., Publisher
Oliver, John W., Professor of History
Orr, Rev. John A.
Palmer, Charles S., Chemist
Parsons, Rev. William, Editor
Patterson, Hannah J.
Peterson, Olof A., Paleontologist
Petty, Rev. C. Wallace
Philips, John McF., Manufacturer
Pigott, R. J. S., Engineer; Researcher
Porter, John L., Corporation Officer
Porter, Stephen G., Congressman
Prather, Thomas J., Lawyer
Pridgeon, Rev. Charles H.
Raschen, John F. L., University Professor
Raymer, Albert R., Railway Official
Reed, David A., Senator
Reed, James C., Professor of Business Law
Reid, Rev. William J., Jr.
Reitell, Charles, Economist
Rhodes, G. P., President, Colonial Steel Co.
Riggs, Norman C., Mathematician
Rittman, Walter F., Chemical and Commercial Engineer
Robertson, Andrew W., Manufacturer
Robinson, Alexander C., Banker
Roessing, Jennie B., Suffragist
Rogers, W. H., Corporate Finance
Rohrbach, Quincy, University Professor
Rook, Charles A., Journalist
Roth, John E., Banker
Rust, Henry B., Corporation Official
Rynearson, Edward, Educator
Rys, C. F. W., Metallurgical Engineer
Saint-Gaudens, H. S., Director of Fine Arts
Schiller, William B., Manufacturer
Seibel, George, Editor
Shaw, George E., Lawyer
Sherman, William O'N., Surgeon
Shipp, F. B., Y. M. C. A. Officer
Sieg, Lee P., Physicist
Silverman, Alexander, Chemist
Siviter, Anna P., Author
Siviter, William H., Journalist
Smith, Cameron C., Steel Manufacturer
Smith, Elva S.
Smith, John H., Civil Engineer
Smith, Sion B., Mining Law
Snowden, J. H., Theologian; Author
Speer, J. Ramsey, Manufacturer
Steiner, Williams K., Organist
Stevenson, William H., Merchant
Storer, Norman W., Electrical Engineer
Sullivan, Patrick J., Congressman
Tait, Edgar W., Lawyer
Tate, John M., Jr., Manufacturer
Taylor, Samuel A., Engineer
Teller, S. A., Social Worker
Thoburn, Rev. James M.
Thompson, Alexander M., Lawyer
Thomson, W. H. Seward, Judge
Thurston, Alice M., Educator
Tillotson, E. W., Jr., Chemist
Trees, Joe C., Oil and Gas

Trinks, Willibald, Mechanical Engineer
Turkle, Rev. Alonzo J.
Turner, Ralph E., Historian
Twomey, Rev. M., Joseph
Tyson, Francis D., Economist
Vance, Selby F., Theologian
Van Etten, Rev. Edwin J.
Venable, William M., Engineer
Voss, Rev. Carl A.
Wadsworth, F. L. O., Engineer; Inventor
Wallace, John J., Clergyman; Editor
Walters, F. M., Jr., Physicist
Wappat, Blanche K. S., Librarian
Wardrop, Robert, Banker
Warner, E. L., Painter
Watters, Rev. Thomas
Weidlein, E. R., Chemical Engineer
Weil, A. Leo, Lawyer
Weir, Ernest T., Manufacturer
Welch, Herbert, Bishop
Wentzel, Wm. F. H., Director of Humane Education
Wherrett, H. S., Plate Glass Manufacturer
White, Jesse H., Psychologist
Whiter, Edward T., Railway Official
Whiting, Phineas W., Geneticist
Whitmer, T. C., Composer; Organist
Wiggins, William D., Civil Engineer
Wilbur, Charles E., Editor
Wilder, Charles W., Educator
Willetts, Ernest W., Medical Doctor
Williams, T. R., Newspaperman
Wilmot, Frank M., Secretary
Wilson, John A., Theologian
Wishart, Rev. William I.
Witherow, Wm. P., Steel Manufacturer
Withers, Robert E., Manufacturer
Wood, E. F., Author; Architect
Worthing, Archie G., Physicist
Wright, Albert B., Economist
Wurts, Alexander J., Electrical Engineer
Wychkoff, Arcalous W., Steel Manufacturer
Yost, Gaylord, Violinist; Composer

POCONO

Hare, Rev. James M.

POTTSTOWN

Rolfe, Alfred G., Headmaster
Wendell, James I., Educator

POTTSVILLE

Althouse, H. W., Mining Engineer
Archibald, James, VI
Halberstadt, Baird, Engineer; Geologist
Luther, Edwin C., Mining Engineer
Palmer, Cyrus M., Congressman
Pugh, William S., Mining Engineer
Richards, Wm. J., Mining Engineer
Sheafer, A. W., Mining Engineer
Silliman, H. I., Editor; Publisher

RADNOR

Atterbury, Wm. W., Railway Official
Bell, John C., Lawyer
Brengle, Henry G., Banker

Noble, Charles P., Medical Doctor
Posey, Wm. C., Ophthalmologist
Young, Charles M., Artist

RAHNS
Rosenberger, R. C., Bacteriologist

RAUBSVILLE
Anthony, Luther B., Editor

READING
Breyfogel, Sylvanus C., Bishop
Bushong, Robert G., Congressman
Casselman, A. V., Church Official
Creitz, Chas. E., Church Official
Croll, Wm. M., ex-Congressman
Derr, Cyrus G., Lawyer
Esterly, Charles J., Congressman
Hagy, Henry B., Banker
Hunt, Rev. Levi C., Educator
Janssen, Henry, Textile Manufacturer
Keator, Alfred D., Librarian
Maurer, J. H., Labor Official
Schaeffer, Paul N., Judge
Teel, Warren F., Educator

RIDLEY PARK
Meeser, Spenser B., Theologian
Wenrich, David H., Zoologist
Yocum, A. Duncan, Professor of Pedagogy

RIEGELSVILLE
Fackenthal, B. F., Jr., Iron Manufacturer

ROCHESTER
Smiley, Rev. William B.

RONKS
Dumont, F. T. F., Consul General

ROSEMONT
Austin, Wm. L., Locomotive Manufacturer
Cunningham, Wilfred H., Banker
Gibbs, George, Author; Illustrator
Jeffreys, Wm. H., Medical Doctor; Author; Missionary
Johnson, Alba B.
Vauclain, S. M., Locomotive Manufacturer

RUSHLAND
Nuse, Roy C., Artist

SAINT DAVIDS
Blythe, Stuart O., Editor; Writer
County, Albert J., Railway Official
Dinkey, Alva C., Steel Manufacturer
Hulme, Thomas W., Railway Official
Kingsley, S. C., Social Worker
Neilson, Lewis, Railway Official
Peck, George L., Railway Official
Robinson, Dwight P., Engineer
Seneff, Edward H., Lawyer
Wilbur, Rollin H., Railway Official

SALLY ANN FURNACE
Esterly, Charles J., Congressman

SALTSBURG
Wilson, A. W., Jr., Educator

SAYRE
Guthrie, Donald, Surgeon

SCRANTON
Amerman, Ralph A., Banker
Crane, Rev. Henry H.
Davis, Reuben N., Museum Director
Fellows, Eugene H., Editor
Frayne, Hugh, Labor Official
Johnson, Rev. David H.
Kaufman, David E., Diplomat
Lynett, E. J., Editor; Publisher
O'Reilly, Thomas C., Bishop
Pattison, William J., Publisher
Seipp, Alice, Artist
Sherwood, H. F., Civic Organizer
Smoley, C. K., Civil Engineer; Educator
Watres, L. A., Lawyer; Banker
Watres, Laurence H., Congressman
Weeks, Ralph E., Educator; Publisher
Weston, Charles S., Banker
Woolworth, Charles S., Merchant

SELINSGROVE
Ahl, A. W., Educator; Author
Follmer, Harold N., Theologian
Manhart, Franklin P., Theologian
Smith, Rev. George M. B., Educator

SEWICKLEY
Baker, Horace F., Lawyer
Bakewell, Donald C., Steel Manufacturer
Clause, William L., Manufacturer
Crutchfield, James S.
Finlay, Walter S., Jr., Engineer
Finley, W. S., Jr., President, West Pennsylvania Electric Co.
Harbison, Ralph W., Manufacturer
Jones, B. F., III, Steel Manufacturer
Lippincott, James, Steel Manufacturer
Lyon, John D., Banker
McCready, Robert T. M., Lawyer
Mitchell, Walter S., Banker
Morrow, J. D. A., Coal Producer
Robinson, Alexander C., Banker
Schuette, Rev. Walter E.
Tate, John M., Jr., Manufacturer
Wardrop, Robert, Banker

SHARON
Ker, Severn P., Steel Manufacturer

SHARON HILL
Burke, Robert B., Educator

SHAWNEE-ON-DELAWARE
Worthington, C. C., Mechanical Engineer
Yates, Cullen, Artist

SHIELDS
Brooks, Frank F., Banker

SHIPPENSBURG

Bower, R. F., Soil Fertility
Lehman, Ezra, Educator
Truscott, F. W., University Professor

SHIREMANSTOWN

Coover, Melanchthon, Theologian
Dennis, L. H., Vocational Education

SINKING SPRING

Bushong, Robert G., Congressman

SLIPPERY ROCK

Blaisdell, Thomas C., College Professor
Eisenberg, J. Linwood, Educator

SPRINGDALE

Alter, George E., Lawyer

SPRING GROVE

Glatfelter, Wm. L., Paper Manufacturer

STATE COLLEGE

Anthony, Roy D., Pomologist
Ash, Percy, Architect
Bonnine, Chesleigh A., Geologist
Boucke, O. Fred, Teacher
Chambers, Will G., College Dean
Chedsey, Wm. R., Mining Engineer
Crockett, Wm. D., Author; Educator
Davey, W. P., Physical Chemistry
Dutcher, Raymond A. Biochemist
Fletcher, S. W., Horticulturist
Forbes, Ernest B., Nutrition Specialist
Gardner, Frank D., Agronomist
Glenn, William S., Medical Doctor
Ham, William R., Physicist
Hetzel, Ralph D., College President
Kern, Frank D., Botanist
Kinsloe, Charles L., Electrical Engineer
Mairs, Thomas I., Educator
Marquardt, Carl E., College Professor
Martin, Asa E., Professor of American History
Peters, Charles C., Professor of Education
Runkle, Erwin W., Psychologist
Sackett, Robert L., Civil Engineer
Stoddart, Charles W., Educator
Struck, F. T., Industrial Education
Watts, Ralph L., Horticulturist
Wendt, Gerald L., Chemist
Whitmore, F. C., Organic Chemistry
Wood, Arthur J., Mechanical Engineer

STRAFFORD

Bikle, Henry W., Lawyer

STROUDSBURG

Palmer, A. M., ex-Attorney-General

SUNBURY

Kline, I. C., ex-Congressman
Lesher, John V., ex-Congressman

SWARTHMORE

Aydelotte, Frank, College President
Bazzoni, C. B., Professor of Experimental Physics
Bonsall, Elizabeth H.
Brewster, Ethel H., College Professor
Bronk, Isabelle, College Professor
Brooks, Alfred M., University Professor
Brooks, Robert C., College Professor
Coleman, Herbert R., Educator
Cons, Louis, Professor of French Literature
Cook, Ernest F., Pharmaceutist; Chemist
Denworth, Katharine M., Educator
Detlefsen, J. A., Physiologist
Dickinson, Asa D., Librarian
Dolman, John, Jr., Professor of English
Downs, Wm. F., Public Utility Executive
Dresden, Arnold, Mathematician
Ellis, William T., Writer
Fergusson, E. Morris, Writer
Fussell, Lewis, Electrical Engineer
Goddard, Harold C., College Professor
Hanny, William F., Cartoonist
Hayes, John R., Librarian
Hill, Reace L., Author
Hoadley, George A., College Professor
Holmes, Jesse H., College Professor
Howland, Arthur C., University Professor
Hull, William I., College Professor
Jones, Arthur J., Professor of Education
Kline, John R., Professor of Mathematics
Ledoux, J. W., Hydraulic Engineer
McClung, Clarence E., Zoologist
McGarrah, Rev. Albert F.
Miller, John A., College Professor
Moore, John P., Zoologist
Pearson, Paul M.
Robinson, Louis N., Economist
Ryan, W. C., Jr., Editor; College Professor
Shero, Lucius R., Professor of Greek
Smith, J. Russell, Geographer
Speck, Frank G., Anthropologist
Swann, Wm. F. G., Physicist
Taylor, Earl H., Writer; Editor
Viehoever, Arno, College Professor
Walter, Wm. E., Editorial Director
Walters, Raymond, Educator; Author
Warren, George W., Dentist
Willits, Joseph H., University Professor

SWISSVALE

DeVitis, M. A., Teacher; Author
Hellmund, R. E., Electrical Engineer

TARENTUM

McVicar, Nelson, Judge

THOMPSON

Miller, John D., Lawyer

TOWANDA

Mercur, Rodney A., Lawyer

TYRONE

Zerbe, Farran, Numismatist

UNIONTOWN

Hudson, Thomas H., Judge
Umbel, Robert E., Lawyer

UPPER DARBY

Anderson, Carlotta A., Teacher, Writer
Chesnutt, N. A., Musician
Hauser, Conrad A., Church Official
Helton, Roy A., Author
Huebner, Grover G.
Mullan, James McE., Denominational Secretary
Olivier, Charles P., Astronomer
Peach, Robert W., Bishop
Taylor, Mills J., Church Official
Wolfenden, James, Congressman
Woody, W. T., Professor, History of Education

VALENCIA

Rosanoff, Martin A., Chemist
Torok, John W. C. T., Bishop

VALLEY FORGE

Burk, Rev. W. Herbert

VILLANOVA

Bodine, Samuel T.
Clothier, Morris L., Merchant
Holland, Charles H., Insurance Executive
Lincoln, Joseph C., Author
McFadden, George, Merchant
Oakley, Amy, Author
Oakley, Thornton, Illustrator
Packard, George R., Insurance Executive
Parker, Alexis du P., Capitalist
Scattergood, J. Henry
Willcox, James M.
White, Beaver, Engineer

WALLINGFORD

Alleman, Gellert, Chemist
Jayne, H. H. F., Archaeologist

WARREN

Ball, Michael V., Medical Doctor
Jefferson, John P., Manufacturer
Lindsey, Edward S., Judge
Mitchell, Harry W., Medical Doctor

WASHINGTON

Baker, Simon S., Educator
Grant-Smith, Ulysses
Leonard, J. W., Oil Producer
Martin, Edward, Lawyer
Martin, George W., Biologist
McGregor, James C., College Professor
Parcell, Malcolm S., Artist
Stewart, John L., Editor
Sweet, A. H., European History
Temple, H. W., Congressman
Weyer, Edward M., Philosopher
Wilson, Rev. Maurice E.

WAYNE

Bayliss, Charles W.
Egbert, Seneca, Medical Doctor
Elmore, Rev. Wilber T.
Holland, Rupert S., Author
Kennedy, David S., Editor
Maxwell, Rev. James A.
Paist, Theresa W.

Stone, John H., Lawyer
Swift, Archie D., Banker
Taylor, A. Meritt
Wiley, Franklin B., Editor

WAYNESBORO

Landis, Mark H., Mechanical Engineer

WAYNESBURG

Stewart, Paul R., College President

WELLSBORO

Cocks, Orrin G.
Dunsmore, Andrew B., Lawyer
Howell, Daniel W.
Kerwin, Hugh L.

WERNERSVILLE

Hill, Samuel S., Medical Doctor

WEST CHESTER

Anderson, Robert F., Mathematician
Bartlett, Rev. Alden E.
Braisted, William C.
Brinton, Christian, Art Critic
Heathcote, Rev. Charles W.
Hergesheimer, Joseph, Author
Herring, John W., Educator
Robbins, Edward R., Educator
Schmucker, Samuel C., Biologist
Sharples, Philip M., Manufacturer
Shortlidge, Jonathan C., Educator

WESTTOWN

Walker, James F., Educator

WHITEMARSH

Edmonds, Franklin S., Lawyer

WILKES-BARRE

Carpenter, E. N., Congressman
Giering, Eugene T., Editor
Huber, Charles F.
Johnson, Frederick G., Publisher
Kirby, Fred M., Capitalist
Laycock, Charles W., Banker
Smith, Ernest G., Publisher

WILKINSBURG

Edgar, Rev. Thomas D.
Hulley, Elkanah B.
Jolly, Rev. Austin H.
McCurdy, Stewart L., Surgeon
McKnight, Rev. Robert J. G.
Miller, Joseph T., Public Utilities
Skinner, Charles E., Electrical Engineer
Taylor, Samuel A., Engineer

WILLIAMSPORT

Bubb, Harry C., Merchant
Burrell, Rev. David deF.
Fisher, Mahlon L., Author
Graff, George E., Publisher
Graham, James B., Banker
Kiess, Edgar R., Congressman
Lamade, Dietrick, Publisher

Long, John W., Educator
Manson, Frederic E., Editor
Thomson, O. R., Howard, Librarian
Walton, Lucius L., Pharmacist

WILMERDING
Miller, John F.

WOMELSDORF
Croll, Rev. Philip C.

WYNCOTE
Collins, Philip S., Publisher
Curtis, Cyrus H. K., Publisher
Gribbel, John, Manufacturer
Harriman, Karl E., Editor
Lorimer, George H., Editor
Main, Rev. William H.
Martin, John C., Publisher
Nash, Edgar S., Editor
Ward, Perley E., Publisher

WYNNEWOOD
Clothier, Wm. J., Coal Merchant
Dufour, Frank O., Civil Engineer

Hall, Reynold T., Naval Officer
Harding, George, Artist
Hires, Charles E., Jr.
Kinnard, L. H., Telephone Official
Meigs, John, Civil Engineer
Yellin, Samuel, Metal Worker

WYOMISSING
Janssen, Henry, Manufacturer
Thun, Ferdinand, Manufacturer

YORK
Brooks, E. S., Congressman
Busser, Ralph C.
Ehrenfeld, Charles H., Chemist
Hogue, Rev. Walter J.
Menges, Franklin, Congressman
Niles, Henry C., Judge
Schmidt, George S., Lawyer
Taylor, Katherine H., Author

YOUNGSTOWN
Scheible, Charles F., Mayor

www.ingramcontent.com/pod-product-compliance
Lightning Source LLC
Chambersburg PA
CBHW070004010526
44117CB00011B/1422